The C.L.R. James Reader

The C.L.R. James Reader

EDITED AND INTRODUCED
BY ANNA GRIMSHAW

First published 1992
Reprinted 1993 (twice)

Blackwell Publishers
108 Cowley Road, Oxford, OX4 1JF, UK

238 Main Street
Cambridge, MA 02142, USA

British Library Cataloguing in Publication Data
A CIP catalogue record for this book is available from the British Library.

Library of Congress Cataloging in Publication Data
James, C. L. R. (Cyril Lionel Robert), 1901–
The C. L. R. James Reader / edited by Anna Grimshaw.
p. cm.
Includes index.
ISBN 0–631–18179–2. —ISBN 0–631–18495–3 (pbk.)
I. Grimshaw, Anna. II. Title.
PR9272.9.J35A6 1992
818—dc20

92–6628
CIP

Typeset by Jim Murray of *Cultural Correspondence*, New York
Printed by T. J. Press, Padstow, Cornwall

This book is printed on acid-free paper

Contents

Preface

The *C.L.R. James Reader* was begun in James's lifetime. It was during the summer of 1988 that James and I started to discuss in detail the contents of a volume which would introduce his work to a new generation of readers. We planned to include a number of key writings from his published corpus and a selection of previously unpublished documents, essays and correspondence.

What was important to us in planning the *Reader* was our sense of the whole. In seeking to escape from the mere chronological documentation of James's life—one of the major problems James had encountered in his attempt to write an autobiography—we agreed that the principle governing the selection of material should be the organic connection between the different pieces.

The introduction to the *Reader* reflects this approach. It is animated by the expansive and yet unifying theme of James's remarkable life. And it is rooted in an understanding of his distinctive method. A fragment from James's autobiography serves as a useful illustration:

> I had been reading from early Aeschylus, Sophocles, Thackeray, Dickens and later Dostoevsky, Tolstoy and a whole list of writers. And I got a conception of human character and the interesting aspects of human personality, and the plain fact of the matter is the middle class people to whom I belonged and among whom I lived were busy trying to shape their lives according to the British idea of behaviour and principles. They were not very interesting. I dare say in time I could have done something with them. But the people who had passion, human energy, anger, violence and generosity were the common people whom I saw around me. They shaped my political outlook and from that time to this day those are the people I have been most concerned with. That's why I was able to understand Marx very easily, and particularly Lenin who was concerned with them. . . . I didn't learn everything from Marxism. When I went to Marxism I was already well prepared. . . . Even in my days of fiction I had the instinct which enabled me to grasp the fundamentals of Marxism so easily and then to work at Marxism having the basic elements of a Marxist view—my concern with the common people.

James's method was essentially empirical. From boyhood he had meticulously gathered information—through observation, reading, research and conversation. His mastery of the concrete details of particular forms of human activity gave him enormous confidence in his approach to the world. It formed the basis for his exploration of ideas; and throughout his life, moving with ease between the general current of world history and the concrete particulars of everyday life, James was able to capture both the complexity and unity of the modern world.

For many years James's work was poorly circulated. During the 1970s, however, books by James became much more easily available, largely as a result of Margaret Busby's initiative in the London-based publishing house, Allison and Busby. In the last decade of James's life most of his full-length works were reprinted; and three volumes of selected writings brought together his articles and essays which had long been buried in obscure publications.

The *C.L.R. James Reader*, while drawing upon these materials, contains much that is new. In particular, it makes available previously unpublished writings from James's personal archive.

A good deal of the work for the *Reader* was built upon earlier projects associated with the James archive. The collection of papers, originally organised and catalogued by Jim Murray in the early 1980s, formed the basis of the exhibition, *C.L.R. James: Man of the People*, held in London in 1986. It also yielded many documents for James's volume, *Cricket*, published later in the same year.

The availability of new materials in the James archive has not just made it possible to fill out the picture of James's remarkable life, to marvel at the sheer productivity of his eighty and more years or to add on a few more labels to the already long list—Pan-Africanist, Marxist, cricket commentator, critic and writer of fiction. What these documents make possible is a *new conception* of that life's work itself. The *Reader* is such an attempt. Its primary purpose is not to offer a representative sample of writings; but to break some of the old categories which fragment and confine James.

We now know more about the scope and precision of James's project. It is, however, the integration of the parts, the weaving of disparate, scattered pieces into a whole, the creation, as James would say, of something new, which will secure and extend the legacy of one of our century's most outstanding figures. This was the basis of James's approach to the work of the great figures—artists, writers and revolutionaries—of history. He knew, too, that it was the challenge of his own autobiography.

The *Reader*, like the autobiography, was unfinished at the time of James's death. In the difficult period since May 1989, I have received a great deal of support from many people. Their contributions, ranging from friendship to financial and editorial assistance, have been invaluable in making possible the completion of this book. Indeed, I like to think of the *Reader* as Jamesian to its core, for its production has grown out of the informal cooperation of individuals organised by the task itself.

In particular, I would like to thank Margaret Grimshaw, Andrew McLaughlin, and David Menzies for their very practical and generous encouragements of my work. Alastair Niven of the Arts Council has offered sound advice and timely support. I would also like to acknowledge the resources made available to James at the end of his life by the Arts Council and the Royal Literary Fund, as these enabled us to begin the *Reader* project. I much appreciate the tenacity and tact of Simon Prosser at Blackwell Publishers. He has persisted in backing the book, despite many obstacles and delays. I am grateful, too, to Silvana Dean for her careful and painstaking work, and to Michael Grimshaw for his help with the James bibliography. Thanks to Ralph Dumain, Casey Hill, David Polonoff, James Scranton, and Shoshana Vasheetz for their diligent editorial work. Associates of the C.L.R. James Institute in New York, particularly Annie Chamberlin, Jerome Hasenpflug, Roderick Thurton, and Kent Worcester have challenged and stimulated the development of many of my ideas. Charles Frederick has made his own special contribution. The friendship of Paul Buhle and Constance Webb Pearlstien has been of great support to me; and I am grateful also to Jeremy McBride, Graham McCann, and Alison Rooper for their unstinting help in all James matters. Keith Hart, my companion and collaborator, has given very generously in many ways to this project. Finally, my special thanks go to Jim Murray whose commitment to James (and myself), both in his lifetime and after his death, has made so many things possible.

Anna Grimshaw
Cambridge

Acknowledgements

The Editor and Publishers would like to thank the following for permission to reprint copyrighted material: The Estate of C.L.R. James; Pantheon Books, a division of Random House, Inc., for 'What is Art' from *Beyond A Boundary* by C.L.R. James, © 1963 by C.L.R. James; Allison & Busby, an imprint of Virgin Publishing, for "From Toussaint L'Ouverture to Fidel Castro" from *The Black Jacobins*, and for "Garfield Sobers" from *Cricket.*

Every effort has been made to trace all copyright holders, but if any has been inadvertently overlooked, the editor and publishers will be pleased to make the necessary arrangements at the first opportunity.

Introduction

C.L.R. James: A Revolutionary Vision for the Twentieth Century

C.L.R. James died in May 1989. His death coincided with the explosion of popular forces across China and eastern Europe which shook some of the most oppressive political regimes in human history. These momentous events, calling into question the structure of the modern world order, throw into sharp relief the life and work of one of this century's most outstanding figures. For James was pre-eminently a man of the twentieth century. His legacy reflects the scope and diversity of his life's work, the unique conditions of particular times and places; and yet at its core lies a vision of humanity which is universal and integrated, progressive and profound.

James's distinctive contribution to the understanding of civilization emerged from a world filled with war, division, fear, suppression and unprecedented brutality. He himself had never underestimated the depth of the crisis which faced modern humanity. In James's view, it was fundamental. It was part and parcel of the process of civilization itself, as the need for the free and full development of the human personality within new, expanded conceptions of social life came up against enhanced powers of rule from above, embodied in centralized, bureaucratic structures which confined and fragmented human capacity at every level. This theme, what James later called the struggle between socialism and barbarism, was the foundation of his life's work. In the early Caribbean phase, it was implicit in his depiction of character and society through fiction and cricket writing; later it became politically focused in his active engagement with the tradition of revolutionary Marxism; until eventually, as a result of his experience of the New World, it became the expansive and unifying theme by which James approached the complexity of the modern world.

C.L.R. James spent his last years in Brixton, south London. He lived simply and quietly in a small room filled with books, music and art. His television set was usually switched on and it stood in the centre of the floor. James recreated a whole world within that cramped space. It was here, too, that he received visitors, those people who sought him out for his practical political advice, for the developed historical perspective and range of his analysis; but, above all, for the sheer vitality and humanity of his vision. From my desk in the corner of that Brixton room I would watch his eyes grow bright and his face become sharp and eager as he responded to questions, moving always with imagination and ease, from the concrete details of particular situations into broader, historical and philosophical issues. Frequently he surprised visitors by asking them detailed questions about themselves, their backgrounds, experiences, education, work, absorbing the information, as he had done throughout his life, as a fundamental part of his outlook on the world. At other times, James retreated; and I watched him sitting in his old armchair, his once powerful frame almost buried beneath a mountain of rugs, completely absorbed in his reading, pausing occasionally only to scribble or exclaim in the margins of the book.

Gradually I became familiar with the different elements of James's method which underlay his approach to the world and left a distinctive mark on all his writing. First of all, James had a remarkable visual sense. He watched everything with a very keen eye; storing images in his memory for over half a century, of distinctive personalities and particular events, which he wove into his prose with the skill and sensitivity of a novelist. Although his passion for intellectual rigour gave a remarkable consistency to the themes of his life's work, his analyses were never confined. He was always seeking to move beyond conventional limitations in his attempt to capture the interconnectedness of things and the integration of human experience.

I. TRINIDAD: 1901-1932

James was the first to acknowledge that the essential features of his perspective had been moulded in the context of his Caribbean childhood and youth. He was born in Trinidad on 4 January 1901; his parents were part of a distinctive generation of blacks—the generation which followed slave emancipation and whose contribution shaped profoundly the future of those small island societies. James's father was a schoolteacher; his mother was, as he described her in *Beyond A Boundary*, ". . . a reader, one of the most tireless I have ever met." The opening page of James's classic book revealed the major influences at work: "Our house was superbly situated, exactly behind the wicket. A huge tree on one side and another house on the other limited the view of the ground, but an umpire could have stood at the bedroom window. By standing on a chair a small boy of six could watch practice every afternoon and matches on Saturdays. . . . From the chair also he could mount on to the window-sill and so stretch a groping hand for the books on top of the wardrobe. Thus early the pattern of my life was set."

Not only did James, through watching, playing and studying cricket, develop at a precociously early age the method by which he later examined all other social phenomena; but also, as a boy, he had responded instinctively to something located much deeper in human experience. Cricket was whole. It was expressive in a fundamental way of the elements which constituted human existence—combining as it did spectacle, history, politics; sequence/tableau, movement/stasis, individual/society.

The importance of literature in James's formation also stemmed from its resonance with his intuitive grasp of an integrated world. James's "obsession" with the novels of Thackeray, particularly *Vanity Fair*, was a decisive part of this developing awareness, and it fed directly into his close observations of the personality in society. He absorbed, too, what may inadequately be called the politics of Thackeray, that sharp satire by which the novelist exposed the petty pretensions and frustrated ambition of middle-class British society. But, more than anything else, James recognised early that literature offered him a vision of society, a unique glimpse of the human forces and struggles which animated history.

James, as a boy growing up in a small colonial society, absorbed everything that European civilization offered to him. He immersed himself in its history and literature, in its classical foundations, in its art and music; but, at the same time he rebelled against his formal schooling, the authority of Queen's Royal College, the island's premier institution, and its British public school masters. He was, as he said many times, "a bright boy"; but he was determined to go his own way and to establish himself independently in the world.

There was a similar mixture of classical and innovative features in the early stories which marked the beginning of James's writing career. Aside from his growing local reputation as a cricket reporter, James had begun, during the 1920s, to write fiction. It was in the style of the novels and short stories of the metropolitan writers, and yet its subject matter, barrackyard life, was new and authentically Caribbean. James was drawn to the vitality of backstreet life, particularly to the independence and resourcefulness of its women. It became the creative source for his first published pieces.

La Divina Pastora (1927) and *Triumph* (1929) establish James's potential as a novelist. Moreover they reveal the foundation of James's imaginative skill in his close observation of the raw material of human life. This closeness to the lives of ordinary men and women was something James consciously developed; but he never shook off his sense of being an outsider, of looking on rather than being a participant in the vibrancy of the barrackyard communities. The early fiction was marked by the memorable characters James created, his stories woven from the rich images he had stored in his mind's eye, the prose brimming with wit and satire as he caught the sounds of the street in his dialogue. These elements he fused into subtle and carefully-crafted narratives.

A technique James used on more than one occasion was to re-work stories which he had heard or which had been told to him. He was particularly fascinated by tales in which the line between the real and the mysterious was blurred, for it was here he recognised that the imagination had greatest scope and opened up to both reader and writer an area of knowledge beyond the limits of the familiar world. Although his life took a different course after his departure from Trinidad in 1932, James never lost his perspective on life as a novelist nor his sense of the strangeness of human experience.

II. BRITAIN: 1932-1938

James sailed to England at the age of 31 with the intention of becoming a novelist. It was a journey many undertook from the colonies. Some sought education abroad, particularly entry into the professions of law and medicine; others were simply hungry for the experiences of a bigger world than the one which circumscribed the familiar society of their youth. For James, an educated black man, the move to England was critical if he was to realise his literary ambitions. He was already a published author. Furthermore he was mature, and confident that his early life in the Caribbean had equipped him with the essential outlook and skills to make his way in the metropolis.

The developed sense James had of himself was conveyed in the first pieces he wrote after his arrival in England—nowhere more strikingly than in the account of the Edith Sitwell meeting he attended in Bloomsbury. Here James again reminded his readers in the Caribbean of his talent as a novelist; but it is much more than that. James, with his fine characterisation, sense of drama and sly wit, set the scene for the encounter between the doyenne of English literary life and the colonial, newly arrived from an island which most of the English had difficulty in locating. As James often remarked, the people he met were generally astonished by his command of the language (adding, usually with a wry grin, that it would have been more astonishing if he hadn't mastered it); but it was his comprehensive and detailed knowledge of European civilization, its art, history, literature and music, which caught the intellectuals, not least Miss Sitwell, by surprise.

The substance of James's exchange with Edith Sitwell, the question of poetic form, offers a glimpse of the early ideas about creativity and technique which James continued to develop over many years. His comments here suggested that he was generally hostile to the innovations of the modern school, particularly given the prominence of form over "genuine poetic fire"; but he worked much more intensively at this relationship, particularly its historical dimensions, within the broader context of his engagement with revolutionary politics. Ironically, though, the commitment James made to a political career meant that he never acknowledged publicly, until much later, the central place of this project in his life's work.

James spent a good deal of his first year in England living in Nelson, Lancashire with his Trinidadian friend, the cricketer, Learie Constantine. Working closely together on Constantine's memoirs, their friendship deepened and they forged a strong political bond around the issue of independence for the West Indies. James's document on this question, much of it drafted before he left Trinidad, was first published with Constantine's help by a small Nelson firm. Later, an abridged form appeared in Leonard Woolf's pamphlet series as *The Case for West Indian Self-Government* (1933).

James's examination of the colonial question had initially focused upon a prominent local figure, Captain Cipriani, whose career he analysed as reflective of more general movements among the people of the Caribbean. The shortened version, however, was not biographical, but concise and factual. It outlined conditions in Trinidad—the population, the social divisions, the form of government—for an audience whose knowledge was severely limited; and yet in its quiet, satirical tone, it was profoundly subversive. James's sharp observations of the cringing hypocrisy and mediocrity among those holding position in colonial society was strongly reminiscent of the style of his favourite novelists, Thackeray and Bennett. This was not surprising, given that his essay, *The Case for West Indian Self-Government,* was rooted in the early phase of James's life; thereafter, his approach to the colonial question was transformed (shown clearly in his polemical piece, *Abyssinia and the Imperialists)* as he became swept up in the political turmoil of pre-war Europe.

The impression James made in English literary circles had, from the beginning, been promising. His job as a cricket reporter on the *Manchester Guardian* increased his public profile, helping him, at first, to publicise the case for West Indian independence; but soon James was swimming in much stronger political currents. His experience of living in Lancashire had exposed him to the industrial militancy of working people. It was also during this time that James began to study seriously the writings of Marx, Engels, Lenin and Trotsky; and the response of his Nelson friends to his developing political ideas acted as a useful reminder of the deeply rooted radicalism in the lives of ordinary men and women. He was made aware, too, of the constant conflict between their pragmatic political sense and developed perspective on the world and the positions taken by their so-called leaders. This division marked James deeply, establishing a creative tension in his own political work for the rest of his life.

James's move to London in 1933 marked the beginning of his career as a leading figure in the Trotskyist movement. His approach to the questions of revolutionary politics acquired a distinctive stamp through his attempt to integrate the struggles of the colonial areas into the European revolutionary tradition. The Ethiopian crisis of 1936 was a turning point, as James was forced to confront the equivocation of the British labour movement in the face of imperialist aggression in Africa. His essay, *Abyssinia and the Imperialists* (1936), was an early acknowledgement of the importance of an independent movement of Africans and people of African descent in the struggle for freedom. It was a position James developed more fully during the second half of the 1930s, particularly through his close collaboration with George Padmore in the International African Service Bureau. But James also drew upon his extensive historical research into the 1791 San Domingo revolution.

The slave revolution led by Toussaint L'Ouverture raised very concretely the question James was seeking to address in his revolutionary politics—not just the nature and course of revolution itself, the changing relationship between leaders and the people; but the dynamic of the struggles situated at the peripheries and those located in the centre. It was a question which turned up in different forms throughout James's career—at times it was posed as the relationship between the proletariat of the imperialist nations and the indigenous populations; at others, as the connection between the struggles of different sections of a single national population.

Since James's arrival in England, he had been actively working on a book about the San Domingo revolution. In 1936 he decided to produce a play, *Toussaint L'Ouverture*, from his drafted manuscript, casting Paul Robeson in the title role. It was a magnificent part for Robeson, given the severe limits he found as a black man seeking dramatic roles; but there were other political considerations which lay behind James's decision to stage the play at London's Westminster Theatre. It was planned as an intervention in the debates surrounding the Ethiopian crisis.

James presented to his audience a virtually forgotten example from the past—of slaves, uneducated and yet organised by the mechanism of plantation production itself, who, in the wake of the French revolution, rose against their masters and succeeded not only in winning their freedom; but, in going on to defeat the might of three colonial powers, secured their victory through independence. At the centre of this outstanding struggle in revolutionary history was the figure of Toussaint L'Ouverture. He was the natural focus for a dramatic account of these tumultuous events; and James's play focused upon his rise and fall as leader of the slaves.

Drama was a form for which James had a particular feel. His lifelong interest in Shakespeare was based on the dramatic quality of the work; and James recognised that theatre provided the arena in which to explore "political" ideas as refracted through human character. It was through the juxtaposition of personality and events that James sought to highlight some of the broader historical and political themes raised by the San Domingo revolution. He hoped to make his audience aware that the colonial populations were not dependent upon leadership from Europe in their struggle for freedom, that they already had a revolutionary tradition of their own; and, as James later made explicit, he wrote his study of the 1791 slave revolution with the coming upheavals of Africa in mind.

The story of Toussaint involved his clash with other remarkable figures of the time, Napoleon, Dessalines, Henri Christophe; but it was equally formed by his relationship with the largely anonymous mass of black slaves. James acknowledged their centrality in the opening of the play. The disappearance of the slaves, however, and James's increasing focus on personalities gradually undermined the vitality and drama of the work. This was something which James, aware of his limitations as a dramatist, was the first to admit; but in many ways, too, it was no accident, for it reflected his particular interpretation of Toussaint's failure as a revolutionary leader.[1]

James remained firmly convinced of the effectiveness of drama as a medium for exploring what he considered to be the key political questions—the relationship between individual and society, the personality in history. Later, in 1944 when he was planning to write a second play based on the life of Harriet Tubman, he recognised the difficulties inherent in such a project:

> The play will represent a conflict between slaves and slave-owners, an exemplification of the age-old conflict between the oppressed and oppressors. It will, therefore, be of exceptional interest in the world of today and particularly of tomorrow. . . . Now the trouble with all such plays written by both amateurs (99%) and talented playwrights (1%) is that either they know the history and the politics, etc., and write a political tract or they write something full of stage-craft, but with no understanding of history and of politics. Politics is a profession. Only people who know about politics can write about it. Politics is made by people, people who live for politics, but who hate, love, are ambitious, mean, noble, jealous, kind, cruel. And all these human passions affect their politics. . . . That is true but that is the appearance. But the essence of the thing is different. Political and social forces change the circumstances in which people live. . . . Now the job is to translate the

economic and political forces into living human beings, so that one gets interested in them for what they are as people. If that is not done, then you will have perhaps a good history, good politics, but a bad play.[2]

James wrote both the play, *Toussaint L'Ouverture*, and his book, *The Black Jacobins* (1938), while he was an active member of the Trotskyist movement. His analysis was deeply marked by his particular political allegiance, though a number of the ideas central to his interpretation of the 1791 slave revolution raised, implicitly, a challenge to certain assumptions which were commonplace on the revolutionary Left. First of all, he cast doubt on the assumption that the revolution would take place first in Europe, in the advanced capitalist countries, and that this would act as a model and a catalyst for the later upheavals in the underdeveloped world. Secondly, there were clear indications that the lack of specially-trained leaders, a vanguard, did not hold back the movement of the San Domingo revolution. These differences were exacerbated by James's study of the Communist International, *World Revolution* (1937).

The problem James, and many others, faced in the 1930s was to define their position as revolutionary Marxists opposed to the Stalinism of Moscow and its British wing, the Communist Party. Trotsky, one of the great figures of the Russian revolution but persecuted and forced into exile after Lenin's premature death, became the focus for this opposition; though what he symbolised, in the struggle against Stalin, was often more important to people like James than their commitment to Trotskyism as such.

Europe's political landscape had been transformed by the Russian revolution. The question of the nature of the Soviet Union dominated debate among intellectuals and activists as the world drew closer to another war, raising again the spectre of revolution in its aftermath. For James and his associates, grouped in small factions operating independently of (and often in opposition to) the organised labour movement, it was imperative to document Stalin's betrayal of the fundamental revolutionary principles upon which the Soviet Union had been founded. *World Revolution* was such an attempt. James relied largely on secondary sources, gathered from across Europe, to build a devastating case. At the core of his interpretation lay Stalin's 1924 pronouncement, "Socialism in One Country"; for at a stroke the international character of the revolutionary movement was undermined and the fate of the fragile new Workers' State was severed from the organisation of the socialist revolution in other parts of the world. The consequences were far-reaching; not just in the barbarities Stalin perpetrated domestically, but also in his suppression, through the Third International, of the workers' movements in France, Germany and Spain.

The method which underlay James's analysis of the Soviet Union and the history of the Communist International was characteristic. He attempted to expose the dialectical interplay between the key personalities, Lenin, Trotsky and Stalin, and the much greater historical and political forces at work in this critical period. These moments of transition, the crisis in government as the old order gave way to something new, became a recurrent theme in James's work—from *World Revolution* and *The Black Jacobins* to his approach, especially during the latter part of his life, to colonial independence and his understanding of Shakespeare.

Although James provided a book badly needed by those on the Left who were opposed to Stalinism, *World Revolution* hinted at serious differences between the author's interpretation of recent historical events and the position of Trotsky. As James stated rather baldly in his analysis of Stalin's rise to power: "What is important is not that Trotsky was beaten, but that he was beaten so quickly." He had put his finger on an issue which later became decisive—the question of the bureaucracy; but there were other unresolved problems. Despite the vigorous discussion in Mexico in 1939 between James and Trotsky on a number of the issues raised by *World Revolution*, James had already begun to chart a new course in the interpretation of the method and ideas of revolutionary Marxism.[3]

At a time when Stalinism was pervasive among the British intelligentsia, James was often reminded that it was his Trotskyist politics which stood in the way of a promising career as a writer, historian and critic. But by 1938 James had moved a long way from his early ambitions. Europe, in turn, now confined his extraordinary energies and intellectual range. He seized the chance to visit the United States; and the conditions of the New World inspired his greatest and most original work.

III. AMERICA AND AFTER: 1938-1956

The purpose of James's trip to America was to address audiences on the political situation in Europe as war approached; and to be a major contributor to the work of the Trotskyist movement on the black question. These topics formed the basis of the nationwide speaking tour which James embarked upon shortly after his arrival in November 1938. It was towards the end of his exhausting schedule, at a meeting in Los Angeles, that James first met Constance Webb. Almost immediately he began his correspondence with her. The first letters from Mexico—evocative, witty and brimming with lively observations of character—were a vivid reminder of James's early aspirations as a novelist; the later exchanges, beginning in 1943, were more intense, indeed passionate, as James sought to break free from the confines of his European background. Something powerful had been unlocked by his experience of America. He sought to articulate it through his exchanges with Constance; and the exploration of the differences between them in background, race, gender and age became a creative force behind their remarkable relationship.

James's correspondence, beginning in 1939 and continuing for over a decade, constitutes a profound meditation on human life. The synthesis he was seeking, the full and free integration of his own personality within the context of his love for a woman, he recognised as a general need among people in the modern world. Consciously employing the dialectical method, James examined the relationship between chance and necessity within his own life. But his letters showed, too, how far he could extend his analysis, from the very personal details of self-discovery to some of the most fundamental questions concerning the future of humanity. At the centre, however, was Constance, the young American woman, who grasped instinctively the connections between those facets of human experience which he had to work hard to bring into an active relationship.

The question of human creativity, the central theme of the letters, not only enabled James to make a direct connection with Constance Webb, particularly through his encouragement of her writing of poetry; but, at the same time, it took him to the heart of the civilization process itself. The developed historical perspective which James brought to bear on the understanding of this process led him to highlight what was distinctive in Constance's creative work. He recognised it as the expression of the experiences of a twentieth century American woman. He saw Constance as a product of the most conscious age in human history; growing up with material advantages unknown to her European counterparts and taking for granted, as the property of everyone, some of the most advanced political ideas known to mankind. Her poetry reflected this. But it also, inescapably at its core, gave expression to the conflict which raged through modern society, nowhere more intensely than in America—the conflict between her highly developed sense of her own unique personality and the form of society which dissipated or stifled all creative energy.

These exchanges with Constance Webb, during the 1940s, cannot be considered apart from the very ambitious project—to understand American society on its own terms—which James had set himself soon after his arrival in the United States. His approach was to see America as a civilization in its own right. But he saw, too, that it contained within its essential features the key to the future of civilization as a whole. For almost a decade James pursued this project privately, while being deeply immersed in more conventional political work which arose through his involvement in the Trotskyist movement. These two areas of his life were kept separate, indeed they often appeared to be in conflict; but the connections between them were profound and released, in James, an explosion of intellectual creativity.

The doubts concerning Trotsky's method and analysis which James had begun to articulate in his work on history were thrown into sharp relief by the crisis posed to the revolutionary movement by the signing, in 1940, of the Hitler-Stalin pact. This raised again—now with great political urgency—the question of the nature of the Soviet Union and whether it could still be defended as a revolutionary society, albeit one with serious flaws. James was plunged into what he later described as "one of the most extreme and difficult crises of my political life."[4]

In order to clarify his position, James embarked on a serious study of the Russian revolution and the development of the Workers' State. Quickly, though, he found himself drawn deeply into questions of philosophy and method, for, as he recognised, "it was not a question of what Russia was, although that was a subordinate question. It was a question of what was the type of Marxism which led to one conclusion and the type of Marxism which led to the other."[5]

Much of James's work was carried out with a small handful of collaborators in a group which became known as the Johnson Forest Tendency. Two of his closest associates were women—Grace Lee, a philosophy Ph.D. and Raya Dunayevskaya, Trotsky's former secretary whose expertise was the Soviet Union.[6] Between them they pooled their different linguistic skills and intellectual training to undertake a comprehensive study of modern history and the dialectic.

In one of his letters to Constance Webb, James gave a valuable picture of their collective working method:

We are at Rae's (Raya Dunayevskaya). Grace, Rae, I and another friend. We have just worked out the basis for the defence of Germany—pointing out its great contribution to civilization in the past and the necessity of its incorporation into the Europe of today—a serious contribution—the only contribution I fear that will be made to any serious understanding of the problem of Germany. It is going to be fine. As we talked I felt very very pleased. One person writes but in the world in which we live all serious contributions have to be collective; the unification of all phases of life make it impossible for a single mind to grasp it in all its aspects. Although one mind may unify, the contributory material and ideas must come from all sources and types of mind. . . . The best mind is the one so basically sound in analytical approach and capacity to absorb, imagination to fuse, that he makes a totality of all these diverse streams.[7]

Towards the end of the 1940s the members of the Johnson Forest Tendency began to publish the results of their intense collaborative exercise. The lengthy essay, *Dialectical Materialism and the Fate of Humanity* (1947) was James's attempt to sort out some of the muddles in Trotskyist thinking—in particular the problem of thought and its relationship to the dynamic of history. He was seeking to clarify the dialectical method—the process by which, what Hegel called "the abstract universal" becomes concrete; and to demonstrate, through its use as a methodological tool, the progressive movement of society. It is one of the very few places, too, that James offered a definition of socialism—the complete expression of democracy—mindful as he always was of its distortion through identification with Stalinism.

This article preceded the much more detailed discussion of method in the documents James wrote from Nevada *(Notes on Dialectics*, 1948). Nevertheless, it covers much of the same ground and its essay form makes more accessible some of the ideas which were critical in James's definition of a new and independent Marxist position.

With tremendous verve and historical sweep, James sets out to trace the development of mankind—the objectification of the subject, the search for completeness, integration, universality. At the centre of his analysis stood the Russian revolution, for it opened a window on this process. It represented an advanced stage in this historical movement; and yet it was still imperfect, not fully realised. Indeed, as James's dialectical method exposed, its very imperfections called forth a response which in its negativity matched the concrete achievements of October 1917:

It is the creative power, the democratic desires, the expansion of the human personality, the record of human achievement that was the Russian revolution. It is these which have called forth the violence, the atrocities, the state organised as Murder Incorporated. Only such violence could have repressed democracy.

For James, however, Stalinist Russia expressed in the most extreme form the contradictions which ran throughout modern society, as the increasing power and self-knowledge of ordinary people came up against enhanced powers of rule from above in the form of bureaucratic structures.

James was aware of these tensions all around him in the United States. It was to be seen nowhere more clearly than in the contradictory position of blacks, their integration and segregation, within American society.

James's work on history and the dialectic thus cannot be separated from his more active engagement with contemporary political questions within the United States. It was difficult, however, for him to play a prominent part in the Johnson Forest Tendency's organisational work, for he had overstayed the limit on his US visa and, after 1940, was forced to operate largely underground. But James continued to write on the race question, developing his understanding of the revolutionary history of America's black population and establishing the independence and vitality of the struggle for basic democratic rights. Not only did James understand the immense political significance of these struggles for America as a whole, for its black communities exposed some of its deepest and most intense contradictions; but he saw too that America's blacks provided the link with the millions of colonial peoples worldwide, struggling to throw off the shackles of imperialist rule. James's statement to the Trotskyist movement, *The Revolutionary Answer to the Negro Problem in the USA* (1948) revealed the clarity with which he understood the political questions it posed; but, at the same time, his interpretation presented to the orthodox Left some of the same difficulties as his earlier work on the San Domingo slave uprising. It was, and remains, a remarkably prescient document.

What James's theoretical and activist work taught him above all was the speed of historical movement. The problem became one of thought. Following Hegel, James contrasted the operation of dialectical thinking, creative reason, with the static categories of understanding which he identified as the fundamental flaw in the Trotskyist method itself. For James, it was revealed most clearly in Trotsky's approach to the nature of the Soviet Union.

The Class Struggle (1950) was an important statement on this question. In putting forward the theory of state capitalism, James and his associates in the Johnson Forest Tendency offered a set of conceptual tools inseparable from the dynamic of historical development, that is, one which matched the development of capitalism itself. In contrast, they concluded that Trotsky and his followers, trapped within the sterile Stalin-Trotsky debate, had separated their understanding of the Soviet Union from the more general movement of modern history, failing thereby to root the analysis of bureaucracy in an understanding of the stage capitalism had reached worldwide.

According to James, the contradictions of the Workers' State were still to be found in the process of production. Nationalisation had transferred the struggle between capital and labour to the level of the state, a characteristic of advanced capitalist systems everywhere, including the United States. In the case of the Soviet Union, however, the Party had become fused with the state.

Having reached this position, James and his associates broke with the notion of the Party as the revolutionary vanguard. The logical development of their analysis was to see that the next decisive stage in history would be the overthrow of the Party itself, the emergence of the people against the structures of bureaucratic rule.

Cumulatively then the philosophical and political conclusions which James reached during his American years made his severance from the Trotskyist movement inevitable. Through his work on history and the dialectic and his engagement with pressing political questions in the United States, particularly the black question, James had identified serious problems in Trotskyist ideas and method. Furthermore he had defined a new position with respect to the nature of the Soviet Union and the role of the vanguard party.

James's commitment to revolutionary Marxism, however, remained unshakeable. He recognised, though, that the tradition in the twentieth century had become distorted and obscured through the bitter struggle between Trotsky and Stalin; and in establishing the foundations of his new, independent Marxist position, James traced his ideas directly from the work of Lenin.

James's fifteen-year stay in the United States is widely acknowledged to have produced his most important work. He often said so himself. Undoubtedly, the documents he wrote as a member of the Johnson Forest Tendency constitute a major contribution to the theory and practice of Marxism, extending the tradition to incorporate the distinctive features of the world in which James lived. But they represent more than this. They made possible the original work which came in the following years.

The year 1950 was a watershed for James. He felt palpably his freedom from the narrow questions of revolutionary politics which had, for so many years, absorbed his energies. At the same time his intellectual confidence was secure, rooted as it was in his mastery of the philosophical foundations of his Marxist perspective. It was reflected in the breadth and urgency of James's later writings; and in his exploration of new questions—questions of art, culture and aesthetics. Although in some ways he was returning to the themes of his early years, his approach was deeply marked by the new and original conception of political life which he had developed by the end of his stay in the United States. It had been shaped decisively by the conditions of the New World. At the centre of this vision was his recognition of the creative energies of ordinary men and women and their critical place in modern history as the force for humanity. If the conventional political work James had carried out in the Johnson Forest Tendency had brought him to this point, it was, above all, his *experience* of living in America which changed and moulded his mature perspective on the world.

What James had discovered in the New World was that the question he considered to lie at the heart of the civilization process itself—the relationship between individual freedom and social life—was most starkly posed. He understood the movement of the modern world to be one of increasing integration. The growing interconnectedness of things through the expansion of communications, the centralisation of capital, the accumulation of knowledge, the breakdown of national boundaries, was mirrored, in his view, by the increasing sophistication and awareness of the human subject. But never before had the individual personality been so fragmented and restricted in the realisation of its creative capacities. James uncovered in America an intense desire among people to bring the separate facets of human experience into an active relationship, to express their full and free individuality within new and expanded conceptions of social life. This was "the struggle for happiness."

James was conscious of the struggle within his own life, for he, too, was seeking integration. It found striking expression in the handwritten note to Constance

Webb which James attached to the back of his essay, *Dialectical Materialism and the Fate of Humanity*. He wrote:

This is the man who loves you. I took up dialectic five years ago. I knew a lot of things before and I was able to master it. I know a lot of things about loving you. I am only just beginning to apply them. I can master that with the greatest rapidity—just give me a hand. I feel all sorts of new powers, freedoms etc. surging in me. You released so many of my constrictions. . . . We will live. This is our new world—where there is no distinction between political and personal any more.

Unfortunately for James the distinction was etched deeply in his personality. It had been reinforced over many years by his involvement in the revolutionary movement, particularly by the difficult conditions under which he had carried out his definitive political work while in America.

Through his relationship with Constance Webb, however, James had begun to understand the logic of his life's course—his struggle against the limits of European bourgeois society, his commitment to the revolutionary movement; and his recognition that in its turn this very movement had confined him and separated essential aspects of his being.

By the late 1940s the tensions between his political role in the Johnson Forest Tendency and his personal commitment to a shared life with Constance Webb were almost tearing him apart. He knew that his future work would take him in new directions; and he felt, acutely, the expansion of his creative powers as he made the leap from Europe to America and shook himself free, at last, from the confines of intellectual and political discourse. His work on American civilization was an attempt to give expression to this newly found freedom.[8]

James began to draft his manuscript, *American Civilization* (originally entitled *Notes on American Civilization)* in 1949. Many of the ideas he had already explored in his private correspondence with Constance Webb; but it was his decisive break with the European tradition (what he called "old bourgeois civilization", with its oppositions between art and culture, intellectuals and the people, politics and everyday life) which enabled him to fuse the different elements—history, literature, popular art and detailed observations of daily life—into a dense work of startling originality. James was seeking to grasp the whole at a particular moment in history; and yet, at the same time, the movement of the narrative, the shift from established literary sources to the lives of ordinary men and women, reflected his understanding of the general dynamic of history. In short, he aimed to distill the universal progress of civilization into a specific contrast between the nineteenth and twentieth centuries. The culture of the intellectuals was giving way to the emergence of the people as the animating force of history.

James's work on American civilization thus contained two parts, bridged by a long chapter on the popular arts. The first half of the manuscript was dominated by a critical reading of the work of Whitman and Melville. Just as James himself had broken with the European forms, so too, he believed, had these two nineteenth-century American writers; and he understood the innovative style and substance of their creative work to give expression to the currents of the new democracy. But in exploring the themes which lay at the centre of their writing, particularly the relationship between individual and society, James was seeking to cast light on the crisis facing modern America. It was his contention that its essential features were anticipated in the work of Whitman and Melville.

Both writers had been witness to the beginning of the modern phase in America's history marked by the Civil War. The old frontier spirit of the early settlers had given way to the new individualism of the captains of industry; and the steady appropriation of the ethos of freedom in the name of market expansion had gone hand in hand with the subjection of the mass of workers to an oppressive economic and social structure. It was here that James located the creative work of Whitman and Melville, observing: "The greatest writers seem to be those who come at the climax of one age, but this is because the new age has grown up inside the old and they are watching both."

The reading James offered of Whitman's poetry highlighted its celebration of individuality. But at the same time James uncovered, too, the intense desire of "this singer of loneliness" for social connection. He argued that if Whitman failed to resolve the contradiction between individual and society in the themes and substance of his poetry, his development of a new form, free verse ("a chant to be sung by millions of men") became the link with his community of fellow Americans.

According to James, Melville from the beginning placed his characters within a social setting. He recognised that the individualism Whitman celebrated, in its extreme forms, threatened to bring about the destruction of society itself. James drew attention to Melville's originality as an artist in his creation of the character Ahab: "Such characters come once in many centuries and are as rare as men who found new religions, philosophers who revolutionize human thinking, and statesmen who create new political forms."[9] This new departure mirrored, for James, Whitman's formal poetic innovation, as both writers, sensitive to the dynamics of a changing world and seeking to give expression to its essential movement, found themselves pushed to the limits of their creative imagination.

But, in arguing for the contemporary significance of Whitman and Melville, the insight they offered into the postwar world, James took great care to stress that they were not writers of "political treatises." His interest was in their distinctive artistic personality. Furthermore, he was attempting to develop a method of criticism which would enable him to expose, through an analysis of creative work itself, hidden currents at work in society and history.

James took this approach further in his book on American civilization. He placed a discussion of the popular arts—soap operas, Hollywood films, detective novels—at the centre of his understanding of modern society; and he used it as the bridge into the lives of the American people. Previously, the presence of ordinary men and women had been glimpsed only through the filter of the intellectual tradition; now, he argued, in the area of popular culture their creative role in the civilization process was for the first time fully revealed.

In a long, passionately argued letter to Bell, James illuminates the ideas and method he was seeking to develop in his work on America. Central was his broad conception of artistic work, his refusal to separate modern popular forms from "high art." James was now tackling the question he had already explored in his correspondence with Constance Webb and which he believed to be critical in the development of humanity, namely the relationship between creativity and democracy.

Conscious of the disdain of the European intellectuals for American culture, James argued for the recognition of America's distinctive contribution to the understanding of civilization. It was his view that American society represented a new stage, its people highly developed and conscious of themselves as never before in history but confronting, in every part of their lives, from the workplace to the most intimate personal relations, the oppressive weight of society. For James the popular arts were something new. They were the expression of what was unique about America in the movement of world society as a whole. He believed that only the mass art forms could encompass all the complexities of modern life, anticipating a future in which art and life were in a close, active, and evolving relationship. They were the powerful symbol of both the triumph and the crisis of the modern world, for they revealed the enormous creative potential inherent in modern society at the same time as they laid bare the tremendous conflicts raging at the core of social life.

James's letter to Bell was part of a series of exchanges he initiated at the same time with other critics. These documents form an integral part of the ambitious project on which he was now embarked. Its first full articulation was *American Civilization.*

The unifying theme which ran throughout the 1950 manuscript, pulling together the disparate parts, was the opposition between democracy and totalitarianism. James was acutely conscious of the particular historical moment which was moulding the next phase of his work. Against the backdrop of the Cold War, as the superpowers faced each other across a ruined Europe and the rhetoric of individual freedom versus state repression reflected the bitter struggle being waged within America itself, James planned a series of books. His concern was no less than the conditions of survival of civilization itself. In a narrow, personal sense, too, James was acutely conscious of the critical moment in his own life as he fought to avoid deportation from the United States.

The integrated vision which inspired his extraordinary manuscript on America emerged then from James's profound grasp of his own sense of history. It was an experience he felt to his core. But the creative synthesis he achieved and expressed in *American Civilization* was tragically short-lived, for the battle raging within James, between his life as a revolutionary in a small political organisation and his need for a fully integrated life, was one he eventually lost. His marriage to Constance Webb foundered and his fight to avoid deportation pulled him back into the old forms of political life.[10]

James's understanding of Melville lay at the centre of his work on America. James's 1950 text as a whole, both in its vision of humanity and in its method, was strongly reminiscent of Melville's finest novel, *Moby Dick*.[11] Later James made his debt to Melville more explicit. He turned his drafted chapter on the nineteenth-century writers into a full-length critical study of *Moby Dick*; and the book, *Mariners, Renegades and Castaways* (1953), became the basis of James's political campaign to avoid deportation from the United States.

In focusing upon one part of his much more comprehensive study of civilization, James hoped to develop his ideas about the creative process in society and history through debate with a number of American and European critics. The passionate tone and sweep of the letters which he wrote during 1953 to Bell, Leyda and Schapiro reveal the scope and urgency of the project beginning to unfold. These early exchanges also establish the elements of James's distinctive approach to questions of art and aesthetics; specifically his acknowledgement of the role of the audience in creative work, his adaptation of Melville's theory of original characters in great literature, and his careful excavations of the process by which life is transmuted into art.

The subjects James raised with literary critics ranged from comic strips to Aeschylus; and yet it is important to recognise that they are located within a single conception of civilization and its evolution.

Two essays written at much the same time, *Notes on Hamlet* (1953) and *Popular Art and the Cultural Tradition* (1954) define more clearly the broad historical contours within which James situated explosions of artistic creativity. For him, the development of the character Hamlet heralded the birth of the modern age—the freedom of the individual, the brilliant entry into history of the Cartesian subject ("I think therefore I am"). The work of the twentieth century filmmakers, however, marked a new stage. The innovative form and substance of film revealed to James what was distinctive about the twentieth century.

James argued that by developing a new form, a mass art form, Griffith, Chaplin and Eisenstein were posing anew the relationship between individual and society. In his view their work, with its panoramic scope and close-up focus, reflected more generally the dialectical movement of the contemporary world. At its centre was the presence of ordinary men and women and their need to express the uniqueness of their individual personalities within the expanded context of world society.

The critical figure in this historical shift from the old world to the new, from Europe to America, from the isolated, fragmented subjects of Proust or Picasso to the power and presence of humanity itself as the creative force in civilization, was Melville. In James's understanding Melville's work formed the bridge. It was part of a tradition which stretched backwards into history ; and yet, for James, Melville was the artist whose work looked to the future.[12] *Moby Dick* with its fusion of nature and society, individual and community, the particular and the universal, was filmic. The broad canvas (the panoramic scope) against which Melville situated individual character (the human personality in close-up) anticipated the creative developments of the twentieth century arts—particularly film.

But Melville's artistic prescience was not accidental. In developing the theory of the original character (". . . a type of human being that had never existed before in the world . . . the character itself becomes a kind of revolving light illuminating what is around it. Everything else grows and develops to correspond to this central figure so that the original character, so to speak, helps the artist create a portrait not only of a new type of human being but also of society and the people who correspond to him"), James was seeking to explore the connections between artistic creativity and moments of fundamental change in society.[13] This became clarified as the relationship between the expansion of democracy (which resulted in new conceptions of the human personality and social life) and creative innovation (which refracted and gave expression to these hidden currents in human history).

Melville's depiction, in *Moby Dick*, of the ship's crew as the symbol of humanity against the destructive power of Ahab and the vacillation of Ishmael, heralded the appearance in the twentieth century of ordinary people as the force for civilization. James exposed the historical antecedents. They were to be found in the work of Shakespeare.

Like Whitman and Melville, Shakespeare wrote at a critical moment in history, as one era gave way to another. It was caught both in the form and substance of his work. For James *King Lear* held the key, being the dramatic culmination of Shakespeare's exploration of the question of government through the history plays and tragedies. Critical was the appearance of a new character, Edgar/Poor Tom—"Edgar, by his origins, by his experiences as Poor Tom and the various crises through which Shakespeare puts him, emerges as the embodiment of a man *not born but shaped by a society out of joint*, to be able to set it right."[14]

It was characteristic of James that, as a prelude to offering his particular interpretation of Shakespeare, he outlined the foundations of his method. This involved taking a position vigorously opposed to the conventional tradition of literary criticism. James began to make explicit the principles which governed his approach in the opening pages of a document known as *Preface to Criticism* (1955). He anchored his critical method in Aristotle's *Poetics*. He took as his point of departure the dramatic quality of Shakespeare's work and made central an understanding of the performance itself, the role of the audience and the development of character and plot. It is not hard to identify here the emergent form of the project which later became *Beyond A Boundary*.

The interpretation of *King Lear* James offered in the later pages of *Preface to Criticism*, and his belief in its central importance as a political play, clarified over the subsequent three decades. In particular, decolonisation and its aftermath threw questions of government, at the heart of *King Lear*, into ever more sharp relief.

IV. THE AFRICAN DIASPORA: 1957-1989

The Gold Coast revolution stood at the centre of the work James carried out during the second part of his life. The issues raised by this landmark in modern history drew him back into active involvement with the Pan-African movement; and, as both his private correspondence and public writings revealed, James was interested in exploring the dynamic connections between different aspects of the black diaspora in order to establish the presence of Africa at the centre of the emerging postwar order. James's letter (to Friends) of March 1957 represents a particularly fine example of his integrated perspective.

Despite the focus provided by the events of decolonisation, it is important, however, not to lose sight of the broader dialectical pattern which marked this phase in James's life—the creative links between his engagement with specific political moments and the much bigger intellectual project he was pursuing concerning the development of democracy in world history. There was constant movement between the two, between the particular and the universal; and, at certain times, James achieved a remarkable original synthesis within his own writing.

The letters on politics which James wrote to his associates in the years following his departure from America focused upon contemporary trends in eastern Europe (specifically the Hungarian revolution), Africa, the Caribbean and the United States. These upheavals raised to prominence the power and presence of ordinary people in the struggle for civilization. Challenging both oppressive political structures and the conventional forms of leadership and organisation, the events of the late 1950s were for James the concrete manifestation of social currents he had anticipated in work carried out a decade earlier. But as these letters show, James also saw their profound connection. Not only did these upheavals underline the general power of ordinary men and women to intervene critically in historical events. They also marked something new and specific—the appearance of black and colonial peoples as a decisive force in the shaping of modern society.

James returned to the Caribbean in 1958 after an absence of twenty-six years. He was highly sensitive to the significance of the historical moment. He saw the approach of independence as a time when fundamental questions concerning government, society and the individual were unusually clarified. Moreover he held that independence offered the populations of the colonial territories a unique opportunity to chart their future, weaving elements from their particular past with broader currents animating the modern world. James raised these issues in his public speeches, writings and journalism during the late 1950s and early 1960s. He was anxious to make the Caribbean people aware that they were indeed at the forefront of the struggle to found the new society—one, James anticipated, which would reflect something fundamental about the movement of world society as a whole.

Three articles James wrote while editor of *The Nation* illustrate these themes and have remarkable unity. First of all, in an important essay on Abraham Lincoln, James raised the most general question posed by independence—the question of democracy. His discussion drew upon his own break with the European tradition and his commitment to the society emergent in the New World. It was here that he saw the future of the Caribbean. Just as Lincoln, responding to a particular moment in history, extended and deepened the conception of democracy, so too, according to James, the Caribbean peoples at independence would emerge as a dynamic force—extending further in the twentieth century the theory and practice of democracy. James left no doubt about his recognition of the power, creativity and capacity for self-organisation among ordinary people. This was the theme of his later article on Carnival. But, for James, nothing gave more concrete focus to this dialectical interplay in modern history than the distinguished career of George Padmore.

Over a period of several months, beginning in late 1959, James published in *The Nation* extracts from his drafted biography of Padmore. What was interesting about Padmore's career was that it encompassed both the early struggles for freedom and democracy by colonial peoples which drew heavily on the European revolutionary movement; and the new, later, phase which was initiated by Nkrumah. The revolution in Ghana established Africa as the creative source for political resistance worldwide. It transformed at a stroke all previously held conceptions of revolutionary praxis. According to James, the work of Padmore, a

West Indian, had been critical in this fundamental shift.

This theme, the relationship between the colonies and the metropolis, James took up again later, exploring it more fully in an appendix to the new edition of his classic work, *The Black Jacobins*. He recognised that questions of nationhood and national identity were at the heart of independence politics; but he had no time for the narrow, small-island mentality of the new Caribbean leaders. Indeed his challenge to them was explicit in the very title of his 1962 appendix, *From Toussaint L'Ouverture to Fidel Castro*.

James's view of the Caribbean was built upon a recognition of its distinctive past, its rich and diverse cultural traditions, its modern peoples; but, above all, he was fascinated by its peculiar place in the evolution of modern society. In *The Black Jacobins* he interpreted the plantation slaves to be among the first proletarians, working with industrial technology in the most advanced sector of Europe's international economy. James believed that Caribbean society two hundred years ago had revealed the critical elements of a world system still in the early stages of its evolution. He understood the island societies at independence to be similarly placed. This lay behind his passionate advocacy of a West Indian federation.

For James, federation became the collective symbol of the search for a new conception of nationhood appropriate to the world of the late twentieth century. At its core was the need to create something new from existing forms. But as he revealed in the conclusion to his appendix, this historical process was also refracted through the creative imagination and found concrete expression in the literary innovations of the Caribbean novelists. James's discussion of the work of Césaire, Naipaul, Lamming and Harris neglects, however, to mention his own highly original work, *Beyond A Boundary*. It was published in 1963, the year following Trinidadian independence.

Beyond A Boundary completed the search for integration which James had begun in the Caribbean some sixty years before. As a boy he had grasped intuitively the interconnectedness of human experience; through political work in Europe's revolutionary movement he developed a consistent method for approaching the complexity of the modern world; but it was his experience of America which enabled him to realise fully his integrated vision of humanity. Thus, it is almost impossible to think of *Beyond A Boundary* apart from his great, unpublished manuscript on American civilization. In both works James achieved an extraordinary creative synthesis, a fusion of the universal movement of world history with a particular moment in contemporary society.

What James gave expression to in this book has to be understood as an extension of the tradition he had already established in his critical work on Shakespeare and Melville. If, according to James, Shakespeare heralded the birth of the individual personality and modern democracy in the creation of the character Hamlet and more fully developed it in *King Lear* (Edgar); if Melville recognised the danger posed by unbridled individualism and set against it the humanity of the crew; if Griffith, Eisenstein and Chaplin founded their creativity in the lives of ordinary men and women; then *Beyond A Boundary* represented the next stage. It broke the existing categories which fragmented the aesthetic experience. Its originality as a study of the game of cricket—and yet *Beyond A Boundary* was neither a cricket book nor an autobiography—symbolised a new and expanded conception of humanity as the black and formerly colonial peoples burst onto the stage of world history.

In the ten years since James's departure from the United States he had been preoccupied with this central question—the relationship between democracy and creativity. It was rooted in his revolutionary Marxism. But James was now charting new areas—he was seeking to clarify some of his general ideas through the detailed examination of artistic explosions within history. He believed that at those moments in history when existing conceptions of democracy were being broken and expanded through political struggle, there was a release of tremendous creative power. Thus the innovation of artists, such as Shakespeare or Michelangelo, Mozart or Melville, Picasso or Jackson Pollock, came out of the struggle at these moments to redefine the human personality. In the twentieth century, however, James believed that what the individual artist in history had struggled to achieve was now the struggle of ordinary people everywhere.

Beyond A Boundary was the product of this intense project. James's analysis of the game of cricket highlighted the direction of his general thesis. The core of the book was the chapter, "What is Art?"—James's exploration of the aesthetic experience. Later he intended to expand these ideas in another book built around an interpretation of photographs of cricketers in action. He wished to investigate here the sculptural dimensions of the game. What James had in mind may be guessed from the many notes and jottings he made at the time he began to write *Beyond A Boundary*. These suggest that he was interested in approaching the player in action as a form of public art, where "man is placed in his social environment in terms of artistic form"; and he was concerned to situate him within a historical tradition which began, in James's view, with the shift from sculpture to tragic drama in early Greece. The cricketer was a modern expression of the individual personality pushing against the limits imposed on his full development by society. It was inseparable, for example, from the artistic impulse James interpreted to lie behind the work of the great twentieth century film-maker, D.W. Griffith, and which he described in the following terms: "It was essentially Greek in spirit, (but) concretely modern. He says always—man in society. His films show individuality in *movement* within a social form historically expressed. It is Shakespeare and Aeschylus over again. The same relation."[15]

James transcended the division between high and popular art in *Beyond A Boundary*. This was something he achieved as a result of his stay in America, and it opened the way for him to excavate the aesthetic dimension of human experience as a single, yet multi-layered experience. It was here James established the area of integration, that creative fusion of individual and community, experience and knowledge, art and everyday life. Moreover, he recognised that what was achieved here was unique. It had profound implications for all other aspects of social existence.

In the years which followed the publication of *Beyond A Boundary,* James traveled widely through Africa and the Caribbean. His energies became focused on the problems of the newly-independent countries. His analyses drew heavily on the work of Shakespeare and Lenin; and it is not surprising to find them linked in the opening paragraph of his essay, *Lenin and The Vanguard Party*. If James had made *King Lear* the basis of his understanding of the question of government (and of the sheer brutality which often surrounded the collapse of the old order), he looked to the work of Lenin for an analysis of the problems of revolutionary transition. Throughout the latter part of his life, James claimed to be actively working on two books: one on Shakespeare and the other on Lenin. He failed, however, to complete either study.

Much of James's discussion of the post-colonial order was anchored in his analysis of the Ghana revolution. But his perspective was much broader, for he understood the birth of the new nations as a transformation in world society as a whole. Thus to analyse the rise and fall of Nkrumah was to cast light on the contemporary form of the age-old problem faced by all revolutionary leaders—the problem of government. For James, no one had addressed this more profoundly and concretely than Lenin.

Against the accumulated record of confusion and distortion surrounding Lenin's contribution to revolutionary praxis, James re-stated his simple, yet profound, insight into the phase of revolutionary transition. He depended heavily, particularly in his 1964 essay *Lenin and The Problem*, upon Lenin's last writings. From these he established the two guiding principles: the abolition of the state and the education of the peasantry; but, as James knew all too well, the new leaders of Africa and the Caribbean had both failed to dismantle the colonial state they had inherited at independence and they had distanced themselves from the popular forces mobilised to create the new society. His early article written for a Caribbean readership, *The People of the Gold Coast* (1960), and the later series of essays entitled *The Rise and Fall of Nkrumah* (1966) indicate the shape of his thesis and the development of ideas James had first articulated in *The Black Jacobins*.

James returned to the United States in the late 1960s. He spent more than a decade teaching in various universities and speaking widely on contemporary events. As his speeches on *Black Power* (1967, 1970) and *Black Studies* (1969) reveal, it was impossible for him to approach the political explosion of America's blacks without a developed historical perspective or an understanding of their dynamic connection with other resistance movements worldwide. The world was now one world. Mindful of his own statement on the black question some twenty years before, James recognised the serious threat such a movement posed to the organisation of society as a whole. It was symbolised, above all, in the adoption of the revolutionary slogans of black and Third World movements by people struggling against oppression worldwide. Even in the midst of the 1968 Paris upheavals, the French students drew much of their inspiration from such symbols as Ché Guevara, Mao, Castro or the Black Panthers; and revealed, in a critical sense, that Europe's place as the centre of revolutionary praxis was decisively over.

Despite the speed of events and the urgency of debate during this period, James remained sensitive to the broader question of the relationship between these intense political struggles and forms of creative expression. His essays on *Sobers* (1969), *Picasso and Jackson Pollock* (1980) and *Three Black Women Writers* (1981) provide the evidence of this continuing interest in the question of democracy and creativity. These pieces are also the reminder of James's distinctive method of criticism—that is, his focus first and foremost upon the artistic work itself. James always insisted upon the integrity of the artistic vision, setting out to master its constituent elements before seeking to situate work of the creative imagination in society and history. His portrait of the West Indies cricketer, Garfield Sobers, is a good example of the approach. What was implicit here, however, was the theme of his later essay on modern art.

James interpreted the form and substance of Picasso's work to be a reflection of the crisis in European civilization, the struggle between humanity and barbarism, between creativity and decay. At its centre was the fragmented human subject amidst war, chaos and destruction. And yet, as James emphasised, in his critical appraisal of *Guernica*, Picasso had placed contradictory images in close juxtaposition. To him this suggested that Picasso *as an artist* could not make up his mind about human nature. He recognised at once the capacity for evil and the tremendous creative potential.

For James the first step taken in the artistic resolution to this crisis was by an American painter, Jackson Pollock. Jackson Pollock had started where Picasso finished—with the destruction and fragmentation of the human subject; but within the abstract nature of his work James found the beginnings of reconstruction, the emergence of humanity, of the active, integrated subject.

Later James saw the black women writers (Toni Morrison, Alice Walker, Ntozake Shange) as an integral part, indeed the most advanced manifestation, of this struggle to achieve "an active, integrated humanism" in the modern world. Their work, like Pollock's, came out of the New World. It represented something new, opening a window on the directions in which modern society was moving.

During his last years James often reflected upon his life's course. Although his strength was slowly, almost imperceptibly, slipping away, he could in conversation often startle his visitors with the brilliance of his insight, his grasp of the details of history, the accuracy of his analysis of contemporary events. He remained a revolutionary to the core. As his whole life and work had shown, there was no limit to how far such a philosophy and method could carry him. His vision of humanity, however, was animated by the simple but profound belief in the creative capacities of ordinary men and women. They were the force for civilization.

PART I

TRINIDAD 1901-1932

1

La Divina Pastora

Of my own belief in this story I shall say nothing. What I have done is to put it down as far as possible just as it was told to me, in my own style, but with no addition to or subtraction from the essential facts.

Anita Perez lived with her mother at Bande l'Est Road, just at the corner where North Trace joins the Main Road. She had one earthly aim. She considered it her duty and business to be married as quickly as possible, first because in that retired spot it marked the sweet perfection of a woman's existence, and secondly, because feminine youth and beauty, if they exist, fade early in the hard work on the cocoa plantation. Every morning of the week, Sundays excepted, she banded down her hair, and donned a skirt which reached to her knees, not with any pretensions to fashion, but so that from seven till five she might pick cocoa, or cut cocoa, or dry cocoa, or in some other way assist in the working of Mr Kayle-Smith's cocoa estate. She did this for thirty cents a day, and did it uncomplainingly, because her mother and father had done it before her, and had thriven on it. On Sundays she dressed herself in one of her few dresses, put on a little gold chain, her only ornament, and went to Mass. She had no thought of woman's rights, nor any Ibsenic theories of morality. All she knew was that it was her duty to get married, when, if she was lucky, this hard life in the cocoa would cease.

Every night for the past two years Sebastian Montagnio came down from his four-roomed mansion, half a mile up the trace, and spent an hour, sometimes much more, with the Perez family. Always he sat on a bench by the door, rolling cheap cigarettes and half-hiding himself in smoke. He was not fair to outward view, but yet Anita loved him. Frequently half an hour would elapse without a word from either, she knitting or sewing steadily, Sebastian watching her contentedly and Mrs Perez sitting on the ground just outside the door, smoking one of Sebastian's cigarettes and carrying on a ceaseless monologue in the local patois. Always when Sebastian left, the good woman berated Anita for not being kinder to him. Sebastian owned a few acres of cocoa and a large provision garden, and Mrs Perez had an idea that Anita's marriage would mean relief from the cocoa-work, not only for Anita, but also for her.

Anita herself said nothing. She was not the talking kind. At much expense and trouble, Sebastian sent her a greeting card each Christmas. On them were beautiful words which Anita slept through so often that in time she got to know them by heart. Otherwise nothing passed between the two. That he loved no one else she was sure. It was a great consolation; but did he love her? Or was it only because his home was dull and lonely, and theirs was just at the corner, that he came down every night?

As the months slipped by, Anita anxiously watched her naturally pale face in the little broken mirror. It was haggard and drawn with watching and waiting for Sebastian to speak. She was not young and her manner was not attractive. The gossiping neighbours looked upon her as Sebastian's property. Even in the little cocoa-house dances (Sebastian never went because he did not dance) she was left to herself most of the time. And then, she loved him.

It came about that Anita's aunt, who lived at Siparia, paid her a surprise visit on Sunday. She had not visited North Trace for years, and might never come back again. Consequently there were many things to be talked about. Also the good lady wanted to know what Anita was doing for herself.

"And when will you be married, *ma chère*?" she asked, secure in the possession of three children and a husband. Anita, aching for a confidante, poured forth her simple trouble into the married lady's sympathetic ear. Mrs Perez expatiated on Sebastian's worldly goods. Mrs Reis, you remember, came from Siparia. "Pack your clothes at once, girl," she said, "you will have to miss this week in the cocoa. But don't mind, I know someone who can help you. And that is La Divina."

Of La Divina Pastora, the Siparia saint, many things can be written, but here only this much need be said. It is a small image of some two feet in height which stands in the Roman Catholic Church at Siparia. To it go pilgrims from all parts of the island, at all times of the year: this one with an incurable malady, that one with a long succession of business misfortunes, the other with a private grudge against some fellow-creature to be satisfied, some out of mere curiosity. Once a year there used to be a special festival, the Siparia fête, when, besides the worshippers, many hundreds of sightseers and gamblers gathered at the little village, and for a week there were wild Bacchanalian carouses going on side by side with the religious celebrations. This has been modified, but still the pilgrims go. To many the saint is nothing more than a symbol of the divine. To more—like the Perez family—it possesses limitless powers of its own to help the importunate. From both parties it receives presents of all descriptions, money, frequently, but oft-times a gift from the suppliant—a gold ring, perhaps, or a brooch, or some other article of jewelry. Anita had no money; her aunt had to pay her passage. But she carried the little gold chain with her, the maiden's mite, for it was all that she had. It was not fête time, and quietly and by herself, with the quiet hum of the little country village in her ears, Anita placed the chain around the neck of the saint and prayed—prayed for what perhaps every woman except Eve has prayed for, the love of the man she loved.

That Sunday night when Sebastian reached Madame Perez's house, the even tenor of his way sustained a rude shock. Anita was not there, she had gone to Siparia, and was not coming back till next Sunday, by the last train. Wouldn't he come in and sit down? Sebastian came in and sat down, on his old seat, near the door. Mrs Perez sat outside commenting on the high price of shop goods generally, especially tobacco. But Sebastian did not answer; he was experiencing new sensations. He missed Anita's quiet face, her steady, nimble fingers, her glance at him and then away, whenever he spoke. He felt ill at ease, somehow disturbed, troubled, and it is probable that he recognised the cause of his trouble. For when Anita landed at Princes' Town the next Sunday, Tony the cabman came up to her and said: "Sebastian told me to bring you up alone, Anita." And he had to say it again before she could understand. During the six-mile drive, Anita sat in a corner of the cab, awed and expectant. Faith she had had, but for this she was not prepared. It was too sudden, as if the Saint had had nothing to do with it.

They met Sebastian walking slowly down the road to meet them. For an hour he had been standing by her house, and as soon as the first cab passed started, in his impatience, to meet her on the way. The cab stopped, and he was courageous enough to help her down. The cabman jumped down to light one of his lamps and the two stood waiting hand in hand. As he drove off Sebastian turned to her. "Nita," he said, shortening her name for the first time, "I missed you, Nita. God, how I missed you!"

Anita was happy, very happy indeed. In her new-found happiness she came near to forgetting the saint, whose answer had come so quickly. Sebastian himself was very little changed. Still he came every night, still Mrs Perez smoked his cigarettes, ruminating now on her blissful future. But things were different. So different in fact that Sebastian proposed taking her to the little cocoa-house dance which was to come off in a day or two. It was the first time that they were going out together since that Sunday. Everybody who did not know before would know now, when they saw Sebastian taking her to a dance, a thing he had never done before. So she dressed herself with great care in the blue muslin dress, and what with happiness and excitement looked more beautiful than she had even seen herself. Then, as she cast another last look in the mirror, she missed something. "How I wish," she said with a genuine note of regret in her voice, "how I wish I had my little gold chain." Here her mother, determined not to jeopardise her future, called sharply to her, and she came out, radiant.

The dance continued till long after five o'clock, but Anita had to leave at three. Sebastian got tired of sitting down in a corner of the room while she whisked around. He felt just a trifle sulky, for he had wanted to leave an hour before, but she, drinking of an intoxicating mixture of admiration, success and excitement, had implored him to stay a little longer. They went home almost in silence, he sleepy, she tired, each thinking the other offended. It was the first little cloud between them.

"It is nothing," thought Anita, "we shall make it up tomorrow night." She thought of something and smiled, but as she peeped at Sebastian and saw him peeping at her, she assumed a more serious expression. Tomorrow, not tonight.

Once inside the bedroom she started to undress quickly, took out a few pins and went to the table to put them down in the cigarette tin in which she kept her knick-knacks. Her mother, who was lying on the bed and listening with half-closed eyes to Anita's account of the dance, was startled by a sudden silence, followed by the sound of a heavy fall. She sprang down quickly, bent over the prostrate form of Anita, and turned to the little table to get the smelling-salts. Then she herself stood motionless, as if stricken, her senseless daughter lying unheeded on the floor. There, in its old place in the cigarette tin, lay a little chain of gold.

1927

2
Triumph

Where people in England and America say slums, Trinidadians said barrack-yards. Probably the word is a relic of the days when England relied as much on garrisons of soldiers as on her fleet to protect her valuable sugar-producing colonies. Every street in Port-of-Spain proper could show you numerous examples of the type: a narrow gateway leading into a fairly big yard, on either side of which run long, low buildings, consisting of anything from four to eighteen rooms, each about twelve feet square. In these lived the porters, the prostitutes, carter-men, washerwomen and domestic servants of the city.

In one corner of the yard is the hopelessly inadequate water-closet, unmistakable to the nose if not to the eye; sometimes there is a structure with the title of bathroom, a courtesy title, for he or she who would wash in it with decent privacy must cover the person as if bathing on the banks of the Thames; the kitchen happily presents no difficulty; never is there one and each barrack-yarder cooks before her door. In the centre of the yard is a heap of stones. On these the half-laundered clothes are bleached before being finally spread out to dry on the wire lines which in every yard cross and recross each other in all directions. Not only to Minerva have these stones been dedicated. Time was when they would have had an honoured shrine in a local temple to Mars, for they were the major source of ammunition for the homicidal strife which so often flared up in barrack-yards. No longer do the barrack-yarders live the picturesque life of twenty-five years ago. Then, practising for the carnival, rival singers, Willie, Jean, and Freddie, porter, wharf-man or loafer in ordinary life, were for that season ennobled by some such striking sobriquet as The Duke of Normandy or the Lord Invincible, and carried with dignity homage such as young aspirants to literature had paid to Mr Kipling or Mr Shaw. They sang in competition from seven in the evening until far into the early morning, stimulated by the applause of their listeners and the excellence and copiousness of the rum; night after night the stickmen practised their dangerous and skillful game, the "pierrots", after elaborate preface of complimentary speech, belaboured each other with riding whips; while around the performers the spectators pressed thick and good-humoured until mimic warfare was transformed into real, and stones from "the bleach" flew thick.

But today that life is dead. All carnival practice must cease at ten o'clock. The policeman is to the stick-fighter and "pierrot" as the sanitary inspector to mosquito larvae. At nights the streets are bright with electric light, the arm of the law is longer, its grip stronger. Gone are the old lawlessness and picturesqueness. Barrack-yard life has lost its savour. Luckily, prohibition in Trinidad is still but a word. And life, dull and drab as it is in comparison, can still offer its great moments.

On a Sunday morning in one of the rooms of the barrack in Abercromby Street sat Mamitz. Accustomed as is squalid adversity to reign unchallenged in these quarters, yet in this room it was more than usually triumphant, sitting as it were, high on a throne of regal state, so depressed was the woman and so depressing her surroundings.

The only representatives of the brighter side of life were three full-page pictures torn from illustrated periodicals, photographs of Lindbergh, Bernard Shaw and Sargent's "Portrait of a Woman", and these owed their presence solely to the fact that no pawn-shop would have accepted them. They looked with unseeing eyes upon a room devoid of furniture save for a few bags spread upon the floor to form a bed. Mamitz sat on the door step talking to, or rather being talked to by her friend, Celestine, who stood astride the concrete canal which ran in front of the door.

"Somebody do you something." said Celestine with conviction. "Nobody goin' to change my mind from that. An' if you do what I tell you, you will t'row off this black spirit that on you. A nice woman like you, and you carn't get a man to keep you! You carn't get nothing to do!"

Mamitz said nothing. Had Celestine said the exact opposite, Mamitz's reply would have been the same.

She was a black woman, too black to be pure Negro, probably with some Madrasi East Indian blood in her, a suspicion which was made a certainty by the long thick plaits of her plentiful hair. She was shortish and fat, voluptuously developed, tremendously developed, and as a creole loves development in a woman more than any other extraneous allure, Mamitz (like the rest of her sex in all stations of life) saw to it when she moved that you missed none of her charms. But for the last nine weeks she had been "in derricks", to use Celestine's phrase. First of all the tram conductor who used to keep her (seven dollars every Saturday night, out of which Mamitz usually got three) had accused her of infidelity and beaten her. Neither the accusation nor the beating had worried Mamitz. To her and her type those were minor incidents of existence from their knowledge of life and men, the kept woman's inevitable fate. But after a temporary reconciliation he had beaten her once more, very badly indeed, and left her. Even this was not an irremediable catastrophe. But thenceforward, Mamitz, from being the most prosperous woman in the yard, had sunk gradually to being the most destitute. Despite her very obvious attractions, no man took notice of her. She went out asking for washing or for work as a cook. No success. Luckily, in the days of her prosperity she had been generous to Celestine who now kept her from actual starvation. One stroke of luck she had had. The agent for the barracks had suddenly taken a fancy to her, and Mamitz had not found it difficult to persuade him to give her a chance with the rent. But the respite was over: he was pressing for the money, and Mamitz had neither money to pay nor hope for refuge when she was turned out. Celestine would have taken her in, but Celestine's keeper was a policeman who visited her three or four nights a week, and to one in that position a fifteen-foot room does not offer much scope for housing the homeless. Yet Celestine was grieved that she could do nothing to help Mamitz in her trouble which she attributed to the evil and supernatural machinations of Irene, their common enemy.

"Take it from me, that woman do you something. Is she put Nathan against you. When was the quarrel again?"

"It was two or three days after Nathan gave me the first beating."

Nathan then had started on his evil courses before the quarrel with Irene took place, but Celestine brushed away objection.

"She musta had it in her mind for you from before. You didn't see how she fly out at you. . . . As long as you livin' here an' I cookin' I wouldn't see you want a cup o' tea an' a spoonful o' rice. But I carn't help with the rent. . . . An' you ain't have nobody here." Mamitz shook her head. She was from Demerara.

"If you could only cross the sea—that will cut any spirit that on you. . . . Look the animal!"

Irene had come out of her room on the opposite side of the yard. She could not fail to see Celestine and Mamitz and she called loudly to a neighbour lower down the yard:

"Hey Jo-Jo! What is the time? Ten o'clock a'ready? Le' me start to cook me chicken that me man buy for me—even if 'e have a so'foot. . . . I don't know how long it will last before 'e get drunk and kick me out o' here. Then I will have to go dawg'n round other po' people to see if I could pick up what they t'row 'way." She fixed a box in front of her door, put her coal-pot on it, and started to attend to her chicken.

Sunday morning in barrack-yards is pot-parade. Of the sixteen tenants in the yard twelve had their pots out, and they lifted the meat with long iron forks to turn it, or threw water into the pot so that it steamed to the heavens and every woman could tell what her neighbour was cooking—beef, or pork, or chicken. It didn't matter what you cooked in the week, if you didn't cook at all. But to cook salt fish, or hog-head, or pig-tail on a Sunday morning was a disgrace. You put your pot inside your house and cooked it there. Mamitz, fat, easy-going, and cowed by many days of semi-starvation, took little notice of Irene. But Celestine, a thin little whip of a brown-skinned woman, bubbled over with repressed rage.

"By Christ, if it wasn't for one t'ing I'd rip every piece o' clothes she have on off'er."

"Don' bother wid 'er. What is the use o' gettin' you'self in trouble with Jimmy?"

Jimmy was the policeman. He was a steady, reliable man but he believed in discipline and when he spoke, he spoke. He had made Celestine understand that she was not to fight: he wasn't going to find himself mixed up in court as the keeper of any brawling woman. Celestine's wrath, deprived of its natural outlet, burned none the less implacably. "I tell you something Mamitz, I goin' to talk to the agent in the morning. I goin' to tell 'im to give you to the end of the month. If only five days . . . I goin' to give you a bath. Try and see if you could get some gully-root and so on this afternoon. . . . Tonight I goin' to give you. . . . An' I will give you some prayers to read. God stronger than the devil. We gon' break this t'ing that you on you. Cheer up. I goin' to send you a plate with you' chicken an' rice as soon as it finish. Meanwhile burn you little candle, say you' little prayers, console you' little mind. I goin' give you that bath tonight. You ain' kill priest. You ain' cuss you' mudder. So you ain' have cause to 'fraid nothin'."

Celestine would never trust herself to indulge in abuse with Irene; the chances that it would end in a fight were too great. So she contented herself with casting a look of the most murderous hate and scorn and defiance at her enemy, and then went to her own pot which was calling for attention.

And yet three months before Mamitz, Celestine and Irene had been good friends. They shared their rum and their joys and troubles: and on Sunday afternoons they used to sit before Mamitz's room singing hymns: "Abide With Me", "Jesu, Lover of My Soul", "Onward Christian Soldiers". Celestine and Irene sang soprano and Irene sang well. Mamitz was a naturally fine contralto and had a fine ear, while Nathan, who was a Barbadian and consequently knew vocal music, used to sing bass whenever he happened to be in. The singing would put him in a good mood and he would send off to buy more rum and everything would be peaceful and happy. But Irene was a jealous woman, not only jealous of Mamitz's steady three dollars a week and Celestine's policeman with his twenty-eight dollars at the end of the month. She lived with a cab-man, whose income though good enough was irregular. And he was a married man, with a wife and children to support. Irene had to do washing to help out, while Mamitz and Celestine did nothing, merely cooked and washed clothes for their men. So gradually a state of dissatisfaction arose. Then one damp evening, Mamitz, passing near the bamboo pole which supported a clothes line overburdened with Irene's clothes, brought it down with her broad, expansive person. The line burst, and nightgowns, sheets, pillow-cases, white suits and tablecloths fluttered to the mud. It had been a rainy week with little sun, and already it would have been difficult to get the clothes ready in time for Saturday morning: after this it was impossible. And hot and fiery was the altercation. Celestine who tried to make peace was drawn into the quarrel by Irene's comprehensive and incendiary invective.

"You comin' to put you' mouth in this. You think because you livin' with policeman you is a magistrate. Mind you' business, woman, min' you' business. The two o' you don't do nothing for you' livin'. You only sittin' down an eatin' out the men all you livin' wid. An' I wo'k hard an' put out me cl's on the line. And this one like some cab-horse knock it down, and when I tell 'er about it you comin' to meddle! Le' me tell you . . ."

So the wordy warfare raged, Celestine's policeman coming in for rough treatment at the tongue of Irene. Celestine, even though she was keeping herself in check, was a match for any barrack-yard woman Port-of-Spain could produce, but yet it was Mamitz who clinched the victory.

"Don't mind Celestine livin' with a policeman. You will be glad to get 'im for you'self. An' it better than livin' with any stinkin' so'foot man."

For Irene's cab-man had a sore on his foot, which he had had for thirty years and would carry with him to the grave even if he lived for thirty years more. Syphilis, congenital and acquired, and his copious boozing would see to it that there was no recovery. Irene had stupidly hoped that nobody in the yard knew.

But in Trinidad when His Excellency the Governor and his wife have a quarrel the street boys speak of it the day after, and Richard's bad foot had long been a secret topic of conversation in the yard. But it was Mamitz who had made it public property, and Irene hated Mamitz with a virulent hatred, and had promised to "do" for her. Three days before, Nathan, the tram-conductor, had given Mamitz the first beating; but even at the time of the quarrel there was no hint of his swift defection and Mamitz's rapid descent to her present plight. So that Celestine, an errant but staunch religionist, was convinced that Mamitz's troubles were due to Irene's trafficking with the devil, if not personally, at least through one of his numerous agents who ply their profitable trade in every part of Port-of-Spain. Secure in her own immunity from anything that Irene might "put on her", she daily regretted that she couldn't rip the woman to pieces. "Oh Jesus! If it wasn't for Jimmy I'd tear the wretch limb from limb!" But the energy that she could not put into the destruction of Irene she spent in upholding Mamitz. The fiery Celestine had a real affection for the placid Mamitz, whose quiet ways were so soothing. But, more than this, she was determined not to see Mamitz go down. In the bitter antagonism she nursed against Irene, it would have been a galling defeat if Mamitz went to the wall. Further, her reputation as a woman who knew things and could put crooked people straight was at stake. Once she had seen to Jimmy's food and clothes and creature comforts she set herself to devise ways and means of supporting the weak, easily crushed Mamitz.

Celestine's policeman being on duty that night, she herself was off duty and free to attend to her own affairs. At midnight, with the necessary rites and ceremonies, Ave Marias and Pater Nosters, she bathed Mamitz in a large bath pan full of water prepared with gully root, fever grass, lime leaves, geurin tout, herbe femmes, and other roots, leaves and grasses noted for their efficacy (when properly applied) against malign plots and influences. That was at twelve o'clock the Sunday night. On Monday morning at eight o'clock behold Popo des Vignes walking into the yard, with a little bag in his hand.

Popo is a creole of creoles. His name is des Vignes, but do not be misled into thinking that there flows in his veins blood of those aristocrats who found their way to Trinidad after '89. He is a Negro, and his slave ancestors adopted the name from his master. Popo is nearing forty, medium-sized, though large about the stomach, with a longish moustache. He is dressed in a spotless suit of white with tight-fitting shoes of a particularly yellowish brown (no heavy English brogues or fantastic American shoes for him). On his head he wears his straw hat at a jaunty angle, and his manner of smoking his cigarette and his jacket always flying open (he wears no waistcoat) will give the impression that Popo is a man of pleasure rather than a man of work. And that impression would be right. He has never done a week's honest work in his life. He can get thirty dollars for you if you are in difficulties (at one hundred per cent) or three thousand dollars if you have a house or a cocoa estate. During the cocoa crop he lurks by the railway station with an unerring eye for peasant proprietors who have brought their cocoa into town and are not quite certain where they will get the best price. This is his most profitable business, for he gets commission both from the proprietors and from the big buyers. But he is not fastidious as to how he makes money, and will do anything that does not bind him down, and leaves him free of manual or clerical labour. For the rest, after he has had a good meal at about half past seven in the evening he can drink rum until six o'clock the next morning without turning a hair; and in his own circle he has a wide reputation for his connoisseurship in matters of love and his catholicity of taste in women.

"Eh, Mr des Vignes! How you?" said Celestine. The inhabitants of every barrack-yard, especially the women, knew Popo.

"Keeping fine."

"Who you lookin' for roun' this way?"

"I come roun' to see you. How is Jimmy? When you getting married?"

"Married!" said Celestine with fine scorn. "Me married a police! I wouldn't trust a police further than I could smell him. Police ain't have no regard. A police will lock up 'is mudder to get a stripe. An' besides I ain' want to married the man in the house all the time, you go'n be a perfect slave. I all right as I be."

"Anyway, I want you to buy a ring."

"Rings you sellin' in the bag? I ain' have no money, but le' me see them."

Popo opened his bags and displayed the rings—beautiful gold of American workmanship, five dollars cash and six dollars on terms. They had cost an Assyrian merchant in Park Street ten dollars the dozen, and Popo was selling them on commission. He was doing good business, especially with those who paid two dollars down and gave him promises of monthly or weekly instalments. If later the merchant saw trouble to collect his instalments or to get back his rings, that wouldn't worry Popo much for by that time he would have chucked up the job. "So you wouldn't take one," said he, getting ready to put away his treasures again.

"Come roun' at the end o' the month. But don't shut them up yet. I have a friend I want to see them."

She went to the door.

"Mamitz!" she called. "Come and see some rings Mr des Vignes sellin'."

Mamitz came into Celestine's room, large, slow-moving, voluptuous, with her thick, smooth hair neatly plaited and her black skin shining. She took Popo's fancy at once.

"But you have a nice friend, Celestine," said Popo. "And she has a nice name too: Mamitz! Well, how many rings are you going to buy from me?"

Celestine answered quickly: "Mamitz can't buy no rings. The man was keepin' her, they fall out, an' she lookin' for a husband now."

"A nice woman like you can't stay long without a husband," said des Vignes. "Let me give you some luck. . . . Choose a ring and I will make you a present."

Mamitz chose a ring and des Vignes put it on her finger himself. "Excuse me, I comin' back now," said Celestine. "The sanitary inspector comin' just now, an' I want to clean up some rubbish before he come." When she came back des Vignes was just going.

"As we say, Mamitz," he smiled. "So long, Celestine!" He was hardly out of earshot when Celestine excitedly tackled Mamitz.

"What 'e tell you?"

"E say that 'e coming round here about ten o'clock tonight or little later. . . . An' 'e give me this." In her palm reposed a red two-dollar note.

"You see what I tell you?" said Celestine triumphantly. "That bath. But don' stop. Read the prayers three times a day for nine days. . . . Buy some stout, Mitz, to nourish up you'self. . . . 'E ain't a man you could depend on. If you dress a broomstick in a petticoat 'e will run after it. But you goin' to get something out o' 'im for a few weeks or so. . . . An' you see 'e is a nice man."

Mamitz smiled her lazy smile.

Celestine knew her man. For four weeks Popo was a more or less regular visitor to Mamitz's room. He paid the rent, gave her money to get her bed and furniture out of the pawn-shop, and every Sunday morning Mamitz was stirring beef or pork or chicken in her pot. More than that, whenever Popo said he was coming to see her, he gave her money to prepare a meal so that sometimes late in the week, on a Thursday night, Mamitz's pot smelt as if it was Sunday morning. Celestine shared in the prosperity and they could afford to take small notice of Irene who prophesied early disaster.

"All you flourishin' now. But wait little bit. I know Popo des Vignes well. 'E don't knock round a woman for more than a month. Just now all that high livin' goin' shut down an' I going see you Mamitz eatin' straw."

But Mamitz grew fatter than ever and when she walked down the road in a fugi silk dress, tight fitting and short, which exposed her noble calves to the knee and accentuated her amplitudes of her person, she created a sensation among those men who took notice of her.

On Sunday morning she went into the market to buy beef. She was passing along the stalls going to the man she always bought from, when a butcher called out to her.

"Hey, Mamitz! Come this way."

Mamitz went. She didn't know the man, but she was of an acquiescent nature and she went to see what he wanted.

"But I don't know you," she said, after looking at him. "Where you know my name?"

"Ain't was you walkin' down Abercromby Street last Sunday in a white silk dress?"

"Yes," smiled Mamitz.

"Well, I know a nice woman when I see one. An' I find out where you livin' too. Ain't you livin' in the barrack just below Park Street? . . . Girl, you did look too sweet. You mustn't buy beef from nobody but me. How much you want? A pound? Look a nice piece. Don't worry to pay me for that. You could pay me later. Whenever you want beef, come round this way."

Mamitz accepted and went. She didn't like the butcher too much, but he liked her. And a pound of beef was a pound of beef. Nicholas came to see her a day or two after and brought two pints of stout as a present. At first Mamitz didn't bother with him. But des Vignes was a formidable rival. Nicholas made Mamitz extravagant presents and promises. What helped him was that Popo now began to slack off. A week would pass and Mamitz would not see him. And no more money was forthcoming. So, after a while she accepted Nicholas, and had no cause to regret her bargain. Nicholas made a lot of money as a butcher. He not only paid the rent, but gave her five dollars every Saturday night, and she could always get a dollar or two out of him during the week. Before long he loved her to distraction, and was given to violent fits of jealousy which, however, were always followed by repentance and lavish presents. Still Mamitz hankered after

Popo. One day she wrote him a little note telling him that she was sorry she had to accept Nicholas but that she would be glad to see him any time he came round. She sent it to the Miranda Hotel where Popo took his meals. But no answer came and after a while Mamitz ceased actively to wish to see Popo. She was prosperous and pretty happy. She and Celestine were thicker than ever, and were on good terms with the neighbours in the yard. Only Irene they knew would do them mischief, and on mornings when Mamitz got up, on Celestine's advice, she looked carefully before the door lest she should unwittingly set foot on any church-yard bones, deadly powders, or other satanic agencies guaranteed to make the victim go mad, steal or commit those breaches of good conduct which are punishable by law. But nothing untoward happened. As Celestine pointed out to Mamitz, the power of the bath held good, "and as for me," concluded she, "no powers Irene can handle can touch my little finger."

Easter Sunday came, and with it came Popo. He walked into the yard early, about seven the morning, and knocked up Mamitz who was still sleeping.

"I t'ought you had given me up for good," said Mamitz. "I write you and you didn't answer."

"I didn't want any butcher to stick me with his knife," laughed Popo. "Anyway, that is all right. . . . I was playing baccarat last night and I made a good haul, so I come to spend Easter with you. Look! Here is five dollars. Buy salt fish and sweet oil and some greens and tomatoes. Buy some pints of rum. And some stout for yourself. I am coming back about nine o'clock. Today is Easter Saturday, Nicholas is going to be in the market the whole day. Don't be afraid for him."

Mamitz became excited. She gave the five dollars to Celestine and put her in charge of the catering, while she prepared for her lover. At about half past nine Popo returned. He, Mamitz and Celestine ate in Mamitz's room, and before they got up from the table, much more than two bottles of rum had disappeared. Then Celestine left them and went to the market to Nicholas. She told him that Mamitz wasn't feeling too well and had sent for beer and port. The willing Nicholas handed over the stuff and sent a shilling for his lady love. He said he was rather short of money but at the end of the day he was going to make a big draw. Celestine cooked, and at about half past one, she, Popo and Mamitz had lunch. Celestine had to go out again and buy more rum. The other people in the yard didn't take much notice of what was an every-day occurrence, were rather pleased in fact, for after lunch Celestine had a bottle and a half of rum to herself and ostentatiously invited all the neighbours to have drinks, all, of course, except Irene.

At about three o'clock Irene felt that she could bear it no longer and that if she didn't take this chance it would be throwing away a gift from God. She put on her shoes, took her basket on her arm, and left the yard. It was the basket that aroused the observant Celestine's suspicions for she knew that Irene had already done all her shopping that morning. She sat thinking for a few seconds, then she knocked at Mamitz's door.

"Look here, Mamitz," she called. "It's time for Mr des Vignes to go. Irene just gone out with a basket, I think she gone to the market to tell Nicholas.

"But he can't get away today," called Mamitz.

"You know how the man jealous and how 'e bad," persisted Celestine. "Since nine o'clock Mr des Vignes, is time for you to go."

Celestine's wise counsel prevailed. Popo dressed himself with his usual scrupulous neatness and cleared off. The rum bottles were put out of the way and Mamitz's room was made tidy. She and Celestine had hardly finished when Irene appeared with the basket empty.

"You see," said Celestine. "Now look out!"

Sure enough, it wasn't five minutes after when a cab drew up outside and Nicholas still in his bloody butcher's apron, came hot foot into the yard. He went straight up to Mamitz and seized her by the throat.

"Where the hell is that man you had in the room with you—the room I payin' rent for?"

"Don't talk dam' foolishness, man, lemme go," said Mamitz.

"I will stick my knife into you as I will stick it in a cow. You had Popo des Vignes in that room for the whole day. Speak the truth, you dog."

"You' mother, you' sister, you' aunt, you' wife was the dog," shrieked Mamitz, quoting one of Celestine's most brilliant pieces of repartee.

"It's the wo'se when you meddle with them common low-island people," said Celestine. Nicholas was from St. Vincent. Grenada and the smaller West Indian islands are looked down upon by the Trinidad Negro as low-island people.

"You shut you' blasted mouth and don' meddle with what don' concern you. It you encouragin' the woman. I want the truth, or by Christ I'll make beef o' one o' you here today."

"Look here, man, lemme tell you something." Mamitz, drunk with love and rum and inspired by Celestine, was showing spirit. "That woman over there come and tell you that Mr des Vignes was in this room. The man come in the yard, 'e come to Celestine to sell 'er a ring, she did promise to buy from 'im long time. Look in me room," she flung the half doors wide, "you see any signs of any man in there? Me bed look as if any man been lyin' down on it? But I had no right to meddle with a low brute like you. You been botherin' me long enough. Go live with Irene. Go share she wid she so' foot cab-man. Is woman like she men like you want. I sorry the day I ever see you. An' I hope I never see you' face again."

She stopped, panting, and Celestine, who had only been waiting for an opening, took up the tale.

"But look at the man! The man leave 'is work this bright Easter Saturday because this nasty woman go and tell 'im that Mr des Vignes in the room with Mamitz! Next thing you go'n say that 'e livin' with me. But man, I never see such a ass as you. Bertha, Olive, Josephine," she appealed to some of the other inhabitants of the yard, "ain't all you been here the whole day an' see Mr des Vignes come here after breakfast? I pay 'im two dollars I had for 'im. 'E sen' and buy a pint o' rum an' I call Mamitz for the three o' we to fire a little liquor for the Easter. Next thing I see is this one going out—to carry news: and now this Vincelonian fool leave 'e work—But, man, you drunk."

Bertha, Olive and Josephine, who had shared in the rum, confirmed Celestine's statement. Irene had been sitting at the door of her room cleaning fish and pretending to take no notice, but at this she jumped up.

"Bertha, you ought to be ashame' o' you'self. For a drink 'o rum you lyin' like that? Don't believe them, Nicholas. Whole day—"

But here occurred an unlooked for interruption. The cabby, hearing the altercation and not wishing to lose time on a day like Easter Saturday, had put a little boy in charge of his horse and had been listening for a minute or two. He now approached and held Nicholas by the arm.

"Boss," he said, "don't listen to that woman. She livin' with Richard the cab-man an' 'e tell me that all women does lie but 'e never hear or know none that does like like she-"

There was a burst of laughter.

"Come go, boss," said the cabby, pulling the hot, unwilling Nicholas by the arm.

"I have to go back to my work, but I am comin' back tonight and I am goin' to lick the stuffin' out o' you."

"An' my man is a policeman," said Celestine. "An' 'e goin' to be here tonight. An' if you touch this woman, you spend you' Easter in the lock-up sure as my name is Celestine an' you are a good-for-nothing Vincelonian fool of a butcher."

Nicholas drove away, leaving Celestine mistress of the field, but for the rest of the afternoon Mamitz was depressed. She was tired out with the day's excitement, and after all Nicholas had good money. On a night like this he would be drawing quite a lot of money and now it seemed that she was in danger of losing him. She knew how he hated Popo. She liked Popo more than Nicholas, much more, but after all people had to live.

Celestine, however, was undaunted. "Don't min' what 'e say. 'E comin' back. 'E comin' back to beg. When you see a man love a woman like he love you, she could treat 'im how she like, 'e still comin' back like a dog to eat 'is vomit. But you listen to me, Mamitz. When 'e come back cuss 'im a little bit. Cuss 'im plenty. Make 'im see that you ain't goin' to stand too much nonsense from 'im."

Mamitz smiled in her sleepy way, but she was not hopeful. And all the rest of the afternoon Irene worried her by singing ballads appropriate to the occasion.

"Though you belong to somebody else
Tonight you belong to me."

"Come, come, come to me, Thora,
Come once again and be . . ."

"How can I live without you"
"How can I let you go!"

Her voice soared shrill over the babel of clattering tongues in the yard. And as the voice rose so Mamitz's heart sank.

"Don't forget," said Mamitz dully. She was thinking that she had only about thirty-six cents left over from the money des Vignes had given her. Not another cent.

But Celestine was right. The enraged Nicholas went back to work and cut beef and sawed bones with a ferocity that astonished his fellow butchers and purchasers. But at seven o'clock with his pocket full of money and nothing to do, he felt miserable. He had made his plans for the Easter: Saturday night he had decided to spend with Mamitz, and all Easter Sunday after he knocked off at nine in the morning. Easter Monday he had for himself and he had been thinking of taking Mamitz, Celestine and Jimmy down to Carenage in a taxi to bathe. He mooned about the streets for a time. He took two or three drinks, but he didn't feel in the mood for running a spree and getting drunk. He was tired from the strain of the day and he felt for the restful company of a woman, especially the woman he loved—the good-looking, fat, agreeable Mamitz. At about half past ten he found his resolution never to look at her again wavering.

"Damn it," he said to himself. "That woman Irene is a liar. She see how I am treatin' Mamitz well and she want to break up the livin'."

He fought the question out with himself.

"But the woman couldn't lie like that. The man musta been there."

He was undecided. He went over the arguments for and against, the testimony of Bertha and Olive, the testimony of the cab-man. His reason inclined him to believe that Mamitz had been entertaining des Vignes for the whole day in the room he was paying for, while he, the fool, was working hard for money to carry to her. But stronger powers than reason were fighting for Mamitz, and eleven o'clock found him in the yard knocking at the door.

"Mamitz! Mamitz! Open. Is me—Nicholas." There was a slight pause. Then he heard Mamitz's voice, sounding a little strange.

"What the devil you want!"

"I sorry for what happen today. Is that meddlin' woman, Irene. She come to the market an' she lie on you. Open the door, Mamitz. . . . I have something here for you."

Celestine next door was listening closely, pleased that Mamitz was proving herself so obedient to instruction.

"Man, I 'fraid you. You have a knife out there an' you come here to cut me up as Gorrie cut up Eva."

"I have no knife. I brought some money for you."

"I don't believe you. You want to treat me as if I a cow." "I tell you I have no knife . . . open the door, woman, or I'll break it in. You carn't treat me like that."

Nicholas's temper was getting the better of him, he hadn't expected this.

The watchful Celestine here interfered.

"Open the door for the man, Mamitz. 'E say 'e beg pardon and, after all, is he payin' the rent."

So Mamitz very willingly opened the door and Nicholas went in. He left early the next morning to go to work but he promised Mamitz to be back by half past nine.

Irene, about her daily business in the yard, gathered that Nicholas had come "dawgin'" back to Mamitz the night before and Mamitz was drivin' him dog and lance, but Celestine beg for him and Mamitz let 'im come in. Mamitz, she noticed, got up that morning much later than usual. In fact Celestine (who was always up at five o'clock) knocked her up and went into the room before she came out. It was not long before Irene knew that something was afoot. First of all, Mamitz never opened her door as usual, but slipped in and out closing it after her. Neither she nor Celestine went to the market. They sent out Bertha's little sister who returned with beef and port and mutton, each piece of which Mamitz held up high in the air and commented upon. Then Bertha's sister went out again and returned with a new coal-pot. Irene could guess where it came from—some little store, in Charlotte Street probably, whose owner was not afraid to run the risk of selling on Sundays. In and out the yard went Bertha's little sister, and going and coming she clutched something tightly in her hand. Irene, her senses tuned by resentment and hate to their highest pitch, could not make out what was happening. Meanwhile Celestine was inside Mamitz's room, and Mamitz, outside, had started to cook in three coal-pots.

Every minute or so Mamitz would poke her head inside the room and talk to Celestine. Irene could see Mamitz shaking her fat self with laughter while she could hear Celestine' shrill cackle inside. Then Bertha's sister returned for the last time and after going into the room to deliver whatever her message was, came and stood a few yards away, opposite Mamitz's door, expectantly waiting. Think as she would, Irene could form no idea as to what was going on inside.

Then Mamitz went and stood near to Bertha's sister; and, a second after, the two halves of the door were flung open and Irene saw Celestine standing in the doorway with arms akimbo. But there was nothing to—and then she saw. Both halves of the door were plastered with notes, green five-dollar notes, red two-dollar notes, and blue dollar ones, with a pin at a corner of each to keep it firm. The pin-heads were shining in the sun. Irene was so flabbergasted that for a second or two she stood with her mouth open. Money Nicholas had given Mamitz. Nicholas had come back and begged pardon, and given her all his money. The fool! So that was what Celestine had been doing inside there all the time. Bertha's sisters had been running up and down to get some of the notes changed. There must be forty, no, fifty dollars, spread out on the door. Mamitz and Bertha's sister were sinking with laughter and the joke was spreading, for other people in the yard were going up to see what the disturbance was about. What a blind fool that Nicholas was! Tears of rage and mortification rushed to Irene's eyes.

"Hey, Irene, come see a picture Nicholas bring for Mamitz last night! An' tomorrow we goin' to Carenage. We don't want you, but we will carry you' husband, the sea-water will do 'is so'-foot good." Celestine's voice rang across the yard.

Bertha, Josephine, the fat Mamitz and the rest were laughing so that they could hardly hold themselves up. Irene could find neither spirit nor voice to reply. She trembled so that her hands shook. The china bowl in which she was washing rice slipped from her fingers and broke into a dozen pieces while the rice streamed into the dirty water of the canal.

1929

PART II

BRITAIN 1932-1938

3

Bloomsbury: An Encounter with Edith Sitwell

I have been living in London for ten weeks and will give what can only be called first impressions. I have been living in Bloomsbury, that is to say, the students' and young writers' quarter. It is as different from Clapham or Ealing suburban, as you can imagine, and is in its way distinctive, so absolutely different from life in the West Indies, that it stands out as easily the most striking of my first impressions. In later articles, I shall go more into detail about such things as have struck me—houses, food, clothes, men, women, the streets, scores of things. But for the present my chief concern will be with Bloomsbury and the Bloomsbury atmosphere. I shall best describe it by not trying to describe it at all, but by merely setting down faithfully the events of three or four days, just as they happened. If there is a lot of "I" and "I" and "I", it cannot be helped. I can only give my own impressions, and what happened to me. To generalize about so large a district and such numbers of people after only ten weeks would be the limit of rashness.

I shall begin with Wednesday the eighteenth of May. I reached home from the city at about half past three having twice sat before food and both times been unable to eat. I knew from long experience that I had a sleepless night before me, and to make matters worse, my right hand which had been going for some time decided finally to go. I tried to write and found that I could not—nervous strain I expect. I went to bed, got out of bed, went to bed again, knocked about the place a bit, tried to read, failed, in fact did not know what to do with myself. But I was in Bloomsbury, so would always find distractions.

Restlessness was the only reason which made me go to a lecture at the Student Movement House by Miss Edith Sitwell. I had promised to go with a girl whom I have met here, extremely interesting, and the only person I have ever met, who, if we are looking down a book or newspaper together, has to wait at the end of the page for me, and not by three or four lines but sometimes by ten. I had almost intended to telephone to say that I was not going, but the prospect of my own company in a room of a Bloomsbury lodging house, aesthetically speaking, one of the worst places in the world, made me decide to summon up some energy and go to hear Miss Sitwell. I went over to my friend's room and met there, herself and another girl friend of hers who had ridden five miles to come to the lecture, and was to ride five miles afterwards to get home. We walked over to the Student House which is a club for London students, white and coloured, but with its chief aim giving coloured students in London an opportunity to meet together and fraternise with English students and with one another. The atmosphere of the place is definitely intellectual, in intention at least.

Now I had heard a lot about Miss Edith Sitwell before. She is supposed to be eccentric, in appearance and manner at least. She and her two brothers, Osbert and Sacheverell, are a family of wealthy people who have devoted themselves to literature (chiefly poetry) and the arts. They have made quite a name for themselves as poets and critics, and although few modern writers have attracted such a storm of hostile criticism, yet that in itself is perhaps a testimony of a certain amount of virility in their work. Today, however, they have won their position and are among the first flight of the younger generation of English writers. Miss Edith Sitwell, I had been told in Trinidad, rather posed. She wore robes, not dresses, and, to judge from her photographs, was not only handsome, but distinctly evil-looking in appearance. She had an underlip that seemed the last word in spite and malice, and in nearly every photograph that I had seen a rebellious lock of hair waved formidably about her forehead.

At a quarter past eight there was the usual whisper and the lady walked into the room. If ever rumour had been lying, this certainly was a case. She did wear robes, some old brocaded stuff, dark in colour with a pattern of some kind. The waist was about six inches below where the waist of the ordinary dress is and the skirt was not joined to the bodice in a straight line but by means of many half circles looking somewhat like the rim of an opened umbrella. Women will know the kind of design I mean. But the chief thing was that she could carry the dress. She is tall and though mature, still slim and the dress fitted beautifully. But even more remarkable than the dress was the face, a thin aristocratic well-formed face, very sharp and very keen. Her eyes too, were bright and keen. The lip I saw later did look spiteful at times but it was only when she shot an arrow at some of her fellow poets and writers, and to speak the truth, she had a good many to shoot. The lock of hair I can say nothing about, because she wore a small white cap which would have kept the most rebellious locks in order. She stood on the little platform to address us, a striking figure, decidedly good looking, and even more decidedly a personality. Perhaps the outstanding impression was one of fitness and keenness together, the same impression I had got from a bronze head of her brother, which I had seen in the Tate.

I do not intend to go into her lecture which consisted partly of readings from her own and other works and partly of short dissertations on certain aspects of modern work, the Sitwells being essentially of the modern school. Her voice was not exceptional and she was rather hoarse but she read well. Most interesting to me however, were the bombs she threw at writer after writer. For a sample, Mr D.H. Lawrence who would be judged by most people as the finest English writer of the post-war period, Miss Sitwell (sparkling with malicious enjoyment) told us that in the course of a lecture at Liverpool she had defined Mr Lawrence as the chief of the Jaeger school of poetry. This was reported in the press and a few days afterwards she received a dignified letter from the famous firm of underwear makers, saying that they had noted her remark and would like to know what she meant by that reference to their goods.

Miss Sitwell replied that she had called Mr Lawrence the head of the Jaeger School because his poetry was like Jaeger underwear, hot, soft and woolly; whereupon the Jaeger Company replied that while their products were soft and woolly they begged to deny that they were in any way hot, owing to their special process which resulted in non-conductivity of heat. Miss Sitwell begged to apologise and asked the Jaeger Company if they could discover a special process for Mr D.H. Lawrence which would have the same effect of non-conductivity. Unfortunately Mr Lawrence died too soon and nothing could be done. That is a sample of the kind of compliment she distributed and it is only fair to say that she and her two brothers if they give hard knocks have received quite as many. Naturally I was very much interested in all this and soon realised that I had done very well to come. But more was to follow. Speaking of D.H. Lawrence, she said that she did not think much of his work, that even his novels were very much overrated, and that she knew a young American writer of 31 or 32 who was a far finer novelist than D.H. Lawrence. However wild horses would not draw his name from her.

Of course that was easy. I told her at once that it was William Faulkner and she rather blinked a bit, though honestly I do not think that there was much in it. Anyone who is really interested in fiction would at least have heard Faulkner's name.

As the evening progressed Miss Sitwell grew more and more animated and told us a story of that very brilliant writer who has just died, Mr Lytton Strachey. To appreciate the story properly, you must understand that Mr Strachey was a very thin, tall man, well over six feet, with a long beard and in appearance the essence of calm, assured, dignified superiority. I had heard of this and fortunately had seen, also in the Tate, first, a portrait of Mr Strachey, full size, which though a mediocre painting, gave one some idea of the man and secondly, a bust which was an admirable piece of work and gave a strong impression of his personality. To return to Miss Sitwell's story. She said that a young composer, a big bustling fellow, whose name she certainly would not tell us, had met Mr Strachey at a party. Two years afterwards he met Mr Strachey at another party, hustled up to him and said, "Hello! I met you at a party two years ago, didn't I?" Mr Strachey drew himself up, pointed his beard in the air, and looking serenely over the head of the intruder on his peace said quietly, "Yes, two years ago. A nice long interval, isn't it?" As soon as the meeting was over I went to her and told her that I hoped I wasn't intruding, but I would be glad to know if her young composer was not Constant Lambert. You never saw a woman look so surprised. She had to admit that it was and wanted to know how in the name of Heaven I knew that.

I do not know Constant Lambert's music at all, but since the re-organisation of the *New Statesman* as the *New Statesman and Nation* he has been writing musical criticism for the new paper, and writes quite well. One day I saw in the *Tatler* or *Sketch* or some picture-book of the kind, a photograph of Mr Constant Lambert and his bride. It was his wife that interested me, however. She was a cute woman with features rather resembling someone whom I knew, and yet no two women could have looked more different. She was rather a striking little woman in her way, and I looked at the photograph for some time, paying little attention however to Mr Lambert himself, who was big and beefy and burly, and looked rather like a prize-fighter. But when Miss Sitwell began her story with this young composer who was so big and who came pushing his way in, then the connection was simple enough. I had one shot and it went straight home.

But before the evening was over, I am afraid I had an argument with the good lady. After the lecture proper, came questions when Miss Sitwell sat down and answered whatever anyone chose to ask. Here she was at her best, showed a wide range of reading, was terse and incisive and every now and then when she got in a particularly good shot which set the house in roars of laughter, her lower lip quivered for a fraction of a second in a fascinating way.

After a while I asked her a question on which I have definite views of my own. There is a lot of experimentation in all modern art today, in technique particularly. People are writing free verse, verse which I believe Shakespeare and Keats and Shelley would find it difficult to recognise as kindred to their own work. Some people say that poetry must find new forms. It is my belief, though only a belief, that a great poet is first and foremost a poet, that is to say a man of strong feeling and delicate nerves, and secondly a technician and interested in technique, as such only as a means of getting the best manner of expressing what he has in him; and I also incline to the belief that if a great poet were born today he could use the traditional forms of verse and write the most magnificent poetry without bothering himself about new forms of poetry and technical experiments and the other pre-occupations of most modern writers. These pre-occupations it seems to me are things of essentially secondary importance. But with the spread of education and multiplication of books, people with little genuine poetic fire, occupy themselves with poetry and thus have to concentrate on technique. Real poetic genius they cannot cultivate, because they have not got it.

At any rate I asked her the question, quite straightforwardly.

"Do you believe that a genuine poet coming into the world today would be able to write great poetry in the old traditional form, the sonnet form for instance." I chose the sonnet particularly. From Sir Thomas Wyatt in the sixteenth century to the present day, Englishmen have written these poems of fourteen lines. Shakespeare and Milton, Keats and Wordsworth, nearly all the great English poets have exercised themselves with the sonnet. Could a modern Shakespeare write a sonnet which would be able to take its place beside the sonnets of Shakespeare or Milton?

Miss S: "To begin with I do not think that any modern sonnets of the first class have been written since the sonnets of Keats and Wordsworth."

Myself: "What about Elizabeth Barrett Browning's *Sonnet from the Portuguese*, particularly the one beginning,'If thou would'st love me, let it be for nought, Except for love's sake only.'"

Miss S: (Shaking her head) "No, as a matter of fact I think that no woman could ever write a really great sonnet. I happen to believe that technique is largely a matter of physique. Pope for instance though an invalid had very strong and beautiful hands . . . and I do not think that any woman is strong enough physically to weight the syllables as a man can in order to strengthen the lines."

Myself: "But you will admit that the *Ode to a Nightingale* and the *Ode to a Grecian Urn* are magnificent poetry."

Miss E.S.: "Yes, certainly."

Myself: "But nevertheless Keats was always very frail."

Miss E.S.: "Of course I do not mean that to write fine poetry a man must be big and strong like a butcher."

It was the reply of a skillful controversialist. The audience was much amused. And as it was her lecture and not mine I let it pass. Nevertheless I think it was pretty clear to a good many in the hall that she was concerned.

But that is not all there is to it. At odd moments I have been thinking over the matter and while I cannot say that she is right I am becoming less and less able to say that she is wrong. Unfortunately for her I happened to hit almost immediately on the chief example which seemed to confound her theories at once. But on close observation even the case of Keats can be defended. Keats' poetry is very beautiful but it is not strong as the work of Shakespeare or Milton is strong; even Shelley, magnificent poet as he is has force and fire, but not strength in the sense that Shakespeare has strength. Take for instance these two lines from one of the sonnets:

> Oh how can summer's honey breath hold out
> Against the wreckful siege of battering days.

Anyone who read that aloud can feel the almost physical weight behind the lines. One does not get it often in Keats and in Shelley. And it is particularly the kind of weight that the sonnet form, compact as it is, needs in order that every line of the fourteen should tell. It is not an easy question, and this is not the place to discuss it. Anyway, after many more questions the regular meeting ended. Then came general conversation in which those who wished went up to the platform and talked to Miss Sitwell while the audience broke up into groups. Students went up and came down, but stranger as I was, I did not go, and was talking to a girl who spoke thirteen languages, when the chairman touched me on the shoulder. Would I give my name and address to Miss S. and would I come up on the platform to speak to her? Certainly, no one was more pleased than I.

Up on the platform Miss Sitwell sat in the centre of a group of students. There was the chairman also and there was a Miss Trevelyan, some relation I believe of the Oxford historian. The talk ran chiefly on the work of the moderns. There is no need to go into what was said, except that Miss Sitwell agreed thoroughly with what I have always felt, that, for instance, to take an outstanding figure among the moderns, while one listens with the greatest interest to the music of Stravinsky, neither he nor any other modern can ever move your feelings as can Bach or Haydn, Mozart or Beethoven. It is the great weakness of most modern work. Well, it ended as all good things have to end. Miss Sitwell promised to send me a book written by her brother in traditional verse. I was bold enough to say that I hoped I would see her again. She said, yes certainly.

We may seem to have got some distance from Bloomsbury. We have not. That is Bloomsbury. Some group or society is always having lectures or talks by some distinguished person who comes and talks and is always willing to do anything for anyone who wishes assistance or guidance of some sort. On the Sunday following Miss Sitwell's lecture, Mr Sidney Dark was to speak. Still later in the term Mr Walter De la Mare is to speak on Modern Fiction. Something of that kind in music, art, literature, architecture, philosophy, history, by the most distinguished persons, day after day. You have your choice. And however distinguished the lecturers, they are always willing to do their very best for anyone who seems more than usually interested. I went to two lectures by Professor Bidet of the University of Ghent on Greece and the Near East. The lectures were in French and I found them rather difficult to follow, but the man was so interesting that I wrote him a short note asking if there were any small books on the subject, or magazine articles which he himself had written. He did not reply at once, but did so when he reached back home. He wrote that he was delighted to have heard from me, that the interest I took in his subject gave him great pleasure, that my writing him about it meant far more to him than anything which he could do for me. He sent me one of his own articles, signed, as a souvenir and told me that although he had not written as yet his book on the subject would soon be published and he would be extremely glad to send me a copy. He does not know me and in all probability never will. There is the case of John Clarke who along with law has been doing literature, and economics, and sociology, and goodness knows what not. He attended a series of lectures on sociology given by Mrs. Beatrice Webb, Lord Passfield's wife. He was not too certain of himself and wrote to her asking for some guidance. He told me that he was surprised at the result. She did not send him information of what books to read, but sent him actual manuscripts, sheets and sheets of her own work. She invited him to tea, filled him with food and knowledge and told him to come again. That is not exactly Bloomsbury, but it is the atmosphere of Bloomsbury. Anyone who lives in this place for any length of time and remains dull need not worry himself. Nothing he will ever do will help him. He was born that way.

1932

4

The Case for West Indian Self-Government

THE ENGLISH IN THE WEST INDIES

A Colonial Office Commission is now taking evidence in Trinidad, the Windward and the Leeward Islands, with a view to the federation of all or some of them. But in these islands today political unrest is widespread and deep, and Sir Philip Cunliffe-Lister, the Secretary of State for the Colonies has consented to the request of a deputation that the Commission be allowed to take evidence on the constitutional question. Yet the merits and demerits of constitutions cannot be fairly adjudged without a thorough understanding of the social constituencies they serve. First, then, to give some account of the people who live in the West Indies, for though the scope of the present Commission is restricted, yet British Guiana (for administrative purposes always considered a part of the West Indies) and Jamaica are closely watching, and the decision of the Colonial Office will powerfully affect opinion and action in these colonies.

The bulk of the population of these West Indian islands, over eighty per cent, consists of Negroes or persons of Negroid origin. They are the descendants of those African slaves who were brought almost continuously to the West Indies until the slave trade was stopped in 1807. Cut off from all contact with Africa for a century and a quarter, they present today the extraordinary spectacle of a people who, in language and social customs, religion, education and outlook are essentially Western and, indeed, far more advanced in Western culture than many a European community.

The advocates of Colonial Office trusteeship would have you believe that the average Negro is a savage fellow, bearing beneath the veneer of civilisation and his black skin, viciousness and criminality which he is losing but slowly, and which only the virtual domination of the European is able to keep in check. Says Lord Olivier:[1]

> In the matter of natural good manners and civil disposition the Black People of Jamaica are very far, and indeed, out of comparison, superior to the members of the corresponding class in England, America or North Germany.

Of their alleged savagery:

> This viciousness and criminality are, in fact, largely invented, imputed and exaggerated in order to support and justify the propaganda of race exclusiveness.

The trustees would have you believe that even when he is not a savage the average Negro is a simple, that is to say, a rather childish fellow. Compare this with Lord Olivier's opinion (among those of a hundred others), that:

> The African races generally have a subtle dialectical faculty, and are in some ways far quicker in apprehension that the average Caucasian. . . .
>
> The African whether at home or even in exile after the great hiatus of slavery,[2] shows practical shrewdness and aptitude for the affairs of local government. His legal acumen is higher than that of the European.

The last argument of the trustees, even when they have to admit the attainments of the Negro, is that he does not produce sufficient men of the calibre necessary for administering his own affairs. Yet Sir Charles Bruce,[3] after his wide experience, could say:

> In the meantime, such has been the energy and capacity of the Afro-European population in the Crown Colonies, where they form the bulk of the general community, that there is no department of government, executive, administrative, or judicial, in which they have not held the highest office with distinction, no profession of which they are not honoured members, no branch of commerce or industry in which they have not succeeded.

Today and at any time during the last forty years such posts as Chief Justice, Colonial Secretary, Puisne Judge, Attorney-General, Solicitor-General and Surgeon-General could be filled two or three times over by local men, most of them men of colour. The Civil Services are over ninety per cent coloured, and even in large-scale business, the white man's jealous preserve, numerous coloured men occupy high and important positions.

It has to be admitted that the West Indian Negro is ungracious enough to be far from perfect. He lives in the tropics, and he has the particular vices of all who live there, not excluding people of European blood. In one respect, indeed, the Negro in the tropics has an overwhelming superiority to all other races—the magnificent vitality with which he overcomes the enervating influences of the climate. But otherwise the West Indian people are an easy-going people. Their life is not such as to breed in them the thirst, the care, and the almost equine docility to system and regulation which is characteristic of the industrialised European. If their comparative youth as a people saves them from the cramping effects of tradition, a useful handicap to be rid of in the swiftly-changing world of today, yet they lack that valuable basis of education which is not so much taught or studied as breathed in from birth in countries where people have for generation after generation lived settled and orderly lives. Quicker in intellect and spirit than the English, they pay for it by being less continent, less stable, less dependable. And this particular aspect of their character is intensified by certain social prejudices peculiar to the West Indies, and which have never been given their full value by those observers from abroad who have devoted themselves to the problems of West Indian society and politics.

The negroid population of the West Indies is composed of a large percentage of actually black people, and about fifteen or twenty per cent of people who are a varying combination of white and black. From the days of slavery, these have always claimed superiority to the ordinary black, and a substantial majority of them still do so (though resenting as bitterly as the black assumptions of white superiority). With emancipation in 1834 the blacks themselves established a middle class. But between the brown-skinned middle class and the black there is a continual rivalry, distrust and ill-feeling, which, skillfully played upon by the European people, poisons the life of the community. Where so many crosses and colours meet and mingle, the shades are naturally difficult to determine and the resulting confusion is immense. There are the nearly-white hanging on tooth and nail to the fringes of white society, and these, as is easy to understand, hate contact with the darker skin far more than some of the broader-minded whites. Then there are the browns, intermediates, who cannot by any stretch of imagination pass as white, but who will not go one inch towards mixing with people darker than themselves. And so on, and on, and on. Associations are formed of brown people who will not admit into their number those too much darker than themselves, and there have been heated arguments in committee as to whether such and such a person's skin was fair enough to allow him or her to be admitted, without lowering the tone of the institution. Clubs have been known to accept the daughter and mother who were fair, but refuse the father, who was black. A dark-skinned brother in a fair-skinned family is sometimes the subject of jeers and insults and open intimations that his presence is not required at the family social functions. Fair-skinned girls who marry dark men are often ostracised by their families and given up as lost. There have been cases of fair women who have been content to live with black men but would not marry them. Should the darker man, however, have money or position of some kind, he may aspire, and it is not too much to say that in a West Indian colony the surest sign of a man's having arrived is the fact that he keeps company with people lighter in complexion than himself. Remember, finally, that the people most affected by this are people of the middle class who, lacking the hard contact with realities of the masses and unable to attain to the freedoms of a leisured class, are more than all types of people given to trivial divisions and subdivisions of social rank and precedence.

Here lies, perhaps, the gravest drawback of the coloured population. They find it difficult to combine, for it is the class that should in the natural course of things supply the leaders that is so rent and torn by these colour distinctions.

For historic and economic reasons, the most important of the other native groups are the white creoles.[4] The white creole suffers from two disadvantages, one of which he understands, and the other of which he probably does not. The first is climate. It seems that the European blood cannot by itself stand the climate for more than two or three generations. Here and there the third and fourth generation may use wealth, early acquired, to bolster mediocre abilities into some sort of importance, but the West Indies, as the generations succeed each other, take a deadly toll of all those families from temperate climates which make their home permanently there.

The second disability of the white creole is less tangible but equally important. He finds himself born in a country where the mere fact of his being white, or at least of skin fair enough to pass as white, makes him a person of consequence. Whatever he does, wherever he finds himself, he is certain of recognition. But with this power goes nothing beside personal responsibility. Englishmen govern the country. The result is an atmosphere which cramps effort. There is not that urgent necessity for exceptional performance which drives on the coloured man of ambition, and the white creole suffers accordingly. But this is not a disease which is easily seen by those who suffer from it, nor is the disease, even when diagnosed, one for which the patient is likely to take the remedy.

Into this community comes the Englishman to govern, fortified (sometimes) by university degrees; and of late years by a wide experience in dealing with primitive peoples in Africa.

His antecedents have not been helpful. Bourgeois at home, he has found himself after a few weeks at sea suddenly exalted into membership of a ruling class. Empire to him and most of his type, formerly but a word, becomes on his advent to the colonies a phrase charged with responsibilities, but bearing in its train the most delightful privileges, beneficial to his material well-being and flattering to his pride. Being an Englishman and accustomed to think well of himself, in this new position he soon develops a powerful conviction of his own importance in the scheme of things and it does not take him long to convince himself not only that he can do his work well—which to do him justice, he quite often does—but that for many generations to come none but he and his type can ever hope to do the work they are doing.

On his arrival in the West Indies he experiences a shock. Here is a thoroughly civilised community, wearing the same clothes that he does, speaking no other language but his own, with its best men as good as, and only too often, better than himself. What is the effect on the colonial Englishman when he recognises, as he has to recognise, the quality of those over whom he is placed in authority? Men have to justify themselves, and he falls heavily back on the "ability of the Anglo-Saxon to govern", "the trusteeship of the mother country until such time" (always in the distant future) "as these colonies can stand by themselves", etc. etc. He owes his place to a system, and the system thereby becomes sacred. Blackstone did not worship the corrupt pre-Reform constitution as the Colonial Office worships the system of Crown Colony government.

"Patriotism," says Johnson, "is the last refuge of a scoundrel." It is the first resort of the colonial Englishman. How he leaps to attention at the first bars of "God Save the King"! Empire Day, King's Birthday, days not so much neglected in England as ignored, give to his thirsty spirit an opportunity to sing the praises of the British Empire and of England, his own country, as its centre. Never does he seem to remember that the native place of the majority of those to whom he addresses his wearisome panegyrics is not England, but the colony in which they were born, in which they live, and in which they will in all probability die.

This excessive and vocal patriotism in the colonial Englishman is but the natural smoke of intensified fires burning within. That snobbishness which is so marked a characteristic of the Englishman at home, in the colonies develops into a morbid desire for the respect and homage of those over whom he rules. Uneasily conscious of the moral insecurity of his position, he is further handicapped by finding himself an aristocrat without having been trained as one. His nose for what he considers derogatory to his dignity becomes keener than a bloodhound's which leads him into the most frightful solecisms.

In Grenada in 1931 there was a very orderly demonstration by all classes of the community against a decision of the Governor. One man who with his family had been invited to Government House for some social function took part in it. The Governor cancelled the invitation, but informed him that the cancellation did not apply to his wife and daughter who could come if they wanted to.

It is not surprising that the famous English tolerance leaves him almost entirely. At home he was distinguished for the liberality and freedom of his views. Hampden, Chatham, Dunning and Fox, Magna Carta and Bill of Rights, these are the persons and things (however misconceived) which Englishmen, undemonstrative as they are, write and speak of with a subdued but conscious pride. It is no accident, the Whig tradition in English historical writing. But in the colonies any man who speaks for his country, any man who dares to question the authority of those who rule over him, any man who tries to do for his own people what Englishmen are so proud that other Englishmen have done for theirs, immediately becomes in the eyes of the colonial Englishman a dangerous person, a wild revolutionary, a man with no respect for law and order, a self-seeker actuated by the lowest motives, a reptile to be crushed at the first opportunity. What at home is the greatest virtue becomes in the colonies the greatest crime.

The colonial Englishman it is fair to say retains some of the admirable characteristics which distinguish his race at home, but he is in a false position. Each succeeding year sees local men pressing him on every side, men whom he knows are under no illusions as to why he holds the places he does. Pressure reduces him to dodging and shifting. Thus it is that even of that honesty which is so well-recognised a characteristic of the English people—but I shall let an Englishman speak: "It is difficult", says Mr Somervell, the historian, "for white races to preserve their moral standards in their dealings with races they regard as inferior." Should Englishmen of fine sensibility stray into the Colonial Service they find themselves drawn inevitably into the circle of their colleagues and soon discover that for them to do otherwise than the Romans would be equivalent to joining a body of outsiders against their own. Thus it is that in the colonies, to quote an English official in the West Indies, "such large and intelligent classes of Englishmen come to have opinions so different from those for which the nation has ever been renowned at home."

THE LEGISLATIVE COUNCIL

The deliberations of an Executive Council are secret. The body in which public interest centres is the advisory Legislative Council, which undoubtedly wields great influence, if not power. The Legislative Council of Trinidad is typical and will best serve as an example. This Council consists of three sections. The first is that of the official members, twelve in number, chosen by the Governor from among the various heads of departments. The second consists of the unofficial members, thirteen in number, partly nominated and partly elected. The third section is not the least important of the three—the Governor, who is in the chair. It will be seen how potent for misgovernment is each of these three sections.

The official section, composed mainly of heads of departments, comprises a solid block of Englishmen with a few white creoles, generally from some other colony. These officials are for the most part strangers to the community which they govern; in Trinidad there have been five Attorney-Generals during the last dozen years. Their position is secure, and their promotion depends not on the people over whom they rule, but on a Colonial Office thousands of miles away. It is not difficult to imagine their bureaucratic attitude. There have been official members of the Trinidad Legislature who over a period of years have sat in the Council, saying nothing, doing nothing, wasting their own time and the time of the public. There is a further unreality, because whenever the Governor wishes he can instruct the officials all to vote in the same way. And the Council becomes farcical when two members of a committee appointed by the Governor receive instructions to vote against their own recommendations. Here today and gone tomorrow, these heads of departments, in clubs and social gatherings mix chiefly with the wealthy white creoles, whose interests lie with the maintenance of all the authority and privileges of the officials against the political advancement of the coloured people. Their sons and daughters intermarry with the white creoles and get employment in the big business houses. From all this springs that alliance so clearly foreshadowed by Cornewall Lewis. "We represent large interests," said the Attorney-General in a recent debate, and every West Indian knows the interest which he and the other officials represent. The local government is the Chamber of Commerce, and the Chamber of Commerce is the local government.

The unofficial members "representing the people" form the second group, and since 1925 they have consisted of six members nominated by the Governor and seven members elected by the people. Formerly the Governor nearly always appointed white men representing business interests. He might as well have appointed a few more heads of departments for all the representation the people got from them.

But it has been the policy of the government for some years past to appoint a few Negroes to these positions. These have usually been Negroes of fair, and not of dark skin. And that type of man, whether on the Council or in the other departments of government, is often a more dangerous opponent of the masses of the people than the Europeans themselves.

In its broader aspect this is no new thing in politics. There is, first of all, the natural gravitation of all men towards the sources of power and authority, and, on far larger stages, parties of privilege have not yet ceased to hire mercenaries to do what would be less plausibly and effectively done by themselves. The West Indian Islands are small and the two easiest avenues of success are the help of the government or the help of the white people. It is, therefore, fatally easy for the nominee to rationalise his self-seeking by the reflection that after all, in such a legislature, he can achieve nothing that the government sets its mind against.

There is yet another consideration no less powerful than the foregoing. These West Indian colonies offer, especially to those no longer young, little in the way of organised amusement, and individuals are thrown back almost entirely on society for recreation. Mr Julian Huxley, after four months' extensive travel in Africa, has written:

> Of a large and important section of white people in Africa, officials as well as settlers, it is not unfair to say that *The Tatler*, *Punch*, a few magazines, detective stories and second-rate romantic novels represent their intellectual and cultural level.

The case in Trinidad is precisely the same, and indeed the shallowness, the self-sufficiency and the provincialism of English colonial society has long been a by-word among cultivated persons. But it keeps itself to itself and thereby becomes exclusive. It is the wealthiest class, lives in the best houses, has the best clubs, organises the best amusements. For the fair-skinned Negro who does not seek much, that society seems a paradise.

But when that is said, though much is said, all is not said. There is first of all the Governor. There have been recent Governors whom the people despised, and rightly. Of one and his entourage it could be said that he represented the butler, his wife the housekeeper, and his ADC the groom. But His Majesty's Representative is sometimes a man of parts, his wife a person of elegance. And whatever qualities they may have are naturally enhanced by the

> . . . power
> Pre-eminence, and all the large effects
> That troop with majesty.

Now and then among the officials one finds a really brilliant man. Of late, members of the Consular Body, and some of the Professors of the Imperial College of Tropical Agriculture, have contributed their fair share to local society. Distinguished visitors often lend both tone and colour to the social dullness of local life. Any unusual social talent of local origin, if it is white, will usually find its way to the top. Thus around the Governor centre a few small groups which, though they will vary in value from time to time, yet whatever they are, are by far the best that the islands can show, for the coloured people, though possessing in themselves the elements of a society of some cultural value (their range of choice being so much wider), are so divided among themselves on questions of colour, based on varying shades of lightness or darkness, that they have been unable to form any truly representative social group or groups. The result is that many a man conscious of powers above the average, and feeling himself entitled to move in the best society the island affords, spends most of his leisure time and a small fortune in trying to get as near to the magic centre as possible, in itself a not too mean nor too comtemptible ambition. The serious flaw in the position of the local man of colour is this, that those to whose society and good graces he aspires are not only Englishmen, but Englishmen in the colonies, and therefore constitutionally incapable of admitting into their society on equal terms persons of colour, however gifted or however highly placed (unless very rich). The aspirant usually achieves only a part of his aim. The utmost sacrifice of money, influence, and dignity usually gains him but a precarious position on the outer fringes of the society which he hopes to penetrate, and he is reduced to consorting with those fairer than himself, whose cupidity is greater than their pride. Others who feel themselves above this place-at-any-price policy stand on their dignity and remain at home, splendidly isolated. Thus it is nothing surprising to find on the Legislative Council three or four coloured men, each a little different in colour, who are more widely separated from one another than any of them is from a white man, and whose sole bond of unity is their mutual jealousy in their efforts to stand well with the governing officials.

These matters would not concern us here except for their unfortunate reaction on the political life of the community.

Not only nominations to the Council but all appointments in the service are made by the government, and the government can, and usually does, point to the number of coloured men it has appointed. But either by accident or design it rarely appoints black men. The appointment of these fair-skinned men seems to depend to a large extent on the way, whether openly or covertly, they dissociate themselves from their own people. But those same arts a place did gain must it maintain. The result is that a more or less intelligent and aspiring minority occupy a position in which they do more harm than good, for to the Colonial Office and the ordinary observer, being men of colour, they represent the coloured people, while the government and the white creole know that when it comes to a crisis these, their henchmen, are more royalist than the king. Some people have endeavoured to see in this a characteristic weakness of the coloured people and a grave reflection on their capacity for leadership. It is not so. Disinterested service actuated by nothing more than a sense of responsibility to one's own best convictions is a thing rare among all nations, and by necessity of less frequent occurrence in a small community of limited opportunities. These men are not so much inherently weak as products of the social system in which they live. Still, whatever the cause of their conduct, its effect is disastrous. Particularly as the government will appoint a dark Negro to a position of importance only when it cannot get a fair one. In this way it builds up in the service a group of men who, however distasteful to Englishmen themselves, are at one with them in their common antipathy to the black. Despising black men, these intermediates, in the Legislative Council and out of it, are forever climbing up the climbing wave, governed by one dominating motive—acceptance by white society. It would be unseemly to lower the tone of this book by detailing with whom, when and how Colonial Secretaries and Attorney-Generals distribute the nod distant, the bow cordial, the shakehand friendly, or the cut direct as many seem fitting to their exalted Highnesses; the transport of joy into which men, rich, powerful, and able, are thrown by a few words from the Colonial Secretary's wife or a smile from the Chief Justice's daughter. But political independence and social aspiration cannot run between the same shafts; sycophancy soon learns to call itself moderation; and invitations to dinner or visions or a knighthood form the strongest barriers to the wishes of the people.

All this is, and has been, common knowledge in the West Indies for many years. The situation shows little signs of changing. The type of constitution encourages rather than suppresses the tendency. But the day that all fair-skinned Negroes realise (as some do today) that they can only command respect when they respect themselves, that day the domination of the coloured people by white men is over. If the white men are wealthy, they will have the influence of wealthy men. If they are able they will have the influence of able men. But they will cease to have the influence of wealth or ability, not because they are wealthy or able, but simply because they are white.

If we neglect the elected members for the time being (a form of attention to which they are well accustomed) there remains now only the Governor in the chair.

At first sight it may seem that the Governor in the chair occupies a merely formal position, but on closer observation it becomes immediately obvious that his position there is as mischievous as those of the other two sections of a Crown Colony legislature. The Governor of a Crown Colony is three things. He is the representative of His Majesty the King, and as such must have all the homage and respect customary to that position. But the Governor is also the officer responsible for the proper administration of the government. The Governor-General of South Africa, like the other Governors-General, is not responsible for the government of the country. The responsible persons are the prime ministers of those countries. In Trinidad the Governor is Governor-General and Prime Minister in one. But that makes only two. When the Governor sits in the Legislative Council he is chairman of that body. The unfortunate result is that when a member of the Council rises to speak he is addressing at one and the same time an incomprehensible personage, three in one and one in three. A member of the House of Commons can pay all due respect to His Majesty the King, submit himself to the proper authority of the Speaker of the House, and yet express himself in uncompromising terms about any aspect of government policy which appears to him to deserve such censure. In a Crown Colony legislature that is impossible. The Governor, being responsible for the administration, is liable to criticism directed against his subordinates. It is natural that he should, it is inconceivable that he would, do otherwise than defend those who assist him in carrying on the affairs of the colony. But should a Governor make an inconvenient admission as the head of the government he immediately assumes one of his other alibis. And in the Council as it is constituted and with the Governor holding the power that he holds, there are never lacking members always on the alert to jump to the defence of the dignity of His Majesty's representative or the respect due to the President of the Chamber, quite neglectful of the responsibility of the head of the administration. In December 1931 one nominated member in the course of his address on a Divorce Bill referred to the part the Governor had played in bringing forward that piece of legislation so unpopular with a certain section:

> It is a pity that Your Excellency did not publish these despatches earlier, so that the public might have known the part Your Excellency has played in respect to this matter. I have no doubt that now the despatches have been published and the atmosphere has been clarified, it will be realised that Your Excellency's share of the responsibility for the presentation of this Bill is absolutely nil.
>
> If I may say so without offence, it would appear that you are regarded by the Colonial Office merely as a servant of the centurion. . . . It must be very humiliating indeed to any responsible officer to find himself in the position in which Your Excellency must find

yourself. . . .

Now that speech erred, if it erred in any way, on the side of temperance. The speaker was forcible, but, nominated brown-skinned Negro in a Crown Colony Legislature, his tone was so respectful as to be almost humble.[5] But not so in the eyes of one member. No. For him the Governor had been insulted. Nor did he wait for a government official to say so. He (himself a brown-skinned Negro) began his own address with a flood of compliment to the Solicitor-General (a white man) for the able way in which he had argued for the Bill and then turned his hose on the Attorney-General (another white man) and complimented him on the able way he had argued against the Bill. Then he switched off to the address of his brother Negro and nominated member: "He referred to the Governor of this Colony in a way ill befitting any member of this Council. . . ."

Nor was he yet satisfied that enough sacrifices had been offered on the altar of the Governor's dignity. Before his speech was finished he found opportunity to make another salaam: "I was pained to listen to his statement in almost flippant language that the Governor of this Colony was the servant of the centurion."

Instances may be multiplied. In his triple position the Governor in the chair exercises a disproportionate influence. His presence is a constant check to free expression of opinion. And a Legislative Council in which a man cannot freely speak his mind is a place fit for academic debates and not for the discussion of the affairs of government.

It is not difficult to imagine the result of all this in the working of the constitution. The government, already so overwhelmingly strong, is without effective criticism or check, and being composed of men who are governing not for the sake of governing, but because they have to make a living, it is not strange that it should be as slack and regardless as it usually is. "Public life is a situation of power and energy. He trespasses upon his duty who sleeps upon his watch and may as well go over to the enemy." There, Burke, as ever, master of political statement, distills for the politician a first principle.

It is the lack of this active vigilance which robs our politics of any reality. Far from being alert guardians of the public weal, the favourite formula of most of these members is: "I beg to congratulate the government." Should an official make a speech of no more than mediocre ability, each one, at some time in his own speech, "begs to congratulate the honourable member". Always they seem to be bowing obsequiously, hat in hand, always the oily flattery, the ingratiating smile, and criticism offered on a silver salver. A person gaining his first impression of politics from a reading of some of these debates would conclude not that it was the sole business of the government to govern properly, but a favour that was being conferred upon the people. It must not be imagined that some of these members have been ciphers of no value on the Legislature. Sometimes they possess great ability or force of personality. They are men of the world enough to know that if to assert themselves too much is a mistake, it would be equally a mistake to assert themselves too little. But they can never have that full weight in public matters which comes from a man like Captain Cipriani, who speaks from his well-known and settled convictions, or from a respected Colonial Secretary who is stating the case from the government point of view. Sometimes they find themselves inadvertently on the wrong side, and it is interesting to see them wriggle out. "Can the government see its way to . . .?" "No." "Couldn't the government . . .?" "No. . . ." "I still think I am right, however, though I beg to congratulate the honourable member who explained the Government's position. It is clear that the government is quite right, too. I beg to congratulate the government. The government will hear nothing more of this from me."

One concrete example must be given of the attitude of these nominated representatives of the people.

From the time that the Imperial College of Tropical Agriculture started its work in Trinidad there were well-founded complaints of discrimination against coloured men. When in April 1930 there came up before the Legislative Council a grant to the Imperial College of 8,500 pounds a year for five years, Captain Cipriani asked the government for a definite assurance that there would be no discrimination. If not, he would oppose the vote. Here for once the underlying reef was showing above the surface, plain, stark, and not to be denied.

The debate continued.

Mr O'Reilly (who had had a brother there): ". . . I do not follow my honourable friend in suggesting that there has been any discrimination at the College. . . ."

Sir Henry Alcazar: ". . . I do not propose to address you on the question of discrimination. . . ."

The Colonial Secretary (reading a statement from the Principal of the Imperial College of Tropical Agriculture): "I am at a loss to know how the idea has occurred that there is a differentiation over coloured students. . . ."

Dr McShine: "Your Excellency, I also supported the desire to have some assurance from the College that the discrimination did not exist or that it was exaggerated, and I am glad to have the explanation, the statement of fact that it is not so. . . ."

Mr Kelshall: "I think that we ought in looking at this subject, to take a long view. . . . But I have the utmost confidence in the Head of the College—Mr Evans—a broad-minded Englishman of the right sort . . . and I do not believe there is at present any ground for complaint in regard to discrimination among the students. . . ."

Mr Wortley (the Director of Agriculture): "I do feel strongly that the reason is not that the College does not wish them, but that for one reason or another the Trinidadians do not wish to go to the College. In other words, other professions and other openings attract them more. . . ."

It remained for the Governor to conclude in the same strain:

. . . We cannot dictate to private companies what appointments they should make, but it appears to me to be very foolish if companies operating in the country do not appoint people that live there, and prefer to go elsewhere to fill appointments. If I can help in this matter I shall certainly do so. (Applause.)

So far the public debate. But what were the actual facts? Mr Gaston Johnston (a coloured man), who was present, did not say anything in the House, but when the meeting was over he told Captain Cipriani that Father English, the Principal of St. Mary's College, had received a letter from Mr Martin Leake, the previous

Principal of the Agricultural College, in which Mr Leake had asked Father English to discourage young men of colour from coming to the Imperial College, because although he, the Principal, had nothing against them, the white students made it unpleasant, which caused a great deal of difficulty.

"My God, Johnston, you mean to say you knew that and not only did not say so yourself, but did not tell me?"

"No, for if I had told you, you would say it and cause a lot of trouble."

Captain Cipriani knew, as every other member of Council knew, the true state of affairs at the College. When he went to England in the July following, he brought the matter to the notice of the Colonial Office. The Colonial Office official listened to him and then took up a copy of Hansard.

"Captain Cipriani, you complain of discrimination. Now, isn't Mr O'Reilly a coloured man? Yes. Now listen to what he says. . . . Isn't Sir Henry Alcazar a coloured man? Now listen to what he says. . . Isn't Mr Kelshall a coloured man? . . . Isn't Dr McShine a coloured man, And this is what he says. . . . Now, Captain Cipriani, what have you come here making trouble about?

Now one can understand the position of the white men who spoke in this debate. One can understand Mr Wortley feeling so strongly that Trinidadians did not go to the Imperial College because they preferred other avenues, for it is an important part of the business of the government official to deprecate any suggestion of colour discrimination, and whenever the opportunity arises, to throw as much dust as possible. The same motives obviously actuated the Governor. How else is it possible to account for his apparent ignorance of the fact that the oil companies would as soon appoint a Zulu chief to some of their higher offices as a local man of colour, whatever the qualifications he had gained at the Imperial College? We can even pass over the irreconcilable conflict of evidence between Mr Evans and his immediate predecessor. Englishmen or white men stand to gain nothing by talk about race discrimination; and on a short-sighted view they stand to lose a great deal. But in this debate, as in every other, what is so pitiful is the attitude of these so-called representatives of the people, who so often hold the positions that they do hold because of their colour. The majority of them hate even more than white men any talk about colour. For if they stand up against colour discrimination they will be noted by the government as leaders of the people, and then good-bye to some of their dearest hopes; while for some it will mean facing in public the perfectly obvious but nevertheless dreadful fact that they are not white men.

That is the Trinidad Legislature. There is no room nor should there be need to go any farther into details of the course of legislation.

The reader may want to know more of that pitiful remnant, the elected members, who form usually about a third of the various legislatures. The usual colour prejudices often divide them; and in any case it takes a man of the courage and strength of Captain Cipriani to hurl himself continuously against the solid phalanx arrayed against him. But the real hopelessness of the situation is best to be seen in Grenada and Dominica. In each of these smaller islands, where the population is more homogeneous and more closely-knit, the local Government has achieved the astonishing feat of uniting both nominated and elected members against itself. In Grenada, both these groups, defeated by the official majority, retired from the Council. Warmly supported by the whole population they have returned, but certainly not to shed tears of happy reunion on the shoulders of the government. In Dominica all the officials, nominated and elected, have refused to go back and though writs have been issued for a new election no one will stand. When, after a time, one man accepted nomination by the government the people burnt his house down. It is in this way that empires prod their citizens into violence and sow the seeds of their own dissolution. Yet though the writing on the walls stretched from Burma to Cyprus, there are those who will not read.

When will British administrators learn the lesson and for the sake of future cordial relations give willingly and cheerfully what they know they will have to give at last? How do they serve their posterity by leaving them a heritage of bitterness and hate in every quarter of the globe? Solution of the problem there is but one—a constitution on democratic lines. This does not necessarily mean a form of government modelled plastically on the English or Dominion systems. Ceylon shows one way, Malta another. The West Indian legislators have their constitution ready. That is not a matter for debate here. But there will only be peace when in each colony the final decisions on policy and action rest with the elected representatives of the people. Hard things are being said today about parliamentary democracy, but the West Indian colonies will not presume to reject it until England and the dominions show them the way. The high qualification for membership of the Council must go. The high franchise, for the power to vote must go. That tight-rope dance, the nominated member, must vanish forever, and the representatives of the people thrown back upon the people.

No one expects that these islands will, on assuming responsibility for themselves, immediately shed racial prejudice and economic depression. No one expects that by a change of constitutions the constitution of politicians will be changed. But though they will, when the occasions arise, disappoint the people, and deceive the people and even, in so-called crises, betray the people, yet there is one thing they will never be able to do—and that is, neglect the people. As long as society is constituted as it is at present that is the best that modern wage-slaves can ever hope to achieve.

For a community such as ours, where, although there is race prejudice, there is no race antagonism, where the people have reached their present level in wealth, education, and general culture, the Crown Colony system of government has no place. It was useful in its day, but that day is now over. It is a fraud, because it is based on assumptions of superiority which have no foundation in fact. Admirable as are their gifts in this direction, yet administrative capacity is not the monopoly of the English; and even if it were, charity begins at home, especially in these difficult times. The system is wicked, because to an extent far more than is immediately obvious it permits a privileged few to work their will on hundreds of thousands of defenceless people. But most of all is the system criminal because it uses England's overflow as a cork to choke down the natural expansion of the people. Always the West Indian of any ambition or sensibility has to see positions of honour and power in his own country filled by itinerant demigods who sit at their desks, ears cocked for the happy news of a retirement in Nigeria or a death in Hong Kong; when they go and others of the same kind take their places, while men often better than they stand outside rejected and despised. And even were the Colonial Office officials ideally suited to their posts the situation would not be better, but worse than it is. For the more efficient they are, the more do they act as a blight upon those vigorous and able men whose home is their island, and who, in the natural course of events, would rise to power and influence. Governors and governed stand on either side of a gulf which no tinkering will bridge, and political energy is diverted into other channels or simply runs to waste. Britain will hold us down as long as she wishes. Her cruisers and aeroplanes ensure it. But a people like ours should be free to make its own failures and successes, free to gain that political wisdom and political experience which come only from the practice of political affairs. Otherwise, led as we are by a string, we remain without credit abroad and with no self-respect at home, a bastard, feckless conglomeration of individuals, inspired by no common purpose, moving to no common end.

"Self-government when fit for it."

That has always been the promise. Britain can well afford to keep it in this case, where evidence in favour is so overwhelming and she loses so little by keeping her word.

1933

5
Abyssinia and the Imperialists

Africans and people of African descent, especially those who have been poisoned by British imperialist education, needed a lesson. They have got it. Every succeeding day shows exactly the real motives which move imperialism in its contact with Africa, shows the incredible savagery and duplicity of European imperialism in its quest for markets and raw materials. Let the lesson sink in deep.

European imperialism has been after Abyssinia for fifty years. What do they want it for? They want it, first of all, for the minerals that are there, to plant cotton, to send some of their surplus population to the highlands, to make the natives buy Lancashire goods, or German goods or Italian goods, as the case might be, to invest money and then tax the native so as to make him pay a steady interest. All this they call developing the country and raising the standard of civilisation. They build a few schools and a few hospitals. Some few of the richer natives get jobs in the government service and come to European universities for education. They are pointed out as evidence of the high standard of civilisation that has been introduced into the native country.

But all the money that the imperialists are making out of the country has to be paid for by labour, and the real sufferers are those millions who, unprotected by trade union organisation or any sort of organised public opinion, are driven off their lands, down into mines at a shilling a day, or working above ground for fourpence a day as in Kenya, with all the special humiliations and degradations that are attached to the African in Africa, not because he is black, but because the imperialist despite his guns and cruisers, is in such mortal fear of the indignation of these people that he builds up in every possible way a wall of defence between himself and them. First of all, he has his cruisers always about, his aeroplanes and his trained soldiers. But in addition he insists always to his own people that they are superior to the exploited races, and he insists always to the exploited races that they are inferior to his own. Thus he reinforces the power of arms by democratizing the mentality of those whom he uses for his purposes both at home and abroad.

Now to this question of Abyssinia. These European imperialists have been after

Abyssinia for fifty years. We have to remember that, because the issue before us today is obscured by the mountain of lies and nonsense which are being wrapped around it. They wanted it for the purposes described above, and they have got it. There is no longer any independence of Abyssinia worth a scrap of paper as far as the imperialists are concerned. The moment the Emperor signed the proposals of the Committee of Five in late September the independence of Abyssinia had vanished. All that Italy, Great Britain and France had been quarrelling about among themselves and with Abyssinia was given to them by those proposals, wrapped round with silver paper labelled "assistance to a weaker nation", and blessed with the holy water of the League. European imperialism was determined to get Abyssinia, and it has got it. Let us trace the steps.

Italy tried in 1896 and was beaten at Adowa and driven out. Abyssinia is a high plateau, strategically very powerful. The people are splendid fighters, so that the imperialists saw they could not steal it as easily as they had stolen the rest of Africa. In 1902 Britain asked for the Lake Tana concession. The Abyssinians refused. In 1906 Britain, France and Italy divided Abyssinia in London by the Tripartite Treaty. When they were finished they sent to tell Menelik, the Emperor of Abyssinia, who told them they could write what they liked in treaties, he remained master of his own country. They sheered off.

In 1915 Britain and France brought Italy into the war by, among other promises, a hint of Abyssinian territory. But when the war was over Britain and France grabbed the German colonies and Italy was left out. In 1919 Italy offered Britain to divide Abyssinia with her. The British government said no, that they did not want to have any power near the Lake Tana concession. Whereupon Italy seeing that Britain was not prepared to divide, conspired with France and dragged Abyssinia by the hair into the League of Nations. This was in 1923. This prevented Britain acting single-handed against Abyssinia as she wanted to do. So in 1925 Britain offered to Mussolini to divide on the same terms that she had rejected in 1919. But Abyssinia threatened to fight, and France supported Abyssinia at the League. Britain and Italy apologised, said they had meant no harm. France, it is to be noted, has a railway from Jibuti in French Somaliland to Addis Ababa. She makes an enormous profit from it, and French goods travel along this railway into Abyssinia. So in as much as France cannot attack Abyssinia herself, she was quite prepared to support Abyssinia to keep the others out.

But by January 1935 France is terribly afraid of Germany. Mussolini has a fine army, and in return for a promise of help against Germany, France "disinterests herself economically" from Abyssinia. In other words gives Mussolini a free hand. In Italy the water is up to Mussolini's nose, and he must find some sort of explanation somewhere or perish. So having squared France, he informs the British that he is ready to talk Abyssinia with them. This was on the 29th January last. The British government would not do a single thing. They would not reply to Mussolini because they did not want to say yes—that could be used in evidence against them—and yet they did not want to say no. Because Abyssinia had been blocking them for forty years, and it was time that she was brought to order. Abyssinia kept on appealing to the League of Nations. Laval would not budge, neither would the British Government. Mussolini meanwhile sent his ships packed with men to Africa. But the Abyssinians would not be frightened, and at last the

British Government had to take notice. The League met and after some negotiations, they appointed Britain and France to discuss with Italy in Paris.

As can be seen from the *Manchester Guardian* of September, in the notes of the foreign correspondent, Britain and France offered Mussolini vast opportunities for exploitation in Abyssinia, but demanded that he should not dominate the country with an armed force. They all would do that together, and the force would be internalised. But Mussolini said no, and when Britain realised that Mussolini meant to establish himself in Abyssinia as firmly as they, for instance, were established in India, they got thoroughly frightened. For Abyssinia, powerfully situated as it is, is in the heart of the British Empire in East Africa, Mussolini would form an army of these splendid Abyssinian fighters, and from there, in the next war, he could march down into any of the British colonies around.

Britain at once sent the fleet to the Mediterranean, started to mobilise the British Army, and seeing that she might have to fight, decided to make it a League War, in defence of collective security, the independence of Abyssinia and a lot of blather of the kind. All the small nations at Geneva, terribly frightened at what is going to happen when Hitler begins, were glad to see Britain standing up for the League at last and wished to support. "Action now" said Eden, sanctions etc etc. The British Government, however, manipulated a scheme known to the world as the Proposals of the Committee of Five, by which Abyssinia would be delivered to them lock, stock and barrel, disarming of the people, all economic concessions, League advisors to govern the country, control of Budget taxes etc.—in fact all that they had been trying to get for fifty years. The Emperor could get no arms and they refused to give him any until he signed. Between the devil and the deep sea he chose the British Government masquerading as the League. Britain was now in a powerful position. Even although France was unwilling she had Mussolini in a serious hole.

She invited him to come in and share in this League mandate. He refused. The League started to impose sanctions, and worse still, the war went badly for Mussolini. The Abyssinians have been defending themselves with great skill and there is little possibility, in fact none, that Mussolini will dominate the plateau which has made the British government so suddenly enthusiastic for the League. Mussolini, therefore, despite all his noise and bluster, showed himself willing to come to terms and take as much as he could without threatening British interests. Forthwith Britain produces the peace plan, giving half of Abyssinia to Mussolini. Once British interests are no longer threatened and they can get their Lake Tana concession, they have no more interest in the League than they had when Japan stole a large piece of China.

What has caused the trouble is that many well-meaning people in Britain took the British government seriously when it announced itself as converted to the League. This sudden reversal has come as a shock, and Baldwin has had to get rid of Samuel Hoare and dodge and shift around and confess that a mistake has been made. One thing however we can take as certain—the British imperialists were prepared to support the League on behalf of Abyssinia and collective security, and even fight, as long as British imperialist interests were threatened. These are now safe, and all that they are concerned with now is dodging out of their promises as quickly as they can! Public opinion is against them. Public opinion on the whole is not aware that by the proposals of the Committee of Five the imperialists have got what they wanted. It genuinely thinks that the League is protecting Abyssinia, and, that accounts for its indignation.

But British imperialism does not govern only the colonies in its own interests. It governs the British people in its own interests also, and we shall see that imperialism will win. It will talk a lot but it will do nothing for Abyssinia. The only thing to save Abyssinia is the efforts of the Abyssinians themselves and action by the great masses of Negroes and sympathetic whites and Indians all over the world, by demonstrations, public meetings, resolutions, financial assistance to Abyssinia, strikes against the export of all materials to Italy, refusal to unload Italian ships etc.

Mussolini, the British government and the French have shown the Negro only too plainly that he has got nothing to expect from them but exploitation, either naked or wrapped in bluff. In that important respect this conflict, though unfortunate for Abyssinia, has been of immense benefit to the race as a whole.

1936

6

The Black Jacobins

CHARACTERS *in order of appearance*
The Prologue:
A Barber
A Lady
Henri Christophe
Jean-Jacques Dessalines
Toussaint L'Ouverture
Madame L'Ouverture
Slaves, white men, drummers, etc.

The Play:
Madame Bullet
Marie-Jeanne
Möise L'Ouverture
M. Bullet
Jean-Jacques Dessalines
Toussaint L'Ouverture
Marat, aide to Dessalines
Max, aide to Möise
Orleans, aide to Christophe
Mars Plaisir, civilian aide to Toussaint
Marquis D'Hermona, a Spanish General
Aide to the Spanish General
First Servant
Second Servant
Tobias Lear, American Consul
General Hédouville of the French Army
General Maitland of the British Army
Henri Christophe
Secretary to Maitland
Celestine, maid to Marie-Jeanne

Colonel Vincent of the French Army
General Bonaparte, First Consul of France
A guard
A secretary to Bonaparte
Samedi Smith, a brigand
A mulatto officer
A French officer
Cathcart
Slaves, soldiers, dancers, drummers, musicians (violinist, flautist, mandolinist.)

SYNOPSIS OF SCENES

All scenes take place in French San Domingo (now the Republic of Haiti) except Act II, Scene 3

THE PROLOGUE: The Slaves, The Barber, The Thief, The Entertainer, The Waiter, The Courier, The Leader.

THE PLAY:

ACT I

Scene 1: Living Room of M. Bullet, a plantation owner: 1791.
Scene 2: Military Headquarters of General Toussaint L'Ouverture: 1794.
Scene 3: Living Room of Tobias Lear, the American Consul, 1798.
Scene 4: Governor L'Ouverture's Headquarters, General Maitland's Headquarters, 1798.

ACT II

Scene 1: Bedroom of Marie-Jeanne, 1800.
Scene 2: Headquarters of Toussaint L'Ouverture, 1800.
Scene 3: Office of General Bonaparte, Les Tuileries, Paris, France, 1800.
Scene 4: Headquarters of Toussaint L'Ouverture, 1802.

ACT III

Scene 1: Headquarters of Dessalines, 1802.
Scene 2: Headquarters of Dessalines, 1803.

The stage is divided into four areas. There is a main central area, two smaller areas—one on each side, and a large area upstage for crowds, banner-bearers, etc. The upstage area is outdoors. In the Prologue it is used for the slaves in silhouette. In the Play it is possible that crowds may assemble at the back and be spoken to from the back of the main central area. Crowds say little but their presence is felt powerfully at all critical moments. This is the key point of the play and comments cannot, must not, be written. It must be felt, dramatically, and be projected as essential to action in the downstage areas. From the beginning, the stage is set for Act I, Scene 1 of the play. The Prologue takes place in and around the setting.

PROLOGUE

Drums begin in blackout. After two phrases, the night sky is illumined.

THE SLAVES

Silhouetted against it are five slaves chained together at the waist. They mime digging with spades. They sing:

Eh! Eh! Bomba! Heu! Heu!
Canga bafio te!
Canga moune de le
Canga, do ki la
Canga, li
(Repeat)

An overseer cracks the whip to stop them. They stop singing and freeze. Blackout. Drums continue for two phrases and stop.

THE BARBER

Lights come up immediately in the central area. (The slaves upstage are still in place, immobile.) A lady sits on a low chair. A well-dressed barber is supervising four slaves. They are dressing the lady's hair. Two stand in attendance, the third, who has been curling it, steps back. The fourth slave steps forward to add the finishing touches and, in doing so, undoes one curl. The lady gives a small cry of disappointment as this happens. The barber, who has been supervising, boxes the face of the fourth slave until he falls to the ground. He cowers as the barber reverses his riding crop. The third slave has mended the damage to the coiffure quickly. The second slave has presented a mirror. The lady smiles and sighs aloud. The barber turns, goes to the lady, pushes away the second slave with his crop, and smiles and bows. The third slave picks up the fourth. They all stand numbly. The barber gracefully accepts the fee and leaves stage left in a flourish. The light fades. Drums start again in blackout. After two phrases the sky is illumined.

THE SLAVES

The five silhouetted slaves mime digging with pickaxes. They sing:

Eh! Eh! Bomba! Heu! Heu!
White man—vow to destroy
Take his riches away
Kill them
Every one
Canga Li.

The overseer cracks his whip. They stop singing and freeze. Blackout. Drums continue for two phrases and stop.

THE THIEF

The lights come up immediately in the area on stage left. (The slaves upstage are still in place, immobile.) A slave is kneeling with his face on the ground. He is held by another slave. A white man stands left of them. Another stands in front of the kneeling slave. There is a sack under the piano behind him. The latter white man speaks: This is outrageous. You have been stealing my neighbour's chickens? *(He hands the neighbour a cat-o-nine-tails.)* Here you are, my dear M. Millet, you may watch him receive one hundred lashes. *(The neighbour takes the whip and hands it to the standing slave. The kneeling slave is jerked to his feet and marched off. The neighbour follows. The white man goes to the door, looks after them, then turns and claps his hands twice. His house slave appears from stage right. The white man points to the sack. The slave picks it up. A chicken clucks from within. The white man says:)* For a change, Madame and I will eat some fried chicken tonight. *(The slave bows as the lights fade. Drums start again in blackout. After two phrases, the sky is illumined.)*

THE SLAVE

The five silhouetted slaves pass heavy boulders slowly from one to the other. They hum the tune of the previous song, slowly and softly. The overseer cracks the whip. They stop humming and freeze; the slaves are bent over with the weight of the boulders. Blackout. Drums continue for two phrases and stop.

THE ENTERTAINER

The lights come up immediately in the small area on stage right. (The slaves upstage have disappeared.) Two white men are talking. One is saying: . . . and when the dancing is over, as a grand finale, we take that old one of mine who has been sick *(the other catches on and mimes an action with three fingers of his right hand shoved down a circle made by the thumb and fingers of his left hand)*, fill him with gunpowder, and blow him to Kingdom Come! *(The other has moved his hands apart with the imagined explosion and they both laugh raucously at this as the lights fade slowly to blackout. Drums start; after two phrases, they stop.)*

THE HOTEL

Lights come up in the stage left area. A waiter, Henri Christophe, is serving drinks to three white men in an Hotel lobby.

WHITE MAN A: Imagine! Only six deputies for San Domingo! The StatesGeneral in France must be crazy.

WHITE MAN B: It was Mirabeau from that black-loving club. "The Friends of the Negro." He had the effrontery to say that if our blacks could not vote, and could be counted in the census, then there were mules and horses in France which could not vote and could be counted in their census.

WHITE MAN C: So unfair! Everyone knows that animals are worth more than blacks.

The others are in accord. The lights fade. A spot remains on Christophe standing to one side. His face is impassive. Then that spot also fades to blackout.

THE FOREST

A patter of drums begins calling for a gathering. The sky is illumined. A blue light comes up in the upstage area where the slaves had been working, Flambeaux light the forest clearing as slaves converge around a speaker standing on a platform. He punctuates his phrases with gasps for breath. Drums fade out.

SPEAKER: My brothers, I have been running all night to tell you. The slaves of the French islands of Guadaloupe and Martinique are fighting their masters. The white slaves in France are fighting their masters. You here in Fort Dauphin, you who have toiled in the fields and got no reward except lashes with the whip; the land belongs to you, your blood and sweat is mixed in the earth. You must join your brothers in revolt, we must fight. . . . *(Two shots ring out. The speaker falls dead. The slaves scatter with their lights. A lone light remains on the fallen speaker with one member of the crowd—Dessalines—bent over him.)*

DESSALINES: *(He looks up with determination and hate on his face. He raises a fist to the sky and shouts.)* We will kill them all. Every one. *(The spot fades to blackout. Silence.)*

THE LEADER

The lights come up on the area stage right. Toussaint L'Ouverture is sitting in a rustic armchair with a book open on his lap. His head is at rest and he stares into the night. His wife enters behind him.

MME. L'OUVERTURE: Old man, why don't you come to bed. It is late.

TOUSSAINT: I can't sleep. There is something frightening in the air. And I have just opened my Raynal to read an even more frightening thing. The book just opened and I looked. The Abbe is saying: "A courageous chief only is wanted." I have read it a thousand times before, but it is as if I had seen it for the first time.

MME. L'OUVERTURE: Toussaint, you still feel this destiny for great things.

TOUSSAINT: Yes, I do. For a long time. Ever since the slave uprisings began. But *what* "great things?"

MME. L'OUVERTURE: Come to bed, Old Toussaint. You're tired.

TOUSSAINT: In a little while. *(Madame L'Ouverture exits. Toussaint looks into the book again, then looks up as the lights fade to a solitary spot on him)* "A courageous chief only is wanted." *(The light fades to blackout.)*

ACT I, SCENE 1: OCTOBER 1791

The living-room of M. Bullet, owner of a slave plantation and many slaves, including Toussaint L'Ouverture. The plantation is a few score miles outside Le Cap, the capital of the French colony of San Domingo in the Caribbean. The slave revolution has broken out in August. The island is in turmoil The time is about half-past two in the afternoon. Madame Bullet is playing a Mozart aria on the piano and singing it. The aria is from Don Giovanni, Act 1: "Vendetta ti chieggio, la chiede il tuo cor."

MME. BULLET:

I demand revenge of you, your heart demands it,
your heart demands it.
Remember the wounds in that poor breast,
Recall the ground, covered, covered with blood,
Should the fury of a just anger, of a just anger
wane in you . . .
I demand revenge of you, your heart demands it,
your heart demands it.

Remember the wounds, recall the blood,
I demand revenge of you, your heart demands it,
I demand revenge of you, your heart demands it. . . .

(The lights come up after the first few bars of this to reveal Madame Bullet at the piano in the central area. At one side of the piano is her companion, a mulatto slave, Marie-Jeanne. Marie-Jeanne is humming, sometimes singing, a phrase when it is often repeated, perhaps in descant. While this is going on, there is, upstage, a subdued humming of "La Marseillaise." "To arms, citizens" seem to be the only words known. There is much repetition, omission, etc., but on the whole the slaves manage a tolerable rendition of the anthem.)

MME. BULLET: Oh, Marie-Jeanne, I wish you could have been with us. Vienna was lovely. Vienna! Some years ago we were lucky enough to be visiting Prague and quite by accident we heard his *Marriage of Figaro*. This time as soon as we reached Paris, we heard that Mozart had written a new opera, *Don Giovanni. (She stands and moves downstage.)* After a few days we heard that *Don Giovanni* was to be performed in Vienna. My husband is a good man. He knew I was dying to hear it and we set off for Vienna almost at once.

(Enter a youth, Möise.)

MÖISE: Madame, M. Bullet is here.

(M. Bullet enters. He wears riding boots and carries a whip. He and his wife embrace, she more ardently than he. The couple break apart and Bullet casts a more-than-interested eye on Marie-Jeanne who has gone slowly to the other end of the room. Madame Bullet looks at each in turn. As soon as she leaves the room, Bullet goes to Marie-Jeanne and embraces her. She submits willingly but is not responsive. The two are still locked together when the half-naked Dessalines enters carrying a drawn sword. He is followed by two or three equally raggedly-dressed slaves carrying staves. Upstage there is a growing murmur of a mass of slaves.)

DESSALINES: *(in a menacing tone)* Master.

(Bullet and Marie-Jeanne draw apart. Bullet is immediately furious, but restrains himself.)

BULLET: What are you doing in here, Dessalines?

(Dessalines steps forward cautiously but definitely, separating Bullet from Marie-Jeanne. He is obviously interested in Marie-Jeanne.)

DESSALINES: Revolution in France. Revolution in San Domingo. Freedom for slaves. Kill Master. Burn down plantation.

(Bullet stands looking at him. Madame Bullet has come to the door, seen what was happening and turned back rapidly.)

BULLET: Well, it has come at last.

(Dessalines turns to the slaves and makes a gesture. More slaves pour in. They start to pull down curtains, etc.)

MARIE-JEANNE: Dessalines. Toussaint! Does Toussaint know what you are doing?

(Dessalines is taken aback. The slaves pause and grow silent. Madame Bullet returns with Toussaint behind her. Toussaint's dress is commonplace, but tidy and neat. He steps forward, all eyes centred on him. He looks around and then speaks)

TOUSSAINT: Dessalines, put that sword away. *(For a moment Dessalines, rebellious, does not know what to do with the sword.)* Give it to Möise.

(Dessalines meekly hands over the sword to Möise.) M. Bullet, you know that the slave revolution broke out in San Domingo over a month ago. All over the North slaves have set fire to the plantations and killed their masters. Now they are free. M. Bullet, you must leave here at once and never return. Otherwise I cannot guarantee your safety. *(Bullet looks at his wife.)* Madame Bullet I shall send by a special guard, with Möise here and my brother Paul. They will take her to her friends in Le Cap. *(To Madame Bullet.)* You will be quite safe with them. You will take certain household effects with you. In two carriages. More than that I cannot do. As for you, Marie-Jeanne, you have to choose. My wife and the children are going to a safe spot in Spanish San Domingo. You can go with my wife or you can go with Madame Bullet to Le Cap. You have to decide now. What will you do?

(Marie-Jeanne, now the centre of attention, is quite composed.)

MARIE-JEANNE: Toussaint, will I be safe from him? *(Pointing to Dessalines)*

TOUSSAINT: *(with a glance at M. Bullet)* If I am taking care of you, you will be safe from everybody.

MARIE-JEANNE: Then I will go with your wife.

(She turns and walks out, without even a glance at the Bullets. Madame Bullet looks at her husband not without malice.)

TOUSSAINT: M. Bullet, I propose to you that you go now. At once. From your camp you will be able to visit Madame Bullet in Le Cap. She will be there tonight by seven o'clock. *(Bullet hesitates for a moment, then leaves. The slaves watch malevolently. Toussaint turns to Madame Bullet.)* Madame will please get ready to leave for Le Cap with your two carriages by four o'clock. *(Madame Bullet hesitates.)* Madame, the life on this plantation is finished.

(Still Madame Bullet does not leave. Finally she speaks:)

MME. BULLET: Toussaint, what is going to happen to you? You have arranged for everyone. But you, where are you going?

(Toussaint looks at her, looks away and then looks at her again.)

TOUSSAINT: Madame, I am going where I belong: to join the revolution.

MME. BULLET: I always knew you would. But you have been very kind to us. I will remember you. Goodbye, Toussaint.

(To the astonishment of all the slaves around, she moves her hand up towards Toussaint's lips. He hesitates for a fraction of a second, then takes her hand in his own and kisses it. At this there is tremendous excitement from the slaves. The light fades on Madame Bullet's exit up the stairs at stage right.)

ACT I, SCENE 2: 1794

Three soldiers are discovered removing the remaining signs of French Colonial gentility from the central area. They are replacing the furnishings with severely functional furniture. They are wearing some semblance of a uniform.

MARAT: All this goddamn furniture to be moved. This is work for slaves.

MAX: They ain't got no more slaves.

MARAT: All right. Not slaves, but fellas to do heavy work. I am a soldier. I am free. What is the use of being free and having to move a piano. When I was a slave I had to move the piano. Now I am free I have to move the piano.

MAX: You used to move the piano for M. Bullet. Now it is for General L'Ouverture.

MARAT: The piano is still a piano and as heavy as hell. *(They take the piano off.)*

(Enter Mars Plaisir, civilian attendant to Toussaint. He is neatly dressed. Max and Marat return with a low bench.)

MARS PLAISIR: The General will be here very soon and you have not prepared the place for his military staff. You, Paul, you promised me.

MARAT: No! Not Paul! Paul was a slave. I told you my name is Marat. That is the name Master Dessalines said I could take. My name is Marat.

(Orleans returns and sets down a Spanish flag.)

MAX: We have no masters any more. You are the Military Aide to Captain Dessalines, Jean is Military Aide to Captain Christophe, and I am Military Aide to Lieutenant Möise. There is no question of masters anymore.

MARS PLAISIR: Now, on behalf of my General, General L'Ouverture, this room must be ready in ten minutes. You know what the General is about time. Tell them where to put the things—Jacques and Jean. Or maybe, Marat, they now have new names, too?

ORLEANS: Yes, I have a new name. I am now the Duke of Orleans.

MARS PLAISIR: *(Good-humouredly)* Good. You are Duke.

ORLEANS: Duke of Orleans. Orleans.

MARS PLAISIR: Orleans. And you Jacques?

MAX: My name is Robespierre. Maximillian Robespierre. Call me Max.

M. PLAISIR: Marat, Max, and Orleans. Ten Minutes. *(He exits.)*

ORLEANS: Where are we going to put these things, Marat?

MARAT: Anywhere outside. Put them in the outhouse. The people who used to sit on these are gone and that is the end of them. *(Max takes out the chair stage right.)*

ORLEANS: *(Sitting on the sofa)* This is too bad. This is a nice chair to sit on. *(He sits comfortably.)*

MARAT: Get up there and get on with it.

(Max returns.)

ORLEANS: *(To Max)* Tell me something. How is the Revolution in France going?

MARAT: *(Intervening)* Just like ours. The white slaves in France heard that the black slaves in San Domingo had killed their masters and taken over the houses and the property. They heard that we did it and they follow us. I am sure in France, the slaves do not move pianos anymore. They make the old Counts and Dukes move them. *(Max has moved upstage of them to pick up the piano stool.)*

ORLEANS: I was talking to Max. What do you think, Max? Max knows a lot he is not saying. Max knows everything. *(Max has halted and turned.)*

MAX: I don't know everything. My Lieutenant, Möise, knows a lot. I listen to what he says.

ORLEANS: Well, how is the revolution in France going. How does your lieutenant Möise see it? What have the slaves got? We've got nothing yet.

MARAT: *(Intervening again with great speed)* Liberty-Equality-Fraternity.

ORLEANS: Everybody says Liberty-Equality-Fraternity. All right, Liberty is when you kill the master; Equality, he's dead and can't beat you again; and Fraternity *(He pauses.)* What is that Fraternity? *(Max listens with foot on stool)*

MARAT: Fraternity. That is very simple. Liberty, Equality . . . Fraternity!

ORLEANS: Yes, I know, but what is Fraternity?

MARAT: You are very stupid. Everybody knows what is Fraternity. Liberty, Equality, and then Fraternity. *(Max exits with stool in disgust.)*

ORLEANS: Yes, Marat, but what is it? Everybody talks about it but nobody says what it is.

MARAT: I just told you.

(Mars Plaisir returns.)

MARS PLAISIR: Well, you all seem to have done very much. The general will be here in two minutes. Hurry up please.

(Marat signals to Max and Orleans. Max exits with him, but Orleans remains.)

ORLEANS: M. Plaisir, tell me. Liberty-Equality-Fraternity. What it means, Fraternity?

(A pause)

MARS PLAISIR: All right. Liberty, slavery abolished; Equality, no dukes, *(To Orleans)* pardon me, Orleans. No counts, no marquises, no princes, no lords, everybody equal. *(Marat and Max return with a plain table and chair.)* And Fraternity, everybody gets together and be friends, nobody taking advantage of anybody, everybody helping everybody else. *(Marat pounces on them.)*

MARAT: That's exactly what I said. Liberty, Equality and then Fraternity, as Mars Plaisir has explained. *(To Orleans.)* Now get that piece of furniture out!

(Toussaint enters with the Spanish General who is attended by an aide.)

TOUSSAINT: General, you can count upon us. I have to repeat: We are devoted to Spain and the King of Spain.

(At the same time near the exit, Orleans, who has been sitting on the one remaining piece of furniture, the sofa, springs to attention. When he sees that Toussaint has not noticed him, he calls Max and together they take the sofa out. Toussaint is in the uniform of a General. In Act I, Scene 1, he was a very human person assuming by instinct an authority that the situation demanded. Now he is every inch a soldier in command. Dessalines is in the uniform of a captain. In the background are a few soldiers, barefooted and somewhat ragged. The Spanish General is nodding in satisfaction at Toussaint's words. The General is about to leave and Toussaint salutes him. The General takes the salute, then embraces Toussaint, and leaves with his aide. Toussaint walks backward and forward, deep in thought. A humming of La Marseillaise begins upstage. Dessalines, Christophe and some soldiers enter humming. After a few seconds the humming is so clear and insistent that Toussaint has to take notice of it. He turns to them. The humming stops immediately on stage only. Dessalines stiffens. Toussaint looks at them for a second and when he speaks his tone is grave.)

TOUSSAINT: Captain Dessalines, go out and stop that song immediately. *(Dessalines goes rapidly. Offstage the humming stops. Dessalines returns.)* Do not sing or hum that song again, either in my presence or alone. We are Africans, and Africans believe in a King. We were slaves and we believe in liberty and equality. But we are not republicans. Do not sing that song again. La Marseillaise is the song of enemies. Our ruler is a king, the King of Spain.

(At this moment, a light appears in the small area on stage right while, simultaneously, the lights fade in the central area. The Spanish General is seen with his aide in the small room.)

SPANISH GENERAL: No, no, no, I don't agree. Toussaint L'Ouverture is one of the purest spirits that can be found in these Godforsaken islands. I am certain of his devotion to the throne and the Crown of Spain. He has given every proof of it. When Spain needed the blacks to fight against the French Government, we offered them guns, ammunition and food; we recognised them as soldiers—as equals—and we asked them only to kill whites—the French. All but Toussaint accepted readily and joined us. Toussaint alone joined us on his own terms. Let me tell you . . .

(The lights in the small room go off and once more the main area is illuminated. Toussaint stands as he was before, opposite to Dessalines and the ragged soldiers. Into the middle of them rushes a young soldier, Lieutenant Möise. He waves a copy of the periodical Le Moniteur over his head He shouts to the soldiers.)

MÖISE: News, citizens! News!

(Möise has not seen Toussaint and his attention is drawn to him by the concentration on Toussaint of Dessalines and the other soldier. Möise therefore turns towards Toussaint. His enthusiasm is momentarily checked by Toussaint's glance.)

TOUSSAINT: Well, Lieutenant Möise, what is this new title by which you are addressing us? Since when have we become citizens? Only members of the French Republic are citizens.

MÖISE: General, we are citizens. I have news. General, let me tell you the news.

(Toussaint seems unwilling to make the concession, but Möise is so enthusiastic and is appealing so strongly that Toussaint partly relents.)

TOUSSAINT: All right, Lieutenant Möise, tell us this news of yours.

(One of two soldiers join the crowd behind Dessalines, and Möise dramatically takes the centre of the stage. He waves the paper in his hands and speaks rhetorically.)

MÖISE: We are citizens, sailors from the ship tell me. They give me a paper and it is here in the paper.

TOUSSAINT: What, Lieutenant, is in the paper?

MÖISE: Former slaves from San Domingo, Bellay *(Looking up)*, black man, *(Reads again)* go to France, to the Chamber of Deputies to represent San Domingo. President of Chamber welcome him and give him Fraternal kiss. President of French Chamber give black slave from San Domingo fraternal kiss. French sailor tell me. And I read it in the paper here. In *Le Moniteur*, the official paper. Slavery in every colony, abolished!

(Möise can speak no longer but continues to wave the paper. There has been a growing hum of excitement while Möise was speaking. Toussaint has listened intently, yet calmly.)

TOUSSAINT: Give me that paper.

(Möise hands it to him and he reads it carefully.)

TOUSSAINT: Möise, you are right. The Convention has abolished slavery. Dessalines.

(Toussaint pats Möise on the shoulder and then talks quietly to him and Dessalines.

Dessalines, summoning two slaves, goes off with Möise. Möise reenters and whispers to Toussaint. Möise stands nearby on his right. After a pause, Dessalines enters pushing in front of him, at sword-point, the Spanish General)

SPANISH GENERAL: General Toussaint, I asked to be brought to you. This savage beast . . .

TOUSSAINT: Marquis, you are my prisoner.

SPANISH GENERAL: Your prisoner?

TOUSSAINT: Yes, a prisoner of the French Republic. I and all of us who you see here are now citizens of the French Republic, one and indivisible. It is here in *Le Moniteur.* The Chamber of Deputies in France has abolished slaves throughout the French Empire.

SPANISH GENERAL: But you are Africans and Africans believe in a King.

TOUSSAINT: We were slaves and slaves believe in freedom.

SPANISH GENERAL: But the San Domingo Government abolished slavery in San Domingo. And you refused to join them. As Africans you swore undying allegiance to a King, the King of Spain.

TOUSSAINT: Marquis, you suffer from the delusion that an African is a special breed of animal different from the rest of the human species. Different he is but only when he is brought across the Atlantic and dumped in the Antilles. Get a chair for the Marquis. He is not holding up very well. *(Christophe brings a chair for the Spanish General. He sits.)* Marquis, my father was a chief in Africa. Before he was captured and brought here he owned slaves. He told me that some Africans—not all, but some—had known and accepted slavery for hundreds of years. But as soon as they came here and saw only black men from Africa were slaves, and because they were black could be nothing else but slaves, one thought became dominant in their minds—freedom! I want you to understand it, Marquis. For unless you do, this island will be an island of blood and graves. Look at these people, General. Some of them understand only one French word—*Liberté. (Möise is now gesturing to the crowd of men, who are eagerly listening.)* They will join anything, or leave anything, for *Liberté.* That is why I can lead them. But the day that they feel I am not for Liberty, the day they feel I am not telling them everything, I am finished. They are all listening to us now. As soon as you and I have finished speaking, they will know what we have said, because Möise, my nephew, is translating what we say into Creole. Many discussions have taken place in front of these men while Möise translated. They know that the Spanish San Domingo Government declared slavery abolished here, that they repeatedly sent to us asking us to join the Republic. But they also understand, Marquis, that when the Government in France abolished slavery, I would be joining them; not before. Now that slavery has been abolished, we go at once. Our soldiers are strategically placed in relation to yours; they have always been. Marquis, your sword please. *(The Spanish General, still dazed, hands over his sword mechanically. Toussaint accepts it with a graceful bow.)* Take him away. No, not you, Captain Dessalines, I have instructed Möise what to do.

(Möise takes the Spanish flag and the Spanish General off. Toussaint exits followed by Dessalines and Christophe. One slave returns the chair to its place behind the table. Another follows Christophe to the exit to ensure that the officers are gone. He returns

to the crowd of slaves who are excitedly conferring among themselves. Other ex-slaves converge from all sides to hear the news. A shout goes up, out of which comes a joyous "La Marseillaise". Drummers enter to accompany the rocking anthem as the men begin to jump up ad lib. Offstage men start a chant that cuts through the repeat of "La Marseillaise". The chant eventually drowns out "La Marseillaise" completely as more sing the former and less the latter.

(When all the men are chanting "Enfin les Français ont donné liberté", a priestess enters with a voodoo container which has three compartments—to hold small jars—and a central lighted candle. She kneels facing the audience in front of the drummers who are seated on a bench. Then three women dancers enter with a new chant, "La Liberté", in counterpoint to the men's chant. Each woman brings in a jar with which they appear to sprinkle the floor. They converge on the priestess and deposit their jars in her container. The drums and chanting stop suddenly. A new rhythm starts immediately. The three women whirl and jerk their bodies in time with it. The men do a simple movement in the background until the women spin off to stage left. Then five of them move downstage in an open-close movement which is stopped by an attendant houngan—voodoo priest—who enters from upstage and makes a diagonal cross with a bull's tail slashing the stage on either side of his path. The five are herded upstage right as the top rhythm changes to a simple insidious phrase.

(As banner-bearing slaves move across upstage, the chief houngan with a cross stuck in the mouth of a gourd floats through a curve upstage right and down. He is preceded by the first attendant bowing before him with the bull's tail. He is followed by two attendant houngans carrying voodoo-branched candle sticks with lighted candles in them. The first attendant stands, then kneels downstage right with a violent torso movement as the chief houngan stands behind him with the cross over his head.

(Two other things have happened while this is going on: Dessalines has returned down left with Mars Plaisir. Dessalines has pushed through the women dancers to stand with hands on hips looking on; a woman—to be known later as Celestine—has entered dancing behind the two candle-bearing attendants. She is followed by the Chief drummer who is executing the top rhythm. Celestine spins into the centre of the stage and there she sees Dessalines. She moves towards him, tempting him to follow her movements. The drummer moves towards them urging them on. Celestine joins forearms with Dessalines and he moves into the dance with her. They then hold hands and do three forehead-to-forehead turns. Breaking this off, both Celestine and Dessalines are dizzy enough to be more susceptible to possession. While Dessalines drifts laterally with his arms out at his sides straight from his shoulders across the stage behind her, Celestine begins trembling with violent jerks of her upper body. She falls to the ground, and begins to roll, still trembling at the knees and shoulders. She rolls up and down stage then stops and trembles violently in one spot as Dessalines drifts down towards her, makes a complete turn with his arms outstretched, raises his left foot, toes pointed downwards, and clenched right fist, and shakes them over her body while showing the whites of his eyes. Mars Plaisir places a hand on the drum of the Chief Drummer. Simultaneously, the drums stop, the candles are snuffed out.)

BLACKOUT.

ACT I, SCENE 3: 1798

During the blackout, the bench of the previous scene is cleared. Then, as the lights return, two servants are seen, one bringing in two chairs, the other with a chair and an American flag. The flag has thirteen stars in a circle on a blue background. There are thirteen stripes, seven red and six white.

1ST SERVANT: You heard anything about the battle?

2ND SERVANT: What battle?

1ST SERVANT: Governor Toussaint and our army are fighting the mulattoes at Jacmel, and the British, they say, are trying to get the mulattoes to join them.

2ND SERVANT: I don't know. I don't care. I am a servant to the American Consul. At the end of the month he pays me my money. That is all I know and that is all I want to know.

1ST SERVANT: He says we are good servants, we work well, and that when he goes to America, he will take us.

2ND SERVANT: That's what he thinks. In America they have slaves. I'm a free man. I am not a slave anymore. I am not going to America or any place where they have slaves. That is all I know. I know nothing else.

(Mr Tobias Lear, the American Consul of San Domingo, enters and looks around the room with approval.)

1ST SERVANT: Can we get anything for you, sir?

LEAR: No. Everything looks satisfactory.

1ST SERVANT: May I get you a drink, sir?

LEAR: No. I am expecting guests. When they arrive . . . *(Voices heard off.)* Ah, if that is General Maitland or General Hédouville, show them in at once. Anybody else, send them away. *(Servants exit. 1st Servant re-enters and announces the visitor.)*

1ST SERVANT: General Hédouville.

LEAR: General, the Representative of the French Government is always welcome on American territory, even though it is in a French colony.

1ST SERVANT: General Maitland. *(He enters.)*

LEAR: General Maitland. I've long wanted to meet the Commander-in-Chief of the British Forces in San Domingo. I am happy, at last, to welcome you to the American Consulate. *(He is obviously nervous.)* Gentlemen, or perhaps I should say, Generals, I know that Britain and France, your respective countries, are at war. But nevertheless you are both on neutral territory and the three of us have to consult with one another about this fantastic Negro, this Toussaint L'Ouverture—now, God help us, Governor of the Colony. *(He sits centre.)*

MAITLAND: *(To Hédouville)* General, was it necessary for the French Government to appoint him not only Commander-in-Chief of the French Army in San Domingo, but Governor of the Colony? We of the British Services could not possibly think of such a thing. *(He sits.)*

HÉDOUVILLE: I know what you mean, and some of us did think that the appointment of a black as Governor was a mistake. But here was the problem: the mulattoes, being half white, educated and privileged, have always felt themselves superior to the blacks. The blacks, being slaves, have always envied the mulattoes. They have never trusted each other. But both the mulattoes and the blacks trust Toussaint. And since the white representatives from San Domingo also urged that Toussaint was loyal to France—we had no choice! With the support of the whites, the mulattoes and the blacks, Toussaint could control the Colony—for France. However, Toussaint has now become too powerful. I've been sent here by the French Government to restrain him. If we could only strengthen the mulattoes, we could maintain a balance. *(He sits.)*

MAITLAND: Today, that problem is being solved for us. General L'Ouverture, I understand, now faces a disastrous military defeat. The mulattoes from all over the island are pouring into Jacmel. He will never take that mulatto stronghold and he will have to retire in disorder. The mulatto Commander at Jacmel, General Pétion, is a mortal enemy of General L'Ouverture, and, if he can, he will not only defeat Toussaint, but destroy his entire army.

HÉDOUVILLE: Gentlemen, since General L'Ouverture is Governor appointed by the French Government, my position is anomalous. I have the authority of a representative of the French Government but no actual power at my disposal. I am in the best position to recognise the threat to the present order which General L'Ouverture represents. I also am informed that he faces defeat at Jacmel . . .

(At this moment, a trumpet sounds. The three jump to their feet obviously startled.)

LEAR: But that is impossible . . .

HÉDOUVILLE: That is Toussaint's trumpet. *(He rushes to a window and looks outside. He comes back and grabs his hat.)* Yes, it is he. Excuse me, gentlemen.

(He makes unceremoniously for the exit on the other side of the room. There is a heavy knock on the door. Enter Christophe, Dessalines and Möise, booted and spurred. They have obviously been riding hard. Möise is applying a handkerchief somewhat carefully to his right eye. Dessalines sits resolutely in the centre chair, puts his foot in the other chair, draws a knife from his boot and begins to peel an orange.)

MAITLAND: Generals, we thought that the Governor had come. It was his trumpet that we heard. What is the news from Jacmel?

DESSALINES: *(Peeling orange)* It was his trumpet. But whenever he comes to Port-au-Prince he always goes to see old Pierre Baptiste. *(Slices top off the orange.)*

MAITLAND: General Baptiste has rendered, I suppose, a great service to the State?

DESSALINES: He is no general. He is over one hundred years old. *(Sucks orange.)*

MAITLAND: The Governor shows great respect for people of advanced age.

DESSALINES: No question of respect. Old Pierre Baptiste is as strong as you or me. Toussaint goes to see him because when they were slaves together and Toussaint was a boy, old Baptiste gave him lessons, taught him to read and write, taught him some Latin out of a book written by a great soldier.

MÖISE: *(To Dessalines)* His name was Caesar. The book was *Caesar on the War in France.*

DESSALINES: I don't know what book it was. Old Pierre Baptiste used to work for some priests. He knew some Latin and he used to teach Toussaint. Now that Toussaint is Governor, and even before, he never comes into Portau-Prince without first going to see old Pierre. When he has made up his mind to do something he always does it, *(Takes last suck on the orange)* nothing stands in his way. *(Throws orange over his shoulder; it narrowly misses Lear.)*

MAITLAND: Most admirable. Obviously the Governor is a man born to govern. But the news . . . *(Möise meanwhile has been wiping his eye more insistently than before. Maitland notices, turns to him.)* General, you are wounded.

MÖISE: I believe I have lost an eye in the service of liberty. Many have lost more for less. Gentlemen, Jacmel has been taken, the army of mulattoes under General Pétion has been completely destroyed. That, I may venture to say, creates an entirely new situation in the country—for us all. I don't know exactly what the Governor has in mind.

CHRISTOPHE: Nobody ever knows.

MÖISE: But I believe that when he heard that there was a sort of conference here, he decided to come at once, although he would not break his rule of going to see old Pierre.

MAITLAND: Quite, quite. Generals, you are high in the service of the Governor. In fact, of the State of French San Domingo. This victory of yours at Jacmel is not unexpected. Just before you came I was telling Mr Lear that General L'Ouverture fights no battles which he does not win. He besieges no town which he does not capture. You remember, Mr Lear, we were talking about that when we heard the trumpet. As a matter of fact, it is in anticipation of just such a result that I came here to talk to the American Consul. Isn't that so, Mr Consul?

LEAR: Yes, yes.

MAITLAND: And I think that I should tell you gentlemen at once, what we have tentatively arrived at. It is obvious that the Governor and his army are now masters of San Domingo. I am able to inform you that His Majesty King George of England has followed through his Ministers the rise of the slaves of San Domingo. His Majesty has long been of the opinion that if the blacks of San Domingo were to achieve complete mastery of the island, then he would welcome the consolidation of black power in a black state. Governor L'Ouverture can establish himself as King. *(Dessalines takes his foot off the chair.)* He would have around him his army, members of the government . . . he could create an aristocracy, and a nobility . . . and so on and so on. We in England have proved beyond the shadow of a doubt that such stability can only be established by a monarchy, a king and royal family and a nobility. His Majesty, King George the Third of England would welcome as his brother, His Majesty King Toussaint L'Ouverture the First of San Domingo. That, Generals, is essentially what I have to tell you—what Mr Lear and I were discussing. I think America will throw its weight in support of this policy.

LEAR: Yes, we have to. The British have military forces and a fleet in this neighbourhood. We have none and we go with them.

DESSALINES: It seems to me . . .

MÖISE: I believe, General Maitland, that such a proposition demands that it be considered first by the Governor. In addition, until he comes, we think that we would like to be alone to consider what will completely alter political relations inside and outside of San Domingo. Perhaps you can let us retire to a room.

MAITLAND: A most reasonable request, but there is no need. It would seem to me that Mr Lear and I should retire and leave you to yourselves, and when the Governor comes, we could return. Mr Lear, do I express your sentiments?

LEAR: I, I agree.

MAITLAND: Well, Generals, we leave you to your discussion.

(Maitland, followed by Lear, leaves the room.)

CHRISTOPHE: Möise, what do you think?

MÖISE: Why do you ask me? You both are Generals of Division, I am only General of Brigade. You are my senior officers.

DESSALINES: Senior officers! Only on the battlefield. In things like this you always know everything.

MÖISE: Only the Governor can decide.

DESSALINES: He will decide but I know what I would do. I don't know the English King, but I know the slaves. We are African people. We like a king. We would like to know that the island belongs to us. Toussaint will be as good a king as anybody. I think we ought to take it.

MÖISE: Take what?

CHRISTOPHE: Dessalines means what the Englishman is offering us. To establish San Domingo as an independent island free of France, with its own king and its own government.

MÖISE: So you mean the British General can give us that?

DESSALINES: Not the British General, he says. The British King.

MÖISE: Christophe?

CHRISTOPHE: I don't know. I think there are strong arguments for and strong arguments against.

MÖISE: You are waiting to hear what Toussaint says.

CHRISTOPHE: That is the kind of nasty remark you are always making.

MÖISE: I am going to tell Toussaint this: We have escaped from the French King. Do we now give ourselves over to the English King?

CHRISTOPHE: He makes an offer. We accept it or we don't. Independence. The Government ours, the army ours, our own king . . .

MÖISE: Yes, and our own aristocracy. A San Domingo nobility. In my district there is the town of Marmalade and there is another town of Turkey. It is a pity that Marmalade and Turkey are not in your provinces. You, Dessalines, could be Duke of Turkey—you make enough noise. And you, Christophe, could be Count of Marmalade. All sugar and spice.

DESSALINES: *(Springing at Möise)* Duke of Turkey! Look here . . . If you weren't wounded, I would put my hands on you. *(Toussaint appears upstage.)* I am no Duke of Marmalade.

MÖISE: Not Marmalade, Turkey. Christophe will be . . . *(They both turn on him.)*

TOUSSAINT: Generals, the Commander-in-Chief is here.

(The three Generals freeze.)

CHRISTOPHE: Ah, Ah, General we have a problem.

TOUSSAINT: *(Drily, as he comes forward)* So I see.

(Christophe clears his throat.)

CHRISTOPHE: Governor L'Ouverture, we met here Consul Tobias Lear talking with General Maitland.

TOUSSAINT: I know. Wasn't Hédouville here?

CHRISTOPHE: No Sir. General Hédouville was not here when we came. But when General Maitland heard that the army of Pétion has been defeated . . .

DESSALINES: Destroyed.

CHRISTOPHE: When he heard that Pétion's army had been destroyed, he said that we could become independent. The British Government would support a black state. We would have a King and he suggested that you, Governor, should be the first king.

DESSALINES: The King of England would welcome you, Toussaint, as his brother.

MÖISE: And don't forget—a black aristocracy, a black nobility, the Duke of Turkey and the Count of Marmalade.

(Dessalines turns away angrily.)

CHRISTOPHE: Governor. General Maitland and the American Consul are in the next room waiting for your reply.

(There is a long silence.)

TOUSSAINT: An offer of independence. To break with France. This is not the first offer, nor will it be the last. In all my military negotiations with General Maitland, he kept on hinting this to me.

DESSALINES: Toussaint, you going to take it? *(A pause. Toussaint does not answer.)* Take it, Toussaint. Make yourself king. If you make yourself king, San Domingo will be ours and French, British, nobody will be able to take it from us.

TOUSSAINT: General Christophe, what is your opinion of this offer? For it is only an offer. Everything depends on what we say.

CHRISTOPHE: Well, I think that the offer is very valuable. On the other hand, to take it means that we run certain dangers. I . . . I . . .

MÖISE: Christophe, how can you be on both sides at the same time. The Governor has asked you your opinion.

DESSALINES: And what is yours, General Möise? *(To Toussaint.)* He is against.

(Toussaint looks enquiringly at Möise.)

MÖISE: The Duke of Turkey has everything mixed up. He doesn't know what I am against. He doesn't know what I am for. Governor, I am against taking anything from the British, either from their general or from their king. They don't own us. They can give us nothing. That is what I am against. But that we should declare ourselves free from the French; that we should make San Domingo a free and independent country; that I am for. Now, whether you should become a king—with your Dukes and Counts, or President of the independent Republic of San Domingo, I am not very sure in my own mind. We will have to ask the people. But if we all four of us and the rest, tell the people that we want to finish with the French, and we want to be free and equal; make San Domingo independent, the people will come with us. The army will be entirely on our side and the French will never be able to take their colony back. But we don't take anything from the British. We don't become independent because the British will help us. We do it because the country belongs to us. We have made it what it is, and we alone can make it what it can be. Nobody else can. That is what I feel. . . .

(A silence.)

DESSALINES: Toussaint?

TOUSSAINT: Möise, let the gentlemen know I am ready.

(Möise exits and returns immediately with General Maitland and Tobias Lear.)

MAITLAND: Governor Toussaint, we are at your service.

TOUSSAINT: General Maitland, and Mr Lear, I feel deeply honoured by this generous offer which countries like Britain and the United States have made to us, we who yesterday were slaves. I would like you to express to His Majesty of England through his Ministers, that his offer of alliance and recognition with a possible King of San Domingo is something that we of San Domingo will never forget. But it will be no surprise to you or to any member of my government that my position today is what it always has been. It is the French Government, the French revolutionary government, which has freed the slaves of San Domingo. No other country in the world has done that or promises to do that. A French colony we are and a French colony we will remain, unless France attempts to restore slavery. That is the faith by which I live and under that banner I hope to die. That is the message which the people transmit to your government—through me, the Governor of San Domingo, their representative. Gentlemen, I expect we shall again be in contact to discuss the many points which are at issue between us.

(He bows and leaves, followed by his Generals. The lights go off in the big room and after a period they are turned on in the small room to the right and the small room to the left. Maitland is dictating to a secretary under a Union Jack and Toussaint is dictating to Mars Plaisir. They are both saying exactly the same thing and are making the pauses for the secretaries to write.)

MAITLAND: The British offer . . .

TOUSSAINT: The British offer is designed to create a split between French San Domingo and the French Government.

MAITLAND: . . is designed to create a split between French San Domingo and the French Government.

TOUSSAINT: However, it must be noted that . . .

MAITLAND: However, it must be noted that this does not mean any support from the British for a free San Domingo.

TOUSSAINT: . . . this does not mean any support from the British for a free San Domingo. That would ruin the whole British Colonial system in the Caribbean.

MAITLAND: That would ruin the whole British Colonial system in the Caribbean. A San Domingo at war with France . . .

TOUSSAINT: A San Domingo at war with France they will support only until the peace. Whereupon . . .

MAITLAND: Whereupon the British will either blockade the island and themselves take it over . . .

TOUSSAINT: . . . or they will collaborate with the French towards restoring the old colonial condition . . .

MAITLAND:. . . mulatto discrimination . . .

TOUSSAINT:. . . and negro slavery.

(The secretaries write, Toussaint and General Maitland watching them. When the writing is finished:)

TOUSSAINT: Send this dispatch to the Minister of Foreign Affairs for the Republic of France.

MAITLAND: Send this dispatch to the Minister of Foreign Affairs of the Kingdom of Great Britain.

TOGETHER: Top secret.

END OF ACT ONE

ACT II, SCENE 1: 1800

A screen to the side of a bed in a small room where Marie-Jeanne lives. There is a table with a bottle of wine and glasses, as well as a small bookcase. Marie-Jeanne is in a dressing gown. General Hédouville is putting on his coat. He pulls the coat down and adjusts the sleeves. Marie-Jeanne helps to button the front. Then she sits on the bed.

MARIE-JEANNE: I suppose you are going now.

HÉDOUVILLE: *(After a pause)* Why do you think so? Even if I had to go, I would like to stay awhile, to talk to you.

MARIE-JEANNE: Why should you want to talk to me?

(Hédouville sits and takes her hand.)

HÉDOUVILLE: Because you make me feel more at home in this wild colony than I have since I left Paris.

MARIE-JEANNE: *(Taking her hand away)* Me! Me make you feel at home? I am a mulatto woman. I am nobody. I was a slave. I was the woman of a French planter. Governor Toussaint was a slave on the same estate. He helps me in any way that he can.

HÉDOUVILLE: You have many books here and you teach young children to read. You were a slave. How were you educated?

MARIE-JEANNE: I was the woman of a plantation owner. His wife liked me.

HÉDOUVILLE: *(Standing and chuckling)* His wife liked you?

MARIE-JEANNE: *(Standing)* Yes, there were many of us mulatto women in that situation, accepted in the house, one of the house-slaves, but spying on the slaves. His wife liked me, taught me to read, and I used to read the books in the house. She even taught me some music. When the revolution came to the plantation, and she had to go, I took some of the books. *(Walks over to the bookcase.)* I have them here. I read them all the time. I have nothing else to do, and I teach the children of the officials to read. Many of the Generals themselves can't even read, far less write.

(Hédouville gets up and walks over to the bookcase. There are some books on the top. He bends over them and, half to himself, speaks.)

HÉDOUVILLE: Molière, Bossuet, Corneille, Racine! *(He flips the pages then turns to look at her.)* You know, I wish we had met under different circumstances.

MARIE-JEANNE: You mean you wish I was a white woman.

(Hédouville puts the Racine down on the chair, puts a knee on it, takes Marie-Jeanne's hand and speaks very earnestly.)

HÉDOUVILLE: No, I don't mean that at all. I wish I had met you in Paris.

Things would have been different if I had met you in Paris.

MARIE-JEANNE: *(Taking her hand away again)* You wouldn't have met me in Paris. I would have been a slave. My mistress promised to take me to Paris one day, but I was a slave.

HÉDOUVILLE: No! No! No! The moment a slave landed in France he was free. The revolution did not create this. That was French law long before the revolution.

MARIE-JEANNE: General Hédouville, you are saying some wonderful things to me. If you are not in a hurry, as you don't seem to be, perhaps you can tell me some of the things I want to know and which only a man who has lived in Paris can tell me. Can I pour you a drink?

(Marie-Jeanne, without waiting for an answer, moves over to the table and pours wine into two glasses. She returns, handing one to Hédouville.)

HÉDOUVILLE: *(Raising his glass)* To my most charming hostess. *(Marie-Jeanne bows gracefully and they drink. Hédouville drains his glass, Marie-Jeanne only sips hers, but pours another glass for him, half of which he drinks at once as she replaces the bottle and returns.)* And now, my dear?

MARIE-JEANNE: I am not educated, *mon General.* I wish to know what a man like you thinks about San Domingo and our new society with slaves now free. And particularly what you think of us, the mulattoes. What will happen to us, now that the mulatto army of the South is defeated? *(She takes a sip of wine from her glass.)*

HÉDOUVILLE: My dear, I occupy a very responsible position in this government, and I shouldn't speak about such things. *(He sips from his glass.)* But, surely you are the kind of person I can talk to. I believe that the mulattoes are in great danger. *(He walks downstage.)*

MARIE-JEANNE: *(Following him)* From the blacks. I knew that. The thing, General Hédouville, is this. We need help. What can we do?

HÉDOUVILLE: I can't suggest anything. *(Moving away from her.)* This is a matter from which I must keep very far.

MARIE-JEANNE: *(Following again)* But all of us believe that you came here to assist the mulattoes to take power, so as to prevent Governor L'Ouverture and the ex-slaves from taking over the colony. But our mulatto army is in retreat. Where does your government stand now?

HÉDOUVILLE: My dear, you seem to understand a great deal. You understand much more than I gave you credit for. I cannot speak for my Government, but this much I can say. The blacks now have the power, but I believe they are too ignorant and too uncivilised to keep it. At the proper moment the French Government, I believe, I cannot see it doing otherwise, would throw all its weight behind the mulattoes.

MARIE-JEANNE: If this were to come to General Pétion's ears, somehow . . .

HÉDOUVILLE: Ah, that I cannot do. But I believe some friend of both the mulattoes and the French Government, could arrange a meeting with General Pétion. I am sure we could come to some understanding. But someone else would have to arrange that, not me. As a matter of fact, this conversation has gone far enough.

(He straightens up and moves over to the table to put down his glass. He takes up

his hat. As he is doing this Marie-Jeanne speaks without looking at him.)

MARIE-JEANNE: We have one problem, General, *(She turns to him)* and that is Toussaint L'Ouverture.

HÉDOUVILLE: Toussaint L'Ouverture. Until he is removed there is no freedom for anybody else in San Domingo. Until he is removed we are all his prisoners. My dear Marie-Jeanne, I must leave you now. *(She nods with understanding of what she has to do to facilitate his leaving. She goes to the back entrance, putting down her glass on the way. She disappears briefly and returns with a nod of clearance. Hédouville bows over Marie-Jeanne's hand.)* I hope to see you soon again, *(He kisses her hand)* and not too much politics.

(As soon as he leaves, Marie-Jeanne, without haste but with decision, sits at the small table and begins to write. While she writes she hums to herself snatches from "Vendetta ti chieggio." She finishes the letter, and calls: Celestine. *As if in answer, there is a violent commotion at the door. She is taken by surprise. She rises, and goes to the entrance, tying her gown about her. Dessalines strides in wearing full uniform including hat and sword. He is pushing the maid, Celestine, ahead of him. Celestine cries:* Madame.)

DESSALINES: *(to Celestine)* Get out of here. *(Celestine flies out of the room. Dessalines turns to Marie-Jeanne.)* I heard that Frenchman was here.

MARIE-JEANNE: Are you paying me a visit, General Dessalines?

DESSALINES: Was that Frenchman here?

MARIE-JEANNE: If you came here to see him, it is clear he is not here.

DESSALINES: I came to see you. You know that.

MARIE-JEANNE: *(Recovering her composure)* Give me your hat, General. *(Dessalines gingerly hands over his hat.)* And your sword. *(Dessalines hands over his sword.)* Sit down, General. *(Dessalines, subdued, sits in the chair that Marie-Jeanne indicates. As he sits on the Racine volume, he jumps slightly, takes it and sets it on the floor. Marie-Jeanne has brought her chair from behind the table and they both sit some distance from each other.)* Well, General, I am delighted that you find time to pay me another visit so soon.

DESSALINES: Marie-Jeanne, this Frenchman, this white man, you are always seeing him?

MARIE-JEANNE: He comes to see me. You come too.

DESSALINES: But you know what he comes for.

MARIE-JEANNE: What do you come for?

DESSALINES: Marie, I tell you again, for him you are just another mulatto woman. I want you to marry me. In the church. I am General of Division now, Marie. Port-au-Prince is my headquarters. I am building a palace there. It will be finished in two months. If you will marry me I will put three hundred men on it and finish in a month. I am Governor of the Province. You will be the wife of the Governor.

MARIE-JEANNE: General Dessalines, I do not want to be the wife of the Governor of a Province.

DESSALINES: *(Standing)* You prefer to be the woman of this Frenchman.

MARIE-JEANNE: I prefer to be what I want to be. You don't own me, General Dessalines. Nobody owns me. Slavery is finished.

DESSALINES: *(Towering over her)* Marie, are you the woman of this man? You were the woman of M. Bullet. You were the woman of the Spanish Marquis. Now you are the woman of General Hédouville. You are the woman of everybody.

MARIE-JEANNE: *(Slipping out from her seat)* Except the woman of General Dessalines.

DESSALINES: *(Following)* What must I do? I don't look at any other woman. I can't. Whenever I want a woman, I think of you. Always. All these women are ready to sleep with General Dessalines and you are ready to sleep with everybody except General Dessalines. Marie, I know I am a savage but I will be everything you want me to be. You only have to tell me. This man, this French man, he is our enemy. If he gets the chance he and those like him will destroy us.

MARIE-JEANNE: I know that.

DESSALINES: You know that?

MARIE-JEANNE: Yes, I do.

DESSALINES: And yet he comes here to see you all the time.

(Marie-Jeanne goes to the table and picks up the letter she has just written. She rips the envelope open.)

MARIE-JEANNE: This letter is the proof of what I think of General Hédouville. And not only what I think, but what I now know.

DESSALINES: What is the use of showing me a letter. You know I can't read.

MARIE-JEANNE: Yes, I know. *(She calls.)* Celestine! *(Her maid appears cautiously.)* Celestine, I want you to do something for me. Here is a letter. You must read it aloud for General Dessalines. As you know, this is the General. He doesn't know how . . . *(Dessalines glowers a warning.)* . . . he doesn't know how well you can read, Celestine. Show him how quickly you have learnt. *(Marie-Jeanne hands the letter to Celestine. Celestine, embarrassed, does not know what to do.)* Read it, child; you know you can.

DESSALINES: Do as you are told, girl.

(Celestine shrinks back. Marie-Jeanne with only one withering glance at Dessalines puts her arm around Celestine and reassures her.)

MARIE-JEANNE: Come, my child, you read for me every day. Read the letter. Begin: "Governor L'Ouverture . . ."

CELESTINE: *(Reading)* Governor L'Ouverture: Your Excellency. This is to inform you that I am now in a position to show the treachery of General Hédouville. Hédouville is ready to intrigue and plot with Pétion and the mulattoes. We can catch him red-handed. I . . .

DESSALINES: That's enough. Go away, you.

(Celestine hands over the letter and picks up her skirt for a rapid exit.)

MARIE-JEANNE: Wait. *(Celestine stops. Marie-Jeanne reseals the envelope.)* Here, Celestine, take this to Mars Plaisir. He is waiting to carry it to Governor Toussaint. Hurry!

(Celestine takes the letter from Marie-Jeanne and, obviously very relieved, rushes out of the room.)

DESSALINES: Marie, what can I say? I understand now what I didn't understand before. We will speak again. I have been trying to learn to read but I can't learn. I have to go but . . . Marie, do something for me.

MARIE-JEANNE: What is it?

DESSALINES: I want you to read . . . you remember. The book you read that night at the reception Toussaint gave. I can't forget it. Read it for me and then I will go.

MARIE-JEANNE: You want me to read for you?

DESSALINES: Yes, that is all I want.

(Marie-Jeanne goes over to him and bends low. He is taken aback. But she is merely picking up the Racine volume from the floor. She stands ready to read.)

MARIE-JEANNE: Marie-Jeanne will read for you . . . Jean-Jacques.

(The lights fade.)

ACT II, SCENE 2: 1800

Toussaint is sitting at a small table. Colonel Vincent, a French Officer, is standing.

TOUSSAINT: Vincent, I have some news for you. I have given General Hédouville notice of dismissal. He must leave by the next boat.

VINCENT: But, sire, he is the representative of the French Government. You cannot dismiss him in that way. The French Government has to recall him.

TOUSSAINT: No. He goes, and he goes at once. He has caused nothing here but disorder, intrigue, disruption of the government and rebellious sentiment in the population. Hédouville has to go. I have placed him under house arrest. *(Vincent is stupefied.)* Sit down, Vincent. Now you have come to talk about the constitution, and if you believe that I sent you away to Spanish San Domingo in order to publish the constitution when you were not here, you are quite right. I did not want you around. You think the constitution is despotic? Constitutions are what they turn out to be.

VINCENT: Sire, whatever the constitution is, what matters is that you have not consulted the First Consul of France. You have had it promulgated officially, you have had it printed and distributed. Which means that for you the matter is settled.

TOUSSAINT: Yes, for me the matter is settled. The constitution swears allegiance to France. For the rest, we govern ourselves.

VINCENT: Yes, General, the constitution swears allegiance to France, but it leaves no room for any French official.

TOUSSAINT: I want a Frenchman to come out and help me govern. But he must recognise the local government. Only a local government can govern. We don't want another Hédouville; we've had enough of them.

VINCENT: But that is independence.

TOUSSAINT: No. That is not independence. We do not seek independence. We are not ready for it. France will be elder brother, guide and mentor. The French Government will send commissioners to speak with me.

VINCENT: *(Standing involuntarily)* But, Sire, I have to remind you that General Bonaparte is not the man to whom one submits a *fait accompli*. Remember, he is First Consul of France.

TOUSSAINT: General Bonaparte is the first man in France and General L'Ouverture is the first man in San Domingo. *(Vincent sits.)*

VINCENT: Sire, you are establishing what amounts to a new dominion.

TOUSSAINT: No, Vincent. What we want is protection. We want to be protected by France. We want to learn from France. France will send capital and administrators to help us develop and educate the country.

VINCENT: What will be the position of the French Government?

TOUSSAINT: The French Government will send commissioners to speak with me.

VINCENT: But the French Government sent Hédouville.

TOUSSAINT: Hédouville came here to govern. No Frenchman can come here to govern. The French Government will send commissioners to speak with me.

VINCENT: This is something entirely new. America has become independent but America is a big country and . . .

TOUSSAINT: You mean that Americans were free men and not slaves. They were white and not black.

VINCENT: General, I did not mean that.

TOUSSAINT: You mean you did not say it.

VINCENT: General, I am speaking in the best interests of you and the exslaves of San Domingo. Tell me which of your comrades deserves promotion and rewards for services to the State; I will recommend them. I have very good contacts in France and if, General, you should feel that there has not been sufficient recognition of the services you have rendered, it will . . .

TOUSSAINT: Vincent, you are the best of the white men who have come here from France. But you are a white man, Vincent. You have never been a slave. You have never felt the degradation of being a black slave. This is not a matter of personal rewards for services rendered. I am a General, I am Commander-in-Chief and Governor of San Domingo, but if I make any serious mistakes all that can go—tomorrow. I will be a hunted fugitive and it will be because I am black and an ex-slave.

VINCENT: But General . . .

TOUSSAINT: Don't interrupt me, Vincent. In San Domingo we are an outpost of freed slaves. All around us in the Caribbean black men are slaves. Even in the independent United States, black men are slaves. In South America black men are slaves. Now I have sent millions of Africans to the United States. You have heard about this. *(Vincent nods reluctantly.)* But it is not to build a fortune for myself so that if anything goes wrong I can escape and live like a rich man. No, Vincent. If this Constitution functions satisfactorily, I intend to take one thousand soldiers, go to Africa and free hundreds of thousands in the black slave trade there and bring them here, to be free and French.

VINCENT: General, I have never doubted your devotion to the cause you represent. What I am telling you is that whatever you are doing, and intend to do, you must get the approval of General Bonaparte.

TOUSSAINT: No, Vincent, I have already done what I intended to do. I have sent a copy of the Constitution to General Bonaparte. *(Vincent is shocked.)* And now, Colonel Vincent *(Toussaint uses the word "Colonel" in such a manner that Vincent rises and stands to attention.)* I hereby relieve you of your post as representative of the French Army in the army of San Domingo. I instruct you to go to France. You have a copy of the Constitution with you. *(Vincent places a hand at his breast pocket.)* You are to recommend it personally to the First Consul.

VINCENT: Sire, it may not be too late. Perhaps if I could go to General Bonaparte and tell him that you have withdrawn the Constitution, and are requesting his approval. Will you withdraw it?

TOUSSAINT: San Domingo may as well withdraw itself from these waters and attach itself to France. You have your orders, Colonel Vincent. I can leave the fate of the Constitution in no better hands than yours. Your long and faithful service to us has now reached its climax. You will be under house arrest until you leave. *(Vincent salutes and turns to leave. He stops and turns back.)*

VINCENT: Sire, before I go, allow me to say one more word about General Bonaparte . . .

TOUSSAINT: Colonel Vincent, the interview is now over.

(The light fades in the area on stage right and comes up in the area on stage left. Vincent crosses the stage to the latter area during the cross-fade to the first ten notes of "La Marseillaise" as played on a flute.)

ACT II, SCENE 3: 1800

The area on stage left represents the First Consul's office in The Tuileries, Paris. General Bonaparte is reading papers with his secretary and an orderly in attendance. There is a guard standing with a bayoneted musket in Colonel Vincent's way. Vincent goes up to the guard and stops.

BONAPARTE: This is the most outrageous document that has ever come into my hands. We shall put these impertinent blacks in their place *(To the guard.)* Let Colonel Vincent come in. *(The guard stands aside to admit Colonel Vincent.)* Colonel Vincent. You, a French Officer, have the audacity to recommend this document for my personal consideration.

VINCENT: Sire, my commanding officer instructed me . . .

BONAPARTE: Commanding officer? Those blacks with epaulettes on their shoulders? They are soldiers of a carnival.

VINCENT: Consul, you are misinformed . . .

BONAPARTE: Here in Paris, I am better informed than you, Vincent, who have been living there for years. Your intelligence has been corrupted by the poisonous atmosphere of that Caribbean island. Your brain needs washing. Do you know that there is a colonist who has offered to capture Toussaint L'Ouverture with sixty grenadiers?

VINCENT: He is bolder than I, for I would not attempt it with sixty thousand.

BONAPARTE: Listen, Mr Secretary, to this Colonel of the French Army. Make notes of this. Colonel Vincent, all the blacks, when they see a real army, they will lay down their arms. They will be only too happy that we pardon them.

VINCENT: You are misinformed, Consul.

BONAPARTE: Vincent, *you* inform me. Mr Secretary, take careful note of what he says.

VINCENT: Sire, the army has soldiers and officers tried and experienced by ten years of constant fighting.

BONAPARTE: "Constant fighting." Take note, Mr Secretary. Constant fighting of ex-slaves against ex-slaves. Slaves in uniform, that's all that they are. Vincent, you are wrong about the strength of that army of blacks. I should have thought that an officer trained in my campaigns would know what an army was. Perhaps you know more about the finances of the colony. I understand Toussaint has salted away forty million francs.

VINCENT: Sire, he has not got forty million francs.

BONAPARTE: Vincent, this Constitution puts him in personal charge not only of the Government and the Army, but of the taxation, finances and trade of the Colony.

VINCENT: Sire, that was to keep his own hand upon the administration and the technical organisation of the country's economy.

BONAPARTE: Note that, Mr Secretary. This ex-slave must handle everything himself. Tell me more about this omnipotent nigger, Colonel Vincent.

VINCENT: Sire, I shall do so. At the head of the resources of what is once more becoming a prosperous colony is the most active and tireless man one can imagine. It is the strictest truth to say that he is everywhere and, above all, in that spot where a sound judgment makes it essential for him to be.

BONAPARTE: He is even more active than I am. Mr Secretary, write that this man works twenty hours a day.

VINCENT: Twenty-two hours a day, Sire. He sleeps only two hours every night.

BONAPARTE: Note, Mr Secretary, two hours every night. We have obviously never had such a miracle in France. Continue, Colonel Vincent.

VINCENT: Sire, the faculty is accorded to him alone of never taking a rest. He enjoys the advantage of being able to start at once with the work in his office after wearisome journeys, to reply to a hundred letters a day, and to tire out his secretaries.

BONAPARTE: Marvelous, Colonel Vincent, marvelous. Tell me. What authority does he have over the men around him? He has obviously completely subordinated Frenchmen.

VINCENT: Sire, he has the art of tantalising and confusing everybody even to deceit; all this makes of him a man so superior to all around him that respect and submission reach the limits of fanaticism in a vast number of heads.

BONAPARTE: *(To secretary)* Have you got that? "Fanaticism in a vast number of heads," the heads of ex-slaves not excluding the heads of officers of the French Army. Go on, Colonel Vincent.

VINCENT: Sire, at your request, I do as you ask. He has imposed on his brothers in San Domingo a power without bounds. He is absolute master of the island and nothing can counteract his wishes, whatever they may be.

BONAPARTE: Excellent. You have told me what I want to know. And now it seems all that is required of me is that I agree with him about the Constitution which he has already made public and thus accept that the colony will become independent.

VINCENT: Sire, he does not aim at independence. He told me repeatedly that he wants the French Government to send commissioners to speak with him.

BONAPARTE: I suspect that the only commissioner he really will accept is myself, and I am occupied with other matters at the present time. You may go,

Colonel Vincent.

VINCENT: Sire, I am asking you to accept the Constitution. I know it is very difficult, but consider the spirit in which it has been made. Toussaint L'Ouverture only wants to secure the future of his people in a constitutional way. Your acceptance of the Constitution would assure him of your friendship and would mean stronger ties between France and the richest colony in the world. General Bonaparte cannot lose prestige in a French colony four thousand miles away. As a matter of fact, Sire, your status would be very much the greater if you supported local opinion and local personalities.

BONAPARTE: Colonel Vincent, I do not wish you to concern yourself any longer over my status with island blacks. You are under arrest. Vincent, go. *(Vincent is led off by the guard. Bonaparte stands and begins to walk up and down.)* Mr Secretary, dispatch these instructions at once. Double the force that has been arranged to go to San Domingo. By double I mean that ten thousand becomes twenty thousand, not ten thousand and as many as possible. Also, I want to make some changes in the command. The Chief of Staff must be Dugua. When I left Egypt for Palestine, he remained and handled a difficult situation efficiently. We will need General Boyer who will be very useful in a tropical territory. And General Humbert. He was in command of the expedition against Ireland. These are men skilled in colonial warfare. Also I want a full list of officers who have taken part in guerrilla warfare in La Vendée. I want to speak to these men all at the same time. Ah, yes. Draft a letter to General Berthier making him personally responsible for the expedition. And, Mr Secretary, inform my brother-in-law, General Leclerc, that I want to see him and my sister, his wife, immediately. Arrange for them to come to dinner. My sister, and the husband of my sister, will give the expedition the prestige that it needs.

(There is a knock. The Secretary goes to attend. He returns.)

SECRETARY: Sire, the orderly wishes to know what should be done with Colonel Vincent.

BONAPARTE: Yes, what shall we do with Vincent? He is a good officer. After a period of re-education in Europe, he can again be of great service. I will send him into exile for a period.

SECRETARY: Yes, Sire, where exactly?

BONAPARTE: Send him to the island of Elba.

(The Secretary bows as the lights fade.)

ACT II, SCENE 4: 1802

Madame Bullet sitting alone on a bench in the office of the Commander-inChief in the central area. Toussaint comes in hurriedly. He kisses her hand and then bends over to embrace her. She turns away.

MME. BULLET: No, Toussaint, that is over. I have come to say goodbye. I want your permission for a passport to go to Paris. I have spent many years of my life in San Domingo. They have been exciting years. First, the revolution, then the abolition of slavery, and then, you. Now it's over. I want to go.

TOUSSAINT: But Madame Bullet . . .

MME. BULLET: *(angrily)* Do not call me that. If you do I shall call you Commander-in-Chief.

TOUSSAINT: Forgive me, Louise, but if you go I shall be left alone. Since I have become Governor, I scarcely have anyone here who I can call my friend. Over the years you have been the only one I can count on.

(Toussaint is once more a very human person. Madame Bullet takes a very stiff attitude.)

MME. BULLET: No! That is not true. There was the Contesse de Noailles. There is the daughter of the man who is Secretary to the military staff. There is that woman who used to live on the big plantation next to ours. No, Toussaint, you will not be alone, you will never be alone.

TOUSSAINT: Louise, you know better than that. You know me very well. I don't run after them.

MME. BULLET: Yes, I know you don't run after them, they run after you. But they always catch you. You are a very attractive man, Toussaint.

TOUSSAINT: Nonsense. They run after the Commander-in-Chief and the Governor of the Colony.

MME. BULLET: And the Commander-in-Chief and Governor of the Colony is quite happy to be persuaded by all these distinguished and handsome women.

TOUSSAINT: Louise, I live amidst constant and imminent dangers and catastrophes. These women distract me for a brief hour. That is all there is to it.

MME. BULLET: I quite believe you. Only all of it added together makes too much for me. I want a passport for Paris. It is over, Toussaint. You have your life to live and I am going to resume my own.

TOUSSAINT: You are going. Everybody wants to go. At least all the white people want to go. Why? We are not treating them in any way that is harsh or revengeful. In San Domingo slavery has been abolished and everybody is free and equal. Tell me, Louise, why do so many of you want to go?

MME. BULLET: I have told you my own reasons, Toussaint. You know that they have nothing to do with politics or race.

TOUSSAINT: Yes, I know. But the others . . .?

MME. BULLET: I cannot speak for the others, but it is said that you will be naming General Möise as your successor. It is said that Möise is the second man in your Government. I believe that if he becomes ruler of San Domingo, all the whites will leave.

TOUSSAINT: So, if General Möise becomes my successor, all the whites will leave.

MME. BULLET: No one understands why you put so much faith in him when he has publicly expressed his disagreement with your policies.

TOUSSAINT: So you believe that Möise is bound to succeed me, that I am bound to him. Louise, my dear Louise, how often have I told you that in serious matters, do not listen to gossip. *(Toussaint becomes stern.)* Möise will never be ruler of San Domingo. I am not bound to him. I am not bound to anybody. Even now, as I am speaking to you, Möise is before a courtmartial on trial for treason.

MME. BULLET: Möise! For treason! Treason to you? Why, Toussaint, even as a boy in the old days he worshipped you.

TOUSSAINT: These are revolutionary times. Who you worship today you are ready to kill tomorrow and sometimes for very good reasons. You see, Louise come and sit over here as you used to, *(She sits)* you see, the country is very unsettled. Many people are quite sure that when the war is over the French will send an expedition to restore slavery.

MME. BULLET: But they will not do that.

TOUSSAINT: We hope not. But today, France is not the same France which abolished slavery. General Bonaparte, the First Consul, does not answer my letters. The country does not know where it stands. Möise is leading a section of the population against me. Möise wants a Declaration of Independence, like the United States. He wants independence, the severance of all connection with the French. *(Mars Plaisir enters.)* Is it General Dessalines?

MARS PLAISIR: Yes, Governor. And he has with him General Möise, and a guard.

TOUSSAINT: Ask General Dessalines to bring in General Möise. *(Madame Bullet rises to leave.)* No, Louise, don't go. Möise knows you.

(General Möise enters between two soldiers. They are Marat and Orleans. General Dessalines is behind him. Dessalines stands behind Möise whose hands are bound behind his back. Möise wears a black patch over one eye; Toussaint stands.)

TOUSSAINT: What is the decision of the court-martial, General?

DESSALINES: Guilty on all counts. Sentence of death. I have the sentence here. It only awaits your signature, Governor.

TOUSSAINT: Give it to me. *(Dessalines hands it over. Toussaint reads and turns to General Möise.)* Möise, I have known you since you were a child. I adopted you as my nephew. You have risen step by step until you have become a General, one of the most important Officers in my army and a Governor of a province. Yet we hear reports from all sides that you are plotting to overthrow my regime. In recent revolts many were shouting "Möise forever." You have been tried for treason, inciting rebellion and imperilling the state, and now you have been found guilty. What have you to say? Why should I not sign this document?

MÖISE: Sign or not, do as you please. I don't care what you do. I am not guilty of any treason. I have not plotted any rebellion. The court-martial knows that. You know that. If people in revolt shout my name it is because they are against your regime and they know I am against it too.

TOUSSAINT: You do not deny your guilt?

MÖISE: What guilt? You speak like a public prosecutor. If to be against your policy is to be guilty of treason, then I am guilty, the most guilty man in San Domingo. But there are many thousands who think as I do.

TOUSSAINT: You are ready to overthrow the government of the country and place us at the mercy of our enemies?

MÖISE: Your policy is placing us at the mercy of our enemies. I don't believe in maintaining the estates and giving them back to the old owners or the new generals. This one here *(Pointing to Dessalines)*, he owns thirty plantations. And he whips the labourers on his plantations as if they were slaves.

TOUSSAINT: That is not true.

MÖISE: It is true. I have investigated it myself and I reported it to you. You have done nothing about it.

TOUSSAINT: General Dessalines, report to General Möise what has been done about this matter.

DESSALINES: *(At attention)* The Governor has informed me by letter and in person that if he heard of a single case on which a labourer was beaten on any of my plantations he would dismiss me from the service or reduce me to the ranks.

MÖISE: Maybe you wrote to him and threatened him. But this brutality against the former slaves goes on all over San Domingo. I will have no part of it, I will speak against it and act wherever I see it or hear of it. The person responsible for it, Governor L'Ouverture, is you. I have said it and I shall continue to say it, court-martial or no court-martial. The country does not know where it stands. Is slavery abolished forever? Or is a French expedition coming to restore slavery? The ex-slaves don't know, the ex-slave owners don't know. I have told you to declare the island independent. Expel all those who do not want to accept it. Assure the ex-slaves that slavery is gone forever. That is what they want to know. Break up those accursed big plantations. As long as they remain, freedom is a mockery. Distribute the lands carefully among the best cultivators in the country. Let everybody see that there is a new regime. That is what I have said and that is what I will stand or fail by.

TOUSSAINT: *(Earnestly)* Ten years ago I took over the island. It was overrun with marauding soldiers and bandits. The Spanish government sent fifty thousand soldiers, the British sixty thousand. We defeated them and drove them out. Production had almost ceased. But I have changed things. Now it is two-thirds of what it was before; all within a year. Except for bandits in the hills I have restored peace and order. All we need now is some help from France.

MÖISE: You are a dreamer. All you will get from Bonaparte is an army to restore slavery. Dessalines knows that. He is always saying it to the people.

DESSALINES: *(Impatiently)* Governor, what about the paper?

TOUSSAINT: Keep him under arrest. I shall sign the order of execution later.

MÖISE: Yes, Toussaint, you shall sign later. You will use your pen like a sword. *(He advances nearer Toussaint.)* But you will see, that until you use your sword like a man *(He is now so close to Toussaint that Dessalines signals to Marat and Orleans, they grab at Möise who, though bound, shakes them off like flies)* until you cut yourself off from all the symbols of colonialism and slavery *(He has taken in Madame Bullet with a withering sweep of his one good eye)* and be truly independent, you will remain just an old man with a dream of an impossible fraternity. *(A mirthless, almost soundless, laugh.)* Pitiful old Toussaint—and his dream.

(Möise turns abruptly and walks off. Marat and Orleans have to hurry to catch up. Dessalines stands looking at Toussaint as if seeing him for the first time, then he too leaves. Toussaint, stunned, begins to walk a few steps downstage like a sleepwalker. He puts a hand to his forehead. Mars Plaisir makes as if to go towards him. Madame Bullet motions to Mars Plaisir that he should leave the room. He exits. Toussaint begins slowly to talk to himself. As he continues what is a self-examination, he gradually becomes more and more excited.)

TOUSSAINT: I adopted him as a son, made him my nephew. He was always the wise one and Möise, the man of books, is now the most popular man in the army. Yet we have to kill Möise. The safety of the state demands that I kill Möise. Everywhere the labourers shout "Long live Möise." Möise says what they think and what I know. And yet the safety of the state demands that we remove him. I have had enough. All I do is crush my own people. People are ready to revolt all over the island. They are right. But revolt to get what? This mock freedom. They shout "Long live Möise!" What they mean is "Down with Toussaint." *(He looks savagely at Louise.)* The blacks want to kill the whites and why shouldn't they. Madame Bullet, why do I protect the whites? Why must I, a black, shoot blacks to protect whites? Always the whites have to be protected. Why? Whites don't love blacks. They tolerate them. That's all. I am a traitor to my own colour. The blacks are beginning to hate me—the whites hate me already.

(Madame Bullet stretches out her hand halfway to Toussaint. He takes no notice of it, intent only on his descent into his depths.)

MME. BULLET: But, Toussaint, the whites have confidence in you. The whites want you to rule.

TOUSSAINT: Madame Bullet, the whites don't want me to rule. I am the person responsible for taking them from up there and putting them where they are today. If they get the chance they will restore slavery tomorrow and make me a slave again. Toussaint L'Ouverture, black man, former slave. Commander-in-Chief of the Army. Governor of the colony. How could whites want me? No. What they want is to be masters again. This slavery demands that a black man be a slave and a white man a master. There was a revolution. The tables are turned. Now the blacks should become masters and the whites should become slaves. That is what ought to be. I am attempting to do the impossible.

(Madame Bullet moves to Toussaint and looks into his eyes with an almost medical concern.)

MME. BULLET: Toussaint, you are not well. What are you saying? How could half a million blacks be masters and twenty thousand whites be slaves?

TOUSSAINT: *(Tormentedly)* Don't ask me. I don't know. All I know is that whatever is, is wrong. *(Madame Bullet leads Toussaint over to the bench. She dries his forehead with her handkerchief. His voice sinks again, but with a curiously bitter nostalgia.)* My wife and I had a small plot of land. We did what M. Bullet told me to do and as long as we did that we were free. Year by year, my wife and I grew closer together, watching over the children. Where are my sons today? I sent them to France, to be educated. General Bonaparte keeps them as prisoners. I write to Bonaparte asking him to send me a commissioner, teachers, priests, skilled workmen—and my children. He does not reply. Bonaparte believes that I will submit to his commands out of fear for my children's safety. He gives me a choice between my love for my sons and my love for my country. And now I have to kill Möise. If he is not silenced, everything is ruined. The Army will mutiny and we will be fighting against one another instead of preparing for a French invasion. God! To go back to my little plot of land with my wife and the boys on a Sunday morning . . . By law I was a slave, but I was free. Now by law I am free, but I am a slave. I am worse; I am a master of slaves. Möise! I have to kill Möise! *(His outburst is over. He is standing. Deeply moved, Madame Bullet moves to him and reaches out to him.)*

MME. BULLET: Toussaint, I know how you must feel. Möise is a very dangerous man; he is dangerous because he believes everything he says. He believes that he is right and you are wrong. He may be naive but he is a brave soldier. You have told me so many times. You trained him yourself. You will do what you think is right, Toussaint. But you do not have to kill Möise. Don't sign that order. Tell me. How can I help you? There have been bad times before now when I have helped you. I will do whatever you want.

TOUSSAINT: Louise, I need your help more than anything else. I need your help. I have written another letter to General Bonaparte, telling him all that we are doing here, that all we need is a word of encouragement and an assurance that the liberties of the people in San Domingo are safe. *(Toussaint turns to her and speaks as if giving commands to his staff.)* Go to Paris, Louise. I will prepare a special letter for you. See General Bonaparte. Tell him that the policy of General L'Ouverture rules San Domingo. France abolished slavery. As long as France is faithful to us, we shall be faithful to France. Go, Louise. A boat leaves tomorrow. Your passport and all the letters will be ready.

(By this time Madame Bullet realises that Toussaint is not thinking of her as much as he is wrapped up in his own plans. She is nodding in agreement.)

MME. BULLET: Yes, Toussaint. Yes, Commander-in-Chief. I will do whatever you say, whatever you want. I will go to Paris tomorrow morning. I will do all that I can to see General Bonaparte, to tell him all you want me to tell him—*(Her tears are too much to be contained and she cannot speak any more. Toussaint realises what he has been doing and tries to make amends.)*

TOUSSAINT: Louise, forgive me. Here you are offering to give me what I needed so much and all I can do is ask you to undertake a political mission. Louise, forgive me, I could not help it.

MME. BULLET: *(Smiling)* Yes, I know you, Toussaint. You could not help it. But remember, I first came to you for a passport. I wanted to go and now I know that I must go. I wanted to get away from you and, as usual, you are doing what I wanted.

TOUSSAINT: And now I will do what we both want: Möise will not be shot. I will send him on a mission abroad.

MME. BULLET: But will he go?

TOUSSAINT: He will have to. Leave it to me. I will see to it.

MME. BULLET: *(Holding his hand)* Toussaint.

(Dessalines bursts into the room with a piece of paper in his hand.)

DESSALINES: Toussaint! The French fleet is here! The message has just come. Hundreds of vessels. They have sent an army. It is war.

(Toussaint moves over to Dessalines and reads the message. He looks up from it.)

TOUSSAINT: So Bonaparte has decided for war. All this uncertainty is over. War it will be. How many ships are there?

DESSALINES: Our watchers have counted five hundred and there are more coming.

TOUSSAINT: France has come to overwhelm us. Dessalines, we must sound the retreat. But before we do, we must use our only weapons: destruction and fire.

DESSALINES: I have already told my men that they must tear up the roads with shot; that they must throw dead horses in all the drinking water; that they must burn and destroy everything. Our soil must not nourish the enemy.

TOUSSAINT: Good. Now we must muster our forces for the retreat, and plan for the counter-attack.

DESSALINES: It will be done, Toussaint. But first . . . the death warrant. *(Toussaint hesitates, looks at Madame Bullet,,who stares back wide-eyed, with a hand at her mouth.)* It is war. Our ranks must be closed. All of us are behind you, Toussaint. And who is not with us is against us. Sign the paper and give it to me.

(Toussaint sits at his desk, picks up his pen and looks at Madame Bullet. Dessalines puts his hand out firmly. Toussaint slowly signs the paper and hands it to Dessalines. Dessalines reaches for it. The lights fade on the tableau.)

END OF ACT TWO

ACT III, SCENE 1

Soldiers are arranging furniture in a plantation living room similar to that of Act I, Scene II. This is Dessalines' unofficial headquarters. Marat (now a Sergeant and an experienced soldier) is seeing that things are in order. Orleans is a corporal. Both are elegantly dressed as befits their rise in rank. Mars Plaisir is standing looking off upstage. Orleans is doing the work.

ORLEANS: Things look pretty bad. Things look pretty bad.

MARAT: You are always seeing the worst of things.

ORLEANS: What could be worse than Governor Toussaint's surrender? Now we are back under the French and . . .

MARAT: Our army is still there. If the French General attempts any nonsense, he will have to deal with us.

ORLEANS: Mars, what did the General say? What is he going to do?

MARS PLAISIR: *(Disturbed from his thoughts)* General L'Ouverture has retired to his plantation. But he is coming here today. I am waiting for him. I don't know what he will do, Orleans.

ORLEANS: In a revolution you never know. In France, they killed the Duke of Orleans, they killed Jean-Paul Marat. They have also killed Maximillian Robespierre.

MARAT: Yes, And here, they shoot our Max, too. After the Governor shot General Möise, Max, his man, had to go. As you say, in a revolution, you never know. But if the French commander attempts to bring back slavery here, the army and the people will drive every Frenchman into the sea.

ORLEANS: Yes, that is what we will have to do. If we can.

MARAT: You and your "if we can." That is what we will do. They can't kill all of us, but we can kill all of them.

(Dessalines, Christophe and Toussaint have entered on these words. Toussaint is in civilian clothes.)

DESSALINES: "They can't kill all of us, but we can kill all of them." Good, Sergeant Marat; for saying that you deserve promotion. Lieutenant Marat, your first duty is to supervise the patrols. If necessary, reinforce them. *(Marat, very pleased, salutes and turns to leave with Orleans.)*

TOUSSAINT: Mars, go with them.

DESSALINES: Lieutenant Marat. *(Marat halts and turns back.)* Have Samedi Smith relieved and sent here. Let him stand near, I will need him soon.

(Marat salutes. Marat, Orleans and Mars Plaisir exit. Dessalines takes some snuff from his snuff-box, sneezes. Christophe goes to the window and closes it.)

DESSALINES: We are quite safe here. Only trusted men are on guard and my wife keeps an eye on them.

TOUSSAINT: Marie-Jeanne is well?

DESSALINES: Too well. Marie-Jeanne insists on fighting side by side with me. And I believe she likes the life in the bush more than all that music and all those books. All night she reads by the camp fire. Thank goodness I never learned to read. *(Dessalines slaps twice on the table. Enter a black peasant. He carries a rifle. Though barefooted and in rags he is undoubtedly a man of authority.)* Say what your name is.

SAMEDI: My name is Samedi Smith.

TOUSSAINT: Samedi Smith. You used to be the leader of a band of people in arms against my government?

DESSALINES: Yes, General. He was one of those whom we used to call brigands, and now the French invaders call them brigands. But there is Macaya at Limbe; Sylla, in the mountains of Plaisance; and Sans-Souci; all formerly enemies of our government. They refused to surrender to us. And now they have refused to surrender to the French.

CHRISTOPHE: But we have made peace with the French! All these men were bandits, gangsters and robbers under Toussaint's regime. They still are bandits. If we and the French really combined our forces we could crush them and then have some law and order.

SAMEDI: We were gangsters once but now we are fighting for freedom. General Leclerc ask us to give up our guns. That we won't do. M. Sonthonax, a white man, used to tell us anybody who ask you to give up your guns, he means to restore slavery. *(He speaks with a certain restraint, looking at Toussaint out of the corner of his eye.)* And the Governor used to tell us so himself. That was before he made peace with General Leclerc.

DESSALINES: Tell the Governor.

SAMEDI: *(Speaking with great animation)* We were short of ammunition, so all of us from the mountain, all around Port-de-Paix, drove out to garrison, killed the white men, burned the houses they had rebuilt, and took possession of the fort. We found twenty-five thousand pounds of powder.

TOUSSAINT: A wonderful feat. But did you get away with all of it?

DESSALINES: All of it. And most of that powder is now in a safe place. Men, women and children loaded themselves with it and carried it off. But you know who was their chief enemy? Christophe! He was sent by Leclerc to cut them off.

CHRISTOPHE: What you expected me to do? From the time General L'Ouverture submitted, and asked us to submit, General Leclerc constantly sends the local Generals to suppress those whom he calls brigands, enemies of the French Government. You suppress them too, General Dessalines. You obey his orders too!

DESSALINES: Yes, I carry out General Leclerc's orders, and I suppress brigands. But I only suppress the ones that disagree with me.

CHRISTOPHE: You believe you can win independence with people like him?

DESSALINES: If we ever win independence it will be with people like him, not with people like you. *(To Toussaint.)* General, all of us believe that although you made peace you were just waiting for the time to move.

(He looks at Toussaint and Christophe, and Dessalines looks at Toussaint also. There is a long silence.)

TOUSSAINT: Samedi Smith! You, Macaya, Jean Panier and all others like you hold the defence of freedom in your hands. I submitted, and asked my generals to submit. It was to prevent the complete destruction of what we have fought so hard to build up. But I insisted that the army should retain its arms. Once the army and the people retain their arms, slavery can never be restored.

DESSALINES: General, the arms of the army are being used against the people. I am afraid of what I see ahead. General, you have led us to victory when the cause, everything, seemed lost. Lead us, now. Say what to do. Whatever you say will be done.

TOUSSAINT: We have to wait and see. I cannot believe that the French Government will attempt to restore the slavery which they and they alone have abolished. General Dessalines, General Christophe. Our people need the help that only France can give. They can't read, they can't write, they have no skills, no knowledge of governing, no knowledge of God. We must hold on and hope that we shall arrive at some understanding. . . . I am no longer a General. I have retired, and only if our liberty is threatened shall I once more place myself at the head of our people. As long as the people have their arms we are safe. *(Toussaint stands. Christophe and Dessalines stand also.)* General Dessalines, we shall meet at my plantation at Ennery on Wednesday morning at nine. I shall wait for you in the usual place. General Christophe, my respects to your wife. Samedi Smith, I remember you. . . . You . . . had been promoted in my division before you took to the hills. . . .

SAMEDI: God bless you, Governor, God bless you.

TOUSSAINT: We all need his blessing. Good night. *(Dessalines moves to go out with him.)* No, Dessalines, Mars will go with me. We shall ride through the night and be in Ennery by morning.

(Toussaint leaves. As soon as he goes, Christophe turns to Dessalines.)

CHRISTOPHE: I have to return to headquarters, General Dessalines. I expect to meet you there, soon.

DESSALINES: Sit down, Christophe. I want to talk to you. Samedi, you and your men wait. I want to see you before you go.

(Samedi salutes and leaves. Christophe sits unwillingly. Coming from upstage are male voices softly in chorus. They sing Samedi Smith's song. Dessalines moves upstage and looks towards the singing. He returns to the table, ignoring Christophe, and takes some snuff. He sneezes. Christophe is obviously uncomfortable.)

CHRISTOPHE: What do you want from me?

DESSALINES: Why do you think I want something of you? *(The chorus from outside becomes clearer and stronger.)* You hear that song?

CHRISTOPHE: No. Yes, of course I hear it.

DESSALINES: You know what it is?

CHRISTOPHE: No, I don't know it. The brigands sing it. It is their song now. They used to sing "La Marseillaise" and the "Ça Ira" but the French soldiers always sing those, so the brigands have started to sing this as their song.

DESSALINES: This is it; listen, Christophe *(He half-sings, half-recites with a pervading irony which sometimes intensifies the interpretation.)*

A l'attaque, brave soldat,
Et qui périt, c'est son affaire,
A l'attaque, grenadier,
Et qui va tomber, reste sur la terre.
Oublier ta maman et ton père,
Et qui périt, c'est son affaire.
Oublier tous tes soeurs et tes frères,
Et qui va tomber, reste sur la terre.
(To the attack, brave soldier,
Who gets killed is his affair.
To the attack, grenadier,
And whoever falls remains on the ground.
Forget your ma, forget your pa
Who gets killed is his affair.
Forget your sister, forget your brothers
And whoever falls remains on the ground.)

(Drumming increases rapidly in tempo.)

CHRISTOPHE: And that means voodoo.

DESSALINES: Absolutely not. *(Shouts.)* Samedi! *(Dessalines goes to the rear of the room and calls in a stentorian voice.)* Samedi! *(At the sound of his voice the drumming stops abruptly. Samedi comes in looking somewhat guilty.)* Samedi, no more of that drumming. No Voodoo. Anybody in my detachment who practises Voodoo will be shot on the spot. No Voodoo and none of that drumming. *(Samedi turns to go.)* A salute, Sergeant Samedi.

(Samedi salutes. Dessalines replies and Samedi retreats.)

CHRISTOPHE: Why have you stopped the drumming? When Toussaint was Governor, he gave those instructions, but those days are over.

DESSALINES: When it came to governing the country, Toussaint was always right.

CHRISTOPHE: But General Leclerc and all the French generals say that the people can drum and dance voodoo as they like. Madame Leclerc is absolutely fascinated by the voodoo. As a matter of fact, in the old days, they say, you were a great voodoo dancer yourself, General Dessalines.

DESSALINES: After one time is another. For instance, now you are for voodoo and you have always been against it. Always in church worshipping their God, Jesus Christ. You also were very stern in putting it down; and if I remember, you would shoot voodoo dancers almost at sight. I heard you say that voodoo prevented the population from becoming good citizens and Christians and warning about liberty and equality and the whole set of principles that come from France.

CHRISTOPHE: Yes, yes. I was merciless against voodoo in my province.

Those were the orders of Toussaint and I believed that voodoo and all that savagery stood in the way of our progress, but today I am for anything that will satisfy the people . . .

DESSALINES: And also satisfy General Leclerc.

CHRISTOPHE: All right, but as I see it, Dessalines, if they want voodoo, let them have voodoo.

DESSALINES: No!

CHRISTOPHE: I have to go now, Dessalines.

DESSALINES: I know. *(contemptuously)* Give my compliments to General Leclerc. But Christophe, I want you to give him a message. From me.

(Christophe sits down again)

CHRISTOPHE: What message?

DESSALINES: I am ordering a concentration of all the forces under my command at Grande Riviere. This is for his ears only. The time of concentration will be on Wednesday morning. At 9 o'clock.

CHRISTOPHE: But on Wednesday morning at 9 o'clock, you are meeting Toussaint at Ennery!

DESSALINES: On Wednesday morning at 9 o'clock I will be in personal command of an operation to clear Grande Riviere and its neighbourhood of brigands. You will tell General Leclerc that Toussaint will be at Ennery. That I leave to you, Christophe. *(Christophe at last seems to understand what Dessalines is saying to him. He rises and begins to take his leave. He reaches the door and in fact has begun to open it when Dessalines speaks again.)* By the way, Christophe, Toussaint, on Wednesday morning, will be alone in the pavilion at the end of the garden. As usual, all his men will be at work on the plantation. 9 o'clock exactly. Remember, he is never early and never late.

(Christophe with understanding dawning in his face, looks at Dessalines for a moment and then, like a man carrying unexpectedly good news, hastens away. Marie-Jeanne enters, her eyes fixed on Dessalines. She is wearing military dress, trousers and high boots, both spattered with mud. But her bodice is frilly and her hair is carefully done. She stands somewhat behind Dessalines, her hands holding the top of the chair. After a period of silence, Dessalines rises, saying half to himself: I must see about . . . He turns to face to Marie-Jeanne. He is startled to see her.)

MARIE-JEANNE: Dessalines, we have to be at Ennery on Wednesday morning. I would be glad if we could leave early on Tuesday so I could spend some time with Madame L'Ouverture and the family.

(Dessalines turns to her with fury. The orchestra quietly but clearly begins to play "Vendetta ti Chieggio la Chiedo il tuo cor.")

DESSALINES: You have been listening! How do you know I am going to Ennery on Wednesday morning? We shall be far from Ennery and you will be with me, Marie-Jeanne. If I hear any more of this from you or anybody else I will kill you.

MARIE-JEANNE: Kill me now. You are a killer. Yes, I was listening. I understand everything. Kill me, Dessalines. Kill me before you go to Grand Riviere. I know—

DESSALINES: You know! What do you know?

MARIE-JEANNE: I know that you are plotting to get Toussaint killed.

DESSALINES: You are a blind fool. Why should I want to get Toussaint killed?

MARIE-JEANNE: To become chief under General Leclerc. To become a house slave once again. I was one, too, remember? I was the woman of M. Bullet. I had to sleep with him and report to him any movement or talk of insurrection among the slaves. I thought, General Dessalines, that we had left all that spying and informing behind. But I see that you want to become the head of the house-slaves. And in the end, Toussaint will be shot. Well, after Toussaint, your turn will come and I will be a house-slave again, to sleep . . .

DESSALINES: Hold your tongue, woman.

MARIE-JEANNE: I will not hold my tongue. That is all I have left. The other day, I, the wife of the great General Dessalines, was driving along the Main Street in Port-au-Prince and I saw M. Bullet standing in the crowd. He saw me, our eyes met, and I know when the old regime is here once more, he will seek me out to become his woman again. During these last days in battle I was near to death many times. I wish I had been killed.

(Dessalines goes to her.)

DESSALINES: Sit down, woman, and listen to me. *(Marie-Jeanne continues to stare at him but makes no move. Dessalines strikes her twice across the face and forces her down into the chair. The orchestra plays the Mozart aria more strongly then ever. However, as Dessalines speaks it gradually declines until by the time he is finished it has died away.)* Sit down, I tell you: I have arranged for Toussaint to be captured, not killed. He will not be killed. General Leclerc has been wanting to put his hands on Toussaint since his surrender. I always told them that if they did without my consent an insurrection would break out at once, all over the island. Now the insurrection is near. The man who stands in the way, Marie-Jeanne, is Toussaint. Don't say a word, woman. It is Toussaint who stands in the way. He will never give the signal the people are waiting for. He still believes in liberty and equality and a whole lot of nonsense that he had learned from the French. All I have learnt from the French is that without arms in my hand there is no freedom. The people still believe that Toussaint is their leader; but I am their leader and when he goes they will know that. From the time he had to kill Möise he has not been the same man. Möise was right. But he had to be shot then. Now the whole thing is changed. Möise's ideas are flourishing in new soil. You see Samedi Smith out there and his men. There are thousands more. When Toussaint is removed they will look to me. And I will lead them. We will drive every Frenchman into the sea. Now you can talk. These last months you were often puzzled at what I was doing. Now you know. *(Marie-Jeanne looks up at Dessalines as if she is seeing him for the first time.)* Toussaint has to go. And it is the French who have to take him.

MARIE-JEANNE: But they will kill him.

DESSALINES: No, they will not kill him. *(Shouting because he is uncertain.)* They will not dare. They will take him straight to the boat that is now in the harbour, it will sail for France at once.

MARIE-JEANNE: *(Still somewhat overwhelmed)* And Madame Toussaint? What will happen to her?

DESSALINES: She will be taken to France with him. And Mars Plaisir, his man, to see after them. They will do what I say. They believe that Dessalines is nothing but an ambitious savage. You believe that too. But now you should know that though I am a savage, I am no fool. The future of this country depends on me. You come with me, Marie-Jeanne, or you will be killed. I will kill you with my own hands.

(There is a long pause during which Marie-Jeanne is obviously adjusting herself to an entirely new situation.)

MARIE-JEANNE: Come here, Jean-Jacques, and sit at my feet as you used to do when we first married. Don't be afraid. You have always been afraid of me. I must set that right. *(Dessalines knows that he has won and he comes docilely and sits at her feet. Marie-Jeanne puts her hand on his head.)* Jean-Jacques, when I married you I was not in love with you.

DESSALINES: I know. I was a barbarian, they used to call me the Tiger. Toussaint told you to marry me in order to civilise me a bit, to make me fit for the high position that I hold. I was General of Division, Governor of a Province and second only to Toussaint, but I could not read and in many things I was still the slave I had always been. That is why you married me, Marie-Jeanne, I know that. Toussaint told you.

MARIE-JEANNE: No, Toussaint never told me that.

DESSALINES: No, I know he never said that. That is a thing Toussaint would never say. But I know, Marie-Jeanne.

MARIE-JEANNE: Jean-Jacques, you listen to me now. When I married you, you were rough and often brutal. But little by little I grew to understand you, the kind of man you were, and your devotion to Toussaint. And these days, fighting with you in the bush, even though you were not telling me what you were doing or why, I fell in love with you, Dessalines. I trusted you completely. Here in San Domingo, people don't trust one another. For the first time in all my life, a man, my husband, meant something to me. In every battle in the bush, I was a person next to you, watching over you, ready to give my life for yours. Life meant nothing to me without you. Nothing. And just then, when I heard you plotting Toussaint's capture, I thought for a moment you had betrayed me, but I understand now. Whatever you say I will do. You will go to Grande Riviere and I, Jean-Jacques, will find my way to the mulattoes and talk to General Pétion. You have often said you wanted someone you could trust to talk to General Pétion.

DESSALINES: That you can. Better than I. Go to him, Marie-Jeanne.

(She stands. Dessalines stands. She puts her arms around his shoulders and leans her head on his breast.)

MARIE-JEANNE: I will win Pétion over. I know the mulattoes are in deadly fear of what will happen to them if slavery is restored. They are waiting on Pétion. We will fight to the end and we will win. They can't beat you, JeanJacques, nobody can. But Toussaint! He took us from nothing, you and me, and made us what we are. It is hard, Jean-Jacques.

DESSALINES: It is hard. The times we live in are hard. *(A pause.)* Tell me that thing I like so much.

(Marie-Jeanne moves away from him and somewhat self-consciously, at least at the beginning, recites.)

MARIE-JEANNE:

I fondly hoped that Heaven above
Would guard a silence to conceal this love.
But my poor heart, twisted and torn with pain
Impels me now to speak, never to speak again.
What were my hopes? I can no longer tell.
Except to know my love was born in Hell.
Achilles did not by any pretended grief
Encourage me to hope for quick relief.
'Twas Heaven itself that with its cruel dart
Applied new torture to my bleeding heart.
To you, that bitter day needs no recall
When both of us were swept into his thrall.
But me, he raped; long hours I lay
Unknowing whether it was night or day.
I fought with storms and when I stemmed the flood,
The arms that circled me were stained with blood.
Doris, I froze. My eyes refused to see
The face that sponsored such brutality.
He led me off. All that remained was pride.
I would not watch him, kept my gaze aside
And then I saw him. There was only calm
In his kind face. It soothed my pain like balm.
My heart declared for him. Instead of fears
I could say nothing except floods of tears

(Now Dessalines joins in and they say the last two lines together, as drums begin very softly in the distance.)

My strength returned, once more I knew my will
I loved him then and now I love him still.

(Dessalines embraces her.)

DESSALINES: You mean they really used to speak like that?

MARIE-JEANNE: Yes, so it says in the book.

DESSALINES: And you say this man was not a General.

MARIE-JEANNE: No. I told you he wrote plays. His name was Racine. The play is called Iphigénie!

(The drums are louder.)

DESSALINES: Well, that suits them in France. In France they write plays. But listen, listen. That is San Domingo. We can't write plays about voodoo!

(Marie-Jeanne stares at him. The lights fade as Dessalines stares back at her.)

ACT III, SCENE 2: 1803

Orleans enters with a huge throne-like chair.

ORLEANS: Things are looking pretty good. Pretty good.

MARAT: Yes, we have come a long way from the days when we used to arrange meetings in the forest. General Dessalines will be the next Governor of San Domingo.

ORLEANS: Yes, if we drive out the French army. If we don't, all of us are done.

MARAT: We must win. General Dessalines does not lose any battles. We, the black people, have the power now.

ORLEANS: Yes, if we defeat the French.

MARAT: Enough of that. You are still with your "if we beat the French." You were a slave and you are fit for nothing else but being a slave. I hear the General.

(As staff enter on one side, the two men move toward the other. A body of officers, soldiers, civilians, etc., enter. They are a government as well as military gathering. Among them is General Christophe. There is a whisper, people saying to each other: He is coming. Here he comes! etc. *General Dessalines enters. He is master of himself and all around him. He is now Commander-in-Chief. He moves to the big chair in the centre of the room, which now has a table in front of it. As he sits, he speaks.)*

DESSALINES: No news from General Pétion yet?

MARAT: Yes sir. He has sent you someone.

DESSALINES: Why didn't you call me? Where is he?

MULATTO OFFICER: Sir, General Pétion sends to say that he expects by the time I reach here, the detachment of General Rochambeau's army in front of him will be defeated. He has them surrounded with their backs against the Gulf of Port-au-Prince.

(Dessalines rises in triumph.)

DESSALINES: That is the end. The mulattoes have not failed us. Friends, the French expedition is finished. They will have to sue for peace. We have won. I knew it. Once we had made up our minds we would have beaten Bonaparte himself. *(He points to the mulatto officer.)* You are a Lieutenant?

MULATTO OFFICER: Yes, sir.

DESSALINES: You are now a Captain. But you are wounded.

MULATTO OFFICER: Yes, General.

DESSALINES: Well, not a Captain, you are now a Major. Christophe, see to it. A proper uniform. Our friends, the mulattoes, have done well. *(Christophe steps forward, takes the officer by the arm and leads him away. Dessalines speaks half to himself.)* I knew we could. *(To the staff.)* By tomorrow morning there will not be a French soldier on this island. *(Marat whispers to Dessalines.)* Bring him in. Bring him in at once. *(Marat goes out and returns with a French officer. Dessalines does not allow the French officer to speak.)* I know what you want. You came here to make negotiations, conditions for a retreat and all that bowing and saluting and games that Toussaint used to carry on with you. No negotiations here, no conditions. Tell your General that he and his army have till four o'clock in the morning to get on their ships and leave our waters. The British fleet is waiting to engage you. But that is your business. You had no right here to begin with. But let your General know that for the last two days I have been preparing red hot shot, and if by tomorrow morning at sunrise the French are not out of every piece of our territory, I shall burn you alive. That is my message. Those are the only negotiations I have to make. Now get out. *(The French officer, terrified, turns and walks out. Dessalines sits at the table working off this anger.)* Now the moment has come. Bring me a French flag. *(A French tri-colour flag is brought to him by*

Orleans. He rises and tears off the white.) Our flag will have no white in it. We will keep the blue for the sea that surrounds and defends us, and I want the red for the blood of the blacks and the mulattoes who have liberated our country. The land is now ours. That is our flag. Now we need a name. No more San Domingo. The name that the Caribs gave to the country before the French came here! What is the name? *(There is a ragged chorus of:* Haiti—*pronounced Ha-ee-tee.)* Haiti! That is our name now. Haiti! *(The crowd take it up and shout:* Haiti! Haiti! Haiti! *Dessalines sits back at the table.)* Now we are independent. We own the soil. We have our own name. We have our own flag. Let us have wine and some music. Call my wife. *(Messengers fly in different directions.)* And now I have to tell you all something. I have been waiting for this moment and now the moment has come. I am going to be Emperor of Haiti. Emperor, not King. They offered Toussaint to be King and he didn't take it. But nobody is going to offer me anything. I, Dessalines, am going to be Emperor of Haiti. Napoleon wants to be Emperor of France. I will be Emperor of Haiti. Dessalines, Emperor of Haiti.

(The crowd is somewhat uncertain at first but, led by Marat, they shout.)

CROWD: Dessalines! Emperor of Haiti! Emperor!

(Dessalines has risen but he sits down again.)

DESSALINES: Now I shall tell you more. Tomorrow, the Emperor will issue a proclamation. The time has come. We are going to kill every white man and woman on this island. They will never be able to restore slavery here because we are going to get rid of all of them. Not one is going to remain. *(His staff is obviously startled and shocked at this proposal. Christophe reenters.)* You fools are not ready for that? Look at what we have had to suffer from these people. Man, woman and child, not one of them is going to be left alive. No more slavery here. That proclamation I shall issue tomorrow, signed by me—Dessalines, Emperor of Haiti. I have learnt to sign my name, Dessalines. I will learn to sign Emperor. All will be killed. All.

(There is a continuing murmur of opposition in the room. Christophe steps forward.)

CHRISTOPHE: General . . .

(Dessalines interrupts him with a roar.)

DESSALINES: Not General, Emperor.

CHRISTOPHE: Yes, Emperor. If you will allow me, your majesty, General Pétion will have to be consulted before such a proclamation is . . .

DESSALINES: Christophe, you are against but again afraid to say so.

CHRISTOPHE: All I am saying, your majesty, is that before you issue a proclamation you should consult General Pétion,

DESSALINES: I will consult him. I will tell him that I have issued a proclamation. That will be enough. He will understand.

CHRISTOPHE: Emperor, that would be the wrong way to show the world your imperial power.

DESSALINES: The Emperor decides what is right and wrong; don't you ever forget that, Christophe. Now that I am Emperor you are head of the army, but no General will ever tell me what to do.

CHRISTOPHE: As your Imperial Majesty decides. Right or wrong.

(A silence in the room, among officers and civilians alike. Dessalines glares at them and they look at him in what is not far from terror. The tension is broken by the

entrance of an orderly. Dessalines addresses him somewhat roughly.)

DESSALINES: What is it?

ORDERLY: There is someone here to see you, sir, Emperor.

DESSALINES: If it is a Frenchman, I will not see him.

ORDERLY: It is not a Frenchman, Emperor. It is an Englishman. His name is Cathcart.

DESSALINES: Show him in

(Cathcart enters. He bows to Dessalines.)

CATHCART: I am Cathcart, General Dessalines, representative of powerful British trading interests. I have my papers here. Everyone is assured of your victory over the French and I have various propositions to make to the rulers of the colony.

DESSALINES: This is no longer a colony, no more French San Domingo. It is the independent state of Haiti and I, Dessalines, am the Emperor of Haiti.

(Cathcart is a little startled. But he is a man of great self-assurance. He bows very low.)

CATHCART: Emperor, I am glad to be one of the earliest to congratulate you on the high position you have assumed. This somewhat affects the proposals I have to make to you. Can I see you in private, Emperor?

DESSALINES: Certainly, you can see the Emperor in private. Go away everybody!

(All turn and leave the room rapidly. Christophe is the last to go and lingers long enough to appraise the situation. Cathcart briefly glances at him, then delicately takes some snuff from the back of his thumb. Dessalines looks on, waiting for a sneeze. Nothing happens. Cathcart offers his snuff-box, but Dessalines declines.)

CATHCART: Emperor, the interests I represent are ready to come to terms with the new rulers, you, about trade with this country. Very special consideration will be given to you in any agreement with Britain. I have all the papers here but there is one consideration for your ear and your ear alone.

(Dessalines is at once suspicious.)

DESSALINES: What is it?

CATHCART: Sir, Emperor, the interests I represent have been expecting that you would defeat the French and chase them out of this island. British and American interests have supported you in your struggle, you know that, but they have told me that there is one necessity before the establishment of beneficial trade relations. That necessity is your vengeance for all that you have suffered. You have to show who is master here. If you do that, we can come to terms. If you do not, we shall not be able to make any permanent arrangements with you. You need our commerce to rebuild the island. These are my instructions.

(Dessalines laughs, rises and shakes him by the hand.)

DESSALINES: That will not be difficult. That is exactly what I intend to do. The proclamation calling upon the population to kill every Frenchman upon the island will be published, *(Pause, as he remembers his exchange with Christophe.)* soon. But sit down. *(He forces Cathcart into a chair.)* Tell me. Why do your "British trading interests" want all the French on the island killed? I know why I am going to kill them. We suffered from them. They made us slaves because they said we were not men. When we behaved like men and fought for our freedom, they called us monsters. Now we behave like they do. But you have not suffered from them. They are white people just like you. I don't understand.

CATHCART: Emperor, you are now head of a state and of course you know the political realities of the day. The British interests that I represent wanted to be quite certain that whoever ruled in Haiti, will not one day restore close relations with the French. After all, you speak their language. You are very French. Restoration of good relations between you and the French would mean the destruction of British trade and influence here. However, if you kill them all, you draw a line of blood between France and your new black country. You and France will never get together again.

DESSALINES: Mr Cathcart, as long as Dessalines is Emperor of Haiti, France and Haiti will remain mortal enemies. But if to kill every Frenchman and woman on the island will also ensure me the friendship of the British, then there is no doubt that it will be done. We understand one another, Mr Cathcart.

CATHCART: Emperor, we understand one another.

DESSALINES: We must celebrate.

CATHCART: Ah, Emperor, one more thing, please. You are of course, certain of the support of all your government in this action? I understand that one of your generals, Henri Christophe . . .

DESSALINES: Christophe will do what I say. He is master of the rest, but I am master of him. Ho there! *(The staff and others come back in. They obviously were just outside.)* You have brought the wine and music? Wine for me and for our new friend, Mr Cathcart. For everybody wine. And some music.

(The musicians enter. Wine is brought in. A toast is drunk, with glasses raised to Dessalines, Emperor of Haiti. Preceded by Orleans, Marie-Jeanne enters. Dessalines greets her.)

DESSALINES: Marie-Jeanne, I am Emperor and you are the Empress. *(Marie-Jeanne stands mystified.)*

MARIE-JEANNE: Empress of what?

DESSALINES: Empress of the new state of Haiti. You will wear a crown. Everybody toasts to the Empress. Marie-Jeanne, Empress of Haiti!

ALL: Marie-Jeanne, Empress of Haiti!

(The toast is drunk, Marie-Jeanne still at a loss. There are sounds of: Dessalines Emperor of Haiti! *from the crowd outside. Dessalines goes to the window and opens it. He shouts down to them.)*

DESSALINES: "Dessalines! Emperor! Haiti!"

(The crowd outside and those in the room are shouting: Dessalines Emperor! Haiti Dessalines! Emperor! Haiti! *They break into song. Waving to them, Dessalines suddenly hears the Samedi Smith song. He backs away from the window slowly, then turns around savagely.)*

DESSALINES: Where is the music I asked for? *(Two violinists, a flautist and a mandolinist step forward.)* A minuet! And play it loudly! Mr Cathcart, I am not only a soldier of many campaigns. I am a fine dancer. Marie-Jeanne, allow me. *(Dessalines and Marie-Jeanne make some steps but suddenly the low singing outside stops. It is replaced by a murmur growing into a tumult. Marat enters and whispers news which spreads so rapidly from person to person that the musicians stop playing the minuet. Dessalines falters in the dance.)* What is it? Play on.

(Marat steps forward.)

MARAT: Emperor, the news just came. Toussaint is dead. He died in prison.

(Marie-Jeanne moves suddenly to the table and knocks over her glass as she seeks support for her body sagging in grief. There is consternation in the room. From Marie-Jeanne comes a silent flow of tears. The crowd outside have started to sing Samedi Smith's song in the style of a mournful chant. Everybody looks at Dessalines.)

DESSALINES: Toussaint L'Ouverture could have been king of San Domingo, but he would not take it. Möise told him exactly what to do, but he killed Möise. I am sorry for him, but we can't do anything about it now. Music there!

(As the minuet hesitantly begins, he steps forward and almost forcibly takes the hand of the weeping Marie-Jeanne to continue the dance. As the lights begin to fade around the periphery of the dance, there is gradual movement off by groups of soldiers. Marat is the last soldier to leave. The musicians then flee as Cathcart remains standing to one side of the dancing and Henri Christophe moves to the right of Dessalines' throne. Marie-Jeanne and Dessalines freeze in a final tableau as the lights fade.)

THE END.

1936

7
Stalin and Socialism

In the Testament, Lenin, as superior to his contemporaries in grasp of men as of politics, had warned the party of a probable split between Trotsky and Stalin. It was, he said, a trifle, but "a trifle as may acquire a decisive significance." Lenin believed in historical materialism but he did not underestimate the significance of individuals, and the full immensity of the consequences are visible today.

Yet, as Lenin, quite obviously saw, the immediate origin of the danger was personal. Lenin did not say so in so many words. The Testament is very carefully phrased, but all through the civil war there had been clashes between Trotsky and Stalin. Stalin, with Zinoviev and Kamenev, who supported him at first, hated Trotsky, but Stalin hated him with a hatred which saw in him the chief obstacle to his power; Zinoviev and Kamenev Stalin knew he could manage. Zinoviev on his part feared Trotsky, but feared Stalin also. He had the idea of balancing one against the other. But he went with Stalin for the time being. What manner of man was this who was so soon to usurp Lenin's position and attempt to play Lenin's part? No man of this generation, few men of any other, could have done this adequately.

Lenin, first and foremost, knew political economy as few professors in a university did. He was absolute master of political theory and practice. He knew the international working class movement of the great countries of Europe, not only their history theoretically interpreted by historical materialism, but from years of personal experience in Britain, France, Germany and Switzerland.[1] He spoke almost faultless German and wrote the language like a second tongue. He was at home in French and English and could read other European languages with ease. Intellectual honesty was with him a fanatical passion, and to his basic conception of allying the highest results of his theoretical and practical knowledge in the party to the instinctive movements of millions, honesty before the party and before the masses was for him essential. The range and honesty of his intellect, his power of will, the singular selflessness and devotion of his personal character, added to a great knowledge and understanding of men, enabled him to use all types of intellect and character in a way that helped to lift the Bolshevik party between 1917 and 1923 to the full height of the stupendous role it was called upon to fulfill. No body of men ever did so much, and how small most of them really were we can realise only by looking at what they became the moment their master left them. Lenin made them what they were. He was sly and manoeuvred as all who have to manage men must manoeuvre. But through all the disagreements of those years which often reached breaking-point he never calumniated, exiled, imprisoned or murdered any leaders of his party. He was bitter in denunciation, often unfair, but never personally malicious. He was merciless to political enemies, but he called them enemies, and proclaimed aloud that if they opposed the Soviet regime he would shoot them and keep on shooting them. But Trotsky tells us how careful he was of the health of his colleagues; hard as he was it is easy to feel in his speeches, on occasions when the party was being torn by disputes, a man of strong emotions and sensitiveness to human personality. In his private life he set an unassuming example of personal incorruptibility and austere living. No man could ever fill his place, but it was not impossible that someone able and willing to act in his tradition could have carried on where he left off, and all knew that Trotsky was best fitted for that difficult post. Lenin had designated him as such in the Testament. But the irony, the cruellest tragedy of the post-war world is, that without a break the leadership of the over-centralised and politically dominant Bolshevik party passed from one of the highest representatives of European culture to another who, in every respect except singlemindedness of purpose, was the very antithesis of his predecessor.

Stalin's personal character is not the dominating factor of Soviet history since 1924. Far greater forces have been at work. But if Lenin's individual gifts were on the side of progress to socialism, Stalin touched only to corrupt. Of political economy he was, and to a great extent is, quite ignorant; in Marxism he and his henchmen are today capable of errors that a raw Social Democrat would not be guilty of. These things will be proved in their place. For the moment it is sufficient to give some significant incidents in his early history.

In January, 1928, Verechtschaks, one of his early companions, gave in the Paris newspaper, *Dui*, some recollections of Stalin in prison.[2] Their authenticity will not be denied by the Stalinists, for in *Pravda* of February 2, 1928, and December 20, 1929, Demian Biedny, a Stalinist scribbler, quoted such scraps as reflected credit on the beloved leader. He did not quote the following. One day a young Georgian was badly beaten by his brother-prisoners in the Benlov prison as a provocateur, a charge which turned out to be false. Later it was discovered that the rumour came from Stalin. On another occasion an ex-Bolshevik knifed and killed a worker whom he did not know but whom he believed to be a spy. The murderer confessed afterwards that Koba (as Stalin was then called) had incited him. At the end of 1901 Koba suddenly left Tiflis. The Georgian Social-Democratic magazine, *Brdzolis Khma* (Echo of Struggle) tells us why. Stalin, by means of slander and intrigue, had attempted to undermine the position of the leader of the organisation. After he had been warned many times he spread still more vicious slander and was unanimously expelled from the Tiflis organisation. This story is told not to blacken his character or cast him for the part of villain. It is of importance because he remains today what he was then, only where in early days he went round whispering and writing letters, from 1924 onwards he had all the resources of a great country at his disposal. The moment Lenin was incapacitated Stalin began to stamp the image of his corrupt and limited personality on the Bolshevik party. There is no inevitability in this. He was one kind of man and Lenin was another. The trial of Zinoviev, Kamenev and the others is no surprise to those who know the history of the Bolshevik party since Stalin has had power in his hands.

One final characteristic will also explain his supreme unfitness for authority in the socialist State. In 1911 he wrote a letter giving his opinion on the struggle Lenin was waging against those who wished to liquidate the revolution and against Trotsky still striving for an impossible unity. "We have heard about the tempest in the tea-cup, the bloc of Lenin-Plekhanov on the one hand, and Trotsky-Martov-Bogdanov on the other. As far as I know the workers incline toward the former. In general, however, they mistrust the emigrés. Why should they bother themselves about them; as far as we are concerned, everyone who has the interest of the movement at heart does his own work. The rest will follow of itself. That is, in my opinion, the best." *(Zaria Vostoka*, 23 December 1925)

He neither knew not cared. There are other instances of his national limitedness, his sneers at the emigrés, his contempt for theory. The Leninism which he has preached so assiduously since 1924 means nothing to him. With the veneer of an Oxford education in England, or a personal fortune in France or America, he would have been an ideal Prime Minister or President. An army of personal advisers and a traditional system would have given him scope for his powers of organisation, and intrigue and ruthless will. He could never have built a mass movement but as a second or successor to a Hitler or a Mussolini he could have found perhaps the best scope for his extraordinary abilities. As guide to a State based on the principles of scientific socialism and formulator of the policies of the Third International, it is impossible to imagine any person more unsuitable. But it is these very qualities and defects that made the bureaucracy instinctively side with him against Trotsky in the struggle that followed.

He was without reputation and had reached where he was by rigidly siding with Lenin on nearly every occasion. In 1905 and October, 1917, he had done little. He had no personal appeal whatever. Nor had Zinoviev and Kamenev. All knew the part they had played not only before October but immediately after, when they had urged a coalition with the Mensheviks and had resigned from the Central Committee on account of their disapproval of the uncompromising policy of Lenin and Trotsky. Lenin had broadcast it to the whole population of Russia. Zinoviev was known to be a coward; his unoriginality earned him the nickname of Lenin's gramophone. Despite a certain popularity, neither he nor Kamenev could rival either Stalin or Trotsky.

Trotsky on the other hand, was, even while Lenin lived, the most brilliant figure in Russia. As far as the strategy of October was concerned, Lenin's had been the guiding hand, but while he was in hiding Trotsky had been the leading figure before the masses in Petrograd. He was the "Man of October." His organisation of the Red Army had given him not only an international reputation but a vast popularity among the peasants. As Commissar for War, travelling from front to front, he had become personally known to and beloved by millions. He was the greatest orator in Europe, and at congresses of the International, delivered the chief address in Russian, German and French, and would then, as War

Commissioner, review the Red Army for the delegates. His pamphlets appealed equally to professors and peasants. Most important of all, he was Lenin's right hand, acknowledged by all as his successor. His personal weakness was imperiousness and a certain inability to function easily with men his equal in status but obviously inferior in quality. He lacked Lenin's comprehensive good nature and homeliness. His very brilliance and audacity in action carried with it a compensating incapacity for that personal manoeuvring at which so many lesser men excel. His great weakness, incapacity in party organisation, did not impede him so long as he was a member of Lenin's great organisation. While Lenin lived he smoothed over all difficulties, and Lenin and Trotksy were two names indissolubly linked together. Stalin, jealous, small-minded but ambitious, lurked in the background and schemed and plotted. He found kindred spirits in Zinoviev and Kamenev. About priority Lenin and Trotsky never quarrelled. After the October revolution, Lenin proposed Trotsky as Chairman of the Council of Commissars. Trotsky saw that the suggestion was preposterous and insisted on Lenin taking his rightful place. They were concerned with policy not with place. But some old Bolsheviks hated this outsider who after opposing their master for years had suddenly walked in and ousted them from the position they thought theirs by right. But to the great masses Trotsky, even when Lenin was incapacitated, had still the prestige of his gifts and achievements and the magic of his close association with Lenin.

Trotsky was not only beloved by the masses, but was popular in the rank-and-file of the party. What had Zinoviev, Kamenev or Stalin ever done to make anyone except their own immediate followers enthusiastic over them? But the three had the party apparatus and the party funds in their hands. Djerzhinsky, who had shared with Stalin Lenin's castigation over the national question, was close to them, and they won over Bucharin in control of the party press. Stalin is supreme in his management of men. The emergency of civil war, blockade and famine, the forcible requisitioning from the peasants in the civil war, the fatigue and passivity of the masses, all these had given power to the party apparatus. Officials in the party were increasingly appointed from above. All over the vast, almost roadless, countryside Soviet officials and party officers held almost unlimited power, subject only to the central authority. While Lenin and Trotsky were immersed in economics, politics and the international revolution, Stalin worked for power.[3] He had had a narrow escape from Lenin. But after Lenin's final incapacitation he bureaucratised the party more and more, Zinoviev, Kamenev and Bucharin helping. What must not be forgotten is that this struggle went on in a narrow circle, so small had the governing group become, even under Lenin. The masses played little part, and Trotsky either could not or dared not bring the masses into it, as Lenin would infallibly have done sooner rather than later. Dissatisfaction began to grow; the party youth resented this tyranny as youth will. Then in September, 1923, with the economic situation critical, two secret societies were discovered in the Bolshevik Party. Measures were instantly taken to suppress them, but such formations were obviously the result of the bureaucratic regime which Lenin had recently attacked so openly and so pointedly. Trotsky brought the struggle into the open. He and many other members demanded that the old resolution on Workers' Democracy be implemented. On October 8, he wrote to the Central Committee pointing out that the apparatus had been bureaucratised by the method of selection instead of election, that the party was now in a dangerous condition and might be taken unawares by a crisis of exceptional severity. He had tried for a year and a half inside the Central Committee, but there had been no improvement, and he felt it his duty to bring the matter to the notice of the party. The reply was typical of that boorishness which has more and more distinguished Soviet politics the more Stalin's influence has increased. The Central Committee said that Trotsky's attacks on the Communist Party, which had continued for "several years," and his "determination to disturb the party," were due to the fact that he wanted the Central Committee to place him and Comrade Kalegaev at the head of industrial life. He was striving for unlimited powers in industry and military affairs and had "categorically declined the position of substitute for Lenin. That evidently he considers is beneath his dignity. He conducts himself according to the formula 'All or nothing.'" Years have not abstracted anything from the coarse personalities of this Government reply to a political accusation by a man who still occupied the position in the socialist States that Trotsky had occupied: the degradation of political life before the party and the masses had begun. But opinion in the party was in those days too strong for Stalin and his clique, and they were finally compelled to pass a resolution binding them to institute workers' democracy. The resolution was unanimously carried. But the three could not put it into operation, for it was the absence of democracy that gave them their power.

Now that Lenin was away, a democratic regime, and Trotsky's authority and moral and intellectual superiority, would automatically place him at the head of the party. Somehow they had to destroy him. Stalin has no principles of any kind, political or otherwise, but Zinoviev and Kamenev lent themselves to this intrigue not only out of personal enmity, but because they feared all that Trotsky stood for. Trotsky wanted to push on with the industrialisation of the country. Zinoviev, notoriously a coward, feared to upset the equilibrium of Soviet economy. Trotsky wanted to utilise the bourgeois technicians as Lenin had always advocated. Stalin opposed this. It was on a similar question, the utilisation of Tsarist officers, that he had intrigued against Trotsky during the civil war, and had been snubbed and suppressed by Lenin. Trotsky was the centre of the intellectuals of the party, of Marxist learning and analysis with its insistence on the necessity of going forward—the permanent reconstruction of the economic basis of the society. Where Zinoviev and Kamenev from temperament stood for caution, Stalin, as his speeches during the next four years proved, undoubtedly did believe (if he ever gave any serious thought to the matter) that if one maintained the Soviet power socialism would come somehow.[4] For these various reasons the three were united in their desire to destroy Trotsky. What Zinoviev and Kamenev did not see was that behind them in this quarrel the party bureaucracy would inevitably range itself; behind the party bureaucracy was the State bureaucracy, and behind these were the capitalist elements in the Soviet Union. There is an observation by Lenin in one of his last articles which shows that he was always aware of the unstable nature of the class relations in the country and feared a split for the very reason that the classes would seize the divisions to align themselves. But neither Zinoviev nor Kamenev nor anyone else could have foreseen the lengths to which Stalin would go in allying himself with reaction in order to destroy Trotsky and the international revolutions for which he stood, and in which they, with all their faults, believed. For the time being they worked to destroy Trotsky.

The resolution had pinned them down. A few days after they got their opportunity. Flushed with his paper victory, Trotsky had written a letter to his own party local with the intention of elucidating the significance of workers' democracy. Without a shadow of malice or personal references he analysed the dangers which beset the party: "Destroying self-activity, bureaucratism thereby prevents a raising of the general level of the party. And that is its chief fault. To the extent that the most experienced comrades, and those distinguished by service inevitably enter into the apparatus, to that extent the bureaucratism of the apparatus has its heaviest consequences on the intellectual-political growth of the young generation of the party. This explains the fact that the youth—the most reliable barometer of the party—react the most sharply of all against party bureaucratism.

It would be wrong to think, however, that the excess of apparatus-methods in deciding party questions, leaves no trace on the older generation, which incarnates the political experience of the party and its revolutionary traditions. No, the danger is great also on this side. It is needless to speak of the enormous significance—not only on a Russian, but on an international scale—of the older generation of our party; that is generally known and acknowledged. But it would be a crude mistake to estimate that significance as a *self-sufficient fact. Only a continual interaction of the older and younger generation within the frame of party democracy* can preserve the Old Guard as a revolutionary factor. Otherwise the old may ossify, and unnoticed by themselves become the most finished expression of the bureaucratisation of the apparatus.[5]

Still pursuing a theoretical analysis he showed how the leaders of the Second International had degenerated from revolutionary Marxism, into Revisionism, and the responsibility which the seniors bore: "we ourselves, the 'old men,' while naturally playing the role of leaders, should recognise the danger, state it openly, and guard against it by fighting against bureaucratism." On this recurrent question, the interaction between the old and the young, no more valuable advice has ever been given to any political party. Stalin, Kamenev and Zinoviev read the document and did not object to its publication in the party press. Kamenev spoke about it without enthusiasm, certainly without hostility.[6] But the very quality of the letter was a sign-post of their approaching eclipse, and suddenly they decided to use it against Trotsky. They accused him of setting the youth against the Old Guard. Stalin began in Moscow. "Whence this attempt to uncrown the Old Guard and demogogishly tickle the youth, so as to open and widen the little rift between these fundamental troops of our party? To whom is all this useful, if you have in view the interests of the party, its unity, its solidarity, and not an attempt to weaken its unity for the benefit of an opposition?" Zinoviev in Leningrad called it an attack on the "direct disciples of Lenin" and the Leningrad Soviet of which he was President passed a condemnatory motion by 3,000 votes to seven with five abstaining. Bucharin followed in the party press. "However, Bolshevism has never contrasted the party with the apparatus. That would be, from the Bolshevik point of view, absolute ignorance, for there is no party without its apparatus."

The "direct disciples of Lenin," "Bolshevism, that is to say Leninism." That was the cue. They had to break the name Trotsky from its inseparable association with the revered name, Lenin. They therefore posed as Leninists, as the heirs and guardians of the true tradition against Trotsky's perversions. That and that only was the origin of Stalin's Leninism. They had begun by calling Trotsky a left Communist. But now they quickly shifted over and called him a Menshevik. For in order to prove that Trotskyism had always been opposed to Leninism they dug down into past history and raked up the old quarrels between Lenin and Trotsky. Now these quarrels had been on two main points, one the organisation question, on which Trotsky had been wrong. But the second was the Theory of Permanent Revolution, and this embodied the whole theoretical basis of the Soviet Union and the Communist International. But Zinoviev and Kamenev followed Stalin and performed prodigies of casuistry. Incapable of even the most primitive theoretical analysis, Stalin, in his simple-minded way, elaborated upon the ideas they put forward. But the management of the campaign of slander, the scope it assumed, its success, these were the contributions of Stalin. His gifts were useless in a revolution. In a period of calm and an internal struggle for power in the apparatus Trotsky was out-generalled from first to last. What is important is not that Trotsky was beaten, but that he was beaten so quickly.

Lenin died in January, 1924, and then followed a campaign on an unprecedented scale which vilified Trotskyism and Trotsky, and prepared the way for removing his supporters. Paul Scheffer,[7] Max Eastman,[8] Louis Fischer,[9] and Walter Duranty,[10] the last two firm supporters of the Stalinist regime, have testified to the nature of this campaign, its baselessness, its dishonesty. No evidence is more valuable than that of Louis Fischer, wholly devoted to the Stalinist regime. In the New York *Nation* of May 2, 1934, he tells how Stalin rewrote "Soviet history, so that Trotsky's role either disappears or becomes besmirched"; how propaganda excited hate against him, "not only in the party and youth but among the general population which once revered him"; how his supporters had to undergo years of "well-nigh intolerable physical, mental and moral suffering." Lenin's eyes used to blaze at any hint of political power used for personal ends. How is this better than bourgeois parliamentarianism, he would ask. Here was the whole power of the State being used to destroy the finest and ablest servants of the revolution. Political reason for this baseness and disloyalty there was at the beginning none. Few of the cynical bourgeois who relate these facts, however, seem to have understood one of its most important aspects for any socialist who understands the part the masses must play in the building of socialism—the degradation of political life and the political thinking of a country already backward. What Lenin in the face of enormous odds had striven for as the only counter to the dictatorship, the political education of the masses, hoping to bring them more and more into control of production, and political activity and understanding as the country developed, all that Stalin, and he is the individual responsible, no sooner in power, began to destroy on a scale that has no parallel in history. To account for this in 1923 purely by the class relationships in the country is to make a geometrical theorem of the materialist conception of history. The process then begun has continued. In the early days—there are still fools who say it—Trotsky was compared to Danton. He was an individualist unable to work with a party. But during the years the full force of Stalin's dictatorship has been used to prove to the Soviet workers that Trotsky, Zinoviev, Kamenev, Rakovsky, Rykov, Tomsky, Bucharin, all their leaders, have at one time or another been guilty of counter-revolution and have plotted to restore capitalism in the Soviet Union. Stalin alone has been good, faithful and true. To the Webbs and other bourgeois philistines, corrupted to the marrow by bourgeois politics, this is merely worth a footnote whereby they show exactly what they mean by socialism. Whatever the future of the Soviet Union, it will be many, many years before political life recovers from this corruption injected from above. Given the defeat of the world revolution degradation was inevitable. But that it took this particular form, and so early, is due to the evil personality of its chief representative.

"Trotsky has always been in the sphere of political questions a mere revolutionary *dilettante.*" So read a sentence from a pamphlet published by the Leningrad Soviet under Zinoviev. And in addition to personal abuse of the fish-wife variety, every sentence that Trotsky had ever written against Lenin or Lenin against Trotsky was raked out and published in unlimited editions. Lenin in his controversies with Trotsky had stated somewhere that Trotsky underestimated the peasantry. The Soviet Union was suddenly overwhelmed with pamphlets, articles and speeches proving that Trotsky underestimated the peasantry. The three conspirators had in their hands the party organisation, the party funds, the party Press—every means of monopolising publicity. Dzherzhinsky and the secret police, the strong centralised control and tradition of disciple, did the rest. Many party members, old Bolsheviks, were bewildered by the charges. But in the confusion their old habits of loyalty to the party induced them to side with the ruling group against Trotsky, who was unceasingly made to appear as someone striving to break party discipline. Discipline, orthodoxy, centralism. This, said Stalin, was Leninism, and used the tradition to cover his aims. All who supported Trotsky and had any influence were dismissed from their posts, the more distinguished sent as ambassadors to foreign countries, others less in the public eye sent to remote parts, the students were dismissed from universities in thousands, and the G.P.U. was active against these new "class enemies," meaning Trotsky's followers. The intellectuals, who were able to investigate all the trumpery about Trotskyism were driven out of the party. The party conference in May was managed with equal ruthlessness and cunning. Krupskaya had given the Troika the Testament to read at the conference. The Central Committee decided that it should not be read but discussed only with the most important party members. The fetish of party unity, party discipline, ceaselessly hammered by Stalin, Zinoviev and Kamenev, stifled criticism.

Lenin had asked that more workers should be introduced into the party. In January Stalin's secretariat selected 100,000 workers all over the country, in May 100,000 more.[11] All were given votes, all voted against Trotskyism.

Trotsky was ill and remained silent. Soon his friends dared not speak, for it might mean banishment to Siberia. Unemployment was rife, and the rank-and-file who would not see and acknowledge the difference between Stalin's Leninism and Trotskyism stood in fear of losing their jobs.

In October came the climax. Trotsky published his articles and speeches of

1917 with a preface on "The Lessons of October," in which, comparing those who opposed Lenin in October, 1917, with the leaders in October, 1923, in Germany, he laid the blame for the failure at the door of the pusillanimous and incompetent German Central Committee. October, 1917, was above all what Zinoviev, Kamenev and Stalin could not have any discussion upon. The book was unofficially suppressed. But the campaign against Trotskyism reached fantastic heights. A flood of articles and pamphlets against Trotskyism was let loose on the Russian public. Electric lights at night advertised "Replies to Trotsky," what Lenin had said about Trotsky, what Trotsky had said about Lenin. Friendly critics have blamed Trotsky for his continued silence. It was not only illness, a stubborn pride, a respect for the dignity of the Soviet State. Under the influence of his profound studies of history he seems for a time to have accepted with too much fatalism this emergence of bureaucratic corruption in a period of revolutionary ebb.

A persecution so cruel, in the name of the socialist revolution for which they had cheerfully risked life and liberty, broke the spirit of many who would have been unshakeable against the counter-revolution. Suicide among the party members became so common that a special investigation had to be made and a report sent to the Central Committee with recommendations to check it. *(Pravda*, October 9, 1924). Lenin was not yet dead one year. Who that knows his record can believe that had he lived such a state of affairs could possibly have existed at that time? In September, 1924, Trotsky's secretary, expelled from the party, committed suicide.

The split to begin with might appear to be a trifle but it was to have a decisive significance. A political struggle of this kind cannot be isolated from its national and international environment. It took four years to drive Trotsky and those who followed him out of the party. The traditions of Leninism were too strongly rooted. Stalin and his faction by their attacks on Trotksy and Trotskyism were driven further and further from Leninism—the theory and practice of international socialist revolution. Trotsky's special contribution to Marxism, the Permanent Revolution, was their special target. But they could not rely on argument and they destroyed physically the Left wing of the party, strengthening thereby the Right. The defence of bureaucratism against workers' democracy caused the Troika to lean still further on the bureaucracy. The proletariat, exhausted by the herculean efforts between 1917 and 1924, had received a crushing blow with the defeat of the German proletariat. The world revolution and all the hopes of 1917 seemed dead. It was bewildered and confused by the sheer weight of the attacks on Trotsky, the man who, more than all others, it associated with October and the defeat of the European counter-revolution. The party bureaucracy in the country which knew without being told where its interests lay. It knew Lenin's views, that Trotsky held them, and that if Trotsky and the Opposition gained power it would mean a cleansing of the party, a cleansing of the government bureaucracy in the manner Lenin had suggested, and a vigilant watch on all bureaucratism. Stalin steadily fused the party and the bureaucracy until today they are undistinguishable. And supporting the party bureaucracy and the bureaucracy in the Soviet government were the new class of kulaks in the country and the traders in the towns.

Under the New Economic Policy the Soviet economy was recovering, but creating inevitably a new capitalist class. Outside, in Europe, capitalism, fed temporarily by American loans, was stabilising itself on the ruins of the German revolution and was reinforcing the growth of reaction in the Soviet Union. The proletariat outside Russia was moving away from revolution to reformism. From much muddle-headed chatter about the imminent revolution Stalin and Zinoviev were compelled to see that capitalism was strengthening itself. Using revolutionary phraseology, but in reality from then and for the next three years the ally of kulak and nepman, against Trotsky and the internationalists, the Soviet bureaucracy crystallised its development and clarified its aims in a new theory that struck at the very basis of all Marxist thinking, the theory that socialism could be built unaided in a single country. When Zinoviev and Kamenev, under pressure from the proletariat of Leningrad and Moscow, recoiled from this theory and its consequences and started to struggle against Stalin, they were helpless. The same methods and machinery which they helped to build for use against Trotsky and Trotskyism were more than efficient for use against Zinovievism. Kamenev was sent abroad, Zinoviev's followers were weeded out, he was dismissed from his positions and Bucharin set up in his place.

Stalin produced his new theory in the autumn of 1924. In the face of elementary Marxism and the whole history of the party Stalin declared that since 1915 (later he made it 1905) Lenin, in opposition to Trotsky and Trotskyism, had always preached that socialism could be built in a single country. In April of that year (1924) in his own book, *Problems of Leninism*, he had written that the organisation of socialist production in the Soviet Union was impossible. For that the assistance of several of the most advanced countries was needed. In October he published a new edition of the book in which the passage was changed to exactly the opposite.

Marx and Engels, said Stalin, had not known that socialism could be built in a single country because they did not know the law of the unequal development of capitalism—one of the first laws learnt by the student of economics, Marxist or otherwise, during the past hundred years.

Lenin had at times spoken of the building of socialism in the Soviet Union. That, after all, was the ultimate aim, and every time he said socialism he could not have been expected to say "the international revolution." His works were diligently scoured. Yet so precise was Lenin's phrasing that in all the thousands of letters and articles that he wrote the Stalinists could find surprisingly little that was of use to them. An article in 1915 was discovered in which, writing of Western Europe and arguing against Trotsky's theory of permanent revolution, he had postulated the organisation of socialist production in a single country. He was writing not of Russia at all and he was arguing against the idea of each working class waiting to act until all the others were ready. That no hint of national socialism was in his mind is proved not only by his writings before 1915 but by scores and scores of passages in his writings down to the last paragraph of the very last article he ever wrote. The passage was torn from its context. In 1923, in an article on Co-operation discussing the political premises for socialism, he said: "have we not all the means requisite for the establishment of a fully socialised socialist society? Of course we have not yet established a socialist society, but we have all the means requisite for its establishment." That was enough for Stalin.

In April, 1925, the new theory was made party policy. Men held up their hands and voted for this as the policy of Lenin. To do otherwise was Trotskyism and already, in the Russia of 1925, party members could see the immediate consequences of Trotskyism much more vividly than the remote results of Stalin's perversions. They voted.

Zinoviev and Kamenev refused to accept what Zinoviev could in those days call Stalin's "opportunist nonsense." Stalin attacked Zinoviev in his clumsy blundering attempts at polemic. It is impossible to build socialism in a single country? "If so, is it worth while to fight for victory over the Capitalist elements in our own economic life? Is it not a natural sequence of Comrade Zinoviev's views, to contend that such a victory is impossible? *Surrender to the Capitalist elements of our economic life*—such is the logical outcome of Comrade Zinoviev's arguments."[12] (original emphases). He indulged in a logical retrospect. "The only puzzle is, why we seized power in October (November), 1917, unless we intended to establish socialism! *We ought not to have seized power in October, 1917*—such is the conclusion to which Comrade Zinoviev's train of argument leads us."[13] (original emphases.) But after this elephantine casuistry he fell back on his strength: "I declare, further, that, as regards the fundamental problem of the victory of socialism, Comrade Zinoviev has taken a line which is opposed to the plain decisions of the Party, as expressed in the resolution. 'Concerning the Tasks of the Communist International and the Communist Party of Russia in conjunction with the Enlarged Executive Committee (the Plenum) of the Communist International'—a resolution adopted at the Fourteenth Party Conference."[14] He used the party machine to create a majority for anything, however absurd, however false, and on that basis he expelled, imprisoned, banished and shot.

To such docility had he bludgeoned the party by April, 1925, that Trotksy and Zinoviev and Kamenev found little support in their opposition. In little more than six months international socialism, the whole basis of Leninism, had been dragged out of the ideological armory by Comrade Stalin, Comrade Lenin's best friend and helper. We must guard against thinking that Stalin himself had made any great change. Neither before 1917 nor after has Leninism meant anything to him. When a young comrade wrote personally to him saying that he had looked through Lenin's works and failed to find any reference to the victory of socialism in a single country, Stalin, in a public report to the party officials in Moscow, replied: "He'll find them some day!"[15] To many people all this argument about socialism in a single country is only tedious nonsense. There could be no greater mistake. It signified the defeat of Trotsky, that is to say of Lenin's international socialism; and the crude violence of the falsification is evidence of the profound changes of which this theory was the outcome and still more the forerunner. The thing to be noted is the extraordinary mastery and speed with which Stalin manoeuvred the party to the new position. With his infallible political insight Lenin, at the beginning of 1923, had pointed his finger at the danger spot. Remove Stalin. As Souvarine *(Stalin)* has so justly pointed out there was a possibility then that the party, having recovered from the civil war and the famine, could, under Leninist leadership, have regenerated itself and moved forward on the socialist road, adapting itself flexibly to the economic circumstances. Between the rising strength of the bureaucracy and the proletarian masses, the party was balancing during 1923. It was the illness and death of Lenin on the one hand, and on the other, the superiority of Stalin to Trotsky in a struggle of this kind, that so quickly and decisively turned the scale in favour of the bureaucracy.

It is convenient here to point out the enormous tragedy for the whole movement of the illness and premature death of Lenin. The growth of the bureaucracy was inevitable. There were bitter struggles ahead. But with Lenin alive the incredible degradation of the Bolshevik party between April, 1923, and October, 1924, is unthinkable. To gain control and introduce his theories, Stalin had to destroy the party. There is a tendency among Trotskyists to exaggerate the economic and social influences at work in the Trotsky-Stalin struggle in 1923. By October, 1923, Trotsky was beaten. Even under Lenin so much power had been concentrated in the upper circles of the party that Stalin could win by his superior gifts of manoeuvre and intrigue. He could never have defeated Lenin in that way. Quite early in 1923 Lenin knew the dangerous range of Stalin's influence, but he could have broken him and intended to do so. And Stalin would have disappeared alone. Zinoviev and Kamenev were never persons to go down fighting for anybody or anything, least of all a Stalin attacked by a Lenin.

Lenin and Trotsky were solid in this matter, and what they said went, not from tyranny but from intellectual power and strength of character. Like attracts like, and they had the best men in the party with them. Whatever the power of the party bureaucracy in 1923, and even of the bureaucracy in the country, Lenin and Trotsky were the ones whom the Red Army, and the masses of Russia, workers and peasants alike, loved and trusted with a blind faith. Such jealously of Trotsky as existed in the old clique, did not among the rank-and-file of the party. And even the old clique acknowledged the superiority not only of Lenin but of Trotsky. In January, 1924, Zinoviev, speaking at the special conference which pretended to investigate the causes of the German failure, paid an involuntary tribute to the very Trotsky whom his Soviet was calling a revolutionary dilettante. The campaign against Trotskyism, of which Zinoviev was one of the chief authors, had been raging for three months. "On the question of the tempo we erred. There is some consolation in that Lenin and Trotsky sometimes erred on this point."[16]

The more one reads Lenin's last writings the more one sees how clearly he saw the danger. An unanswered question is, why Trotsky never used the army, which was devoted to him. He did not realise early enough the deep menace of Stalin. He thought first of the unity of the party, he did not want to appear anxious to step into Lenin's shoes. Instead of mobilising his considerable support to do what Lenin had said, and remove Stalin, Trotsky tried to collaborate with Stalin. To understand a problem is to be half-way on the road to solution. Lenin saw it to the end and it is our belief that he would have gone to the masses, using the people, in the army and in the Soviets, against the bureaucracy. Circumstances were driving him to repair another error—too great a concentration of power in the summits of the party. Whenever he was in difficulties he looked below, and his head was already turned that way. He had dominated his party for twenty years. In April, 1923, despite Stalin's intrigues, he was still unquestioned master of it with even Stalin mortally afraid of him, of even an article by him. Without the world revolution the bureaucracy was bound to grow. But to think that with Lenin alive and well, with Trotsky head of the Red Army, and the thousands of old Bolsheviks in the party who followed Lenin and Trotsky, but in reality Lenin, to think that Stalin, or any other bureaucrat for that matter, could have slipped into the power without years of struggle, without even the final resort to force, is to show a complete misconception of what Lenin started out to do and did, when he wrote that with an organisation Russia could be overturned.

Lenin was not only Lenin. He was Lenin plus the Bolshevik party, still intact despite the inroads made upon it, with enormous reserves of strength in the masses of the people. To explain all, as too many do, by economic and social forces, is grossly to simplify a complex problem. Let us not forget that those who were the antithesis of Lenin from the first found their most potent weapon in using his name. They at least had no illusions about what Lenin, his party and his tradition, meant to the majority of the Russian people. The very strength of his leadership was its weakness, for when he went the party, built around him, almost instinctively clung to the centre he had dominated, but which, without him, was already heading for reaction.[17]

If anything will emerge from this book, it is not only the strength of principles but the power of leadership. The first helps the second. The party of international socialism rose with Lenin and died with him. This is not to deny Marxism. Lenin would have fought the bureaucracy, would have conquered it with the help of the world revolution, would certainly have kept it in check for years. But nobody else could. And yet Marxism, while giving full value to the role of remarkable individuals in history—and Stalin, in his own corrupt way is one of the most remarkable men in modern history—yet offers the only conclusive logical explanation of the events we have just outlined. For the working class movements in Western Europe had begun on an international revolutionary basis in the First International, had each raised, through its own weakness against capitalism, a bureaucracy. These bureaucracies, with criminal short-sightedness, had gradually succumbed to surrounding circumstances, become penetrated with bourgeois ideas, crushed the revolutionary elements, and then decided each to build socialism peacefully in its own country, had revised its theories to suit, and by the logic of events had deserted internationalism at the great crisis of 1914. In the same way the bureaucracy in Russia having gained a victory over the powerful international revolutionary tradition and sections in the Workers' State, succumbed to its weakness against the temporary stabilisation of capital which began in 1924, deserted internationalism for national socialism, and using its influence on the world working class movement, is preparing it for a still more colossal betrayal than that of 1914. That is the way that history works. So for historical materialism.

But the national socialists might have won in 1917. If Lenin had not reached Petrograd in April, 1917, international socialism would probably have lost, despite the work of the previous thirty years. Lenin was out of it in 1923, and international socialism had lost this time almost before the battle had begun. We deny emphatically that so complete a defeat at such a time was "inevitable," and shall have no difficulty in pointing out the immediately ruinous influence which Stalin exercised on the Communist International.

1937

PART III

AMERICA AND AFTER 1938-1956

8

Letters to Constance Webb

AUGUST 26, 1943

At last I am able to write to you. You got my night-letter I hope. I left New York the next day and am now out of town, living alone by the sea, absolutely alone. For the most part I sit here, read a little and just keep still. I have not written because I could not write—just that literally. It is a long story. I'll tell it to you.[1]

Two years ago, three in fact, April 1940, I left Los Angeles. I was on the verge of my first serious illness. For the last half of 1940 I was in a bad way. I went to hospital for an operation, but two days before there was a division of opinion among the doctors and I finally decided not to go ahead. An operation might or might not cure the ulcer and the risk was too great. I came out in December very much shaken. I started writing and had a bad year, working but ill half the time, though keeping it to myself. In addition to the stomach trouble I had nervousness of the fingers—writing with great difficulty. It was very trying because I have never had so much to say as during the last few years. However, I made good use of the illness. I made a thorough study of Capital—at last, and thought of you much during it.

Late in 1941 I left New York and went into the wilderness for ten months—a tremendous experience involving thousands upon thousands of workers, black and white, and much traveling over hundreds of square miles. The whole thing passed off splendidly; but, when I came back, I was seriously ill—that was August 1942. I was in bed and out until December 1942 when I fell ill in the street, was lifted home and operated upon that very night. My ulcer had perforated. The operation was completely successful. I made a marvelous recovery and, after a few weeks of recuperation, I started working again. I dictate most of my work now. Writing is sometimes very difficult. These few days were pretty bad. But I am better now than I have been for years.

The foregoing might make you think that the last three years have been miserable for me. Far from it. I am very strong really, but have taken advantage of it and now I am having trouble to readjust myself. It is clear that I need someone to take care of me but I am highly individualistic in my habits and personal outlook and, unless I feel that I can share my life completely with someone, I am unable to contemplate even the idea of a temporary association. I will marry a wife, neither a nurse nor a cook.

But while this illness and the unsatisfactory circumstances of my personal life have worn me down somewhat, on the other hand these last three years have been very wonderful for me. I have, at last, got hold of Marxism, economic *(Capital)* and philosophical (Hegelian dialectic). I don't know all I want to know, but I have covered the ground. Not only in theory but as a result of it, in my daily work, I can really see that I am in command of things. These last three years have been the most exciting intellectually of my life and, if I could have studied only because I was ill so much, I don't regret it. I welcome it. I have a few close collaborators; they are young, full of enthusiasm and are doing magnificent work. At the same time, bourgeois society goes so rapidly to pieces in Europe and Asia that we feel we are on the verge of great events. I feel my enforced isolation and semi-retirement. But that I cannot overcome. So I submit philosophically. There have been great battles and some of it has been wearing, but that is politics.

SEPTEMBER 1, 1943

I got your letter at 12. I came home and started to write. Then I decided to stop and swim. The house is on the water when the tide is in. I got into trunks and sat for an hour dangling my feet in the water—thinking, thinking of the European revolution, of the Negro question, and of one Constance, actress. I was looking at my feet in the water and then out across the Sound, and my thoughts just went their own way. I have just dipped and am back again.

You write, "I read every book I could find on acting" and, again, "I was a monomaniac about acting". Sister, that is life and living and finding yourself. Stick to it and squeeze it dry. The feelings that surge and must be expressed are the pulsations of a life within you more powerful than in the average person. All people have it. Capitalism stifles it. But with some it is so powerful that it breaks through. You achieve or you don't achieve. But the thing that matters is to live your life, to express yourself as long as it is not ignoble or mean or actuated by cheap motives such as getting a lot of money. You seem uncertain about understanding what you are doing and why. Some pseudo-Marxist has been getting at you, telling you that what you should do is join a party and work in a factory? Just tell them to go to hell, that's all. I worked at literature for years and made my own way to where I am. Nobody taught me; and, thank Heaven, I find that I am still making my own way while so many others are floundering around.

During the last years, illness and other difficulties have caused me to spend a certain amount of time at the pictures. I rather despised them—Hollywood, I mean. I don't any more. The rubbish I look at would astonish you. I can sit through almost anything. When it is very bad I see why it is bad. I have seen *Now Voyager* six times and will see it, if necessary, six times more. The reason? I work at home. At times I must stop. The only thing that keeps me quiet is the movies. So at all hours of the day or night I go where there is a picture, often the nearest. That is why I see some over and over again. I am learning plenty, I can assure you. If you were near I'd talk to you about it, day after day; and, being a woman and quick, you'd teach me much that I am missing. But meanwhile here goes.

The movies, even the most absurd Hollywood movies, are an expression of life, and being made for people who pay their money, they express what the people need—that is, what the people miss in their own lives. That explains a great deal I think. Why the popularity of the Western? Because young people who sit cramped in buses and tied to assembly lines terribly wish they could be elsewhere. They may not be conscious of it; yet, when they see it they respond. That is the fundamental principle. Like all art, but more than most, the movies are not merely a reflection, but an extension of the actual—an extension along the lines which people feel are lacking and possible in the actual. That, my dear, is the complete secret of Hegelian dialectic. The two, the actual and the potential, are always inseparably linked; one is always giving way to the other. At a certain stage a crisis takes place and a complete change is the result. We can take that up another time.

Now, as I watch the movies and the stars and see who is popular and who not, certain things begin to emerge. The great stars are all characteristic people, selected by the masses who pay their dimes, because they represent something that the people want. Charles Boyer and his predecessor Rudolf Valentino. American women in particular are fascinated by Boyer, a typical representative of the Latin-Gallic civilisation. He is not merely a great lover. The people do not express themselves clearly. He is a Latin gentleman, smooth, cultured, suave, with an air about him that is the result of a thousand years of European civilisation. I would love to watch him with you in the same picture three or four times and work it out thoroughly. Jean Gabin in French pictures is a finer actor than Boyer. He is a failure here, I think, for one reason—he is a tough guy; and Americans have their own Clark Gable and Humphrey Bogart. That is the real American type, as different from Boyer as men could be. But this type also the American people want and they get it. At least when they see it, they seize it. Note Ronald Coleman, before Boyer. He is English—not as finished as Boyer but reserved, no fanny-slapping, "hello baby," type; slightly insipid if you ask me, but full of appeal to people who would love sometimes to be treated with courtesy and restraint and a certain grace.

The women are equally characteristic. For the exotic charmer, they rush to Greta Garbo and Marlene Dietrich. The three women who today are really at the head of their profession—Bette Davis, Ingrid Bergman, and Greer Garson—are a wonderful study in types. Ingrid Bergman is a Scandinavian, a typical representative of one of the very finest examples of European bourgeois civilisation. The Scandinavian countries and Denmark acting as food producers or agents for the great imperialist powers had all the advantages and none of the responsibilities (great armies, navies, colonial oppression, excessive political corruption, etc.) of imperialism. Hence they produced some of the finest people in bankrupt Europe. Note how closely Greer Garson approximates to Ronald Coleman, though she is, in my opinion, a better craftsman than he. But Bette surpasses them both in my opinion. This American woman has something that neither of these representatives of the older civilisation have—a tremendous vitality. She is not so fine a person as Ingrid Bergman is, you can feel it, and

Greta Garbo achieves some extraordinary effects with the greatest economy of means; but Bette Davis is simply terrific at her best. She sweeps on like a battleship.

Lana Turner is no fool, but she is the eternal bed-companion. There is always one on the screen. Men want such. But Ginger Rogers is more interesting. She has a wonderful figure, though I have noticed how lousy she looks in evening dress. Style she has none; but she is plain, honest-to-goodness, American lower middle-class—one of the people, and the American people love her for it. I don't mind the silly pictures she plays in; I see what she represents. Jean Arthur is another, a highly skilled young woman who aims at portraying a social type—I think more consciously than do most of the others.

Now, my dear Constance, I may have seemed to have wandered far from you. I don't think so and I am sure you don't. You seemed to have been traveling along the same road; you inside, I outside, a fellow traveler so to speak. It appears to me that success depends on two things: 1. what you have in you; 2. what the public wants. The second seems beyond your control. It isn't. The more powerfully you develop yourself, the more you strive to bring out all that is in you, the more genuinely yourself you are; for being yourself in any arts is a hell of a job (I know that my dear C., I have seen and felt the process at work). The more you express your own genuine personality, the easier it is for people to recognise that you express something which is inside of them. Often they don't know it. The artist, writer, actor, painter expresses something by strenuous effort. And people say "Yes, that's wonderful." They mean "I have felt that all along."

This house, the platform, wind, air, sun and the sea, and the sound in front and to right and left. My table is filled with a mass of papers and cuttings about the war. The surroundings are commonplace—not even a radio or a phonograph, and yet I sit here and you are 3000 miles away and it is a wonderful day. You know, periodically, I stop and think. How wonderful life can be! Not could be, in the future. But now. By the way. Last night I was reading *Romeo and Juliet*. Balcony scene. Did you do Shakespeare? How wonderful life can be, even in the midst of a crashing civilisation. I am sitting and watching the water and feel a strange inability to say what I want to say. Let me try again. I am political. I live at present in the daily expectation of the beginning of an upheaval in Europe, marking the beginning of the socialist revolution. I think of that many hours every day. It keeps me alive. It governs my every activity. I feel life is worth living on account of that. I want to give every drop I have in me to help the cause on. And yet if someone were to say wish two wishes, I would say, 1. the socialist revolution and, 2. to sit on the platform with Constance and watch the evening sun go down. The connection may seem to some monstrous. It isn't. Somehow the intensity of a personal experience, even at this distance, the sense of beauty and companionship, which are so very rare, such things when exercised only in imagination and over a continent's distance, seem to give a personal meaning and significance to the great struggles opening up in Europe. If you don't understand me, I'll try again another time. I don't often try to express myself this way. I am, as all the world knows, very reserved. Maybe that is why you mean so much to me. People are always seeking self-expression and where they can find it they stay. It is hard to find.

1943 (NO DATE)

The truth is far more powerful than these half and half fakers can work out.

I (forgive the ego) fought battles with intellectuals on *Song to Remember*. I had one standard—great art had been brought to the proletariat. I judge every picture, for pictures are for the people, by that first. Most pictures are vulgar. This one, even if vulgar (and there is a case for this one) was vulgar + Chopin. Imagine people sneering at the Iturbi vulgarisations—as if that mattered, and note the cheap, weak defence.

Iturbi will have a place in the history of culture. He went to Hollywood. The others didn't.

The picture exceeded in results my greatest hopes. Not only in Hollywood but everywhere the masses loved it. I'll talk to you about the picture itself one day. But the social facts are: the great music companies sold so much that they are ready to subsidise pictures around the great composers. On the way are Beethoven, Rachmaninov, Rimsky-Korsakov. Music, great music, will become a possession of the people. *It is revolutionary*. Why? Because the more the technical discoveries of capitalism bring culture to the masses, the more they resent the degradation and humiliation of their role in *production*—the grinding slavery of the machine.

Again. Today an intelligent worker sees the same films, reads the same best-sellers, hears the same radio speeches, same newspapers, etc., as the bourgeoisie. An intelligent working class girl can dress and look like anybody else, more or less. The gap between the classes is becoming increasingly narrow. If even the great millions are down below, the fact that the more favoured representatives of their class can reach out to these things, makes the desire for them not utopian but something that can be got by a 30% increase in wages. Thus the musical "renaissance" is part of the development of the proletariat.

Finally the logical method is important. Note how it happened. A Hollywood director notes the great success of the Tchaikovsky Concerto in B minor in *The Great Lie*. He, *to make money*, works on a new kind of musical. He produces this film. Why? *Because the masses are craving for something new*.

Now if the masses didn't like it, the idea would have died. *They gobbled it up*. This proved that, among all the novelties being presented to them, *they wanted this*. Result—they get more and more. In two years they will know about *music*. Lenin would have loved this. He said once, "We must get millions of reproductions of the great pictures and distribute them so that the proletariat will get culture—know what the bourgeoisie knows." Thus we see a great dialectical law—the capitalist seeking profit, or Marlene Dietrich seeking publicity with pants, opens up an avenue through which the masses recognise something and at once appropriate it—there are all sorts of distortions but yet [it is] a step forward. Thus the chance, the appearance, the accident, is the capitalist seeking profit. The social necessity, the social movement, is the mass grabbing at culture as today it grabs at everything it can.

So history moves. Where class relations are where they are today, things of accidental importance can have great repercussions. It looks like chance but it is social necessity, and every great necessity expresses itself by chance. We'll see this law often—it is a great discovery of Hegel and the life-blood of Marxism.

1944 (NO DATE)

I agree. Her weakness you analyse perfectly. (Muriel Rukeyser). What she and her type represent, that too you see. Modern man runs away from the deeper emotions. Society and science are so developed that he can no longer hide from himself what is and what ought to be. So his art becomes increasingly more abstract and his emotions undergo a similar transformation. All this is very sound but needs history, a knowledge of literature and of philosophy, to develop as it should be developed. But even with all this, no one is really any good without creative insight. (That is a bad phrase for insight is a creative act.) That you have. The world is simply waiting for work of that kind.

But there is something more important for you. *Why does M.R. write that way?* She learnt from the creators of modern verse. But she is "proletarian," she is at least "progressive." She wants to be read by thousands, hundreds of thousands. Yet she writes as she does. Simplifying her images wouldn't do it. If the images were "right" they wouldn't have to be simplified. Every poet, or most, until they are mature, has to work like hell to perfect his style. But that effort for perfection is needed even with straightforward verse as Houseman. No, the images, the form, the finished work (it must be finished in more senses than one) are the final expression of the mind. The mind is sensitive and strong. It absorbs a certain type of impression and rejects others. These are transmuted into a complete personality. Soon the personality begins to select images and impressions. That it is begins to impose its own stamp on what it meets. The outside world still shapes the personality however—until growth stops. But the process is a dual one. Now who is Rukeyser? What were her original gifts? What life does she live? Who are her friends? What are her aims in life? What dominates her?

I don't know. But I can sum it up—my guess—in a phrase. She is probably *for* the working class but not *of* it. There are two people who are very important in this connection. Engels was a Manchester business man. He dressed well, was at home in any drawing-room, rode to hounds (he said he was preparing for the revolution—the cavalry) and led a bourgeois life. But that was on the surface only. Every thought, every line he wrote was permeated with the spirit of the working-class. *His mind lived in that world.* He was a great scholar. He made no concessions to the uneducated in his serious work. But somehow in the most abstruse of his reasonings you are conscious of the fact that the role of his class dominates him. Now I suggest M.R. does not think that way. W.H. Auden and that bunch. They, none of them think that way. So they can simplify their images as much as they please—they cannot get very far towards being popular in the best sense of that word. Another is Gorky. He was a man of letters, revolutionary, but living the life of a man of letters. But he came from the people and remained one of them. In his case all his early life, the formative years, had been spent with them. In Engels's case you have a mind that in its youth grasped intellectually the importance of the workers so powerfully, and spent so much of his life developing the ideas, that his bourgeois life never touched him.

To be "popular," to do what you want your poetry to do, you cannot "simplify," and if organically you do not think in terms of the people, then your popularisation will become either sentimentality or blood and thunder shrieking of the r-r-r-revolution. This is not "prophecy." It is a logical argument. Now in your work *since you came*, there is little of this in it before, shows that you have a powerful impulse in the right direction—not right, because I think that is right, but because if the poetic or "personality" impulse is not that way—then the work will be infallibly like M.R. or that type. No. The poet today who will be popular must have the highest standards, must *not* write down, must work out his images and ideas and stick by them, however strange and new they are. But if he is organically of the people, then the work will be popular in the best sense and, if not read immediately in thousands, must ultimately get the ear of the people. Poetry for the workingman. Yes! But the poet must be so much a part of his time, and that today means particularly in the U.S.A., the hopes, ideas, aspirations, weaknesses of the great democracy, the great mass, that altho' he writes of love's young dream or dialectical materialism, the mass of the people will in time feel it to be their own. That is why I have tried to tell you over and over again.

You have all the signs, all, of the truly creative personality, you are in the best environment of the age, that orientation to the working class, not as something to save you, but as something you feel part of (without that we have the T.S. Eliots, then the Audens—*who have done their work*). All that you have. But, the individual today is so subject to the life of society that your problem is the development of yourself. You write a sentence that makes me feel to squeeze you: "Ordinary man must feel the impact with no effort on his part and be stirred into the realization that he is MAN (with capitals because of the greatness)." That is the whole secret of present society. It took me years to learn. The productive capacity is solved. The problem is not a higher standard of living or no employment. The problem, and dear lady, this will rejoice your heart, the strictly scientific, economic problem, the solution of the capitalist crisis, lies in precisely the recognition of man as MAN. That is Marxism, that is Marx's philosophic theory, that is his economic theory, that is his political theory. The act out of the revolution makes him man. In these days when your mind is opening you will have to feed it, and strengthen it and exercise it continuously in that direction. The difficulties in your way I have told you about. You will have to fight it out. I'll help. But the fight is yours.

1944/45 (NO DATE)

Glory be! Where did you spend Sunday? I discovered by my well-organised system that you were out of town. So was I. I spent it at Long Island. You remember the house on the L.I. Sound from which I wrote you my first letter last August. Well! I came out this weekend, exhausted from an article I had written during the last few days.[2]

The house is on the water and I lay in bed looking at the stars and listening to the water. It was wonderful. I remembered the weeks I spent here, when I first re-made communication with you. It was quite an anniversary. Everything so still—a relief after the weeks of abusing Laski.

Today some English people turn up. They are living here. I spent a lot of time with them last summer. The wife knows Laski very well and we abused him heartily. We talked about England and the old Europe that is gone.

I know Normandy well enough. I spent a holiday there in the fall of '38. A country hotel—I was translating Souvarine. I knew a girl in Rouen who came over every morning at 9, helped me in the translation. We had lunch and dinner and walked in the woods. I took her to the bus at 9, and went back and read Maupassant until I fell asleep. Now that countryside is being torn to pieces. The trees will never grow again, not for decades. And the girl—I don't know if she is alive. I have her picture. She was half-Norwegian, half-French. I think she went to Norway. If she did, then she has, I am almost certain, been killed in the underground movement. I know the type—very quiet, with a slow smile, but as determined as hell. She wouldn't give way to Nazis. I remember it all well because that very October I sailed for New York.

Later tonight I was talking with Lyman who has traveled all over Western Europe. I told him of how I loved Paris—of having dinner with a friend in a restaurant on the left-bank, from which we could see Notre Dame—the wonderful food, the quiet, the overshadowing cathedral. I asked him if I was mistaken, but I had an impression that nowhere did I ever feel the same atmosphere in America. He is American through and through, but he said no—it didn't exist here, and he told me of Florence, where Clarke's men will soon be. What will happen to Europe I don't know. I know what I hope, but *that* Europe is gone. Even if capitalism should last for some time, it can never be the same again. There are things I regret, things I would have loved to show you one day. I hope to God they do not destroy Paris—Bastille Square, the Tuileries, the Louvre, the Luxembourg, Champs Elysées, the Arc de Triomphe, Montmartre, Place Blanche, Place de l'Opera. The sense of history in every inch, the wonderful food, the social grace of the French people, their pride in their famous capital, the book shops (they say more book shops in Paris than in the whole of England), the open book shops on the Seine—a great capital throbbing above and when you look over the bridges on the Seine down below white sand and people—fishing! To say nothing of Versailles, which is the most wonderful place in the whole world I think.

But though old France is going, the France that meant so much to European civilisation will not perish. It is being reborn in the spirit of the great masses of the French people. They resisted and they led the peasants and the middle classes. The other day a member of the Underground said at the Assembly in Algiers that France had never had a free uncensored press until the underground press. That sentence will live in history—it lights up the whole fraud of class relations. Today the French masses are not dominated by the French bourgeoisie—and they reject the Germans. Thus, with their minds clear and able to think their own thoughts, they have recreated the nation underground so to speak. The press is brilliantly written—such wit, such style, such fire, and the merciless satire of the French. No advertisements, no libel action, no big overhead, anybody who has a typewriter and is prepared to risk his neck can write and publish, and everybody reads. There are literary journals, journals on the arts, poetry, music, political differentiation, all sincere, powerful, vivid, and free as never before despite the soldiers of Hitler and the police of Laval. How Roosevelt hates them! He is terribly afraid of the people who are maintaining the best traditions of the nation, but in a revolutionary manner, potentially dangerous to all.

Voilà. Enough. The night is mysterious, as it always is, though in town we lose the sense of it. To sit on the little portico (a large deck across the front of the house, overlooking the water) and look out across the water, mixing hosannas to Nature divine with anathemas to the mosquitoes. There are not too many though, and we'll make still another contact with another aspect of life. Those in favour say Aye. Nello (loudly and firmly) Aye. And you?

P.S. Lyman left early this morning and Freddie and I are still here. It is raining—such rain as you never *see* in town. It beat down upon the water and churned it up and the wind and rain roared together at the little house and the big dark clouds closed over as if to say: Go ahead. Beat them up. Blot them out. I'll prevent anybody from seeing. For the few minutes I had a very strong sense of what primitive man must have felt in the face of Nature. For we can never recapture that sense of being entirely at the mercy of natural forces. For a moment we can get a flash-back. That's all. But the mechanised world is too much with us. Now it's all over, for a time at any rate, and I can see at the other end of the Sound the *aeroplane* hangar of the Vanderbilts. I shall go into the village and use the *telephone*, I'll take the *train* in; and by *bus* or *subway* home, where I'll turn on the *electric light* and the *radio*. Nature in its original form cannot dominate man, but what W.B. Yeats calls "mechanised nature," i.e. capital, the means of production, that dominates man entirely now, and he will conquer it as he conquered primitive Nature or this far more dangerous enemy will destroy him. Now somehow or other the poet must feel this menace and translate it into terms which his fellow creatures in this age will understand. People are waiting eagerly for a voice or voices. By poetry I mean nothing narrow. It was said of Rachel, the great French actress, that when she sang the Marseillaise you could see the gaunt, hungry, marching masses of Paris and Marsailles. Somehow we have to get it into our bones today some feeling, some sense of the great forces at work in modern society and then express them through our personality such as it is. This modern world; our world. As for a moment I caught a glimpse into the thought processes of primitive man, and even the Greeks, it made me see only the more clearly what our world is *not*. For Heaven's sake, do not misunderstand me. Shelley, the passionate idealist and lover of political liberty, wrote:

> I am the daughter of
> earth and water
> and the nursling of the
> sky
> I pass through the pores
> of the ocean and
> shores
> I change but I
> cannot die.

He was a master of Greek, Latin, German, French, Spanish and Italian. He hesitated whether to become a poet or a metaphysician. So that out of his intense awareness of his own time and his technical mastery and knowledge of his art came the power of his work, and its strangeness. I wrote for Heaven's sake, do not . . . Sorry. It was rude. But, you know, one lives in a world of controversy, of statement and counter-statement and, alas, deliberate mis-statement. So unless one is very careful or if one is in the least tired, the routine of the particular mind asserts itself and Juliet or Cleopatra becomes the recipient not of emotional responses and spontaneous communications of mind to mind and heart to heart but of arguments. "For Heaven's sake do not misunderstand me!" Too bad. But so we are, what with the world we live in and the things and persons it makes of us. Now, you, fair lady, by some trick of fate, humanise this intellectual barbarian that is me, not with the restraint and reserve that I formally exercise towards people in general, but for other reasons, quite, quite, other reasons.

Now I am going to do my work. In reality I always write about politics, or nearly always. The ordinary arguments about this and that group are so sterile. Neither understands what it is talking about. A political attitude today is a philosophy of life. Little by little, and then with sudden flashes of insight that complete in a minute the work of a year, one masters the fundamental movements of our age, sees it in relation to past and future and becomes intellectually and emotionally a part of it. So that when a man comes along and talks about a progressive capitalism, or another babbles about a new faith, or still a third talks about suppression of rights as if it were something you could turn on or off at will, then the reaction should be deep, immediate and not only social but personal. Otherwise all the good will and energy in the world means only mischief and corruption. Hence Laski talks the utmost nonsense about T.S. Eliot and James Joyce. So, however far I may seem to leave politics, I am really on that subject, i.e., an understanding of society. Once and for all, goodbye.

1944 (NO DATE)

What is a poet? I'll explain. When I lived in the West Indies I lodged once with a woman, a Mrs. Roach. She was not educated. She spoke English with the French *patois* accent of the peasant people. She was a gentlewoman, but language was not her strong point. She had a brother, a drinking, shuffling, guitar-playing idler, Francis. Francis would not work and what was worse got himself one day into trouble with the police for keeping a brothel or helping to keep one. Mr Roach was the City Cashier, and this would have meant a terrific scandal. And Mrs. Roach, a woman with a high sense of social propriety and a very moral woman in addition, was outraged. Passing through the yard I heard and saw her talking to Francis.

She had a shawl around her shoulders and she stood straight like a tragic actress. She said, "Our parents brought us up together, Francis, spent time and money on us. But from youth you went your gambling, guitar-playing way. Wine and women, that has been your life. You have disgraced yourself and disgraced us enough; and now you may have to go to jail for keeping a brothel. Look at the white hairs on your head, Francis. Are you never going to change? Thank God, our dear parents don't live to see you as you are," etc., etc.

She had never spoken like that before. I never heard her speak that way again.

But for the moment she had uninterrupted fluency, a wonderful rhythm, dramatic pauses, etc. I, a very literary person in those days, listened amazed. What caused it? Intense emotion, it was bursting in her, and a subject she knew well, had long meditated upon. At various times she had said this and thought that about Francis; other people had discussed it with her. Then under a powerful stimulus, this last disgrace, she became for the moment a poet. She was on a very high level of emotion and to batter Francis into some sort of discipline she needed a very high level of expression. She found it. Perhaps for once in her life—perhaps two or three times. Then she slipped back to her old level.

The poet, my dear, is so constructed that this height which ordinary people reach only on rare occasions, is the general level of his or her consciousness. That is the quality of the personality. Mrs. Roach had to speak to Francis. If she didn't she would burst. You know the expression. Same with the poet. He has to speak. But inasmuch as we are social creatures, his need of expression takes certain forms which others have used—thus he or she writes verse, free or rhymed, wants it published in a magazine or journal of poetry—all the things which poets do. But all that is merely form. Two thousand years ago he would have played a harp and sung songs. The thing that matters is the urgent need to express the personality. There is nothing wrong, in the slightest, with that. You are a piece of earth, matter, with a highly-charged consciousness. By means of such, when the consciousness is of a superb character, e.g. Marx, Hegel, Shakespeare, Tolstoy, Michelangelo, society as a whole is moved forward. Science, art, literature, philosophy—these are part of the means of production. Yes, exactly that. People see their world and understand it and themselves better and humanity moves forward. The personality has greater or lesser gifts—nerves, will, desires, strong heart, etc. But the society around shapes the person. A great poet in the eighteenth century can do no better than Pope. The age is the "Age of Reason". Shakespeare would have been a Pope. We express ourselves best when we express some powerful social current. One day I'll tell you how closely Shakespeare was related to his time, to the rising bourgeoisie, how much his own work owes to it. He lived among them—he merely expressed the tumultuous thoughts they were thinking. He was superbly gifted. But his age was bursting with new ideas, new desires, new sensations. It educated him in general. But he educated it in particular. By merely living among his people he learnt what they had to say. His high tension, his need for expressing it, dramatised it so that they could see and hear and feel. From highest to lowest that is the relationship between the artist and his age. But of recent years this relationship has become clarified to an unusual degree. . . .

We now approach the question of what you should specifically study and how. It isn't easy because strictly speaking you can really study only what appeals to you, either in the sense that it is immediately attractive or, although it is drudgery, you feel deep down inside that there is something here which you must study. That is and remains true. At the same time, however, you are as we have agreed 1) American, 2) you are not an academician as Shelley, T.S.Eliot, or Auden, 3) you have instinctively a certain orientation towards the workers at a time when they are filling the social and political stage and affecting every kind of art or thought. This dictates a certain trend in reading and study, i.e., in thinking.

Fortunately the Whitman essay said half of what I had to say. You should read it repeatedly.

The sonnets, rhymed verse, concentration on the beloved as inspiration, etc., mark a poetic expression of a certain stage in human society. It is connected with forms of language, with a continuing literary tradition, etc. But the dividing lines are clear. The sixteenth century in Britain saw the maturing of the magnificent blank verse form—the Shakespearean. I believe that this form, so sharply opposed to the stanzas of Chaucer, marked the greater freedom of expression which was required by a new and more expanded society. Shakespeare and the Elizabethans needed a new verse form to express a new world. After that outburst, verse slowly swung *back* to the artificial couplets of Pope. Listen

> Know well thyself, presume
> not God to scan.
> The proper study of
> mankind is man.

and again

> Some men to business, some to
> pleasure take.
> But every woman is at heart
> a rake.

The verse is the verse of an ordered society. They have left behind them the Shakespearean blank verse line. But immediately after the French Revolution, Keats, Shelley, Wordsworth and Coleridge broke away from the type of verse Pope and the eighteenth century specialised in—the change had been coming a long time—and once more English verse became a medium of great freedom.

I am sticking here to England, and I am stating *briefly* general ideas which would have to be formulated with many qualifications in a formal thesis. *But of their general validity I have no doubt at all.* Now the importance of Whitman is this. He consciously saw that the society of America, *without the European roots* and more democratic in its social life than any European society, needed a new verse form. *He was a great student of the European tradition.* Don't forget that please, miss. He knew he couldn't start afresh. *He knew and said that without them he could not have written as he did.* He was neither ignoramus nor dilettante. But he broke clean away and every year sees his work growing in importance. He is the greatest literary force in America because he broke so consciously. *At the end of his career*, the Symbolist movement in France started the revolt against the traditional bourgeois verse from which has come Yeats, Eliot and the whole modern school. Note something specifically American. Whitman broke away *in confidence*; the Europeans broke away in disgust. Why did Whitman not have a greater influence? This is a historical question. In the nineteenth century there was real popular government in the U.S.A. The big bourgeoisie did not dominate as yet. It really seemed as if democracy could function. Unfortunately the Civil War victory let in big industry. And the popular masses were slowly disciplined by big capital. Thus the social system became more and more like the European.

After the war America made one notable contribution—the fiction of Hemingway. He broke the literary convention and brought the speech of "the people" not only into dialogue but into his very narration.

Today it seems to me that the studious American poet, with the power and devotion can take verse a long long way. The American democratic tradition, the life of the country today, the power of the workers, the approach of a new social order based on the working class, demand new forms. But you can't sit and make those up. Whitman knew European verse, he knew America, *he participated in its struggles*, he knew American democracy both in theory and practice, and soaking himself in these he caught something of the spirit of the country and this gave him his style.

Now you have to do the same. The traditional verse you must read and study. The democracy of today is workers' democracy. The America of today is the most wonderful country in the world, its problems, the problems of the people, must be your problems, the philosophy of the working-class movement you must understand, and as you live these things, deeply and sincerely, they will express themselves in your writing—even in love lyrics. This does not mean joining anything. But it does mean that your thoughts, your ideas, your hopes, must move in a certain direction. *Get that right*, strengthen your mind, develop it, exercise it, in that way, and according to your talent, it will express itself in the verse. Is that clear? Now to be more precise. Do I say Read this or Read that or Read the other? No. But I say, e.g., See what you can get out of Whitman, read books about him, if you find him interesting, try to place him in American history. Follow him as far as your mind leads you.

To sum up. You have to read such books and investigate such problems as will give your mind the background, breadth, and impetus necessary to attempt to do for America today what Whitman did in 1860. *He was very conscious.* You have to be far more conscious than he. The age demands it. But the age also provides the material and the social premises. The various points for elaboration are innumerable. To take one. Whitman emphasized that he wrote as an individual. That is not accidental. Bourgeois society is essentially the production of individuals. Today the individual can be individual only so far as he is a member of a collective unit. The individuality of today is a higher individuality but it rests on a very conscious collectivity. Everywhere you see it. A worker in 1860 had as his highest aim to become his own boss. That was the American dream. Today he may say that in words (though he rarely does) but his aim is through his union to gain collective benefits. No one can sit down and write verse expressing that. But to see it and feel it, and understand it makes a poet write in a different way. And so on, and in various multiple ways. If I am not mistaken your acting method is the same. It is all a reflection of the age. . . .

AUGUST, 1944

One day I'll tell you how after the French Revolution, the revolt against Hume led through Kant, Fichte, Schilling, Hegel and Feuerbach to Marx, step by step, with an inevitable logic culminating in the doctrine of the class struggle. It is a fierce doctrine, harsh and unforgiving, chiefly, however, because the ruling class makes it so.

What is most exciting is that the sequence from Hume to Marx which I have been studying for the last three years and which has had an effect on my thinking and on my personal life beyond all explanation, this I find repeated with an almost photographic exactitude in modern poetry. Yes, modern poetry! The sequence from T.S.Eliot to Auden, Spender and Cecil Day Lewis is a repetition of the sequence from Hume to Marx. It is and must be so, for the human mind having said A must say B. I would never have looked at it at all, not unless I was ill, but for you. And the sequence I would never have discovered but for W.B.Yeats. Some years ago he wrote an essay which I read lately and have been reading steadily since. *He knows poetry*. That was his job. He analysed it with the eye of a master. And as he traced stage by stage the development, there before me was the classic philosophical sequence. Hegel had traced it in ancient philosophy, had himself been the completion of the greatest example of it, and now here it is again. The perfect exemplification which Yeats gives in his analysis was a great thrill for me. In fact it is so far the best exemplification. And there in the very heart of it, tangled up inextricably with it, is yourself, living, warm, and lovely. Do you see why I call you my little miracle? One day we'll have a jam session—you and me. It will begin with philosophy—the method of thought, i.e., logic, the inevitable development of ideas, and we'll reach poetry by that road. Then we'll see as clear as day what the concept class means and what the absence of it has meant to poetry. Always remembering however that the poet reacts to life *emotionally*—and without that, though he were the wisest man in the world, he could not write a line of verse. But the more humanity develops the more the emotional response depends upon a conception of the world which does not so much guide the poetry, but releases and expands the personality, integrates it, opens horizons, and thus gives the emotional responses a range and depth and power impossible otherwise. This, sweetheart, is to live. When the disciples asked Christ about the world to come and the places they were to get in it, he told them, "The Kingdom of Heaven is within you." They could not understand. They just *couldn't*. The glory of life in our age is that this intense, individual, personal life can, in fact, must be lived, in harmony with the great social forces that are now striving to carry humanity over the last barrier. When I say I love you, it comes from very, very far.

JANUARY 5, 1944

Enclosed I send you the programs of *Othello*. I am thrilled at the idea of your doing Shakespeare with (John) Carradine. Fight for it, Constance. Fight hard to make it. It is presumptuous for me to give you advice, but I think I understand something about Shakespeare. I want you to know what I think.

The other day I saw an interview with Carradine in the press. He said that he and the late John Barrymore used to read Shakespeare. He read too "colloquially", in J.B.'s opinion. In his, J.B. read too lyrically. Both were *wrong*. Pardon me the dogmatism. I have felt Shakespeare in my bones too long and am studying him once more. I have also seen some superb Shakespearean actors and I have some opinion.

The English tradition is the best. It aims at preserving the Shakespearean rhythms, the finest in the world, and *at the same time* making them natural. In other words, you have to do what both Carradine and J.B. were doing. It is hard, hard as the devil, but it can be done. I heard J.B. do a speech from *Hamlet* and another from *Richard III* on discs. He was theatrical. The best I know is Forbes Robertson on some old Columbia records. Get them if you can. He is old, but rhythm and expression are perfectly matched. To do this is a triumph. It is worth doing. Shakespeare in drama and Beethoven sonatas in music are the supreme test. Few succeed. If you would care for me to listen to some discs and send them to you let me know.

You see, I saw the *Othello*. It has created a tremendous stir here. In my opinion it, particularly Paul (Robeson), was lousy. Not one of them, except at odd moments, had the Shakespearean rhythm—not one. I was shocked because Margaret Webster and Uta Hagen were both trained in England. To hear John Gielgud or Edith Evans is to hear a miracle of rhythmic beauty and naturalness. Without the first, there is no Shakepeare.

Robeson was rotten. He is a magnificent figure, a superb voice, and, as usual with him, at moments he is overwhelming. But in between his lack of training, his lack of imagination, were awful. For long periods he stood in one spot and *said* the lines, just said them. Dynamic development of the part, there was none except the crudest. And Shakespeare is dangerous for the amateur. Without strong feeling you slip immediately into melodrama. A great actor gives a grand sweeping performance in effect, but every line means something. Every phrase can stand by itself. It is built up into a whole. For long periods Robeson lacked grip. I knew he was just going to shout at the climax. I wish I could see it with you two or three times. How I would love to. Then I'd tell you what I think and you'd help put me right.

What made R's failure so noticeable was a magnificent performance by Jose Ferrer. Never once was he just swimming along with the stream. I never saw him working hard or sweating. He had an all-over mastery. But he had both the imagination and the discipline to make every line tell. I have never seen anything better. EXCEPT: The rhythm of Shakespeare was entirely absent. You know in one scene, after Iago has planted the poison in O's heart, Shakespeare makes him soliloquise: "Not poppy, nor mandragora, nor all the drowsy syrups of the world, shall ever medicine thee to that sweet sleep which thou owedst yesterday."

Now lines like these are a test. Shakespeare did not write that music for fun. The music emphasises the dramatic climax. It must ring. You must hear it. Where on the film an orchestra emphasises the dramatic values, Shakespeare orchestrates himself. Ferrer didn't have it. Just as in a film if the music came suddenly to a climax at the correct moment and then died away again, so it must be in Shakespeare. I have heard Gielgud do the Hamlet lines: "Angels and ministers of Grace, defend us." Dramatic passion and lyric beauty were fused. You could not separate them.

One thing the play has done, however. It shows that Othello was a black man—who felt his colour and his age were a handicap to him. The mess that colour can cause in happy married life was particularly clear, and the whole American Negro question was highlighted by the play. *Politically* it is a great event. It was also very interesting. I could see it often again. It was a distinguished performance, and Robeson's remarkable gifts and personality were very much worth watching. But the play on the whole fell short. A word on Desdemona. She is frail and young and sweet; then, when righteous indignation forces her to stand up to him, there is a terrific clash. You should tremble for her. Even at times her fire and innocence should enrage and yet overawe Othello, only for his rage to mount higher. What should break her is her inability to convince him she has not been unfaithful. You should get a glimpse of this spirit in her defiance of her father, and it should come out in the quarrels between them. That would give the last acts a grim power. But Uta H simply bungled it up properly, or rather Margaret Webster did, for the responsibility is hers. Desdemona is a "revolutionary". She crossed the colour line. She spurned the rich and curled darlings of Venice. She married a middle-aged man. She ran away to do so. She is a modest maiden but she has a fiery spirit. When Othello turns on her, she should, after a time, *fight back*. That spirit must appear again. She loves him but she must resent his accusations. The Moor, as he usually is, is a big man, a soldier, a terrible-looking African (in his rages) and she is as Uta Hagen was, bowed down before O. She was merely pathetic. Someone had poisoned Othello against her. That was all. It all depended upon the plot, upon the trick that Iago played. That wasn't good enough.

Successful as the play is, it could have lifted off the roof if Desdemona with technique and insight and imagination had been able to rise to the necessary heights. I repeat. It was not merely the trick, the plot. You should have been able to see her very personality making Othello mad.

You see, my dear Constance, Shakespeare, like Beethoven, is a man who has not yet been fully grasped by bourgeois society.

The world made a great stride forward in the seventeenth century. Bourgeois society began. Religion was the dominant mode of feudal society. Dewey (although he didn't know what he was doing) removed religion from heaven to earth, from the priests and the Church to the heart of the individual man. The first great bourgeois writer was Shakespeare and coming when he did, he posed for the first time the relation of the individual to society. Hamlet remains forever the prototype of what we know today as the petty-bourgeois liberal or radical. In politics, for instance, he is for the revolution, he sees it intellectually, but he cannot bring himself to take part in such violence. He ruins himself and all around him. The Jewish problem—it is perfectly posed in the *Merchant of Venice*. The race question, and with it the marriage of a middle-aged man to a young girl. The demagogue and the masses—*Julius Caesar*. Today society is profoundly different from Shakespeare's day. But it is bourgeois society. And whereas in feudal days the Church decided what was right and what wrong, with bourgeois society the individual has to decide. Today more and more the great classes make the decisions, but the conflicts are sharper than ever, in fact they are at breaking-point. Now Shakespeare was a dramatist, no sociologist, so he individualised them. Every man looking on them today can see them not only in individual but in social terms. Yet whatever society is, each man must make his individual choice. So today we see these plays and in them is mirrored the life of society. The artist therefore can play them and the managers stage them with a penetration and breadth that comes from 300 years of social experience. As Hegel says somewhere, an old man repeats the same prayers that he did as a boy but now they are pregnant with the experience of a lifetime. So today we look at Shakespeare but we have not solved the problems he posed and we can see them as he never could. And in this period of world-shaking crises they are all around us, insisting on solution as never before.

Finally, the more I think of Shakespeare and Beethoven, the more I see that the rhythms and the tonal qualities (of B) are organic to their work. They felt the tragic quality of society, Shakespeare after the Reformation and Beethoven after the French Revolution. The rhythms are a response, deep and tragic, to the tragic quality of life in all periods of great social ferment. There is a well-known piano piece by Beethoven that children play, *Fur Elise*. Listen to it. You hear something never heard in music before or since; same with Shakespeare. You see now why I think you should as an artist move heaven and earth to work at these plays. Whoever after years of work grasps them, penetrates into them, and recreates them for this age, will be doing the work of a giant. I know that you have it in you. I read your letters and I see that. You see Carradine and make him take you, just make him. Then you'll come to N.Y. and we'll read the plays and you'll do parts for me to see and you'll be graceful and lovely and full of power and I'll be terribly happy; and if I can tell you a few things which will help you see deeper into them, I am sure that when I see you there are many many things I'll understand about Shakespeare for the first time.

Take care of yourself, mind you.

1944 (NO DATE)

A modern woman, a woman born after the Russian revolution and World War I, a woman born in America, is a certain type of person. Her relationship with a man, even in her own mind, is something different from that of a person who grew up in a different age. The generation before her had to fight the theoretical battle for sex equality. This generation hasn't got to fight that battle; *it grew up with it in its bones*. If, and when, through personal weakness or difficult circumstances, it capitulated, *it was conscious of defeat*. When a woman of 1924 submitted to the dictation of another will, however much disguised, however sincerely, her submission was, to a large degree, a battle within her own head; for she had grown up fighting if she was a progressive woman at all. The suffragettes fought a revolutionary struggle (and I am sure had a fine time). This generation is different. It has grown up looking upon this freedom as normal, as accepted. I have seen submission, after keeping itself quiet for a dozen years, break out in the most furious revolt. I know two women, sisters in their thirties, who tell me "that they don't want to be bothered with any husband". A man, yes. A man they must have; but they will not stand nonsense from any man. The men they meet are " normal" men, who want a wife and kids. What these women are saying, in reality, is that they want a husband who does not relegate them to a secondary position where they have to submit their will to his. One has been married twice; the other, once. They are not intellectuals. They have merely arrived at a certain maturity and, unbeknown to themselves, are expressing the changed position of women in the modern age. That is the ordinary, regular, normal, type of woman. Some of them make the best of it, as a wife, "*because of the children*". Over and over again I see this and hear it. I regret to say that many men I have known want kids as the surest way to keep the wife quiet. Very often, however, the woman loves the man. Her deepest instincts are aroused by him. And life in capitalist society being what it is, she suppresses something that is smaller for what is to her larger. Fifty years ago Shaw saw that clearly in Candide. Fifty years ago! In backward England. Candide was still a wife, Marchbanks wanted to worship her; and she was to share the dramatic, high-lighted, ups and downs of the life of an artist, an adventure. That is still, very often, the conflict today.

With the increasing opportunities that modern production (and the development of ideas based upon it) gives to women, a new type of woman arises. She is called a career woman. The name is stupid but nevertheless very revealing. A man is never a career man. That is his right and privilege. He can have his career, and the finest fruit of his successful career is wife and children. But the woman is called career woman because her "career" in modern society demands she place herself in a subordinate position or even renounce normal life. The social dice are loaded against her; and the plain fact of the matter is that they are loaded, not only in the economic opportunities, *but in the minds of men*. The men cannot take it. I know my own sex reasonably well. With the best will in the world, a man, a good man, unconsciously demands that a woman submit to him. It is what he wants that matters in the end, not what she wants. Some men are crudely egotistic. Others are not. They believe in equality; but the practice of society dominates them. It must, as long as they do not consciously oppose it. Nevertheless,"the career woman" can fight and, given real ability and luck, can *sometimes* win through.

But if a woman is an artist, then God help her! Virginia Woolf, no mean artist in her own way, and a woman who had every advantage, social and financial, has summed it up in the very title of her book on this subject. It is called *A Room of One's Own*. That is what a woman, who is an artist, wants—a room of her own. It is the devil's own job to get it. A surprisingly large number of women, who are physically and emotionally normal, just go their way and take love as male artists do—as strictly subordinate affairs, sweeping them out of themselves for a time, but pushing it into its place as soon as it interferes with them. They are not satisfied with that, as a rule; but society being what it is, and men being what they are, they make their own adjustment. They do not think in social terms. They are not socialists. They are not acting for or on behalf of society at all. They are acting for themselves, seeking to live their own personal lives. But their personal lives are what they are because of social changes and social movements. Those who do it instinctively, and battle for their own way, are expressing a social movement which is highly progressive. Those who do it, conscious of what it means to society, of what they represent, are very much stronger (the individual life becomes part of a collective movement). They express themselves more clearly to themselves and to others; becoming, in their own way, and in their own sphere, fighters for a new society. It isn't that one does this or that "for socialism". No. One does this or that because in society as it is today, a substantial number of people express themselves and live the life that is in them. They refuse to be bound by the old traditions or ideas. The very fact that these people appear in increasing numbers is a sign of the break-up of the old society and the emergence of the new—both of which take place at the same time and are one movement. It is not "I would do this—for you, but I have to do this for socialism." It is, "I must do this, for myself, and not to do it is treason to myself, and to the others who are all fighting with me in this sphere, and to all the millions who in their various ways, are fighting their battles, which together constitute the struggle for the new society."

So it is for the "career woman"; so much the more for an artist—a woman conscious of gifts. Socialistic or not, she must fight for the development of herself. It is a duty she owes to the fact that she has gifts. But, and this is your case, if the woman is completely conscious of the social movements, identifies herself with one part of it, and finds that she has a talent which can help, then that is argument enough. Nothing must stand in the way. Nothing at all. There are two reasons, both intimately connected. First of all, one has a duty, the highest and most difficult type of duty, the self-imposed, which springs from no external compulsion. It comes from "inside". but this powerful impulse from "inside" is merely the response of a resonant, sensitive personality to what is taking place outside. That is the essence of the personal question. As a result of this, however, an individual becomes more powerfully individualistic than ever. The stronger the collective force which the individual is expressing, the more powerfully individualistic the individual becomes in that he or she cannot suppress that individuality for another individual. One may try to, may succumb to temptation, to strong personal feeling, one may, for a time, feel reconciled, one may gradually become reconciled, and even be "happy". But if the original impulse is strong and organic to the personality—then a hell of a mess is the result. There is always the gnawing consciousness of a wasted life, frustration, sometimes a resentment that lies dormant and grows with the years. Candide can give up and live. But if Candide were herself an artist and a creative person, then utterly apart from the sense of duty (which is particularly strong in an artist in 1944, with a social bent.) I say that, purely from a personal point of view, there is danger. To put it crudely, the very attempt to secure a "happy", "personal" life may be the road to life-long personal unhappiness. It all depends upon the personality.

But the personal life remains. It will not be suppressed. If suppressed it wears the artist down. Of that there is no question at all. Some compromise is necessary. It is always so in life. The point is: which matters most to the individual person. I should say that the ultimate decision as to whether a particular choice was successful or not does *not* rest with the person. If society moves forward, the collective movement is fighting, great decisions being taken, great sacrifices borne, the person who has "retired" is miserable. If, however, the social hopes are set back, no progress is being made, then "retirement" is more acceptable.

Now a last point—philosophical, but for that reason more profound than the rest. Today our world—for the conscious ones—is becoming more and more fluid on the surface and more serious below. Take as an example, verse. Where before the rigid forms disciplined the poet externally, today the free verse gives an enormous range, allows far greater power; but there is a trap for those who have not got a powerful, internal discipline. In reality it is much, much harder to write superb verse in the modern style than in the old style. "Society" gives more privileges, even to the writer, but demands greater responsibilities. Same in social life. Formal manners are much looser. The result is that real social distinction depends far more on character and natural consideration and tact than when everyone was a little Emily Post.

Marriage is the same. The old relationship was simple. The woman was to be faithful. The man was not to neglect her. They compromised; but the lines were broadly established. Today, *among people who can afford it*, that is going. Both he and she have greater freedom. But this freedom only means that the mutual bond below is infinitely more powerful than anything the old relationship could show.

1945 (NO DATE)

News. Wonderful news. I went to Richard Wright's house as soon as I spoke to you. I was "cautious" because he was just outside the booth. We talked for one and one-half hours. First, he has broken with our friends (the Communist Party of America)—told me with emphasis that he has no political affiliations whatever. But I am not rejoicing in the ordinary political manner.

It is from what he told me. For years I have wanted to talk to him more than to anyone else in America (political and literary). From his books I felt that he understood the Negro question. I was equally confident that no one else I knew did, except a few people whom I had preached to for years. I knew I was right because, first of all, the Old Man (Leon Trotsky) had always said that he had never *studied* the question, but from all he had seen and heard it seemed to him that the intellectuals and the Marxists in America were *wrong* on this question. Secondly, I knew Amy Garvey, the wife of Marcus, and she knew the whole thing inside out, with her political limitations of course. Thirdly I had done close study of the San Domingo Revolution, and had learnt the essence of the question there.

Richard Wright, with an artistic sincerity for which I could have kissed him, has worked his way to a real grasp, and is now engaged in correcting the proofs of a book for which the whole intellectual public is going to abuse him fiercely. He tells me that he is almost completely isolated, and I think he sees quite clearly the chances that his reputation will suffer a serious setback. But he is confident of his truth and he is giving all he has. It was a wonderful meeting.

I knew about him—though I didn't know how far he had gone. But he didn't know that I held the same views. Briefly the idea is this, that the Negro is "nationalist" to the heart and is perfectly right to be so. His racism, his nationalism, are a necessary means of giving him strength, self-respect and organisation *in order to fight for integration into American society*. It is a perfect example of dialectical contradiction.

Further, however, the Negroes represent a force in the future development of American society out of all proportion to their numbers. The repression has created such a frustration that this, when socially motivated, will become one of the most powerful social forces in the country.

Finally, neither white America *nor black America* has faced the Negro question for the deep fundamental thing that it is in the life of the *nation* as a whole.

He has worked to it artistically, I through history. But our conclusions are identical. If you have read *Native Son* and remember Bigger Thomas, compare him to the Peter I outlined to you—frustrated, fierce, unreasonable, overstepping the bounds. I have been wavering about writing a book. But I shall hesitate no longer. By the time they have recovered from his autobiographical novel *(Black Boy)*, I shall hit them across the eyes with a historical study. You should have seen him grinning all over as I told him what I thought of his work and how long I had wanted to tell him but had avoided him. This is just an hors d'oeuvre. The real letter follows.

By the way, Richard Wright was rather despondent. But he is wrong. The tide is turning. His own work is evidence. So is mine. What pleased me with him is that although he sees it as an individual artist, he drew the full and complete conclusion and went at it with the throttle open. You know, history does move. The thing is to see it.

Let us try and see if we can get the fundamental, the essential question right. It isn't easy. But until that is right, nothing is stable and one fumbles along.

What are the standards, ideas, values, by which we live? By "we", I mean society as a whole, which expresses them through the individual personality, its conflicts and the problems faced by every living soul (writer, actress, revolutionary, worker, waitress) to the extent that he or she is conscious. Unfortunately for some, we live in a conscious age. This is not just because it is an age of revolutionary upheavals where every "accepted" idea is in question—all accepted ideas are in question whenever social conflicts reach the period of explosion. The distinctive feature of our age is that mankind as a whole is on the way to becoming fully conscious of itself. All the great revolutionary periods—the Renaissance, the Reformation, the French Revolution—meant some further progress towards more complete consciousness. We are now on the eve, historically speaking, of a complete realisation of the purpose, meaning, and potentialities of human existence.

Your business in life is to find yourself. Whoever suggests to you or hints that you "ought" to have remained in or should join a serious political organisation, is an idiot. A man or woman should do that for one reason, and one reason only, because that is the way he or she *must* live. People who do not feel that compulsion have no right whatever even to think of it. The average number at most of those who feel that way in bourgeois society was in France, in 1937, 300,000 out of 40 million; Germany, in 1932, 400,000 out of 60 million; Russia, in *October 1917*, 200,000 out of 170 million. It will never be proportionately more, never. It is usually much less. But every educated person, every serious artist, every young person today has to come to some conclusion about the world. It *ends* with conflicts about Stalinism and Trotskyism. It does not begin there.

We are the fruit of 2000 years—not to go back further. The classical world was very different from ours. The large mass of men were slaves. They were not considered as human. Today every person is theoretically a human being, with human rights. They are often deprived of these rights. But at least, theoretically, they are ours. It took the ruin of the Graeco-Roman civilisation to establish that. Christianity was a revolutionary movement which said that every man and woman (for there were terrific fights before women too were included—the cult of the Virgin Mary is no accident), was equal in the sight of God, all were his children. We may not all be Christians; but, theoretically today, every man has the possibility to be as good as any other man.

After the establishment of that principle we had centuries of semi-slavery and serfdom, and the growth of a new civilisation of the Middle Ages. Its greatest exponent was St. Thomas Aquinas. Life was very poverty-stricken in those days. Nature dominated man. He could not master it, so he lived in expectation of the future life where the theoretical equality and happiness would be made real. One thing, however, St. Thomas expressed was the *unity* of civilisation under one God, and His representative the Catholic Church. Europe has never lost that concept. But it was only ideal. Today, however, for Europe and the world, it has become a compelling necessity. Civilisation will be unified or it will perish from imperialist wars. The ideal has become real. Then came the humanists of the Renaissance—Erasmus, Petrarch, Sir Thomas More, and others. They established that the good life should not only be celestial but human—here on earth—hence *humanists.* This was a tremendous advance, due of course to the developing process of production.

The next great stage is the Reformation. The movement that began with Dewey established man's right to decide his own course to heaven and, as far as possible, his own course on earth; and it established *individual responsibility*. For St. Thomas, humanism and individual responsibility were not only impossible but heresy. He could not have understood those things at all.

Let us go a little more quickly. The American Revolution (Declaration of Independence) and the French Revolution went further. They proclaimed liberty: the *political* rights of man.

By the middle of the nineteenth century we have something new; the rights not of man in general, but of *labour*, the working man. Marx led this current of thought.

Today, in advanced countries, labour of right demands universal *higher* education, safety from unemployment, state medical attention—you know them all. Now look at that worker whom you see in the subway, the bus, or moving properties in the theatre. An ordinary person, full of prejudices, not knowing very much, etc. Viewed historically, however, he is an extraordinary person. He believes:

1. That he is as good as any other man. He is a worker because he has no money, etc.; but the road to anything is theoretically open to him. This was the driving force of *Christianity* when it was a revolutionary force.

2. He thinks that somehow or other, and this is true above all in Europe, that the civilisation of our day must somehow become unified. Two world wars and one great depression have taught him that. St. Thomas's great theoretical principle is now a matter of life and death with the average worker in the street.

3. He may call himself a Catholic, but he is a confirmed *humanist.* He believes that the good life is here, on earth.

4. He lives and works side by side with Catholics, Methodists, Episcopalians, etc., and would not dream of persecuting his fellow-worker for his religion. He may, for political reasons, use religion or be stimulated to use religion as a weapon. But he never thinks of religious persecution purely for the sake of religious persecution. It took Europe almost a century of blood and destruction to learn that. St Thomas, fine intellect and splendid vision that he had, could not have understood this at all.

5. The worker believes in the Rights of Man. Before the end of the eighteenth century, the finest minds of civilisation did not believe that. Millions of workers are far more advanced here than, e.g., Spinoza.

6. The idea that all men have a right to the best possible education, that unemployment and medical attention, etc. are the concern of the State, these things would have seemed like madness to Kant and Hegel. They could not have understood it.

Thus today the average advanced worker accepts as legitimate certain human and social values which make him, as a human being, infinitely superior to these men of past ages, infinitely his superior in intellect, learning, and nobility of character. His values, instinctively and weakly as he holds some of them, are the only values that count today. I repeat. There are no other values of any significance whatever. The slow accumulation, century by century, of the thoughts of the great philosophers, which they could only hold often as ideals, are now the common property, *as a matter of everyday life*, of millions upon millions of ordinary people. The tremendous ferment in India, China and Africa shows that, owing to the progress of technology (steamship, plane and radio), the poverty-stricken, starving backward millions of Oriental peasants are demanding these things for themselves. People call this a materialistic civilisation. So it is. But its true significance is that things which hitherto a few idealists and sometimes certain classes preached in distorted form, are today the desires of the masses everywhere. *"Idealism" is being forced into material form in the lives of the people.* There never was a more highly civilized age than ours—never were the basic ideals of a good full life so desperately desired by so many people.

By a dialectical law which one day, we shall, I hope, talk about, this unprecedented movement towards a more profound civilization finds itself in terrible conflict with the existing social order. It always has been so. Fascism is nothing more than the attempt to suppress it. People say this, but do not appreciate its full significance. The German Fascists struck at every principle I have outlined—men were *not* theoretically equal, the good life was not for man but for the state, etc. But, in the crisis, certain startling truths emerged. What people thought was the heritage of *all* civilisation was defended only by the working class. (They defended it badly, but they did their best.) Not only the capitalists but the middle classes to a large degree showed that in the crisis, desperate for a way out, they were willing to abandon everything. The teachers, the journalists, the actors, the clerks, the whole bunch in large numbers, followed the Fascists. *The workers did not.* They were taken by surprise in Germany. But in Spain, for instance, they fought magnificently. *They alone were uncompromising defenders of the great heritage.* I am not idealising them. They defended it because it was their daily lives they were defending. For you and me, as a class grouping, democracy in its fullest sense was, or seemed to be, an ideal. The European middle classes were prepared to let it go because they were suffering so much. The workers, *precisely because they were suffering*, could not let it go. All theories must be proved by practice. Mussolini and Hitler had all the power they needed. Look at what they have done to Italy and Germany. To make it personal. You are interested in artistic expression. But the Fascists, in crushing democracy, ruined the artistic life of the nation. There is no art today without freedom. And without the freedom of the workers *there is no freedom for anybody.* That we all must hold fast to.

Let me explain it as concretely as I can, using the great experiences of the last dozen years.

In America we have about 13 million organized workers. With all their faults they are the most fanatical defenders of freedom of speech, freedom of organization, the Rights of Man, etc. They must be. They know nothing of Martha Graham, of Eugene O'Neill, of Hemingway, of Ernst and Dali, of the men who are sincerely striving in philosophy, in political economy etc. But if the workers should be defeated and lose their privileges, then so cohesive is the structure of modern society that everything else goes. No work in any of the arts or sciences (this has been proved) can be done in a totalitarian state. Once the workers' power is gone, a blight descends *and must descend.* The men who have to keep the workers quiet in a modern society must control film, radio and press; and see that they serve these ends.

Martha Graham, O'Neill and the rest, who perhaps do not think of workers at all, can think, work and develop solely because the workers' organizations exist. The peculiar thing is neither group worries over much about the other (except for a few here and there). But the intellectual consciousness of society rests with the mass, that and the great heritage of Western civilisation.

Now anyone who thinks at all must know this and never forget it. More than that—his duty is wherever possible to try and make the workers conscious of it. The more conscious they become, the safer the great values of civilisation are. Always, always, always, the task is to develop the consciousness, the independence, the sense of destiny, the sense of responsibility, among the masses of the people. Anything else serves the forces of reaction which aim at the destruction of this enormous power which faces them.

The relation I have outlined here is broad and rough. In reality it is very intimate, affecting personal lives, sex relations of the most intimate kind, the development of personality and so on. As Wright and I talked tonight, point after point came rushing out—about Negroes chiefly. But I see evidence for these ideas every day, in the voices of people, the songs they sing, the clothes they wear, and the terrible struggle for self-expression, self-realisation. Most folks give up. One reason is because they do not comprehend historical necessity. As Engels says: freedom is the recognition of necessity. The necessity within which a modern life can be truly and fully lived is the recognition of what the working class means in a modern society, to be able to trace this relation in all its ramifications (they are innumerable) and to live up to them bravely, courageously, and with the inner confidence which it brings. Compromises one has to make; but with a clear understanding one knows pretty soon how far one can go. In all forms of art today, all, this consciousness guides the people who ten years from today will amount to something. Details of this I'll talk to you about in time, when we can. It isn't easy to grasp. It took me years and years. But I have it now and I don't care two damns for the opposition. I am sure "inside". If for you to be sure "inside" takes you away from me, then sister, go in peace. You have to live your own life, which will bring you nearer or further away.

Thanks for the picture. It is lovely—closer to you than anything I have yet seen, but not quite you. It looks sophisticated and aloof; but somewhere in it is some of your child-like simplicity. You know there are two kinds of simplicity—the simple direct one you have sometimes, and the same simplicity which is the result of much experience and strenuous living. All artists have the first. No one can be an artist without it. All great artists arrive at the second. That is their maturity. So Marx and Lenin by tremendous studies and experience arrived at profundities which expressed the thoughts and aspirations of the simplest workers. So, as I believe I have written to you, Hegel says that an old man repeats the prayers he repeated in childhood, but now with the experience of a lifetime.

Ten years ago I talked about the workers. Today I say the same. But God! What a difference. Same with a woman, love, happiness. I am going to bed now, 3 o'clock. Take care of yourself. Remember that whatever happens to you happens to me.

1946 (NO DATE)

Christ have mercy, where were you on Sat'y night. Tonight. In fact an hour ago. We saw *Love Letters.* My second time. It was an experience. I am a fan of Jennifer Jones. She has a marvelous face, and a great talent. Her face is all bone-structure, curves and planes, Negroid and Mongolian; wide eyes, a good strong nose, wide mouth and a lovely curved cheek-bone. She has the goods. Now the film is typical, good bits, cheap sentiment, etc. But this time I was struck by what J.J. was doing with her lines. They were commonplace. But in emotional scenes by sheer acting, emotional power but restraint, she gave them a genuine poetic quality. Over and over again it happened. Then it struck me. *This is our modern poetry*. Remember T.S. Eliot and his poetry coming back to ordinary speech. Now Dryden did it—and Wordsworth, whom *we must read*, did it—and stated the case in the Preface to *Lyrical Ballads*. Now we have come to a new age. The symbolists and the free versifiers have prepared the ground. We havc said this before. But there before us, before me, the thing was being done. Naturally everything contributed. But I grew terribly excited because I know that what by voice, intonation, inflexion, gesture, etc. She was doing, you are doing by plain pure writing. Yours is a thousand times harder. But it is the same thing. She is your age, older probably, but your generation. She is bourgeois and as far as I know hasn't an idea in her head. What she is doing will vanish. But the particular quality I find in your poetic work I found distinctly in her treatment of the trite lines she had to say.

We must see the thing together and I hope you will see what I mean. I missed it completely the first time. But it was as clear as day to me this time.

We do not speak here of Shakespeare. But we feel that way and we have to use the prosaic sharp disjointed urban speech of our time and make people feel as Shakespeare wrote. Wordsworth did it in his day. Now, more deeply all are into it. J.J. was using the actress's arts. But *chiefly* rhythm and inflection. Now I am seeing every day that rhythm is an expression of the human "soul", which is of course social. But the great rhythms of history—the Greek hexameter, the Elizabethan blank verse, the heroic couplet, all are social. But as Hegel shows, the modern ones are connected with social development, and therefore connected with each other in a process of development. I shall trace them with you, I have it *I think*. Sufficient for the time being to say that the rhythm is the rhythm inherent in a particular language, i.e., in a particular culture, which is constantly being distilled from the particular stage of "normal" speech at the time. Thus when we read Wordsworth, and the poems that matter are not many and simple, we shall see a rhythm that is related to Pope behind him and Tennyson after him. It is, I feel, English, and the gradual discovery by a nation of its most intimate language—a growing to maturity. That is why in Eliot there are all these poets, these quotations (and even more so in Ezra Pound). He feels the need but lacking a positive *universal*, his very rhythms are chaotically and crudely introduced. His universal is not merely not positive, it is negative, destructive, not *creative*, lacking perspective. Now I think that your rhythms today can express, not negatively, but positively and coherently all the previous ones fused. The basic structure will be simple speech, the poetic quality Jennifer Jones was getting across. But I have noticed in many places a return to rhyme and rhythms of previous times. Stravinsky does the same in his work (written in the style of Bach here, Mozart there, Rachmaninov there); Joyce does it—but they all do it critically, evocatively, expressing nostalgia. But today the people's speech, the basic common language, distilled into poetic rhythm (and of course imagery) becomes the basic structure, while all sorts of echoes of previous rhythms and the things they represented can become not only echoes but positive expressions towards the freedoms, powers, sentiments, etc., of previous generations enjoyed by only a few. All that of course is beyond Sister Jennifer. She is no poet. But that, in expressing in her own way a strongly felt artistic emotion, she should so strongly remind me of the things you are doing, was a revelation that makes me feel only too clearly that you are expressing something that belongs to this generation, that is deep down in it.

The logical working out of it hits me with great force because I was working on the incomparable Hegel and applying his ideas to English poetry. I am a bit scared that when you listen you will not hear (and see) what I heard. But we must try. Remember the last pages of Dick's *Black Boy*. It is the same sort of thing. Now previously (I think this sums it up) they got to that only exceptionally, only in very high and social moments. Now that is our regular, only it is much closer to the ordinary. But we reintroduce our modern distillation of their old ones.

9

Dialectical Materialism and the Fate of Humanity

Mankind has obviously reached the end of something. The crisis is absolute. Bourgeois civilisation is falling apart, and even while it collapses, devotes its main energies to the preparation of further holocausts. Not remote states on the periphery but regimes contending for world power achieve the most advanced stages of barbarism known to history. What civilised states have ever approached Nazi Germany and Stalinist Russia in official lies, official murder and the systematic brutalisation and corruption of their population? Only a shallow empiricism can fail to see that such monstrous societies are not the product of a national peculiarity (the German character) or a system of government ("communism") but are part and parcel of our civilisation. Everything that has appeared in these monstrous societies is endemic in every contemporary nation. Millions in the United States know that Nazi Germany and Stalinist Russia will have nothing to teach the American bourgeoisie when it finds itself threatened by the revolutionary American workers seeking the complete expression of democracy which is socialism. The dream of progress has become the fear of progress. Men shrink with terror at the hint of scientific discoveries. If it were known tomorrow that the crown of human technical achievement, the processes of manufacturing atomic energy, had been lost beyond recovery, this scientific disaster would be hailed as the greatest good fortune of decades.

But the seal of the bankruptcy of bourgeois civilisation is the bankruptcy of its thought. Its intellectuals run to and fro squealing like hens in a barnyard when a plane passes overhead. Not a single philosopher or publicist has any light to throw on a crisis in which the fate not of a civilisation but of civilisation itself is involved. The Keynesian theories are now part of the history of economics. The ridiculous "four freedoms" of the late President Roosevelt take their place with the Three Principles of Sun Yat-Sen (the father-in-law of Chiang Kai-shek), the thousand years of Hitler's Reich and the "socialism in a single country" of Stalin. The chattering of Sidney Hook and Harold Laski is stunned into silence by the immensity of their own inadequacies. Thought has abdicated. The world is rudderless. All illusions have been destroyed. "Man is at last compelled to face with sober sense his real conditions of life, and his relations with his kind." And in face of this the bourgeoisie has nothing to say.

The method of thinking is rooted in society. Bourgeois thought has collapsed because bourgeois society has collapsed. We have learnt by hard necessity the truth of the following dictum of Trotsky: "Hegel in his *Logic* established a series of laws: change of quantity into quality, development through contradictions, conflict of content and form, interruption of continuity, change of possibility into inevitability, etc., which are just as important for theoretical thought as is the simple syllogism for more elementary tasks." (Trotsky, *In Defence of Marxism.)*

Hegel defines the principle of Contradiction as follows: "Contradiction is the root of all movement and life, and it is only in so far as it contains a contradiction that anything moves and has impulse and activity." *(Science of Logic*, translated by Johnson and Struthers, volume 2, page 67.) The first thing to note is that Hegel makes little attempt to prove this. A few lines later he says: "With regard to the assertion that contradiction does not exist, that it is non-existent, we may disregard this statement."

We here meet one of the most important principles of the dialectical logic, and one that has been consistently misunderstood, vilified or lied about. Dialectic for Hegel was a strictly scientific method. He might speak of inevitable laws, but he insists from the beginning that the proof of dialectic as scientific method is that the laws prove their correspondence with reality. Marx's dialectic is of the same character. Thus he excluded what later became *The Critique of Political Economy* from *Capital* because it took for granted what only the detailed argument and logical development of *Capital* could prove. Still more specifically, in his famous letter to Kugelmann on the theory of value, he ridiculed the idea of having to "prove" the labour theory of value. If the labour theory of value proved to be the means whereby the real relations of bourgeois society could be demonstrated in their movement, where they came from, what they were, and where they were going, that was the proof of the theory. Neither Hegel nor Marx understood any other scientific proof. To ask for some proof of the laws, as Burnham implied, or to prove them "wrong" as Sidney Hook tried to do, this is to misconceive dialectical logic entirely. Hegel complicated the question by his search for a completely closed system embracing all aspects of the universe; this no Marxist ever did. The frantic shrieks that Marx's dialectic is some sort of religion or teleological construction, proving inevitably the victory of socialism, spring usually from men who are frantically defending the inevitability of bourgeois democracy against the proletarian revolution.

So convinced a Marxist as Trotsky reminded the revolutionaries in 1939 that Marxists were not fatalists. "If", said he, "the international proletariat, as a result of the experience of our entire epoch and the current new war, proves incapable of becoming the master of society, this would signify the foundering of all hope for a socialist revolution, for it is impossible to expect any other more favourable condition for it." The Marxian expectation of socialism arising from the contradictions of capitalism would have proved itself to be utopia.

The law of contradiction is what for the moment we can call a "hypothesis" for the grouping of empirical facts. All men use hypotheses for the grouping of facts. That is what logic consists of. The bourgeois hypotheses are for the most part unconscious. They are the inevitability of bourgeois society, natural division of labour, more particularly of men into capitalists and workers, constantly expanding technical progress, constantly expanding production, constantly expanding democracy, constantly rising culture. But during the last thirty years, these have crumbled to dust in their hands. They have no hypotheses they can believe in and that is why they cannot think. Historical facts, large and small, continuously deliver shattering blows at the foundation of their logical system. Nothing remains for them but the logic of the machine gun, and the crude empiricism of police violence.

Quite different is the mode of thought of Marxism. It understands its own logical laws. For Marxists, the fundamental logical law is the contradictory nature of all phenomena and first of all human society. The dialectic teaches that in all forms of society we have known, the increasing development of material wealth brings with it the increasing degradation of the large mass of humanity. Capitalism, being the greatest wealth-producing system so far known, has carried its contradictions to a pitch never known before. Thus it is that the moment when the world system of capitalism has demonstrated the greatest productive powers in history is exactly the period when barbarism threatens to engulf the whole of society. The anti-dialecticians stand absolutely dumbfounded before the spectacle of the mastery of nature for human advancement and the degradation of human nature by this very mastery. The greater the means of transport, the less men are allowed to travel. The greater the means of communication, the less men freely interchange ideas. The greater the possibilities of living, the more men live in terror of mass annihilation. The bourgeoisie cannot admit this, for to admit it is themselves to sanction the end of the bourgeois civilisation. Hence the complete paralysis of bourgeois thought. Yet never was thought of a fundamental character so necessary to mankind. As our political tendency has recently written:

> It is precisely the character of our age and the maturity of humanity that obliterates the opposition between theory and practice, between the intellectual preoccupations of the "educated" and of the masses. All the great philosophical concepts, from the nature of the physical universe (atomic energy) through the structure and function of productive systems (free enterprise, "socialism", or "communism"), the nature of government (the state versus the individual), to the destiny of man (can mankind survive?), these are no longer "theory", but are in the market-place, tied together so that they cannot be separated, matters on which the daily lives of millions upon millions depend. *(The Invading Socialist Society)*

Never were such universal questions asked by the whole of the civilised world. Never have such inadequate answers been given. All that the bourgeoisie can answer is the purely technical question of the manufacture of atomic energy, and it wishes that it could not.

Now it is precisely because this contradiction of society has reached its farthest point in Stalinist Russia that the dialectical materialist analysis of Russia is the most important key to the perspective of world civilisation.

The second law of dialectical materialism is the change of quantity into quality. At a certain stage a developing contradiction, so to speak, explodes, and both the elements of contradiction are thereby altered. In the history of society these explosions are known as revolution. All the economic, social and political tendencies of the age find a point of completion which becomes the starting-point of new tendencies. The Russian revolution is one such explosion. But the examination of the Russian revolution involves both the laws of development through contradictions and the change of quantity into quality.

Let us examine the Russian revolution in some of its most important features, such as would be agreed upon by most observers, excepting the diehard reactionaries.

The revolution was the greatest outburst of social energy and creativity that we have yet seen. Previously the French revolution had astonished mankind by the rapidity and grandeur of its achievements. So much so that to this day 14 July 1789 is the date in all probability most widely known among the great majority of mankind. But the Russian revolution exceeded the French. A combination of workers and peasants, the lowest classes of mankind, tore up an established government by the roots and accomplished the greatest social overturn in history. Starting from nothing, they created a new state, created an army of millions, defended the new regime against famine, blockade and wars of intervention on all fronts. They reorganised the economy. They made Russia a modern state. They passed and tried honestly to carry out a series of laws on popular education, equality of women, repudiation of religious superstition, sexual sanity, workers' control of production, all of which constituted the greatest potential democracy and enlightenment that the world had ever seen. They organised a world-wide Communist International devoted to the achievement of the same ideals in the entire world. The gradual decline and final failure are treated in the text. But the accomplishments are history, imperishable and of permanent significance for mankind. Taken in its entirety the heroic period of the Russian revolution is the most glorious episode in human history.

Lenin, the leader of the revolution, claimed always that one of the greatest achievements was the establishment of a new type of democracy, the Soviets of Workers', Soldiers' and Peasants' Deputies, which was able to unloose the creative energies of the great masses of the people. Their mere administration of the state in his opinion would make the further existence of capitalism impossible. This administration by the masses is "not yet" socialism, but it is no longer capitalism. "It is a tremendous step towards socialism, a step from which, if complete democracy is retained, no backward step towards capitalism would be possible without the most atrocious violence perpetrated upon the masses". *(The Threatening Catastrophe)*

Capital, in the form of state capital, once more rules in Russia. Democracy has not been retained. But this has been done only at the cost of the condition foreseen by Lenin. The most atrocious violence has been perpetrated upon the masses of the people. Thus, the Russian revolution, as it has developed and declined, shows us the two most violent extremes that we have known in history. It is only dialectical materialism that can unite these extremes in logical and intelligible connection. It is the creative power, the democratic desires, the expansion of human personality, the record of achievement that was the Russian revolution. It is these which have called forth the violence, the atrocities, the state organised as

Murder Incorporated. Only such violence could have repressed such democracy.

One can see the glint in the eye of the enemy of the proletarian revolution. Without perspective, himself, intellectually helpless before the contemporary barbarism, indulging in nonsensical opposites like Yogis and Commissars, or searching diligently in his own writhing insides for the solution to the problems of the world, he hastens to use the fact of the Russian degeneration as an unanswerable argument against the ideas of Bolshevism. Patience, my friend, patience. "Bolshevism", says Trotsky, "is above all a philosophy of history and a political conception." Without the philosophy, the political conception falls to the ground. We have to get to the philosophy step by step. We have arrived at this much. The atrocious violence and crimes which now distinguish the state of Stalin are the necessary and inevitable response to the revolutionary fervour and democratic organisation and expression of the Russian people. Not the Russian people in general, however, but the Russian people as they had developed and expressed themselves in the socialist revolution of 1917. This is not merely a Russian phenomenon. The Russian revolution is a climax to a series of revolutions which have moved according to certain laws. Briefly: The British revolution in the seventeenth century embraced only small sections of the population—some revolutionary bourgeois, petty-bourgeois farmers and yeomen and a small number of artisans, and others in the few and small towns. They could not create the new but they could destroy the old. The work of the revolution having been accomplished the counter-revolution, heir to the new social order, established itself by a mere invitation to Charles II to return. A handful of people only were punished. With the development of economy and its socialisation, i.e. the increasing inter-relation of all classes in production, the French revolution embraces the great mass of the nation. The revolution destroys feudalism and establishes the modern state. Its basic work accomplished, "order" must be restored to society by the counter-revolution, the heirs to the new regime, but this time there are millions of aroused people. It is the great body of the nation which is to be disciplined. No mild return of royalty, no forgiveness, no mutual amnesty. Only the military police-dictatorship of Napoleon can hold this country down. The contradiction between the revolution and the counter-revolution has sharpened.

Society established itself on new foundations. But the contradiction between the classes grows. If the revolution in Russia was the broadest and deepest development of the revolution of the seventeenth century, the Stalinist regime is the similar development of the counter-revolution. The German revolution of 1918 did not overthrow bourgeois property. But the German proletariat, infinitely larger and more highly developed than the Russian, had a long history of democratic achievement and organisation behind it. After the revolution, its organisation continued and expanded. That is why the Nazi counter-revolution was as brutal as it was. But if the German proletariat in 1918 had established a Soviet state embracing workers, agricultural proletarians and semi-proletarians, the lower ranks of the petty-bourgeoisie and the sympathetic intelligentsia, then logically speaking one of two things would have happened. Either the new democratic formation would have gone on from strength to strength awakening the deepest reserves of social power and aspirations of the already highly-developed

German people and spreading throughout Europe; either this or something else. The atrocities and the violence which would have been needed to suppress a successful German proletarian revolution and the response it would have awakened in the German and other European peoples would have exceeded the crimes of Hitler as much as Hitler exceeded the crimes of Napoleon.

The pervading barbarism of the Stalinist regime, therefore, is not to be attributed to this or that weakness in the theory of "communism", or some partial aspect of the Stalinist state. Stage by stage, wc have seen the revolution and the counter-revolution develop in Europe over the centuries. At each new stage of development, both the revolution and the counter-revolution assume a new quality with the new quality of the social development. Precisely because the Russian revolution assumed a new quality in attempting to establish a universal democracy, the Russian counter-revolution assumes a new quality of universal barbarism in the sense that it embraces all aspects of the Russian state.

At this stage, to try to separate progressive aspects from so comprehensive and all-pervading an enemy of human development as is the Stalinist state, is to strike down the dialectical method at the root. Hegel understood the limits within which one could designate a corruption as partial:

> The Reformation resulted from the *corruption of the Church*. That corruption was not an accidental phenomenon; it is not the mere *abuse* of power and domination. A corrupt state of things is very frequently represented as an "abuse"; it is taken for granted that the foundation was good—the system, the institution itself faultless—but that the passion, the subjective interest, in short the arbitrary volition of men has made use of that which in itself was good to further its own selfish ends, and that all that is required to be done is to remove these adventitious elements. On this showing the institute in question escapes obloquy, and the evil that disfigures it appears something foreign to it. But when accidental abuse of a good thing really occurs it is limited to particularity. A great and general corruption affecting a body of such large and comprehensive scope as a Church is quite another thing. . . . The corruption of the Church was a native growth. *(Philosophy of History)*

The Russian revolution is the completion of a historical process, the development of class society. Its relation to past revolution can be illuminated by the laws of changes of quantity into quality. The British revolution, although it pointed the road for the rest of Europe, was only to a subordinate degree of international significance. The French revolution shook the whole of Europe to its foundations and established the logical lines along which revolution and counter-revolution would struggle in Europe for the succeeding century. It is in the very nature of modern society and the Russian revolution that Russia today is symbolical of the whole fate of modern civilisation. There is no further stage. Either the revolution succeeds in encompassing the whole of the world or the whole of the world collapses in counter-revolution and barbarism. The whole path of Western civilisation for two thousand years has reached an ultimate stage in Russia. There is no by-pass. There is no third alternative.

Therefore, as dialectical materialists, we do not bewail nor do we underestimate or in any way attempt to minimise the monstrous character of the Stalinist regime.

We repudiate utterly any idea that what is there has any socialist character whatever. But we draw from it for Russia itself and for the whole world an ultimate, a universal conclusion. The barbarism is not to come. It is there.

In our previously quoted pamphlet, we have written:

> The unending murders, the destruction of peoples, the bestial passions, the sadism, the cruelties and the lusts, all the manifestations of barbarism of the last thirty years are unparalleled in history. But this barbarism exists only because nothing else can suppress the readiness for sacrifice, the democratic instincts and creative power of the great masses of the people.

Those are the two forces in conflict. The philosophy of history which is Bolshevism bases itself upon the destruction of the barbarism by the inevitable triumph of the socialist revolution. There are even revolutionaries who deny this. For them it is not scientific to believe in inevitability. Such a belief implies that dialectic is a religion or mysticism. For them the correct scientific attitude is to reserve judgement. Yet these very ones turn out to be the mystics and the practitioners of an ill-concealed religiosity. If they recognise the bankruptcy of bourgeois democracy, if they accept the need for universality in the masses, if they recognise that barbarism is the only force that can suppress this need, then to refuse to accept the inevitability of socialism leaves only one of two choices. Either the inevitability of barbarism, that is to say, the acceptance of the principle of inevitability which they have just rejected or the hope, the faith, the belief that history will offer some way out of the impasse. This is the denial of a philosophy of history, that is to say, the denial of a method of thought, for which the only name is irrationalism or mysticism.

The deniers of the inevitability of socialism can be routed both historically and logically.

Marx developed his philosophical doctrines in the years which preceded the 1848 revolutions. The revolution was obviously on the way. Yet society was dominated by the experience of the great French revolution which had achieved such miracles but had failed to achieve universality (liberty, equality and fraternity), and despite all its sacrifices and bloodshed, had ended in the triumph of the counter-revolution. The experience of 1830 had only multiplied both the fears and the hopes which had been engendered by the colossal experience of the French revolution. In this period, so similar to ours, philosophy came out of the study, particularly in Germany, and attempted to give some answers to the problems that were shaking society.

The utopian socialists of all stripes were distinguished precisely by this, that they argued interminably about the possibility as opposed to the inevitability of the socialist revolution. They were tortured by these doubts because, after the experience of the French revolution and its obvious failure to relieve the conditions of the great masses of the people, they themselves had lost faith in the inevitability of socialism. Which is only another way of saying the inevitability of the achievement by the people of complete self-expression, complete democracy, socialism. In so far as their beliefs were the result of theoretical speculation, they had, in the words of Marx, lost the capacity to draw from the experience of man's past in order to establish perspectives for man's future.

The result was a complete chaos, disorder, confusion in their own thoughts with an absolute inability to meet the challenge of the approaching revolution. It was into this ulcer that Marx drove the knife of scientific socialism. Bolshevism is a philosophy of history. Marx first clarified himself philosophically. As he wrote to Ruge in 1843:

Almost greater than the outer obstacles appear in the inner difficulties. For although there is no doubt about the "whence", there prevails the more confusion about the "whither". Not only has a general anarchy broken out among the reformers; each of them also must himself confess that he has no exact conception of what ought to be. Precisely in this is the advantage of the new movement, that we do not anticipate the new world dogmatically but intend to find the new in the criticism of the old world. Up to now the philosophers have had the solution of all riddles lying in their desks and the dumb exoteric world had only to gape in order for the ready-baked pies of wisdom to fly into their mouths. Philosophy has become worldly, and the most decisive proof of this is that philosophic consciousness has been drawn into the anguish of the struggle not only superficially but thoroughly.

If the construction of the future and the preparation for all time is not our affair, it is all the more certain what we have to complete at present, i.e., the most relentless criticism of all existing things, relentless both in the sense that the criticism fears no results and even less fears conflicts with the existing powers.

We face the same situation today in the radical and revolutionary movement. In 1947, however, not only is philosophy worldly. In the face of the universal character of the crisis, the world is driven to become philosophical. It is compelled to examine in their nature and in the totality of their relations (that is to say, philosophically), economics, politics, science and even the very nature of the universe and society. All agitation about the possibility of barbarism, third alternatives, the mysticism of the inevitability of socialism, these are no more than what they were in Marx's day, only infinitely more so: terror before the destructive contradictions of modern society, doubts of the capacity of the proletariat to resolve them. This amounts to no more than a defence of bourgeois society in so far as bourgeois society still can provide thinkers with freedom enough to substitute the analysis of their own thoughts for a positive intervention in the chaos of society.

So far historically. Logically, the inevitability of socialism is the absolute reverse of religion or mysticism. It is a consciously constructed necessity of thought. As we have quoted in the article on *Historical Retrogression*, Hegel recognised that without holding fast in thought to your ultimate goal, it is impossible to think properly.

To hold fast the positive in its negative, and the content of the presupposition in the result, is the most important part of rational cognition: also only the simplest reflection is needed to furnish conviction of the absolute truth and necessity of this requirement, while with regard to the examples of proofs, the whole of Logic consists of these. *(Logic*, vol. II, p. 476)

Precisely because they held fast to the presupposition of the inevitability of bourgeois society, the bourgeois thinkers in the early days of capitalism made their tremendous contributions to the science of human thought. Even without philosophical perspective, the bourgeoisie at least has one reality, maintenance of power against the workers and rival bourgeoisies. But without presupposing the inevitability of socialism, that is to say, without thinking always in terms of the victory of the masses, thinking among those hostile to bourgeois society must become a form of scholasticism and gnosticism, self-agitation and caprice.

Over a hundred years ago, Hegel said that the simplest reflection will show the necessity of holding fast the positive in the negative, the presupposition in the result, the affirmation that is contained in every negation, the future that is in the present. It is one of the signs of the advanced stage of human development that this is not longer a mere philosophical but a concrete question. To anyone that does not accept bourgeois society, the simplest reflection shows that it is impossible not only to think but to take any kind of sustained positive action in the world today unless one postulates the complete victory of the great masses of the people. What is this but the exemplification in life of the logical theory, the inevitability of socialism?

The Stalinist state, the Nazi state, and in their varying degrees all states today, based upon property and privilege, are the negation of the complete democracy of the people. It is this state which is to be destroyed, that is to say, it is this state which is to be negated by the proletarian revolution. Thus, the inevitability of socialism is the inevitability of the negation of the negation, the third and most important law of the dialectic.

I have said earlier that the laws of the dialectic are "hypotheses". Any Deweyite pragmatist who is rubbing his hands with joy at this "reasonable" Marxism is in for rude disillusionment. "Dialectics", said Lenin, "is the theory of knowledge of (Hegel and) Marxism." So far I have been dealing with it as a theory of knowledge, as a mode of thought, examining more or less empirically contemporary society and the Russian revolution, and showing how by means of the dialectical approach, some order, some perspective, some understanding come out of them, showing equally why the bourgeoisie can make no sense of anything except to hold on to power.

But Marx's hypotheses were not hypotheses in general. They were not empirically arrived at, tentatively used, discarded if not satisfactory, experimental or instrumentalist. They were logical abstractions organised according to the *method* of Hegel and reflecting *the movement of human society*. This is no simple matter. But it has remained obscured and neglected too long.

The dialectic is a theory of knowledge, but precisely for that reason, it is a theory of the nature of man. Hegel and Marxism did not first arrive at a theory of knowledge which they applied to nature and society. They arrived at a theory of knowledge from their examination of men in society. Their first question was: What is man? What is the *truth* about him? Where has he come from and where is he going? They answered that question first because they knew that without any answer to that general question, they could not think about particular questions.

Both Hegel and Marx in their different ways believed that man is destined for freedom and happiness. *They* did not wish this (or they did, that does not matter). They came to this conclusion by examining man's history as a totality. Man for Marx was not Christian man nor the man of the French revolution (nor Stalin's bloodstained secret police). The concept of man was a constantly developing idea which was headed for some sort of completeness. When Marx said that with the achievement of the socialist revolution the "real" history of humanity will begin, he was not being rhetorical or inspiring (or optimistic). He was being strictly and soberly scientific.

The truth is the whole. The whole, however, is merely the essential nature reaching its completeness through the process of its own development. Of the Absolute it must be said that it is essentially a result, that only at the end is it what it is in very truth.

Thus Hegel in the *Phenomenology of Mind*; Marx worked on the sample principles. The essential nature of man was becoming clear only as it approached its completeness in bourgeois society. It is in bourgeois society that we could see what man really is. And it is "only at the end" of bourgeois society that we can see what man is in very truth. Thus it is in the contemporary barbarism that can be seen most clearly what is the "real" nature of humanity. The need and desire for socialism, for complete democracy, for complete freedom, that is the "real" nature of man. It is this which explains his past. But it could be expressed within the concrete circumstances of past ages only to the degree that objective circumstances allowed. Did man, therefore, suffer through all those centuries to produce completed man? The defenders of bourgeois society are ready to defend and rage over all these unjustified sufferings of past mankind in their die-hard opposition to the proletarian revolution which will relieve present mankind. They will get nothing to comfort themselves with. "The truth is the whole." All the various stages constitute the nature of man. Continues Hegel: "And just in that consists its nature, which is to be actual, subject or self-becoming, self-development." Man is the subject, that which is developing itself. The subject becomes more and more real, and therefore the truth about man becomes deeper and wider, more universal, more complex, more concrete. Complete universality, complete democracy in the sense that every man is able to do what every other man does, this is the ultimate stage. The Russian revolution was an imperfect, limited, handicapped but nevertheless decisive step in this direction. The nature of man, therefore, becomes the search for this completeness and the overcoming of the obstacles which stood and stand in its way. Past history therefore becomes intelligible and what is more important, the road to the solution of the overwhelming problems to the present day becomes open.

If today we say that now we know what is the "real" man, it is because we see him as a totality, as the result of his whole past. But from there we make another step. The terrible crisis of civilisation is the result of the fact that man is at last real, he has become himself, completely developed. But the old type of world which developed him cannot contain him. He must burst through it. That world was a world in which he was subjected to nature. It was in the subjection of nature that he fully realised himself, a continuous negation of the obstacles which impeded his development. That being accomplished, his real history will begin. He negates all that has previously impeded him, i.e. negated him, in the full realisation of his inherent nature. Socialism is the negation of all previous negations. It is obvious that these are large conceptions. But the death of a world civilisation is not a small thing.

The conception being stated, it is now necessary not to prove it (only life can do that) but to show where it came from.

Western civilisation, and therefore, the Hegelian dialectic begins with Christianity.[1] It was Christianity which established universality in its most abstract form, that very universality which we are now seeing concretely striving for expression in the proletariat all over the contemporary world. The very early or "primitive" Christians attempted a universality that was extremely concrete, commonalty of goods and absolute equality. But it soon collapsed. The abstract universality was established by that historical Christianity which superseded the Roman Empire. Christianity united all men, before birth, in the universality of original sin, and after death, in the possibility of universal redemption in heaven. Thus it carefully avoided a concrete universality. It was the religion of the millions who had been released from slavery by the collapse of the Roman Empire. The narrow straitened circumstances of their material lives were compensated for by the subjective conception of an after-life in which all their material needs would be satisfied or, better still, there would be no need for material satisfactions at all. But, extreme abstraction though it was, man is for the first time established as universal man. Hegel expresses the idea in all its fullness in the *Philosophy of History*:

> Man, finite when regarded *for himself*, is yet at the same time the Image of God and a fountain of infinity *in himself*. He is the object of his own existence—has in himself an infinite value, an external destiny. Consequently, he has his true home in a supersensuous world—an infinite subjectivity, gained only by a rupture with mere natural existence and violation, and by his labour to break their power from within. . . .

These conditions are not yet a concrete order, but simply the first abstract principles, which are won by the instrumentality of the Christian religion for the secular state. First, under Christianity slavery is impossible; for man as man—in the abstract essence of his nature—is contemplated in God; each unit of mankind is an object of the grace of God and of the Divine purpose; "God will have all men to be saved." Utterly excluding all speciality, therefore, man, in and for himself—in his simple quality of man—has infinite value; and this infinite value abolishes, *ipso facto*, all particularity attaching to birth or country.

This is what Hegel calls an abstract universal. The history of humanity is no more than this abstract universal becoming concrete. International socialism is the concrete embodiment of the abstract principle of Christianity. And Christianity appeared and international socialism is now appearing because they are of the very nature of man. To call the recognition of this teleology and religion is a sign of the greatest ignorance, or, is not ignorance, but a determination at all costs to defend bourgeois society against the philosophy of Bolshevism today so as not to have to defend it against the revolutionary masses tomorrow. To have been Christian and to be socialist is an expression of the need for concrete universality which is not so much in as of the very nature of man. And dialectic bases itself upon this precisely because it is not religious and not teleological. If this, scientifically speaking, is not the nature of man, then what do the opponents of dialectic offer instead? Either man has expressed these desires and these aims by accident, i.e. they have no significance whatever, for he might have expressed entirely different aims and had entirely different needs, and may do so tomorrow. Or these needs and aims are not the nature of man but came from some outside agency or God.

It is only in the sense described above that dialectic speaks of freedom and happiness being the purpose of man's existence. Purpose, not in the religious sense, but in the sense that if we examine man's history through the centuries he has sought these aims. It is difficult therefore to say what other purpose his existence has, and the anti-dialectician is left with the alternative that man's life has no purpose at all, which is only another way of accommodating one's self to the existing society, bourgeois society.

The logical principle of universality contains within it a logical contradiction, the contradiction of abstract and concrete. This logical contradiction is a direct reflection of the objective circumstances in which the men of early Christianity lived. Their physical and material circumstances were on the lowest possible level. And therefore, to make their existence a totality, they had to fill it out with this tremendous abstraction. Thus is established the basic logical contradiction in the universal between concrete and abstract, between objective and subjective, between real and ideal, between content and form. But both together form a whole and have no meaning apart from each other. They are opposites but interpenetrated. To Christian man, the conception of heaven was *real* and *necessary*, an integral part of his existence in the objective world. Those who accuse dialectics of being a religion understand neither dialectics nor religion. The history of man is his effort to make the abstract universal concrete. He constantly seeks to destroy, to move aside, that is to say, to negate what impedes his movement towards freedom and happiness. Man is the subject of history. "(The) subject, (man) is pure and simple negativity." This is a cardinal principle of the dialectical movement. The process is molecular, day by day never resting, continuous. But at a certain stage, the continuity is interrupted. The molecular changes achieve a universality and explode into a new quality, a revolutionary change.

Previous to the revolutionary explosion, the aims of the struggle can be posed in partial terms, possibility. It is the impossibility of continuing to do this that interrupts the continuity.

The revolution, precisely because it is a revolution, demands all things for all men. It is an attempt to leap from the realm of objective necessity to the realm of objective freedom.

But in the limited objective circumstances to which the low level of productivity has confined society, what is demanded by, of and for all men, only some men can have. The concrete universality, therefore, becomes the property of some men, a class. They are therefore compelled to use objective violence against those excluded and to substitute an abstract universality for the concrete universality of which the mass has been deprived. But the absence of concrete universality from the whole also limits the universality of the few. Their own concrete universality therefore begins to be limited and its limitations substituted for by abstractions. This is the Hegelian process of "mediation". The new state established after the revolution, the ideology which accompanies it, are a form of mediation between abstract and concrete, ideal and real, etc.

The mediation usually assumes the form of the state power, and the specific ideological combinations of abstract and concrete to bind the new relations are developed by the philosophy of the age. A new equilibrium in the process of the development of man has been established. At a later stage, the same developing process will be repeated in the attempt to negate the actual stage of man previously established. There will be the mass revolution for undifferentiated universality, the class differentiation in its realisation, the splitting of the nation into opposing factors, and the attempt to realise in ideology the reconciliation of the opposing factors. Man is not only what he does but what he thinks and what he aims at. But this can only be judged by the concrete, what actually takes place. The truth is always concrete. But it is the concrete viewed in the light of the whole. In the decisive page of the preface to the *Phenomenology*, Hegel writes:

> As subject it is pure and simple negativity, and just on that account a process of splitting up what is simple and undifferentiated, a process of duplicating and setting factors in opposition, which (process) in turn is the negation of this indifferent diversity and of the opposition of factors it entails. . . . It is the process of its own becoming, the circle which presupposes its end as its purpose, and has its end for its beginning, it becomes concrete and actual only by being carried out, and by the end it involves.

Marx is expressing concretely just this concentrated Hegelian generalisation when he says:

> For each new class which puts itself in the place of one ruling before it is compelled, merely in order to carry through its aim, to represent its interest as the common interest of all the members of society, put in an ideal form, it will give its ideas the form of universality and represent them as the only rational, universally valid ones. The class making a revolution appears from the very start, merely because it is opposed to a *class*, not as a class but as the representative of the whole society; it appears as the whole mass of society confronting the one ruling class. It can do this because, to start with, its interest really is more connected with the common interest of all other non-ruling classes, because under the pressure of conditions its interest has not yet been able to develop as the particular interest of a particular class. Its victory, therefore, benefits also many individuals of other classes which are not winning a dominant position, but only in so far as it now puts these individuals in a position to raise themselves into the ruling class. . . . Every new class, therefore, achieves its hegemony only on a broader basis than that of the class ruling previously, in return for which the opposition of the non-ruling class against the new ruling class later develops all the more sharply and profoundly. Both these things determine the fact that the struggle to be waged against this new ruling class, in its turn, aims at a more decided and radical negation of the previous conditions of society than could all previous classes which sought to rule.

This organisation of historical development did not fall from the sky. It is the result of the concept of the dialectic worked out by Hegel and without the dialectic it could not be done at all. It is this Hegel that Burnham calls the "arch-muddler" of human thought. It is from the examination of this process, the developing conflicts between abstract and concrete, subjective and objective, the abstract universal assuming a certain content which becomes concentrated in a special form, the form gradually becoming infused with a new content until it can contain it no longer and explodes, it is from the examination of all this in society and nature but particularly in its ideological reflection in philosophy that Hegel works out the significance of categories and the movement of his *Logic*. Just as Marx's economic categories were in reality social categories, just in the same way the logical categories, contradictions, etc., of Hegel were a reflection of social categories and social movement. Hegel, and for very good reasons of his time, led his *Logic* into an impossible and fantastic idealism about world-spirit, etc. But the basis of his work was solidly materialistic. He himself explains that:

> The community of principle which *really* links together individuals of the same class and in virtue of which they are similarly related to other existences, assumes a *form* in human consciousness; and that form is the thought or idea which summarily comprehends the constituents of generic character. Every universal in thought has a corresponding generic principle in Reality, to which it gives intellectual expression or *form*. *(The Philosophy of History)*

Marx and Engels knew this. They could carry over the Hegelian dialectic into a materialistic form because it had been derived originally not from religion but from a study of the stages of man in nature and society and the reflection of these stages in human thought. The dialectic of negativity, the negation of the negation, the inevitability of socialism are a culmination in logical thought of social processes that have now culminated in contemporary society. You look in vain in writings of Hook, Professor of Philosophy at New York University and Burnham, a member of the same faculty, for the slightest understanding of this.

The beginning of this process for the modern world is Christianity and the beginning "presupposes its end as its purpose". For Hegel, these stages are the work of the universal spirit. Marx here is his diametrical opposite. Marx is a dialectical *materialist.* For him, and right from the very start, *these concrete revolutionary stages are the work of the great masses of the people forever seeking the concretion of universality as the development of the productive forces creates the objective circumstances and the subjective desires which move them.*

Hegel could see the abstract universal, the relation between abstract and concrete in historical Christianity and the developing relation in human history. Marx saw that, but because he was closer to the end, he could see more of the "real" man. Because he had seen the revolutionary *proletariat*, he was able to complete the dialectical analysis of previous stages by the recognition of the role of the revolutionary *masses.* These appear at the very beginning of history.

In his introduction to *Class Struggles in France*, Engels writes:

> This party of revolt, of those known by the name of Christian, was also strongly represented in the army; whole legions were Christian. When they were ordered to attend the sacrificial

ceremonies of the pagan established church, in order to do the honours there, the rebel soldiers had the audacity to stick peculiar emblems—across on their helmets in protest. Even the wonted barrack cruelties of their superior officers were fruitless. The Emperor Diocletian could no longer quietly look on while order, obedience and discipline in his army were being undermined. He intervened energetically, while there was still time. He passed an anti-Socialist, I should say anti-Christian, law. The meetings of the rebels were forbidden, their meeting halls were closed or even pulled down, the Christian badges, crosses, etc., were like the red handkerchiefs in Saxony, prohibited. Christians were declared incapable of holding offices in the state, they were not to be allowed even to become corporals. Since there were not available at that time judges so well trained in "respect of persons" as Herr von Koller's anti-revolt bill assumes, the Christians were forbidden out of hand to seek justice before court. This exceptional law was also without effect. The Christians tore it down from the walls with scorn; they are even supposed to have burnt the Emperor's palace in Nicomedia over his head. Then the latter revenged himself by the great persecution of Christians in the year 303, according to our chronology. It was the last of its kind. And it was so effective that seventeen years later the army consisted overwhelmingly of Christians, and the succeeding autocrat of the whole Roman Empire, Constantine, called the Great by the priests, proclaimed Christianity as the state religion.

The Christian revolutionaries, however, were not struggling to establish the medieval papacy. The medieval papacy was a mediation to which the ruling forces of society rallied in order to strangle the quest for universality of the Christian masses. In one sense the papacy merely continued the Roman Imperium, and, in Hobbes's phrase, was indeed "no other than the ghost of the deceased Roman Empire sitting crowned upon the grave thereof".

But it was much more than that. Primitive Christianity had begun as a mass revolt that had sought to establish the community of men upon earth. By the time of Gregory the Great, when the papacy began to take over the functions of the declined and fallen Roman Empire, the papacy was beginning its career as a combination of the Empire *and the tremendous impact of the mass revolution.* It was the ghost of the Roman empire and living symbol of Christ on Earth. Heaven was too abstract to satisfy completely the masses of the people. The Church guaranteed them, in return for obedience, the happy future life. But it also took care of the life on earth, and performed the functions of teacher, protector and provider for the poor and sick and needy. It mediated between society and heaven and between the secular rulers of society and the masses. It succoured the poor and was a centre of learning and the improvement of agriculture. In the method by which it was established, in its mediation, of contending classes and its manipulation of concrete abstract, the medieval papacy, as the culmination of the Christian revolution, contains in embryo all the development to the modern age. The dialectical materialist method, the product of a stage nearer to the end, is infinitely superior to Hegel's dialectic. Constantly, contemporary events throw a penetrating light into the past and thereby illuminate the future. It is, for example, the concrete history of the last thirty years of proletarian revolutions that for the first time makes it possible to grasp fully the meaning of Renaissance. But the dialectical materialist study of the Renaissance drives the last nail in the coffin of those who hesitate before the conception of the negation of the negation, the inevitability of socialism and the dictatorship of the proletariat.

The leading ideological characteristic of the early Renaissance can be usefully designated by the popular term "humanism". The medieval towns produced a brilliant civilisation. With the growth of wealth, chiefly a result of commercial capitalism, there arise classes of men whom the early Christian contradiction between objective and subjective, abstract and concrete, is no longer tenable. It is not merely a question of objective wealth. The idea of universality becomes more concrete because of the "energetic position which man is sensible of occupying in his subjective power over outward and material things in the natural world, in which he feels himself free and so gains for himself an absolute right." (Hegel, *Philosophy of History*)

The papacy is itself mediated. It became humanised, i.e. more completely secular, and thus took the road to its own ruin. St. Thomas Aquinas had already begun the rationalisaton of faith, making it reasonable by a brilliant and profound misuse of the writings of Aristotle. Dante, whom Engels calls one of the first modern men, though profoundly religious, wished to substitute Emperor for Pope. The national monarchy begins to substitute for the papal authority.

So far so good. But, and here the Marxist dialectic sharply departs from the Hegelian, the new universal was established and took its form by such violent revolutions of the European proletariat as Europe did not see again until the period which opened in 1917. It is only recently that bourgeois historians have begun to recognise these. The historians of the socialist society will in time make of this one of the great chapters of human history.

As always in critical periods, there were a series of peasant revolutions in Europe throughout the fourteenth century. They were of tremendous range and power, some of them semi-socialistic. But they were not decisive. The decisive revolutions were revolutions of the workers and the petty bourgeoisie of the towns. If the phrase had not already been appropriated by Marxists for the revolution of the socialist proletariat, it would be perfectly correct to say that within the various municipalities the workers aimed at, consciously, and in some few cases actually achieved, the dictatorship of the proletariat.

In the last half of the fourteenth century, these revolutions swept from one end of Europe to another. In Salonika, the sailors and the artisans ruled the rich, the landowners, the commercial magnates and the clergy for ten years. In Italy, the struggle between the "fat" and the "thin". In Bologna, in Genoa, in Sienna, the masses sought to obtain absolute mastery of municipal power. In Florence, under the leadership of Michel Lando, they organised the celebrated revolt of the Ciompi and established the dictatorship of the proletariat whom they called "God's people". Rome and other towns saw similar battles. But it was in the Lowlands, in towns of Ghent, Ypres, and Bruges that the workers made the most desperate efforts to establish their own dictatorship. Revolutionary history badly needs a study of the incidents which centre around the van Artevelde family. Over and over again during a period of decades, the workers rose. More than once they established their dictatorship, they proclaimed an equality of fortunes and the suppression of all authority except the authority of people who live by manual labour. They repeatedly defeated the flower of feudal chivalry. It is reported that in Ghent, the workers went so far as to plan the complete extermination of the bourgeoisie and the nobles with the exception of children of six years of age. In the German towns of Cologne, Strasbourg, Aix-la-Chapelle, Lubeck, Stettin and many others, in Barcelona, Valencia, and the other towns in Spain, the same desperate battles took place. The working class and its allies closest to it fought for fifty years all over Europe to establish proletarian democracy. Why they failed to achieve substantial successes was due not only to the low level of production but the fact that they fought only as members of isolated municipalities. Some of them indeed aimed boldly at an international proletarian revolution. But their time was not yet.

Let Boissonade, a bourgeois historian, speak in the concluding paragraph of his *Life and Work in Medieval Europe*. The reader should read carefully and note particularly the words we have underlined:

For the first time the masses, ceasing to be mere herds without rights or thoughts of their own, became associations of freemen, proud of their independence, conscious of the value and dignity of their labour, *fitted by their intelligent activity* to collaborate in all spheres, political, economic, and social, in the *tasks which the aristocrats believed themselves alone able to fulfil*. Not only was the *power of production multiplied a hundredfold by their efforts*, but society was regenerated by the incessant influx of new and vigorous blood. Social selection was henceforth better assured. It was thanks to *the devotion and spirit of these medieval masses that the nations became conscious of themselves, for it was they who brought about the triumph of national patriotism*, just as their local patriotism had burned for town or village in the past. The martyrdom of a peasant girl from the marshes of Lorraine saved the first of the great nations, France, which had become the most brilliant home of civilisation in the Middle Ages. *They gave to the modern states their first armies*, which were superior to those of feudal chivalry. *Above all, it was they who prepared the advent of democracy and bequeathed to the labouring masses the instruments of their power, the principles of freedom and of association.* Labour, of old despised and depreciated, became a *power of incomparable force in the world*, and its social value became increasingly recognised. It is from the Middle Ages that this capital evolution takes its date, and it is this which makes this period, so often misunderstood, and so full of a confused but singularly powerful activity, the *most important in the universal history of the labour before the great changes witnessed by the eighteenth and nineteenth centuries.*

This was the working class five hundred years ago. They were not proletarians in the modern sense. They were, for the most part, free workers in the guilds. They did not function within the socialised organisation of modern labour. But note, Messrs. anti-dialecticians and anti-Marxists, that these workers, five hundred years ago, all over Europe, believed that they were "fitted by their intelligent activity to collaborate in all spheres, political, economic and social in the tasks which the aristocrats believed themselves alone able to fulfil". That is what the millions of proletarians all over the world today believe. They will fight for it. We believe they will succeed. You believe what? Their ancestors of five hundred years ago were not as developed as are the workers of today. But they fought for complete equality, for complete democracy, for universality. They failed, but they established the foundations of what we know as liberalism. Some of you still live on it, thin fare though it has become. The bourgeoisie had the feudal lords, in terror of these workers, rallied behind the absolute monarchy and the national state. Both humanism and the national state of the absolute monarchy were mediations of the mass proletarian desire for universality no longer in heaven but on earth. Humanism was the substitution of a liberal culture for the rich in place of the complete self-expression desired by the workers; the national state, disciplining the church, supplemented the concrete objective protection of wealth by abstract subjective claims of being the arbiter of justice, the guardian of law and order, and the protector of all the people. The contradictions, the antagonisms in the quest for universality had grown sharper than ever.

So, Messrs. doubters and sceptics and sneerers at dialectic, you will begin to see perhaps that what dialecticians believe in is not the result of religion. We have a certain conception of the nature of man based on history. When Marx and Engels wrote about the proletarian revolution in connection with the negation of the negation, when they wrote that in the present stage of society, man would either achieve this revolution or society would tear itself to pieces, they were being guided not by the dislocations of Marx's "psyche" as Edmund Wilson thinks or by any Hegelian triads or historical religiosity, as is the opinion of Burnham and Hook. It was a logical deduction from the experience of history. The struggle of the masses for universality did not begin yesterday. An intellectual like Dewey believes that men's quest is the quest for certainty. The intellectual believes that all men are intellectuals. That is wrong. Men seek not intellectual certainty. The quest is the mass quest for universality in action and in life. It is the moving force of history. And history has reached a climax because this quest has reached a climax.

Space compels rapid compression of the next great stages in the process of social development—the Protestant reformation and the French revolution. Rising capitalism expropriated the agricultural labourer and in the creation of wage-labour threw the masses further back from universality than they had ever been. Humanism had dragged universality from heaven down to earth and had by that made the contradiction between real and ideal an intolerable antagonism. The new proletariat could not play any great part in the struggles of the Protestant reformation, as the mature workers of the medieval towns had done. Hence the classes which took the lead were the bourgeoisie, the petty bourgeoisie and the peasants. Let us concentrate on one outstanding and familiar example, the English revolution.

The Puritans give us the key to the understanding of the whole period in the light of the struggle for democracy. The revolution of Dewey had shattered forever the claims of the Pope as mediator between God and man. It placed the responsibility for the individual's moral salvation squarely on the individual man. As Hegel put it: "This is the essence of the Reformation: Man is in his very nature destined to be free", and in his own peculiar but profound manner he sums up modern history. "Time, since that epoch, has had no other work to do than the formal imbuing of the world with this principle, in bringing the Reconciliation implicit (in Christianity) into objective and explicit realisation." If you stand it on its head, and say that the objective development of man in society has been the various stages through which various classes have sought to realise the freedom implicit in Christianity, a great truth will have been grasped.

But the mass of men do not think, and certainly do not act according to those terms. The Puritans of town and country, petty-bourgeois, and semi-proletarian, shut off from freedom by the state, attempted to establish democracy in religion. The sects each attempted to form a social community in which the individual would exercise the new freedom, unlimited except by the equal freedom of other men. James I of England did not misunderstand them one bit. He knew what their anti-Ecclesiasticism meant. To all their arguments for religious freedom he invariably croaked in reply, "No Bishop, no King." Their weakness was a social weakness, the lack of organisation which reflected the scattered character of their labour. But when the big bourgeoisie and some liberal aristocrats started the revolution, and the small farmers and small masters of the towns organised in the army, the Puritans showed what social passions were hidden behind their psalm-singing. In 1646, tired of the vacillations of their bourgeois and aristocratic leaders, they seized the person of the King and held him as a hostage. They then began negotiations with Cromwell and in the twin documents, the agreement of the People and the Heads of the Proposals, they put forward a programme for such a parliamentary democracy as was not even put forward in England until the Chartist movement two hundred years later. They put it forward to Cromwell; and in the discussion with Cromwell and his brother-in-law, Ireton, they raised the property question as a barrier to democracy in the most plain-spoken manner. These were not the Levellers, and the Diggers, who were the extreme left. These were the main body of the army. They were suppressed by a combination of fraud and force, but Cromwell, striking to the left, was compelled to strike at the right also. Charles I was executed and the monarchy was destroyed. In the familiar phrase, it was not monarchy but royalty which returned at the restoration. Monarchy in Britain was gone forever, destroyed by the religious democrats. They held power for eleven years, but as always, and particularly in this case, they were too few to represent the nation and the old process of mediation once more took place. They had cleared the way for capitalism, and nowhere was the antagonism sharper between developing capitalism and the masses of the nation than in England.

The history of the French revolution is familiar to all Marxists and the conclusions for our main argument are therefore easy to draw.

The intervention of the masses, its range and power, the social desires, the capacity for achievement and sacrifice, revealed itself to an educated Europe which had not dreamt that the shabby exterior of workers and peasants and the common people hid such colossal energies and such social needs. The quest for universality was no longer a secret. Liberty, equality and fraternity were the slogans of the revolution. If the Reformation had sought to establish a "democratic" freedom of religion, the French revolution attempted to establish a social freedom of political democracy. If out of the individual's responsibility for his own salvation, there had leapt democracy, out of his political freedom, there leapt communism. Robespierre's dictatorship was an attempt to establish the reign of virtue. But the French masses, not only Babeuf, saw and were ready for what was needed, drastic regulation and even confiscation of the property of the rich. The modern problem was posed. But it was the old problem in a new and more aggravated, a more contradictory form.

When the French revolution was over and men had time to think, it was seen that the revolution of reason and the mighty struggle for liberty, equality and fraternity had left men farther apart than ever before. Behind the formal equality before the law, capitalist production was accumulating wealth at one pole and misery, subordination and degradation at the other on a scale hitherto unknown. The universality of men, honour, loyalty, humanism, liberty, equality, fraternity, democracy, these were as abstract to the mass of men as the heaven of the early Popes. These ideals had a certain existence among the ruling classes, but thinking man could see that the needs and deprivations of the excluded mass reached with devastating effect upon the humanity of the rulers. The masses had tried to make a state a popular state. The result had been the creation of a monster such as had never been seen before and far surpassed in range and power the state of absolute monarchy. It was in the throes of this contradiction which was shaking all Europe that Hegel, the culmination of the German classical philosophers, set himself to study the problem of human destiny and elaborated a theory of knowledge. Hegel recognised what men were striving for and he recognised that the French revolution was a climax in this struggle.

Hegel understood Adam Smith and Ricardo. He understood the fragmentation and dehumanisation of man in the process of capitalist production. Many of Marx's most famous pages in *Capital* have as their direct origins some of Hegel's descriptions of the workers in capitalist industry. This was, for Hegel, the final insuperable barrier to any community of association among men. Hence universality for the mass of men was impossible. By means of his dialectical method he drew the necessary conclusions. We who live toward the end in the epoch of Hitler and Stalin can understand Hegel's conclusions better than most men of previous generations, with the exception of Marx.

Universality for the mass of men was impossible. Only the state, said Hegel, could embody universality for the community. But, in particular, the state was a defence against the revolutionary masses. Hegel had seen them and their activities in European history and now the French Revolution had shown that nothing could ever come of it. So it had been and it would ever be. At each stage, a few chosen individuals represented the abstract spirit of mankind. Universality had to be restricted to these. This was the basis of Hegel's idealism. But with the clear insight of a great scholar of both past and contemporary history, and by his mastery of his method, he analysed and drew his analysis to its conclusion. The state would have to organise production. The chaos of capitalist production would have to be disciplined by organising the separate industries into corporations. The state would be the state of the corporations. Universality being impossible to all men, the state bureaucracy would embody universality and represent the community. Hegel did not know the modern proletariat. He operated therefore on the basis of the inevitability of proletarian subordination. But grant him that premise and his dialectical method shows that he made an astonishing anticipation in thought of the inevitable end of bourgeois society—the totalitarian state. Hegel must not be misjudged. He wrote and propounded in the name of freedom and Reason. But those who today sneer at him and his dialectics are not fit even to wipe the dust off his books. To this day, except for the writings of the great Marxists, no single writer since the French revolution has so much to say that is indispensable to modern thought and particularly modern politics.

This is where Marx began. It was as impossible to go any farther along the road of Hegel as it is impossible to go farther than the totalitarian state of contemporary history. Beyond both lies only decay. Marx had to abandon the quest for universality or find a new basis for it.

A long line of European thinkers, Ricardo, Fourier, Saint-Simon, Feuerbach, and the classical economists, the ferment in Europe which preceded the revolutionary outburst in 1848, and, what Hegel had never seen, the emergence of the proletariat as an organised social force—these gave to Marx, already a master of Hegel's system, the impetus to the new system. Men had sought universality in heaven, in the freedom of religion, in the freedom of politics. Politics had failed. Neither Hegel nor Marx ever had any illusions about bourgeois democracy as a solution to the unquenchable desires and aspirations of men.

Nothing is more indicative of the philosophical character of Marxism and its organic continuity of the tradition of the great philosophers of Europe than the method by which Marx dismissed democratic politics. For Marx bourgeois democratic politics was a fraud, but like all the great panaceas from Christianity on, it was an expression of the perennial need historically conditioned. The productive process of capitalism denied any real community to men. And democratic politics, like religion, was a form of mediation by which men gained the illusion that they were all members of one social community, an illusion of universality. How not to remember Hitler's insistence that his tyrannical regime represented the folk community. The more the Nazi regime deprived the masses of all human rights, the more imperative it was to substitute an abstraction of abstractions to create the totality of existence, a sense of universality, without which men cannot live.

Marx reversed Hegel at all points. It was not an intellectual construction. Men were doing it and had been doing it all around him for years.

Hegel saw objective history as the successive manifestation of a world spirit. Marx placed the objective movement in the process of production. Hegel had been driven to see the perpetual quest for universality as necessarily confined to the process of knowledge. Marx reversed this and rooted the quest for universality in the need for the free and full development of all the inherent and acquired characteristics of the individual in productive and intellectual labour. Hegel had made the motive force of history the work of a few gifted individuals in whom was concentrated the social movement. Marx propounded the view that it was only when the ideas seized hold of the masses that the process of history moved. Hegel dreaded the revolt of the modern mass. Marx made the modern proletarian revolution the motive force of modern history. Hegel placed the future guardianship of society in the hands of the bureaucracy. Marx saw future society as headed for ruin except under the rulership of the proletariat and the vanishing distinction between intellectual and manual labour.

That was the conflict. That is the conflict today. The proletariat, said Marx, is revolutionary or it is nothing. The proletariat, he said, will conquer or society will destroy itself. The bureaucracy as conceived by Hegel he subjected to a merciless analysis. Let the reader think of Hitlerite Germany and Stalinist Russia and see how profound, how realistic, how anticipatory of the absolute crisis was the battle between the last of the great bourgeois philosophers and the first philosopher of the proletarian revolution. The smug anti-dialecticians have not yet caught up with this conflict between the masters of dialectic over a hundred years ago.

Hegel's conception of history is nothing other than the speculative expression of the Christian-German dogma of the opposition of spirit and manner, God and the world. This opposition expresses itself within history, within the human world itself, as a few chosen individuals, active spirits, confronting the rest of humanity, the spiritless mass matter. Hegel's conception of history presupposes an abstract or absolute spirit which develops itself so that humanity is only a mass bearing this spirit unconsciously or consciously. Within the empirical exoteric history, he sees a speculative esoteric history. The history of mankind is transformed into the history of the abstract spirit of mankind, beyond actual men.

Parallel with this Hegelian doctrine, there was developed in France the theory of the doctrinaires proclaiming the sovereignty of reason in opposition to the sovereignty of the people, in order to exclude the masses and rule alone. The result is that if the activity of the actual masses is nothing more than the activity of a mass of human individuals, the abstract universality, reason, spirit, possesses abstract expression exhausted in a few individuals. It depends upon the position and the strength of imagination of each individual whether he will pass as representative of "spirit".(Marx, *The Holy Family)*

Hegel had observed the unconscious development of the process of mediation. The bureaucracy of his corporate state was a conscious final mediation. Marx, in the *Critique* of Hegel's *Philosophy of Right* took up the challenge. The passage which follows might have been strange or difficult twenty years ago, not today. The reader must remember that both Hegel and Marx had common pre-suppositions—the recognition of the quest for universality, the recognition that the French revolution had brought the perpetual mediation of the growing contradictions to some final stage. The essence of the passage is that while Hegel believed that the bureaucracy can and must be a mediation for universality, Marx shows that the contradiction between objective and subjective, between ideal and real, concrete and abstract, has now reached such a stage, that the universality of the bureaucracy can have no reality. The quest for universality, embodied in the masses, constituting the great mass of the nation, forbids any mediation. The bureaucracy is compelled to become objectively the embodiment of the crassest materialism and subjectively, in its words, the embodiment of the crassest hypocrisy.

Here is the passage with certain words emphasised:

The "state formalism" which the bureaucracy is, is the "state as formalism" and as such formalism Hegel has described it. Since this "state formalism" is constituted as actual power and its own material content becomes itself, *it is self-understood that the "bureaucracy" is a network of practical illusions or the "illusion of the state". The bureaucratic spirit is a thoroughly Jesuitical theological spirit. The bureaucrats are the Jesuits and theologians of the state. The bureaucracy is the "republique pretre".*

Since the bureaucracy is essentially the "state as formalism", it is this also in its purpose. Thus the actual purpose of the state appears to the bureaucracy as a purpose against the state. The spirit of the bureaucracy is the "formal spirit of the state". *It makes therefore the "formal spirit of the state" or the actual emptiness of spirit of the state into a categorical imperative.* The bureaucracy thus is driven to the final end and purpose of the state. Since *the bureaucracy makes its "formal" purpose into its content, it gets into conflicts everywhere with the "real" purposes. It is therefore necessary to substitute the form for the content, the content for the form. The purposes of the state are transformed into administrative ones or the administrative purpose into state purposes. The bureaucracy is a circle out of which no one can get.* Its hierarchy is a hierarchy of knowledge. The apex entrusts to the lower circles insight into particular things, and the lower circles entrust to the apex insights into the universal and thus they mutually interchange.

The bureaucracy is the imaginary state besides the real state, the spiritualism of the state. *Everything therefore has a double meaning, a real one and a bureaucratic one*, as knowledge is double, real knowledge and bureaucratic (also the will). The real essence is handled according to its bureaucratic essence, according to its other worldly spiritual essence. *The bureaucracy has* the essence of the state, the *spiritual essence of society in its possession, it is its private property*. The general spirit of the bureaucracy is the secret, the mystery, guarded internally through the hierarchy, externally as the closed corporation. The apparent spirit of the state, the opinion of the state, appear therefore to the bureaucracy as a treason to its mysteries. *Authority is therefore the principle of its knowledge, and deifying of authority is its principle. Within itself, however, spiritualism becomes a crass materialism, the materialism of passive obedience, of belief in authority, the mechanism of fixed formal behaviour, fixed principles, observations, traditions.* As for the individual bureaucrat, the purpose of the state becomes a private purpose, a hunt for higher posts, for careers. First, he regards real life as material, for the spirit of this life has its exclusive existence in the bureaucracy. The bureaucracy must therefore proceed to make living as material as possible. Secondly, it is material for itself, i.e. so far as it becomes an object of bureaucratic handling, for its spirit is prescribed to it, its purpose lies outside of it, its existence is the existence of administration. The state exists henceforth only as fixed spirits of various offices, whose connection is subordination and passive obedience. *Actual science appears as without content, actual life is as dead, for the imaginary knowing and imaginary living pass as the essence.* The bureaucrat must therefore believe Jesuitically with the actual state, be this Jesuitism now conscious, or unconscious. It is, however, necessary that as soon as his opposite is knowing, he also achieve self-consciousness and purposeful Jesuitism.

That is the political anatomy of the Stalinist bureaucracy. In the review *After Ten Years*, I could touch only briefly (such are the trials of political minorities) upon the dehumanisation of the Russian bureaucracy itself. The Russian bureaucracy, as the Nazi bureaucracy in its time, represents essentially the opposition to the universality of the people in every single sphere of life. As the same article says:

In socialist society or in a society transitional to socialism, politics, science, art, literature, education all become truly social. The *individual* is able to exercise his gifts to the highest capacity, to become truly universal, because of the essentially *collective* life of the society in which he lives. Look at Stalinist society. No individual is more "political" than the individual in Stalinist society. Nowhere are art, literature, education, science, so integrated with "society". This is the appearance. In reality, never before has there been such a prostitution of all these things for the corruption and suppression of the direct producer, with the resulting degradation of the producers and managers alike.

Hitler called his state the truest democracy, his community was the folk community of the whole nation. His regime was "socialism". The Stalinist regime goes farther. The state possesses all the virtues. The internationalist conception of the human welfare is maintained through the connection with the corrupt and depraved communist parties and the constant appeal to the masses of the world. The state guarantees a "genuine" democracy, a "*genuine*" freedom of speech. Science, art and literature, like production, exist only to serve all the people. The state only administers the property which is the possession of all the people. Liberty, equality (within reason) and fraternity, honour, loyalty, chivalry, geniality, are the possession of all the people (except the Trotskyists). The leader is the leader because he possesses all these qualities to a superlative degree. Any oppositionist to the slightest of these claims becomes immediately an enemy devoid of all these virtues and fit only for extermination. The totality of the abstraction is to be explained only by the totality of the deprivation. Today this state is not only confined to Russia as an isolated phenomenon. It is spreading. Trotsky taught that the growth of the Stalinist state was due to the struggle over consumption. We cannot accept this at all. The Stalinist state is the completest expression of the class state—not the distorted beginning of something new but the culmination, the final form of the old. To believe that this state has roots only in consumption and not in the whole productive system is to saddle the concepts of Marxian socialism with a burden which they cannot indefinitely carry. The Stalinist state is a class state, a culmination of the old, not in any shape or form the beginning, however distorted, of the new.

Of precisely the same genre are the abstractions of the bourgeois democracies, different not in quality but only in the degree. Phrases like the "century of the common man" and the "four freedoms" are abstractions to satisfy the suppression of objective needs. The League of Nations of 1919 becomes the United Nations of 1947. The more concrete the negation of the need, the more abstract, empty and flamboyant becomes the subjective mediation.

There is a school of Marxists today who preach the ridiculous doctrine that in Russia today politics governs production. In reality, production governs politics. In appearance, the state takes hold of capital. In reality, capital takes hold of the state, and upon the mediation of the antagonisms of social and political life is superimposed and the antagonisms of capitalist production itself. In its most developed form, it is state capital.

It is this modern state, the negation of universality for so many millions, which is to be negated. The negation of this is the negation of the negation. The agent of this negation is the revolutionary proletariat. When the modern millions take hold of this state, they negate the root of their degradation, production itself, for to control the state of state capitalism is to control production itself. At this moment, the state begins to wither away.

I can sum up best by a quotation from an article I wrote in *New International* of June 1944:

But the outstanding feature of the contemporary world is that the *principles* for which Christianity stood in its best days are now regarded as matters of life and death by the average worker. This is no accident at all though we can only state the facts here. European civilisation must become a unity? Hundreds of millions of European workers know that this must be achieved or the continent will perish. Equality of nations? That, too, the great masses of Europe passionately desire, not as an ideal but to be able to live in peace. A central government to represent the interests of all? As late as 1935, Lord Cecil could get eleven million votes in a plebiscite in Britain supporting the idea of a League of Nations. And when workers say a League of Nations and collective security they mean it. And that early attempt to succour the poor, to help the afflicted, to teach the ignorant? The great mass of the workers in European countries conceive of Labour Parties as doing just that, within the conditions of the modern world.

Our anti-dialecticians believe the negation of negation and the inevitability of socialism are religion. But when one attempts to penetrate into *their* philosophy of history, one increasingly meets a vacuum or the most arbitrary combinations of historical phenomena, tied together by bits of string, by subjective analysis and a crude determinism which even sometimes has the presumption to call itself Marxism. For us there is no philosophy of history without Marxism, and there can be no Marxism without the dialectic. In the article quoted above, I continued:

He who would exhibit the Marxist method must grasp the full significance of that early uprising of the masses when Christianity proclaimed its message. We must watch not only the primitiveness and simplicity of its aims but their comprehensive scope. Then by slow degrees, through the centuries, we see one part of the aim becoming concrete for one section of the population, and then another part for another section. Ideas arise from concrete conditions to become partially embodied in social classes and give rise to further interrelations between the spiral of real and ideal, content and form. This is the dialectic to which Marx gave a firm materialistic basis in the developing process of production. As society develops, the possibilities for individual development of man become greater and greater, but the conflict of classes becomes sharper and sharper. We stand today at an extreme state of these interrelated phenomena of social development. When a modern worker demands the right of free speech, the right of free press, of free assembly, continuous employment, social insurance, the best medical attention, the best education, he demands in reality the "social republic". Spinoza and Kant would stand aghast at what the average worker takes for granted today. But he does not demand them as an individual or in the primitive manner the early Christian did. In America, for instance, there are some thirteen million workers organised for nothing else but the preservation and extension of these values. These are the values of modern civilisation. They are embodied in the very web and texture of the lives of the masses of the people. Never were such precious values so resolutely *held* as necessary to complete living by so substantial and so powerful a section of society. Socialism means simply the complete expansion and fulfillment of these values in the life of the individual. This can only be attained by the most merciless struggle of the whole class against its capitalist masters. The realisation of this necessity is the final prelude to full self-consciousness.

You still believe, gentlemen, that these ideas and conclusions are the result of a dialectical religion? Go your way. God be with you. Amen.

Bolshevism is above all a philosophy of life and a political conception. The political conception is the organised preparation for the proletarian revolution. Lenin was the originator of Bolshevism, the Marxism of our time. The world was to be saved by reason, but reason lay not in the heads of philosophers and intellectuals but in the actions of the masses. The world as we know it, under the control of its present masters, is unreasonable, chaotic, lacking in energy and creative force, gangrenous, barbarism. For Lenin, reason, order, historical creativeness, lay precisely in the forces which would destroy the old world. This is how he saw the councils of the workers, the soviets, and the revolutionary actions of the masses in 1905:

The old power, as a dictatorship of the minority, could maintain itself only by the aid of police stratagems, only by preventing and diverting the masses from participating in the government, from controlling the government. The old power persistently distrusted the masses, feared the light, maintained itself by means of deception. The new power, as a dictatorship of the overwhelming majority, could and did maintain itself only by winning the confidence of the great masses, only by drawing, in the freest, broadest, and most energetic manner, all the masses into the work of government. Nothing hidden, nothing secret, no regulations, no formalities. You are a working man? You wish to fight to liberate Russia from a handful of police thugs? Then you are our comrade. Choose your delegate at once, immediately. Choose as you think best. We shall willingly and gladly accept him as a full member of our Soviet of Workers' Deputies, of our Peasants' Committee, of our Soviet of Soldiers' Deputies, etc., etc. It is a power that is open to all, that does everything in sight of the masses, that is accessible to the masses, that springs directly from the masses; it is the direct organ of the masses and their will. Such was the new power, or rather its embryo, for the victory of the old power very soon trampled upon the tender shoots of this new plant. *(Selected Works*, vol. VII, pp. 252-3)

There are innumerable people opposed to bourgeois society, as they think, but who fear the uprising of the proletarian masses from that passive obedience, which is precisely the basis of bourgeois society. They want socialism but want to be sure of order, system, reason. Lenin had a different conception of where order was to be sought:

When the history of humanity moves forward at the speed of a locomotive (the petty-bourgeois intellectual) calls it a "whirlwind", a "deluge", the "disappearance" of all "principles and ideas". When history moves at the speed of a horse and cart he calls it reason, system. Then the masses themselves, with all their virgin primitiveness, their simple, rough determination, begin to make history to apply "principles and theories" directly and immediately, the bourgeoisie takes fright and wails that "reason is thrust into the background". (Is not the very opposite the case, you philistine heroes? Is it not precisely in such moments of history that the reason of the masses is displayed rather than the reason of single individuals? Is it not precisely at such times that reason of the masses becomes a living, active force, and not an armchair force?) When direct action by the masses is crushed by shootings, executions, floggings, unemployment and famine, when the bugs of professorial science, subsidised by Dubasov, crawl out of the cracks and begin to speak on behalf of the people, *in the name of the masses*, and sell and betray the interests of the latter to a privileged few—the knights of philistinism imagine that an epoch of peace and calm progress has set in, that "the turn of sense and reason has now come again. *(Selected Works*, vol. VII, pp. 260-1)

The bourgeois world is rejected completely. Only what destroys it is reasonable. But the reason of the masses was not merely destructive. It was destructive of the *bourgeois world*. But it was itself a "mighty creative force".

The point is that it is precisely the revolutionary periods that are distinguished for their greater breadth, greater wealth, greater intelligence, greater and more systematic activity, greater audacity and vividness of historical creativeness compared with periods of philistine, Cadet, reformist progress. But Mr Blank and Co. picture it the other way about. They pass off poverty as historical-creative wealth. They regard the inactivity of the suppressed, downtrodden masses as the triumph of the systematic activity of the bureaucrats and the bourgeoisie. They shout about the disappearance of sense and reason, when the picking to pieces of parliamentary bills by all sorts of bureaucrats and liberal "penny-a-liners" gives way to a period of direct political activity by the "common people", who in their simple way directly and immediately destroy the organs of oppression of the people, seize power, appropriate for themselves what was considered to be the property of all sorts of plunderers of the people in a word, precisely when the sense and reason of millions of downtrodden people is awakening, not only for reading books, but for action, for living human action, for historical creativeness. *(Selected Works*, vol. VII, pp. 261-2)

This is creative reason during the revolution and this is creative reason after the revolution. Readers of the following articles in this pamphlet and of the documents of our tendency will know that for us the economic planning of the new society must be the result of the same creativeness and energy of the masses expressed through their soviets, their councils, their party or parties. As we have shown in our pamphlet this was Lenin's conception. For us therefore, once the masses in Russia were totally subordinated to the bureaucracy, then capital as an economic force resumed sway, and objective economic law reasserted itself. The proletarians of the fourteenth century failed, but the masses today begin from a society in which the socialisation of the labour process is the dominant feature of the economy. The education, the training, the discipline, the social awareness, the material and spiritual needs of the great millions have reached astonishing proportions. These are the new economic forces. They are worldwide. If the earlier revolutions were outstanding peaks in a world in which the periphery was large, backward and stagnant, it is not so today. Disparate as are the economic levels of the United States and China, the world is today one system and a social unit. The need for universality of the individual man is only part of the need for universality in the world at large; "only with this universal development of productive forces is a *universal* intercourse between men established which produces in all nations simultaneously the phenomenon of the 'propertyless' mass (universal competition), makes each nation dependent on the revolutions of the others, and finally has put world-historical, empirically universal individuals in place of local ones." Thus Marx in *The German Ideology*, in 1846. Today we are at the end.

It would be a grave mistake not to attempt to show, however briefly, the theoretical link between these concepts and the practical activity of building a revolutionary organisation. The dialectician is often seriously thrown back by the fact that the great masses of the workers do not seem to think in a way that corresponds to these ideas. He should remember that the number who thought of socialist revolution in Russia in February 1917 was pitifully few. There was not one single republican in France on 14 July 1789. How many of the Founding Fathers advocated independence in 1776? The anticipations of these ideas accumulate and then under suitable conditions explode into a new quality.

But with the masses the matter goes even deeper. *They do not think as intellectuals do and this intellectuals must understand.* In one of his most remarkable pages Lenin confesses that at a critical moment of the Russian revolution he was performing the most critical of all tasks, evaluating the events of July in order to change the policy and organisation of the Bolshevik Party. He was living with a working-class family. The hostess placed bread on the table. "Look," says the host, "what fine bread. 'They' dare not give us bad bread now. And we had almost forgotten that good bread could be had in Petrograd." Let Lenin himself continue:

> I was amazed at this class evaluation of the July days. My mind had been revolving around the political significance of the event, weighing its importance in relation to the general course of events, analysing the situation that had given rise to this zigzag of history and the situation it would create. And debating how we must alter our slogans and party apparatus in order to adapt them to the changed situation. As for bread, I, who had never experienced want, never gave it a thought. Bread to me seemed a matter of course, a by-product, as it were, of the work of a writer. Fundamentally, the mind approaches the class struggle for bread by a political analysis and an extraordinarily complicated and involved path.
>
> But this representative of the oppressed class, although one of the better-paid and well-educated workers, took the bull by the horns with that astonishing simplicity and bluntness, with that firm resolution and amazingly clear insight, which is as remote from your intellectual as the stars in the sky. *(Selected Works*, vol. VI, pp. 280–81)

The key phrase in this passage is "although one of the better-paid and well-educated workers". Better paid and well-educated workers are very often corrupted by bourgeois education. It is the great millions, very often unorganised in unions but "disciplined, and united and organised by the very mechanism of capitalist production" itself that constitute the most heroic, the most self-sacrificing battalions of the new social order. They do not approach great questions by a complicated and involved path "as intellectuals do. Their most effective method of expression is action, corresponding to the astonishing simplicity, bluntness . . . firm resolution and amazingly clear insight" of their speech when they do speak. For long years they appear entirely subordinated to bourgeois ideas and the place bourgeois society has reserved for them. But they have their own ideas and in the continuous crisis and catastrophic decline of society, they have in recent decades repeatedly entered upon the field of history with world-shaking effects. Since 1917, no lasting victory has been theirs but the future is with them or there is no future.

Revolutionary politics consists of a conscious relating of the needs of the objective situation to the state of development of the masses. But decisive always is the objective situation, the world of today, and a superficial conception of the stage of development of the masses can be a terrible trap for the unwary. The objective conditions of our world demand universal solutions. It is absolutely impossible to propose a proletarian programme to counter the imperialism of the "Marshall Plan" without counterposing an international plan of socialist economic construction. That is the world in which we live.

In Europe, adequate wages, stable prices, food, housing and heating are no longer partial questions. Any reasonable satisfaction of the needs of the people demands a total reorganisation of the economy, a plan for continental rehabilitation, and close association with the economic power of the United States. Peace is indivisible. The need for universality stretches out from the hearth to the whole world.

But the same need exists intensively. It is the crime of capitalism that it uses men only partially. Labour bureaucracies which call on men only for votes or sending telegrams, are only partially mobilising vast stores of creative energy which are crying for release. Bankrupt economies which cannot mobilise the universal contained in modern man are doomed to remain bankrupt. That and nothing else but that can rebuild the vast wreck which is the modern world. Objectively and subjectively the solution of the crisis demands a total mobilisation of all forces in society. Partial solutions only create further disorders in the economy; partial demands, as such, because they are abstractions from the reality, lead only to disappointment; partial demands by leaders on the workers fail to mobilise their energies and leave them with a sense of frustration and hopelessness. Thus not only the concept but the need for universality reigns throughout all phases of society.

This was the constant theme of Trotsky before he was murdered in 1940. In previous periods the socialists fought for partial demands and held before the masses the social revolution as a distant goal. Today those days are over. The revolutionaries hold always before the masses the concept of the proletarian revolution but do not neglect to snatch this and that partial demand to better the position of the toilers and mobilise them for the final struggle.

This only is reason. The modern intellectual, once he breaks with bourgeois conceptions, finds a vast new world of ideas open before him. But he can pursue and present these ideas in their inner essence only with the inevitable universality of the revolutionary proletariat in mind. Without this there is no dialectic, and without dialectic, thought soon bogs down in the chaotic disintegration of the modern world. Quite different is it with the dialectical materialist. In his boldest flights, he is conscious that he will not exceed the real history of humanity which is being prepared by the revolutionary masses.

1947

10

The Revolutionary Answer to the Negro Problem in the USA

The decay of capitalism on a world scale, the rise of the CIO in the United States, and the struggle of the Negro people, have precipitated a tremendous battle for the minds of the Negro people and for the minds of the population in the US as a whole over the Negro question. During the last few years certain sections of the bourgeoisie, recognising the importance of this question have made a powerful theoretical demonstration of their position, which has appeared in *The American Dilemma* by Gunnar Myrdal, a publication that took a quarter of a million dollars to produce. Certain sections of the sentimental petty bourgeoisie have produced their spokesmen, one of whom is Lillian Smith. That has produced some very strange fruit, which however has resulted in a book which has sold some half a million copies over the last year or two. The Negro petty bourgeoisie, radical and concerned with communism, has also made its bid in the person of Richard Wright, whose books have sold over a million copies. When books on such a controversial question as the Negro question reach the stage of selling half a million copies it means that they have left the sphere of literature and have now reached the sphere of politics.

We can compare what we have to say that is new by comparing it to previous positions on the Negro question in the socialist movement. The proletariat, as we know, must lead the struggles of all the oppressed and all those who are persecuted by capitalism. But this has been interpreted in the past—and by some very good socialists too—in the following sense: the independent struggles of the Negro people have not got much more than an episodic value and as a matter of fact, can constitute a great danger not only to the Negroes themselves, but to the organised labour movement. The real leadership of the Negro struggle must rest in the hands of organised labour and of the Marxist party. Without that the Negro struggle is not only weak, but is likely to cause difficulties for the Negroes and dangers to organised labour. This, as I say, is the position held by many socialists in the past. Some great socialists in the United States have been associated with this attitude.

We, on the other had, say something entirely different.

We say, number one, that the Negro struggle, the independent Negro struggle, has a vitality and a validity of its own; that it has deep historic roots in the past of America and in present struggles; it has an organic political perspective, along which it is travelling, to one degree or another, and everything shows that at the present time it is travelling with great speed and vigour.

We say, number two, that this independent Negro movement is able to intervene with terrific force upon the general social and political life of the nation, despite the fact that it is waged under the banner of democratic rights, and is not led necessarily either by the organised labour movement or the Marxist party.

We say, number three, and this is the most important, that it is able to exercise a powerful influence upon the revolutionary proletariat, that it has got a great contribution to make to the development of the proletariat in the United States, and that it is in itself a constituent part of the struggle for socialism.

In this way we challenge directly any attempt to subordinate or to push to the rear the social and political significance of the independent Negro struggle for democratic rights. That is our position. It was the position of Lenin thirty years ago. It was the position of Trotsky which he fought for during many years. It has been concretised by the general class struggle in the United States, and the tremendous struggles of the Negro people. It has been sharpened and refined by political controversy in our movement, and best of all it has had the benefit of three or four years of practical application in the Negro struggle and in the class struggle by the Socialist Workers' Party during the past few years.

Now if this position has reached the stage where we can put it forward in the shape that we propose, that means that to understand it should be by now simpler than before; and by merely observing the Negro question, the Negro people, rather, the struggles they have carried on, their ideas, we are able to see the roots of this position in a way that was difficult to see ten or even fifteen years ago. The Negro people, we say, on the basis of their own experiences, approach the conclusions of Marxism. And I will have briefly to illustrate this as has been shown in the Resolution.

First of all, on the question of imperialist war. The Negro people do not believe that the last two wars and the one that may overtake us, are a result of the need to struggle for democracy, for freedom of the persecuted peoples by the American bourgeoisie. They cannot believe that.

On the question of the state, what Negro, particularly below the Mason-Dixon line, believes that the bourgeois state is a state above all classes, serving the needs of all the people? They may not formulate their belief in Marxist terms, but their experience drives them to reject this shibboleth of bourgeois democracy.

On the question of what is called the democratic process, the Negroes do not believe that grievances, difficulties of sections of the population, are solved by discussions, by voting, by telegrams to Congress, by what is known as the "American way".

Finally, on the question of political action, the American bourgeoisie preaches that Providence in its divine wisdom has decreed that there should be two political parties in the United States, not one, not three, not four, just two: and also in its kindness, Providence has shown that these two parties should be one, the

Democratic Party and the other, the Republican, to last from now until the end of time.

That is being challenged by increasing numbers of people in the United States. But the Negroes more than ever have shown—and any knowledge of their press and their activities tells us that they are willing to make the break completely with that conception.

As Bolsheviks we are jealous, not only theoretically but practically, of the primary role of the organised labour movement in all fundamental struggles against capitalism. That is why for many years in the past this position on the Negro question has had some difficulty in finding itself thoroughly accepted, particularly in the revolutionary movement, because there is this difficulty—what is the relation between this movement and the primary role of the proletariat—particularly because so many Negroes, and most disciplined, hardened, trained, highly developed sections of the Negroes, are today in the organised labour movement.

First the Negro struggles in the South are not merely a question of struggles of Negroes, important as those are. It is a question of the reorganisation of the whole agricultural system in the United States, and therefore a matter for the proletarian revolution and the reorganisation of society on socialist foundations.

Secondly, we say in the South that although the embryonic unity of whites and Negroes in the labour movement may seem small and there are difficulties in the unions, yet such is the decay of Southern society and such the fundamental significance of the proletariat, particularly when organised in labour unions, that this small movement is bound to play the decisive part in the revolutionary struggles that are inevitable.

Thirdly, there are one and a quarter million Negroes, at least, in the organised labour movement.

On these fundamental positions we do not move one inch. Not only do we not move, we strengthen them. But there still remains in question: what is the relationship of the independent Negro mass movement to the organised labour movement? And here we come immediately to what has been and will be a very puzzling feature unless we have our basic position clear.

Those who believed that the Negro question is in reality, purely and simply, or to a decisive extent, merely a class question, pointed with glee to the tremendous growth of the Negro personnel in the organised labour movement. It grew in a few years from three hundred thousand to one million; it is now one and a half million. But to their surprise, instead of this lessening and weakening the struggle of the independent Negro movement, *the more the Negroes went into the labour movement, the more capitalism incorporated them into industry, the more they were accepted in the union movement. It is during that period, since 1940, that the independent mass movement has broken out with a force greater than it has ever shown before.*

That is the problem that we have to face, that we have to grasp. We cannot move forward and we cannot explain ourselves unless we have it clearly. And I know there is difficulty with it. I intend to spend some time on it, because if that is settled, all is settled. The other difficulties are incidental. If, however, this one is not clear, then we shall continually be facing difficulties which we shall doubtless solve in time.

Now Lenin has handled this problem and in the Resolution we have quoted him. He says that the dialectic of history is such that small independent nations, small nationalities, which are powerless—get the word, please—*powerless*, in the struggle against imperialism *nevertheless* can act as one of the ferments, one of the bacilli, which can bring on to the scene the real power against imperialism—the socialist proletariat.

Let me repeat it please. Small groups, nations, nationalities, themselves powerless against imperialism, nevertheless can act as one of the ferments, one of the bacilli which will bring on to the scene the real fundamental force against capitalism—the socialist proletariat.

In other words, as so often happens from the Marxist point of view from the point of view of the dialectic, this question of the *leadership* is very complicated.

What Lenin is saying is that although the fundamental force is the proletariat, although these groups are powerless, although the proletariat has got to lead them, it does not by any means follow that they cannot do anything until the proletariat actually comes forward to lead them. *He says exactly the opposite is the case.*

They, by their agitation, resistance and the political developments that they can initiate, can be the means whereby the proletariat is brought on to the scene.

Not always, and every time, not the sole means, but one of the means. That is what we have to get clear.

Now it is very well to see it from the point of view of Marxism which developed these ideas upon the basis of European and Oriental experiences. Lenin and Trotsky applied this principle to the Negro question in the United States. What *we* have to do is to make it concrete, and one of the best means of doing so is to dig into the history of the Negro people in the United States, and to see the relationship that has developed between them and revolutionary elements in past revolutionary struggles.

For us the centre must be the Civil War in the United States and I intend briefly now to make some sharp conclusions and see if they can help us arrive at a clearer perspective. Not for historical knowledge, but to watch the movement as it develops before us, helping us to arrive at a clearer perspective as to this difficult relationship between the independent Negro movement and the revolutionary proletariat. The Civil War was a conflict between the revolutionary bourgeoisie and the Southern plantocracy. That we know. That conflict was inevitable.

But for twenty to twenty-five years before the Civil War actually broke out, the masses of the Negroes in the South, through the underground railroad, through revolts, as Aptheker has told us, and by the tremendous support and impetus that they gave to the revolutionary elements among the Abolitionists, absolutely prevented the reactionary bourgeoisie—(revolutionary later)—absolutely prevented the bourgeoisie and the plantocracy from coming to terms as they wanted to do.

In 1850 these two made a great attempt at a compromise. What broke that compromise? It was the Fugitive Slave Act. They could prevent everything else for the time being, but they could not prevent the slaves from coming, and the revolutionaries in the North from assisting them. So that we find that here in the history of the United States such is the situation of the masses of the Negro people and their readiness to revolt at the slightest opportunity, that as far back as the Civil War, in relation to the American bourgeoisie, they formed a force which *initiated* and *stimulated* and *acted as a ferment*.

That is point number one.

Point number two. The Civil War takes its course as it is bound to do. Many Negroes and their leaders make an attempt to get incorporated into the Republican Party and to get their cause embraced by the bourgeoisie. And what happens? The bourgeoisie refuses. It doesn't want to have Negroes emancipated.

Point number three. As the struggle develops, such is the situation of the Negroes in the United States, that the emancipation of the slaves becomes *an absolute necessity*, politically, organisationally and from a military point of view.

The Negroes are incorporated into the battle against the South. Not only are they incorporated here, but later they are incorporated also into the military government which smashes down the remnants of resistance in the Southern states.

But, when this is done, the Negroes are deserted by the bourgeoisie, *and there falls upon them a very terrible repression.*

That is the course of development in the central episode of American history.

Now if it is so in the Civil War, we have the right to look to see what happened in the War of Independence. It is likely—it is not always certain—but it is *likely* that we shall see there some *anticipations* of the logical development which appeared in the Civil War. They are there.

The Negroes begin by demanding their rights. They say if you are asking that the British free you, then we should have our rights, and furthermore, slavery should be abolished. The American bourgeoisie didn't react very well to that. The Negroes insisted—those Negroes who were in the North—insisted that they should be allowed to join the Army of Independence. They were refused.

But later Washington found that it was imperative to have them, and four thousand of them fought among the thirty thousand soldiers of Washington. They gained certain rights after independence was achieved. Then sections of the bourgeoisie who were with them deserted them. And the Negro movement collapsed.

We see exactly the same thing but more intensified in the Populist movement. There was a powerful movement of one and one quarter of a million Negroes in the South (The Southern Tenant Farmers' Association). They joined the Populist movement and were in the extreme left wing of this movement, when Populism was discussing whether it should go on with the Democratic Party or make the campaign as a third party. The Negroes voted for the third party and for all the most radical planks in the platform.

They fought with the Populist movement. But when Populism was defeated, there fell upon the Negroes between 1896 and about 1910 the desperate, legalised repression and persecution of the Southern states.

Some of us think it is fairly clear that the Garvey movement came and looked to Africa because there was no proletarian movement in the United States to give it a lead, to do for this great eruption of the Negroes what the Civil War and the Populist movement had done for the insurgent Negroes of those days.

And now what can we see today? Today the Negroes in the United States are organised as never before. There are more than half a million in the NAACP, and in addition to that, there are all sorts of Negro groups and organisations—the churches in particular—*every single one of which is dominated by the idea that each organisation must in some manner or another contribute to the emancipation of the Negroes from capitalist humiliation and from capitalist oppression.* So that the independent Negro movement that we see today and which we see growing before our eyes is nothing strange. It is nothing new. *It is something that has always appeared in the American movement at the first sign of social crisis.*

It represents a climax to the Negro movements that we have seen in the past. From what we have seen in the past, we would expect it to have its head turned towards the labour movement. And not only from a historical point of view but today concrete experience tells us that the masses of the Negro people today look upon the CIO with a respect and consideration that they give to no other social or political force in the country. To anyone who knows the Negro people, who reads their press—and I am not speaking here specially of the Negro workers—if you watch the Negro petty bourgeoisie—reactionary, reformist types as some of them are in all their propaganda, in all their agitation—whenever they are in any difficulties, you can see them leaning toward the labour movement. As for the masses of Negroes, they are increasingly pro-labour every day. So that it is not only Marxist ideas; it is not only a question of Bolshevik-Marxist analysis. It is not only a question of the history of Negroes in the US.

The actual concrete facts before us show us, and anyone who wants to see, this important conclusion, that the Negro movement logically and historically and concretely is headed for the proletariat. That is the road it has always taken in the past, the road to the revolutionary forces. Today the proletariat is that force. And if these ideas that we have traced in American revolutionary crises have shown some power in the past, such is the state of the class struggle today, such the antagonisms between bourgeoisie and proletariat, such, too, the impetus of the Negro *movement toward the revolutionary forces*, which we have traced in the past, is stronger today than ever before. So that we can look upon this Negro movement not only for what it has been and what it has been able to do—we are able to know as Marxists by our own theory and our examination of American history that it is headed for the proletarian movement, that it must go there. There is nowhere else for it to go.

And further we can see that if it doesn't go there, the difficulties that the Negroes have suffered in the past when they were deserted by the revolutionary forces, those will be ten, one hundred, ten thousand times as great as in the past. The independent Negro movement, which is boiling and moving, must find its way to the proletariat. If the proletariat is not able to support it, the repression of past times when the revolutionary forces failed the Negroes will be infinitely, I repeat infinitely, more terrible today.

Therefore our consideration of the independent Negro movement does not lessen the significance of the proletarian—the essentially proletarian—leadership. Not at all. It includes it. We are able to see that the mere existence of the CIO, its mere existence, despite the fakery of the labour leadership on the Negro question, as on all other questions, is a protection and a stimulus to the Negroes.

We are able to see and I will show in a minute that the Negroes are able by their activity to draw the revolutionary elements and more powerful elements in the proletariat to their side. We are coming to that. But we have to draw and emphasise again and again this important conclusion. If—and we have to take these theoretical questions into consideration—if the proletariat is defeated, if the CIO is destroyed, then there will fall upon the Negro people in the US such a repression, such persecution, comparable to nothing that they have seen in the past. We have seen in Germany and elsewhere the barbarism that capitalism is capable of in its death agony. The Negro people in the US offer a similar opportunity to the American bourgeoisie. The American bourgeoisie have shown their understanding of the opportunity the Negro question gives them to disrupt and to attempt to corrupt and destroy the labour movement.

But the development of capitalism itself has not only given the independent Negro movement this fundamental and sharp relation with the proletariat. It has created Negro proletarians and placed them as proletarians in what were once the most oppressed and exploited masses. But in auto, steel, and coal, for example, these proletarians have now become the vanguard of the workers' struggle and have brought a substantial number of Negroes to a position of primacy in the struggle against capitalism. The backwardness and humiliation of the Negroes that shoved them into these industries is the very thing which today is bringing them forward, and they are in the very vanguard of the proletarian movement from the very nature of the proletarian struggle itself. Now, how does this complicated interrelationship, the Leninist interrelationship express itself? Henry Ford that if he were so inclined.

The Negroes in the Ford plant were incorporated by Ford: first of all he wanted them for the hard, rough work. I am also informed by the comrades from Detroit he was very anxious to play a paternalistic role with the Negro petty bourgeoisie. He wanted to show them that he was not the person that these people said he was—look! he was giving Negroes opportunities in his plant.

Number three, he was able thus to create divisions between whites and Negroes that allowed him to pursue his anti-union, reactionary way.

What has happened within the last few years that is changed? The mass of the Negroes in the River Rouge plant, I am told, are one of the most powerful sections of the Detroit proletariat. They are leaders in the proletarian struggle, not the stooges Ford intended them to be.

Not only that, they act as leaders not only in the labour movement as a whole but in the Negro community. It is what they say that is decisive there. Which is very sad for Henry. And the Negro petty bourgeois have followed the proletariat. They are now going along with the labour movement: they have left Ford too. It is said that he has recognised it at last and that he is not going to employ any more Negroes. He thinks he will do better with women. But they will disappoint him too. . . .

Let us not forget that in the Negro people, there sleep and are now awakening passions of a violence exceeding, perhaps, as far as these things can be compared, anything among the tremendous forces that capitalism has created. Anyone who knows them, who knows their history, is able to talk to them intimately, watches them at their own theatres, watches them at their dances, watches them in their churches, reads their press with a discerning eye, must recognise that although their social force may not be able to compare with the social force of a corresponding number of organised workers, the hatred of bourgeois society and the readiness to destroy it when the opportunity should present itself, rests among them to a degree greater than in any other section of the population in the United States.

1948

11
The Class Struggle

The Stalinist theory is, despite zigzags, logical and consistent. Like every theory of all exploiters it is the theory of the rulers, the result of their struggles with the direct producers whom they exploit, and of competition with other rulers. The theory justifies Stalinist exploitation of the Russian workers. It can be used as a weapon against the traditional bourgeoisie in the struggle for the domination of the world working-class movement, without impairing the positions of the rulers inside Russia. It fortifies this position in the minds of the public which is interested in these questions and the members and fellow-travelers of the Stalinist parties.

The theory itself is an adaptation of the pre-Marxian petty-bourgeois ideology from Kant to Sismondi and Proudhon to the specific conditions of state-capitalism. That we shall go into later. But then as now its purpose can be summed up in a phrase—the radical reorganisation of society with the proletariat as object and not as subject, i.e. with no essential change in the mode of labour. The crisis of world capitalism, a hundred years of Marxism, thirty years of Leninism, impose upon this theory, as a primary task, the need to destroy and to obscure the theory of class struggle in the process of production itself, the very basis of Marxism and of the proletarian revolution.

The Stalinists did not arbitrarily "choose" this theory. Politics on the basis of the analysis of property is of necessity the struggle over correct policy and the correction of "evil". Social division, if not rooted in *classes*, automatically becomes a selection of personnel. The criterion not being a criterion of class becomes automatically a criterion according to competence, ability, loyalty, devotion, etc. This personnel, comprising many millions, the Stalinists have enshrined in the 1936 constitution under the name of "our socialist intelligentsia". The most competent, the most able, most loyal, most devoted, the elite become the party. The instrument of the party is the state. The corollary to disguising the rulers of production as "our socialist intelligentsia" is the Stalinist denunciation of bureaucracy as inefficiency, red tape, rudeness to workers, laziness, etc.—purely subjective characterizations.

The first task of the revolutionary International is clarification of this term, bureaucracy. The Stalinists take advantage of the fact that Marx often used the term, bureaucracy, in relation to the mass of state functionaries. But with the analysis of state-capitalism by Engels, the word bureaucracy began to take on a wider connotation. Where Engels says, "Taking over the great institutions for production and communication, first by joint-stock companies, later on by trusts, then by the state," he adds: "The bourgeoisie demonstrated to be a superfluous class. All its social functions are now performed by salaried employees" *(Socialism, Utopian and Scientific)*. These are bureaucrats.

The moment Lenin saw the Soviet, the new form of social organisation created by the masses, he began to extend the concept, bureaucracy, to include not only officials of government but the officials of industry, all who were opposed to the proletariat as masters. This appears all through *State and Revolution* and, in its most finished form, in the following:

We cannot do without officials *under capitalism, under the rule of the bourgeoisie*. The proletariat is oppressed, the masses of the toilers are enslaved by capitalism. Under capitalism democracy is restricted, cramped, curtailed, mutilated by all the conditions of wage-slavery, the poverty and the misery of the masses. This is why and the only reason why the officials of our political and industrial organisations are corrupted—or more precisely, tend to be corrupted—by the conditions of capitalism, why they betray a tendency to become transformed into bureaucrats, i.e. into privileged persons divorced from the masses and *superior to* the masses.

This is the *essence* of bureaucracy, and until the capitalists have been expropriated and the bourgeoisie overthrown, *even* proletarian officials will inevitably be "bureaucratised" to some extent.

Lenin's whole strategic programme between July and October is based upon the substitution of the power of the armed masses for the power of the bureaucrat, the master, the official in industry and in politics. Hence his reiterated statement that if you nationalize and even confiscate, it means nothing without workers' power. Just as he had extended the analysis of capitalism, state-capitalism and plan, Lenin was developing the theory of class struggle in relation to the development of capitalism itself. This strengthened the basic concepts of Marxism.

Marx says:

The authority assumed by the capitalist by his personification of capital in the direct process of production, the social function performed by him in his capacity as a manager and ruler of production, is essentially different from the authority exercised upon the basis of production by means of slaves, serfs, etc.

Upon the basis of capitalist production, the social character of their production impresses itself upon the mass of direct producers as a strictly regulating authority and as a social mechanism of the labour process graduated into a complete hierarchy. This authority is vested in its bearers only as a personification of the requirements of labour standing above the labourer. *(Capital*, Vol. III)

This is capitalist production, this hierarchy. The special functions are performed "within the conditions of production themselves by special agents in opposition to the direct producers". These functionaries, acting against the proletariat in production, are the enemy. If this is not understood, workers' control of production is an empty phrase.

With the development of capitalism into state-capitalism, as far back as 1917, Lenin, in strict theory, denounced mere confiscation in order to concentrate his whole fire upon the hierarchy in the process of production itself, and to counterpose to this, workers' power. It thus becomes ever more clear why the Stalinists in their theory will have nothing whatever to do with state-capitalism and rebuke and stamp out any suggestions of it so sharply. The distinction that Lenin always kept clear has now developed with the development of capitalism over the last thirty years. It has now grown until it becomes the dividing line between the workers and the whole bureaucratic organization of accumulated labour, science and knowledge, acting against the working class in the immediate process of production and everywhere else. This is the sense in which the term bureaucracy must be used in Russia.

It is upon this Leninist *analysis* that the theory of state-capitalism rests and inseparable from this theory, the concept of the *transition* from social labour as compulsion, as barracks discipline of capital, to social labour as the voluntary association, the voluntary labour discipline of the labourers themselves. Lenin, in *The Great Beginning*, theoretically and practically wrote an analysis of labour in Russia which the development of society *on a world scale* during the last thirty years now raises to the highest position among all his work on Russia. This must be the foundation of a Marxist approach to the problems of economics and politics under socialism. In that article Lenin did two things:

(a) established with all the emphasis at his command that the essential character of the dictatorship of the proletariat was "not violence and not mainly violence against the exploiters." It was the unity and discipline of the proletariat trained by capitalism, its ability to produce "a higher social organization of labour";

(b) analysed the communist days of labour given to the Soviet state and sought to distinguish the specific social and psychological characteristics of a new form of labour, and the relation of that to the productivity of labour.

With all its mighty creations of a Soviet state and Red Army, and the revolution in the superstructure, it is here that the Russian socialist revolution could not be completed. The "historical creative initiative" in production, the "subtle and intricate" relations of a new labour process—these never developed for historical reasons. But there has been a vast development of capitalism and of the understanding of capitalism all over the world since the early days of the Russian revolution. The British Chancellor of the Exchequer, the Stalinist bureaucracy, the whole capitalist class in the US (and in the US more than anywhere else)—all declare that the problem of production today is the productivity of labour and the need to harness the human interest, i.e. the energy and ability of the worker. Many of them are aware that it is the labour process itself which is in question.

What they see partially, contemporary Marxism must see fully and thereby restore the very foundations of Marxism as a social science.

It is in the concrete analysis of labour inside Russia and outside Russia that the Fourth International can find the basis of the profoundest difference between the Third International and the Fourth International. The whole tendency of the Stalinist theory is to build up theoretical barriers between the Russian economy and the economy of the rest of the world. The task of the revolutionary movement, beginning in theory and as we shall see, reaching to all aspects of political strategy, is to break down this separation. The development of Russia is to be explained by the development of world capitalism and specifically, capitalist production in its most advanced stage, in the United States. Necessary for the strategic task of clarifying its own theory and for building an irreconcilable opposition to Stalinist, it is not accidental that this method also is the open road for the revolutionary party to the socialism inherent in the minds and hearts, not only of the politically advanced but the most backward industrial workers in the United States.

It is for this reason that the analysis of the labour process in the United States must concern us first and only afterwards the labour process in Stalinist Russia.

Roughly, we may attribute the decisive change in the American economy to the last part of the nineteenth century, taking 1914 as a convenient dividing line. After World War I the Taylor system, experimental before the war, becomes a social system, the factory laid out for continuous flow of production, and advanced planning for production, operating and control. At the same time there is the organization of professional societies, management courses in college curricula and responsible management consultants. Between 1924 and 1928 there is rationalization of production and retooling (Ford).[1] Along with it are the tendencies to the scientific organization of production, to closer coordination between employers, fusion with each other against the working class, the intervention of the state as mediator and then as arbiter.

For the proletariat there is the constantly growing subdivision of labour, decrease in the need of skills, and determination of sequence of operations and speed by the machine. The crisis of 1929 accelerated all these processes. The characteristic, most advanced form of American production becomes Ford. Here production consists of a mass of hounded, sweated labour (in which, in Marx's phrase, the very life of society was threatened); and this production only by means of a hired army (Bennett) of gangsters, thugs, supervisors who run production by terror, in the plant, in the lives of the workers outside production, and in the political control of Detroit. Ford's regime before unionisation is the prototype of production relations in fascist Germany and Stalinist Russia.

But—and without this, *all* Marxism is lost—inextricably intertwined with the totalitarian *tendency* is the response of the working class. A whole new layer of workers, the result of the economic development, burst into revolt in the CIO. The CIO in its inception aimed at a revolution in production. The workers would examine what they were told to do and then decide whether it was satisfactory to them or not. This rejection of the basis of capitalist economy is the preliminary basis of a socialist economy. The next positive step is the total management of industry by the proletariat. Where the Transitional Programme says that the "CIO is the most indisputable expression of the instinctive striving of the American workers to raise themselves to the level of the tasks imposed upon them by history", it is absolutely correct. The task imposed upon them by history is socialism and the outburst, in aim and method, was the first instinctive preparation of the social revolution.

Because it was and could not be carried through to a conclusion, the inevitable counterpart was the creation of a labour bureaucracy. The history of production since is the corruption of the bureaucracy and its transformation into an instrument of capitalist production, the restoration to the bourgeoisie of what it had lost in 1936, the right to control production standards. Without this mediating role of the bureaucracy, production in the United States would be violently and continuously disrupted until one class was undisputed master.

The whole system is in mortal crisis from the reaction of the workers. Ford, whose father fought the union so uncompromisingly as late as 1941, now openly recognises that as far as capitalism is concerned, improvements in technology, i.e. the further mechanisation of labour, offers no road out for the increase of productivity which rests entirely with the working class. At the same time, the workers in relation to capitalism resist any increase in productivity. The resistance to speed-up does not necessarily mean as most think that workers are required to work beyond normal physical capacity. It is resistance by the workers to any increased productivity, i.e. any increase of productivity by capitalist methods. Thus, both sides, capital and labour, are animated by the fact that for each, in its own way, the system has reached its limit.

The real aim of the great strikes of 1946 and since is the attempt to begin on a higher stage what was initiated in 1936. But the attempt is crippled and deflected by the bureaucracy, with the result that rationalization of production, speed-up, intensification of exploitation are the order of the day in industry.

The bureaucracy inevitably must substitute the struggle over consumption, higher wages, pensions, education, etc., for a struggle in production. This is the basis of the welfare state, the attempt to appease the workers with the fruits of labour when they seek satisfaction in work itself. The bureaucracy must raise a new social programme in the realm of consumption because it cannot attack capitalism at the point of production without destroying capitalism itself.

The series of pension plans which have now culminated in the five-year contract with General Motors is a very sharp climax of the whole struggle. This particular type of increase in consumption coordinates the workers to production in a special manner after they have reached a certain age. It confines them to being an industrial reserve army, not merely at the disposal of capital in general but within the confining limits of the specific capitalist factory which employs them. The effect, therefore, is to reinforce control both of employers and bureaucracy over production.

But along with this intensification of capitalist production and this binding of the worker for five years *must* go inevitably the increase of revolt, wildcat strikes, a desperate attempt of the working class to gain for itself conditions of labour that are denied to it both by the employers and labour bureaucracy. While the bureaucracy provides the leadership for struggles over consumption, it is from the workers on the line that emerges the initiative for struggles over speed-up. That is precisely why the bureaucracy, after vainly trying to stop wildcat strikes by prohibiting them in the contract, has now taken upon itself the task of repressing by force this interruption of production. It expels from the unions workers who indulge in these illegal stoppages, i.e. who protest against the present stage of capitalist production itself. The flying squads, originated by the union for struggle against the bourgeoisie, are now converted by the bureaucracy into a weapon of struggle against the proletariat, and all this in the name of a higher standard of living, greater consumption by the workers, but in reality to ensure capitalist production.

The increase of coercion and terror by the bureaucracy increases the tendency of the workers to violent explosion. This tendency, taken to its logical conclusion, as the workers will have to take it, means the reorganisation of the whole system of production itself—socialism. Either this or the complete destruction of the union movement as the instrument of proletarian emancipation and its complete transformation into the only possible instrument of capital against the proletariat at this stage of production.

This is the fundamental function of the bureaucracy *in Russia*. Already the tentative philosophy of bureaucracy in the United States, its political economy of regulation of wages and prices, nationalisation and even planning, its ruthless political methods, show the organic similarity of the American labour bureaucracy and the Stalinists. The struggle in the United States reveals concretely what is involved in the Stalinist falsification of the Marxist theory of accumulation, etc., and the totalitarian violence against the proletariat which this falsification protects.

In the recent coal strikes, despite the wage and welfare gains of the miners, the heads of the operators declared that control of production had been restored to them by the two-year contract. C.E. Wilson, president of General Motors, hailed the five-year settlement as allowing the company "to run our own plants," and as "the union's complete acceptance of technological progress". Reuther hailed the General Motors settlement as a "tremendous step forward" in "stabilizing labour relations at GM". An editor of *Fortune* magazine hailed the contract as the harbinger of "new and more meaningful associative principles" with the corporation as "the center of a new kind of community".

The Stalinist bureaucracy is the American bureaucracy carried to its ultimate and logical conclusion, both of them products of production in the epoch of state-capitalism. To reply to this that the bureaucracy can never arrive at maturity without a proletarian revolution is the complete degradation of Marxist theory. Not a single Marxist of all the great Marxists who analysed state-capitalism, not one ever believed capitalism would reach the specific stage of centralisation. It was because of the necessity to examine all tendencies in order to be able to mobilise theoretical and practical opposition in the proletariat that they followed the dialectical method and *took these tendencies to their conclusions as an indispensable theoretical step*. In the present stage of our theory it is the scrupulous analysis of production in the United States as the most advanced stage of world capitalism that forms the indispensable prelude to the analysis of the labour process in Russia.

The Russian revolution of October 1917 abolished feudalism with a thoroughness never before achieved. The stage was therefore set for a tremendous economic expansion. Lenin sought to mobilise the proletariat to protect itself from being overwhelmed by this economic expansion. The isolated proletariat of backward Russia was unable to do this. The subsequent history of the labour process of Russia is the telescopic re-enactment of the stages of the process of production of the United States; and, added to this, the special degradation imposed upon it by the totalitarian control of the bureaucracy and the plan.

The Russian revolution in 1917 substituted for the authority of the capitalist in the factory the *workers' control of production*. Immediately there appeared *both* the concrete development of self-initiative in the factory *and* the simplification of the state apparatus outside. There was workers' control, with some capitalists as owners, but *mere* owners. Production conferences, not of bureaucracy but of workers, decided what and how to produce. What capitalists there remained seemed to vanish into thin air once their economic power was broken, and workers' control was supplemented the following year by nationalisation of the means of production. The red thread that runs through these first years of workers' rule, workers' control, seems to suffer a setback under war communism in general and with order 1042[2] in particular. It takes less than a year for the workers to force a change, and the all-important trade union debate of 1920 follows. Lenin fights successfully both Trotsky, the administrator, and Shlyapnikov, the syndico-anarchist, and strives to steer a course in consonance with the Declaration of the Rights of the Toilers, that only the masses "from below" can manage the economy, and that the trade unions are the transmission belts to the state wherein "every cook can be an administrator".

In the transition period between 1924 and 1928 when the First Five-Year Plan is initiated, the production conferences undergo a bureaucratisation, and with it the form of labour. There begins the alienation of mass activity to conform to specified quantities of *abstract labour* demanded by the plan "to catch up with capitalism." The results are:

(a) In 1929 ("the year of decision and transformation") there crystallises in direct opposition to management by the masses "from below" the *conference of the planners*, the engineers, economists, administrators; in a word, the specialists.

(b) Stalin's famous talk of 1931 "put an end to depersonalisation". His "six conditions" of labour contrasted the masses to the "personalised" individual who would outdo the *norms of the average*. Competition is not on the basis of creativity and Subbotniks[3] but on the basis of the *outstanding* individual (read: bureaucrat) who will devise norms and have others surpass them.

(c) 1935 sees Stakhanovism and the definitive formation of an aristocracy of labour. Stakhanovism is the pure model of the manner in which foremen, overseers and leadermen are chosen in the factories the world over. These individuals, exceptional to their class, voluntarily devote an intensity of their labour to capital for a brief period, thus setting the norm, which they personify, to dominate the labour of the mass for an indefinite period.

With the Stakhanovites, the bureaucratic administrators acquire a social base, and alongside, there grows the instability and crisis in the economy. It is the counterrevolution of state-capital.

(d) Beginning with 1939 the mode of labour changes again. In his report on the Third Five-Year Plan, Molotov stressed the fact that it was insufficient to be concerned merely with the mass of goods produced. The crucial point for "outstripping capitalism" was *not the mass* but the *rate* at which that mass was produced. It was necessary that per capita production be increased, that is to say that each worker's productivity be so increased that fewer workers would be needed to obtain an ever greater mass of goods. Intensity of labour becomes the norm.

During the war the norm turned out to be the most vicious of all forms of exploitation. The Stalinists sanctified it by the name of "socialist emulation". "Socialist emulation" meant, firstly, that the pay incentive that was the due of a

Stakhanovite was no longer the reward of the workers as individuals, once they *as a mass* produced according to the new raised norm. In other words, the take-home pay was the same despite the speed-up on a plantwide basis. Secondly, and above all, competition was no longer limited to individual workers competing on a piecework basis, nor even to groups of workers on a plantwide basis, but was extended to cover *factory against factory*.

Labour reserves are established to assure the perpetuation of skills and a sufficient labour supply. Youths are trained from the start *to labour as ordered.* The climax comes in 1943 with the "discovery" of the conveyor belt system. This is the year also of the Stalinist admission that the law of value functions in Russia.

We thus have:

1918: The Declaration of the Rights of Toilers—*every* cook an administrator.

1928: *Abstract* mass labour—"lots" of it "to catch up with capitalism".

1931: Differentiation within labour—"personalised" individual; the pieceworker the hero.

1935: Stakhanovism, *individual competition* to surpass the norm.

1936-37: Stalinist constitution; Stakhanovites and the intelligentsia *singled out* as those "whom we respect".

1939-41: *Systematisation* of piecework; factory competing against factory.

1943: "The year of the conversion to the conveyor belt system."

Whereas in 1936 we had the singling out of a ruling class, a "simple" division between mental and physical work, we now have the stratification of mental and physical labour. Leontiev's *Political Economy in the Soviet Union* lays stress not merely on the intelligentsia against the mass, but on specific skills and differentials, lower, higher, middle, in-between and highest.

If we take production since the Plan, not in the detail we have just given, but only the major changes, we can say 1937 closes one period. It is the period of "catching up with and outdistancing capitalism" which means *mass* production and relatively simple planning. But competition on a *world* scale and the approaching Second World War is the severest type of capitalist competition for world mastery. This opens up the new period of per capita production as against mere "catching up". Planning must now include productivity of labour. Such planning knows and can know only machines and *intensity* of exploitation. Furthermore, it includes what the Russians call *rentable'nost'*, that is to say profitability. The era of the state helping the factory whose production is especially needed is over. The factory itself must prove its worthiness by showing a profit and a profit big enough to pay for "*ever-expanded*" production. And that can be done only by ever-expanded production of abstract labour in mass *and in rate.*

Nowhere in the world is labour so degraded as in Russia today. We are here many stages beyond the degradation which Marx described in *General Law of Accumulation.* For not merely is the Russian labourer reduced to an appendage to a machine and mere cog in the accumulation of capital. Marx said that the reserve army kept the working labourer riveted to his martyrdom. In Russia, because of the power to plan, the industrial reserve army is planned. Some 15 million laborers are planned in direct forced labour camps. They are organized by the MVD (GPU) for production. The disciplinary laws which began with reduction in wages for coming 15 minutes late have as their final stage, for lack of discipline, "corrective labour", i.e. the concentration camp.

What the American workers are revolting against since 1936 and holding at bay, this, and nothing else but this, has overwhelmed the Russian proletariat. The rulers of Russia perform the same functions as are performed by Ford, General Motors, the coal operators and their huge bureaucratic staffs. Capital is not Henry Ford; he can die and leave his whole empire to an institution; the plant, the scientific apparatus, the method, the personnel of organization and supervision, the social system which sets these up in opposition to the direct producer will remain. Not inefficiency of bureaucrats, not "prestige, powers and revenue of the bureaucracy", not consumption but capital accumulation in its specifically capitalist manner, this is the analysis of the Russian economy.

To think that the struggle in Russia is over consumption not only strikes at the whole theory of the relationship of the superstructure to the productive mechanism. In practice, today, the crisis in Russia is manifestly the crisis in production. Whoever is convinced that this whole problem is a problem of consumption is driven away from Marxism, not towards it.

It was Marx's contention that the existence of a labouring force compelled to sell its labour-power in order to live meant automatically the system of capitalist accumulation. The capitalist was merely the agent of capital. The bureaucrats are the same. Neither can use nor knows any other mode of production. A new mode of production requires primarily that they be totally removed or totally subordinated.

At this point it is convenient to summarize briefly the abstract economic analysis of sate-capitalism. We have never said that the economy of the United States is the *same* as the economy of Russia. What we have said is that, however great the differences, the fundamental laws of capitalism operate. It is just this that Marx indicated with his addition to *Capital* dealing with complete centralisation of capital "in a given country".

"A given country" meant one specific country, i.e. the laws of the world-market still exist. If the whole world became centralised then there would be a new society (for those who want it) since the *world market* would have been destroyed. Although *completely centralised* capital "in a given country" can plan, it cannot plan away the contradictions of capitalist production. If the *organic composition* of capital on a world scale is 5 to 1, moving 6 to 1, to 7 to 1, etc., centralised capital in a given country *has to keep pace with that*. The only way to escape it would be by a productivity of labour so great that it could keep ahead of the rest and still organise its production for use. Such a productivity of labour is impossible in capitalism which knows only the law of value and its consequence, accumulated labour and sweating proletarians. That is precisely why Engels wrote that though formally, i.e. abstractly, complete state property could overcome the contradictions, actually it could not, the "workers remain proletarians". The whole long dispute between underconsumption and rate of profit theorists has now been definitively settled precisely by the experience of Russia.

Lenin in 1917 repeated that state-capitalism without the Soviets meant "military penal labour" for the workers. The Soviet power was the road to socialism. The struggle in Russia and outside is the struggle against "military penal labour" and for the Soviet power. The revolt which gave birth to the CIO prevented American capital from transforming the whole of American production and society into the system which Ford and Bennett had established. This monstrous burden would have driven capital still further along the road of accumulation of capital, domination over the direct producer or accumulation of misery, lowered productivity, barbarism, paralysis and gangrene in all aspects of society. That was Germany. That would be the plan, the plan of capital, and with state property it is more free than before to plan its own ruin.

The totalitarian state in Russia prevents the workers from making their social and political experiences in open class struggle. But by so doing, it ensures the unchecked reign of capital, the ruin of production and society, and the inevitability of total revolution.

The decisive question is not whether centralisation is complete or partial, heading towards completeness. The vital necessity of our time is to lay bare the violent antagonism of labour and capital at this definitive stage of centralisation of capital. Whether democratic or totalitarian both types of society are in permanent decline and insoluble crisis. Both are at a stage when only a total reorganisation of social relations can lift society a stage higher. It is noteworthy that in the United States the capitalist class is aware of this, and the most significant work that is being done in political economy is the desperate attempt to find some way of reconciling the working class to the agonies of mechanised production and transferring its implacable resistance into creative cooperation. That is of educational value and many of its findings will be used by the socialist proletariat. In Russia this resistance is labelled "remnants of capitalist ideology" and the whole power of the totalitarian state is organised to crush it in theory as well as in fact.

We shall see that upon this theoretical analysis the whole strategy of revolutionary politics is qualitatively differentiated from Stalinist, inside and outside Russia. The Stalinists seek to establish themselves in the place of the rival bureaucracy. The rival bureaucracy seeks to substitute itself in the place of Stalinist. The Fourth International must not seek to substitute itself for either of these, not after, not during nor before the conquest of power. Theory and practice are governed by the recognition of the necessity that the bureaucracy as such must be overthrown.

We can now come to a theoretical conclusion about the question of plan and with it, nationalisation. For the capitalist mode of labour in its advanced stages, the bureaucratic-administrative plan can become the greatest instrument of torture for the proletariat that capitalism has yet produced. State property and total planning are nothing else but the complete subordination of the proletariat to capital. That is why in *The Invading Socialist Society* we summed up our total theory in two points, the first of which is:

"1. It is the task of the Fourth International to drive as clear a line between bourgeois nationalisation and proletarian nationalisation as the revolutionary Third International drove between bourgeois democracy and proletarian democracy."

All theory for our epoch must begin here.

But aren't state property and the plan progressive?

State property as such and plan as such are metaphysical abstractions. They have a class content. Aren't trusts progressive, Lenin was asked in 1916. He replied:

It is the work of the bourgeoisie to develop trusts, to drive children and women into factories, to torture them there, corrupt them and condemn them to the utmost misery. We do not "demand" such development; we do not "support" it; we struggle against it. But *how* do we struggle? We know that trusts and factory work of women are progressive. We do not wish to go backwards to crafts, to pre-monopolist capitalism, to domestic work of women. Forward through the trusts, etc., and beyond them toward socialism! *(The Bolsheviks and the World War)*

We reply similarly. This is Marxism—the antagonism of classes. Under capitalism, private or state, all science, knowledge, organization, are developed only at the expense and degradation of the proletariat. But at the same time capitalism organizes the proletariat for struggle. We do not "demand" or "support" plan. We proposed to substitute proletarian power and subordinate plan to the revolutionary struggle of the proletariat.

Where does orthodox Trotskysim stand on this? Every member knows the answer. Nowhere. Its conception of plan is summarized in the slogan in the Transitional Programme: "The plan must be revised from top to bottom in the interest of the producers and consumers."

The capitalist plan cannot be revised except in the interests of capital. It is not the plan that is to be revised. It is the whole mode of production which is to be overthrown.

The whole analysis is in terms of (to use the underlined phrases of the Transitional Programme) "*social inequality*" and " *political inequality*". In *The Revolution Betrayed* the chapter entitled "The Struggle for Productivity of Labour" deals with money and plan, inflation, rehabilitation of the ruble. It says that analysis of Stakhanovism proves that it is a vicious form of piecework. But it soon returns to the question of the ruble. And it finally ends on the note that the Soviet administrative personnel is "far less adequate to the productive tasks than the workers". Therefore, what is needed is more competence, more efficiency, less red tape, less laziness, etc. If the Russian bureaucracy were more efficient, more scientific, etc., the results for the Russian proletarian would be worse.

The chapter "Social Relations in the Soviet Union" in *The Revolution Betrayed* deals with the privileges, wages, etc. of the bureaucracy in relation to the worker. Neither in the Transitional Programme nor *The Revolution Betrayed* does analysis of the worker in the production process find any place, except where in the Programme the slogan is raised, "factory committees should be returned the right to control production". In the analyses of orthodox Trotskysim there are a few references here and there to creative initiative being needed at this stage. That is all.

All the slogans in the Transitional Programme do nothing more than demand the restoration of democracy to where it was in 1917, thereby showing that the whole great experience of thirty years has passed orthodox Trotskysim by. World capitalism has moved to the crisis and counterrevolution in production. The programme for the reintroduction of political democracy does no more than reintroduce the arena for the reintroduction of a new bureaucracy when the old one is driven out.

But, after all, production relations must include somewhere workers, labour, the labour process—the place where the population is differentiated by function. The World Congress Resolution *(Fourth International*, June 1948) quotes from *The Revolution Betrayed* an elaborate summary by Trotsky of his own position in 1936. The worker in the labour process is not mentioned. The resolution asks: what alterations have to be made in the analysis following the development of the past eleven years? It begins:

"... the social differentiation is the result of bourgeois norms of *distribution*; it has not yet entered the domain of ownership of the means of production."

The struggle out of which the CIO was born, the domination of the machine, the drive for greater productivity, what about that? The orthodox Trotskyist in 1950 would have to reply: the question is not a question of production. It is a question of collective ownership; it is a question of the thieving bureaucracy taking for itself consumption goods which belong to the workers; it is a question of whether the bureaucracy passes laws of inheritance; it is a question in 1950 as it was in 1934 of whether the tendency to primitive accumulation will restore private property, etc. etc. Is this an injustice to orthodox Trotskyism? If it is, then *what* would it reply, and where is any other reply to be found?

1950

12
Whitman and Melville

Because of the peculiarly free conditions of democracy in the United States, the American intellectuals as a social group were the first to face as a practical question the beginnings of a problem which has been fully recognized during the last twenty years—the relation of individualism to democracy as a whole. By contrast, in Europe, this question was narrowed and concretised by all sorts of special conditions. Thus Dostoyevsky, Flaubert, Rimbaud had precise problems to deal with and the universality of their work emerges from the concreteness of the conditions. Problems were posed for the American writers in a very different way—hence the vagueness and the uncertainty of their work, its inability to achieve significant form or, where it did as in Hawthorne, the narrowness and limitations showed. But now, as society faces its fundamental problems, the work of these writers assumes a new significance. Their only rival is the Russian literature of the last century and, while it serves no purpose to make invidious comparisons, this much can be said—world war one made the writings of the Russians familiar to the general modern reader; world war two already seems to have lifted American literature of the mid-nineteenth century to a new level.

Whitman is the most comprehensive of the American intellectuals of this period, one of the most unusual figures in the realm of literature and an American who is the opposite pole to Melville. Like Melville he embodies American and international characteristics; like Melville what he represents, what he expressed is clearer than ever today. But whereas Melville grows from year to year, Whitman shrinks. This poet, with the reputation of having devoted his life and work to the struggle for American and world democracy, may yet end by being excoriated by the popular masses everywhere, if they take any notice of him at all. He is, on the surface, an enigmatic figure. But there is no enigma about him really. We have to ignore all the things Whitman said about himself and depend entirely upon the literature as literature—by watching that we shall be able to reconstruct the real Whitman.

As an artist, Whitman is first, last and nothing else but a lyric poet, self-centred, individualistic, in the tradition of the great individualistic Romantic writers and poets—from Rousseau through Wordsworth, Keats and Shelley to Lamartine,

DeVigny and Debusset. All this shouting, and real hoarse-voiced shouting it is, about democracy is only because of this.

European Romantic individualism everywhere was expressed as a revolt against the domination of industrial civilisation. Industrial civilisation created the need for individualism, free enterprise and free institutions; but, at the same time, created horrible conditions for the great masses of men. It subjected sensitive intellectuals to such wealth and power above and such misery below, that they declared their own soul's suffering, defiance, solace to be the only reality worth cultivating—that was Rousseau, Keats, Shelley, Byron and, in various ways, the succeeding generations of poets.

Whitman was the same. This must be firmly grasped or he will be terribly misunderstood and his real significance, for us, completely lost. But this individualistic Romantic was an American, and he could find neither feudalism nor oppressive capital nor any striking combination of both to revolt against. Furthermore, America in 1850 was traditionally, and actually, a land of equality and heroic individual achievement. Whitman accepted it.

His most perfect poem, the one in which he is master of all his power and his inspiration, is *Out of the Cradle Endlessly Rocking*. It is a purely Romantic poem—his own personal loss of a dear friend, set in the memory of an incident of childhood where a bird lost its mate. The apotheosis is a glorification of death. No European poet has surpassed it. In one important sphere, style, he breaks new ground. It is the kind of poem Whitman was always master of—a social, not a literary, fact. Undoubtedly the greatest of American poets, he had nothing more to say than the retreat from society to the individual experience which has distinguished European poetry for 150 years. In another masterpiece, *Crossing Brooklyn Ferry*, the duality in Whitman which lifted him to his highest (and ultimately ruined him as a poet) is at its best. There is a marvellous fusion of nature, people, present and future generations and himself; but himself is not a part of it, though, he wants to be, terribly wants to be. Here, this American separates himself from his European counterparts. He, and this is a fundamental part of the modern American character, a product of the whole country, is an isolated individual. But he craves free association with his fellows. The old heroic individualist activity was going and Whitman, the intellectual, passionately wanted to be one with his fellow-men:

> Just as you feel when you look on the river and sky, so I felt;
> Just as any of you is one of the living crowd, I was one of a crowd;
> Just as you are refresh'd by the gladness of the river and the bright flow,
>   I was refresh'd;
> Just as you stand and lean on the rail, yet hurry with the swift current, I
>   stood, yet was hurried;
> Just as you look on the numberless masts of ships, and the thick-stem'd
>   pipes of steamboats, I look'd.

Whitman there managed the fusion. When he came into contact with life at some point where he felt himself at one with his fellows, his personal lyricism, although intensely personal, assumes concreteness and a genuinely national note.

Hence the complete success of his poems on Lincoln; similarly there are some very fine poems in *Drum-Taps* when he writes of the Civil War.

That is one part of Whitman's work—the lyrics and their form; the other, is, as poetry valueless, but extraordinarily significant as a portrait of the United States between 1850 and 1914. Whitman tried to prove that, contrary to Europe, in America all men were knitted together by a common bond of Democracy with a capital D; that, not only all men in America were equal but all men all over the world were really equal, and in time, one generation, fifty generations (it did not matter) would all be equal with the equality of equal Americans. He was for revolutions in Europe because they would make Europeans equal as Americans were equal.

Whitman developed special poetical methods of his own to overcome the potent fact that men were not equal; and, as time went on, he adopted every shibboleth of the time to maintain, in his verse, the fantastic thesis. Americans "en-masse" did not read and would not read Whitman. It was not that he was too deep—he was too shallow. They believed and would accept rhetoric about equality from public orators, newspaper editorials and the like; but when it was presented as poetry, they would have nothing of it.

In *Carol of Occupations* occurs a typical Whitman passage, ridiculous as poetry, but not to be ignored:

> Manufactures, commerce, engineering, the building of cities, every trade
> carried on there, and the implements of every trade.

Skip a dozen lines, we are still at it:

> Every-day objects, house-chairs, carpets, bed, counter-pane of the bed,
> him or her sleeping at night, wind blowing, indefinite noises.

It is funny at first, then irritating, and then the full significance breaks in, as you remember scores of such passages enumerating things; and enumerating people. Here is a man desperately striving to make contact with his fellow-men at their daily work and play. He mentions hundreds of them, trying to show that he knows what they do; that whether they are thieves, prostitutes, Negroes, bakers, cooks, workers, he is one with them. But one who is one with everybody is one with nobody. Whitman is alone; he has no sense of belonging to any section of society, no class to which he belongs, no class which he is against. His catalogues and shouting are a tale told by an idiot, full of sound and fury; but they do not signify nothing. Whitman showed the American individualistic passion and the craving to mingle with all his fellow-men—the American dream which had been a reasonable reality and which was going to become a universal reality. The greatness of the effort and the poverty of the result show equally the greatness of the need and the impossibility of its realisation in the America Whitman knew. The greatest of American poets, he wrecked himself trying to achieve the impossible. That still remains the basic social need of the vast majority of the American people. And because Whitman knew his own isolation, the new isolation of the intellectual, he sought ceaselessly in his verse to bridge the gap. He ran away to the whole world.

Look at a page of *Salut au Monde*. You will see Arab, Mexican, Cossack, Thames. . . . Look at the next page, Rocky Mountains, Pyrenees, Mount Hecla, Anabmacs, Madagascar; and so it goes. In between are sometimes fine passages, but with the whole world for the workingman, Whitman struggles desperately to make some contact, a contact that eludes him.

There is a logic to such colossal efforts to achieve the unachievable. Whitman, baffled, but no rebel at heart, discovered Science and Industry (both with capital letters) as the means whereby his precious individuality would be attained. In his *Song of the Exposition* he writes:

> Mightier than Egypt's tombs,
> Fairer than Grecia's, Roma's temples,
> Prouder than Milan's statued, spired Cathedral,
> More picturesque than Rhonist castle-keeps,
> We plan, even now, to raise, beyond them all,
> Thy great cathedral, sacred Industry—no tomb
> A keep for life for practical Invention.

A captain of industry, a financier, set out to make money, to create industry for profit. He never claimed to be making a nation of great individuals or, if he did, he was not serious about that. The politicians between 1865 and 1892, when Whitman died, are not remembered today by anybody; they contributed nothing to individualism, free or unfree. Yet this writing of Whitman's was exactly what a skillful publicist on their behalf would have written—visionary ideals of individual freedom and concrete subordination to the reality of the prevailing regime.

Another of Whitman's revolutionary discoveries was sex or, as he called it, animality. But today Whitman's revolutionary attitude towards sex is a damp squib. It is no use saying it was revolutionary in its day. Melville's homosexual episode between Ishmael and Queequeg is as fresh and far more significant today than the day it was written. It is because Melville was not exploiting individuality; he was describing fundamentally what he had observed among many men.

Whitman preached also the equality of women. To the end of his days he believed that he had made the workingman and the working woman the centre of his literary innovation.

What is the actuality? Science, industrial development, the recognition of sex, of the body beautiful, equality for women, the equality of the workingman, all led by Democracy with a capital D. What are these but the ideals by which "progressive" America lived during the period that Mark Twain called "The Gilded Age".

What is the reality? People view with terror the development of Science. The growth of the Cathedral of Industry has resulted in problems undreamt of by Whitman. The social ideas of other poets become outmoded and unimportant; but his have never sunk into oblivion. They have remained. But they have remained in a manner which shows us how much and how little Whitman represented. Today in the "cold war" the picture of America which is being presented to the world by the rulers of America, is Whitman's picture. Free individuals, free enterprise, science, industry, Democracy—that is the Voice of America; and this, at a time when every thinking mind in America is pondering over the outcome of precisely what these terms signify for America and human civilisation. The very attempt to represent these as ideals for the whole world is no more than an extension of Whitman's *Salut au Monde* and *Passage to India*. His "body beautiful", "body electric" and "seminal wetness" are the reservoir from which advertisers of foods, toothpaste, vitamins, deodorants, draw an unending source of inspiration by which to cheat and corrupt the American people. As Cyril Connolly,the English critic, reports in his magazine *Horizon*, he found where one would least expect it, among the rulers of America, serious probing into the realities behind these slogans and doubts of their validity. They are all there in Whitman. He couldn't write poetry about them. Nobody could. But he set them down.

And individuality? It has disappeared; that is the history of American since Whitman—the disappearance of the individuality he celebrated and the need for it, greater than ever.

Now this attitude of Whitman's was not mere Philistinism. It was an evasion as is proved first and foremost by nothing else than the miserable poetic character of his work in this sphere. It was an evasion because Whitman knew the political world of his day. A few years before *Leaves of Grass* appeared in 1855, he had written in a pamphlet unpublished until 1928, the following appreciation of politics, and he was, remember, a practising journalist:

> Whence then do these nominating dictators of America year after year start out? From lawyers' offices, secret lodges, backyards, bed-houses and bar-rooms . . . from the running sores of the great cities; thence to the national, state, city and district nominating conventions of these States, come the most numerous and controlling delegates. Who are they personally? Office-holders, office-seekers, robbers, pimps, exclusives, malignants, conspirators, murderers, fancy-men, port-masters, custom-house clerks, contractors, kept-editors . . .

Whitman was caught and swept away by the grandeur of the national awakening in 1860, and to this day he achieved the heroic only in celebration of the Civil War and the victory of national union. But before 1860 Whitman had discovered the means whereby he could avoid the realities which pressed in on him. He mastered the art of substituting the individual for anything that was too difficult for him to overcome in reality. He develops a trick whereby nothing is what it is, but means something else. In 1856, in *As I Sat Alone by Blue Ontario's Shore*, he writes:

> O I see now, flashing, that this America is only you and me
> Its power, weapons, testimony are you and me,
> Its crimes, lies, thefts, defections, slavery are you and me
> Its Congress is you and me—the officers, capitols, armies, ships are
>   you and me,
> Its endless gestation of new States are you and me,
> The war—that war so bloody and grim—the war I will henceforth

forget—was you and me,
Natural and artificial are you and me,
Freedom, language,poems, employments, are you and me
Past, present, future, are you and me.

This was a perpetual manoeuvre of Whitman. Constitutions, laws, institutions, things—none of these were real. The real things were individuals, you and me; over and over again he does it.

This characteristic of Whitman's opens a broad road to another significant aspect of one of the most comprehensive and powerful personalities of the nineteenth century, and therefore to the nineteenth and twentieth centuries. The characteristic of Whitman just noted is a gigantic symbolism, but the symbolism of evasion. This refusal to face things, the mass of things which dominate modern life, has dominated the poetic literature of the last third of the nineteenth century and the twentieth century. Its technical roots may be in Poe, its literary and social base is in this practice of Whitman. It has been used by poetic individualists, men who have turned away from the world or expressed their rage against it in strictly individual terms—Verlaine, Rimbaud, T.S.Eliot, and even prose writers like Joyce. It has been degraded into the preoccupation with technique and special symbols, which now distinguish the majority of poets who write for a coterie.

This turn of the individual into himself was inherent in Whitman from the beginning. It might have appeared earlier and he might have pursued it to its conclusion, anticipating Rimbaud and the others, but for the national unity of the Civil War which solved his doubts and made him feel that here the fullness of individuality would be realised. In the early poems, Whitman's tendency to turn into himself is present and is linked closely to a sombre preoccupation with Death. His *Song of the Open Road* is a splendid poem, an early one, which has appealed to lovers of the full and free life everywhere. But in it Whitman has left his preoccupation with the mass—you only have to compare him with Shelley, who was a genuine, if frustrated, democrat.

In all the exuberance of the *Open Road*, Whitman, the super-democrat, is calling to a select few:

You shall not heap up what is call'd riches,
You shall scatter with lavish hand all that you earn or achieve,
You but arrive at the city to which you were destined—you hardly settle
 yourself to satisfaction, before you are call'd by an irresistible call
 to depart,
You shall be treated to the ironical smiles and mockings of those who
 remain behind you;
What beckonings of love you receive, you shall only answer with
 passionate kisses of departing,
You shall not allow the hold of those who spread their reach'd hands
 toward you.

Later on in the same poem he says:

My call is the call of battle—I nourish active rebellion;

He nourished nothing of the kind. He shared to the full his countrymen's delusive belief, based on America's early history, that America in its mere existence, was a rebellion. His rebelliousness is a personal sentiment but, like his other songs, to European revolutionaries, Whitman's rebelliousness was an individualistic gesture and nothing more. He had no sense whatever of rebellion as a social movement. He, and all who thought as he, would leave the workingmen and go to follow the *Open Road*. There is contained in the *Open Road* and much of his writing an element of exclusiveness, of an elite, the few who would live their own lives, irrespective of the harsh reality.

Whitman as a historical figure has drunk to the dregs his failure to solve the contradiction contained in his own position. If you insist on individualism as he did and then seek it in industry, science, etc., in general, not only are you used by those who control science, industry, etc. Individualism elevated to this position and unable to find a road inevitably turns in upon itself and makes itself and its accumulated misery the norm of society. The end of this is Existentialism, the gloomy doctrine of modern Europe which has so many devotees among intellectuals in the United States. Still another expression of the tendencies of Whitman has received perhaps the strangest embodiment of all—by no modern social group is Whitman more admired than the American representatives of the totalitarian barbarism of Russia. The American Communist Party, in their self-interested hyprocritical use of American tradition, has made him their own. That combination of frenzy in praise of Democracy (with the capital D) and the complete abstractness of Whitman's poetical treatment of it, Whitman's messianic conception of poets as the great individuals to lead the nation—all this finds in them a response which seems far more than merely a total failure.

Was his poetical work for democracy then a total failure? No. He was, in his way, a genuine democrat, in that he began with a vision of what early America had produced—a conviction of the worth of the individual as an individual in work and play and all aspects of life, and the recognition that this individual could only find his fullest expression with other individuals equal to himself. The roads to which his failure led are evidence of his passion in seeking his aim, a passion still held by his countrymen above all other people. He failed because he tried to embrace all, took Democracy in general as synonymous with the growth of America. But if he succeeded as a poet only where he spoke of himself and his sorrows, he left behind the impact of his passion for his fellow-men in the verse form he perfected.

For fine as these poems are, Whitman's chief claim to fame is not the poems themselves. This American writer felt in all his bones that America was different from Europe. He felt that America needed a poetry that was characteristic of America, a poetry of the people, written by a poet who in himself as an individual represented the people and thereby was fitted to write for them. His whole life showed that this, above all, moved him. The result is that there, expressing his strongest and finest emotion, he did succeed. He felt the need for a new medium, free verse, and he worked at it. He was no slap-dash writer who never blotted a line, but a devoted artist, seeking to create a new democratic form. The paradox of his career is that though he had little that was really new to say, his passion to identify himself with his fellow countrymen did enable him to create a new social medium.

Whitman's form is his profoundest contribution to literature, and it is here again that American writers of the mid-nineteenth century have struck chords whose significance can only be recognised today.

Hegel has drawn attention to the fact that the verse of the ancients did not rhyme, and was a verse which depended upon quantity, pure and simple; giving a tremendous flexibility of the individual line. He claims that this type of verse represented the one-ness of the individual Greek with the social phenomena of life and the objects that Greek life dealt with. The Greek was a part of his society. Greek society did not know the individual separate from it—hence the plasticity of the poetry, which while rhythmic in form, sought to shape itself to the object described.

The growth of individualism in European society destroyed this. The individual, conscious of his isolation, could not allow the verse to seek to follow the object. The recurrent rhythm and the rhymes at the end of the line, characteristic of modern poetry, were the concrete contact of the subjective individual with what otherwise would have escaped him. He had a need that the educated Greek or Roman did not have. In the first great revolutionary age of modern times, when the individual felt himself representative of society, we have the formation of the national languages. Calvin, Dewey and the early English translators of the Bible, religious leaders all, led this transformation.

At the moment when England was preparing to introduce secular society as opposed to feudal, Shakespeare and the Elizabethan dramatists, broke with rhyme and introduced blank verse, which in the hands of its greatest masters, remains to this day unsurpassed as a poetic medium, both for depth and flexibility. It was closer to the plasticity of the Greeks and Romans than anything we have seen before or since. With the end of the Elizabethans, its greatest period was gone; and it has since known nothing but decline. The genuine passion of the isolated Whitman to get into contact with his fellowmen and the character of his fellowmen, produced another great stage in the development of poetic language.

Whitman's verse can express, as he expressed, the most intimate personal feelings, using as all new languages must do, the intimate nuances of the past. But it is also a chant, a chant to be sung by millions of men. It is popular, yet in the hands of a master, it can be subtle and intricate beyond the elaborate verse forms that preceded it. If some day all men will be educated and feel the need of expression in verse, some such form as Whitman used will be the medium. It has been, as so much that he did, taken up and made into the most precious of verse forms by modern masters; but all the schoolchildren in the United States who write, use it. His passion for identification did find some permanent expression, but not in the same sense he intended.

Herman Melville is the exact opposite of Whitman, at least in his great book *Moby Dick*. Melville's greatness and superiority are due to the fact that, stirred by the critical period, he did the very things that Whitman did not do. He described with absolute precision various individuals in their social setting, the work they did, their relations with other men. This led him to see that individualism in certain sections of America had become one of the most dangerous vices of the age and would destroy society.

Melville saw each man separately, concretely; but in all his individuality and all his relations. His insight came from the fact that he saw all men in this way and, because of this, he saw all in relation to Nature. In *Moby Dick*, Melville was the counterpart of Whitman. He sought not the violent self-expression of individuality which is so peculiarly American, but that conviction of the need for communication with all types of men which is also so peculiarly American. Many European intellectuals write for common men, organise for them, will readily die for them—do everything for them, except meet them as men. Melville described common men as they have been described in no modern literature; but he saw no way for them to form a harmonious society and drew a society which would crash to its doom by individuals.

Melville wrote *Moby Dick* in 1851. As is well known, it is a story of a whaling vessel led by a manaical captain which pursues a white whale so intemperately that the ship is lost with all on board except one survivor. Melville was bitter in his protest that his book was not some miserable allegory, and the general tenor of his meaning is correct. An allegory concretises and imprisons the universal. Melville's book is symbolic—it gives indications and points of support by which the innermost essence and widest reaches of the universal may be grasped.

Melville painted a picture of the society of his day—not merely the society of America, but all of society. He indicated very clearly where he thought it was heading. At the end of the book the last sight of the ship shows an eagle, the symbol of America, caught in an American flag being nailed down, without possibility of escape, to the mast by the blows of an American Indian. It is impossible to speak more clearly. The social perspectives, however, are not completely hopeless. The survivor is not saved merely for the purpose of relating the story; he is saved by a coffin, prepared by the request of another savage and fitted for its ultimate purpose so deliberately by the author as to exclude any idea that this is accidental. It is enough that while Melville sees no solution to the problem of society, he does not say that there is none. He can see none.

The mysticism of life which Melville deals with, and which some writers pay great attention to, is not the most important part of the work. Mysticism is an expression of the inability to arrive a rational solutions of the problems of nature and society. Melville's whole book shows that this is what concerned him, man and his relation to Nature; and, as a result, man in relation to his fellows, social man.

This is the significance of the white whale—Nature in relation to the active life of man. The white whale must be seen as a symbol, not as an allegory, as Melville insists. For it is precisely a symbol which offers the widest variety of reference and interpretation. Unlike Dostoyevsky, Melville places his symbolic characters in a very concrete environment, the environment of an industry, of men doing the daily business of the modern world. Melville is to this day unique in his portrait of an industry. Where else does anything like this appear in literature? Certainly not in the sprawling, over-emotional novels of Zola, nor in the modern propagandist novels, nor in the romantic sea-stories of Conrad. Not one great novelist even faintly approaches the realistic description of the process and personnel from the signing up of Ishmael and Queequeg, the preparation of the *Pequod* by the owners, to the final catastrophe. Melville's sense of society was American—the opposite of the talkers, reasoners, arguers of Dostoyevsky.

The *Pequod* was doing a legitimate business, one of the greatest industries of the middle of the nineteenth century. This cannot be over-emphasised for it is of the essence of Melville. Furthermore, Melville takes care to show that there had been whales which had terrorised whalers, and there had been captains who in the way of business, had sought out and destroyed such whales. Thus Ahab's manaical quest is merely the exaggeration, the intensification beyond reason, of the legitimate and, in fact, necessary pursuits of men. This is precisely why it is so terrible and so dangerous.

This legitimate activity symbolises the perpetual relation of civilised man with Nature. The whale was the most striking of living things which man had to subdue in order to have civilised lives. The whale is not a mere fish. The conquest of the air and the mastery of atomic energy are symbolised by the whale. The symbol as such could appeal more easily to men in 1851, than to our own day when the contact with Nature is so much more mechanised, complicated and scientific. But Melville has that relation in mind. Man must perpetually seek to conquer Nature, to bend it to his will. And Nature is malevolent, making him pay a heavy toll, and creating such strains and stresses in his character as can turn him into a monomaniac.

Melville carries the symbolism further. He divided society as a whole into two spheres—the stable society of the land and the society of the sea, the shifting boundaries of man's need to go further and ever further. How Melville does this, however, is characteristic and very important for understanding the particular method to be used in this book. Melville is not a social scientist; he is an artist, first, middle and last. A great artist is not a politician and his social and political ideas are to be deduced from his artistic work. Melville, as a matter of fact, was not even an ardent Northerner in pursuit of the war with the South; but no man had more sympathy for the great masses of the slaves and primitive peoples than he. This is to be seen in his work, not in such political views as he expressed.

Melville shows what the sea means for him in the strange and haunting episode of Bulkington. Bulkington first appears in Chapter III, a sailor who has just landed, a superbly handsome man, a Southerner, a man reserved, with deep problems of his own but loved by his fellow-sailors. Then in Chapter XXIII Bulkington reappears, in a brief chapter, wholly devoted to him. Ishmael sees him at the helm on a bitterly cold winter's night:

> I looked with sympathetic awe and fearfulness upon the man, who in mid-winter just landed from a four years' dangerous voyage, could so unrelentingly push off again for still another tempestuous term. The land seemed scorching to his feet.

Then come three clauses which are, in reality, a brief poem in the elegiac style of the Greeks:

> Wonderfullest things are ever the unmentionable; deep memories yield no epitaphs; this six-inch chapter is the stoneless grave of Bulkington.

No novelist anywhere can surpass Melville at such moments. The power of the poetry derives not only from the monumental weight of the words but the dramatic setting. Bulkington appears no more in the book.

Then Melville states what for him man's life means:

> Know ye, now Bulkington? Glimpses do ye seem to see of that mortally intolerable truth; that all deep, earnest thinking is but the intrepid effort of the soul to keep the open independence of her sea; while the wildest winds of heaven and earth conspire to cast her on the treacherous slavish shore?
>
> But as in landlessness alone resides the highest truth, shoreless, indefinite as God—so, better is it to perish in that howling infinite, than be ingloriously dashed upon the lee, even if that were safety! For worm-like, then, oh! who would craven crawl to land! terrors of the terrible! is all this Bulkington! Bear thee grimly, demigod! Up from the spray of thy ocean-perishing—straight up, leaps thy apotheosis!

That is the sea for Melville, the unknown that man must continually seek to know. Death and destruction face him, but man, men who matter, cannot resist. Moby Dick is merely the active principle in the sea, Nature, the unknown, which is in constant conflict with man. *Moby Dick* is a baffled, defeated, but not a hopeless book.

Ishmael, the writer of the story, is an individualist intellectual who goes to sea because he is sick at heart. Ahab is the individualist whose individualism imperils all of society. Bulkington is an individual, superb person, physically and in the effect of his personality; yet he is a Southern mountaineer, turned ordinary sailor and loved by his fellow sailors. Melville has greater respect for no one in the book. He recognizes the significance of the type. It holds the future of man in its hands, the things that for Melville matter. But Melville can only describe him as from a distance and praise him. He can do nothing else with him. We shall appreciate the significance of this when we see later where Melville openly confesses his bafflement.

Melville, as is known, describes every detail of whale-fishing, the conversion of the ship into a factory at sea for the extraction and storage of oil. One of his profoundest and most far reaching symbolical episodes is based upon this. But his book is often misunderstood because critics take the tiresomeness of his endeavour, never lost sight of for a moment, to root the madness of Ahab in the normal.

Again Melville's style is at its most magnificent when he describes the course of the *Pequod* in its chase after Moby Dick. The struggle then is the struggle between man and Nature, as old as historical time and as wide as the world. But though less obvious, Melville is equally concerned with the relations between man and man, relations which man must enter into, in order to pursue his destined task. Once more the ship symbolizes the whole world, in which are portrayed the most characteristic social types, with the most delicately shaded individual types of character to represent the organic types of Melville's day. They are in their way skilled workmen; but Melville repeatedly calls them a heathen crew, renegades, castaways, the scum of the earth. Yet again in a manner to himself this American writer invests them with dignity. They do their work splendidly, the ship is kept in fine shape, the whole crew does its daily work heroically, to recall De Tocqueville's phrase. Melville draws the reader's attention to it:

But this august dignity I treat of, is not the dignity of kings and robes, but that abounding dignity which has no robed investiture. Thou shalt see it shining in the arm that wields a pick or drives a spike; that democratic dignity which, on all hands, radiates without and from God! Himself! The great God absolute! The centre and circumference of all democracy! His omnipresence, our divine equality.

But it is not only that he says so. The whole treatment shows an absolutely unique objectivity about ordinary labor, without sentimentality which cannot be found in any other novelist.

Having laid his basis, so to speak, Melville then portrays a social stage higher, the picked men, the highly skilled harpooners who represent the skilled craftsmen so characteristic of the economy of his time. There was no necessity whatever for Melville to do what he does. He gives this vastly important role to three savages, Queequeg, a cannibal from the South Seas, Tashtego, an American Indian and Doggo, an African giant. They are the representatives of the three continents where primitive men were still found. Here again Melville's unbounded sympathy and admiration within a strictly realistic framework is unique in literature. The men are masters of their craft, brave and skillful as virtuosos. But over and over again they perform the bravest acts, far beyond the line of duty. Whenever anything remarkable is done, one of them does it.

As if that there were not enough, Melville makes Queequeg into one of the most carefully realised characters in the book. He is an admitted cannibal but he has left his country to learn from civilisation to go back to teach his people. Ishmael, the narrator, the soul-sick intellectual, finds in Queequeg a friend and a brother, and the opening pages describe a thinly disguised homosexual relationship between the two in a manner that is as plain and yet as inoffensive as it could possibly be.

It is obvious that these savages do key work in the whaling business, that Queequeg is a distinguished personality; but he is a savage, a cannibal. If, in addition to his grand physique, his skillful work and his noble character, he were a civilized human being, then there would be some hope for the world which Melville sends to its doom. But splendid as he is, the primitive Queequeg cannot save society. Melville, in the person of the distraught Ishmael, can admire and love. It is not difficult to see the significance of this for the world of today and the whole problem of world civilization.

Next in the hierarchy are the three American mates—Starbuck, Flask and Stubb, capable men all; but differentiated with a marvelous skill.

Now the question that Melville poses is: Why did this ship's crew not revolt, put Ahab in irons or kill him, and thus save the ship and crew? This problem, so pregnant today, is handled by Melville with unique insight and mastery, and the subtlety of the relation between Ahab and the crew, and Ahab and the mates is a political study of rare discrimination. No generation but our own could have appreciated this. Melville himself poses the question, but says that crews had been known to revolt against captains, adding that the men of the *Pequod* were perfectly capable of it. One of his most telling strokes is his statement that the crew were not only mongrel, renegades, castaways and savages; but that they were "morally enfeebled also by the incompetence of mere unaided virtue or rightmindedness in Starbuck, the invulnerable jollity of indifference and recklessness in Stubb, and the pervading mediocrity of Flask." The relations between Starbuck, a brave, honest, conscientious man and Ahab are a most important part of the book.

Melville was deeply concerned with the inability of the crew to put an end to the mad captain by revolt. In Chapter LIV he breaks his narrative to introduce a story and goes to great length to give the impression that it is true. It could not be accidental that Melville made this known to Ahab's crew and gave them every indication of what they should do. Why didn't they do it? Here Melville does a most extraordinary thing. He says frankly that he doesn't know. Ahab inspired his men with his hate of the white whale; the whale seemed to the men also "in some dim unsuspected way . . . the gliding great demon of the seas of life." But why should this be so, "all this to explain would be to dive deeper than Ishmael can go." Melville cannot understand why. It should be obvious by now that behind this marvellous sea story, this writer was digging into problems of far greater social significance for us today than were Flaubert, Dostoyevsky and Rimbaud.

And yet the study of Ahab is a masterpiece—perhaps so far the only serious study in fiction of the type which has reached its climax in the modern totalitarian dictator. Here we must pause to get our literary and sociological points of reference clear. Melville was not writing a political tract for 1950 nor for the times he lived in. But he was looking at society as a whole, painting it in as comprehensive a series of relations as he could. He saw the characteristic social types of his day and because he lived at a turning point, he saw also a characteristic social type of the age which was to follow.

This, in fact, seems to be the condition of many of the greatest works of the genuinely creative writers. Dante summed up not only the Middle Ages, but saw more clearly the new secular age; Balzac, temperamentally and politically admired the aristocracy, but although he disliked it, he was fascinated by the new bourgeoisie and his imagination was stimulated by the new men and their impact upon the old society. The greatest example of this is Shakespeare. He held all the ideas of the radical aristocracy; but he came at the turning point, just before the Puritan revolution of individualism. How great passions could shake men who had escaped the rigid roles of feudalism—this more than anything else was what interested Shakespeare. Hence the great tragedies and the tragedy, above all, of Hamlet who could not decide. The greatest writers seem to be those who come at the climax of one age, but this is because the new age has grown up inside the old and they are watching both.

This was the case with Melville. The old heroic individualist America he knew; but he could see, as artists see, that the old, individualism was breeding a new individualism—one which would destroy society. The prototype of this was Ahab. The modern dictator whose prototype he is, is best exemplified by Adolf Hitler.

It is necessary to stop again and make clear what we are doing. Melville did not write political treatises. The modern dictator arises from economic and social circumstances profoundly different from those of Melville's day. Nevertheless, the greatness of a writer is revealed by the fact that peering and probing until he finds what he considers the fundamental types of his own period; he portrays what we, in later years, can see are the ancestors of what exists in our own world. We are therefore entitled to, in fact we have to, with the knowledge that we have gained through the development of history and our own experiences, examine earlier writers and see how much they saw that was permanent and enduring.

In this respect Ahab is an astonishing character in fiction. He is not only the individualism that Melville saw and feared, run mad. Contrary to Dostoyevsky, Melville places the individualism in opposition to a representative section of the society of his time. In addition, and here he touches Dostoyevsky, he shows the conflicts within Ahab himself. Before we attempt briefly to indicate some of the main facets of this character and activity, it must be remembered, that no historical character like Ahab had yet appeared on the American social and political scene; but he has appeared in Europe. Hitler is not only an individual. A man like Hitler could only appear when an essential number of people, representing the type, had become a social grouping, representing vast social forces. If there had been no outstanding social and political figure like Ahab in the United States, among large sections of the population, and particularly in the popular art and literature of the day, figures of this type—vulgarised but essentially the same—are more and more becoming the dominant type of hero in the United States.

First of all, Ahab's relations with his men and his employers. Ahab is an executive, he is captain of a vessel and a very skillful and able whaling captain. His employers would not have countenanced for one moment, as Melville says, this mad chase of Ahab's. His mates were against him. Nothing is more pathetic than the relationship of Starbuck, the honest conscientious man, to Ahab. Starbuck is the only man who challenges Ahab and tries to turn him back, talks to him of the ease and comforts of life at home. Ahab dominates him by sheer force of personality. At a certain stage when Starbuck sees that Ahab is, as he says, going to ruin the lives of perhaps thirty men, he takes a gun and goes towards Ahab's cabin to shoot him. But he cannot do it. Inside he hears Ahab talking in his sleep about his quest and he gives way. When Ahab takes to the boat for the last fight against Moby Dick, he places Starbuck in charge of the ship and thereby places his life in Starbuck's hands. The other mate, Stubb, is told by Ahab to get out of his cabin. Ahab threatens to kick him down. But Stubb, who admits that he has never been treated in this way before, accepts it—dominated also by the overpowering personality and will of Ahab.

Profound, far-reaching and subtle are the relations between Ahab and the men. It is impossible here to go through stage by stage the manoeuvres of Ahab with the crew; sufficient to say that very early he recognised the danger:

> Ahab was now entirely conscious that . . . he had indirectly laid himself open to the unanswerable charge of usurpation; and with perfect impunity, both moral and legal, his crew if so disposed, and to that end competent, could refuse any further obedience to him, and even violently wrest from him the command.

This occurs as early as Chapter XLV, when there are still two-thirds of the book to go and the reader of this outline must accept, for the time being, that the rest of the book is a manual of political practice between a dominant political figure and the officers and ranks whom he must dominate. Every change of atmosphere in the men, every doubt, every enthusiasm is used by Ahab in order to maintain control. At a certain stage the men are doubtful and suspicious, but so certain, so domineering, so overwhelming is Ahab's concentration on his purpose that they dare not raise the question with him, and his mates move around unable to look at him.

The main purpose of Melville's book in his own mind was the struggle between men and Nature. That must be admitted. But with his vast experience of the world and his immense insight and a certain comprehensiveness, which distinguish the selectivity of a great artist, Melville attempted to paint a rounded picture, to symbolise the world as he knew it in this whaling story. This accounts for the great attention he paid to the social, and what I am calling the political, structure of his symbolical presentation. After a hundred years, as repeatedly happens with great books, the book, so to speak, can be seen by us in a manner which amounts to a reversal of the particular emphasis which Melville may have had in mind when he wrote. We cannot attempt to see the book as precisely as when Melville wrote it. The greatness of the writing is due to the fact that, while his original purpose is not in any way diminished (we today, for instance, in the conquest of atomic energy and the accomplishments of science and the deadly destruction they seem to hold for society, can appreciate more than ever what Melville calls the demonism in the world),—nevertheless the accuracy and insight of the social structure which he built, and the social and political significance of his characters assume for us a significance which perhaps they did not have for him. They are a testimony to the depth and accuracy of his observations and the profundity of his imagination. Melville understands the manner in which a dominating will and an immense concentration can overpower men who do not resist it with an equal will and force. He thereby has penetrated to the heart of the secret of the mechanism by which political power is grasped and wielded today in a period of revolutionary changes.

Finally there is the character of Ahab himself. Ahab's madness is effective, because, as must be insisted upon, it is a madness which is just one stage beyond the normal activities of man. The crew, as Melville points out again and again, shared some of his aspirations and to some degree sympathised with his aims. Even Ishmael, the educated intellectual, feels the demonism in Nature as represented by the White Whale and feels also the spell of Ahab's personality, so that even he for a time, is captivated and shouted with the rest of the crew. Melville insists that Ahab's individualism is just a part of what every man feels, but which has been allowed to run away with itself and hence is so dangerous. Ahab further attempts to convey the impression that his hatred of the White Whale is due to the fact that Moby Dick ate off his leg. Melville knows that that is not so. He shows quite clearly that Ahab, with his enormous will and instinct to dominate, is merely the result of an exasperation with the insoluble moral and intellectual problems with which the society of his day faced him.

It is necessary to get this clear. For nearly seventy years after *Moby Dick*, individualism in the shape of captains of industry ran wild in the United States. But *Moby Dick* has begun to come into its popularity only since world war one. Ahab represents far more the new individualism which captured American after the Civil War. With an almost mathematical logic, Melville took individualism to the extreme limit of what it could accomplish and then faced it with the crisis which he inevitably foresaw would result. He could see that as in every age society presented serious men with profound problems, there was ahead a tremendous crisis and there would appear the type of Ahab (that was all he saw). Quite early Melville makes us aware of what Ahab represents and what the White Whale represents to Ahab:

> . . . in his frantic morbidness he at last came to identify with him, not only all his bodily woes, but all his intellectual and spiritual exasperations. The White Whale swam before him as the monomaniac incarnation of all those malicious agencies which some deep men feel eating in them, till they are left living on with half a heart and half a lung . . . all evil, to crazy Ahab, were visibly personified and made practically assailable in Moby Dick. He piled upon the whale's white hump the sum of all the general rage and hate felt by his whole race from Adam down; and then, as if his chest had been a mortar, he burst his hot heart's shell upon it.

Ahab represents not merely man in general, but the individualistic man of the nineteenth century at a stage where he faces the insoluble nature of his problems both with Nature and society. That is where modern man has reached today. And if in Ahab's day, Ahab felt it more than all the others and thereby gained the domination through his will, Bulkington felt it also and Ishmael, the intellectual. So, in their various ways, did many of the crew. Today we have reached a stage where this consuming rage with the social and psychological problems of society is eating away at the whole of humanity. However, society is not the same. Where Ahab, the dominating executive felt it most, today it is the great masses of the people in whom it stirs. Melville saw it, understood it and painted it with what we can now see was a marvellous clarity.

The final aspect of Ahab's character is the fact that he is a human being. We do not live far enough removed from a man like Hitler to be able to understand the real secrets of the power which he wielded over men, for politics, although the sum total of economic and social forces, is made by individual men. Ahab gains Starbuck's sympathy because he confessed to him that he did not understand why he was so torn and driven. For forty years he had been a whale man, forty years he tells Starbuck of suffering and privation. What is the cause of it? It is precisely the need of man to live, to work, to struggle for his existence, constantly to go on further, which is the basis of Ahab's madness. Finally Ahab comes to the conclusion that it is fate, it is the destiny of man so to act and he, Ahab, is merely fulfilling destiny. It is impossible to understand the modern social and political world without real and genuine insight into this aspect of modern society. In the end, as inevitably happens to these men—beginning upon the basis of the ordinary needs of mankind, driven by the dominating will to positions of authority, feeling in time that the immense catastrophes and social upheavals are merely the result of inevitable destiny—they reach the stage where they see themselves as chosen instruments and ungoverned by any law. Melville draws the picture of modern tormented man, driven by the inevitable desire to solve his problem, bringing the whole world down with him—all this with a combination of realism and symbolism unmatched in the works of any author of the nineteenth and twentieth centuries.

The last word, so far as the social significance of the book is concerned, must be with Ishmael in which is perhaps the book's most remarkable page. The *Pequod* has been converted into a factory at sea; the factory is aglow, the oil is boiling; it is night and Ishmael, the intellectual, suddenly feels that the whole spectacle is not within the bounds of reason: "The burning ship drove on, as if remorselessly commissioned to some vengeful deed." See what can easily pass for a picture of the more primitive type of industry, but which was characteristic of much of the unskilled industry of Melville's time.

The hatch, removed from the top of the works, now afforded a wide hearth in front of them. Standing on this were the Tartarean shapes of the pagan harpooners, always the whaleship's stokers. With huge pronged pole they pitched hissing masses of blubber into the scalding pots, or stirred by the fires beneath, till the snaky flames darted, curling, out of the doors to catch them by the feet. . . . As they narrated to each other their unholy adventures, their tales of terror told in the words of mirth; as their uncivilized laughter forked upwards out of them, like flames from the furnaces . . . the harpooners wildly gesticulated with their huge pronged forks and dippers; as the wind howled on, and the sea leaped, and the ship groaned and dived, and yet steadfastly shot her red hell further and further into the blackness of the sea, and the night, and scornfully champed the white bone in her mouth and viciously spat round her on all sides; then the rushing *Pequod*, freighted with savages, and laden with fire, and burning a corpse, and plunging into that blackness of darkness, seemed the material counterpart of her monomaniac commander's soul.

It is impossible to say more clearly that modern industrial society was going to its doom and that Ahab's madness was the result of this society. Finally, in this very chapter, Melville brings out clearly the character of Ishmael, the intellectual. He is the man without will. He is the man who sees Ahab's madness, is swept up by it, is intelligent enough to oppose it; but like Melville himself, has no substitute, no force with which to oppose the mad captain. That night Ishmael is at the helm. He can see nothing ahead but disaster.

Melville saw, and indeed on the basis of his experiences, could see no solution whatever; but it is noticeable that this American, this product of the heroic individualism of 1776 to 1850 had no sympathy whatever with intellectualism or escapism of any kind. The society was doomed, and he sent it to its doom. Ahab knew what he wanted; and Melville not only admires Ahab, but has nothing but scorn for the intellectual without will. The book begins with Ishmael stating that he has reached a stage where he could no longer stand the world, then he goes to sea. But in a remarkable chapter, "The Masthead", Melville deals once and for all with the soul-sick. Ishmael climbs up the mast to do his share, but up there he keeps a "sorry guard", "the problem of the universe is revolving in him". He is up there deep in thought and revelling in his sorrow, so to speak, revelling in his intellectual problems; but Melville, with that sarcastic yet genially Shakespearean humour which he uses so often, soon puts him in his place, making him say of anyone so loftily perched:

There is no life in thee, now, except that rocking life imparted by a gently rolling ship; by her, borrowed from the sea, by the sea, from the inscrutable tides of God. But while this sleep, this dream is on ye, move your foot or hand an inch, slip your hold at all; and your identity comes back in horror. Over Descartian vortices, you hover. And perhaps, at mid-day, in the fairest weather, with one half throttled shriek you drop through that transparent air into the summer sea, no more to rise forever. Heed it well, ye Panthesis.

Melville had no use for the ivory tower, nor would he have had for those for whom the problems of the universe revolve in their own insides. The point is that he knew the type.

There must be a final point on his style. Buffon says that the style is the man; and that is true. But the really great man is the society. And therefore, through remote refractions, the style is more than the man. It is the society too.

It has been noted that Melville is very strongly influenced by, among other writers, Shakespeare and Sir Thomas Browne. Melville's *Moby Dick* is truly Shakespearean in the geniality and breadth of its humor. But Shakespeare's influence on Melville is, in my opinion, a social matter. Shakespeare came on the eve of a great change in the society of his country. He expressed the immense vitality of an age which was finishing and another which was about to begin. He felt the individualism and its ramifications which were to distinguish European society for hundreds of years. It is clear that Melville felt the same about the America of his time, clear that he viewed the new man with the same interest, insight and, at the same time, fearful admiration with which Shakespeare feared Macbeth, Othello and Lear. At the same time, the influence of Sir Thomas Browne is very strong. Browne in his *Urn Burial* expressed a learned historical scepticism of the very vitality which so attracted Shakespeare. Browne seems to say that history in the end worked out only to dead bones and a tomb. I do not think it at all surprising that both these authors influenced Melville to the extraordinary extent that they did. He was conscious of the immense vitality and dangers of the individualism which he saw about to rise to a new and unprecedented stage. But he was conscious also, as Browne was conscious, of the inevitable end of all things:

"all collapsed and the great shroud of the sea rolled on as it rolled five thousand years ago."

1950

13
Letters to Literary Critics

I. MY DEAR BELL,

You told Saul Blackman that you liked parts of my book *(Notes on American Civilization)* you read, but that you hoped, when I spoke about my admiration for comic strips, I was speaking with my tongue-in-cheek. First I would never speak tongue-in-cheek to the general public. Beyond that, this matter of American comic strips involves a great deal of my outlook on modern society. My perspective on artistic development in the civilization of the United States is rooted in comic strips, soap opera, and jazz; the gangster film; the television comedians; and especially the great men of the movies up to 1930. My ideas of art and society, like my specifically literary criticism, are based upon Aristotle and Hegel. I doubt if there are many beside professional scholars who read and re-read Aeschylus and Shakespeare as much as I; but it is precisely these studies that have led me to see comic strips and soap operas as I do. You see at any rate that my attitude is not an idiosyncrasy or some sort of mental game.

Some years ago I suffered from a type of insomnia and marked out a routine which I followed about four or five nights a week for months. I went to the movies on 42nd Street at midnight, got home about three and slept till nine. I awoke tired and turned on an old radio by my bed, which would only give one of two stations satisfactorily. One of these programs was a soap opera which I listened to morning after morning, carelessly at first, but with a fascination that never ceased to grow. At that time Allied troops were marching on Paris from the south of France. One soap opera dealt with an American soldier in this army. He was wounded. He was nursed by a Frenchwoman who was attracted to him. Also in the plot were the adventures of his wife. She had gone into business, in the office of a factory doing war work. She was attracted to her boss who was attracted to her. Also in the family was a younger sister who, in the disrupted home-life, fell in with gangsters and was saved in the nick of time.

The thing lasted for months. I remember that when a holiday came, either July 4th or Thanksgiving, the soap opera was right up to date both in France and in the United States; and we all, in France and America, players and listeners, celebrated the national holiday together. There were other operas too that I listened to, but this was the one that mattered. This is what struck me. Every day for fifteen minutes, there was being reproduced an approximation of what was the living experience of millions of American soldiers and their families split apart by the war. *Every day*. I can imagine that millions listened in as I did, every day, and saw themselves and their families and their friends in a form of artistic representation. As "art" it was good or bad—I do not care; and some of it, I thought, was very good. But it was new, this daily attempt to chart the emotional and artistic needs of a vast population. It is new, and it is here to stay. It is symbolic of a new pattern of art in relation to society. If the quality is not good, that does not matter to me in the least. If and when great artists take the people seriously, they will transform these entertainments into works which will satisfy the most exacting.

Hemingway and Faulkner are the culmination of a general tradition lasting centuries and specifically of 150 years of the novel. The soap opera, I repeat, belongs to us of the twentieth century and to America above all. Modern American fiction I read with interest, but I do not believe it has anything special to communicate to the world; still less does poetry or drama; its music (Copland etc.)I find similarly uninteresting; its painting I know little about and care less. I cannot conceive of any serious person believing that in America today there is art, or the promise of art, which will regenerate the artistic world. The art of America, like the art of Europe during the last 20 years, I find decadent and without any promise whatever. You can trace the decline in poetry beginning with Baudelaire, through Rimbaud to the bankruptcy of today. That is why I look with an interest that grows with the years at the immense vitality and the new forms by which the American mass, using modern technology, interests and amuses itself. If the other is an end, this is, for me, a beginning.

I am going to develop these ideas more fully in my work on American civilization. I want to begin with two of the greatest periods that we know of in the history of art. In common opinion they are, first, the Greek dramatists, and secondly, the Elizabethans. What were the circumstances under which these works were produced? The great drama of Aeschylus, Sophocles, and Euripedes was first and foremost a popular drama. The whole Athenian nation, or rather the whole city-state was there, from the highest officials down to those slaves who were allowed to come.

It was not a solemn performance. The Athenian masses, many of whom I suppose were illiterate, stamped and shouted and booed and carried on as much as the masses of people in New York do at Ebbets Field or the Yankee Stadium. At one time the prizes, for as you know this was a competition, were decided by popular vote. Afterwards, some judges were appointed, chosen by lot. But even this choosing by lot did not mean that a certain number of qualified people really decided, because it is stated that the rank-and-file were so violent in their partisanship, this one for Sophocles, the other one for Aeschylus, etc. as the case might be, that they intimidated the judges and the judges used to decide in accordance with what was obviously the sentiment of the spectators of the time. You can be sure the competing artists knew whom they had to please.

The dramatists dealt with topics which had an obvious contemporary application. Indeed Aristophanes satirized Cleon,the dictator, so savagely in one of his plays that Cleon brought him up for libel. It is a lesson in irony to compare what Greek drama is today—the subject of studies in universities or precious performances in small theaters in London, Paris and New York—with what it was in the days when it was created—a tremendous popular production in which the people themselves were vitally interested and settled who should win the prizes. I would like to mention, by the way, that Plato for certain, and I think Aristotle also, fumed with rage at the role the masses of the people played in all this. If they had had things in their hands, they would not have organized anything like the masterpieces that have come down to us. The power came from the Athenian democracy. When democracy declined the great Athenian drama declined with it.

The conditions in which the Shakespearean drama was produced were quite similar. Shakespeare was another John Ford or D.W.Griffith. He was a writer for his company, in which he had invested his money. He wrote plays so that they might attract an audience which would pay and enable the company to make a profit. Shakespeare was a very great artist. But the medium in which he worked, the procedures by which his plays were brought to public notice, were essentially a matter of business and an attempt to attract the attention of masses of people in London. As among the Greeks, *the whole nation* from the highest to the lowest was represented in the Shakespearean audience. But the majority of them were the working people and apprentices of London; and Shakespeare's success or failure depended on them. They paid their pennies and came to see. They loved the drama. They followed Ben Jonson and Beaumont and Fletcher and Greene and the rest of them. But for these people, the greatest of all was Mr Shakespeare and for twenty years they gave him almost unstinted support. Half the credit for his plays should be given to those people who allowed Shakespeare's genius to flourish and develop by their constant appreciation. About these productions there was not the slightest scholasticism or culture or intellectualism in the way we use these words. They were not the preserve of educated people. In fact the scholastics attacked these plays and proved by Aristotle that they were bad. And when the price went up from a penny to sixpence so that the common people could no longer go, the great Elizabethan drama collapsed.

In the early days of the modern film, in the days of Chaplin, D.W. Griffith and the early Keystone comedies, you had a new art being shaped and its foundations laid in much the same manner that the Greek and Elizabethan tragedians laid the foundations of their drama. The movies were new, as new as Aeschylus was new. They were a genuine creation—they had no models to go by. To succeed they had to please the people.

There is something in the works of this early period of the movies that makes its best work the masterpieces of our day. I do not know any finer movie than Griffith's *Birth of a Nation*, where he takes the Civil War from beginning to end including the pre-war and post-war periods. He has an eye for masses of men in the countryside that I have seen equalled only in paintings by one of the Breughels; his battle scenes, his domestic pictures, his historical vignettes, his energy and his tenderness are all mastery. But what makes him a supreme master is the epic breadth and the historical imagination that you find in the great war novel of

Tolstoy or in Homer's *Iliad.* Compare it with Clark Gable and Vivien Leigh in their soap opera, *Gone With The Wind.* And, if his work is not faithful history, what epic is?

Is there any art in the twentieth century which can compare with the art that Charlie Chaplin developed and built up until somewhere about the middle of the thirties when he began to decline? These are the masterpieces of the twentieth century and they were produced by artists who were unknown, men who displayed an unexpected ability to create artistic form. And they did it in their attempts to please the popular mass. There was not the slightest trace of critical appreciation in the days when these men gathered their dollars how they could and hurled themselves into the business of film-making. I believe that, when the history of the twentieth century comes to be written, it is not names like Hemingway and Joyce and D.H. Lawrence and the rest who will dominate accounts of its art. Future historians will write that in the twentieth century a new art began, and that the great masterpieces of the age, both in form and in impact upon the generations that they served, were the films of Chaplin and Griffith.

These movies in their day were no doubt treated with the same lack of interest by critical intellectuals as comic strips are being treated today. The movies were new in that they were conditioned by the suffrage of the whole nation. The same quality of newness distinguishes the soap opera, the comic strip and jazz music because of the peculiar conditions of the twentieth century—the impact of the mass audience on the one hand and the fact that some artists set out to fill the needs of this vast population.

I have picked up here and there some information about comic strips. Al Capp states that the comic strip was at first what its name declared it to be. It was a strip designed to make people laugh. But somewhere about 1931, one of those sharp-eyed newspapermen, sensing something in the population, told Chester Gould that he was now ready for what finally became the Dick Tracy comic; and it is something to read how Gould was told to draw the bullets entering into people, all the paraphernalia of cruelty and sadism that we know so well today. Why did it come just then? I believe that, as a result of the depression, rage, anger and bitterness were surging through the people of the United States; and the savage comic strip of Chester Gould supplied some sort of artistic expression of this. Since that time, as Capp said, the comic strip has changed completely and now it has joined the great band of representations of shooting, plotting, murdering, police-chasing thieves and gangsterism which is one of the most significant features of artistic production today.

At the same time there is expressed in strips not only gangster and police activities of people like Tracy and others, but also the lives of the great masses of the people, the things they would like to do. Joe Palooka must be the aim and the aspiration of God knows how many millions of young American boys, who would like to be champion of the world and live a pleasant and interesting life.

The people *need* these things. Is this *all* the people need? I do not say that for one minute. Given more freedom, would the people need more, would they attempt to penetrate more deeply into the life among them, would the things that they look at have to be of a different quality? I haven't the slightest doubt of it. But I cannot believe that it is accidental or something passing that there is this response in the early 1930s to a profound change in the attitude of the population and a corresponding change in the things at which they look. That what took place in the comic strip is not at all accidental is, in my opinion, proved by the gangster film.

The gangster film is one of the finest achievements of the modern American movie and it began more or less about 1931. That also, it seems to me, is a product of the depression. Now it is quite a phenomenon when some of the finest and most popular artists of the day, people like James Cagney and Edward G. Robinson, movie directors of the greatest skill and all the tremendous forces and technical talents of the industry are brought to bear to show in movie after movie the career of a gangster. In the last minute or two he is shot down to prove that crime does not pay, a gesture to morality. But the last minute or two does not matter in the least. The concentration of all these forces upon portraying this type of character corresponds to certain needs of the American population which is looking on. The gangster film has also been an immense success abroad. Cyril Connolly states that Americanism after the depression in Europe, as far as art is concerned, means the gangster film.

And finally, to clinch the argument, I want to take the detective novel. The gangster film made its concession to civic morality in the last minute. But civic morality produced a far deeper expression, I mean the type of tough detective who was developed with such consummate skill by Dashiell Hammett and Raymond Chandler. He (most often in the cinematic person of Humphrey Bogart) took law and order in his own hands. In my opinion he completes what the gangster film begins. And both of them are historical phenomena of great importance. They are examples of the tremendous frustration of individualism in the United States.

This country was built upon the idea of freedom of the individual personality. As far as I know, nowhere in the world was this achieved to the degree that it was achieved in the United States in the early days. But over the last few decades the power and weight of the collective organization of society have come to be in mortal conflict with individual free expression. Both the gangster, who at any rate is an individual and exercises his individual capacity to the fullest degree, and the detective, the individual who takes over from the state the task of ridding society of this gangster, are both examples of the denial of individual freedom of the American people, a frustration of which they have become acutely conscious during the last 20 years.

I hope some day to show that the artistic limitations of the gangster school are due to the fact that they are the product of social defeat and the narrowness of despair. They are men of the depression. Griffith was not. And Chaplin could satirize the shibboleths and pretenses of society as freely as he did because they were obvious enough for all to see and were not as yet part of a sense of universal crisis. The boldness and creative sweep of Griffith came from an enormous reservoir of social confidence. But the men of the depression are limited because there are other passions in the American people besides thwarted individualism. In *Mariners, Renegades and Castaways* I give my view that American society is driven by the fundamental conflict between the need for individual self-expression and the enormous need for collective association. This is the fundamental conflict in the world at large, though it has nowhere reached the pitch of sharpness that it has in the United States.

But this the movies do not touch except negatively. It is a sign of the deep antagonism of industrial relations in the United States and of the influence that the masses of the people have on the media which depend on their quarters, that there seems to be a common agreement not to touch the question of labour relations. The movie people realize that they would have to satisfy those who finance them; yet they understand that the American people will not go for any overt pro-boss propaganda. So that both of them, by an armed truce, agree that all such matters will be left untouched. *Birth of a Nation* had all the ferocity, the cruelty, the destructiveness of a real civil war. I don't believe that anyone today can dare to conceive any such picture. Classes, race, associations, embassies of foreign nations (not to forget the foreign market)—all would crowd into the blank sheet and fill it before he wrote a line.

I want to say a few words about jazz music. I have listened to it for several decades now. At the same time, as an amateur, I have paid a great deal of attention to the great composers. The most startling experience of my musical and artistic life is the level of musicianship of the great popular bands of the United States. Mozart and Beethoven would be at home in our modern concert halls. But I believe popular music in the United States would astonish them. It is difficult for me to conceive that at any time in history there has ever been a music of such quality, shared in so spontaneously and easily by the great mass of the population, as the bands and records of Louis Armstrong, Benny Goodman, Lionel Hampton and heaps of others. Their musicianship, I have been told by musicians, has reached a high pitch. And it depends entirely upon popular support and popular interest.

I have noticed in the United States a great number of people, and especially young people, untrained in formal music, whose ear and sense of musicianship, sense of timing, combinations of tone, color, etc. have been developed to an extraordinary pitch by the interest that most of the younger generation seems to have in the popular musicians. Here is an extraordinary development of popular culture such as never has existed before.

Furthermore, there is in the development of jazz from decade to decade, or even from year to year, a clear response to changes in the moods and attitudes of the American people, which in turn reflect economic and social development. Again the Depression marks the dividing line. They do not compose the songs they did before 1929 (or a few years after). They do not even play in the same way. To me *this* is what matters in the world of art today. Owing to the increasingly social organization of life and the corresponding technological changes and opportunities, the popular artists working for the mass are expressing powerful currents of thought and feeling as never before in a way that is quite new.

I said earlier that artistic quality does not interest me very much. Nevertheless, I know no greater artists in the twentieth century than Charlie Chaplin and D.W. Griffith. Two years ago I saw *City Lights* about five times in seven days to test my responses. It was more beautiful the last time than it was the first. And I felt the same general emotions that I feel when reading plays like *Twelfth Night* or *As You Like It*. I never miss Dick Tracy unless I cannot help it. Not for Tracy himself. He and his adventures do not interest me much. But over the years I have noticed a gallery of strange characters in Chester Gould's drawings that are to me a remarkable illustration of the types of citizens and types of lives in the United States as I have grown to know the country better and to be more familiar with the people. Again, I have the same feeling that I have had looking over old volumes of Hogarth's prints dealing with life in eighteenth century London.

What interests me is not the question of quality, but rather the form. Aeschylus, as far as we know, invented tragedy and tragic masterpieces at one and the same time. The regular account is that he took the *popular* Dionysian *festivals* and used them as a basis for the invention of his tragedy. But some deny this and say that the form originated with peasants who amused themselves in the countryside with primitive drama. Be that as it may, there is a whole horizon between the early attempts of Aeschylus and such a staggering masterpiece as *The Oresteia*. With Shakespeare a lot of work had been done by others and himself before he achieved his mature style. If, as I believe, new forms of art have been created over the last forty years, then sooner or later, when the people are able to express themselves more fully and completely, say more clearly what they want, and art is rid of its present social limitations, I see no reason at all why the most gifted artists should not express themselves in these forms. I read that Picasso is very much interested in comic strips. I am not surprised.

I mention here only two of my ideas. Suppose a man like Daumier had been given the freedom to organize a unit (like Disney, another great modern) and choose his artists for producing a strip about what he pleased. Is it unreasonable to think that under modern conditions that result would be something unprecedented in the world of art, both as form and as social communication? I cannot help believing that that great artist, with his insight into society and politics, would have accepted the form for its daily impact on so many millions and achieved miracles. Goya the same. (And yet a strip is not a cartoon. As a rule a cartoon deals with an event. Strips deal with human characters with whom you can identify yourself, and the form is infinitely freer and more flexible than the cartoon.) I take another example. Imagine a first-class draughtsman with an acute social and political sense who had a free hand to draw a strip of the life of a Negro family in the United States. I don't believe he would last two weeks. The whole country would be in an uproar. Do not think that I see merely political and social ideas being injected into the strip by good drawing. Not at all. For me the form is a natural, coming from deep instincts among the people. And the great artist who feels that develops the form.

I have no need to be reminded of the achievements of Western civilization in the realm of culture. Why then do I call European culture a poison? I refer specifically to that considerable body of American intellectuals who believe that they are the defenders of the culture of Europe against the masses of the American people. I can imagine nothing more intellectually pernicious and self-destroying. Today in 1953, European culture, like European civilization and in fact all western civilization, has reached a dead end. It has nothing more to say. And American writers and artists, like the fellows abroad, have nothing to say. Certainly many of them write very well and periodically one or the other registers with great force some aspect of contemporary life. But does anyone believe that new forms of art that matter to our century can be found in the way e.e. cummings prints his verse on the page? That O'Neill has discovered new forms of drama? That Tennessee Williams holds in his hand a future for the drama? They can be called new only from the narrowest and most superficial point of view.

I do not believe any such thing. The Greek drama was *new*. Elizabethan tragedy was *new*. The modern novel in the hands of Samuel Richardson was *new*. The nineteenth century Russian novelists added a new dimension to the novel. Pascal made the French language into modern prose. Rousseau gave it color and feeling and sensitivity. All these were expressions of vast social changes. But the twentieth century has seen the culmination of changes which make our world different from the past as no previous age has ever differed from its past. And all that I see *new* in art is movies, comic strips, soap operas, etc.

I believe that the distinguishing feature of the civilization of the twentieth century is the fact that the masses have entered upon the stage of history. And those people are most successful as individual artists, political leaders, etc., who recognize this. The totalitarians recognize it. But only for the purpose of perverting and crushing, distorting and using for their own destructive purposes, the new forces, movements and ideas and passions which have been let loose in our century. I cannot believe that the incessant soul-searching and wailing and misery that distinguishes so much of modern literature expresses any future. To me it is the end of something, the end of a civilization, and particularly the domination of the literary work of that civilization by intellectuals. That for me is old. These intellectuals actually have believed that they are the world. Thus they give to themselves and their writings between 1920 and 1930 the title of "The Lost Generation". They, that infinitesimal minority, may have been lost. Did the hundreds of millions of young people living in that decade consider themselves in any way to be a lost generation? I see no sign anywhere that they did.

I believe then that the forms in which these new passions and needs can be expressed are already clearly before us, although thwarted by the limitations of the very society that has helped to produce them. I say that what Western civilization reveres as culture is poison because, among other reasons, it is permeated by the idea that culture is a matter of "education". How educated were the Greeks who shouted and stamped and gave Aeschylus the prize thirteen times? Some people accept the fact that it is the interest, the ideas, the needs and the passions of the masses of the people that are going to be, for good or ill, dominating features in the civilization of the future. They agree that this is inevitable, but what conclusions do they draw from that? They foresee or they hope that the future of art rests with the time when the masses of the people will be educated and when a sufficient number of them will have learned to go to concerts and appreciate Beethoven or read Shakespeare regularly and have learned to appreciate T.S. Eliot. Only upon this basis do they see the possibilities of an expanding culture. I consider that view not only wrong but absolute death. It has no foundation whatsoever in the history of society or art.

There are, I suppose, a thousand American cities with people of more education than there were in Athens of the fifth century BC. There are more educated American people, I expect, who see movies in a week than the total who saw Shakespeare's plays during his working lifetime. Yet compare Aeschylus,

Sophocles, Euripedes and Shakespeare with the best that we can do. The disproportion is fantastic. So I cannot begin to believe that the future of art rests with the masses of people learning to appreciate art in the terms that intellectuals understand this today. I believe that the future of art rests with the development of great individual artists (or groups) working on the forms which people in the United States have demonstrated that they really want today, or in such new forms as may arise.

You see, therefore, that I am serious when I speak about my interest in comic strips and the life of the people in the United States. This does not mean, by the way, that the great art of the past will be ignored by the modern masses. The people of the United States are not interested in culture for culture's sake. Here again I have watched them. They are ready to go to see *Julius Caesar* and judge Shakespeare on his merits. When the time comes and the operas of Mozart are presented in forms that appeal to them, they will make their judgement and accept them. I believe they will accept a great deal. Some years ago a film was produced called *A Song To Remember*. I found it enormously interesting and did not share the hostility which many lovers of Chopin and people who have studied Chopin's life greeted it. What astonished me was that immediately afterwards the book shops were denuded of their lives of Chopin. Millions of gramophone records of his music were sold; and sheet music and copies of his works could not satisfy the demand. But the American people accept it not as culture, rather as something which they find interesting. If they don't find it interesting, they let it pass without a qualm.

This is the division between the culture of the intellectuals and educated people and the desire of the mass to interest itself and amuse itself and be stimulated. It was never so sharp as in the much-vaunted nineteenth century. And it is this division which in my opinion the twentieth century has to break down. I see in the United States a very clear, immensely interesting current of activity and mass response which seems to me to be the road of the future. If there is any other road, I would be glad to hear of it. This is the one that I see and that I am interested in. And the great power of the American people in this matter is due to the size of the country, to the high development of technology and, above all, what so many people abuse the American masses for, to the absence of traditional culture. That which so many, including Americans, consider the greatest weakness of the American people, I consider to be their greatest strength. It is their lack of traditional culture that enables them to decide what they want and to support it with that freedom and vigor which is missing in other countries, particularly in Europe.

Note that this popular art which is produced and has reached its highest development under American conditions is received with immense popularity all over the world. It is a sign that there is something here that deeply appeals to the masses of the modern world.

I must say a few words about the social limitations of this popular art. Let me take as an example a new phenomenon, the comedians on television. Now anyone familiar with Aristophanes, Rabelais and Molière knows that their comic genius is rooted in the unashamedly farcical. I have been watching men like Sid Caesar, Milton Berle, Red Buttons, Red Skelton, Jackie Gleason and Wally Cox (Mr

Peepers). I am astonished that week after week, every seven days, these men produce their skits, full of wit, humor, observation of life, knowledge of human nature, often aiming good-natured and sometimes savage satire at the absurdities of the age. Some of them are highly gifted in various ways, singing, dancing, miming well enough to be able to gain the particular effects that they want. If one were to make a selection of the best things that are being produced, there would result a body of work which could stand comparison with that of any humorists of any generation except the very greatest masters. As is customary in America, where the cult of personality is carried to such a pitch in everything, the show revolves around one individual. The idea that it is the writers who give them the material is absurd. The writers write for the personalities or the types of personalities that these comedians have already developed.

I find something characteristic of our age in the combination of organization and personality which goes into the weekly presentation of these shows—the vast audiences, the close relation between these audiences and popular moods and the performers, writers, etc. I see that Robert Sherwood is to write some truly cultured plays for television. And to do this he stipulated that he have "absolute freedom". And I turned to *Omnibus* one day and saw Brian Aherne and somebody playing the love scene from *Henry V*. All this I conceive to be culture and a serious attempt to "raise the tone" of television. To each his own. It will raise the tone or lower the tone, but it will be the same tone, and these are tones that Europeans will always sing better than Americans. I prefer the comedians.

But are they incipient Swifts or Molières of the twentieth century? No, they are not. It is because of the social limitations from which they suffer, limitations that Aristophanes, for one, did not suffer from. The weakness is that they cannot, for example, touch seriously upon politics and the great social conflicts that characterize our age. This is the strangle-hold. Politics, in its most comprehensive sense, is more important to us than to any preceding civilization except perhaps the Athenian Greeks. But it is taboo. One slip and a comedian can ruin himself for good. But Aristophanes ran riot among the gravest social and political problems of his day. In *Tartuffe*, Molière pilloried the religious hypocrite. Our popular artists have to keep away from all this, from labor and capital, from socialism and fascism, from war and peace, from religion, from the merciless characterization of not only great political figures but even distinctive and important social types.

We talk about political freedom. But in these modern mass media, which are so perfectly adapted for immediate communication to 20 million people, the artist is limited as never before. Strangely enough the Greek drama, though subsidized by the state, was free! The comic dramatists in particular thought nothing was sacred. I do not believe that the Greeks would have objected to *Birth of a Nation* as a reconstruction of history. Instead some liberal dramatist would have produced *his* play on the subject. And Aristophanes might have ridiculed *both* plays, and the Civil War, and, if he felt like it, made a mockery of Abraham Lincoln. I believe that if our popular comedians had that freedom, and I hope they will have it some day, then evening after evening, the millions would tune in to see the topics of the day torn apart. Sid Caesar or Red Buttons may not be men of the calibre of Swift or Anatole France; but I am quite satisfied that in these forms they have worked out and been given the freedom (or at least the consciousness of backing) that an artist must have, and out of them can spring artists as great as any we have ever known.

For the great artist is but an individual who embodies in himself some mighty social current of thought and feeling. And there are some new and mighty currents of thought and feeling abroad in our world. Never before was the possibility of social communication so great. The proof of all this is in the future. But the future is not born all at once. It exists in the present. The thing is to know where to look. And this letter can do no more than indicate to you where I am looking, why I look there, and what I see. Allow me to say at least this, that in art, as well as in politics, I am a profound believer in what is so lightly called by so many democracy.

P.S. I do not believe that the present popular art forms are necessarily or even probably the forms in which a great new culture will express itself. I am pretty certain that no gifted and modern artist of today can pour his content into these forms, that Sartre or someone else can, for example, begin to write artistic soap operas. I know that great and new and enduring art forms are not developed in that way. First some distinctively new content takes hold of these forms and in realizing itself transforms them. Secondly, the imagination and technique of a great artist are shaped by new content and new forms. He attains his maturity in them, and then the explosive creations begin.

Why am I so certain that the old forms are outmoded? First, the general curve of decline can be traced from Rousseau to the present day. Writers have been writing more and more about less and less. I shall conclude with the case of Sartre. He published a few years ago a pathetic book, *What is Literature?* Sartre's chapter headings tell the whole story. 1. What is Writing? 2. Why Write? 3. For Whom Does One Write? 4. Situation of the Writer in 194?

There is much profundity and great brilliance in this illuminating book. In it he says of the French writers: "We are the most bourgeois writers in the world. Well housed, decently dressed, not so well fed, perhaps; but even that is significant; the bourgeois spends less on his food, proportionately, than the workman; much more for his clothes and lodging. All of us, moreover, are steeped in bourgeois culture. . . . But as for us, we were used to literature long before beginning our first novel. To us it seemed natural for books to grow in a civilized society, like trees in a garden. . . . We knew from the time we were adolescents the memorable and edifying features of great lives. . . . Thanks to these models and recipes, from our childhood on the career of a writer seemed to us magnificent, though without surprises; one is promoted partly by merit, partly by seniority. That's what we are. In other respects, saints, heroes, mystics, adventurers, angels, enchanters, executioners, victims, as you like. But first of all, bourgeois. There's no shame in admitting it. And different from one another only in the way we each assume this common situation."

There you have it, by the most distinguished man of letters in Europe today, himself a product of the most highly cultivated and the oldest literary tradition in Europe. They are encased at birth. For decades they wrote well by fighting the traditions, but even that is now exhausted. That is why I call that whole cultural tradition poison.

The final proof is Sartre's prescription. This highly educated and gifted man proposes that the way out is for writers to embrace the working class, to express the aspirations of the proletariat, etc., etc. That he should write such nonsense is evidence of the pitiable position literature is in. Great literature, great art, is not produced in that way, and Sartre more than anyone else must know that. Shakespeare expressed the great new concept of bourgeois individualism perfectly, but he did not "turn to" the bourgeoisie. He lived at a time when these new social forces were expressing themselves in a million ways, large and small; when the clash between the old and the new was taking place on every side; and he saw these things and wrote. He was one of the new men, the forces that shaped them were shaping him, and out of all this his creative imagination shaped his unique figures and techniques. This process of shaping society and the artist I see at work in the fields I have indicated. Only the future will tell.

June 1953

II. MY DEAR LEYDA

What exactly do you think of my book? [*Mariners, Renegades and Castaways*] You praise it for its fire and drive; but add that fire should not drive out logic. You stop there. Where is my logic weak? If it has fire, unity, drive—where do these come from? You imply that it is due to my "feelings", because of my imprisonment. My dear fellow, my book was planned that way. The book meant all that to me from the start. Why else would I write a book on Melville? I am primarily interested in the social crisis of our time. I studied literature *and* criticism for years, but then I dropped them for political writing. Nevertheless I continued to read certain classics. The divorce between criticism and life haunted me. Aeschylus, Shakespeare, Milton—I felt them real and living; T.S.Eliot, I.A. Richards and the rest of the critics—fine intellects (I was trained enough to see that), but remote. Over the years I have bridged the gap. Melville and my public audience did that for me. This is not "feelings". It is work, method. It is good or bad; but don't ignore or evade it.

I am perfectly aware of the aesthetic foundations on which *my* criticism is based. This means that I am also aware of the fact that my book is an uncompromising challenge to the prevalent schools of critics and, in particular, to the Melvilleans. I don't want them to be kind to me. Hell! No. My book is not kind to them. From the start it faces the reader with this—if James is right, or rather, justified, then something is terribly wrong with the others. The Communists' social criticism is little but political brutality, and the psychoanalysts seem to me to be flogging their own horses (the ineradicable evil in human nature and the need to submit). I believe that by my method, both society and literature are equally illuminated.

Look at what I have done in a popularly written book. I have put forward a theory of *characters in great fiction.* It is chiefly Melville's, but it is rooted in Aristotle and Hegel. I have already delivered lectures on this question, beginning with Aeschylus *(Oresteia* and *Prometheus Bound)*, then on Shakespeare, Milton, Rousseau and the characters of Dostoyevsky's *Karamazov* and *The Possessed*. Each great character is rooted in his own age. The changes in social development are reflected in them—that is what makes the characters "original". Furthermore, they are logically connected with each other. I show Hamlet's relation to Lear; the relation of Hamlet and Lear to Satan; I see Rousseau as a bridge; then I take Melville's characters; and finally those of Dostoyevsky. From Hamlet through Ishmael and Pierre to Stavrogin is a *continuous line*.

When Murray says that Ahab is Milton's Satan, he shows to perfection the method I am challenging. I do not wish to hold him down to a single sentence in an essay, for I have no use for such niggling criticism. I know that Murray has said, in the introduction to *Pierre*, that Ahab is the superbest prophecy of the essence of fascism that any literature has produced. Wonderful. That is exactly what I think; but for that very reason that Ahab cannot be Satan.

Satan is Milton's portrait of a type he had grown to fear and hate—"new men", men who all through the eighteenth century would destroy the foundations of all established government, authority and order. Milton would have pointed to Robespierre and said, "I told you so. I knew this would be the end." The defiance, the rage, the passion are similar; but in each century the form is specific and individual. This form is the essence of literature. I place Ahab *where he belongs*. I begin there. The artist does that instinctively; the critic, however, must do it consciously and clearly. I, the critic, insist on this and it explains why I so sharply delineate the social roots of Melville's characters and all literary characters.

Each historic rebel, rebels against something very specific and it takes a specific literary form, precisely because of its specific social character. If you do not bear this in mind, literary form becomes a mere mould into which something is poured. Ahab is a man of the nineteenth century; and yet, at the same time, Melville is doing what Aeschylus, in *The Oresteia* and *Prometheus*, and Shakespeare, in *King Lear* do—they see the whole of the past in the present. Their world is horizontal, covering the known world, and vertical, bringing as they do imaginative conceptions of history which they boldly place in the contemporary world. Artists do this by creative instinct; they are summing up all civilization and all history in these works. We, the critics, must keep the distinctions clear.

My book, in a sense, is a critical manifesto. Everything hangs on putting the characters and the author where they belong. Orestes, Hamlet and Pierre each have a similar problem to settle; but just look at what happens to each in the concrete work—Orestes goes mad, but wins out with the direct help of Religion and Politics; Hamlet barely succeeds and ends in personal ruin; Pierre is a disastrous failure and shrivels up. Why these differences?

Aeschylus, devoted to the democracy, if a little nervous of its excesses, was writing for an audience which shared his fundamental ideas. At the end of the Libation Bearers (Act II), Orestes was in the same mess as Hamlet and Pierre; but in Act II Aeschylus boldly brought Athena and Apollo to his rescue. He and his age believed in them, and without their intervention, the play would have petered out. By contrast, *Shakespeare could not bring anything directly to Hamlet's rescue*. In 1600, Hamlet, the new man, the man of original instincts, the intellectual, of free individual speculation, was already outside society. He was not one of its fundamental forces. Aeschylus and Orestes were not outside society, and that is why Shakespeare can conclude *Hamlet* only by artistic brutality. For me, social criticism and literary criticism are indistinguishable. You are startled, I am sure;

but I have begun, so I must finish.

Let us, bearing Ahab in mind, stick to Hamlet. Why is he the character he is? He is the new type of man, the modern intellectual and some of him is in *every* modern man. His greatest period is the 17th and eighteenth century; but with Rousseau his isolation begins; Melville completes his complete collapse; Dostoyevsky his total degradation. Orestes was no intellectual. He made the transition from the blood feud, organic society, to the Greece of law, public responsibility, democracy. He is similar to Hamlet only in the terrific breakdown of personality; but the particular content and forms are in the age and the author, the author's relation to the age and his own place in it. I want you to note that Aeschylus was a complete man, a complete citizen in that profoundly social age. Prometheus is a completely social man. Shakespeare, on the other hand, was perhaps the first of the intellectuals, the first who made his living by going directly to the public. He was in touch with the Court and with the people; but he was outside. In *Henry V*, *Julius Caesar*, then *Hamlet* and *Lear*, you see Shakespeare tracing the intellectual type, going at it over and over again. The majority of critics of the last few years recognize that *Lear* is a social play. Feudalism, a conception of society as a whole, was going down before the doctrine of Goneril, Regan and Edmund—*each for himself.* The intellectual could talk and protest, but he could not effectively influence affairs (the plot). In *Macbeth*, *Hamlet* and *Lear*, Shakespeare is in trouble around Acts 3 and 4. He is structurally successful only in *Othello*. Othello is another of these men seeking his own individual road. He is a professional soldier, an alien, and very much outside of society. Instead of the old medieval organic society, Othello elevates not each for himself, but a woman as his guiding star. He is one of the first Romantics. In the structure, style, etc., of this play, Shakespeare achieves perfection, for it is easier than the others because the individualist is more or less like other men. But in the other plays Shakespeare cannot conclude—in *Hamlet* he brings in a foreigner, Fortinbras; in *Lear* he brings in the forces of the King of France; in *Macbeth*, the forces of the King of England. Without these external forces, "evil" would conquer. Serious literary criticism is social criticism. Aeschylus could call on Religion and Politics, Shakespeare could not. His characters could not either. But Shakespeare did have some confidence in society as a whole. The intellectual, the individualist, was at the beginning of a great historical career. Melville chronicled their decline. He sent them to the bottom of the sea, but he had a social perspective. It is in every line of *Moby Dick*, positively and negatively, and it belongs to the twentieth century.

Moby Dick is magnificent in structure. The technique is the technique of a world that once more must be seen as an integrated whole—the individual, technology, society, Nature. There are scenes of Shakespearean grandeur, but they are given to crazy Ahab. It is the panorama of social activity, Nature and, above all, the crew which, with the dramatic episodes, are fused into a whole. There is nothing like this anywhere. Dostoyevsky never encompasses this; in him, Nature is absent. Melville has fused all. When an author writes pages after pages about social activity, the critic must find out why. This is what is new in Melville; though the moment he isolates an intellectual, as Pierre, his form goes straight back to the form of Shakespeare, but without the movement and vitality.

When people suggest or hint I attribute to Melville ideas that he could not possibly have had, or that he was interested mainly in the human condition and not in political prophecy or economic relations, they show merely that they have a very superficial conception of politics and economics.

I want to take Murray again. In his introduction to Pierre, he says specifically: "*Moby Dick*, for instance, was the superbest prophecy of the essence of fascism that any literature produced." To me *that* is what matters *in 1953.* When you look at the paragraph you will see that Murray claims that Ahab represented "the forces antithetical to the cultural compound of Puritanism, rationalism, materialism, which were lurking, barbarized by repression, in the heart of Western man, biding the moment for their eruption." I go along with this. He says splendidly: "It would be a fatal mistake to regard his autobiographical writings mainly as egotistical exhibitions of purely personal experiences." Both here and in the essay, Murray is aware of the precise, specific situation of Ahab; but, whereas in the treatment of Pierre he is historically precise, in the essay he gives the impression that Ahab is a generalized archetypal figure, a representative of universal human nature.

I claim, however, that Melville knew precisely what produced Ahab. I analyze what *Melville wrote* about Ahab—his eating, sleeping, the isolation of command, his bitterness at the promise of science and its inability to solve the problems of the human personality, etc. Ahab is a Prometheus in a social age unsuited to the type—in that sense, he is "archetypal" if you will. Melville seemed to say *today* Prometheuses are no longer viable; but to see that, you have to be aware of the crew and its constant opposition to the individualist on all sorts of things, large and small. I know of few more thrilling moments in literature for a modern reader, one of us, than when Melville says that the crew is composed of renegades from all over the world. He knew what he was doing so clearly—compare Whitman. Whitman in his poetry is a continuation of individualism, magnificent too, with a desperate desire to find a community. He has the same preoccupation as Melville; but Whitman celebrates individualism where Melville attacked it. Whitman adds the world community one by one, adding them remorselessly by trade and nationality. Melville cuts through all this and fuses the whole into one; but it is the same preoccupation—the individual and the need for community. Melville also saw further than Whitman into the social types around him and hence this glorious book, this literary creation, *Moby Dick*.

I want to continue for a moment with structure and style. Note the tremendous pace of the Shakespearean drama and that incomparable blank verse line. A new world of movement was expressing itself here. Why drama? Because the clash of social forces—the new individual versus the old world order and authority—was direct, the forces were interlocked. Each side could *speak for itself.* As Shakespeare gained an adequate conception of the character, the poetry becomes indistinguishable from the drama. The attitude to the life of Ahab and the crew are far from that. They are not expressed in drama, because the two are not in direct conflict. Melville is the mediator, he has to be, and that accounts for his technique, structure, style. I could not go into all these things in my book; but I laid the basis for future discussion.

I strive for a social criticism which will illuminate the text. I say categorically that the work of Aeschylus is the result primarily and fundamentally of the age he lived in, *his own life* in it and his reactions to it, and the prevailing sentiments of the people for whom he wrote. In the six authors I chose for my Columbia lectures, I took each in relation to his age and I took up structure, plot, style and showed the relations to the problems of the age *as they presented themselves to the artists*. I examined what the great artist used of tradition and what he created. That is the only proof.

Let me repeat it. Melville heralded the age when once more the individual had to be integrated with society, with Nature, and now with technology. Hence his attempt to include *everything* and relate everything to everything else in *Moby Dick*. Note that *Moby Dick*, in its effort to catch everything, can be seen as a gigantic scenario—so an artist's material and needs push him forward into the technique of a new age. For me, these questions are fundamental to a modern criticism. My "feelings" have nothing to do with this. I had mobilized myself to fight a battle in criticism, not the Government for pushing me around.

Let me take my ideas further, for once you begin you have to go on. An impressionist critic is to be judged by his results, all criticism should be. The psychoanalysts have a method; but I say that to the extent you speculate on the unconscious, and make that your main emphasis, to that extent you destroy the book the author wrote. Moreover, you say what he did not say—and in Melville's case, what he took great care not to say. For Melville, Moby Dick, the whale (I take my life in my hands and push out into the open sea) symbolizes nothing—zero—a big fish in the sea; that's all. It is Ahab and Ishmael who make these fantastic symbolisms; and Melville is superb in the way he contrasts their fantasies with the objective naturalism of Moby Dick. Moby Dick is, after all, a wrinkled forehead and hump. I have shown where this symbolizes science and the weight of the past; but only in Ahab's crazy head. Melville himself will have nothing to do with that. He said so. He was mortally afraid at Moby Dick being taken for an allegorical figure. That for him was crucial. When you look at his structure you see that Ishmael writes "as one of the crew", a strictly realistic account of Moby Dick. The combination of realism and superstition, but always with a basis of historical truth, is superbly done and very consciously done. That is how it was. You can feel Melville's sympathy with the sailors and his own superb reporting of the crew—objective, realistic, and their superstitions based on that; Ahab and Ishmael, each with his own preoccupation. The subtle changes of style and yet the total mastery—the swift transitions from reporting to psychology, to metaphysics—these are the themes of the novel; but the actual Moby Dick is the first one, the Moby Dick of the crew.

We also have Melville, in his constantly recurring proofs and descriptions of how a sperm whale can smash a ship, openly safeguarding what he considers the main danger spot. Why? Because unless this is accepted, the reader will see Moby Dick as Nemesis or *deus ex machina*. Melville knew that if this was done, then his book was ruined. He has told us what happened—you get a character, an original character, and once you see it, you see everything else differently. Mark his words *(The Confidence Man*, Chapter 44): "So that, in certain minds, there follows upon the adequate conception of such a character, an effect, in its way, akin to that which in genesis attends upon the beginning of things." A whole *new world* swims before the writer's eyes. Character and surroundings have a life of their own. To mistake this for allegory, is to ruin it. That is why Melville gets so mad at the idea that he was constructing something to prove a point. My position is that any criticism which does not make that clear is bound to misinterpret Melville.

This brings me to my final point. What must a critic do, today, in 1953, when he wishes to assess a classical, non-contemporary, author? I say that he *must* get into his own head what were the social and political assumptions of the work he is studying. *Not* whom the artist voted for, *not* what parties he joined, or anything of the kind; but what his creative work showed to be the assumptions on which he *wrote.* Plain biography here can be misleading. You remember Robinson Crusoe? Defoe had an interesting political career in the superficial sense. It is not very important. What matters is that Robinson, on his desert island, behaved exactly as a British bourgeois would have behaved—in his thoughts, in his plans, in his work, in every Goddamn thing. It is there on the page. In that period Defoe assumed them instinctively. They were the foundations of his mind. By politics I do not mean whether he was Whig, Tory or Dissenter; he was bourgeois. *From his book I see that.*

Now, I repeat, a *modern* critic has to *begin* there. If he does not, he does not belong to our age. Hazlitt did not have to, nor Coleridge, nor Bradley. They lived in an age in which concern with individual character was part of the total intellectual climate. They did very fine work. Those days, however, are over; *that* work is done. *We* have to *begin* with the social ideas. I do not say that a critic has to write about that aspect. God forbid. He writes about what he pleases. But this is the mental framework of our age. The critic who ignores it will find himself pursuing single aspects until he finds himself way out of contact with anything or anybody, other than his own coterie. I cannot go into it here except to repeat (with Melville) that the age of individualism is over. The intellectual must once more be incorporated with the universal. It is a profound subject *today.*

I hope you get what I mean by my attempt to relate structure (Aeschylus, Shakespeare, Melville) to the age, as it is reflected in the life and work of the writer. Here the text is primary and the equipment needed by the critic unlimited. For example, look at Melville's treatment of the crew. Look at the adjectives he uses about them. Every time he touches their work his pen flows and glows. Why? Watch, too, Ishmael's language. Over and over again he is combining the land and sea. He wants the adventurousness of the sea and the stability of the land—not the land of Manhattan and New Bedford, but the land of adventure. Hence his recurring similes of the prairie and the sea. He knows, though, that the prairie is, or soon will be, exhausted. This is in *Mardi* as plain social analysis. The literary leads to the social, the social back to the literary. Note Melville's metaphors in dealing with Steelkilt, with the white horse in the whiteness chapter. You will see, as in many other places, that Melville's historical conceptions when expressed in literature are always in terms of a human type. He has a vision of man at his best in previous days—tall, handsome, "bluff-browed", God-like Israel Potter in his prime. That type is gone. Its descendants are Ahab, Ishmael, Stubb and Flask. Melville seeks a new social integration. It is not literally historical. The history is transmuted into literary creations; but they are, in his conceptions, historically and logically connected.

The critic works at the text and reveals the social assumptions of the author. Did Melville have this or that in mind? It is a ridiculous and heavily motivated question. I, in 1953, read his text and rebuild his often unstated assumptions, remembering always that he is an artist and expresses his assumptions in literary form. I do not read his letters and his life to understand his work; rather, I read his work to understand his letters and life. Praise God that we know so little about Shakespeare's life. This kind of working back to the author's unstated assumptions is for me the first necessity. I say that when I do that and look at his work and our world I see certain things which are of fundamental importance today. There is confusion about the word "politics". Melville had a *philosophical* conception of the crew. Where could mankind find what Ahab, Ishmael and the others had lost? I show from his books how, in pursuing his own aims, he transformed the crew of *Typee* into the crew of *Moby Dick*, from a bunch of debauched drunkards and criminals into the men of tragic graces.

I shall end this long letter with one point. Look at that scene with the magnetic lights—way out at sea the boundaries of civilization, magnetic lights flashing, Ahab seeking a greater, fuller, more satisfying contact with life. Normality, responsibility, in the person of Starbuck is saying: "I want to go home. Let us go home," back to the normal, the established, to the world of Nantucket, New Bedford and Manhattan. The officers and the crew, the rest of the world, are standing by and looking on, aware that their fate is involved; but, as they have been trained, they leave it to their betters to decide. How is it possible not to feel that the world Melville knew, had left what it had achieved and was in a no-man's land, seeking to pierce something beyond? The whole world—Bildad, Peleg, New Bedford patricians, the *Pequod*, officers, crew, all the world of 1851 and the specter of pagan barbarism, Fedallah there also. I cannot argue about this. You feel it or you don't. And if you feel it, you have to ask—no man's land between what and what? Think of another superb scene at the beginning of the voyage when the *Pequod* sets out with old Bildad singing the hymn and Ishmael, as usual, hoping to find some spot where he will have both sea and land; then they stop, the boat goes back and the *Pequod* plunges forward. Surely a society is going somewhere, from somewhere, seeking something. What society, going where, seeking what?

I have tried to answer. I do not say that I have said everything. Melville had a lot to say about religion. I leave it out. Why? He was a poor theologian; religion does not interest us today as it did his generation; and most important, it was not vital to the book. You cannot write on Dante and leave out religion. You can do it with Melville. I insist that you must have a basis for criticism. I have given mine and I find that it does not lessen Melville. It raises him. It enables me to read his books whole, and it helps me to pose and solve strictly literary problems.

So will you please tell me, quite frankly. What do you think of my book?

7 March 1953

III. MY DEAR SCHAPIRO,

The question of *Lear* recurs. For me, Shakespeare's characters are an embodiment of the assault upon the ordered conception of the medieval world (God, Nature,

Society, Reason, State, Church, etc.) attacked in the cause of free individualism. It has been demonstrated over and over again that the key word in *Lear* is Nature. It was no longer beneficent. This is what Lear discovers and this is the significance of the storm. His world (that is to say, the medieval world) has fallen to pieces. I find the same in *Prometheus Bound* and in *Moby Dick*—what man has hitherto considered his presiding beneficence is now discovered to be an enemy. The cause is objective, but the representative feels it subjectively. Hence in all three works, there is the *scene* of desolation, the defiant figure out in the open, and there are the representative figures of the poor, the disinherited, the mass. The very setting shows that man is once more without a conceptual home.

In each case the defiant figure mercilessly attacks the old ways and speaks of the new. Lear's attack on the old regime is clear enough—he condemns *everything*. It seems that you disagree with me when I say that Lear outlines the new. Let us stick to the new. Lear proposes a new distribution of income in favour of the poor. We cannot take that lightly. Granville Barker thinks it is the climax of the play; so do I. It means a redistribution of income. Swinburne went so far as to call it socialism; he is entirely wrong. This is the seventeenth century, the beginning of enterprise and individualism.

Lear, and all other Elizabethans, considered Nature the keystone of their structure. If the concept is in ruins, then it must be examined. Hence Lear asks: "Is there any cause in Nature which creates people like Goneril and Regan?"; and, dramatically emphasized, "What is the cause of thunder?" Edwin Redgrave in his volume *Literature and Society* says that in *Lear* two societies are in conflict—the old society and the society of each for himself. Many modern critics accept that.

In *Prometheus Bound*, Prometheus is in conflict with the king of Gods and men directly; Lear is in conflict with Elizabethan Nature through his conflict with Goneril and Regan; Ahab, in Moby Dick, is in conflict with fire as the source of power. In each case an established conception, the established conception, has been found wanting by the defiant rebel. This is why Lear denounces the thunder and lightning for joining with his daughters. Previously he thought Nature was on his side. He denounced Cordelia in the name of Nature, he cursed Goneril in the name of Nature; but now it seems that Nature has joined with his evil daughters. He wavers, it is true, in his conception of Nature—even in the storm scene; but the change in his attitude is decisive.

Danby, the author of *Shakespeare's Doctrine of Nature*, is very detailed about all this; but he does not know what to make of Lear. He thinks that Lear, in his despair, is harking back to the old medieval communist ideas. I believe he is wrong. Lear's behavior in Act I shows that he is an individualist, for he puts his own feelings above the state and the family. When I examine the storm scene I see that—1. Nature is no longer beneficent and *therefore* it must be examined afresh, scientifically, in the nature of Goneril and the cause of thunder; 2. income must be distributed not according to estates, but according to social need; and 3. Lear creates a tribunal of the Fool and the madmen, which he calls a Great Council, and asks it to judge Goneril and Regan, the reigning monarchs. Later Lear says of evil-doers, "None does offend. None." No one is personally responsible for his evil deed.

I say that here is the creed of liberal humanitarianism for two hundred and fifty years to come. In his utter revulsion against the society, which had cast him out, Lear lets his thoughts run—and they run in that direction. Danby and the others miss this. There are two societies, the old one and the free struggle of Goneril and Regan. Shakespeare knows that the Gonerils and Regans will win in the end, that the old society is doomed; but he introduces a third, Edgar, who belongs to neither. Edgar is a liberal intellectual, outside of both, a former prosperous yeoman who has been cast down into the ranks of the agricultural vagrants. The play is packed with Elizabethan social types; and there was no more urgent a social problem in Shakespeare's day than the number and condition of these vagrants.

The critics have not penetrated as yet into the real concreteness of *Lear*. For that we, today, have to recreate for ourselves some pictures of what was new in Shakespeare's day and Shakespeare's own relation to it. I think the key is the great and immediate success of *Hamlet*. Hamlet is an intellectual, the first of the moderns, in drama what Descartes, Hobbes and Locke are in philosophy. His virtue (and his vice) is his love of intellectual speculation, and that in a world where his special business is to think primarily of his social responsibilities. Hamlet *questions* every accepted canon of his day in the light of his own individual response to it. My contention is that he was, to his first audiences, an exciting figure who said what all were more or less thinking. He was the embodiment of one of the greatest of the new freedoms—freedom of the individual intellect. Shakespeare had been watching and working on this type for years—you see it in Henry V, then Brutus; but he really gets hold of the character in Hamlet. *Lear* is the end result of all this intellectual speculation, since Shakespeare carries to a logical conclusion all the doubts and queries of *Hamlet*. But in his fundamental understanding of this type, lies the well-known weakness of structure in *Hamlet* and *Lear*. At the end of Act III, *Lear* is past its climax; *Hamlet* is concluded by a tour de force. This type, in action and words, could pose fundamental questions and, for two centuries and a half, it would do so; but it could not resolve them. The problems raised are all resolved externally.

One question remains—for us, the most important one. I say that Lear speaks with the vision of centuries to come. What do Lear's ravings amount to? Remember that he repeats them in Act IV and that Shakespeare, to make doubly sure, says them, all over again in the sub-plot of Gloucester. It is, I repeat, the creed of liberal humanitarianism. Social life no longer has divine or natural sanction. Man is "unaccommodated man." Men will have to *investigate* Science and Nature. Crime and poverty are objective things with objective causes. The poor have character and, perhaps, as good a judgement as the rich and educated. Finally, and this is embedded in the very structure of the play, in the new world *there is no real place for the intellectual*. The new world is a world of unrestrained struggle for power. Lear has no place in it. Cordelia has no place in it; and Edgar, who rules in the end, assumes his duties as a man sentenced to a lifetime of hard labor.

This is how I see Lear. He realizes clearly the breakdown of the old system. Wounded by it, as Ahab was wounded, he goes mad and in his impaired ravings he outlines the creed by which intellectuals will live for centuries to come. It is not outlined as a creed, except in two fundamental attitudes—first, that men of good will had to turn to the poor, the humble, the disinherited (Lear says it and Gloucester repeats it); and second, that men of good will had no social standards to live by, other than their own individual sense of right and wrong and their sense of personal integrity.

The real difficulty, as I see it, is confusing our view of Shakespeare with his own ideas and the people he wrote for. We today can see his work as we can see Melville's—with a perspective gained by history; but Melville's theory of original characters enables us to bridge the gap. Shakespeare observed and then, as great artists will, pursued certain indications to the end. How much did his audiences see? I believe that they saw, or rather felt, as much as we—and perhaps more, though in a different way. The elements from which Hamlet and Lear came were all around them, existing in themselves—a very concrete reality, enabling them to follow emotionally the speculative ranging of Shakespeare in a way that we cannot. Poor Melville had no audience. His real audience were the mariners, renegades and castaways; but they could not read. I cannot help noting that once Shakespeare had done *Lear*, he was through with great tragedy and, I feel that, in a similar way, *Moby Dick* was an end.

The decision in my case is still pending; but as soon as I hear anything I shall let you know.

9 March 1953

IV. DEAR PROFESSOR KERMODE,

I listened last evening to your talk on *King Lear* on BBC2. I would call it a careful summary of where critical opinion in Britain stands today on this play. That view is, in my opinion, not merely critically misguided but, to put it bluntly, gives an utterly false view of what *King Lear* is about. It encapsulates the misunderstanding of Shakespeare which is rampant in English criticism.

I shall now proceed to outline the arguments for my view, and I do it under two headings—a) the play itself; and b)the play as the summation of Shakespeare's lifelong concern with what was for him the major function of government.

a)The play itself.

Structurally *King Lear* is the finest of Shakespeare's plays. With a professor like yourself, I can afford to be brief. Act I poses the problem and establishes the selfishness, the violence (and viciousness) of *King Lear*. A most genuine beginning of a play of horrors. Act II shows Lear being punished for his deficiencies. Act III transfers from the scenes of those who govern to the open heath. Emphasis is usually placed there on Lear's denunciations of nature and society (purposely lacking in effective substance). But the real significance of Act III is the confrontation between Lear and Poor Tom.

The play can be made or lost in Act III. I propose the following consideration for any producer. A contemporary play begins with two acts portraying the grandeur and decadence of a President of the United States. Act III then shows the President in confrontation with a tramp of the lowest order in one of the public parks. There one would have the constituents of a play of which the whole world could be aware. That is what Shakespeare is doing, but I regret to say that while I have seen many performances of this play and read an infinite number of analyses, nowhere has it been made clear to me what Shakespeare is writing about. In the first three acts the characters and confrontations are posed; in Act IV the drama moves on. There is no need to go into it here, except that Shakespeare brings in a thoroughly crazy Lear to state certain positions of the most advanced extremity in the seventeenth century and still vibrant in contemporary thought.

On women: "But to the girdle do the Gods inherit. Beneath is all the fiends." Shakespeare on this basis would have had an intimate discussion with Freud. On the great image of authority: "A dog's obeyed in office." On that image of authority, Shakespeare could have a very close discussion with Marx and Lenin, the discussion centering around perhaps the most shattering line in all Shakespeare: "None does offend, none, I say none; I'll able 'em."

The play undoubtedly portrays humanity descended to its very dregs; but it is not defeatist. At a certain stage Gloucester, inevitably, asks Edgar: "Now, good sir, what are you?" and Edgar replies: "A most poor man, made tame to fortune's blows; Who, by the art of known and feeling sorrows, Am pregnant to good pity."

Nothing can be more unlike the political murderfest of the totalitarian states of eastern Europe. *Lear* is not a defeatist play. From its very degradation Shakespeare creates dramatic and effective events and a personality indicating the heights which mankind can achieve. Once this is grasped, line after line of the play hits with tremendous force. Edgar plays six different personalities before he becomes the ruler. That is Shakespeare's dramatic statement of a ruling democracy. But unless Shakespeare's central thesis is grasped, the play degenerates into a collection of significant episodes, forcibly knit together by all sorts of psychological, at times, theological unifiers.

b) The play as summation of Shakespeare's concern with the rejection of monarchy and the search for a replacement.

In Hamlet, Shakespeare poses what was for him at the time an insoluble question—the time is out of joint and Hamlet bewails that he "was born to set it right." The key word there is "born". That is Shakespeare's problem. No one can be "born" to govern, particularly when the times are out of joint. In *Othello* a man outside the ruling class finds it open to him on account of his wife; but this outsider cannot make it and the nobility of character is not enough. Shakespeare is at the question again in *Macbeth.* Success corrupts Macbeth; but in Act IV, Scene 3, Shakespeare shows us Malcolm on the one hand enumerating the crimes of one unfit to govern and, on the other, at the end stating: "The king-becoming graces. As justice, verity, temperance, stableness, Bounty, perseverance, mercy, lowliness, Devotion, patience, courage, fortitude."

That statement, however, is abstract. Shakespeare now has to demonstrate these necessities of government in a person, and that he does in Edgar. Edgar, therefore, is the climax of decades of political seeking (and dramatic presentation) by Shakespeare. Any performance of *Lear* which does not make Edgar the centre of its progression is certain to find itself exploring psychological backwaters and avoiding the plain highway by which Edgar leads us out of the collapse and decay of government (The Tragedy of King Lear) to authority and democracy based on experience.

To this I would like to add that the general public grasp the significance of

King Lear far more than the critics do. Up to World War I the most popular play was *Hamlet*; but with the crisis into which the world entered in 1914–1918, *Hamlet* has gradually been displaced, and today the decisive work of Shakespeare is the tragedy of *King Lear*. But that work will only receive its full power when people realise that Edgar, by his origins, by his experiences as Poor Tom, and the various crises through which Shakespeare puts him, emerges as the embodiment of a man not born but shaped by a society out of joint, to be able to set it right.

P.S. To play Edgar in those terms is a colossal task, none more colossal in our time. I propose Vanessa Redgrave.

15 September 1982

14

Notes on *Hamlet*

A recent critic has said that Shakespearean criticism is a jungle, a wilderness and a forest; and the wildest part is the jungle of modern criticism on *Hamlet*. Mr Redgrave says that of the great tragedies *King Lear* is the only one in which two ideas of society are directly confronted and the old generation and the new are set face to face, each assured of his own right to power. This is false. All the great tragedies deal with precisely this question of the confrontation of two ideas of society and they deal with it according to the innermost essence of the drama—the two societies confront one another within the mind of a single person. It is true of Hamlet, as Mr Granville Barker sees when he says Hamlet is a man adrift from old faiths and not at anchor in the new. It is true of Macbeth; it is above all true of Lear.

There is little that is vague in the confrontation of Lear, on the one hand, and Goneril and Regan on the other. It is the stock formula of Hollywood when it aims at dramatising social conflicts. Mr Shaw did the same; and that is why, even in *Saint Joan*, his characters are all nineteenth century intellectuals expressing social needs and social ideas. This is the mould into which Communist critics of literature force great art. Shakespeare grappled with a far more fundamental problem, the problem of human personality. The only play in which he mastered it is *Othello* and that is why in structure and language, *Othello* is the most perfect but the most limited of the four great tragedies.

Shakespeare found himself in *Hamlet*. He had been approaching the problem, the dramatic problem, for some time. Already in *Henry V* the warrior king is affected by grave doubts as to the relation between his social function and his personality as a human being. But this is no real conflict. In *Richard II* the same problem dominates, but Richard is not a great tragic character. He is too much of a piece. His language breaks no new categories. His images revolve around a fixed framework. Brutus is closer; but we are still a distance from high tragedy. The real antithesis of Brutus is not in himself; it is outside of him—Mark Anthony, the ruthless and unscrupulous man of action who deals with a critical situation.

It is in *Hamlet* that these currents meet. Hamlet has a situation to deal with, a situation that is far clearer than the one Mark Anthony handled with such success. In his mind he knows what he ought to do. His position, his training, his sense of duty, his personal affections and the spirit of his father, embodiment of the old regime—all are telling him what he ought to do. But he himself, his sense of his own personality, is in revolt, against this social duty. That in itself, however, would not be sufficient to make *Hamlet* what it is—the central drama of modern literature. What gave Shakespeare the power to send it expanding through the centuries was that in Hamlet he had isolated and pinned down the psychological streak which characterised the communal change from the medieval world to the world of free individualisation.

This was nothing less than the freedom of the individual mind. *I think therefore I am.* Descartes, Hobbes, Bacon, Locke, Spinoza, Newton, the Royal Society—these men laid the scientific foundations of the modern world by investigation and speculation which they considered to be free. And free they were, not only in relation to the previous age, but also because they were not bounded by the conditions of their existence; they were not aware of these limitations. This colossal change in the organisation of social function was the very basis of individual personality. But from the start it was inseparable from a tension between individual freedom and social responsibility. To the extent that any modern man thought at all, he was subject to this tension. And it was nowhere greater than in the man for whom freedom of thought and speculation became a specialised function—the intellectual.

This was Hamlet, the embodiment of the conflict between social duty and freedom of thought. And because in him the sense of social duty was still strong, stronger than it would be again for over three centuries, and the liberation of free individual speculation was a dawn, more wonderful than mankind has known since that time, in him the two tendencies were balanced in a tension that finally destroyed him but created an imperishable drama, a great recording of a model stage in the development of civilisation.

That is the "politics" of *Hamlet* and the very word evokes the inadequacy of the conception. When Coleridge talks of *Hamlet* as an example of the weakness of too much intellectual speculation, he reduces the play to a vulgar psychological problem case. Shakespeare may have thought that he was painting human nature in general; but his eyes were glued on reality, the conflict between the old and the new. And because the new was of such immense significance for human personality and Shakespeare found it, he could make Hamlet into the most brilliant human being the world has ever known. Mr Madariaga speaks of Hamlet's egotism as if it were reprehensible; and reprehensible it would be in the twentieth century. In the seventeenth it was revolutionary. Hamlet questioned everything. He speculated on philosophy, on religion, on science and the stars in their courses, on the relations of kings to countries and of monarchy to the common people, on the changing relations between different classes of society, on drama and the art of acting, on the style of State papers and the form of the language, on love and friendship, on the vanity of human wishes and, now that the old uncertainties were gone, on man's individual attitude to death. He observed and speculated and generalised on all these things in relation to human personality and above all his own.

I am concerned here only with those elements of Hamlet's character which constitute his originality, the originality of the new type of human being who has come into the world. Hamlet is the precursor in human personality of the supremacy of reason, of rationalism; and the essence of rationalism is the communication of ideas. He needs to communicate. If Hamlet soliloquised so much, one reason is he loved to soliloquise. These thronging ideas sprang from the need and possibility and necessity of expressing them. If he is the ancestor of all the philosophers and formulators of rationalist thought, he is the embodiment of the intellectual's need to communicate. The orator who sways the public, the journalist who informs it, the essayist who expresses a view of life seeking a response in his audience—all these can feel in Hamlet a kindred soul.

He complains that he reads only words, and that he can only unpack his heart with words. But the whole of the second soliloquy rests on the fact that the player[1] can express himself in an abstract cause with such great effect, while Hamlet, with such a motive and a cue for passion, can do nothing. Hamlet would have liked "to drown the stage with tears, and cleave the general ear with horrid speech, make mad the guilty and appall the free, confound the ignorant, and amaze indeed the very faculty of eyes and ears" (Act 2, scene 2). But all he can do is speak to himself, not with mighty words and phrases, but in common curses like a whore. When he is dying he begs Horatio to tell everyone the real truth.

Aristotle placed thought in its proper place—in a dramatic character. It gives the motives for action; but it is subordinate to the action itself. But for Hamlet the process of thought is his conception of action. And modern scholarship has done an inestimable service in putting the idea that a tragic character must have some flaw in his character into a fitting subordinate place in Aristotle's thought. The habit of thought was no flaw in Hamlet's character. It was his character. If it was a flaw, it was a flaw in the whole construction of civilisation from the sixteenth century onward. And inevitably, with this polarisation of action and thought in social function and personality, there developed in the men of thought a sense of isolation, of impotence, of melancholy, because you wandered through eternity, you voyaged in strange seas of thought, alone; that is to say, with an ever-growing consciousness of the divorce between the boundless exhilaration of thought and its divorce from reality. All who read the original thinkers felt it. Hamlet felt this. The intellectual was an organic part of rationalist society and Hamlet is the organic intellectual. That is why the character endures.

How did Shakespeare come to draw this character? To say his great genius or his great knowledge of human nature is to say nothing. Anyone can say that. He drew Hamlet so powerfully because there were Hamlets all around him. If he had been an ancient Greek or a dramatist at the Court of Louis XIV, he would not have drawn Hamlet. As for himself, his whole life, working and thinking, was passed in the very situation and in the very circumstances which produced Hamlet. We know quite enough of Shakespeare's life; and Shakespearean criticism would be thrown back a quarter of a century if there were suddenly discovered correspondence between himself and his wife, or worse still, between himself and his father; or himself and his children. All this is insignificant in comparison to the fact that Shakespeare was himself the first intellectual whose life has been shaped by the communication of ideas to the general public. He knew in his own life the background of what he shaped into Hamlet.

The intellectuals of two types of society met in him. Shakespeare was an intellectual of the medieval tradition in that he enjoyed both royal and aristocratic patronage. But he was primarily a member of a business corporation which produced plays, invested in costumes and stage property, and built a theatre. He knew the rulers and the men of affairs, but he did not live by them. He practised the new freedom of thought and expression in a milieu which made it very clear to him that thought was one thing and the effective organisation and activity of society something else. Not a few years, but a gulf, separated Shakespeare from Sir Phillip Sidney, Spenser, and in the dim distance, Chaucer, the court official.

The supreme artists—Aeschylus, Dante, Shakespeare, Melville, Dostoyevsky—have always been men whose own personal lives, lived in the decisive social milieu of their time, could thus become the source of their most profound conceptions. Ben Jonson thought that Shakespeare was not of an age but for all time. Not quite. Shakespeare was for all time precisely because he was so much of an age. But he was fortunate in his age. Shakespeare then was a man of a certain place in society who observed and drew men of a certain social place in society, both author and characters being products of certain changes in society. It is as absurd to label this an "economic interpretation" as to call it Shakespeare's "politics". It was Shakespeare's good fortune to live in an age when the whole economic and social structure was in the throes of revolutionary change on a colossal scale. But Shakespeare, like all the supreme artists, was more concerned with human character than any artist before or since, because it was precisely in his age that human personality first assumed its most striking and individualistic forms.

A recent American study of Twelfth Night has convincingly demonstrated that every character in that play is tied closely to a particular stratum in the Elizabethan social structure, as if Shakespeare were making a survey for a government department. The play is seen to be about the fear of Elizabethans for the threatened security of their society. For those to whom literature is a game or an escape from harsh reality—and no less so when the escape is into regions of eternal truth and eternal beauty—the intrusion of these ideas into the warm tear-drops about Viola is a sacrilege. At least that is Shakespeare's "politics". The more profound aspects are elsewhere.

The great dramatist himself would be quite mystified at this almost universal attitude. Shakespeare's actual politics have nothing to do with the case. That he was on the side of Essex, that he shared the views of Elizabethans on the need for despotism, that he had sympathy for the masses of the people but believed their entry into politics was always disastrous, all this has no significance whatever for the creation or the appreciation of his plays. These views he shared with hundreds of thousands or even millions of his countrymen and they are in no way decisive. If they were, he would live as a great political philosopher. The trouble is that the views of contemporary politics expressed by Shakespeare, Dostoyevsky and their peers are usually in direct opposition to the whole tenor of their creative work. And it could not be otherwise. They begin with these views. The creative work of Shakespeare, the portrayal of the new individuality, was destined to blow sky-high his commonplace conceptions of contemporary government and politics; not government and politics in general, but the kind of government and the kind of politics he knew.

1953

15

Popular Art and the Cultural Tradition

I propose to show that artistic creation in the great tradition of Aeschylus and Shakespeare finds its continuation today in films by D.W. Griffith, Charlie Chaplin and Eisenstein.

I shall also make some remarks about the function of literary criticism in relation to these films.

Film critics often write as if Griffith invented techniques as Edison invented the electric light. But the film techniques which Griffith created are the result of the extended interests, awareness, needs and sensibilities of modern men.

Our world of the twentieth century is *panoramic.*

Contemporary society gives man a sense, on a scale hitherto unknown, of connections, of cause and effect, of the conditions from which an event arises, of other events occurring simultaneously. His world is one of constantly increasing multiplicity of relations between himself, immense mechanical constructions and social organizations of world-wide scope. It is representation of this that demanded the techniques of *flashback, cross-cutting* and a camera of extreme mobility.

Along with this panoramic view we are aware today of the depths and complexities of the individual personality, as opened up by Freud and others.

This finds its most plastic representation in the *close-up.*

Modern content demanded a modern technique, not vice versa. What is the content that this technique serves? Ours is an age of war. D.W. Griffith's *Birth of a Nation* portrays the American Civil War, the first great modern war. Ours is an age of revolution. The *Birth of a Nation* is the first great epic of a modern nation in revolutionary crisis. And reactionary as is his attitude to the Negro, in his famous scenes of the organization of the white-shirted Ku Klux Klan, Griffith gives us a portrayal, to this day unsurpassed, of the rise of the Fascistic movements which are so characteristic a feature of our age. In this film he unfolds the history of our epoch. The date is 1915.

The two masterpieces of Griffith bear the stamp of an artist in the grand manner.

In periods of historical transition man seeks to integrate in the present his conceptions of his past and his expectations of the future.

Time present and time past
Are both perhaps present in time future,
And time future contained in time past.[1]

It is a common characteristic of the great artists at the height of their powers. Aeschylus in the *Oresteia,* Dante in the *Divine Comedy,* Shakespeare in *King* Lear, Victor Hugo in *Legende des Siecles,* Melville in *Moby Dick.* But no age has been so conscious of the permeation of the historical past in the actual present as our own, and no modern artist has attempted such a colossal integration of the historical past as Griffith in *Intolerance.* In this film he shows us the fall of Babylon, the story of Christ, the religious crisis in Europe in the 16th century, the struggle between capital and labour, and the story of a family of unemployed in a big city.

The means he uses show the same insight into the needs of our century. Today, in mid-century, as we look back and forwards, we can see that our age is dominated by a sense of the immense accumulation of institutions and organised social forces which move with an apparently irresistible automatism. Yet at the same time it is an age more than ever conscious of the inviolability of the single human personality. The sub-title of *Intolerance* is *Love Through the Ages.* In reality Griffith gives a portrait of the individual in desperate struggle against the constantly increasing power of social forces.

Griffith writes the epic of the ordinary man. The lyric poet of the ordinary man is Charlie Chaplin, from his beginnings up to *City Lights.* (For me after that, there is still genius but genius in decline.) The Tramp is himself the modern individual, inviolable in the midst of the cruelties and pretenses of modern society. But how does he convey this inviolability? Modern aesthetics, in its search for the secret of form, has neglected perhaps the most remarkable manifestation of it that our society has created. Chaplin is, above all, an actor. And certainly within the memory of man living, no one has seen a performer more fully equipped, both in his individual virtuosity and his sense of himself in relation to the whole. It is by the perfection of his form that Charlie, the Tramp, becomes a heroic individual, representing all humanity.

The existentialists have never surpassed Chaplin in their emphasis on the fact that the essential existence of man is in the violent struggles that take place in him over the most elementary details of his everyday existence. But they, like the Freudians, are overwhelmed by these problems.The Tramp always emerges from them, not necessarily victorious, but always undefeated.

Why?

I believe that it is because Chaplin played for a mass popular audience. Chaplin and Griffith, like Aeschylus and Shakespeare, had to please the mass audience.

We have therefore to examine this audience.

The mass popular audience of Griffith and the early Chaplin lived in an atmosphere of social freedom and absence of traditional restraints characteristic of the growth of the United States. It enjoyed the most advanced technology in the world and the greatest possibilities for formal education and social mobility. The beginning of the century in the United States saw the growth of the cheap popular newspaper and the inclusion of the great masses of the people in the hitherto restricted stream of general intellectual communication. It was precisely in this period that there sprang into sudden existence the popular arts which, characteristic of American civilization, have been welcomed by the common people all over the world, the comic strip (culminating in the work of Walt Disney) and jazz music. It was this public for which the early film was produced.

These new popular arts seemed very far removed from the work of the great artists in Europe. Yet I believe there is a bond and one whose significance will grow with time. Proust, Picasso, Joyce, Stravinskv, T.S. Eliot (and also Bergson and Freud) are united in this, that they seem to have had as their common purpose the complete destruction of the values of 19th century civilization.

An examination of the popular art of the early 20th century of the American mass will show that they were no less hostile to the values of the 19th century, and particularly to romanticism. The two masterpieces of Griffith[2] and the films of Chaplin are only one proof of this. But while in the European art of the 20th century the impression is of doom, an undefeated buoyancy pervades the American popular art, despite its frequent crudenesses and brutality. It is this buoyancy, which finds its most characteristic expression in the work of Chaplin.

The mass popular audience, however, must not be considered as being separate from the nation. If the mass was decisive, yet the audience for which Griffith and Chaplin produced was a national audience. It was the depression in 1929 which opened the split in the national consciousness in the United States. And with that began a period of decline for the film.

No less characteristic of modern society than the mass audience in the large industrial cities is the great industrial corporation. I believe it to be of immense significance for the study of aesthetics that the artistic productions of Griffith and Chaplin were created by typical modern corporations, with their hierarchical organization, their thousands of mass employees, their financial manipulations and the extent and variety of their relations with their public. In other words the artists, the medium and the audience, were an organic part of the social structure of their day. (Contrast this with the isolation of a Valéry or a Joyce)

The third of the great masters is Eisenstein, but what I have to say about him will be better said later. I prefer immediately to take up the other point that I stated at the beginning, that a modern aesthetic—an aesthetic of the 20th century—must base itself upon modern popular art and above all, the modern film. In the light of what we have observed about Griffith and Chaplin, let us look at Shakespeare. Shakespeare was a script writer for a dramatic company, and the modern screen writer has more interest in his script than Shakespeare seems to have had in his. Whenever I read that school of critics who persistently treat Shakespeare as if he were engaged in writing cosmic profundities for philosophic minds, I say to myself: if indeed it were so, it is very strange that he did not take more care to see that these were printed.

Full of philosophical profundities as he might be, the artistic company through which and for which Shakespeare worked was a commercial company, (like Griffith's and Chaplin's) characteristic of the new forms of industry of the time. He and the actors had their money invested in it. They had to please a mass popular audience. If they didn't please it, like Griffith and Chaplin, they would go bankrupt.

To continue this line of investigation we therefore have to examine this audience carefully. It was one of the greatest audiences that an artist ever had. First, it was a national audience composed of all classes. At the time of Shakespeare's death the national consciousness had not been split by the Civil War. But the great body of the audience consisted of artisans, apprentices and students, the mass popular audience of the London of that day. From these Londoners, within a generation after Shakespeare's death, came some of the cadres of Cromwell's army. From them came the cadre of that great political party, the Levellers. From that stratum came some of the men who founded the United States. This class of men was permeated with the great new idea of free individualism, and all of Shakespeare's great tragic characters are essentially individualists who are in conflict with the corporate society of medieval Europe. Even the puritans who bitterly opposed the theatre were themselves an extreme form of this individualism. Every thinker was prepared to stand on the corner of the street and expound his individual interpretation of the scriptures.

Hamlet is an individualist, a man of free enterprise. But I have to separate myself from the vulgarities of Stalinist criticism. Hamlet is not a rising capitalist. His activity, the freedom of his enterprise, is intellectual. For him thought is a form of action. To think freely, to examine, to speculate, that was a new force in society in 1600. And Hamlet is torn between the need for action as a member of a corporate society and his need to examine, to speculate on everything in sight, and above all, on his own individual personality.

The individuality of Hamlet is the individuality of the intellectual. In every succeeding generation the intellectual has been caught between these two compulsions, to act within the precise and limiting conditions of society or to preserve his intellectual being by wandering through continually expanding seas of thought alone. That is why the play has achieved increasing significance through the ages, particularly for the cultivated, the intellectuals.

Now the relation between Shakespeare and Griffith and Chaplin is this. The modern novelists and the modern poets are at the tail-end of that tradition which had its magnificent beginning in *Hamlet.* But Griffith and Chaplin and Eisenstein have broken out of it. I am not making futile comparisons between the relative aesthetic values of Shakespeare and Chaplin. What I am drawing attention to is that Shakespeare in giving artistic embodiment to the intellectual tradition in *Hamlet* was seeking to please his mass popular audience. And Griffith and Chaplin have broken out of that tradition, now in decay, because they sought to please their mass popular audience. They deal with an individual too, but the individual they deal with is not an intellectual. He is the common man, everyman, the lowest possible denominator. The Tramp could not be lower in the social scale. Griffith would not even give names to any of his fictional characters in *Intolerance.*

With Aeschylus I can be even more brief.

The organisation for which he worked was a state organisation, whose structure was characteristic of the social political organisation of the Greek city-state.

His audience was truly national. It was also truly popular, the overwhelming majority being that extraordinary social phenomenon, the political democracy of 5th Century Athens. This mass audience, directly or indirectly, decided who were the victors in the dramatic competition. I am sure that I have seen somewhere that Aristotle or Plato, or both, disapproved of this literary criticism by the populace. But this audience gave Aeschylus the prize thirteen times and I don't see how Aristotle and Plato and their friends could have done any better.

For this popular audience (and it seems that it was extremely partisan and very noisy) Aeschylus wrote *The Oresteia* which is admittedly the greatest drama of ancient times and for me personally the greatest play that has ever been written.

Here we have to note only that Orestes is not Hamlet nor is he the ordinary man of Chaplin and Griffith, overwhelmed by institutions. Prince though Orestes is, his crisis was the crisis of the normal Greek citizen caught between the old tribal society and the new order of democratic government by law.

We can now see the umbilical cord that enables us to bring together such diverse names: revered artists of the cultural tradition, like Aeschylus and Shakespeare, and modern popular favourites like Griffith and Chaplin. In their ways they give three stages in the development of the relationship of the individual man to his social environment which is the true history of humanity.

I am not confusing aesthetics with history. Aesthetics is the study of artistic form. And the form of the film both illustrates and is illustrated by the history of the dramatic classics. In the art of the Greek city state, where individual and universal have achieved some balanced relation, it is the chorus upon which the whole dramatic action depends. In the drama of the modern free individualist, it is the soliloquy. It is because the individual is dominant in life that he can take the liberty of explaining to the audience not only his open but his secret motives, the motives of everyone in sight and anything which is needed to advance the drama. It is in our world, the world of vast institutions and the helpless individual, that Griffith's close-up tells us the facts about the individual that the individual does not know himself.

But these relationships are even more subtle. We have lost the chorus which was the audience on the stage. But the modern director moves his camera always with a view to whether he wishes the audience to be directly involved in the middle of the action or for some artistic reason to be removed from it. Never before has the audience been so directly a constituent of the process of artistic creation. The recent film production of *Julius Caesar* is for me as arresting, as startling, as revealing a commentary on our own age and on Shakespeare as I have seen in a lifetime of reading and study of the plays. To oppose to these considerations comparisons between the relative values of the work of Shakespeare or of Griffith is entirely irrelevant, not to say stultifying.

It is now that I want to say a few words about Eisenstein. If Griffith and Chaplin refused to deal with the heroic individual of free enterprise (either in action or in thought) but dealt with the individual as symbolic of the mass, Eisenstein goes further. He makes the mass itself his hero. All criticism must begin from the individual impulse. And for my part, from the very first time I saw *Battleship Potemkim* many, many years ago, the scene on the steps of Odessa has not been the greatest scene in the film. I was fascinated by the spectacle of the thousands upon thousands of people bursting from all parts of the screen on their way towards the body of the dead sailor. And the years have only confirmed this first impression. And I believe that it is this discovery, of a new category, in dramatic creation that accounts for the formal perfection and simplicity, of the structure of *Potemkin*. But Eisenstein was never to repeat it. Like Aeschylus he worked for a state organisation. But unlike Aeschylus the final verdict on his work was not the verdict of the mass popular audience but of the central committee or its representatives.

Here it is convenient to point out the infinite complexity of some of the problems which for the most part I am merely stating here. I will take only one. It seems to me that Eisenstein had to satisfy a committee. The Russian working class, the basis of the mass audience in Russia, was separated from the rest of the nation in its own consciousness and in the consciousness of the Russian artist of that time. I have made clear my belief that (judging empirically from history) this conscious separation of the classes seems to be an obstacle in the way of the greatest creation. I am concerned with it here for its effect on form. The more I see of *Potemkin,* the more it brings to mind, of all people, Racine. It is true that the 20th century sees infinitely more in Racine than did the 18th and the 19th. Perhaps we are beginning to understand what his audience saw. Be that as it may. In *Potemkin* as in *Phedre* I see the result of an artist who knows precisely the clearly defined audience for whom he is working, and I note the same in *The Mother* of Pudovkin.

Formal perfection is not necessarily the most inclusive mode of expressing what is there to be expressed. *Potemkin* was a very early creation of Eisenstein. But this artist teeming with ideas was denied a natural development. And as I read the fascinating account of his theories in Marie Seton's recent biography, *I* am more than ever convinced that the tragedy of the whole brilliant Russian school was that they were not able to test their theories by the suffrage of the popular mass.

I am now in a position to make some remarks on criticism today. Modern criticism has to reckon with the fact that modern man, the ordinary everyday citizen, feels that he requires to know his past in order to understand his present. This knowledge he can learn only in art, and above all, in literature. So that criticism today has a popular function to perform. It will cease being merely culture or perish. The great creative works of Aeschylus and Shakespeare, which I have taken here as examples, were not produced as culture. And it is noticeable that the greatest of all literary critics, Aristotle, did not know drama as culture but as a popular art.

What is one distinguishing characteristic of Aristotle's criticism, especially today since the development of psychoanalysis? It is the theory of catharsis. Through the pity and terror which the audience feels, these passions are purged from them. The importance of this theory to me is that Aristotle had in mind and could not have had in mind anything else but the great body of the political democracy of Athens. In other words, he had in mind the Athenian form of the modern film audience. I believe that to be the source of the enduring value of his *Poetics.* I go further, I believe that *we* of the 20th century will get closer to an understanding of the *Poetics* of Aristotle by a study of it in relation to the modern film and its audience. By it also we will understand more clearly than previous generations where we have left the *Poetics* behind. Plato, in his hostility to the poets, was obviously motivated also by the mass character of the Greek audience. In this study modern literary criticism can find its true function.

Since Aristotle and Plato and the decline of the Greek city-state, criticism of necessity no longer has the mass popular audience as the center of its conceptions. It is the modern film which has restored this possibility.

I am not speaking of social consciousness. No philosopher was more conscious of society than Hegel. His philosophy was completely permeated with a conception of humanity developing through different social stages to complete self-realisation. His aesthetics is the culmination of his system, but it is the culmination of his system because he believed this complete selfrealisation was impossible in the objective world. That is why he placed its realisation in intellectual activity, specifically art and religion. The Romanticism of disoriented men of genius like Rousseau, Chateaubriand, Wordsworth, Keats, Shelley, and the whole French Romantic movement was only the actuality of what was arrived at by a man so entirely different from them as Hegel. Aristotle might have that problem in his politics and longingly contemplate refuge in a community of kindred souls. He did not have it in aesthetics.

That problem is still with us.

I want to take as an example English criticism of Shakespeare. Coleridge lifted Shakespeare criticism to great heights by the romantic interest in individuals, both in the characters of the plays and the uniqueness of the gifts of the great artists. But once he and his colleagues, Lamb and Hazlitt had done that, there was nothing left to be done in that field but a mere repetition according to personal insight, idiosyncracy and the capacity to generate enthusiasm of the critic. English criticism of Shakespeare has not recovered from it to this day. The great advances that have been made have been in the field of scholarship. A reviewer has recently said in the *Times Literary Supplement* of Shakespeare criticism that it is a jungle. Of integration there has been none.

Integration there will have to be. Nothing on earth can prevent the coalescence of the cultural tradition with the popular audience. The question is: How? It can be done according to the directives of that great literary critic, the late Zhdanov, or of that other great literary critic, Mao-Tse-Tung. Possible deficiencies in criticism are more than atoned for by the power of the totalitarian press, and if that is not sufficiently convincing, the secret police. But the democracies have no reason to be complacent. In America the divorce is complete. American criticism lives almost entirely in little magazines read only by students and professors. A great government corporation, like the British Broadcasting Corporation, frankly divides its cultural programme into two parts, the Third programme for the cultivated and popularisation for the mass.

As far as France is concerned, I have constantly in my mind the conclusion of Jean Paul Sartre's otherwise very illuminating book *What is Literature?* Here he puts forward the doctrine that for literature to be saved, writers must write for the masses on behalf of the proletarian class struggle in order to advance mankind on the road to socialism. That is the way to produce party resolutions, not great literature. But it is significant evidence that serious criticism on its present basis either retires into the clique or the coterie, or in its desperate effort to reach the masses of its own free will arrives at conceptions leading to totalitarianism.

I do not propose to give any advice to creative artists. I believe, however, that if Aeschylus, Shakespeare or the author of *Tartuffe* and *Don Juan* (I am not sure of Racine) came back today, they would take one glance around and immediately buy a plane ticket for Hollywood, in order to make contact with the popular audience of the world.[3] But to critics and to all interested in the cultural tradition, what I have to say amounts to this. Today the tradition can only be renewed in the place where the tradition was created, in an art intended for the popular mass audience.

I have confined myself to the classic films. It is not that there are no modern films worthy of critical notice, for example, the Italian school which sprang up after the nation purged itself of totalitarianism. There are good modern films. There are bad ones. But whether they are good or bad, the medium deals with that range and variety of modern sensibilities from which it originated.

If the film however has declined, as it undoubtedly has, the reasons, I think, are not artistic but social. At the root is the depression which deprived the artist of that national audience which it seems is inseparable from great creativity. And the other reasons spring from the first. Griffith could treat, for example, the subject of capital and labour with the utmost freedom. But today, in the United States, for instance, or for that matter anywhere, so tense is the relation between the different classes, and so highly organised their representative institutions, that immense areas of social experiences have no opportunity to be presented on the screen. In this respect Aeschylus and Shakespeare had infinitely greater freedom than any modern film director. The poet or novelist is free. The film director is not. He needs it far more than they. His creative imagination is stunted from the very beginning. The solution of that is not an aesthetic question. It is a question of politics.

1954

16

Preface to Criticism

Literary criticism today means nothing to anybody except literary critics. Never before have scholars piled up such mountains of information necessary for criticism or discovered such a variety of technical instruments as during the last quarter of a century; yet never before have critics been so incapable of integrating it into any coherent system or method.

But contemporary literary criticism, if it has no integrated method, has achieved certain effects. Some of them represent a complete repudiation of all previous opinion—cultivated and commonplace—as has ever been achieved by criticism before. It has been, for example, a common opinion that the plays of Shakespeare were written for dramatic performance; but following the opinions of Mr L.C. Knight, Dr Leavis and Mr Wilson Knight, with a glance at Mr William Empson—some of the most eminent of contemporary Shakespearean critics—one reviewer gave his own judicial opinion: "That there is something valuable in the sheer dramatic structure, underneath the words, seems to be shown both by Mr Kenneth Tynan's effective staging, some years ago, of the bad quarto of *Hamlet* and by Mr Marlon Brando's performance as Antony in the film of *Julius Caesar*—a performance which was in many ways a powerful and moving one, though Mr Brando was incapable of speaking Shakespeare's lines in a way that brought out their rhythms, their sonorities, or even the finer subtleties of their poetic sense." It seems that one school of modern criticism has found the proof that there is something valuable in the dramatic structure of Shakespeare, in one staging of the bad quarto and a performance by a Hollywood actor incapable, as indeed he was, of saying the lines properly. If modern criticism has repudiated its ancestors, it is equally certain that this judgment would be repudiated by every English critic from Ben Jonson to Bradley, including Charles Lamb, the great apostle of Shakespeare in the study rather than on the stage.

What is most remarkable is not only the judgment itself; but the casual manner in which it is uttered. The critics have done this work so well that the writer has no idea of the utterly fantastical character of what he is saying. It is not surprising that along with these ideas goes an equally light-hearted repudiation of what have long been regarded, in many quarters, as the fundamentals of critical practice.

Another editorial in the *Times Literary Supplement* (which claims, and justly, that it represents the middle body of opinion) gives the following recommendation of a translation of Aristotle's *Poetics*: "What has Aristotle today to teach such a reader? . . . perhaps he would learn . . . of the primary importance, in much literary creation, of construction or design; of having, for instance, one story to tell, not a set of fragments of several stories, and of telling it as coherently as possible without irrelevant additions. . . . Aristotle could usefully recall the attention of young writers to the part played by conscious planning and hard thinking, in at least many major works, to the beauties of proportion and coherence, and to the whole vast problem of literary structure". If that is what Aristotle has to contribute to "the whole vast problem of literary structure", then he has no more to say than any instructor who undertakes to teach the writing of saleable fiction by post in ten easy lessons.

My view is, on the contrary, that any integration of contemporary literary criticism must begin with Aristotle—the first and still the greatest of literary critics. His stature derives from his method which is completely comprehensive and completely integrated. It is not merely of historical importance. Today, more than ever, it is the indispensable foundation of any serious reorganisation of contemporary criticism. Modern critics do not understand him because, unlike Aristotle, they do not root their criticism in the world in which they live.

Aristotle's premises, commonplace for centuries are as follows: 1. the audience; it is purged of pity and fear by the spectacle on the stage, and 2. the drama, Aristotle insisted upon the central importance of what he called the plot. Modern commentators, in particular, have never known what to do with this, so much so that Hollywood directors and Miss Dorothy Sayers have been able to appropriate it as the justification of their practice. The principle which unifies Aristotle's ideas is the popular audience, whose modern counterpart crowds into the cinema in every modern city. This was the dramatic audience of Aeschylus, Sophocles and Euripedes. Aristotle knew of no other and could conceive of no other.

We can begin by examining Aristotle's theory. Actors, imitating actions, as though they were living it themselves in the emotions of a popular audience facing a situation in which they feel themselves to be profoundly involved—this is the beginning of the plot. The middle excites the emotions of the audience to the highest pitch. Fundamental questions have been posed and deep emotions have been aroused. There must, therefore, be fundamental solutions. This is the end, when the audience must be satisfied in accordance with the expectations that have been raised. To Aristotle, the most ingenious plot of a novel by Miss Sayers would have been an ingenuity and nothing more; for there was nothing to involve the nation in the serious consideration of what mattered to it as a social unit. Perhaps a detective novel is not a reasonable example; but to Aristotle and the Greeks, novels like *Mrs Dalloway* or *In Remembrance of Things Past* or *Ulysses*, likewise could pose no problem which would immediately make the whole nation feel that it was involved, and, in that sense, it would be weak in plot, having neither beginning, middle nor end.

A contemporary critic might think that this would prove the limitations of Aristotle's theory; rather, it is proof of the limitations and narrowness forced upon the world of literature by the development of modern society. To Aristotle, literature for the popular audience, dealing with things that concern it vitally, was not easier but more difficult than literature for cultivated persons. For him, the construction of a plot to express this was the most important part of artistic creation. That is why he could say that poetry was more philosophical and of higher value than history. Such a work of literature, for such an audience, was the history of the nation at a certain time in its development. It is from there that we have to begin. Where the modern critic from Saint Beuve to T.S.Eliot conceives of literature as a form of culture for the cultivated and popular art as some form of relaxation or anodyne for the common people, Aristotle choosing between the epic (which was narrated before a cultivated audience) and tragedy (performed before a popular audience) came down squarely on the side of tragedy as artistically superior.

The schools of contemporary criticism make no sense whatever of the Greek drama, far less Aristotle. Sir Gilbert Murray, writing of Aeschylus, says that the Greek tragedians as a whole were poets of ideas, and of bold ideas; poets like Milton, Shelley or Victor Hugo, not like Shakespeare. He finds Aeschylus occupied with the struggle between God and man's conscience. To believe this, is to believe that the audience of the Greek drama was enthralled, excited and driven to partisanship by philosophical ideas. No such popular audience has ever existed or will exist. We touch here one of the mountains that modern criticism carries on its back—the belief that the greatest poets are men using drama for the expression of ideas. Shakespeare was not, neither was Aeschylus; and it is the mark of the inferiority of Milton or Shelley that they used poetic forms as a vehicle for ideas.

We might have expected that the critical school which operates under the banner of Stalin/Zdhanov/Mao-tse-tung to have some understanding of the audience. One of its most eminent representatives, Mr G.D.Thomson, author of the learned and valuable *Aeschylus and Athens*, says that the audience at the city of Dionysia was not a cross-section of the community; but the community itself associated for the performance of a collective ritual act. That is true; and it is the foundation of the greatness of both the dramatists and of Aristotle's literary criticism. But on the same page Mr Thomson tells us that the great plays of Shakespeare were not "immediately and consciously related to the social movement of his time". It would seem that for Sir Gilbert Murray's conception of the Athenian drama as a vehicle for the propagation of ideas, Mr Thomson has merely substituted literature as a vehicle for the propagation of economic and political programme.

In reality, there is here the whole difference between the nineteenth century and the world we live in. Sir Gilbert Murray at least never loses sight of the work. If he considered the mass audience at all, it was with some vague liberal idea that some day, with the spread of education and democracy, more and more of it would be able to learn to appreciate the ideas of Aeschylus and Milton. This remoteness from the contemporary popular audience resulted in a similar remoteness from the popular audience of Aeschylus and in his book, Murray has not one word to say about it. Mr Thomson, however, has discovered that the modern popular audience can no longer be ignored. In literature as in politics, this means that it is seen as a receptacle into which to pour advanced ideas. Mr I.A. Richards, another critic who years ago discovered the popular audience, aimed to emancipate it, not by the abolition of private property, but by using literature as a means of bringing some order and balance into the chaos of its impulses. It is the revolt against these critics, back to the thing of value in itself, which has produced the magists, the textualists, the metaphoricals, the cultists of ambiguity and the whole formalist school. In seeking, however, to defend the work itself from all alien influences they isolate it from the social movement and they end by destroying it. When Mr Empson has analysed the significance of the word "all" in *Paradise Lost* or Mr Wilson Knight or Mr Traversi has analysed the plot of *Lear* as "an expanded image", there remains only Mr Empson, Mr Knight and Mr Traversi. The works themselves have disappeared.

It is in its relation to a popular audience that modern criticism will find the beginning of the integration of the ever-accumulating mass of knowledge; but it is no easy matter for us in this century to grasp the relation between audience and work which was so simple and natural to the Greek audience and critic or to Shakespeare and his Elizabethan audience.

A great work of art bears its meaning on its face. The meaning can change from one generation to another; but when Shakespeare wrote his plays, and they were produced and acted, author, performers and audience understood what the play was about. They did not have to take a text home and work at it. They could disagree, but they knew what they disagreed about. Contemporary criticism has not arrived at the most elementary agreement of what *Lear* signifies or, worse still, *Hamlet*. Olivier's Hamlet, within a few minutes, makes it clear to the audience that Hamlet's trouble is that he is in love with his mother. Hamlet, from the first, was a popular play and that means that it had for its audience a clear meaning. People might differ as to their attitude to that meaning, but the confusion about what the play means today is a sign of weakness, not of strength. We should know what we think, even if men of the twenty-first century may think something else. The first condition for this is the restoration of the popular audience as an integral part of the conception in the writing and production of a play. It is one of the triumphs of modern scholarship that during the last fifty years the text, the stage and the acting of Shakespeare's plays are now in a fair state of restoration. Nevertheless there is one constituent which can never be restored—the Elizabethan audience, the most important element in the production and criticism of Shakespeare's plays; but its substitute can be found in the popular audience of today.

The modern audience goes to films; and recently a serious version of *Julius Caesar* has been produced. The general standard of characterisation was low and the film was held together by the performance and mastery of the Shakespearean verse line by John Gielgud, aided on a lower plane by Marlon Brando. I saw the film twice in New York and half a dozen times in London, both in the city and in the suburbs. In every case the audience was held spell-bound to the end of Mark Antony's oration, but then the interest declined and finally collapsed. The producers knew that the film was collapsing, for at this point they introduced on the screen a printed explanation of the stage that had been reached. Not knowing what to do next, they fell back on a big battle scene in which all the resources of the cinema were used—only to make Shakespeare's play more tiresome than ever.

The producers are not to be blamed. Shakespearean criticism has never known what to make of the last two acts of *Julius Caesar*. It is possible for the critics, working in their studies, to devise such explanations as "the spirit of Caesar" continuing to dominate after his death; but, I believe, that every popular audience in the world, at any time in history, would be acutely conscious of the fact that the last two acts of the play were a wash-out. It is, of course, possible to say that Shakespeare wrote a bad play; though we have to accept that only as a last resort.

The solution is to be found in a consideration of the Elizabethan audience. Like every popular audience, it shared with its authors certain presuppositions which were as native to it as the clothes it wore. One of these fundamental presuppositions was the safety and stability of the state and the influence of the actions of great persons upon the state. An audience would follow the fortunes of Cassius, Brutus, Mark Antony and the rest; but it would never lose sight of the fact that the play had to settle the problem of the government of Rome. Century by century, with the development of individualism and parliamentary government, western civilization has lost that consciousness. Now it is returning and has returned already in the totalitarian states. In this matter the Elizabethan audience was far closer to the popular audience in a modern totalitarian state than it is to the audience in a democracy. Nineteenth century criticism saw Shakespearean characters as individuals and followed their fate as the fate of individuals; and this tradition has persisted. If one looks at Cassius and Brutus as individuals, nothing can save the last two acts of *Julius Caesar* from being a dramatic failure; but neither Shakespeare nor his audience saw it that way.

As soon as Mark Antony is left alone with Caesar's body, he makes a tremendous denunciation of Caesar's murderers and the prophecy of revenge. It is one of the most powerful, most dramatic soliloquies in all of Shakespeare. This, for the Shakespearean audience was a sign that something was finished and something else was about to begin. Immediately a servant announces the approach and importance of Octavius Caesar. Octavius Caesar is the new ruler of Rome. To the deaf, stumbling, epileptic Caesar, the old ruler, is contrasted this young, formidable, self-contained young man, mature beyond his years. After Mark Antony has succeeded in sending the crowd to destroy the conspirators, a servant again announces that Octavius Caesar is near. All this the producers of the film, who so far had followed Shakespeare with exemplary faithfulness, left out and thereby robbed themselves of a million dollars in addition to the expense of their quite unnecessary battle.

Soon we shall see Octavius Caesar; and here the play will stand or fall, as so many of Shakespeare's plays do, by the production. Caesar is old and decrepit, Cassius is lean and hungry, Mark Antony is given to sports and taking long chances in politics, Brutus is academic and prosy. All talk incessantly. Octavius Caesar is a man of few words, but every word he utters carries weight and establishes him as the one who will bring order out of chaos.

I have taken *Julius Caesar* because it is now universally known as a play and because criticism and production, following criticism, has consistently failed to see it as a successful play. But what is true of *Julius Caesar* is infinitely more true of the most famous plays of Shakespeare—*Hamlet* and *King Lear*. Only those who have had to wade through the best of modern critics have any idea, not of the differences, but of the confusion which exists about these plays.

Criticism of *Lear* persists as an example of a proud old man who is humbled by adversity until he learns humility. Let me say at once that to write a play whose beginning is the crisis in a great state caused by the folly of its ruler, to see this crisis develop through anarchy, violence, murder, madness, civil war and the death of guilty and innocent alike and, then to have as an end, as a culmination, as a means of catharsis, a reconciliation between the old man and his daughter—we do not need Aristotle to see that this is an unreasonable, not to say, ridiculous interpretation of the play. We nod our heads at the philistinism of the generations which until 1838 completed *Lear* by marrying Edgar to Cordelia; but they were more consistent than we. They played *Lear* as a drama of individual character and, felt, justly, that as such, the ending Shakespeare gave to it was unreasonable.

The modern popular audience turned away from the last act of *Julius Caesar* and in doing so, it was right and the producers, following the critics, were wrong. We are accustomed to noting how Shakespeare wastes not a second in placing before us essential characteristics of the important persons in his plays. It is due to our preoccupation with individual character and the remoteness from us of an organic concern with the fate of the state, that we do not note that in the great tragedies Shakespeare in his first scene, sometimes the first sentence, always places before us a crisis in the state. It is so in *Julius Caesar*, in *Hamlet* and in *Lear*. If we accept that in his most serious plays, Shakespeare always begins by telling his audience that the state, that is to say, the fate of society is involved, then we can most easily grasp the role of the last act. There the question stated at the beginning is resolved and resolved in the only manner that a popular audience would accept it, that is, resolved dramatically on the stage. An audience would watch the individual hero fascinated; but they could expect at a certain stage that the community with a mass of characters on the stage would discipline him. For the Elizabethans, the very structure of the stage, with its long projection into the audience, could separate the individual character out from the stage community, but the conclusion of the play would see his return to find his properly subordinate place in the community as a whole.

1955

PART IV

THE AFRICAN DIASPORA 1957-1989

17
Letters on Politics

I. 18 NOVEMBER 1956

The news of the last days from Hungary has come to a climax this morning. We have now seen what, in my opinion, is the decisive turning point in modern history. The first was the Paris revolution of 1849; the second was the Commune; the third was the Russian October Revolution. This Hungarian revolution is the last, and incomparably the greatest, of them all.

If you look at the *Sunday Times* editorial you will see that the bourgeoisie knows that something final has happened to Stalinism which it calls the World Revolution. That is doomed. The editor also sees that the proletarian revolution is unconquerable; but he does not recognise *that* as the World Revolution. So much the worse for him.

Before the first proletarian revolution, Marx in 1848 drew the conclusion of the dictatorship of the proletariat. It was abstract. He refused to concretise it. When the Commune took place he said, "There, *that*, is the dictatorship of the proletariat." Now we today are faced with the task of drawing the conclusions from this greatest of all revolutions, and doing so in a manner that restores revolutionary Marxism to the place which it had lost—the vanguard of political thought as a guide to action. The proposed ten page pamphlet is not enough; we have to do something on the scale of Marx writing about the Paris Commune.

These are the things that are new—new in that they have appeared in full flower where they were only embryonic before:

1. The working class, in backward Hungary, is at the head of the nation. You will see that the *intellectuals* have called for a government of workers' committees and freedom fighters, with a musical composer as a figurehead—presumably to give tone. This is new and the historical process has no farther to go. This is the historical dialectic at its clearest. For whereas formerly the intellectuals and the vanguard party fanatics recognised that only the workers could overthrow the regime, they took it for granted that only they could rule. But they have been driven to call for rule by workers' committees, because the revolution has so destroyed the bourgeois state that it is obvious that nothing else but the workers

can rule. Hungary, *whatever happens*, has established this once and for all.

2. The writer of the *Sunday Times* editorial talks about human bravery, readiness to die etc. He is a follower of the Trotskyites. The reasons for this endurance are the character of capitalism in its form of state capitalism. *We* have to root the bravery in the contemporary social structure.

3. Following from the above points is the disappearance of "the Party" and "the unions". The Party has consistently led workers to disaster since 1922. If the Party, any party, had been in charge, it would have ruined the revolution. Furthermore, if even it had been successful in overthrowing the regime, no party in the world would have dared to fight the Russians a *second* time, or decided on the general strike which is unparalleled in the whole history of revolution.

You see what has to be written. These conclusions have to be drawn from the modern world and their development, since 1848, traced in a strictly dialectical manner. I believe that the whole of Central Europe, including West Germany, wants to break with the Russian alliance, to have nothing to do with the western powers and to build socialism on the basis of workers' power. As I write, an irrational but overwhelming feeling comes over me that I wish Lenin was alive today. Not to do anything, but to see it—just to see how the proletariat is now the only class that has programme, policy and will; while the others pass resolutions and stand impotent, cowardly and utterly degraded. Note, too, that North Africa is boiling. France is on the verge of a catastrophic crisis and the Arab states are blowing up pipelines, blocking the Suez Canal, etc.—torn between the intrigues of the United States, Britain and France on the one hand and Russia on the other. Nasser and the others will not last long. The Communists are very strong in certain countries of the Middle East, but one must learn to understand history. After Hungary, they cannot hold power anywhere near Europe for long. There will be defeats, setbacks, compromises; but the permanent revolution is on its way once more. It is the permanent revolution not of 1848 or 1917, but of 1956.

Read, read, read. Read till your eyes swim; get yourselves right, hold meetings, keep on holding them. To aim high and far is not the problem, for that is not what distinguishes those who accomplish. It is the planning, the organisation, the attention to detail, the tenacity that count.

P.S. In the face of the clarity and power of the Hungarian worker, we have the following: Tito's now thoroughly exposed phoney revolution and his speeches on both sides; Gomulka fighting the Polish people because they want to break as completely as the Hungarians, but he, too, wants to be on both sides; Kingsley Martin who says that the future depends on Russia this weekend, "if the world has a future"; *The Observer* says that the future of the world depends on the decisions of the Russian leaders; another newspaper that the future of the world depends on Eisenhower's vision, from his golfing record that vision doesn't seem too good. The Hungarian workers say get out and stay out. That is politics today.

II. 10 FEBRUARY 1957

The books are pouring out and, as usual, the French are way in advance of everybody else. I was waiting for one in particular—Sartre's magazine, Sartre having finally split from the Communist Party. He is far and away the most distinguished writer in France; and he has recognized that the time was ripe for a total statement of views. In his special Hungarian issue, you have his views on the Russian Revolution—where it has come from, where it is today and where he thinks it is going. It is absolutely imperative that any organisation must make its position on this question clear, showing where de-Stalinisation and the suppression of the Hungarian revolt comes from and where it is going. Sartre has vision enough to feel and to see what is required at this moment.

The introduction to the mass of documents on the Hungarian revolution which Sartre presents gives a summary of the significance of the revolution for the future development of the revolutionary struggle. What Sartre understands is that today people want original documents—they want to hear and to see what the Hungarians experienced. Sartre gives them 200 pages of it and, further, the extracts and the writing are on the whole concerned with freedom, liberty of thought, the stifling of thought. To an old-fashioned Marxist it may seem that this is merely the intellectuals' preoccupation with the need for free expression. It is not so; and in the writings of the Hungarian intellectuals in the stormy period which preceded the revolution, you will see the passion for freedom of information, freedom of thought and freedom from lies.

But Sartre's Hungarian issue is a catastrophe as far as Marxism and the revolution are concerned, for these people are revolutionaries and they are Marxists. There is no question about that. They are intellectuals and do not try to hide it; but they are carrying on a battle among the intellectuals of France against the Communist Party which has a tremendous influence among them. The battle they are carrying on, as always in France, is the battle that others are going to be carrying on after them when they catch up.

Why then do I call the issue a catastrophe?

In those 500 pages, Sartre himself has a page and a half about workers' councils, perhaps three pages. The editor who writes the article on Stalinism does not, I think, mention the workers at all. The writer of the introduction to the Hungarian documents bases himself upon the working class, but he is concerned with denouncing Stalinism and envisaging a future in which the workers in general will play the decisive role. But the worst is yet to come. In the 200 pages of documents, I think there are about 15 pages which deal with the workers from a sort of intellectual point of view. That is all. There is not a single document issued by the workers' councils or any of the revolutionary organisations in Hungary. The thing is fantastic to read and see the good will and the revolutionary spirit, the attempt to apply Marx; and yet the complete futility of the whole thing as an explanation of what is taking place today or an illumination of the future.

Let me give you one single fact worth all the 500 pages of Sartre's book and which, by the way, in its total effect is and must be completely reactionary. It is the greatest single fact of the revolution, arising out of the formation of the workers' councils and the role of the proletariat. The revolution began on 23rd October and the demonstration was asking for no more, if as much, as a solution to the Hungarian question on the lines of Gomulka in Poland. The fighting began, however, and we know how Nagy was compelled, in response to the workers' demands, to carry the programme way beyond what Gomulka had asked for in

Poland. On 31st October, the Soviet tanks appeared to withdraw finally from Budapest; then on 4th November they counter-attacked. The revolution had had three brief days in which to envisage the future.

Now this is the fact. In the course of those three days, the freedom fighters realised where the danger lay for the future of socialism in Hungary. To quote Sartre himself, they were afraid of the resurrection of the ancient political formations, or it is possible that they were scared of what might happen in an ordinary parliamentary election. These people proposed to form a great party of the revolution which would include the Christian and petty bourgeois Right, former members of the small-proprietors party, social-democrats and Communists. They had actually begun to plan it and to carry out discussions when the Russian army returned and they had to stop and start fighting again.

Beginning from a demonstration on 23rd October, which was asking for freedom and democracy, within a week it had gone to the extreme limits that a programme could go for national freedom, and within three days it was working out an entirely unprecedented political formation in order to meet the dangers foreseen. This is to sum up in oneself the whole of the revolutionary past of the proletariat and to open out the road to the future.

At times I feel overwhelmed by the whole business and as I see the thing so clearly I wonder if I shall have the physical strength to do what is required. Sartre and the rest of them do not know and cannot recognize the significance of what has taken place. We are in a position to do so. I recommend to you to go through our material and pick out those places where we said that the party of the future would be such a mass party as would make the idea of a vanguard party a patent absurdity. But, we have to recognize that boldly as we thought, we never envisaged that the party of the future would deliberately bring Catholics as Catholics, small proprietors as small proprietors, social-democrats and Communists into one grand party. The proletariat, and you can be sure that the initiative came from them, can accomplish more for theory in one week than theoreticians in 20 years. They saw a problem and they took the concrete steps necessary to finding its solution. All the weeping and wailing about the difficulties that the revolution faced from the counter-revolution, how it all fades away in the face of this astonishing demonstration of the realism and the boldness with which the workers of today faced the problems they know they have to deal with.

I want now to pass on to Sartre and his colleagues. They are not only very important for us; but also because what the French are thinking today, the British think the day after and the American intellectuals come labouring behind about a week late. Sartre believes that Russia is and always has been a workers' state. His policy, however, for France is that it is necessary to de-Stalinize the Stalinist party. He sees the future of France as dependent upon a united front between the Communist Party and the Socialist Party. Do not misunderstand Sartre. Sartre is not afraid of the revolution. Like so many intellectuals today, he is way beyond the intellectuals whom Trotsky used to have so much pleasure in denouncing. One of the things events in Poland and Hungary have shown us is that today the intellectuals are part of the revolution and feel themselves as such. It is our business to break away consciously from the limitations which we had imposed upon ourselves during the past two or three years and address them directly with the consciousness that they are part of the revolution. The decisive point is this. Whereas the Hungarian freedom fighters see quite clearly that the reorganisation of the old parties will inevitably result in the regeneration of the old quarrels in the old form, Sartre sees the salvation of France in the united front between these same damned parties that have ruined the revolution and corrupted the proletariat for over thirty years. Insofar as theory is responsible, we may say that, while Sartre and the other intellectuals have read Trotsky, the Hungarian freedom fighters have not.

I ask myself—what is the central issue around which everything revolves, allowing us to relate all the tendencies of the revolution and the counter-revolution? We touched on it in *State Capitalism and World Revolution;* but now we have to bring it right out. The central principle where we must begin is that in Lenin's day the proletariat still functioned through its parties, unions and co-operatives. Lenin saw the significance of the soviets, but, in harmony with economic relations, he saw the necessity for a party, a political party, a revolutionary party. It was essentially a party which was removed from the factory floor and from the other areas where people work. Today, however, we have to make it clear that we live in a new epoch. The difference between this epoch and the one in which Lenin lived and worked is that the centre of production, and therefore the centre of social and political power and progress, lies in the shop floor organizations of the working class and workers' councils in every branch of national activity. It is the shop floor organisations which save bourgeois production from complete chaos, for in defending themselves the working class brings order where there would be none. These organisations are a new form of society, not only of production. It is because the unions and the labour parties represent a previous stage of society that the conflict between them and the shop floor organisations is so sharp. The old organizations do not merely subjectively suppress the energy and latent power of the proletariat; but they must be seen and represented as direct obstacles to national production. Many see the anarchy of production in private property and the market; we have to show the anarchy of production in the conflict between shop floor organisations and the representatives of bourgeois society, whether on the side of management or the bureaucratic organisation of labour.

The full significance of this appears in what has happened in Poland and Hungary in regard to the Plan. In the democratic organisation of society, the working class in its shop floor organisations is able to have some influence upon the organisation of production and the protection of labour. Marx made this point clear, in a way we did not understand, when he said that it was the democratic organisation of the proletariat in the middle of the last century which forced the factory acts, and thus saved capital from its ruinous pursuit of profit which was destroying society, not labour, at its very source. The catastrophe which has overtaken the planners in Poland and Hungary is due to the fact that they were able to impose their will upon the proletariat. It has resulted precisely in the destruction of society. Poland and Hungary were literally driven into the ground, and Eastern Germany is in much the same situation today.

Now that is precisely the situation in production which Trotsky never saw and which enabled him to talk all his rubbish about the Plan and the party. Sartre is a complete Trotskyite. He has no conception whatever of an organic conflict between the Russian proletariat and the Russian bureaucracy. Therefore, for him, Russia despite everything, is socialism—and he says so without equivocation. For the same reason he sees in France the working class parties as having in their hands the solution to the future of France. As long as Sartre fails to see the organic conflict between the shop floor organisations on the one hand and management and the labour bureaucrats on the other, he will remain exactly where Trotsky remained all his life.

Previously our ideas about shop floor organisations and their conflict with those who claimed to represent the workers were theory. We could only point to anticipations of them in the past. Now that is over. The Hungarian revolution allows us to pose a concrete reality.

The position of Sartre is not merely the position of an intellectual. I am positive that his ideas are more or less the ideas of the vast majority of the French proletariat, even its most active sections. All the doubts, the hesitations that they feel are in Sartre's article. He is honest enough to put them down, but in the end he says that this is the best, the only realistic, way out. That was precisely the mentality of the Hungarian workers on the day the revolution started. Within ten days they had reached the stage where they were ready to form a party consisting of the Catholics on the Right and Communists on the Left. The longer I live, the more I understand Lenin. In France and elsewhere to write and speak as Sartre does at this time, is to reinforce the most backward ideas and conceptions of the proletariat. He and his kind think that it is progressive to attack the Stalinists, and it does a certain amount of good; but fundamentally it reinforces the Stalinists and the social-democrats because it remains within the same framework in which they function.

The Hungarian revolution, as every revolution has done, breaks the old framework of thought. One must not believe that the Hungarian workers were suddenly visited by bright ideas during a few days of revolution; that is not the point at all. The ideas that they developed were inherent in their experience and in their years of suffering under the regime. They knew the way out, though it seemed impossible to realise; but as soon as they had struck the first blow and the immediate barrier was down, they followed their thoughts right through to the end. That also was a revolutionary process.

To sum up. In 1933 Trotsky was asking for the united front between the Communist Party and the Social Democrats in Germany. Both those parties were already dead. In 1957 Sartre, and I suppose all the others, had nothing else to put forward—although those parties were not only dead, but rotten. The program in 1933, as today, should have been the blowing up of both parties by the unified working class, unified in the process of production, and other freedom fighters wherever they are.

There is a danger that these analyses may seem remote from conditions in the United States. Completely wrong. They are not remote from Russia. They are not remote from America. They are more sharply posed in both those countries than anywhere else. The American bourgeoisie knows that; that is why it supported McCarthyism and still uses the terror. Let us get this Hungarian revolution right and all else will follow.

III. 20 MARCH 1957

Dear Everybody,

The general perspectives and the particular tasks are such as to require complete understanding by *everyone*.

1. The *year* 1956 was decisive. That is now as clear as day. The ferment here is like a bubbling volcano. Everywhere the same. That I shall treat in detail over the coming period.

2. You have to prepare all your affairs, with scrupulous attention to detail and a *fixed programme*. We here have to do our share. The most important thing is to realise *concretely* a political line.

3. I propose to postpone the Hungarian pamphlet for 4–6 weeks and do instead a 70,000 word book on Ghana. Why? The structure of the book will tell you why.

i) My own observations and impressions of the trip. I met *people*. The university student who served as ADC; the man who drove my car. I met their parents, families. The attendants in the hotel. Civil servants. Ministers. A mass of *people*, seen through the dialectic. Strict observation of human individuals in their social and historical setting. I saw and understood more in fourteen days than people who have been studying the subject for fourteen years. It sounds wild, but I am sure it is because of that that the politicians spent so many hours with me in that busy time, and are looking forward to the book as the first satisfactory exposition of what has happened there. They will give all possible assistance.

ii) I propose to review past writings particularly *Black Jacobins*. I shall quote and show how clearly the future was foreseen there, when practically everybody thought they were crazy. (Read in particular pp. 314–316; p. 11; p. 222.) I shall draw the argument to a head.

iii) I shall review Nkrumah's book and break completely with, or rather develop qualitatively the theoretical premises of the *Black Jacobins* and the Leninist theory of the colonial revolution. The African revolution (as a process) is no longer to be seen as supplementary to or subordinate to the revolution in Western Europe. I shall examine it in relation to the French Revolution; the Russian; the Chinese and the Hungarian.

The chief point is *The Party* (now draw a deep breath). At the height of the movement the Party consisted of about a million people in a population of five million. Now it is about five hundred thousand which is astonishing enough. It would mean in the U.S. a party of fifteen million people by arithmetical calculation. Socially calculated it would mean thirty or forty millions.

I hope you realise what that means in terms of our theory. The way power was achieved was beyond all praise. *I shall deal with it in detail.* Now for part iv.

iv) The party is in mortal danger. The danger is that it will succumb to the fact that it is now a government party, a ruling party subject to the corruption that has overtaken all revolutionary parties that rule. The kind of "corruption" that the critics are talking about, financial, etc. I shall treat with the utmost contempt. In twenty-four years Ghana will not achieve the corruption that takes place in twenty-four hours.

This is the kind of thing and there are plenty of them, that has to be driven home and so place the Ghana question in an entirely new framework.

No, the danger is more deeply rooted. It can be overcome in only one way: the revolution must be permanent. This can manifest itself in the following ways.

1. Ghana must become the centre of the struggle for African liberation. That Nkrumah has made absolutely clear. So far, so good. But

2. The very backwardness of Ghana makes it able to start its social and political life in accordance with the most advanced conceptions of the twentieth century. I shall detail them. Farming co-operatives in Denmark and Belgium; collectives in Israel; shop stewards movement in England (I shall need help here) but you see the idea. The *state must take the initiative.*

In colonial countries even more than in advanced countries, the weakness of the economy compels the state to initiate new projects. All the colonial countries now must follow India in what they call a socialist pattern of society.

What we have to say is that the party being what it is in Ghana, the new state must take the lead not only in organising the economy from above but in initiating new social relations from below.

It must be repeated that if it does not work along these lines, nothing can prevent it from becoming a government party divorced from the population.

There are also the democratic instincts and practices of the African tribes, not those damned chiefs with their feathers and umbrellas and stools, made into petty tyrants by the British Government, but the old tribal method of appointing them by election and throwing them out if they were unsatisfactory.

To sum up. The Ghana Government must break at once with the idea that its task is to show the imperialists that they have learnt to govern in the British tradition. Instead they must break right out of that tradition and to aim at being a modern socialist society, or rather to build in that direction. *They cannot succeed by themselves*. But they must start, or they will be overwhelmed by their own backwardness. That is the issue. To achieve that, to grapple with it continuously is much harder than to achieve power.

3) How concretely? The decisive question is the future of the party. It is a government, it must rule, the country is appallingly backward. Yet it must aim high and far, or succumb. The great antagonism is between the party as party and the party as government. The party must maintain its ideological domination over the party as government.

A continuing struggle. What we can do is to make them and the public aware of it. To pose it this way, lift it out of the colonial status both for themselves and for people in Britain and the U.S., for the first time gives them the opportunity to see this question in international and social and not in provincial terms.

4) We can be more concrete.

a) The party must lead the proletariat and the unions. Otherwise the proletariat as sure as day will in time split the party, and take away the leadership of all the masses, pushing the Government into the arms of the big companies and the conservative professional classes who hate it now. (I went to Tankard, a modern port, with a proletariat of ten thousand. You could have picked up any one of them and dropped him in Detroit. My conversations with them will have to wait.)

b) They will have to let the British and American public know what they are doing. The British public wishes them well and feels a sort of paternal interest in them which it does not feel for example towards India. If they can show that they are not content with "independence" but are, despite their poverty and backwardness, aiming at the most advanced conceptions of a modern society, they will create a vast reservoir of good will, concrete desire to help, and, for the first time, educate the British public in particular as to what was involved in the colonial relationship and what must now be the relationship between a contemporary society of an advanced character and the backward countries. For they are backward. Let no one have any doubt about that. You only have to look at the strides Britain, for example, is making in atomic energy for industrial purposes or a powerful industrial structure like the Ruhr in Germany and then compare cocoa farmers in Ghana to realise the gap.

One sure sign will be when young people here begin to emigrate to Ghana. We must work for this. I shall here.

The same with the U.S. and the U.S. Negroes. I shall expect from you all a statement as to what is the attitude of the American Negroes in particular to Ghana. Particularly I want to know the attitude of the proletariat towards emigration.

The old conception and the new face each other. Formerly three types of people went to Africa: 1. imperialists to conquer and rule; 2. officials at high salaries; 3. missionaries to work hard, teachers, etc. But these last were dominated by the imperialists. The "missionary spirit" is still very strong in Puritan Britain. Now they can go without the taint and corruption of imperialism.

c) The most important point. Nkrumah (who is a splendid fellow) has formed a Socialist Youth Society in the party, to study socialism, etc., and help educate the party and the people. We shall point out that *they* have to be the most advanced section of the population *intellectually*. In this sense. They have to study the dialectic, Stalinism, Greek democracy, *everything*. They must be able to hold their own in any international conference. The Government must protect them even against itself. They must make the university above all a battleground. The party youth must continually be a challenge to the Government, the union leadership and the university. They must be a totality, intellectuals, worker youths, farmer youth. Their function is to maintain and develop the flow of ideas, so that the party leadership can never be overwhelmed by the routine tasks of government which embrace you so much on all sides that they kill all political initiative unless they are consciously fought.

I also intend to bring in a section on the Negro struggle in the U.S.

Now it should be clear what this book can be. We shall put forward our whole program in a most concrete context, for Ghana and for everybody else. . . .

IV. 25 MARCH 1957

I have stopped everything to do this because, in my opinion, it is extremely urgent that you study it and penetrate as deeply as possible into what I have been trying to say over the last week or two.

Yesterday, the Reverend Luther King and his wife had lunch with us and stayed here from 12.30 until nearly 5 p.m. With us was George Lamming, the West Indian writer who has just received a distinguished literary prize, the

Somerset Maugham award of five hundred pounds for his book, *In the Castle of My Skin*. The award demands that the winner must travel and he is going to Ghana. There was also with us Dr David Pitt, who is likely to be the first West Indian or African to run for Parliament. He too was in Ghana.

After about two hours of general conversation, Luther King and his wife began to speak about the events in Montgomery, Alabama. I shall include a chapter on their experiences in a book on Ghana, and as I give you an account here of what he said, I shall introduce one or two parallels from the Ghana experiences. The more I look at this, the more I see that we are in the heart of a new experience which demands the most serious analysis.

One Thursday, on a day in December, a woman was arrested in Montgomery, Alabama, for travelling on the bus in a seat reserved for white people. The woman resisted and, to this day, says she does not know why she did. Thousands of Negroes had obeyed the regulations for many years. A local trade union leader went down and bailed her out and called up Dr King suggesting that they should "do something". It was the kind of statement that is made a hundred times a month in various parts of the South, whenever one of these outrages takes place. This time, however, King called up a few of the better class Negroes and parsons in the community, and they called a meeting for the Friday. About 60 of them, upper class Negroes, got together and they decided to call for a boycott. The idea was not entirely new, because some months before a girl of 15 had defied the bus regulations and people had spoken of the necessity of doing something and had talked about the boycott—but it passed, as so many of these things pass. They decided to call for the boycott and started off at once to inform people not to travel on the buses from Monday morning. The news spread, and on the Monday morning there began one of the most astonishing events in the history of human struggle. The Negro population of Montgomery is about 35,000. From the Monday morning and for about a year afterwards, the percentage of Negroes who boycotted the buses was over 90%. The Commissioner of Police and the head of the Bus Company have stated that never on any day did more than 35 people ride the buses.

In addition to calling for the boycott, the committee had called a meeting on Monday evening at the church of the Reverend King. When they saw the tremendous success of the boycott they were nervous about going through with the meeting. King says that they thought along the following lines—the boycott had been a tremendous success and if they decided to have a meeting and nobody turned up, or very few people, then the whole movement would be exposed as a failure. (At some other time I shall give my own experience of what the failure for a movement in the South can mean. It is usually the signal for fierce reprisals by the whites.)

King and the others, however, decided that they would go through with the meeting. From about 3 o'clock in the afternoon there were people waiting to get into the Church for the meeting at 7 p.m. The church itself could hold only a few hundred people; but there were thousands packed around it, though luckily the church had loudspeakers so that they could hear. Half an hour before the meeting began, King (who had been elected chairman of the committee) left the company and went outside for half an hour's meditation. He recognised that this movement had to have some political policy to guide it. He had had no idea whatever of being a leader for the struggle of his people—he was a young man of 28 years of age; he had read philosophy and he had read also the philosophy of Gandhi, but with no specific purpose in view. In the course of the half hour's meditation, the idea came to him that what was needed to give this movement a social and political under-pinning, was the policy of non-violence; but, as he explained, non-violence as he conceived it, had nothing passive about it. While it stopped short of armed rebellion, it was incessantly active in its attempt to impress its determination and the strength of its demands upon those whom it is directed.

King worked out his policy in the half hour and submitted it to no committee. There was no time. When he was called upon to speak without any notes, he delivered his address and, from that moment, he became the guiding principle of the movement.

King was elected chairman of the committee by a unanimous vote. He himself had had someone else in mind to propose. It turned out that they had thought of him as chairman because in his preaching he had always emphasised a social gospel, that is to say, preaching with an emphasis on the improvement of the social situation of the community and not with the emphasis on individual salvation. That was all, but it had singled him out in the minds of his fellow preachers and other members of the upper class Negro community who formed the committee.

After that, the movement was on its way and, for one whole year, never looked back until the victory was won. It is one of the most astonishing events of endurance by a whole population that I have ever heard of. There are other details which on another occasion I shall go into; but there are a few points I want to make at once:

1. The always unsuspected power of the mass movement.

Some of you may have beside you Padmore's book, *Africa: Britain's Third Empire*. Now Padmore is one of the most forward looking and inwardly confident of all those who have interested themselves in Africa. If you look on page 207 of this book, which bears the date May Day 1948, you will see that Padmore is still thinking that "the strained relationship which existed between the chiefs and intellectuals . . . is giving way to a united effort between the chiefs and the people". I do no injustice to George when I say that as late as 1948 he shows no knowledge or indication of the tremendous power of the mass movement which the CPP would soon unloose. At that time the movement had taken the form of the boycott of European and Syrian merchants, and later the march of the ex-servicemen who had been shot down. Nkrumah and five others were arrested and deported for six weeks. It was only one year later, in June 1949, that the CPP was formed and launched with a rally of 60,000 people. When it did get underway, just as the masses in Montgomery, Alabama, it never looked back.

2. The significance of the leadership.

a) At first sight it would seem that Nkrumah had had a long training; whereas King had had none at all. This is undoubtedly true and the question of the various trends of thought which contributed to the development of Nkrumah is an extremely important one which in the book I shall go into detail. But, with all due regard to the small scale of the Montgomery occasion and the much larger scale of the action of the CPP in Ghana, the similarities between the two, in my opinion, are greater than the differences. King's programme was created on the spur of the moment, so to speak. Further, in chapter 10 of his autobiography, it is obvious that if even Nkrumah was closer in his own mind as to what positive action meant, not only did the Government not understand it, but the public did not either. On pages 110 and 112 you can see the frantic haste and the circumstances in which Nkrumah wrote, for the first time, a pamphlet with the significant name, *What I Mean By Positive Action*. In other words, both of them put forward decisive programmes which the crowd caught up, almost in passing. You will note, too, how close the idea of positive action is to King's spontaneous conception that non-violence was in reality the opposite side of an unceasing attack upon the enemy.

b) The critical moment in the history of the CPP is the decision at Saltpond to break with the UGOC. All who have studied this episode, a highly important one, know that Nkrumah and the leadership had more or less decided, for the time being, not to break. It was the rank and file delegates and the crowd outside who practically dragged Nkrumah from the conference hall and told him to go inside and resign. I am positive at these and other critical moments, when the leaders seemed to waver, that it was always the demonstration by the mass of its force, determination and its confidence in them, which enabled them to take the forward step.

You note the similar situation with the Montgomery committee on the Monday afternoon, when they were ready to call the whole thing off, but were impelled to go on by the thousands who were lining up since the afternoon for the meeting that they had called that night.

By the way, just as in Ghana, the historical accidents are for the most part on the side of the advancing mass movement. Some of them are as funny as hell. A coloured servant took one of the leaflets to her white mistress on the Saturday morning. She, the mistress, called up the local newspaper and the whites, anxious to know what these Negroes were up to, published it. A lot of Negroes who had not heard anything, and could not possibly have heard in time, learnt about what was involved from this gratuitous stupidity of the white newspaper. Again—the rumour spread that some Negroes were intimidating others from riding the buses; the commissioners of police, in order to prevent this, appointed two motor cycle riders to go along with each bus, and the sight of them scared off all those Negroes who may possibly have had the idea of taking the bus.

3. The masses, the party and the leadership.

I wish to begin here with Leon Trotsky's attitude to the relation of mass party and leadership. His article, *The Class, the Party and the Leadership*, deals with this question in relation to the Spanish revolution and he goes to great lengths to try to explain how the leadership betrayed the revolution. It is, and was, quite clear that the anarchists at various times were able to seize power. It was in the streets for them to pick up.

However, basic to Trotsky's whole conception is his idea that the proletariat needs a long experience, and its cadres, a long period in which they can get to understand one another and to appreciate the intricacies of politics. All this is entirely false and proof lies not only in historical study, but in the experience of the Gold Coast revolution, of Montgomery, Alabama and in the Hungarian revolution. Trotsky's great mistake was to believe that the masses in 1956 or 1946 were at a similar level of development as the masses in 1903 or 1917. The most astonishing thing about the Gold Coast revolution is the fact that the masses of the people, in a few months, recognised Nkrumah as their leader and were prepared to go to the end with him. In Montgomery, Alabama, they recognised King as their leader in a few hours and were prepared to go to the end with him. In Hungary I doubt if they recognised any particular person as the leader at all; yet they went to the end, organising and recognising the leadership as they went along. We must never forget that they had won; the counter revolution inside Hungary was totally defeated and the revolution was suppressed only by foreign tanks.

What is the conclusion to be drawn? That the general level of the mass movement both in the advanced and backward countries is such that it recognises immediately any leadership which is saying the things it wants to hear. There is no need for a ten year preparation. I hope no-one underestimates the tremendous inner power of a movement which results in 99% of a population refusing to ride in the buses for over a whole year. The achievement of the Gold Coast masses, of the people in Montgomery, Alabama, in the Hungarian revolution (different as were their spheres), is a warning to all revolutionaries not to underestimate the readiness of modern people everywhere to overthrow the old regime.

It is highly significant that in each case the relationship of the leaders to the mass is something that springs up practically overnight; and the leaders learn as they go along. All thinkers and theorists about revolution will have to pay attention to the sudden-ness and the rapidity of the political development. The roots of this, I am convinced, are in the universal social and political situation in the world in general and in the masses in particular since the end of world war two. The strength of these leaders is that in a specific situation they recognised this and rode the whirlwind.

What precisely are the constituents of the world situation? You will find some of the answers in a review of Nkrumah's autobiography by Lord Attlee *(The Spectator*, 8 March 1957). He misunderstands the whole situation empirically as thoroughly as Trotsky does theoretically. He compares Nkrumah to Grantley Adams and Norman Manley of the West Indies. Could there be any greater misunderstanding of a political figure? He says again that the influence of Gandhi upon Nkrumah leads him to reject violence as a means of achieving his ends. This type of "influence" is, in my opinion, not only meaningless but absurd.

In my view Nkrumah recognised that in the objective relationship of forces in the Gold Coast, if he could mobilize the people sufficiently, the ruling power had so slight a base that it was bound to retreat. In other words, Gandhi did not "influence" Nkrumah. Non-violence represented an ideological covering for a shrewd appreciation on the part of Gandhi of the real relation of forces in India. A similar grasp of objective relations led Nkrumah to see in Gandhism an ideology suitable to the political struggle as he envisaged it.

In the course of my discussions with King, I pointed out that on more than one occasion he was on the extreme edge of the most violent and bloody struggles in Alabama. He admitted it. The same situation presented itself as in the Gold

Coast. But the fact that, in the end, they were able to win their objective by their original policy was due to their correct appreciation of the relationship of forces, and not to any theoretical belief in the absolute validity of non-violence.

Attlee shows the high point of misunderstanding when he says that had the Indian Congress Party shown as much wisdom as the men of Ghana, they might well have had Indian independence and, quite possibly a united India, a decade earlier. Absolutely and completely false. The British Government of 1947, whether of Labour or Conservative, cannot possibly be compared with the British Government of 1937. They retreated in 1947 because their inner confidence was gone. To suppress the revolution in India by force would have raised a storm at home. Furthermore, the Indian people did not look at them with the same eyes in 1937 as they did in 1947.

The whole world lived through a period of fundamental revolution between 1939 and 1945. It is the business of leaders to sense, to recognise and act upon this basic change, a great historical change, in the relationship of forces. Since world war two, Nkrumah, King and the Hungarian factory workers who led the Hungarian revolution have been the men who show the clearest recognition of this. It is this which must be analysed and the general theory of revolutionary struggles brought up to date by their experiences.

You will see that I am not accepting a theory of non-violence as any fundamental theory for our time. What I am concerned with here is the light it throws on the relationship of forces in the postwar world. This I am convinced, whether they agree to it or not, was the fundamental conception which governed the ideological conclusions, strategy and tactics of the leaders of the movements we have been discussing. The revolutionary movement on the whole, and the Marxist movement in particular, will be making a fundamental mistake if it does not recognize these movements for what they are—a form of revolutionary struggle characteristic of our age—and if we allow ourselves to be misled by this label of non-violence which has been pasted upon it. It can cause a lot of confusion unless we look beyond the surface and see the tremendous boldness, the strategic grasp and the tactical inventiveness, all fundamentally revolutionary, with which particular leaders handled it.

V. LETTERS TO MAXWELL GEISMAR

13 March 1961

I am vastly pleased that a critic of your status likes my novel, *Minty Alley*. The "human" aspect of it which surprises so many people is the basic constituent of my political activity and outlook. Quite recently I had to deliver a blast at a West Indian bureaucrat whose behaviour was not only politically, but personally, offensive to me. In a highly political document I wrote as follows—

My first response was a human one. The day I recognise that my instinctive response to any political situation is not a human one, then I know that my time for retiring has come, since all that I would do afterwards would be bureaucratic and fraught with mischief. Callousness with rulers is an occupational disease. It is the human responses that have to be worked out into politics. You respond as a human being instinctively, and afterwards you work out a political line. In the immeasurable cruelties of the age in which we live (the most cruel in human history), a politician has to watch, above all, himself; but it is much better if his colleagues, and still more, his party, watch him.

I cannot conceive of *modern* politics otherwise.

P.S. I have been in a fine mess for some weeks now, trying to get my mind clear about Dreiser's *American Tragedy*. The movie, *A Place in the Sun*, did as much as anything else to confuse me and I haven't got with me the books on American literature which you kindly presented me. I combed your *American Moderns* which I have with me, but the essay on *Sister Carrie*, which I found in the book, did not have much on *American Tragedy*. You see I feel that Dreiser in naming his book *American Tragedy* definitely meant to distinguish it from previous types—for example, European, Greek, etc. But I feel somehow that the book does not penetrate to the basis of American life, and that in his concern with religion, education and so on, Dreiser did not penetrate to the bones which the great writers do. Yet, you say that he is the most distinguished of all of them. I am going to grapple with the book and place it in relation to Tolstoy and Dostoyevsky. More of this later.

11 April 1961

In spite of myself, and all that I have to do, my mind has been increasingly occupied these past weeks with my conception of the American character and American literature.

I do not believe that any literature is an accurate reflection of society at a particular time, it is certainly not a bare reflection; but, I know no better means of estimating what were the particular features of an age. Let me try again. The normal everyday life of a society, I find as a rule unreflected in great literature; what I do find, over and over again, is a summing up of a past period and an outline of what is to take place during generations to come.

I have in mind an essay on the American character as I have known it and as I have seen it reflected in American literature. I have read your book, *American Moderns*, many times, but the book which seems to solve a lot of problems is Styron's *Lie Down in Darkness*. I have given his novel and your estimate such a going-over as I don't believe I have given to modern literature for many years. Styron seems to prove my case. This is my case.

Dostoyevsky, in searching for remedies to what he thought was a Russian disease, exposed the dilemma—in fact, the insoluble crisis of a non-socialist world.(Dostoyevsky, of course, had no real understanding of socialism.) His greatest book, from the point of social personality, is *The Possessed*; for here he draws pictures of the contemporary types, our contemporaries, who, unable to accept life in liberal bourgeois society, have filled the ranks of the Stalinists and Fascists all over the world. We cannot forget that, in France, until De Gaulle cheated them, there were 150-odd members of the Communist Party in the French parliament and a massive political and social organisation to correspond. These people and the types who formed the basis of Hitler's party are a contemporary type. Massive parties could not be formed unless there were hundreds of thousands of people, not only receptive but ready for this kind of organisation and brutality.

Hannah Arendt understood this and, despite, its other weaknesses, this is the imperishable value of her book, *The Origins of Totalitarianism.*

André Gide lectured on Dostoyevsky in the 1920s without mentioning the Grand Inquisitor; yet Dostoyevsky claimed that the Grand Inquisitor episode, in *The Brothers Karamazov*, was the climax of his work. And he was right. The Grand Inquisitor told Christ plainly that his return would not be accepted by those who ruled in his name. He told him plainly that the rulers of Christianity were now ruling according to the words and doctrines of Satan—pretending, of course, that these were the doctrines of Christ. Dostoyevsky meant to say, and all his work showed it, that the ideas and ideals which had animated man since the dawn of the Illumination could not work any longer; and that the personality of men could only find harmony with social activity and logic if they adapted these ideas, contrary to the ideas of liberalism, progress and, ultimately, socialism. He was in my view absolutely correct. His characters are the first prototypes of the evil bodies of men who have been dominating the world in the last thirty years or so. Some of them are rabid anti-Communists and defenders of democracy; nevertheless the type is universal and they are to be found in great numbers in the United States.

Their appearance, however, in American literature is very different from the way they have appeared in Europe. I shall have to take it in jumps, but I am sure you will follow me.

What do people in Europe say about American literature? What do they say about the character of Americans? They say that they lack the sense of the tragic; sometimes they add, that the American character is juvenile. This is written and said by very serious people. I do not know that not to have a sense of the tragic is a lack, a fatal weakness. What is this sense of the tragic? It is, in my opinion, a sense of the inability of man in society to overcome the evil which seems inseparable from social and political organisation. To have a sense of the tragic, is to be aware of this and to judge humanity by the degree to which man is able to struggle against this overriding doom; to establish moral and psychological domination over the feeling of impotence and futility which it would otherwise impose. The American people of today most certainly have not got this sense of the tragic in the manner that it has pervaded, and still pervades, European literature.

Modern America, and particularly since the Civil War, simply refuses to accept a tragic view of life. Modern Americans don't see why this should be—they refuse to accept. Prohibition is one example of this; Kinsey's statistics are another. Europeans have a background of acceptance of a certain indefinable dominance of the unknown over the known. At times they break out of it; but only to settle down to it again, after a period in which some real progress is made. The American character does not reconcile itself to this, for it is dominated by the idea of the Illumination, with its perspective of life, liberty and the pursuit of happiness. The longer I live, the more I see that Americans begin by taking that pursuit of happiness with a deadly seriousness and in a manner that Europeans do not.

All this, I hope is not too startling to you. I have been at it for any years and the background is those Columbia lectures I gave on the human personality in great tragedy.

The break with Europe in literature came with Hawthorne, Melville and Co.; and this, D.H. Lawrence, to his eternal credit, recognised and dealt with very fully in his *Classic American Literature*. For me, as you can well understand, the most outstanding figure is Melville. Melville was suffused with the European attitude, the prose rhythms and literary associations of classical English literature. Ahab was breaking out of this—he wasn't going to take any more of that. His insanity lay in the fact that he was determined to solve a problem which the average European would have accepted as insoluble (or would have attempted to solve only in strict terms of insanity, such as Lear or in terms of revulsion, Dostoyevsky).

Here enters an entirely new consideration. One of the dominant characteristics of American life, as I have known it, is nostalgia. This explains the American behaviour to children which so shocks Europeans. By the time Americans are in their early twenties, they have begun to recognise that the ideals, the pursuit of happiness, upon which they had been raised are unattainable. Despite the high standard of living, the satisfaction that they have been led to believe American society will give begins to shrink away as a fantasy. Recognising that happiness, though pursued, is unattainable, Americans first of all attempt to give children everything that could possibly make them happy. They themselves, however, continue to live with a terrible undercurrent of anger and frustration at the difference between what life really is and what they have been led to believe.

The great break in American literature does indeed come with Mark Twain and *Huckleberry Finn* with its flat, declarative sentence. But it comes, as far as I have been able to see, because Mark Twain represents the disillusionment, the sharp break with the natural ebullience, energy, humour and genius for literature which is characteristically American. He turned backwards and made *Huckleberry Finn* what it was because he embodied, as great writers do, a national experience.

Now the particular interest which I have had in Styron's book arises from the fact it is redolent with nostalgia for childhood experiences. *Lie Down in Darkness* paints a picture of social unhappiness and dissatisfaction, unrelieved, I am sorry to say, by any serious attempt on the part of the characters to meet their problems and overcome them. You find that Styron does not condemn; and you also state that the literary moral, so to speak, of his book is the decay which inevitably follows the refusal to leave behind the dreams and aspirations of childhood. I find that I, not so much, disagree with you, but think differently.

My reaction to most of the characters in the book is that they are undisciplined people who have no conception of any inner sense of discipline. What is worse is I find that Styron himself is very close to them in his sympathy with their incapacity to achieve some sort of compromise with life and reasonable happiness. Unless I am very much mistaken, I find that you had to search for a moral axis to Styron's book.

You must understand that all these ideas I am writing down have been reasonably clear in my mind for a long time. The difference between the Europeans and the Americans is very great indeed. I have to put it crudely—Americans expect to be happy; they want to be happy; they see no reason why they should not be happy. When it turns out that, despite material promises which they know are for many of them reasonably satisfactory, happiness continues to elude them, then their fury and frustration is the fury and frustration that permeates Styron's book. All this for me has enormous social and political implications—one of them is that Americans have never shown themselves inclined to pursue the type of politics that Europeans pursue with such pertinacity.

Let me sum up brutally. The Americans do not have internal moral axes to which they feel they must conform in the way that so many Europeans do. As D.H. Lawrence says—they do not wish to be saved. They do not wish to know that they have fought the good fight with all their might; they do not wish to know that in regard to what the world considers good, they have lived the good life even though from day to day they have suffered, put up with compromises which hurt but which are to be accepted in view of the larger issues which have to be served.

The average American wants to be satisfied in the things that he is doing from day to day and in his personal relations with people, to a degree far beyond what the average European thinks possible. I am not going to say for one minute that he is wrong—not me. One thing is certain—that if he does make an attempt to change the society in which he lives, he is not going to be put off with the statistics of production or the high ideals or how much poverty has been eliminated. He will want to know and to feel that his life, from day to day, from hour to hour, has been substantially altered and that the pursuit of happiness is now realisable.

18

Lincoln, Carnival, George Padmore: Writings from *The Nation*

I. ABRAHAM LINCOLN: THE 150th ANNIVERSARY OF HIS BIRTH

We of the West Indies have very little that is at the same time bright, outstanding and recognised in our history. We shall have to construct our own hall of fame from the foundations up. But we have one advantage. We are starting late, and our nationalism, firm in its rightness, will have nothing narrow about it. Toussaint L'Ouverture, Dessalines and Christophe of Haiti come easily to mind. But no West Indian pantheon will ever be able to omit from its panels the name of Simon Bolívar, the Liberator of Latin America. We believe also that in good time the name of Abraham Lincoln will be a similar household word to our children.

Lincoln has been known to our people chiefly as the Great Emancipator, the American statesman who liberated the slaves. To a people to whom their own liberation from slavery forms such an important stage in their history, this hailing of Lincoln as the Great Emancipator was natural. The time for that is past. Lincoln's chief claim to greatness is not that he emancipated four million slaves. It is that he preserved the Union, kept the United States as one country. Today, in the age of planes and of missiles, guided and unguided and misguided, all who live in the Americas are better able to understand the perils we would have been in if America had gone the way of Europe, and the outlying territories had become, as they certainly would have become, a hunting ground and cockpit for two or three powerful American states. One of them is giving us enough trouble as it is. Two or three of them would have reduced us to the fate of Belgium and Holland, Malta and Cyprus.

Lincoln has an even greater claim on our attention than the preservation of the Union and emancipation of the slaves. He was the champion of democracy, such a champion as it has rarely had in all its brief and troubled modern history.

As we grow towards maturity we shall learn to see him in perspective, putting first things first. Our complete emancipation will mean that we shall see ourselves first as citizens of the world, and only secondarily as coloured people who see all history from the point of view of our own deliverance. That is some distance away yet, you cannot force such developments, but Lincoln offers an opportunity to broaden our perspectives and incorporate new conceptions into the body of ideas by which we live and grow.

Ideas have a life of their own, and the ideas of Lincoln have changed greatly in the twentieth century. At first he was hailed rather uncritically as the Great Emancipator. Then came the Communists who introduced a new and for a time very effective counter-blast to Lincoln worship. They publicised his letter to Horace Greeley, August 22nd 1862: "If I could save the Union without freeing any slave, I would do it; if I could save it by freeing all the slaves, I would do it, and if I could save it by freeing some and leaving others alone, I would also do that."

The inference was clear. That he freed the slaves was only a by-product of his struggle to save the Union. This view is entirely false, and we shall devote the limited space at our disposal to showing exactly where Lincoln stood, more precisely, where he began and where he ended, in relation to slavery and the Civil War. The full stature of the man will emerge as one of the greatest statesmen the world has ever known.

The Civil War was begun over this question: who was to develop the vast territories west of the Mississippi. If the slave states, then that would mean greater power for them in the central government in Washington. This the North and Middle East were determined to prevent. They were quite prepared to let the South keep the slaves it had. But more slave states? No. That was the policy on which Lincoln won the election in 1860.

His own attitude to Negroes was complicated and no one will understand Lincoln's work and his greatest speeches, above all the Gettysburg Address, unless he grapples with this question firmly. Lincoln believed that Negroes were of an inferior mould to white people and he said and wrote this often enough. At one time he considered sending them all back to Africa, after the Civil War was finished. Yet Frederick Douglass, the great Negro abolitionist and orator, used to say that Lincoln was one of the few white men who, when he talked to you, did not make you feel that you were a Negro. You find the same attitude to slavery. But he had no sympathy with the Abolitionist Movement led by William Lloyd Garrison, the greatest of all American journalists, Wendell Phillips, the greatest of all American orators, Frederick Douglass, John Brown and others. That movement shook the whole of the United States and precipitated the Civil War. Lincoln would have nothing to do with it. When the new party, the Republican Party, which was to lead the North to victory, when this party was formed in 1856, Lincoln did not join it. He came in only later.

The South began the war and Lincoln had no choice. The Abolitionists pressed him to declare slavery abolished. He refused. Religious denominations pressed him. He refused. As late as September 13, 1862, this answer to a deputation gives a priceless picture of his mind: "I admit that slavery is at the root of the rebellion, or at least its *sine qua non*. The ambition of politicians may have instigated them to act, but they would have been impotent without slavery as their instrument. I will also concede that emancipation would help us in Europe and convince them that we are incited by something more than ambition. I grant further that it would help somewhat in the North, though not so much, I fear, as you and those you represent, imagine. Still, some additional strength would be added in that way to the war,—and then, unquestionably, it would weaken the rebels by drawing off their labourers, which is of great importance; but I am not so sure that we could do much with the blacks. If we were to arm them I fear that in a few weeks the arms would be in the hands of the rebels; and indeed, thus far, we have not had arms enough to equip our white troops. I will mention another thing, though it will meet only your scorn and contempt.There are fifty thousand bayonets in the Union armies from the border slave States. It would be a serious matter if, in consequence of a proclamation such as you desire, they should go over to the rebels. I do not think they all would,—not so many indeed, as a year ago, nor as six months ago; not so many today as yesterday. Every day increases their Union feeling. They are also getting their pride enlisted, and want to beat the rebels. Let me say one thing more: I think you should admit that we already have an important principle to rally and unite the people, in the fact that constitutional government is at stake. This is a fundamental idea, going down deep as anything."

By January 1, 1863 he had changed his mind and the Proclamation was issued, a caution document, emancipating only those slaves who were already out of the jurisdiction of their masters.

You will have noted that Lincoln was doubtful of the capacity of the former slaves to fight. Led by the Abolitionists and other radicals, the free Negroes and ex-slaves fought a terrific battle against the Lincoln administration to be allowed to take arms. They won, and created one of the sensations of the war by their bravery and self-sacrifice in battle. By December 8, 1863 in the annual message to Congress Lincoln wrote that the Negro soldiers were not inferior to others, and before the war was over he was to say that without Negro soldiers and Negro labour in the areas of battle, the North would lose the war. This is the growth of Lincoln, and now we can understand how it was that, elected a second time to the Presidency during the war, at his Inaugural Address, he uttered these words, as ferocious a denunciation of slavery and determination to abolish it as has ever been made: "Fondly do we hope, fervently do we pray, that this mighty scourge of war may speedily pass away; yet if it be God's will that it continue until the wealth piled by the bondman's two hundred and fifty years of unrequited toil shall be sunk, and until every drop of blood drawn with the lash shall be paid by another drawn with the sword, as was said three thousand years ago, so still it must be said that the judgments of the Lord are true and righteous altogether."

They are tremendous words. They frighten the timid and the conservative to this day. The writer of this article knows of no similar declaration at any time by any head of state who had assumed power by traditional and not revolutionary means. Lincoln not only meant them. He wrote later that he thought the Second Inaugural the best thing he had ever done and the one that would last longest. He also recognised that it was not popular.

Now we can look with fresh eyes at the Gettysburg Address. Lincoln expected to make the traditional lengthy oration. Instead he read this from two or three sheets of paper. He took no particular trouble to be heard. Thousands were present but his voice was barely audible beyond a small circle of those who were near. He does not mention slavery. He does not mention Negroes. He does not even directly mention union. His theme, stated in the first sentence, is the equality of men. Can a nation built on that endure? That is what the war is about. He calls upon the American people to dedicate themselves to this.

In the United States there was no problem of democracy for white people. If they had been white there would have been no civil war. He was telling them that they would have to include the Negroes in their democracy. He knew the terrible struggles ahead after the war would be won. He knew that now his vision was far ahead of the nation as a whole so he said what he had to say quietly and left it to history. But the determination to lay all the wealth the slave had built in ruins rather than let slavery continue and to pay back every wound of the whip with a wound of the sword, shows the feelings that moved in Lincoln when he delivered the Gettysburg Address. Many Americans do not understand this at all. And as for the British, a famous British authority on the United States, Viscount Bryce, prepared an anthology of Lincoln's speeches and writings for a well-known series of British classics. He printed the Second Inaugural, and omitted the passage dealing with the unrequited labour of the slave, the whip and the sword. We need not think he was dishonest. He simply could not understand Abraham Lincoln. We who have lived in this twentieth century, the century of catastrophes, can understand him better. In the history of human emancipation he stands in the first rank. West Indians will do not him but ourselves honour by making him one of our national heroes and living in constant companionship with his life and work.

Lincoln, the orator, the writer, is a model made to order for the politicians and publicists of an underdeveloped country. He grew up in the raw and backward Middle West, his schooling was small—he was essentially self-educated; he was a grown up man before he became in any way familiar with the political and literary figures of the day. Yet it is doubtful if his greatest speeches, two of which we print in our editorial columns, have been surpassed. And in one significant respect, he stands pre-eminent. Burke, Demosthenes, Pericles may have excelled him in range and sustained power. None of them has his simplicity. Any child can understand Lincoln, and never more so than, as on these two occasions, when he is at his most profound. This directness and simplicity he undoubtedly owed to the fact that he had grown to maturity in a semi-rural community where the first necessity of any speaker was not to go beyond the range of his hearers. All those who are continually bemoaning the backwardness of the common people would do well to meditate on this. We have referred earlier to the tremendous range and majesty with which, in the Second Inaugural, he made known his determination to bring the whole house down rather than compromise with evil. But the passage should never be read or quoted by itself. For immediately after this awesome declaration he makes one of the most beautiful transitions in all literature, a parallel to which can be found only in great music: "With malice towards none, with charity for all, with firmness in the right . . ." Read the two passages together aloud and you will see and feel, not art, but a statement expressing the profoundest feelings of a nation at one of the high moments of its existence.

We may seem to give undue prominence to Lincoln's speeches. This is no matter of intellectual or literary "culture". With them we are dealing with the history of civilisation in general and with the material which contributes to a just appraisal of the United States today.

The world's greatest speeches (and in time we shall most certainly print some of them in *The Nation*), these speeches have come and can come only at rare moments in the life of a nation. In the Civil War America was making the great transition from the old to the modern world. After years of war the nation found itself shaken and divided to its very foundations. All veils, pretences, illusions and hypocrisies had been stripped off. The whole world was watching. All knew that not only the fate of the United States but much of the future of the world would depend on the outcome of the great conflict. It was the first modern war, and is still the greatest civil war that the world has ever known. These were the circumstances in which Lincoln rose to speak. We have given an outline of the slow stages by which he arrived at his final determination, his patient refusal to go further than where he thought the nation had reached. Now by 1863 (The Gettysburg Address) and still more by 1865 (Second Inaugural) he felt that the fundamental forces in the world at large were with him. It was a great occasion, and his greatness lies in that he was equal to it. The democratic creed had had worthy expounders before him. None ever had so dramatic a stage, so comprehensive an audience. The long agitation and bloody battles which had preceded the Civil War, the rise of the Abolitionist Movement, the war itself, had sifted the forces of the nation, faced them with the sternest reality, and as a result of all this Lincoln could declare that the war was for democracy and however dreadful the cost, would continue until the shame of slavery had been wiped away. There indeed was the Voice of America. That was what the American nation, when it was forced to choose, had chosen. We of his generation have seen the shocking spectacle of McCarthyism, we are watching the convulsions that shake the country in its attempt to wipe away the disgrace of American persecution of Negroes. We in the West Indies have special reasons to be vigilant in our exposure and denunciation of these horrors. But no one who has studied the history of the United States in this, the period when the bones of the nation were laid bare, can doubt that ultimately the time will come when the American people will say as they once said: We now face the ultimate reality, these things must come to an end and whatever the price we have to pay we shall finish away with them.

7 February 1959

II. CARNIVAL

There is an undercurrent of attack on the Carnival festival. Now that the Government has taken it over and it is clear that it is going to be a dazzling success, we can expect this undercurrent to grow.

These carpers ought to be demolished at once, so that we shall be able to continue with our discussions and preparations and organisation of Carnival, without being bothered by them.

First of all, anyone who looks at the world today will see that the entertainment industry plays an enormous role in the economic and social life of every country in the world and none more so than the most advanced countries. Sometimes allied with the entertainment industry but in reality separate from it, is sport. Side by side with the expansion of popular democracy over the last hundred years has grown this expansion of entertainment and sport.

It is being more and more understood today that such activities represent a necessary part of human existence. "Entertainment" and "sport" are not merely relaxations from living which you take when you have time and money. They are a necessary part of civilised life.

A second point. Educators for some time now have been very concerned to teach children art appreciation. But side by side with this, and not necessarily divorced from it, is the far more important drive to make them practice art themselves. Not so much with the idea of becoming gifted, but because this also is a necessary part of a fully human existence.

So-called savage cultures experience this. We are just learning it. Finally, one of the greatest problems of modern life is the divorce between labour, ordinary activity, and the practice or appreciation of what interests them for its own sake. It is commonly believed that the abstract artist of today and the whole trend of modern art during the last 50 or 75 years are a direct result of the divorce in modern civilisation which creates the divided personality.

Now when we look at Carnival we have the extraordinary spectacle of entertainment, sport, free competition, and the practice of the arts to one degree or another, being carried on by a populace; in fact, by all sections of the population, without any inculcation from above, without any educational instruction, without any encouragement or stimulus by philosophically-minded person or persons who are interested in the arts as such.

You have colour, line, individual and mass representation, elementary drama, music, popular ballads, such a mass of creative activity as staggers the observer who knows how hard educators work to try to inculcate these things. All this is, from any point of view, an extraordinary social phenomenon and anyone who decries it or sneers at it is most probably merely venting his rage and anger at the development of the Trinidad people. It is not at all accidental that the full expansion of Carnival as we know it today, has taken place side by side with the expanding development of democracy and nationalism.

Carnival, we say, is a national festival. A simple affair? There are countries in the world, five, fifteen times as wealthy as Trinidad, which would give a substantial portion of their wealth to have a national festival, a festival in which the great masses of the people naturally and spontaneously take part, expressing themselves in the innumerable variety of ways in which the people of Trinidad do. This is nothing to be tolerant of or to be tolerant to. It is something to rejoice at and be thankful for. Very few countries have it.

We have not seen the best of Carnival yet by a long way. It is only now that the Government is going to settle down seriously to organise that we are going to see the full possibilities of this extraordinary social and artistical form which has sprung from the depths of the people of Trinidad and which they have tenaciously pursued despite official discouragement against some of its most characteristic features.

Here is another of the innumerable facts of Carnival. An enormous amount of work, of sheer hard labour, goes into the preparation and organisation of these Carnival shows and particularly of the Carnival bands. Work is work. It may be work for money; or it may be work purely for the love of it. But it is work. It is time and energy expended. People calculate the amount of money that is spent on Carnival. The thing to note, however, is the amount of work that is done.

In addition to the work, there is the immense organisation and self-discipline that are shown. Hundreds of people get together in order to organise a display of a certain kind, put themselves under a leader, make all the necessary preparations, make their displays for two days and then, after a period, settle down to do it again. The thing to note is that it is self-organisation. This, too, is another astounding phenomenon.

It is impossible at the present time to tell precisely what is the origin of this national festival. A great national movement is always difficult to analyse precisely, especially since, till the recent move towards national independence and nationalist pride, the best educated minds were usually concerned with everything except what was under their very noses. But it is fairly certain, and there are many historical precedents to help us, that the amount of work and the amount of independent organisation that go into Carnival were a form of self-activity of the masses of the people, a reaction against the perpetual preaching of foreign doctrines and foreign celebrations. Deprived of carrying on normal social and political activity they built something of their own. People, especially in the modern world, have a natural tendency to organise things that they are interested in; to carry on some sort of social activity by themselves. In many countries the social activity takes the form of political organisation, or of social work of some kind. We know very little of Carnival really. It is fairly certain that ultimately the sociological investigators and the psychologists will find that a great deal of what has been done and what is being done in the preparation and organisation of Carnival is the diversion of energies which would normally have been spent on ordinary social work. This goes very deep into the history of islands like Trinidad and others in the West Indies which are westernised without any nationalisation of their own. Carnival should be investigated along the lines of a substitution by the people for some national activity which was independent of the social life, of the national festivals and other national activities which were imposed on them from outside. All these things are matters to be investigated. But those are the lines of investigation. We shall do our share.

One final word. It is perfectly clear that all the Government has to do is to assist this precious and valuable tendency to independent work, to independent activity, to independent organisation, to express itself to the full. In other words, the more skilfully the Government organises, the more powerfully this independent activity will be able to express itself more independently than ever. There are pitfalls, but there is every sign that the PNM Government understands the essentials of the problem. In any case it will take a very powerful Government to organise to such a degree as to suppress this which has fought for its existence for so long and has now come to full flower.

Although Carnival may be said to be associated with entertainment, with sport, with a precious artistic development which creates and does not sit down merely to appreciate, there is still another aspect to it. People are always denouncing the people of Trinidad as being lazy, etc. Let the heathen rage. Carnival shows that when they are interested, they are incredibly energetic. If in the future there should be some sort of crisis in these areas as took place, for example, in Western Europe in the war. Or if the Government is able, as it may have to do, to impress the people with the necessity for some great national effort, then once the people are convinced that the effort that they are being called upon to make is worth making, that it is for a good cause, and is led by people they can trust, then we can be certain that the energy, the creativity and the capacity for independent organisation which they show in Carnival will very easily be transferred to another object. We can see in the Carnival the possibility (we do not go any further than possibility) of such a national mobilisation, as would put to shame all efforts that have hitherto been made in industrial and social activity.

21 February 1959

III. NOTES ON THE LIFE OF GEORGE PADMORE

On the evening of the day that he received the news, Dr Kwame Nkrumah, then Prime Minister of Ghana, broadcast to the nation on the death of George Padmore. He said: "George Padmore was, in my view, one of the greatest fighters against colonialism of our modern times. . . . One day, the whole of Africa will surely be free and united and when the final tale is told, the significance of George Padmore's work will be revealed."

Two years earlier, in 1957, when Dr Nkrumah invited him to become his adviser on African affairs, Padmore had more knowledge of African political movements and more personal contacts and relations with African politicians than any man living. He was a Marxist and a revolutionary, and for thirty years this West Indian had one main purpose in life—the emancipation of Africa from foreign domination.

Padmore, whose real name was Malcolm Nurse but like many revolutionaries had early adopted a pseudonym, was born in Trinidad in 1904. His father, Hubert Alphonso Nurse, was a rather unusual figure in his day. He was a black man, but he had gained a post in the Department of Education, a distinction which did not then often fall to men who were not white, or at least light in complexion. His ability, however, got him into trouble and after continuous friction, Nurse was either dismissed or he left. He also became a Moslem, a most unusual step for a West Indian black. I remember him living in a small room, almost entirely surrounded by books from floor to ceiling. I had never seen so many books before in a private house. Mr Nurse gave lessons there and I often visited him with my father and heard him hold forth. During vacations George and I spent long hours together and our chief recreation was going, day after day, to swim in the Arima river.

In Trinidad at this time, around 1910, there was little political activity; nationalist agitation, there was none. The young men of our class were highly literate and vocal, but not in such matters as politics and unionism. It was only in 1923 that the first elections were held for a small minority of the Legislative Council. In 1920 Captain Cipriani, a French Creole, started a combined labour and political mass organisation; but it was not very effective at the beginning. The influential ideas in the island came from the United States—books by Booker T.Washington and Dr Du Bois and, later, Marcus Garvey's paper *The Negro World*. The paper was banned, but all of us read it. Socially racial lines were clear. The whites, the browns and the blacks kept their own company. The best positions were shared very unequally by the first two, though there was no official segregation. It was on the black as opposed to the brown middle class that the discrimination fell hardest; and George was a member of that class. But white, brown and black, we had all gone to school together; in our separate clubs we played games in public competitions together; and somehow there was a sense of accommodation on all sides. A race riot was unthinkable. Yet a proud and sensitive black man could feel a sense of intolerable restriction, particularly because you were powerless to do anything about a situation that all classes seemed to accept as the natural order. This was the background of the young man who left Trinidad for the United States in the mid 1920s.

Padmore first went to Fisk University and later to Howard, the black university in Washington D.C. By this time he had become a militant revolutionary. One day Esme Howard, the British Ambassador, was due to pay a visit to Howard University. In those days that was a great event and the black professors prepared a distinguished welcome for their visitor. Padmore, however, had had printed a set of leaflets which described in fierce terms the oppression of British imperialism in Africa. When the procession of dignitaries appeared, he suddenly stepped out from among the students and threw the leaflets in front of the British Ambassador, some say into his face. Padmore was not expelled as one would expect, but he abandoned his academic career and he next appeared as a paid functionary in the American Communist Party.

George adopted the Communist doctrine completely and became very expert in it. People who knew him then agree that he was a great militant—active, devoted and fearless. The complaint of George, and most of the other blacks in the Communist Party, was that the leaders never understood that the Negro question had racial connotations which demanded special consideration by a political organization—however much this organization might aim to work for the equality of all mankind. This was the problem which formed the axis of George's career as a Marxist. Nevertheless, whatever the doubts were about George's strict Communist orthodoxy on the Negro question, by 1930 he was created head of the Negro department of the Profintern, with his headquarters in the Kremlin. He held that post until 1935, and if he had done nothing else his place in black history would still be safe.

Up to 1918 blacks, as a whole, played no particular role in world politics. The world was not conscious of them except as objects. Blacks were not conscious of themselves. A spirit of frustration, humiliation, rebellion is not political consciousness. The man who made both blacks conscious of themselves and the world conscious of blacks as a force to be reckoned with in world politics was a Jamaican, Marcus Garvey. By 1925/26 Garveyism as a force was finished, but the political problem represented by black people had been placed before the world once and for all. Henceforth it had to be taken into consideration in all calculations on a national as well as international scale.

It is a most extraordinary thing that the next great step in the international organization and mobilisation of blacks, was taken by yet another West Indian, George Padmore. What Padmore did between 1930 and 1935 was to organize and educate the black masses on a world scale in the theory and practice of modern political parties and modern trade unionism. Up to 1945, the end of the second world war, there was hardly a single African leader still active who had not passed through the school of thought and organisation which George directed from Moscow. Tens of thousands of black workers in various parts of the world received their first political education from the paper he edited, *The Negro Worker*. It gave information, advice, guidance, ideas about black struggles on every continent. All movements need an ideology, a body of ideas and information to which effort can be related and which has significance beyond that which is immediately visible. This *The Negro Worker* gave to hundreds of thousands of active blacks; and while the educated in Trinidad, for example, were sunk in the acceptance of ideas inculcated through British imperialism, Uriah Butler and the workers of the oil-fields were nourishing themselves on illicit copies of Padmore's paper and preparing for the outburst which was to launch the West Indies on the paths of nationalism and democracy. It developed too, the consciousness among blacks that they were part of an international movement. It must be remembered that men in Mombasa, Lagos, Port of Spain, Port au Prince, Dakar struggling to establish a trade union or political organization, often under illegal conditions and under heavy persecution, read and followed with exceptional concern the directives which came from the trusted centre in Moscow. George acquired an extraordinary skill, of which I was many times the witness in later years, of understanding a situation from the slenderest data and writing a programme, outlining a policy and indicating a line of action by which untaught and inexperienced blacks in a particular situation could direct themselves. This was his work.

One of Padmore's early achievements was the international conference of revolutionary black workers held in Hamburg in 1930. It was the first such conference which had ever been convened and to get the delegates together, George travelled over half the globe. As he wrote in his first book, *The Life of the Negro Toilers*: "At this conference, Negro delegates from different parts of Africa, the United States, West Indies and Latin America, not only discussed trade union questions, but dealt with the most vital problems affecting their social and political conditions, as for example, the expropriation of land by the imperialist robbers in Africa; the enslaving of toilers through Pass laws and other anti-labour and racial legislation in Africa; lynching, peonage and segregation in the United States; as well as unemployment, which has thrown millions of these black toilers on the streets, faced with the spectre of starvation and death."

Everybody says these things nowadays; but in 1930 George was giving them currency. If it is true that he had the power and the money of the powerful Russian state behind him, in some of the places he had to go and the things he had to do, nothing, not even Russia, could protect him. I still marvel at the courage, the world-wide historical vision, the political knowledge and organizational skills which moved in George at that time only 26 years old.

I went to England in 1932, knowing little or nothing of all this. At first I stayed with Learie and Norma Constantine in Nelson, Lancashire; but the following spring I went to London to live. I was a cricket reporter for the *Manchester Guardian* while I educated myself politically. One day a friend told me that there was a meeting in Gray's Inn Road and a great black communist had come from Europe to speak. I was going to every meeting in those days and the race aspect of the matter was an added attraction. I went and found about fifty people, mostly blacks, in a small hall; we waited for some time and then in stepped George Padmore, accompanied by one or two of his associates. I was amazed and delighted.

He spoke to the audience about struggles all over the world. Although he was a very good speaker, he was not a great orator; but what he had was authority. I was struck by the admiration and awe with which the audience listened and looked at him. He had been lucky to get out of prison into which the Nazis had put him as soon as they came into power. Many of his audience knew the risks he took in daily life, but he rarely spoke about it and always briefly. It was part of his profession, that was all.

That night after the meeting, George and I had a reunion. Life is much stranger than fiction. He told me that a year before he had been in London looking for lively recruits to take to Moscow to be trained; and he said that if he had met me he would most certainly have asked me. I did not tell him that if he had asked me in 1932 I most certainly would have gone with him. In 1932 I knew nothing of Communism, but by 1933 things were different. I was speaking a great deal on West Indian self-government and similar matters, but I had not entered politics as yet. Nevertheless I was reading hard and was already a long way towards becoming a Trotskyist. Between Communism and Trotskyism there was a line of antagonism and conflict stained with blood, incredible cruelties, murders and death. We were now swimmers in waters deeper and more turbulent than the Blue Basin of the Arima river. Although powerful currents were driving George and me apart, the early days at home and our common interest in African emancipation kept us together. We never once quarrelled. After that night I did not see George again, until one day, early in 1935, he came unexpectedly to my flat, pale and drawn, to tell me that he had broken with the Kremlin and would henceforth be living in London. From that time on we worked closely together.

Between 1928 and 1935 the whole policy of the Russian state, and the Communist International which it controlled, was based on the theory of imminent world revolution. George was aware of the struggle between the Stalinists and Trotskyists over policy, both internal and external; but it didn't seem to affect him or his work in any way. His main targets were Britain, France, Belgium and Italy as the leading imperialist powers in Africa and all his propaganda, in harmony with the policy of the Communist International as a whole, was directed against them. But by the beginning of 1935 Stalin was orienting Russian foreign policy and that of the Communist International in a new direction. Russia aimed to form some sort of alliance with Britain and France against Germany, Japan and Italy and part of the price Russia had to pay was the cessation of anti-imperialist propaganda. George Padmore was informed that the policy had to be changed. The Negro Worker was to preach that the main enemy of the African and of the democratic and progressive societies in the world, were the Fascists, particularly Germany and Japan; but to preach to Africans that their main enemies were Germany and Japan (who had no colonies in Africa) and that Britain, France and

Belgium were to be looked upon as friends of democracy was to make a nonsense, not only of all that George had been preaching for years, but of the actual situation in Africa at that time. Many Communist functionaries, the vast majority, made the change and followed the new Kremlin orientation. For George it was an unspeakable betrayal and he refused point-blank to do it.

For some months, after his appearance in London in 1935, George had a very hard time. The Communists persecuted him and vilified him with great bitterness; but despite the fact that the whole Stalinist machine was put in motion, both George's reputation and his political standing remained firm. Stalinism never shook the confidence in him of black people as a whole; what was shaken was the confidence of blacks in Communism. George lived to become an even more powerful enemy of imperialism than when he had at his disposal the immense resources of the Russian state and the Communist International.

George came to England when the Ethiopian crisis was just beginning. He was immediately in the thick of it. I believe that from the time of his break with Moscow, George had made up his mind to continue his efforts on behalf of colonial emancipation with specific concentration on Africa; but that under no circumstances would he ever again join any European or worldwide organisation in which black or colonial peoples did not have the dominant and controlling role. As time went on, I saw this more in his actions than in his words. George was no colonial specialist in the sense that he concerned himself only with colonial or African affairs; rather he read and studied everything political—China, India, Russia, Latin America—and he was as interested and familiar with the politics of Britain as anyone practising in British politics. But he would not join anything and instead formed organizations of his own.

The first organization, however, in which George began to function on his arrival in London was one which I organized—the International African Friends of Ethiopia (IAFE). It was the response of Africans and people of African descent to the rape of Ethiopia by Mussolini. For the first and last time I was the chairman of a colonial organization in Britain; ever afterwards, any such group dealing with African affairs saw George as chairman as of right. The IAFE had as its leading members Jomo Kenyatta, Wallace Johnson, Amy Garvey and others and we created a tremendous stir. Almost at once George began his life-long work of going round labour organisations, semi-revolutionary groups, trade union conferences or other groups who wanted to hear about the colonial issue and he began again the tireless correspondence with all the people and organisations he knew abroad. When the Ethiopian question subsided, the organisation would probably have fallen apart; but George took it over and transformed it into the International African Service Bureau (IASB). The IASB became the centre of anti-imperialism and the struggle for African emancipation in London; George was its chairman and I was editor of the journal we printed and distributed to every address we could find.

Our protest meetings and our resolutions which we sent to organisations in Britain and abroad had this virtue—they prevented anyone being able to say that people were "satisfied" with the colonial situation or "apathetic". George's articles for his newspapers and his correspondence kept the situation alive. We were always on the alert to feed information to Members of Parliament willing to ask questions in the House; and we wrote letters to the press, usually trying either the *New Statesman* or the *Manchester Guardian.* If we were lucky, we got one in five published but there was usually Fenner Brockway editing the *New Leader* to give us a helping hand. On every issue, when *The Times* and the big Conservative press, the Colonial Office, the Stalinists, the Labour Party put forward their side, we saw to it that the anti-imperialist case was put forward. George made the IASB into a genuine political force, yet our main weapon was propaganda. We wrote books and got them published—George published *How Britain Rules Africa* and later, *African and World Peace*; I completed *The Black Jacobins* and *The History of Negro Revolt*; Kenyatta wrote *Facing Mount Kenya*. We became so well known that in time leftist labour groups and unions would write to us for speakers. Eventually we rented the upper floor of a large building where we held meetings and had rooms for strangers visiting London. All this cost money. We dug into our shallow pockets, but it was Makonnen, a young man from British Guiana, who got most of the money. How he managed to maintain an operation of this kind is still beyond my comprehension, but he took it on his shoulders and did a colossal job, even cooking and cleaning the building himself.

George lived for the Bureau—his capacity for work was of the highest but it made severe demands. He earned a precarious living by his writing; he spent countless hours with people from Africa and all over the world, his encyclopaedic knowledge, his enthusiasm, his eagerness to explain, his hospitality drew them like a magnet. He talked like a torrent, but always to an end—an article, a resolution, a manoeuvre with the Colonial Office, an avenue for some propaganda in the British press. Politics, and above all, revolutionary politics frequently makes men hardened and indifferent to normal human relations. There was never a trace of that in George. He could be harsh, and even brutal, particularly at political treachery and he could get furious at the mere idea of certain things. But indifference, cruelty, ingratitude, betrayal, I never saw a trace in him, despite the fact that he had seen and known brutality such as few men had actually experienced.

It was largely the West Indians who made the African question a live question in British politics and this state of affairs continued until Nkrumah came to London in the early 1940s. The working out of the theory which shaped the revolution in the Gold Coast, its achievement of independence under the name of Ghana and with it the total rout of all imperialist pretensions to continue to rule in Africa—all this was Padmore's immense theoretical contribution to the politics of our time. I have spent a good deal of my life reading and studying the history of revolution; but the achievement by Nkrumah remains the most systematically planned and executed revolutionary strategy that I know of. In the preparation for this, George Padmore's work achieved perhaps its greatest victory.

Between 1930 and 1945 all of us saw African emancipation as dependent upon the breakdown of imperialist power in Europe. Armed rebellion was sure to be crushed unless the imperialist powers were impotent; and this could only be the result of revolutions within the metropolitan powers themselves. The theory is most unambiguously stated in my book, *The Black Jacobins* and few challenged it. Everyone, revolutionaries and conservatives expected the war and out of the war, revolutionary upheavals. We, in the Bureau, based our calculations and all our work on this.

When Nkrumah arrived in London from the United States, he walked into a political milieu which for nearly ten years had been devoted to the study and documentation of the question of African emancipation in itself, and in relation to world politics. George Padmore embodied in his person a theoretical and practical Marxism for Africa, a Marxism purged of the contemporary corruption. Nkrumah was consumed with one passion, the emancipation of Africa. He brought with him the equipment for political action on a grand scale—in addition to his academic studies and personal experience in American labour, he had absorbed into his predominantly African consciousness all that America, and particularly the American black struggle for equality, had had to teach. Between Nkrumah and Padmore, a new theory and programme of action was devised for the freedom of Africa.

The need for a political reappraisal arose from the fact that, contrary to our pre-war speculations, nowhere had the proletariat of the metropolitan powers overthrown the imperialist state. The actual struggle of the Africans now had to depend on themselves alone. The Marxist foundation of the Bureau remained unshakeable; but Nkrumah was a great student of Gandhi and his theory of passive resistance, and he and George worked out a policy, whatever its origins, which was new. The full responsibility was placed on the African population. The plan was to stretch the constitutional declarations of the European governments to the limit. First and foremost a party had to be organised and under its influence, the leaders, without ever doing anything against the law, would work with and help strengthen the trade unions, the co-operatives, peasant associations, every kind of African organization and mobilize them all under the banner of national independence. If, and when, this was done, the movement would on a certain day call a general strike and face the colonial government with the population embattled but peaceful. The calculation was that if the organization was comprehensive enough and solid enough, the government would be paralysed; and, even if it wanted to, would not have the forces to undertake bloody repression. The demonstration would be internationally publicised and continued government by the colonial power would become impossible. Armed insurrection was not entirely repudiated. It was held in reserve, but only if the new orientation failed.

All this came to a head in the Manchester Pan African Conference of 1945 attended by nearly 300 delegates, most of whom came from African political parties and unions. The theoretical ideas were now rooted and nourished in predominantly African personalities, active in forms of struggle in Africa itself and fortified by an African leader, Kwame Nkrumah. Two years after the Manchester conference Nkrumah, armed with theory and practical experience, went to the Gold Coast, wrote out his plan and began to organise. When he returned home in 1947, following twelve years abroad, he embodied in himself a great heritage of political and social experience from Europe, the United States and, through Gandhism, Asia. Few modern statesmen have had this thorough international education and training; and at the centre, in the crucial years, was George Padmore. If George had done nothing after the 1945 conference, he had done enough. The African revolution was on its way. This is how self-government and independence began in Africa; the legend that the British Colonial Office patiently "taught" the

Africans of the Gold Coast to govern themselves is a bubble which badly needs pricking.

Nkrumah's plan depended upon the completeness with which the mass movement was organised. Sufficient to say that when, in 1949, he called his Constituent Assembly, of some seventy-five organizations of all kinds in the country, seventy-three were represented. The Assembly was a public meeting in Accra and there were 90,000 people present. Shortly after, Nkrumah declared what he called Positive Action. A general strike paralysed all economic and social life for a week. Then Nkrumah called it off. From start to finish he had perfect control of this vast movement. The Government never had the opportunity to use violence, except against individuals here and there. Everything was strictly constitutional and yet devastatingly revolutionary. The colonial government put Nkrumah in jail, but they were beaten. They had to take him out again and make him head of the government.

1959-60

19
From Toussaint L'Ouverture to Fidel Castro

Toussaint L'Ouverture is not here linked to Fidel Castro because both led revolutions in the West Indies. Nor is the link a convenient or journalistic demarcation of historical time. What took place in French San Domingo in 1792-1804 reappeared in Cuba in 1958. The slave revolution of French San Domingo managed to emerge from

> . . . The pass and fell incensed points
> Of mighty opposites.

Five years later the people of Cuba are still struggling in the same toils.

Castro's revolution is of the twentieth century as much as Toussaint's was of the eighteenth. But despite the distance of over a century and a half, both are West Indian. The people who made them, the problems and the attempts to solve them, are peculiarly West Indian, the product of a peculiar origin and a peculiar history. West Indians first became aware of themselves as a people in the Haitian Revolution. Whatever its ultimate fate, the Cuban Revolution marks the ultimate stage of a Caribbean quest for national identity. In a scattered series of disparate islands the process consists of a series of uncoordinated periods of drift, punctuated by spurts, leaps and catastrophes. But the inherent movement is clear and strong.

The history of the West Indies is governed by two factors, the sugar plantation and Negro slavery. That the majority of the population in Cuba was never slave does not affect the underlying social identity. Wherever the sugar plantation and slavery existed, they imposed a pattern. It is an original pattern, not European, not African, not a part of the American main, not native in any conceivable sense of. that word, but West Indian, *sui generis*, with no parallel anywhere else.

The sugar plantation has been the most civilising as well as the most demoralising influence in West Indian development. When three centuries ago the slaves came to the West Indies, they entered directly into the large-scale agriculture of the sugar plantation, which was a modern system. It further required that the slaves live together in a social relation far closer than any proletariat of the time.

The cane when reaped had to be rapidly transported to what was factory production. The product was shipped abroad for sale. Even the cloth the slaves wore and the food they ate was imported. The Negroes, therefore, from the very start lived a life that was in its essence a modern life. That is their history—as far as I have been able to discover, a unique history.

In the first part of the seventeenth century, early settlers from Europe had made quite a success of individual production. The sugar plantation drove them out. The slaves saw around them a social life of a certain material culture and ease, the life of the sugar-plantation owners. The clever, the lucky and the illegitimate became domestics or artisans attached to the plantation or the factory. Long before the bus and the taxi, the small size of the islands made communication between the rural areas and the urban quick and easy. The plantation owners and the merchants lived an intense political life in which the ups and downs of sugar and in time the treatment and destiny of the slaves played a crucial and continuous role. The sugar plantation dominated the lives of the islands to such a degree that the white skin alone saved those who were not plantation owners or bureaucrats from the humiliations and hopelessness of the life of the slave. That was and is the pattern of West Indian life.

The West Indies between Toussaint L'Ouverture and Fidel Castro falls naturally into three periods: I. The Nineteenth Century; II. Between the Wars; III. After World War II.

I. THE NINETEENTH CENTURY

The nineteenth century in the Caribbean is the century of the abolition of slavery. But the passing of the years shows that the decisive patterns of Caribbean development took form in Haiti.

Toussaint could see no road for the Haitian economy but the sugar plantation. Dessalines was a barbarian. After Dessalines came Christophe, a man of conspicuous ability and within his circumstances an enlightened ruler. He also did his best (a cruel best) with the plantation. But with the abolition of slavery and the achievement of independence the plantation, indelibly associated with slavery, became unbearable. Pétion acquiesced in substituting subsistence production for the sugar plantation.

For the first century and a half of Haiti's existence there was no international opinion jealous of the independence of small nations; no body of similar states, ready to raise a hue and cry at any threat to one of their number; no theory or aid from the wealthy countries to the poorer ones. Subsistence production resulted in economic decay and every variety of political disorder. Yet it has preserved the national independence, and out of this has come something new which has captured a continent and holds its place in the institutions of the world.

This is what has happened. For over a century after independence the Haitians attempted to form a replica of European, i.e., French civilisation in the West Indies. Listen to the Haitian Ambassador, M. Constantin Mayard, in Paris in 1938:

French our institutions, French our public and civil legislation, French our literature, French our university, French the curriculum of our schools. . . .

Today when one of us [a Haitian] appears in a circle of Frenchmen, "welcome smiles at him in every eye." The reason is without doubt that your nation, ladies and gentlemen, knows that within the scope of its colonial expansion it has given to the Antilles and above all to San Domingo all that it could give of itself and its substance. . . . It has founded there, in the mould of its own national type, with its blood, with its language, its institutions, its spirit and its soil, a local type, an historic race, in which its sap still runs and where it is remade complete.

Generation after generation of the best sons of the Haitian élite were educated in Paris. They won distinctions in the intellectual life of France. The burning race hatred of pre-independence days had vanished. But a line of investigators and travellers had held up to international ridicule the hollow pretensions of Haitian civilisation. In 1913 the ceaseless battering from foreign pens was reinforced by the bayonets of American Marines. Haiti had to find a national rallying-point. They looked for it where it can only be found, at home, more precisely, in their own backyard. They discovered what is known today as Négritude. It is the pervading social ideology among politicians and intellectuals in every part of Africa. It is the subject of heated elaboration and disputation wherever Africa and Africans are discussed. But in its origin and development it is West Indian, and could not have been anything else but West Indian, the peculiar product of their peculiar history.

The Haitians did not know it as Négritude. To them it seemed purely Haitian. Two-thirds of the population of French San Domingo in Toussaint's time had made the Middle Passage. The whites had emigrated or been exterminated. The Mulattoes who were masters had their eyes fixed on Paris. Left to themselves, the Haitian peasantry resuscitated to a remarkable degree the lives they had lived in Africa. Their method of cultivation, their family relations and social practices, their drums, songs and music, such art as they practised and above all their religion which became famous, Vodun—all this was Africa in the West Indies. But it was Haitian, and the Haitian élite leapt at it. In 1926 Dr Price Mars in his famous book, *Ainsi Parla L'Oncle (This is What Uncle Said)*, described with loving care the way of life of the Haitian peasant. Rapidly, learned and scientific societies were formed. The African way of life of the Haitian peasant became the axis of Haitian literary creation. No plantation labourer, with free land to defend, rallied to the cause.

The Caribbean territories drifted along. At the end of the nineteenth century, Cuba produced a great revolution which bears the name "The Ten Years' War." It produced prodigies—no West Indian pantheon but will have among its most resplendent stars the names of José Martí the political leader and Maceo the soldier. They were men in the full tradition of Jefferson, Washington and Bolívar. That was their strength and that was their weakness. They were leaders of a national revolutionary party and a national revolutionary army. Toussaint L'Ouverture and Fidel Castro led a revolutionary people. The war for independence began again and ended in the Platt Amendment of 1904.

It was just one year after the Platt Amendment that there first appeared what has turned out to be a particular feature of West Indian life—the non-political writer devoted to the analysis and expression of West Indian society. The first was the greatest of them all, Fernando Ortiz. For over half a century, at home or in exile, he has been the tireless exponent of Cuban life and *Cubanidad*, the spirit of Cuba. The history of Spanish imperialism, sociology, anthropology, ethnology, all the related sciences are his medium of investigation into Cuban life, folklore, literature, music, art, education, criminality, everything Cuban. A most distinctive feature of his work is the number of solid volumes he has devoted to Negro and Mulatto life in Cuba. A quarter of a century before the Writers' Project of the New Deal began the discovery of the United States, Ortiz set out to discover his native land, a West Indian island. In essence it is the first and only comprehensive study of the West Indian people. Ortiz ushered the Caribbean into the thought of the twentieth century and kept it there.

II. BETWEEN THE WARS

Before World War I Haiti began to write another chapter in the record of the West Indian struggle for national independence. Claiming the need to recover debts and restore order, the Marines, as we have seen, invaded Haiti in 1913. The whole nation resisted. A general strike was organized and led by the literary intellectuals who had discovered the Africanism of their peasants as a means of national identity. The Marines left, and Negroes and Mulattoes resumed their fratricidal conflicts. But Haiti's image of itself had changed. "Goodbye to the Marseillaise,") a famous phrase by one of the best-known of Haitian writers signifies the substitution of Africa for France in the first independent West Indian state. Africa in the West Indies would seem to have been evoked by an empirical need and accidental circumstance. It was not so. Long before the Marines left Haiti, the role of Africa in the consciousness of the West Indies people had proved itself to be a stage in the development of the West Indian quest for a national identity.

The story is one of the strangest stories in any period of history. The individual facts are known. But no one has ever put them together and drawn to them the attention they deserve. Today the emancipation of Africa is one of the outstanding events of contemporary history. Between the wars when this emancipation was being prepared, the unquestioned leaders of the movement in every public sphere, in Africa itself, in Europe and in the United States, were not Africans but West Indians. First the unquestioned facts.

Two black West Indians using the ink of Négritude wrote their names imperishably on the front pages of the history of our time. Standing at the head is Marcus Garvey. Garvey, an immigrant from Jamaica, is the only Negro who has succeeded in building a mass movement among American Negroes. Arguments about the number of his followers dispute the number of millions. Garvey advocated the return of Africa to the Africans and people of African descent. He organised, very rashly and incompetently, the Black Star Line, a steamship company for transporting people of African descent from the New World back to Africa. Garvey did not last long. His movement took really elective form in about 1921, and by 1926 he was in a United States prison (some charge about misusing the mails); from prison he was deported home to Jamaica. But all this is only the frame and scaffolding. Garvey never set foot in Africa. He spoke no African language. His conceptions of Africa seemed to be a West Indian island and West Indian people multiplied a thousand times over. But Garvey managed to convey to Negroes everywhere (and to the rest of thc world) his passionate belief that Africa was the home of a civilisation which had once been great and would be great again. When you bear in mind the slenderness of his resources, the vast material forces and the pervading social conceptions which automatically sought to destroy him, his achievement remains one of the propagandistic miracles of this century.

Garvey's voice reverberated inside Africa itself. The King of Swaziland told Mrs. Marcus Garvey that he knew the name of only two black men in the Western world—Jack Johnson, the boxer who defeated the white man Jim Jeffries, and Marcus Garvey. Jomo Kenyatta has related to this writer how in 1921 Kenya nationalists, unable to read, would gather round a reader of Garvey's newspaper, *The Negro World*, and listen to an article two or three times. Then they would run various ways through the forest, carefully to repeat the whole, which they had memorised, to Africans hungry for some doctrine which lifted them from the servile consciousness in which Africans lived. Dr Nkrumah, a graduate student of history and philosophy at two American universities, has placed it on record that of all the writers who educated and influenced him, Marcus Garvey stands first. Garvey found the cause of Africans and of people of African descent not so much neglected as unworthy of consideration. In little more than half of ten years he had made it a part of the political consciousness of the world. He did not know the word Négritude but he knew the thing. With enthusiasm he would have welcomed the nomenclature, with justice claimed paternity.

The other British West Indian was from Trinidad, George Padmore. Padmore shook the dust of the cramping West Indies from his feet in the early 1920s and went to the United States. When he died in 1959, eight countries sent representatives to his funeral, which was held in London. His ashes were interred in Ghana; and all assert that in that country of political demonstrations, there never has been a political demonstration such as was evoked by these obsequies of Padmore. Peasants from remote areas who, it could have been thought, had never heard his name, found their way to Accra to pay the last tribute to this West Indian who had spent his life in their service.

Once in America he became an active Communist. He was moved to Moscow to head their Negro department of propaganda and organisation. In that post he became the best known and most trusted of agitators for African independence. In 1935, seeking alliances, the Kremlin separated Britain and France as "democratic imperialisms" from Germany and Japan, making the "Fascist imperialisms" the main target of Russian and Communist propaganda. This reduced activity for African emancipation to a farce: Germany and Japan had no colonies in Africa. Padmore broke instantly with the Kremlin. He went to London where, in a single room. He earned a meagre living by journalism, to be able to continue the work he had done in the Kremlin. He wrote books and pamphlets, attended all anti-imperialist meetings and spoke and moved resolutions wherever possible. He made and maintained an ever-increasing range of nationalist contacts in all sections of African society and the colonial world. He preached and taught Pan-Africanism and organised an African Bureau. He published a journal devoted to African emancipation (the present writer was its editor).

This is no place to attempt even a summary of the work and influence of the most striking West Indian creation between the wars, Padmore's African Bureau. Between the wars it was the only African organisation of its kind in existence. Of the seven members of the committee, five were West Indians, and they ran the organisation. Of them, only Padmore had ever visited Africa. It could not have been accidental that this West Indian attracted two of the most remarkable Africans of this or any other time. A founder-member and a simmering volcano of African nationalism was Jomo Kenyatta. But even better fortune was in store for us.

The present writer met Nkrumah, then a student at the University of Pennsylvania, and wrote to Padmore about him. Nkrumah came to England to study law and there formed an association with Padmore; they worked at the doctrines and premises of Pan-Africanism and elaborated the plans which culminated in Nkrumah's leading the people of the Gold Coast to the independence of Ghana. This revolution by the Gold Coast was the blow which made so many cracks in the pieces of African colonialism that it proved impossible ever to stick them together again. With Nkrumah's victory the association did not cease. After independence was signed and sealed, Nkrumah sent for Padmore, installed him once more in an office devoted to African emancipation and, under the auspices of an African government, this West Indian, as he had done in 1931 under the auspices of the Kremlin, organised in Accra the first conference of independent African states, followed, twenty-five years after the first, by the second world conference of fighters for African freedom. Dr Banda, Patrice Lumumba, Nyerere, Tom Mboya, were some of those who attended the conference. Jomo Kenyatta was not there only because he was in jail. NBC made a national telecast of the interment of his ashes in Christiansborg Castle, at which Padmore was designated the Father of African Emancipation, a distinction challenged by no one. To the degree that they had to deal with us in the period between the wars, many learned and important persons and institutions looked upon us and our plans and hopes for Africa as the fantasies of some politically illiterate West Indians. It was they who completely misconceived a continent, not we. They should have learned from that experience. They have not. The same myopic vision which failed to focus Africa is now peering at the West Indies.

The place of Africa in the West Indian development is documented as few historical visions are documented.

In 1939 a black West Indian from the French colony of Martinique published in Paris the finest and most famous poem ever written about Africa, *Cahier d'un retour au pays natal* (Statement of a Return to the Country Where I was Born). Aimé Césaire first describes Martinique, the poverty, misery and vices of the masses of the people, the lickspittle subservience of the coloured middle classes. But the poet's education has been consummated in Paris. As a West indian he has nothing national to be aware of. He is overwhelmed by the gulf that separates him from the people where he was born. He feels that he must go there. He does so and discovers a new version of what the Haitians, as had Garvey and Padmore, had discovered: that salvation for the West Indies lies in Africa, the original home and ancestry of the West Indian people.

The poet gives us a view of Africans as he sees them.

> . . . my Négritude is not a stone, its
> deafness a sounding board for
> the noises of the day
> my Négritude is not a mere spot of
> dead water on the dead eye of
> the earth
> my Négritude is no tower, no cathedral
>
> it cleaves into the red flesh of the
> teeming earth
> it cleaves into the glowing flesh of
> the heavens
> it penetrates the seamless bondage of
> my unbending patience
>
> Hoorah for those who never invented
> anything
> for those who never explored anything
> for those who never mastered anything
>
> but who, possessed, give themselves up
> to the essence of each thing
> ignorant of the coverings but possessed
> by the pulse of things
> indifferent to mastering but taking the
> chances of the world. . . .

In contrast to this vision of the African unseparated from the world, from Nature, a living part of all that lives, Césaire immediately places the civilisation that has scorned and persecuted Africa and Africans.

> Listen to the white world
> its horrible exhaustion from its
> immense labours
> its rebellious joints cracking under
> the pitiless stars
> its blue steel rigidities, cutting
> through the mysteries of the
> flesh
> listen to their vainglorious conquests
> trumpeting their defeats
> listen to the grandiose alibis of their
> pitiful floundering

The poet wants to be an architect of this unique civilisation, a commissioner of its blood, a guardian of its refusal to accept.

> But in so doing, my heart, preserve
> me from all hate
> do not turn me into a man of hate of
> whom I think only with hate
> for in order to project myself into
> this unique race
> you know the extent of my boundless
> love
> you know that it is not from hatred
> of other races
> that I seek to be cultivator of this
> unique race. . . .

He returns once more to the pitiful spectre of West Indian life, but now with hope.

> for it is not true that the work of man
> is finished
> that man has nothing more to do in the
> world but be a parasite in the world
> that all we now need is to keep in step
> with the world
> but the work of man is only just beginning
> and it remains to man to conquer all
> the violence entrenched in the recesses
> of his passion
> and no race possesses the monopoly of beauty,
> of intelligence, of force, and there
> is a place for all at the rendezvous
> of victory. . . .

Here is the centre of Césaire's poem. By neglecting it, Africans and the sympathetic of other races utter loud hurrahs that drown out common sense and reason. The work of man is not finished. Therefore the future of the African is not to continue not discovering anything. The monopoly of beauty, of intelligence, of force, is possessed by no race, certainly not by those who possess Négritude. Négritude is what one race brings to the common rendezvous where all will strive for the new world of the poet's vision. The vision of the poet is not economics or politics, it is poetic, *sui generis*, true unto itself and needing no other truth. But it would be the most vulgar racism not to see here a poetic incarnation of Marx's famous sentence, "The real history of humanity will begin."

From Césaire's strictly poetic affinities we have to turn our faces if even with distinct loss to our larger general purpose.[1] But *Cahier* has united elements in modern thought which seemed destined to remain asunder. These had better be enumerated.

1. He has made a union of the African sphere of existence with existence in the Western world.

2. The past of mankind and the future of mankind are historically and logically linked.

3. No longer from cxternal stimulus but from their own self-generated and independent being and motion will Africa and Africans move towards an integrated humanity.

It is the Anglo-Saxon poet who has seen for the world in general what the West Indian has seen concretely for Africa.

> Here the impossible union
> Of spheres of existence is actual,
> Here the past and future
> Are conquered, and reconciled,
> Where action were otherwise movement
> Of that which is only moved
> And has in it no source of movement—

Mr Eliot's conclusion is "Incarnation"; Césaire's, Négritude.

Cahier appeared in 1938 in Paris. A year before that *The Black Jacobins* had appeared in London. The writer had made the forward step of resurrecting not the decadence but the grandeur of the West Indian people. But as is obvious all through the book and particularly in the last pages, it is Africa and African emancipation that he has in mind.

Today (but only today) we can define what motivated this West Indian preoccupation with Africa between the wars. The West Indians were and had always been Western-educated. West Indian society confined black men to a very narrow strip of social territory. The first step to freedom was to go abroad. *Before they could begin to see themselves as a free and independent people they had to clear from minds the stigma that anything African was inherently inferior and degraded.* The road to West Indian national identity lay through Africa.

The West Indian national community constantly evades racial categorisation. After Ortiz, it was another white West Indian who in the same period proved himself to be the greatest politician in the democratic tradition whom the West Indies has ever known.

Arthur Andrew Cipriani was a French Creole in the island of Trinidad who came into public life as an officer in a West Indian contingent in World War I. It was in the army that many of the soldiers, a medley from all the British West Indian islands, for the first time wore shoes consistently. But they were the product of their peculiar history. The speed with which they adjusted themselves to the spiritual and material requirements of a modern war, amazed all observers, from General Allenby down. Cipriani made a reputation for himself by his militant defence of the regiment against all prejudice, official and unofficial. To the end of his days he spoke constantly of the recognition they had won. By profession a trainer of horses, it was only after much persuasion that, on his return home after the war, already a man over forty, he entered polities. He at once put himself forward as the champion of the common people, in his own phrase, "the barefooted man." Before very long this white man was acknowledged as leader by hundreds of thousands of black people and East Indians. An utterly fearless man, he never left the colonial government in any doubt as to what it was up against. All who ever heard him speak remember his raising of his right hand and his slow enunciation of the phrase, "If I raise my little finger . . ." Against tremendous odds he forced the government to capitulate on workmen's compensation, the eight-hour day, trade union legislation and other elementary constituents of democracy. Year after year he was elected mayor of the capital city. He made the mayoralty a centre of opposition to the British Colonial Office and all its works.

Cipriani always treated West Indians as a modern contemporary people. He declared himself to be a socialist and day in and day out, inside and outside of the legislature, he attacked capitalists and capitalism. He attached his party to the British Labour Party and scrupulously kept his followers aware of their privileges and responsibilities as members of the international labour movement. Cipriani was that rare type of politician to whom words expressed realities. Long before any of the other territories of the colonial empires, he not only raised the slogans of national independence and federation of the British West Indian territories, he went tirelessly from island to island mobilising public opinion in general and the labour movement in particular in support of these slogans. He died in 1945. The islands had never seen before and have not seen since anything or anybody like him.

The West Indian masses jumped ahead even of Cipriani. In 1937, among the oil field workers in Trinidad, the largest proletarian grouping in the West Indies, a strike began. Like a fire along a tinder track, it spread to the entire island, then from island to island, ending in upheaval at the other end of the curve, in Jamaica, thousands of miles away. The colonial government in Jamaica collapsed completely and two local popular leaders had to take over the responsibility of restoring some sort of social order. The heads of the government in Trinidad and Tobago saved their administrations (but earned the wrath of the imperial government) by expressing sympathy with the revolt. The British Government sent a Royal Commission, which took much evidence, discovered long-standing evils, and made proposals by no means unintelligent or reactionary. As usual they were late, they were slow. Had Cipriani been the man he was ten years earlier, self-government, federation and economic regeneration, which he had advocated so strenuously and so long, could have been initiated then. But the old warrior was nearly seventy. He flinched at the mass upheavals which he more than anyone else had prepared, and the opportunity was lost. But he had destroyed a legend and established once and for all that the West Indian people were ready to follow the most advanced theories of an uncompromising leadership.

III. AFTER WORLD WAR II

Cipriani had built soundly and he left behind a Caribbean Labour Congress devoted to federation, independence and the creation of an enlightened peasantry. But what has happened to Castro's Cuba is inherent in these unfortunate islands.

In 1945 the Congress, genuinely West Indian, joined the World Federation of Trade Unions. But in 1948 that body split into the World Federation of Trade Unions of the East and the International Confederation of Free Trade Unions of the West. The split in the international split the Caribbean Labour Congress and it lost its place as the leader and inspirer of a genuinely West Indian movement. The British Colonial Office took the coloured middle class under its wing. These gradually filled the Civil Service and related organisations; they took over the political parties, and with the parties, the old colonial system.

What is this old colonial system? It is the oldest Western relic of the seventeenth century still alive in the world today, surrounded on all sides by a modern population.

The West Indies has never been a traditional colonial territory with clearly distinguished economic and political relations between two different cultures. Native culture there was none. The aboriginal Amerindian civilisation had been destroyed. Every succeeding year, therefore, saw the labouring population, slave or free, incorporating into itself more and more of the language, customs, aims and outlook of its masters. It steadily grew in numbers until it became a terrifying majority of the total population. The ruling minority therefore was in the position of the father who produced children and had to guard against being supplanted by them. There was only one way out, to seek strength abroad. This beginning has lasted unchanged to this very day.

The dominant industrial structure has been the sugar plantation. For over two hundred years the sugar industry has tottered on the brink of disaster, remaining alive by an unending succession of last-minute rescues by gifts, concessions, quotas from the metropolitan power or powers.

SUGAR MANUFACTURERS' "GRIM FUTURE"

From our Correspondent

Georgetown, Sept. 3

The British West Indies Sugar Association's chairman, Sir Robert Kirkwood, has stated here that cane sugar manufacturers were facing a grim future and the position was reaching a stage where beet sugar production should be restricted to provide cane manufacturers with an enlarged market. Sir Robert pointed out that Britain's participation in the European Common Market should be no threat to sugar manufacturers in the region provided preferences under the Commonwealth sugar agreement were preserved.

You would be able to read the same in any European newspaper at regular intervals during the last two hundred years. Recent official reports on the life and labour of the plantation labourer are moved to language remarkably similar to that of the non-conformist agitators against plantation slavery. There are economists and scientists today in the West Indies who believe that the most fortunate economic occurrence would be a blight that would destroy the sugar cane completely and thus compel some new type of economic development.[2]

As they have been from the first days of slavery, financial power and its mechanism are today entirely in the hands of metropolitan organisations and their agents.

Such a Westernized population needs quantities of pots, pans, plates, spoons, knives, forks, paper, pencils, pens, cloth, bicycles, buses for public transport, automobiles, all the elementary appurtenances of civilisation which the islands do not manufacture, not forgetting MercedesBenzes, Bentleys, Jaguars and Lincolns. In this type of commerce the dominating elements are the foreign manufacturers and the foreign banks. The most revealing feature of this trade and the oldest is the still massive importation of food, including fresh vegetables.

The few industries of importance, such as oil and bauxite, are completely in the hands of foreign firms, and the local politicians run a ferocious competition with each other in offering inducements to similar firms to establish new industries here and not there.

As with material, so with intellectual necessities. In island after island the daily news is entirely in the hands of foreign firms. Radio and television cannot evade the fate of newspapers.

In 1963 the old colonial system is not what it was in 1863; in 1863 it was not what it had been in 1763 or 1663. The fundamentals outlined above, however, have not changed. But for the first time the system is now threatened, not from without but from within, not by communism, not by socialism, but by plain, simple parliamentary democracy. The old colonial system in the West Indies was not a democratic system, was not born as such. It cannot live with democracy. Within a West Indian island the old colonial system and democracy are incompatible. One has to go. That is the logic of development of every West Indian territory, Cuba , the Dominican Republic, Haiti, the former British colonies, the former French colonies, and even Puerto Rico, the poor relation of the wealthy United States.

The supreme wrong of West Indian politics is that the old colonial system has so isolated the ruling classes from the national community that plain, ordinary parliamentary democracy, *suffused with a sense of national identity*, can remake the islands.

Statistics of production and the calculations of votes together form the surest road towards misunderstanding the West Indies. To which for good measure add the antagonism of races. The people of the West Indies were born in the seventeenth century, in a Westernized productive and social system. Members of different African tribes were carefully split up to lessen conspiracy, and they were therefore compelled to master the European languages, highly complex products of centuries of civilisation. From the start there had been the gap, constantly growing, between the rudimentary conditions of the life of the slave and the language he used. There was therefore in West Indian society an inherent antagonism between the consciousness of the black masses and the reality of their lives, inherent in that it was constantly produced and reproduced not by agitators but by the very conditions of the society itself. It is the modern media of mass communication which have made essence into existence. For an insignificant sum per month, the black masses can hear on the radio news of Dr Nkrumah, Jomo Kenyatta, Dr Julius Banda, Prime Minister Nehru, events and personalities of the United Nations and all the capitals of the world. They can wrestle with what the West thinks of the East and what the East thinks of the West. The cinema presents actualities and not infrequently stirs the imagination with the cinematic masterpieces of the world. Every hour on the hour all variations of food, clothing, household necessities and luxuries are presented as absolutely essential to a civilised existence. All this to a population which over large areas still lives in conditions little removed from slavery.

The high material civilisation of the white minority is now fortified by the concentration of the coloured middle classes on making salaries and fees do the work of incomes.

Sometimes a quarter of the population is crowded into the capital city, the masses irresistibly attracted by the contrast between what they see and hear and the lives they live. This was the tinder to which Castro placed a match. Historical tradition, education in the sense of grappling with the national past, there is none. History as taught is what it always has been, propaganda for those, whoever they may be, who administer the old colonial system. Power here is more naked than in any other part of the world. Hence the brutality, savagery, even personal cruelties of the regimes of Trujillo and Duvalier, and the power of the Cuban Revolution.

This is the instrument on which perform all West Indian soloists, foreign or native. Take the French West Indian islands of Martinique and Guadeloupe. The colonial administration declared and acted for Vichy, the mass of the population for the Resistance. Vichy defeated, the islands whole-heartedly became departments of France, anxious to be assimilated into French civilisation. But the hand of the Paris administration, notoriously heavy in the provincial administrations of France itself, is a crushing weight on any attempt to change the old colonial system. Today the mass of the population, disillusioned, is demanding independence. Their students in Paris are leading the struggle with blood, with boldness and with brilliance available to all who use the French language.

The British system, unlike the French, does not crush the quest for a national identity. Instead, it stifles it. It formed a federation of its Caribbean colonies. But the old colonial system consisted of insular economies, each with its financial and economic capital in London. A federation meant that the economic line of direction should no longer be from island to London, but from island to island. But that involved the break-up of the old colonial system. The West Indian politicians preferred the break-up of the Federation. Two of the islands have actually been granted independence. The Queen of England is their queen. They receive royal visits; their legislatures begin with prayers; their legislative bills are read three times; a mace has been presented to each of these distant infants by the Mother of Parliaments; their prominent citizens can receive an assortment of letters after their names, and in time the prefix "Sir." This no longer lessens but intensifies the battle between the old colonial system and democracy. Long before the actual independence was granted, large numbers of the middle classes, including their politicians, wanted it put off as far into the distance as possible. For the cruiser in the offing and the prospect of financial gifts and loans, they turn longing eyes and itching feet towards the United States.

The Caribbean is now an American sea. Puerto Rico is its show piece. Puerto Rican society has the near-celestial privilege of free entry into the United States for their unemployed and their ambitious. The United States returns to the Puerto Rican Government all duty collected on such staple imports as rum and cigars.

American money for investment and American loans and gifts should create the Caribbean paradise. But if the United States had the Puerto Rican density of population, it would contain all the people in the world. Puerto Rico is just another West Indian island.

In the Dominican Republic there is no need to go beyond saying that Trujillo had gained power by the help of the United States Marines and all through the more than quarter-century of his infamous dictatorship he was understood to enjoy the friendship of Washington. Before the recent election of his successor, Sr. Juan Bosch, the French newspapers stated as an item of news that members of the left in the Dominican Republic (names were given) were deported to Paris by the local police, who were assisted in this operation by members of the FBI. Trujillo gone, Duvalier of Haiti is the uncrowned king of Latin American barbarism. It is widely believed that despite the corruption and impertinence of his regime, it is American support which keeps him in power: better Duvalier than another Castro.

Such a mass of ignorance and falsehood has surrounded these islands for so many centuries that obvious truths sound like revelations. Contrary to the general belief, the Caribbean territories taken as a whole are not sunk in irremediable poverty. When he was Principal of the University of the West Indies in Jamaica, Professor Arthur Lewis, former head of the faculty of economics at Manchester University and at the time of writing due to head the same faculty at Princeton, tried to remove some cobwebs from the eyes of his fellow West Indians:

> This opinion that the West Indies can raise all the capital it needs from its own resources is bound to shock many people, because West Indians like to feel that ours is a poor community. But the fact of the matter is that at least half of the people in the world are poorer than we are. The standard of living in the West Indies is higher than the standard of living in India, or China, in most of the countries of Asia, and in most of the countries of Africa. The West Indies is not a poor community; it is in the upper bracket of world income. It is capable of producing the extra 5 or 6 per cent of resources which is required for this job, just as Ceylon and Ghana are finding the money they need for development by taxing themselves. It is not necessary for us to send our statesmen around the world begging for help. If help is given to us let us accept it, but let us not sit down and say nothing can be done until the rest of the world out of its goodness of heart is willing to grant us charity.[3]

The economic road they have to travel is a broad highway on which the sign posts have long been erected. Sr. Juan Bosch began his campaign by promising to distribute the land confiscated from the baronial plunder of the Trujillo family. His supporters rapidly transformed this into: "A house and land for every Dominican." Not only popular demand and modern economists, but British Royal Commissions during the last sixty years, have indicated (cautiously but clearly enough) that the way out of the West Indian morass is the abolition of the plantation labourer and the substitution, instead, of individual landowning peasants. Scientists and economists have indicated that an effective industry is possible, based on the scientific and planned use of raw material produced on the islands. I have written in vain if I have not made it clear that of all formerly colonial coloured peoples, the West Indian masses are the most highly experienced in the ways of Western civilisation and most receptive to its requirements in the twentieth century. To realise themselves they will have to break out of the shackles of the old colonial system.

I do not propose to plunge this appendix into the turbulent waters of controversy about Cuba. I have written about the West Indies in general and Cuba is the most West Indian island in the West Indies. That suffices.

One more question remains—the most realistic and most pregnant question of all. Toussaint L'Ouverture and the Haitian slaves brought into the world more than the abolition of slavery. When Latin Americans saw that small and insignificant Haiti could win and keep independence they began to think that they ought to be able to do the same. Pétion, the ruler of Haiti, nursed back to health the sick and defeated Bolívar, gave him money, arms and a printing press to help in the campaign which ended in the freedom of the Five States. What will happen to what Fidel Castro has brought new to the world no one can say, but what is waiting in the West Indies to be born, what emerged from the womb in July 1958, is to be seen elsewhere in the West Indies, not so confused with the pass and fell incensed points of mighty opposites. I speak now of a section of the West Indies of which I have had during the past five years intimate and personal experience of the writers and the people. But this time the people first, for if the ideologists have moved closer towards the people, the people have caught up with the ideologists and the national identity is a national fact.

In Trinidad in 1957, before there was any hint of a revolution in Cuba, the ruling political party suddenly declared, contrary to the declaration of policy with which it had won the election, that during the war the British Government of Sir Winston Churchill had given away Trinidad property and it should be returned. What happened is one of the greatest events in the history of the West Indies. The people rose to the call. Mass meetings and mass demonstrations, political passion such as the island had never known, swept through the population. Inside the chains of the old colonial system, the people of the West Indies are a national community. The middle classes looked on with some uncertainty but with a growing approval. The local whites are not like whites in a foreign civilisation. They are West Indians and, under a strong impulse, think of themselves as such. Many of them quietly made known their sympathy with the cause. The political leader was uncompromising in his demand for the return. "I shall break Chaguaramas or it will break me," he declared, and the words sprouted wings. He publicly asserted to mass meetings of many thousands that if the State Department, backed by the Colonial Office, continued to refuse to discuss the return of the base, he would take Trinidad not only out of the West Indian Federation but out of the British association altogether: he would establish the independence of the island, all previous treaties entered into under the colonial regime would automatically become null and void, and thus he would deal with the Americans. He forbade them to use the Trinidad airport for their military planes. In a magnificent address,"From Slavery to Chaguaramas," he said that for centuries the West Indies had been bases, military footballs of warring imperialist powers, and the time had come to finish with it. It is the present writer's opinion (he was for the crucial period editor of the party journal) that it was the response of the population which sent the political leader so far upon a perilous road. They showed simply that they thought the Americans should quit the base and return it to the people. This was all the more remarkable in that the Trinidad people freely admitted that Trinidad had never enjoyed such financial opulence as when the Americans were there during the war. America was undoubtedly the potential source of economic and financial aid. But they were ready for any sacrifices needed for the return of the base. They were indeed ready for anything, and the political leadership had to take great care to do or say nothing which would precipitate any untoward mass intervention.

What was perhaps the most striking feature of this powerful national upheaval was its concentration on the national issue and its disregard for all others. There was not the slightest trace of anti-American feeling; though the British Colonial Office was portrayed as the ally of the State Department and the demand for political independence was well on the way, there was equally no trace of anti-British feeling. There was no inclination towards nonalignment, not even, despite the pressure for independence, anti-imperialism. The masses of the people of Trinidad and Tobago looked upon the return of the base as the first and primary stage in their quest for national identity. That they were prepared to suffer for, if need be (of this I am as certain as one can be of such things) to fight and die for.

But in the usual accompaniments of a struggle against a foreign base, they were not in any way concerned. Not that they did not know. They most certainly knew. But they had had a long experience of international relations and they knew precisely what they wanted. Right up the islands, the population responded in the same way to what they felt was a West Indian matter. The press conference of the political leader was the most popular radio programme in the West Indian islands. It was 1937-38 all over again. "Free is bow you is from the start, an' when it look different you got to move, just move, an' when you movin' say that is a natural freedom make you move."[4] Though the British flag still blew above them, in their demands and demonstrations for Chaguaramas they were free, freer than they might be for a long time.

The West Indian national identity is more easily to be glimpsed in the published writings of West Indian authors.

Vic Reid of Jamaica is the only West Indian novelist who lives in the West Indies. That presumably is why he sets his scene in Africa. An African who knows the West Indies well assures me that there is nothing African about Reid's story. It is the West Indies in African dress. Whatever it is, the novel is a *tour-de-force.* African or West Indian, it reduces the human problems of underdeveloped countries to a common denominator. The distinctive tone of the new West Indian orchestra is not loud but it is clear. Reid is not unconcerned about the fate of his characters. The political passions are sharp and locked in murderous conflict. But Reid is detached as no European or African writer is or can be detached, as Garvey, Padmore, Césaire were not and could not be detached. The origin of his detachment appears very clearly in the most powerful and far-ranging of the West Indian school, George Lamming of Barbados.

Confining ourselves strictly to our purpose, we shall limit ourselves to citing only one episode from the latest of his four powerful novels.

Powell, a character in *Season of Adventure*, is a murderer, rapist and altogether criminal member of West Indian society. Suddenly, after nine-tenths of the book, the author injects three pages headed "Author's Note." Writing in the first person he accounts for Powell.

Until the age of ten Powell and I had lived together, equal in the affection of two mothers. Powell had made my dreams; and I had lived his passions. Identical in years, and stage by stage, Powell and I were taught in the same primary school.

And then the division came. I got a public scholarship which started my migration into another world, a world whose roots were the same, but whose style of living was entirely different from what my childhood knew. It had earned me a privilege which now shut Powell and the whole *tonelle* right out of my future. I had lived as near to Powell as my skin to the hand it darkens. And yet! Yet I forgot the *tonelle* as men forget a war, and attached myself to that new world which was so recent and so slight beside the weight of what had gone before. Instinctively I attached myself to that new privilege; and in spite of all my effort, I am not free of its embrace to this day.

I believe deep in my bones that the mad impulse which drove Powell to his criminal defeat was largely my doing. I will not have this explained away by talk about environment; nor can I allow my own moral infirmity to be transferred to a foreign conscience, labelled imperialist. I shall go beyond my grave in the knowledge that I am responsible for what happened to my brother.

Powell still resides somewhere in my heart, with a dubious love, some strange, nameless shadow of regret; and yet with the deepest, deepest nostalgia. For I have never felt myself to be an honest part of anything since the world of his childhood deserted me.

This is something new in the voluminous literature of anti-colonialism. The West Indian of this generation accepts complete responsibility for the West Indies.

Vidia Naipaul of Trinidad does the same. His Mr Biswas writes his first article for a newspaper.

DADDY COMES HOME IN A COFFIN

U.S. Explorer's Last Journey

On Ice by M. Biswas

. . . Less than a year ago Daddy—George Elmer
Edman, the celebrated traveller and explorer—
left home to explore the Amazon.

Well, I have news for you, kiddies.

Daddy is on his way home.

Yesterday he passed through Trinidad.

In a coffin.

This earns Mr Biswas, former agricultural labourer and keeper of a small shop, a job on the staff of this paper.

Mr Biswas wrote a letter of protest. It took him two weeks. It was eight typewritten pages long. After many re-writings the letter developed into a broad philosophical essay on the nature of man; his son goes to a secondary school and together they hunt through Shakespeare for quotations and find a rich harvest in *Measure for Measure*. The foreigner may miss this bland reproduction of the *modus operandi* of the well-greased West Indian journalist, politician, prime minister.

Mr Biswas is now a man of letters. He is invited to a session of local literati. Mr Biswas, whose poetic peak is Ella Wheeler Wilcox, is bewildered by whisky and talk about Lorca, Eliot, Auden. Every member of the group must submit a poem. One night after looking at the sky through the window Mr Biswas finds his theme.

He addressed his mother. He did not think of rhythm; he used no cheating abstract words. He wrote of coming up to the brow of the hill, seeing the black, forked earth, the marks of the spade, the indentations of the fork prongs. He wrote of the journey he had made a long time before. He was tired; she made him rest. He was hungry; she gave him food. He had nowhere to go; she welcomed him. . . .

"It is a poem," Mr Biswas announced. "In prose."

. . ."There is no title," he said. And, as he had expected, this was received with satisfaction.

Then he disgraced himself. Thinking himself free of what he had written, he ventured on his poem boldly, and even with a touch of self-mockery. But as he read, his hands began to shake, the paper rustled; and when he spoke of the journey his voice failed. It cracked and kept on cracking; his eyes tickled. But he went on, and his emotion was such that at the end no one said a word. . . .

The West Indian had made a fool of himself imitating American journalism, Shakespeare, T. S. Eliot, Lorca. He had arrived at truth when he wrote about his own West Indian childhood, his West Indian mother and the West Indian landscape. Naipaul is an East Indian. Mr Biswas is an East Indian. But the East Indian problem in the West Indies is a creation of politicians of both races, seeking means to avoid attacking the old colonial system. The East Indian has become as West Indian as all the other expatriates.

The latest West Indian novelist is one of the strangest of living novelists. Beginning in 1958 he has just concluded a quartet of novels.[5] He is from British Guyana, which is a part of the South American continent. There are nearly 40,000 square miles of mountains, plateaux, forest, jungle, savannah, the highest waterfalls in the world, native Amerindians, settled communities of escaped African slaves—all largely unexplored. For fifteen years, over this new territory, Wilson Harris worked as a land surveyor. He is a member of a typical West Indian society of 600,000 people which inhabits a thin strip of coastline. Harris sets the final seal on the West Indian conception of itself as a national identity. On the run from the police a young Guianese, half-Chinese, half-Negro, discovers that all previous generations, Dutch, English, French, capitalists, slaves, white and black, were expatriates.

. . . All the restless wayward spirits of all the aeons (who it was thought had been embalmed for good) are returning to roost in our blood. And we have to start all over again where they began to explore. We've got to pick up the seeds again where they left off. It's no use worshipping the rottenest tacouba and tree-trunk in the historic topsoil. There's a whole world of branches and sensations we've missed, and, we've got to start again from the roots up even if they look like nothing. Blood, sap, flesh, veins, arteries, lungs, heart, the heartland, Sharon. *We're the first potential parents who can contain the ancestral home.* Too young? I don't know. Too much responsibility? Time will tell. We've got to face it. Or else it will be too late to stop everything and everyone from running away and tumbling down. And then All the King's Horses and all the King's Men won't be able to put us together again. Like all the bananas and the plantains and the coffee trees near Charity. Not far from here, you know. A small wind comes and everything comes out of the ground. Because the soil is unstable. Just pegasse. Looks rich on top but that's about all. What do you think they say when it happens, when the crops run away? They shrug and say they're expendable crops. They can't begin to see that it's *us*, our blood, running away all the time, in the river and in the sea, everywhere, staining the bush. *Now* is the time to make a newborn stand, Sharon; you and me; it's up to us, even if we fail on our knees and *creep* to anchor ourselves before we get up.

There is no space here to deal with the poet in the literary tradition, or the ballad singer. In dance, in the innovation in musical instruments, in popular ballad singing unrivalled anywhere in the world, the mass of the people are not seeking a national identity, they are expressing one. The West Indian writers have discovered the West Indies and West Indians, a people of the middle of our disturbed century, concerned with the discovery of themselves, determined to discover themselves, but without hatred or malice against the foreigner, even the bitter imperialist past. To be welcomed into the comity of nations a new nation must bring something new. Otherwise it is a mere administrative convenience or necessity. The West Indians have brought something new.

Albion too was once
a colony like ours. . . .

. . . deranged
By foaming channels, and the vain
expanse
Of bitter faction.

All in compassion ends.
So differently from what the heart
arranged.

Passion not spent but turned inward. Toussaint tried and paid for it with his life. Torn, twisted, stretched to the limits of agony, injected with poisonous patent medicines, it lives in the state which Fidel started. It is of the West Indies West Indian. For it, Toussaint, the first and greatest of West Indians, paid with his life.

1962

20

'What Is Art?'

I have made great claims for cricket. As firmly as I am able and as is here possible, I have integrated it in the historical movement of the times. The question remains: What is it? Is it mere entertainment or is it an art? Mr Neville Cardus (whose work deserves a critical study) is here most illuminating, not as subject but as object. He will ask: "Why do we deny the art of a cricketer, and rank it lower than a vocalist's or a fiddler's? If anybody tells me that R.H. Spooner did not compel a pleasure as aesthetic as any compelled by the most cultivated Italian tenor that ever lived I will write him down a purist and an ass." He says the same in more than one place. More than any sententious declaration, all his work is eloquent with the aesthetic appeal of cricket. Yet he can write in his autobiography: "I do not believe that anything fine in music or in anything else can be understood or truly felt by the crowd." Into this he goes at length and puts the seal on it with: "I don't believe in the contemporary idea of taking the arts to the people: let them seek and work for them." He himself notes that Neville Cardus, the writer on cricket, often introduces music into his cricket writing. Never once has Neville Cardus, the music critic, introduced cricket into his writing on music. He finds this "a curious point". It is much more than a point, it is not curious. Cardus is a victim of that categorization and specialization, that division of the human personality, which is the greatest curse of our time. Cricket has suffered, but not only cricket. The aestheticians have scorned to take notice of popular sports and games—to their own detriment. The aridity and confusion of which they so mournfully complain will continue until they include organized games and the people who watch them as an integral part of their data. Sir Donald Bradman's technical accomplishments are not on the same plane as those of Yehudi Menuhin. Sir John Gielgud in three hours can express adventures and shades in human personality which are not approached in three years of Denis Compton at the wicket. Yet cricket is an art, not a bastard or a poor relation, but a full member of the community.

The approach must be direct. Too long has it been impressionistic or apologetic, timid or defiant, always ready to take refuge in the mysticism of metaphor. It is a game and we have to compare it with other games. It is an art and we have to compare it with other arts.

Cricket is first and foremost a dramatic spectacle. It belongs with the theatre, ballet, opera and the dance.

In a superficial sense all games are dramatic. Two men boxing or running a race can exhibit skill, courage, endurance and sharp changes of fortune; can evoke hope and fear. They can even harrow the soul with laughter and tears, pity and terror. The state of the city, the nation or the world can invest a sporting event with dramatic intensity such as is reached in few theatres. When the democrat Joe Louis fought the Nazi Schmelling the bout became a focus of approaching world conflict. On the last morning of the 1953 Oval Test, when it was clear than England would win a rubber against Australia after twenty years, the nation stopped work to witness the consummation.

These possibilities cricket shares with other games in a greater or lesser degree. Its quality as drama is more specific. It is so organized that at all times it is compelled to reproduce the central action which characterizes all good drama from the days of the Greeks to our own: two individuals are pitted against each other in a conflict that is strictly personal but no less strictly representative of a social group. One individual batsman faces one individual bowler. But each represents his side. The personal achievement may be of the utmost competence or brilliance. Its ultimate value is whether it assists the side to victory or staves off defeat. This has nothing to do with morals. It is the organizational structure on which the whole spectacle is built. The dramatist, the novelist, the choreographer, must strive to make his individual character symbolical of a larger whole. He may or may not succeed. The runner in a relay race must take the plus or minus that his partner or partners give him. The soccer forward and the goalkeeper may at certain rare moments find themselves sole representatives of their sides. Even the baseball-batter, who most nearly approaches this particular aspect of cricket, may and often does find himself after a fine hit standing on one of the bases, where he is now dependent upon others. The batsman facing the ball does not merely represent his side. For that moment, to all intents and purposes, he is his side. This fundamental relation of the One and the Many, Individual and Social, Individual and Universal, leader and followers, representative and ranks, the part and the whole, is structurally imposed on the players of cricket. What other sports, games and arts have to aim at, the players are given to start with, they cannot depart from it. Thus the game is founded upon a dramatic, a human, relation which is universally recognized as the most objectively pervasive and psychologically stimulating in life and therefore in that artificial representation of it which is drama.

The second major consideration in all dramatic spectacles is the relation between event (or, if you prefer, contingency) and design, episode and continuity, diversity in unity, the battle and the campaign, the part and the whole. Here also cricket is structurally perfect. The total spectacle consists and must consist of a series of individual, isolated episodes, each in itself completely self-contained. Each has its beginning, the ball bowled; its middle, the stroke played; its end, runs, no runs, dismissal. Within the fluctuating interests of the rise or fall of the game as a whole, there is this unending series of events, each single one fraught with immense possibilities of expectation and realization. Here again the dramatist or movie director has to strive. In the very finest of soccer matches the ball for long periods is in places where it is impossible to expect any definite alteration in the relative position of the two sides. In lawn tennis the duration of the rally is entirely dependent upon the subjective skill of the players. In baseball alone does the encounter between the two representative protagonists approach the definitiveness of the individual series of episodes in cricket which together constitute the whole.

The structural enforcement of the fundamental appeals which all dramatic spectacle must have is of incalculable value to the spectator. The glorious uncertainty of the game is not anarchy. It would not be glorious if it were not so firmly anchored in the certainties which must attend all successful drama. That is why cricket is perhaps the only game in which the end result (except where national or local pride is at stake) is not of great importance. Appreciation of cricket has little to do with the end, and less still with what are called "the finer points" of the game. What matters in cricket, as in all the arts, is not finer points but what everyone with some knowledge of the elements can see and feel. It is only within such a rigid structural frame that the individuality so characteristic of cricket can flourish. Two batsmen are in at the same time. Thus the position of representatives of the side, though strictly independent, is interchangeable. In baseball one batter bats at a time. The isolated events of which both games consist is in baseball rigidly limited. The batter is allowed choice of three balls. He must hit the third or he is out. If he hits he must run. The batter's place in the batting order is fixed—it cannot be changed. The pitcher must pitch until he is taken off and when he is taken off he is finished for that game. (The Americans obviously prefer it that way.) In cricket the bowler bowls six balls (or eight). He can then be taken off and can be brought on again. He can bowl at the other end. The batting order is interchangeable. Thus while the principle of an individual representing the side at any given moment is maintained, the utmost possible change of personnel compatible with order is allowed. We tend to take these things for granted or not to notice them at all. In what other dramatic spectacle can they be found built-in? The greatness of the great batsman is not so much in his own skill as that he sets in motion all the immense possibilities that are contained in the game as structurally organized.

Cricket, of course, does not allow that representation or suggestion of specific relations as can be done by a play or even by ballet and dance. The players are always players trafficking in the elemental human activities, qualities and emotions—attack, defence, courage, gallantry, steadfastness, grandeur, ruse. This is no drawback. Punch and Judy, Swan Lake, pantomime, are even less particularized than cricket. They depend for their effect upon the technical skill and creative force with which their exponents make the ancient patterns live for their contemporaries. Some of the best beloved and finest music is created out of just such elemental sensations. We never grow out of them, of the need to renew them. Any art which by accident or design gets too far from them finds that it has to return or wither. They are the very stuff of human life. It is of this stuff that the drama of cricket is composed.

If the drama is very limited in range and intricacy there are advantages. These need not be called compensating, but they should not be ignored. The long hours (which so irritates those who crave continuous excitation), the measured ritualism and the varied and intensive physical activity which take place within it, these strip the players of conventional aspects, and human personality is on view long enough and in sufficiently varied form to register itself indelibly. I mention only a few—the lithe grace and elegance of Kardar leading his team on to the field; the unending flow of linear rhythm by which Evans accommodated himself to returns from the field; the dignity which radiates from every motion of Frank Worrell; the magnificence and magnanimity of Keith Miller. There are movie stars, world-famous and rightly so, who mumble words and go through motions which neither they nor their audience care very much about. Their appeal is themselves, how they walk, how they move, how they do anything or nothing, so long as they are themselves and their particular quality shines through. Here a Keith Miller met a Clark Gable on equal terms.

The dramatic content of cricket I have purposely pitched low—I am concerned not with degree but kind. In addition to being a dramatic, cricket is also a visual art. This I do not pitch low at all. The whole issue will be settled here.

The aestheticians of painting, especially the modern ones, are the great advocates of "significant form", the movement of the line, the relations of colour and tone. Of these critics, the most consistent, the clearest (and the most widely accepted), that I know is the late Mr Bernhard Berenson. Over sixty years ago in his studies of the Italian Renaissance painters he expounded his aesthetic with refreshing clarity. The merely accurate representation of an object, the blind imitation of nature, was not art, not even if that object was what would commonly be agreed upon as beautiful, for example a beautiful woman. There was another category of painter superior to the first. Such a one would not actually reproduce the object as it was. Being a man of vision and imagination, the object would stimulate in him impulses, thoughts, memories visually creative. These he would fuse into a whole and the result would be not so much the object as the totality of the visual image which the object had evoked in a superior mind. That too, Mr Berenson excluded from the category of true art (and was by no means isolated in doing so): mere reproduction of objects, whether actually in existence or the product of the sublimest imaginations, was "literature" or "illustration". What then was the truly artistic? The truly artistic was a quality that existed in its own right, irrespective of the object represented. It was the line, the curve, its movement, the drama it embodied as painting, the linear design, the painterly tones and values taken as a whole: this constituted the specific quality of visual art. Mr Berenson did not rank colour very high; the head of a statue (with its human expression) he could usually dispense with. It was the form as such which was significant.

Mr Berenson was not at all cloudy or mystifying. He distinguished two qualities which could be said to constitute the significance of the form in its most emphatic manifestation.

The first he called "tactile values". The idea of tactile values could be most clearly grasped by observing the manner in which truly great artists rendered the nude human body. They so posed their figures, they manipulated, arranged, shortened, lengthened, foreshortened, they so articulated the movements of the joints that they stimulated the tactile consciousness of the viewer, his specially artistic sense. This significance in the form gave a higher coefficient of reality to the object represented. Not that such a painting looked more real, made the object more lifelike. That was not Mr Berenson's point. Significant form makes the painting life-giving, life-enhancing, *to the viewer*. Significant form, or "decoration", to use his significant personal term, sets off physical processes in the spectator which give to him a far greater sense of the objective reality before him than would a literal representation, however accurate.[1] Mr Berenson does not deny that an interesting subject skilfully presented in human terms can be interesting as illustration. He does not deny that such illustration can enhance significant form. But it is the form that matters. Mr John Berger of the *New Statesman*, ardent propagandist of socialist realism in art, claims that what is really significant in Michelangelo is his bounding line. The abstract artists get rid of the object altogether and represent only the abstract form, the line and relations of line. If I understand Mr Berger aright he claims that all the great representational paintings of the past live and have lived only to the degree that their form is significant—that, however, is merely to repeat Mr Berenson.

The second characteristic of significant form in Mr Berenson's aesthetic is the sense of "movement".

We have so far been wandering in chambers where as cricketers we are not usually guests. Fortunately, the aesthetic vision now focuses on territory not too far distant from ours. In his analysis of "movement" Mr Berenson discussed the artistic possibilities and limitations of an athletic event, a wrestling match. His exposition seems designed for cricket and cricketers, and therefore must be reproduced in full:

> Although a wrestling match may, in fact, contain many genuinely artistic elements, our enjoyment of it can never be quite artistic: we are prevented from completely realizing it not only by our dramatic interest in the game, but also, granting the possibility of being devoid of dramatic interest, by the succession of movements being too rapid for us to realize each completely, and too fatiguing, even if realizable. Now if a way could be found of conveying to us the realization of movements without the confusion and the fatigue of the actuality, we should be getting out of the wrestlers more than they themselves can give us—the heightening of vitality which comes to us whenever we keenly realize life, such as the actuality itself would give us, *plus* the greater effectiveness of the heightening brought about by the clearer, intenser and less fatiguing realization. This is precisely what the artist who succeeds in representing movement achieves: making us realize it as we never can actually, he gives us a heightened sense of capacity, and whatever is in the actuality enjoyable, he allows us to enjoy at our leisure. In words already familiar to us, he *extracts the significance of movements*, just as, in rendering tactile values, the artist extracts the corporal significance of objects. His task is, however, far more difficult, although less indispensable: it is not enough that he should extract the values of what at any given moment is an actuality, as is an object, but what at no moment really is—namely, movement. He can accomplish his task in only one way, and that is by so rendering the one particular movement that we shall be able to realize all other movements that the same figure may make. "He is grappling with his enemy now," I say of my wrestler. "What a pleasure to be able to realize in my own muscles, on my own chest, with my own arms and legs, the

life that is in him as he is making his supreme effort! What a pleasure, as I look away from the representation, to realize in the same manner, how after the contest his muscles will relax, and the rest trickle like a refreshing stream through his nerves!" All this I shall be made to enjoy by the artist who, in representing any one movement, can give me the logical sequence of visible strain and pressure in the parts and muscles.

Now here all of us, cricketers and aesthetics, are on familiar ground. I submit that cricket does in fact contain genuinely artistic elements, infinitely surpassing those to be found in wrestling matches. In fact it can be said to comprise most of those to be found in all other games.

I submit further that the abiding charm of cricket is that the game has been so organized that the realization of movement is completely conveyed despite the confusion and fatigue of actuality.

I submit finally that without the intervention of any artist the spectator at cricket extracts the significance of movement and of tactile values. He experiences the heightened sense of capacity. Furthermore, however the purely human element, the literature, the illustration, in cricket may enhance the purely artistic appeal, the significant form at its most unadulterated is permanently present. It is known, expected, recognized and enjoyed by tens of thousands of spectators. Cricketers call it style.

From the beginning of the modern game this quality of style has been abstracted and established in its own right, irrespective of results, human element, dramatic element, anything whatever except itself. It is, if you will, pure decoration. Thus we read of a player a hundred years ago that he was elegance, all elegance, fit to play before the Queen in her parlour. We read of another that he was not equal to W.G. except in style, where he surpassed The Champion. In *Wisden* of 1891 A.G. Steel, a great player, a great judge of the game and, like so many of those days, an excellent writer, leaves no loophole through which form can escape into literature:

The last-named batsman, when the bowling was very accurate, was a slow scorer, but always a treat to watch. If the present generation of stone-wall cricketers, such as Scotton, Hall, Barlow, A. Bannerman, nay even Shrewsbury, possessed such beautiful ease of style the tens of thousands that used to frequent the beautiful Australian ground would still flock there, instead of the hundred or two patient gazers on feats of Job-like patience that now attend them.

In 1926 H.L. Collins batted five hours for forty runs to save the Manchester Test and Richard Binns wrote a long essay to testify among much else that Collins was never dull because of his beautiful style. There is debate about style. Steel's definition clears away much cumbersome litter about left shoulder forward and straight bat: "no flourish, but the maximum of power with the minimum of exertion". If the free-swinging off-drive off the front foot has been challenged by the angular jerk through the covers off the back foot, this last is not at all alien to the generation which has experienced Cubism in posters and newspapers advertisements.

We are accustomed in cricket to speak of beauty. The critics of art are contemptuous of the word. Let us leave it aside and speak of the style that is common of the manifold motions of the great players, or most of them. There are few picture galleries in the world which effectively reproduce a fraction of them—I am sticking to form and eschewing literature and illustration. These motions are not caught and permanently fixed for us to make repeated visits to them. They are repeated often enough to become a permanent possession of the spectator which he can renew at will. And having held our own with the visitor from the higher spheres, I propose to take the offensive.

And first I meet Mr Berenson on his own ground, so to speak. Here is John Arlott, whose written description of cricket matches I prefer to all others, describing the bowling action of Maurice Tate.

You would hardly have called Maurice Tate's physique graceful, yet his bowling action remains—and not only for me—as lovely a piece of movement as even cricket has ever produced. He had strong, but sloping shoulders; a deep chest, fairly long arms and—essential to the pace bowler—broad feet to take the jolt of the delivery stride and wide hips to cushion it. His run-in, eight accelerating and lengthening strides, had a hint of scramble about it at the beginning, but by the eighth stride and well before his final leap, it seemed as if his limbs were gathered together in one glorious wheeling unity. He hoisted his left arm until it was pointing straight upwards, while his right hand, holding the ball, seemed to counter-poise it at the opposite pole. Meanwhile, his body, edge-wise on to the batsman, had swung its weight back on to the right foot: his back curved so that, from the other end, you might see the side of his head jutting out, as it were, from behind his left arm. Then his bowling arm came over and his body turned; he released the ball at the top of his arm-swing, with a full flick of the wrist, and then plunged through, body bending into that earth-tearing, final stride and pulling away to the off side.

All these things the textbook will tell you to do: yet no one has ever achieved so perfectly a co-ordination and exploitation of wrist, shoulders, waist, legs and feet as Maurice Tate did. It was as if bowling had been implanted in him at birth, and came out—as the great arts come out—after due digestion, at the peak of greatness which is not created—but only confirmed—by instruction.

Because most people think always of batting when they think of cricket as a visual art another description of a bowler in action will help to correct the unbalance.

From two walking paces Lindwall glides into the thirteen running strides which have set the world a model for rhythmic gathering of momentum for speed-giving power. Watching him approach the wicket, Sir Pelham Warner was moved to murmur one word, "Poetry!"

The poetry of motion assumes dramatic overtones in the last couple of strides. A high-lifted left elbow leads Lindwall to the line. The metal plate on his right toe-cap drags through the turf and across the bowling crease as his prancing left foot thrusts directly ahead of it, to land beyond the popping crease. This side-on stretch brings every ounce of his thirteen stone into play as his muscular body tows his arm over for the final fling that shakes his shirtsleeve out of its fold. In two more strides his wheeling follow-through has taken him well to the side of the pitch. Never had plunging force and science formed so deadly an alliance.

We may note in passing that the technique of watching critically, i.e. with a conception of all the factors that have contributed to the result, can be as highly developed and needs as many years of training in cricket as in the arts. But I do not want to emphasize that here.

What is to be emphasized is that whereas in the fine arts the image of tactile values and movement, however effective, however magnificent, is permanent, fixed, in cricket the spectator sees the image constantly re-created, and whether he is a cultivated spectator or not, has standards which he carries with him always. He can re-create them at will. He can go to see a game hoping and expecting to see the image re-created or even extended. You can stop an automobile to watch a casual game and see a batsman, for ever to be unknown, cutting in a manner that recalls the greatest exponents of one of the most difficult movements in cricket. Sometimes it is a total performance branching out in many directions by a single player who stamps all he does with the hallmark of an individual style—a century by Hutton or Compton or Sobers. It can be and often is a particular image—Hammond's drive through the covers. The image can be a single stroke, made on a certain day, which has been seen and never forgotten. There are some of these the writer has carried in his consciousness for over forty years, some in fact longer, as it is described in the first page of this book. On the business of setting off physical processes and evoking a sense of movement in the spectator, followers of Mr Berenson's classification would do well to investigate the responses of cricket spectators. The theory may be thereby enriched, or may be seen to need enrichment. To the eye of a cricketer it seems pretty thin.

It may seem that I am squeezing every drop out of a quite casual illustration extracted from Mr Berenson's more comprehensive argument. That is not so. Any acquaintances with his work will find that he lavishes his most enthusiastic praise on *Hercules Strangling Antaeus* by Pollaiuolo, and the same artist's *David Striding Over the Head of the Slain Goliath*. In more than one place *The Gods Shooting [arrows] at a Mark* and the *Hercules Struggling With a Lion*, drawings by Michelangelo, are shown to be for him the ultimate yet reached in the presentation of tactile values and sense of movement, with the consequent life-giving and life-enhancing stimulation of the spectator. Mr Berenson, in the books I have mentioned, nowhere analyses this momentous fact: the enormous role that elemental physical action plays in the visual arts throughout the centuries, at least until our own. Why should he believe that Michelangelo's projected painting of the soldiers surprised when bathing would have produced the greatest masterpiece of figure art in modern times? I have been suggesting an answer by implication in describing what W.G. brought from pre-Victorian England to the modern age. I shall now state it plainly.

If we stick to cricket it is not because of any chauvinism. The analysis will apply to all games. After a thorough study of bull-fighting in Spain, Ernest Haas, the famous photographer, does not ignore the violence, the blood, the hovering presence of death, the illustration. Aided by his camera, his conclusion is: "The bull fight is pure art. The spectacle is all motion. . . . Motion, the perfection of motion, is what the people come to see. They come hoping that this bull-fight will produce the perfect flow of motion." Another name for the perfect flow of motion is style, or, if you will, significant form.

Let us examine this motion, or, as Mr Berenson calls it, movement. Where the motive and directing force rests with the single human being, an immense variety of physical motion is embraced within four categories. A human being places himself physically in some relation of contact or avoidance (or both) with another human being, with an animal, an inanimate object, or two or more of these. He may extend the reach and force of his arms or feet with a tool or device of some kind. He propels a missile. He runs, skips, jumps, dives, to attain some objective which he has set himself or others have set for him. In sport there is not much else that he can do and in our world human beings are on view for artistic enjoyment only on the field of sport or on the entertainment stage. In sport cricket leads the field. The motions of a batter in baseball, a player of lawn tennis, hockey, golf, all their motions added together do not attain the sum of a batsman's. The batsman can shape to hit practically round the points of the compass. He can play a dead bat, pat for a single, drive along the ground; he can skim the infielders; he can lift over their heads; he can clear the boundary. He can cut square with all the force of his wrists, arms and shoulders, or cut late with a touch as delicate as a feather. He can hit to long-leg with all his force or simply deflect with a single motion. He can do most of these off the front foot or the back. Many of them he can do with no or little departure from his original stance. The articulation of his limbs is often enough quite visible, as in the use of the wrists when cutting or hooking. What is not visible is received in the tactile consciousness of thousands who have themselves for years practised the same motion and know each muscle that is involved in each stroke. And all this infinite variety is from one base, stable and fixed, so that each motion in its constituent parts can be observed in its detail and in its entirety from start to finish.

The batsman propels a missile with a tool. The bowler does the same unaided. Within the narrow territory legally allowed to him there is, as Mr Arlott on Tate has shown, a surprising variety of appeal. He may bowl a slow curve or fast or medium, or he may at his pleasure use each in turn. There have been many bowlers whose methods of delivery has seemed to spectators the perfection of form, irrespective of the fate which befell the balls bowled. Here, far more than in batting, the repetition conveys the realization of movement despite the actuality. Confusion is excluded by the very structure of the game.

As for the fieldsmen, there is no limit whatever to their possibilities of running, diving, leaping, falling forward, backwards, sideways, with all their energies concentrated on a specific objective, the whole completely realizable by the alert spectator. The spontaneous outburst of thousands at a fierce hook or a dazzling slip-catch, the ripple of recognition at a long-awaited leg-glance, are as genuine and deeply felt expressions of artistic emotion as any I know.

You will have noted that the four works of art chosen by Mr Berenson to illustrate movement all deal with some physical action of the athletic kind. Mr Berenson calls the physical process of response mystical.[2] There I refuse to go along any further, not even for the purpose of discussion. The mystical is the last refuge, if refuge it is. Cricket, in fact any ball game, to the visual image adds the sense of physical co-ordination, of harmonious action, of timing. The visual image of a diving fieldsman is a frame for his rhythmic contact with the flying ball. Here two art forms meet.

I believe that the examination of the stroke, the brilliant piece of fielding, will take us through mysticism to far more fundamental considerations than mere life-enhancing. We respond to physical action or vivid representation of it, dead or alive, because we are made that way. For unknown centuries survival for us, like all other animals, depended upon competent and effective physical activity. This played its part in developing the brain. The particular nature which became ours did not rest satisfied with this. If it had it could never have become human. The use of the hand, the extension of its powers by the tool, the production of a missile at some objective and the accompanying refinements of the mechanics of judgment, these marked us off from the animals. Language may have come at the same time. The evolution may have been slow or rapid. The end result was a new species which preserved the continuity of its characteristics and its way of life. Sputnik can be seen as no more than a missile made and projected through tools by the developed hand.

Similarly the eye for the line which is today one of the marks of ultimate aesthetic refinement is not new. It is old. The artists of the caves of Altamira had it. So did the bushmen. They had it to such a degree that they could reproduce it or, rather represent it with unsurpassed force. Admitting this, Mr Berenson confines the qualities of this primitive art to animal energy and an exasperated vitality. That, even if true, is totally subordinate to the fact that among these primitive people the sense of form existed to the degree that it could be consciously and repeatedly reproduced. It is not a gift of high civilization, the last achievement of the noble minds. It is exactly the opposite. The use of sculpture and design among primitive peoples indicates that the significance of the form is a common possession. Children have it. There is no need to adduce further evidence for the presupposition that the faculty or faculties by which we recognize significant form in elemental physical action is native to us, a part of the process by which we have become and remain human. It is neither more nor less mystical than any other of our faculties of apprehension. Neither do I see an "exasperated vitality" in the work of the primitive artists. The impression I get is that the line was an integral part of co-ordinated physical activity, functional perhaps, but highly refined in that upon it food or immediate self-preservation might depend.

Innate faculty though it might be, the progress of civilization can leave it unused, suppress its use, can remove us from the circumstances in which it is associated with animal energy. Developing civilization can surround us with circumstances and conditions in which our original faculties are debased or refined, made more simple or more complicated. They may seem to disappear altogether. They remain part of our human endowment. The basic motions of cricket represent physical action which has been the basis not only of primitive but of civilized life for countless centuries. In work and in play they were the motions by which men lived and without which they would perish. The Industrial Revolution transformed our existence. Our fundamental characteristics as human beings it did not and could not alter. The bushmen reproduced in one medium not merely animals but the line, the curve, the movement. It supplied in the form they needed a vision of the life they lived. The Hambledon men who made modern cricket did the same. The bushmen's motive was perhaps religious, Hambledon's entertainment. One form was fixed, the other had to be constantly re-created.

The contrasts can be multiplied. That will not affect the underlying identity. Each fed the need to satisfy the visual artistic sense. The emphasis on style in cricket proves that without a shadow of a doubt; whether the impulse was literature and the artistic quality the result, or vice-versa, does not matter. If the Hambledon form was infinitely more complicated it rose out of a more complicated society, the result of a long historical development. Satisfying the same needs as bushmen and Hambledon, the industrial age took over cricket and made it into what it has become. The whole tortured history of modern Spain explains why it is in the cruelty of the bull-ring that they seek the perfect flow of motion. That flow, however, men since they have been men have always sought and always will. It is an unspeakable impertinence to arrogate the term "fine art" to one small section of this quest and declare it to be culture. Luckily, the people refuse to be bothered. This does not alter the gross falsification of history and the perversion of values which is the result.

Lucian's Solon tells what the Olympic Games meant to the Greeks. The human drama, the literature, was as important to them as to us. No less so was the line, the curve, the movement of the athletes which inspired one of the greatest artistic creations we have ever known—Greek sculpture. To this day certain statues baffle the experts: are they statues of Apollo or are they statues of athletes? The games and sculpture were "good" arts and popular. The newly fledged democracy found them insufficient. The contrast between life under an ancient landed aristocracy and an ancient democratic regime was enormous. It can be guessed at by what the democracy actually achieved. The democracy did not neglect the games or sculpture. To the contrary. The birth of democracy saw the birth of individualism in sculpture. Immense new passions and immense new forces had been released. New relations between the individual and society, between individual and individual, launched life on new, exciting and dangerous ways. Out of this came the tragic drama. After a long look at how the creation of the Hambledon men became the cornerstone of Victorian education and entertainment, I can no longer accept that Peisistratus encouraged the dramatic festival as a means of satisfying or appeasing or distracting the urban masses on their way to democracy. That would be equivalent to saying that the rulers of Victorian England encouraged cricket to satisfy or appease or distract the urban masses on their way to democracy. The Victorian experience with cricket suggests a line of investigation on the alert for signs both more subtle and more tortuous. It may be fruitful to investigate whether Peisistratus and his fellow rulers did not need the drama for themselves before it became a national festival. That at any rate is what happened to the Victorians.

The elements which were transformed into Greek drama may have existed in primitive form, quite apart from religious ceremonial—there is even a tradition that peasants played primitive dramas. However that may be, the newly fledged Greek democrat found his need for a fuller existence fulfilled in the tragic drama. He had no spate of books to give him distilled, concentrated and ordered views of life. The old myths no longer sufficed. The drama recast them to satisfy the expanded personality. The end of democracy is a more complete existence. Voting and political parties are only a means. The expanded personality and needs of the Victorian aspiring to democracy did not need drama. The stage, books, newspapers, were part of his inheritance. The production of these for democracy had already begun. What he needed was the further expansion of his aesthetic sense. Print had long made church walls and public monuments obsolescent as a means of social communication. Photography would complete the rout of painting and sculpture, promoting them upstairs. The need was filled by organized games.

Cricket was fortunate in that for their own purposes the British ruling classes took it over and endowed it with money and prestige. On it men of gifts which would have been remarkable in any sphere expended their powers—the late C.B. Fry was a notable example. Yet even he submitted to the prevailing aesthetic categories and circumscribed cricket as a "physical" fine art. There is no need so to limit it. It is limited in variety of range, of subject-matter. It cannot express the emotions of an age on the nature of the last judgment or the wiping out of a population by bombing. It must repeat. But what it repeats is the original stuff out of which everything visually or otherwise artistic is quarried. The popular democracy of Greece, sitting for days in the sun watching *The Oresteia*, the popular democracy of our day, sitting similarly, watching Miller and Lindwall bowl to Hutton and Compton—each in its own way grasps at a more complete human existence. We may some day be able to answer Tolstoy's exasperated and exasperating question: What is art?—but only when we learn to integrate our vision of Walcott on the back foot through the covers with the outstretched arm of the Olympic Apollo.

1963

21

Lenin and the Vanguard Party

Next year is the 400th anniversary of the birth of Shakespeare. It is also the 40th anniversary of the death of Lenin. Will there be any controversy about either of them in the British Labour movement? As far as I can judge not a thing. Tired repetition or routine rehashing of old doctrines is not controversy. If even you are debating two pages of Roman history, controversy is always about what is contemporary. You haven't got to prove this. It either is so, or is not. For example:

The theory and practice of the vanguard party, of the one-party state, is not (repeat not) the central doctrine of Leninism. It is not the central doctrine, it is *not* even a special doctrine. It is not and it never was. In forty years it would be as easy to prove (and be equally wrong) that the United States of Europe had always been the central doctrine, or became a special doctrine, of the Tory party.

Bolshevism, Leninism, did have central doctrines. One was theoretical, the inevitable collapse of capitalism into barbarism. Another was social, that on no account of its place in society, its training and its numbers, only the working class could prevent this degradation and reconstruct society. Political action consisted in organising a party to carry out these aims. These were the central principles of Bolshevism. The rigidity of its political organisation came not from the dictatorial brain of Lenin but from a less distinguished source—the Tsarist police state. Until the revolution actually began in March 1917, the future that Lenin foresaw and worked for was the establishment of parliamentary democracy in Russia on the British and German models. His party would be an opposition party in a parliament which, he calculated, would be dominated by bourgeois politicians. The anti-Leninists, in reality they are anti-Marxists, can attribute all sorts of psychological impulses or needs to Lenin. All fiction. Bolshevism until 1917 might agree with Kautsky against Bernstein but it accepted in every kind of state, even the Soviet state, not only the co-existence of labour, but of bourgeois political parties. *On this Lenin never altered his view.* Where he differed from the parliamentary democrats was in his certainty that in Russia parliamentary democracy would be achieved only by revolution. Bolshevism looked forward to a regime of parliamentary democracy because this was the doctrine of classical Marxism: that it was through parliamentary democracy that the working class and the whole population (I say the whole population) was educated and trained for the transition to socialism.

Bolshevism, however, believed that the overthrow of Tsarism was not a mere matter of overthrowing a government. Russia needed also to abolish landlordism and to abolish the oppression of the nationalities. These tasks the revolution and only the revolution could accomplish.

What upset the scheme was the cyclonic intervention into these important matters of the proletariat and the peasantry (organised into the army). They rapidly organised themselves into Soviets. People who continue to place the responsibility for the one-party totalitarian state on Lenin's dictatorial brain are opening themselves wide to devastating queries as to what exactly do they mean by democracy? The revolutionaries and the reactionaries in Russia of 1917 did not indulge in any constitutional or logical metaphysics. The Bolsheviks saw that if they wanted to carry out any programme at all power had to go to the Soviets. The anti-Bolsheviks knew what this would mean and laid all their stress on the Constitutional Assembly and other parliamentary procedures. It was as simple as that: where would the power be? I do not propose to enter into the rights and wrongs of what happened: in Europe, after the experiences of 1917-1963 we ought to know. What I want to establish without a shadow of a doubt is that Lenin never had as a central thesis of Marxism the establishment of the one-party state. His central concern was never the party. So as to facilitate controversy I want to repeat, central to his ideas was never the party, never, never, never. It was the proletariat and the work he believed it and it alone could do. He believed that the Soviet state opened out immense new opportunities for the immense new responsibilities placed on the proletariat. That was and is the central doctrine of Leninism. And to this all his ideas and activities about the party were strictly subordinate. Let us get that clear.

Lenin never babbled and he was particularly careful of his words at Party conferences and more particularly in relation to programmes. How many people I would like to know have ever seen, far less meditated on his address to the Eighth Party Congress in 1917?

First, Lenin's belief in the Soviet.

> Nobody will deny that in the matter of true, not paper, democracy, in the matter of enlisting the workers and peasants, we have done more than has been done or could be done by the best of the democratic republics in hundreds of years. It was this that determined the importance of the Soviets, it was owing to this that the Soviets have become a slogan for the proletariat of all countries.

He then shows how subordinate a position the political party holds not only in his theory but in his practice and his recommendations.

> But this in no way saves us from the fact that we are up against the inadequate culture of the masses. We do not regard the question of disenfranchising the bourgeoisie from an absolute point of view, because it is theoretically quite conceivable that the dictatorship of the proletariat may suppress the bourgeoisie on every hand without disenfranchising the bourgeoisie. This is theoretically quite conceivable. Nor do we advance our constitution

as a model for other countries. All we say is that whoever conceives the transition of socialism without the suppression of the bourgeoisie is not a Socialist. But while it is essential to suppress the bourgeoisie as a class, it is not essential to deprive them of the suffrage and of equality. We do not want freedom for the bourgeoisie, we do not recognise equality of exploiters and exploited, but in the programme we treat this question from the standpoint that measures such as the inequality of workers and peasants are by no means prescribed by the constitution. They were embodied in the constitution after they were already in actual practice.

His talk of suppression of the bourgeoisie refers only to capitalist ownership of the commanding heights of the means of production, and there is ample proof that in regard to this, in Russia, he was the most cautious of men.

Above all Lenin was guided by the actions of masses of people.

It was not even the Bolsheviks who worked out the constitution of the Soviets; it was worked out against themselves by the Mensheviks and the Socialist-Revolutionaries before the Bolshevik revolution. They worked it out in the way it had been worked out in practice. The organisation of the proletariat proceeded much more rapidly than the organisation of the peasantry, which fact made the workers the bulwark of the revolution and gave them a virtual privilege. The next task is gradually to pass from these privileges to their equalisation. Nobody drove the bourgeoisie out of the Soviets before the October Revolution and after the Bolshevik revolution. The bourgeoisie themselves left the Soviets.

Similar thinking can be found on almost every page of his writings and speeches. But, the Menshevik historians and the parliamentary democrats are waiting with their megaphones. Lenin, they thunder, suppressed the Constituent Assembly; Lenin at the first Congress of the Communist International in 1919 laid down the principles of the vanguard party and these led straight to . . .

Pardon me, gentlemen. I admit that Lenin's doctrines were very new and very difficult. Not only were they misused by a barbarian like Stalin (applause from Krushchev). They were never completely grasped, never at any time, by Trotsky (louder applause by Krushchev). But there is no excuse for not understanding them today (stormy applause from Krushchev and all who support him, including the party propagandists, 1963).

I repeat: there is no excuse today for babbling nonsense about Leninism, the Vanguard Party and the totalitarian state. In 1917 the Bolshevik Party consisted, I believe, of 78,000 members. And the majority of them were not very good Bolsheviks, not even good proletarians. In a population of over 150 million what else could they be but a vanguard? Lenin saw that and drew the conclusions. In 1945 in Italy the Communist Party had over three million members. It completely controlled the organised trade union movement. In France the situation was not too different, and for a time the French Communist newspaper, *L'Humanite*, was the most widely sold daily newspaper in France.

To believe that Bolshevism, or to be more precise, Leninism, would under the circumstances advocate or preach the theory of the vanguard party is to continue slander of Leninism, but not to his theory of the party (that is no longer viable) but to his central doctrine—the role of the proletariat in the preservation of society from barbarism. To interpret Leninism as the advocacy of a vanguard party of three million is nearly as bad as the doctrine of Goebbels that Christ was not a Jew. Objective circumstances in Russia forced Lenin into a certain position. He accepted it without apologising for it. He knew what he was doing and he knew also, for he said it many times, what he was not doing. His doubts about it, not only for other countries but for Russia, he made public many, many times. What is really happening is not a mistake, no such thing. This falsification of Leninism is a weapon of the West against the East and a weapon of Khrushchev-Stalin against Russia and satellites.

Next year Lenin will have been dead forty years. What he stood for has almost vanished. Imagine what has happened to poor Shakespeare in ten times as many years. What has this to do with political controversy and Lenin? Simply this. Who should govern, what he should aim at, what philosophy of society he should adopt, what should be a political leader's personal philosophy in a time of revolution, who are the political types he is likely to meet, on all this and the exposition of it, Shakespeare stands second to none, neither to Aristotle, to Rousseau nor to Marx. He is surprisingly close to Lenin. The labour movement could do worse than initiate controversy on this and similar subjects. It will begin to relearn why it exists.

1963

22
Lenin and the Problem

The countries known as underdeveloped have produced the greatest statesmen of the twentieth century, men who have substantially altered the shape and direction of world civilisation in the last fifty years. They are four in number: Lenin, Gandhi, Mao Tse-tung and Nkrumah. They are not merely gifted individuals and effective politicians. They of the underdeveloped must be seen against the background of the developed civilisation of their times. The very words underdeveloped and advanced need some definition. It is a commonplace of contemporary life to be horrified at the fact that the Hitler regime murdered six million Jews. That is only part of the gruesome history. By 1941 Hitlerism ruled and tortured and massacred its enemies from the Bay of Biscay to Eastern Poland. Since the twentieth congress of the Russian Communist Party, it is possible to say without dispute that Stalinism was doing the same from Eastern Poland to Vladivostok. Thus a vast area of civilisation had degenerated into elementary barbarism, primitive cruelty and disregard of human life, of ordinary common decency. The rest of the advanced countries of Western civilisation need to be seen within the context of this frightful reality. For a century, the United States had perpetrated against millions of its citizens a civil and psychological brutality of which it itself is only now becoming fully aware. James Baldwin popularly regarded at home as well as abroad as the effective spokesman against the century old persecution of Negro Americans, has unequivocally stated that the problem is not a problem of the black skin—it is a sickness in American civilisation itself which has expressed and expresses itself in the persecution of the Negro population.

France killed eighty thousand in Madagascar and fought to the end to preserve its domination of Indochina, Morocco, Tunis and Algeria. Just a few miles across the Mediterranean, France killed a million Algerians, a million of a total population of ten million people, equivalent in terms of the United States to the extermination of the Negro population. Obviously the need of French civilisation at all costs to continue its domination was very great. The great mass of the British people have been the sanest in Europe for many years. But they have need to be on guard against what remains in Britain which formerly made hewers of wood, drawers of water and subordinate helots of hundreds of millions of Indians and over a hundred million Africans. What remains hidden in contemporary Britain we do not know, only that Britain is a part of Western civilisation more obviously so every day. That civilisation now contemplates itself frantically seeking to detonate the powers of what self-destruction it so assiduously cultivates. On the whole we can say with confidence that the powers and creativeness which the political leaders of the underdeveloped countries have so signally shown, spring from the fact that they represent something new in the world, the rejection of the role on which a dominant civilisation for centuries had built itself, and without which it sinks deeper and deeper into moral and political decay.

Whatever the faults and blunders of the underdeveloped countries, they represent something new in a decaying world and the importance (not necessarily the judgement) of Lenin is that he first raised the banner and organised the revolt against what we have seen and experienced from 1914 to 1964. It is therefore a historic need to examine as scrupulously and objectively as possible what the leader of the first underdeveloped country seeking to make the transition thought: what he hoped to do, what he believed he had done, and the directions for the future he left behind him. There are many values in such a procedure when scrupulously carried out. One of them is that it does not imperatively demand an estimate of the success or relevance of his achievements. That debate began before Lenin became a world figure, continues to the present day and will continue. The reader will maintain, develop or even change his own opinion. Yet the facts, the facts within the terms prescribed, are as clear as it is possible for the statements of the head of a revolutionary state to be. They are worth examination first because the internal problems posed and tackled are still the problems faced by all underdeveloped countries. In Africa no less than elsewhere.

Secondly. his view of the problems as he saw them, and the solutions he proposed, have disappeared from history as completely as if they were Etruscan hieroglyphics carved on stone. Lenin's recommendations to his party for the consolidation of the Soviet state were two: (1) The reconstruction of the governmental apparatus which, he said, despite the name soviet, was no more than an inheritance from tsarism; and (2) The education of the almost illiterate peasantry.

There is no but or maybe. He says there are two essential points and then names these two. They cannot be said to be forgotten, because they have never been noticed.

The reason for this I can indicate with confidence and certainty born of a fully documented experience—my own. Twenty-five years ago, I wrote a history of the period.[1] I am certain that in preparation for the work, I read the relevant passages. But today I can find no concern with them on the numerous sympathetic pages I devoted to Lenin's ideas. I must simply have read them and passed them by. And my experience is that all other students of the period and writers on it have done the same. I was for years active among the leading Trotskyists: no Trotskyist that I knew ever even spoke, far less wrote of them. I translated from the French nearly a thousand pages of the life of Stalin by Boris Souvarine, a book based on personal acquaintance with the Russian leaders and the Russian scene of Lenin's day, and mastery of all available material. These ideas of Lenin's are barely mentioned. In a wide acquaintance with Trotsky's voluminous writings on Lenin and revolutionary Russia. I have found no treatment of them. In authoritative and extensive examinations of the whole Russian revolution by Isaac Deutscher and E. H. Carr, you find the same blank incomprehension. None of us says that Lenin was wrong, that these ideas marked a decline in his mental powers due to the illness which killed him. Simply the modern world is so constituted that it cannot take seriously such political recommendations as the construction of an honest and efficient government, and the education of an illiterate peasant population. These were not accidental or psychological utopias. They were, in Lenin's view at least, the summation of his life's experience and studies, and his six years' experience as leader of the Russian revolution. A decent, honest government and the education of an illiterate peasantry. Those were the last words of Leninism.

The last period begins with the victory of the Russian revolution over the invasion by Britain, France, the United States, Japan, etc. At its tenth congress in 1921, the Bolshevik Party posed the question: we have made a proletarian revolution aiming at socialism; we have for the moment defeated invasion, what shall we do now with this state of which we find ourselves the masters? The Leninist Bolshevik Party was the most highly politically educated and self-conscious party in history, and this debate is the greatest political debate that I know. The only thing to compare with it is the debate at Putney between Cromwell and Ireton on the one side, and the revolutionary soldiers of the army on the other. The problem of the Puritan revolutionaries was of the same scope as the problems that faced the Bolsheviks—now that they had defeated the former rulers, what political and social form were they to give, what were they to do with the country of which they were now the masters? We are concerned here only with tracing the growth of Lenin's ideas to their incredible climax.

The first thing to be noticed in this Marxist is his empiricism and his frank admission of it. For years before the revolution and immediately after October, Lenin had insisted that Russia, an underdeveloped peasant country, was not ready for socialism. Socialism he always saw as the organisation of an advanced economy by the state—the economy of advanced countries or some substantial part of them.

Now, after three years of civil war, the Bolsheviks found themselves with a national economy originally backward and now almost destroyed but organised on communist lines. War communism was the name it bore, and to the end of his days Lenin could not say definitely whether the civil war had pushed them into it or whether in a rush of enthusiasm (initiated by the necessities of war) they had plunged into a communist experiment for which the country was unsuited:

> The peasantry demands a practical demonstration of the ability of the workers who own the factories, the works, industry, to organise exchange with it. On the other hand, an immense agrarian country with bad means of communication, boundless spaces, different climates, different agricultural conditions, etc., inevitably presupposes a certain freedom of turnover for local agriculture and local industry, on a local scale. In this respect we made many mistakes; we went too far; we went too far along the road of nationalising trade and industry, of stopping local turnover. Was this is a mistake? Undoubtedly.

In this connection we did much that was simply wrong, and it would be a great crime not to see and realise that we did not keep within proper limits. Some of the things, however, we were compelled to do by necessity; up to now we have been living under such conditions of furious and incredibly severe war that we had no other alternative but to act in a wartime manner in the sphere of economics. The miracle was that a ruined country was able to hold out in such a war. The miracle did not come from heaven, it arose out of the economic interests of the working class and the peasantry, who performed this miracle by their mass enthusiasm; this miracle repulsed the landlords and the capitalists. At the same time. it is an undoubted fact, and we must reveal it in our agitation and propaganda, that we went further than was necessary theoretically and politically. (Report on the Tax in Kind at the Tenth Party Congress, *Selected Works*, Vol. IV, pp. 112-13.)

An examination of a country in the throes of revolution, any examination which is not aware that much that happens is unforeseen, unexpected, and cannot be logically explained even by the participants themselves, is sure, in Milton's phrase, to make confusion worse confounded. How they had got themselves into that hopeless confusion Lenin never worked out. The most urgent task was to get out of it, and when revolt broke out in Russia, with a startling abruptness, Lenin abandoned government regulation of peasant production and trade and introduced the New Economic Policy. Contrary to what is now popularly (and even learnedly) believed, to Lenin this economic policy was not in any sense of the word new. As far back as May 1918,[2] he had urged on the party and the population the necessity and validity of what he called state capitalism.[3] In April 1921 speaking after the Tenth Party Congress, he quoted, literally, the 1918 speech to the extent of ten pages.[4] He was always making references to this 1918 speech, and in the last months of his life, he referred to it again: "Whenever I wrote about the New Economic Policy I always quoted the article on state capitalism which I wrote in 1918."

More indication of the way he thought, of the totally unprecedented problem which his government faced—unprecedented then—were some of the personal expressions, *obiter dicta* (and rebukes) which he introduced into the great debate of 1921. As is familiar, Trotsky, acutely aware of the magnitude of the economic crisis, wanted to make the trade unions a part of the state. That, he argued, was not only imperative for Russia of 1921, in a workers' state it was legitimate Marxism.

Equally well-known is Lenin's refusal to accept this drastic regimentation of the Russian working class. Russia, he said, was not *quite* a workers' state. The debate is, or ought to be, familiar. What is not so well-known is how, in a mass of confused action and conflicting proposals on all sides, Lenin arrived at his view of the root cause of the crisis in which the party found itself. We babble sometimes with great profundity of analysis and learning (sometimes with less) of the learned considerations by which politicians arrive at crucial decisions. Here is Lenin himself telling us what enlightened him, what gave him his insight into this historic moment in a great historical conjunction.

That is why, when the "scrap started" at the Fifth All Russian Conference of Trade Unions, November 2-6, 1920 (and that is exactly where it started), when immediately after that conference—no, I am mistaken, *during* that conference—Comrade Tomsky appeared before the Political Bureau in a high state of extraordinary excitement and, fully supported by Comrade Rudzutak, who is the calmest of men, began to relate that Comrade Trotsky at that conference had talked about "shaking up" the trade unions, and that he, Tomsky, had opposed this—when this happened, I immediately and irrevocably made up my mind that the essence of the controversy was one of policy (i.e. the trade union policy of the party) and that Comrade Trotsky was entirely wrong in his dispute with Comrade Tomsky over his policy of "shaking up" the trade unions; for, *even if it were partly justified* by the "new tasks and methods" (Trotsky's thesis 12), the policy of "shaking up" the unions at the present time and in the present situation cannot be tolerated because it threatens a split.

This was the profoundly human and personal origin of the profundities of political and philosophical analyses which Lenin developed before the debate was ended.

Other observations are equally relevant to any consideration of politics at any time. This is about Trotsky's proposals:

Take this controversy as you like, either as it arose at the Fifth All-Russian Conference of Trade Unions, or as it was presented and directed by Trotsky himself in his pamphlet-platform of 25 December; you will see that Trotsky's *whole* approach, his whole trend, is wrong. He has failed to understand that it is necessary and possible to approach the trade unions as a school even when one raises the subject of "Soviet trade unionism", even when one speaks of production propaganda in general, and even when one puts the question of "coalescence", of the trade unions participating in the management of industry, in the way Trotsky does. And as regards the latter question, in the manner in which it is presented throughout Trotsky's pamphlet-platform, the mistake lies in the failure to understand that the trade unions are a *school of administrativetechnical management of production*. Not "on the one hand a school and on the other hand something different" but *from all aspects*, in the present controversy, with the question as now presented by Trotsky, *trade unions are a school*, a school of unity, a school of solidarity, a school for learning how to protect one's interests, a school of management, a school of administration. Instead of understanding and rectifying this fundamental error of Comrade Trotsky's, Comrade Bukharin made a ridiculous little amendment: "On the one hand . . . on the other hand."

Let us approach the question still more concretely. Let us see what the present trade unions are as an "apparatus" for the management of production. We have seen from incomplete returns that about nine hundred workers—members and delegates of trade unions—are engaged in the management of production. Increase this figure tenfold if you will, or even a hundredfold; as a concession to you and in order to explain your fundamental mistake, let us even assume such an incredibly rapid "advance" in the near future—even then we get an insignificant number of those directly engaged in *management* compared with the general mass of six million members of trade unions. And from this it is still more clearly evident that to concentrate all attention on the "leading stratum" as Trotsky does, to talk about the role of the trade unions in production and about managing production, without taking into account the fact that 98.5% *are learning* (6,000,000 - 90,000 = 5,910,000 = 98.5% of the total) *and will have to learn, for a long time*, means committing a fundamental mistake. Not school *and* management, but school of management.

This is Lenin's thesis all through. The backwardness of Russia imposed on the party the necessity of teaching and above all teaching themselves. We have to administer. But the main business is to teach:

Even in ten years' time we shall probably have to say that not all our party and trade-union workers have sufficient industrial training, just as in ten years' time not all the party, trade-union and War Department workers will have sufficient military training. But we have made a *beginning* with industrial training by the fact that about a thousand workers, members and delegates of trade unions, participate in the work of management boards, and manage factories, head offices and higher bodies. The fundamental principle of "industrial training" of the training of *ourselves*, of the old underground workers and professional journalists, is that we ourselves set to work, to study our own practical experience in the most careful and detailed manner in accordance with the rule: "Measure your cloth seven times before you cut." Persistent, slow, careful, practical, and businesslike testing of what this thousand has done; still more careful and practical correcting of their work and advancing only after the usefulness of the given method, the given system of management, the given proportion, the given selection of persons, etc. has been fully proved—such is the basic, fundamental, absolute rule of "industrial training"; and it is precisely this rule that Comrade Trotsky breaks with all his theses, the whole of his pamphletplatform, are such that by their mistakes they have distracted the attention and forces of the party from practical "production work" to empty and vapid word-spinning.

For Lenin the backwardness of an underdeveloped country imposed on the party the necessity of teaching and above all teaching themselves.

It is not my business here to go into any detail about Russian economic development, and more particularly the development of agriculture. That would involve controversy of which there is enough already and material abounding. I shall stick to the continuous development and progression of Lenin's political ideas. On 17 October 1921, he delivered a report to the Second All-Russian Congress of Political Education Departments. Now of all political organisations, the Russian Bolshevik government believed in the necessity of the political education of the Russian people, especially in the new doctrines of Marxism, of socialism. The operative word here is *not* Marxism; it is *not* socialism. It is education.

Lenin was coldly if not brutally realistic:

Raising the level of culture is one of our most immediate tasks. And this is the task of the Political Education Departments, if they can serve the cause of "political education", which is the title they have adopted for themselves. It is not difficult to adopt a title. but how about acting up to it? Let us hope that after this Congress we shall have precise information about this. A commission for the liquidation of illiteracy was set up on 19 July 1920. Before coming to this congress, I deliberately read the decree establishing this commission. It says: All-Russian Commission for the Liquidation of Illiteracy. Let us hope that after this congress we shall receive information about what has been done in this sphere, and in how many gubernias, that we shall receive a precise report. But the very fact that it was found necessary to set up an Extraordinary Commission for the Liquidation of Illiteracy shows that we are (what is the wildest term I can use for it?), well, something like semi-savages, because in a country that was not semisavage it would be considered a disgrace to have set up an Extraordinary Commission for the Liquidation of Illiteracy. In such countries illiteracy is liquidated in schools. There they have tolerable schools, where people are taught. What are they taught? First of all they are taught to read and write. But if this elementary problem has not yet been solved, it is ridiculous to talk about a New Economic Policy.

The reader will I hope allow me to interject here a solitary observation. The day that I hear of one political leader of an underdeveloped country speaking in these terms to a political gathering of his own people (and publishing it), my confidence in the future of underdeveloped countries would take a great bound forward.

Russia, you must remember, was a country of many universities, publishing houses, a wide variety of established journals. Beginning with Pushkin, born in 1801, right up to Chekhov, who died in 1904, Russia had produced men who even outside of Russia were acknowledged as the greatest artists of the nineteenth century. All this Lenin ignored. His concern was the people, the common people: "First of all they are taught to read and write. But if this elementary problem has not been solved, it is ridiculous to talk about a New Economic Policy."

This was no chance remark, no individual aside. Lenin then proceeded to make his first summation of the three principal enemies now confronting Soviet Russia "irrespective of one's departmental functions".

The three enemies were: "the first—communist vanity; the second enemy—illiteracy, and the third enemy—bribery." The thing to note is that none of these are psychological appraisals about the weakness of men, nor the vices of the instincts (according to the depth psychologists), nor the lack of experience in democracy (beloved by the Western liberal), nor the lack of character (beloved by the European reactionary). These are strictly social defects of a historical origin. The vanity Lenin speaks about is the political conceit of a member of the governing party, employed in a government institution, who believes that he can solve the urgent problems affecting millions of people, by issuing government decrees.

Next illiteracy. "An illiterate person", Lenin decrees, "is outside politics, he must first of all be taught the alphabet. Without that there can be no politics. Without that, there are only rumours, gossip, fables and prejudices, but not politics."

Finally, there is bribery, or to use the more modern and comprehensive term—corruption. Corruption, in Lenin's view, rises on the soil of illiteracy.

Some time after his speech, Lenin grew physically much worse, but before he took to his bed, never to leave it again, he was able to address the Party Congress once more, and in the course of this address, he referred to the mess the government was in, and the responsibility for it. *Nobody was responsible!*

It would be unfair to say that the responsible communists do not approach their tasks in a conscientious manner. The overwhelming majority of them, ninety-nine per cent, are not only conscientious: they proved their loyalty to the revolution under the most difficult conditions before the fall of tsarism and after the revolution; they literally risked their lives. Therefore it would be radically wrong to seek for the cause in this. We need a cultured approach to the simplest affairs of state. It must be understood that is a matter of state, of commerce, and if obstacles arise one must be able to overcome them and take proceedings against those who are guilty of red tape. I think the proletarian courts will be able to punish, but in order to punish, the culprits must be found. I assure you that in this case no culprits will be found. Look into this business, all of you; no one is guilty. all we see is a lot of fuss and bustle and nonsense. . . . Nobody has the ability to approach the business properly; nobody understands that affairs of state must be approached not this way, but that way.

What Lenin was looking at were the defects of a system, a society, a backward society which corrupted good men.

Before we come to the last words, the summary of a lifetime, we have to know what he was seeing—only then shall we be able to understand what he said and why. At the Eleventh Party Congress, Lenin told Russia (and the world) his reflections on where Soviet Russia had reached and where it was going:

Well, we have lived through a year, the state is in our hands; but has it operated the New Economic Policy in our way during the past year? No. But we refuse to admit this. It did not operate in our way. How did it operate? The machine refused to obey the hand that guided it. It was like an automobile that is going, not in the direction of the man who is driving it, but in the direction desired by someone else, as if it were being driven by some secret, illegal hand. God knows whose, perhaps that of a profiteer, or of a private capitalist, or both. Be that as it may, the car is not going in the direction the man at the wheel imagines.

We now approach his last writings—three articles.

The three articles are the climax of Lenin's reflections on what the underdeveloped country was to do with its unprecedented control of the economy. These are reflections on what we must remember was an entirely new and entirely unprecedented phenomenon. It began in 1921; in 1922 illness drove Lenin from his desk. By the early months of 1923, he had lost the power of speech, and his last three articles represent his last will and testament. We do not assume any loss of intellectual power. The very last article of the three, "Better Fewer, but Better", is perhaps as fine a production (and as famous) as ever came from his pen. The articles contain much that is new, either never said before or giving entirely new emphasis to objectives stated before but not made fundamental. He had no opportunity to translate these ideas into political action. (We have therefore to watch the articles, not only in themselves, but in the light of what has happened since.)

The first article, dated 4-6 January 1923, is entitled, "On Cooperation", Lenin states at once that precisely because of the New Economic Policy, the cooperative movement "acquires absolutely exceptional significance"—such words he did not use lightly. His new point is that since state power is in the hands of the working class—and he at once concretises this claim "since this state power owns all the means of production"—the only task that remains to be done is to organise the population in cooperative societies. It is no wonder that from that day to this the words and the new ideas contained in them seem to elude, to baffle all commentators. Lenin is very serious, for he goes on to say:

When the population is organised in cooperative societies to the utmost, the socialism which formerly was legitimately ridiculed, scorned and treated with contempt by those who were justly convinced of the need for the class struggle, for the struggle for political power, etc. automatically achieves its aims. But not all comrades appreciate the enormous, boundless significance that the organisation of Russia in cooperative societies now acquires.

Enormous, boundless. He had not spoken about the cooperatives like that before. In fact, speaking on the Food Tax on 14 April 1921, he had given a distinctly different appreciation of the cooperatives.[5] Cooperatives have now become all that is necessary for the building of socialism, first, from the aspect of principle, and secondly, underlining the words, Lenin makes clear what he is getting at and the reason for this new orientation: from the aspect of the transition to the new order (socialism) he has found "the means that will be *simplest, easiest, and most intelligible for* the peasantry."

This for Lenin is not only important. Everything else, economic planning, the organisation of the state, is subordinate to the response of the small peasants, whom Lenin will later remind us constitute nine-tenths of the population of Russia. They are what matters. "It is one thing to draw up fantastic plans for building socialism by means of all sorts of workers' associations; but it is quite another thing to learn to build it practically, in such a way that every small peasant may take part in the work of construction." Lenin now makes a criticism of the NEP which he has mentioned at various times but which he now states was the central mistake in that perpetually discussed new orientation. The mistake was that they forgot to think about the cooperatives, they are underestimated, their "enormous significance" is forgotten.

No directive on the Russian economy was ever raised by Lenin with greater force and greater emphasis. None has been so signally ignored. Before we are finished we shall see why.

As was his way, especially when introducing something new, Lenin now proceeds to deepen the argument. Every new social system arises with the assistance of a new class. The new class he has in mind for the new Russia is the peasantry. The state must give the cooperative peasants a bonus but not for any kind of cooperative trade. The assistance, Lenin says, he underlines the words, must be for cooperative trade in which "*real masses of the population really take part*". The whole point is to "verify the intelligence behind it, to verify its quality.

Lenin knows that the kind of participation he has in mind is today beyond the peasant population. It will take one or two decades. It will require universal literacy, the population must acquire the habit of reading books. (Here we see why, in his address to the Political Education Departments, he laid such heavy stress on illiteracy.) The Russian peasant trades in an Asiatic manner. He has to learn to trade in a European manner. This task of instructing them he recommends should be undertaken with new enthusiasm. The emphasis now must be on educational work. There is some highly original and highly significant phrasing: if we confine ourselves "entirely to economic internal relations", the weight of emphasis is certainly shifted to educational work. The literacy Lenin is now talking about is not primarily concerned with politics or what in the English-speaking world is known as culture. It is the precondition of economic progress.

How unambiguous Lenin is can be seen in the final paragraph in this brief article. Two main tasks constitute the epoch. The first we shall come to in a moment. But the second drives home what Lenin believes he has now securely established: "The second is to conduct educational work among the peasants. And the economic object of this educational work among the peasants is to organise them in cooperative societies. If the whole of the peasantry were organised in cooperatives, we should be standing firmly with both feet on the soil of socialism."

There are immense difficulties in the way of this cultural revolution but the difficulties are "of a purely educational (for we are illiterate) and material character (for in order to be cultured we must have reached a certain level of development of the material means of production, we must have a certain material base)."

Let us carefully avoid what may be viewed sceptically as a biased interpretation. There is no need to interpret, we can only presume that Lenin means what he says.

How deadly serious (and systematic) he was is proved by the next article which is dated three weeks later, 23 January. We remember that he defined the number of tasks which constituted the epoch as two. Educational work among the peasants had been the second. The first had been in its way quite as uncompromising and quite as new.

> The two main tasks which confront us constitute the epoch: the first is to reconstruct our apparatus, which is utterly useless, and which we took over in its entirety from the preceding epoch; during the five years of struggle we did not, and could not, make any serious alterations in it.

It is to this reconstruction of the governmental apparatus that Lenin now addresses himself. The form it takes is a series of proposals addressed directly to the Twelfth Party Congress. As we grasp the precision of the proposals we see that if Lenin had been well enough to attend the Congress, these proposals would have dominated its energies and attention in the same way that in 1921 the Trade Union question had dominated the Tenth Congress. The first thing Lenin does is to condemn the whole Soviet government as nothing more than a survival of the old tsarist government (notoriously, by the way, the most backward government in Western Europe): "With the exception of the People's Commissariat for Foreign Affairs, our state apparatus is very largely a survival of the old one, and has least of all undergone serious change. It has only been slightly repainted on the surface, but in all other things it is a typical relic of our old state apparatus."

That is where we begin; there should be no minimising of what Lenin means to say. These are soviets, and the government departments are headed by Bolsheviks and Communists. But the whole thing is rotten. It is not that the new Soviet government is unworkable. It is that under the thin covering of new forms the old tsarist apparatus still remains. Thus in the view of Lenin (a view entirely unique) it was not the new Bolshevism but the old tsarism from which Russia, after six years, was bleeding. The regime faces a crisis comparable to the most dangerous moments in the Civil War. We have to bear in mind the article on cooperation. The tremendous task posed there will have to be carried out by the new government that Lenin proposes. Lenin proposes that the Congress attempt the reorganisation of one government department, just one, and this one, the Workers' and Peasants' Inspection. And here we run right up against one of the great historical perversions of our times. The Stalin and Trotsky conflict and the debate which has followed it has confused and even obscured what Lenin tried to do at this Congress. His proposals and the article that followed particularised Stalin as the most offending bureaucrat, and his department, the Workers' and Peasants' Inspection, as the most offensive department in the government. But Stalin is not and never was the main issue, though it was in those terms that Trotsky and Stalin represented the conflict to Russia and the whole world. Lenin was not concerned with Stalin but with the whole Russian apparatus of government. And we must know what the Workers' and Peasants' Inspection was intended to be and why it is the whole apparatus of government Lenin has in mind and not primarily Stalin.

In January 1920, long before the Civil War was over, Lenin had addressed a memorandum to Stalin on his Commissariat, copies of which had been sent to other members of the government. Instructions on the reorganisation of the Workers' and Peasants' Inspection had been issued by the Central Committee. Lenin wanted Stalin to add the following points. The whole Workers' and Peasants' Inspection should aim at abolishing itself. Its function should be to introduce a section of the Workers' and Peasants' Inspection in all departments of state control and then cease to exist as a separate department.

Lenin's additions read suspiciously like a totally new reconstruction of whatever the Central Executive may have had in mind. The object of the department is to enlist all the toilers, men "and particularly women" in the work of the Workers' and Peasants' Inspection.

Local authorities should compile lists of all (except office employees) who should take part in the work of the inspection in rotation. The department should exercise "wider" control over the accounting of products, goods, stores, materials, fuel etc. Lenin obviously had in mind a continuously spreading inspection and checking of every sphere of government by workers, especially women, "all women".

Gradually peasants were to be invited from the local districts to take part in the work of state control at the centre. Peasants were to be invited to take part "unfailingly", "nonparty peasants".

Lenin may have been a utopian dreamer. That question is not being debated here. What is certain is that he did not have utopian ideas before and while he aimed at power, only to be transformed by power into a one-party totalitarian dictator. If his ideas were utopian then it is clear that after six years of power, he turned to them as the sole solution of the mess into which the Soviet government was sinking, had already sunk. That he saw the problem as Trotsky v. Stalin is a totally false view of this which seemed to him the greatest crisis the Soviet state had hitherto faced. The Central Control Commission was a purely party body which was responsible for the discipline and control of party members all over the country. Lenin proposed to amalgamate this party body with the government departments of the Workers' and Peasants' Inspection.

The Congress was to elect from seventy-five to a hundred workers and peasants as new members of the Central Control Commission. These elected persons were to be selected on the same principles, subjected to the same tests, as the members of the Central Committee. This severe selection was due to the fact that those chosen were to enjoy the same rights as the members of the Central Committee.

Let us see where we are now. For this is Lenin's organisational counterpart to a political policy such as the education of tens of millions of illiterate peasants. We have now organised in one body what was originally two distinct bodies, to which is added a new one. The bodies are:

(1) The Central Committee of the Bolshevik Party which in reality politically controls all aspects of life in Russia. Its most important sub-committee is the Political Bureau, the actual rulers of Russia. There is also an organisation committee, a secretariat, etc.

(2) The Central Control Commission of the Party so far has had nothing to do with government. It will have seventyfive to a hundred new members, workers and peasants. Lenin proposes that the staff of the Workers' and Peasants' Commissariat should be reduced in number to three or four hundred. This reduced personnel should be put to the strictest tests in regard to (a) conscientiousness, (b) knowledge of the state apparatus. They should also undergo a special test in regard to their knowledge of the principles of the scientific organisation of labour in general and of administrative and office work in particular. Then comes a revealing admonition. These highly trained, carefully chosen and specially paid members of the staff should "perform purely secretarial work" for the members (workers and peasants) of the Workers' and Peasants' Inspection and the new members of the Central Control Commission. The workers and peasants are to do the inspection. The staff is to do what they are told.

If Lenin's ideas were utopian, he was completely and wholeheartedly utopian. What does Lenin expect to gain by this organisational reconstruction?

Two things.

First, the prestige of the Workers' and Peasants' Inspection will be enormously increased as these workers and peasants go round inspecting and checking the activities of all government functionaries. They will have the authority and meet with the respect that will come to them from being full members of the ruling organisation of Russia.

Secondly, the Central Committee and the Central Control Commission in their two-monthly meetings will more and more assume the character and function of a superior party conference. This will increase the "methodical, expedient and systematic" organisation of its work and it will help to add to its contacts with really broad masses.

This is Lenin all over, the broad comprehensive democratic aims and the tight but tentative organisational structure by which the work will be begun. How will it work out? That would be seen. His whole method was summed up in his quotation from Napoleon on War: "*On s'engage et puis on voit*." Napoleon was the most meticulous planner of military campaigns who ever lived. But after the plan was made: you engage, and then you see.

If we want to understand the stage at which Lenin's ideas had reached (and also the past and the future development of an undeveloped country), one must now pay special attention to the violent, absolutely unbridled condemnation and abuse which Lenin continues to shower on the Russian apparatus of government after six years of Bolshevik rule. It is not Stalin who is responsible for this. The whole party is responsible. The enemy consists of those who advocate "the preservation of our apparatus in the impossible and prerevolutionary form in which it exists to the present day."

Lenin makes other technical recommendations, but the main point of his proposals is the reorganisation proposed. It seems that the proposal was not eagerly received and by 2 March Lenin unloosed his consuming detestation and repudiation of the Russian form of government, a repudiation which had been disciplined but ill-concealed in the original proposals. The first five years of the Bolshevik Russian revolution have "crammed their heads with disbelief and scepticism". For a socialist republic the culture of Western European bourgeois states would be too modest an aim. But as a start they should be satisfied with getting rid of "the particularly crude types of pre-bourgeois, bureaucratic or serf-culture" which they have. The present form of government in Russia is "so deplorable, not to say outrageous" that "we must come to our senses in time." The Russian apparatus does not deserve the name of socialist, Soviet, etc. Such elements of decent government that they have are ridiculously small and to build a decent apparatus will take "many, many years."

To continue with this drastic criticism of the Soviet government, the most drastic ever made, Lenin tells his party members that "we must set ourselves the task first of learning, second of learning, and third of learning. . . . We have been bustling for five years trying to improve the state apparatus, but it was mere bustle, which during the five years, only proved that it was useless, or even futile, or even harmful. This bustle created the impression that we were working; as a matter of fact, it only clogged up our institutions and our brains."

This is the road that they must follow.

"It is better to get good human material in two years, or even in three years, than to work in haste without hope of getting any at all." Lenin reaches lengths of advocacy and desperation hitherto untouched by him. Nothing that might happen in Russia would have surprised the man who wrote:

> I know that it will be hard to follow this rule and apply it to our conditions. I know that the opposite rule will force its way through a thousand loopholes. I know that enormous resistance will have to be offered, that devilish persistence will have to be displayed, that in the first year at least, the work in this connection will be hellishly hard. Nevertheless I am convinced that only by such work shall we be able to achieve our aim, and only by achieving this aim shall we create a republic that is really worthy of the name Soviet, Socialist, etc.

The extremity of what might legitimately be called desperation is reached in the following sentence: "If we cannot arm ourselves with patience, if we are not prepared to spend several years on this task, we had better not start on it."

This is not an ill-considered angry remark. It follows directly upon this sober evaluation:

> Either it is not worthwhile undertaking another of the numerous reorganisations that we have had, and therefore we must give up the Workers' and Peasants' Inspection as hopeless,

or we really set to work, by slow, difficult and unusual methods, and testing these methods over and over again, to create something exemplary, which will win the respect of all and sundry for its merits, and only because rank and calling demand it.

If the party is not ready to throw itself into this gigantic task, with the necessary energy and patience, then it had better leave it alone. The government apparatus of a country was not something to play with.

We will not go into Lenin's exceptionally severe requirements for the training of the functionaries needed for this gigantic and, even in the eyes of its founder, almost impossible operation. One thing we can say. It was a task which he saw as big as the October revolution. It was possible that it could be carried through, at least initiated, projected on lines which would have inspired the nation with a new national purpose. But only Lenin could have done it. Today, after forty years, I have never read or heard anyone who seems to have understood even what Lenin had in mind. What we have to understand is the tremendous break with all his previous conceptions—a break in its way as gigantic as the break in March 1917 when with the perspective of the bourgeoisdemocratic revolution, and the new conception of power to the soviets, on the way to the proletarian socialist revolution. Before we conclude with the unmistakable evidence, both positive and negative, of what he said and what he did not say, of this dynamic new perspective, we think it would be well to establish once and for all the unparalleled gravity of the situation as he saw it: "In essence, the question stands as follows: either we prove now that we have learnt something about state construction (we ought to have learnt something in five years) or we prove that we have not matured for that sufficiently. If the latter is the case, it is not worth while starting on the task."

What then were the changes in the basic and guiding ideas within which Lenin had worked certainly from 1905 and particularly since 1917? He always believed and often said that any serious and notable change in the social and political constitution of Russia came from the proletariat or from the masses, only when the masses take part does real politics begin. This was his creed. Now in the face of the threatening catastrophe of all he had worked for, he faced the fact that what was required the proletariat could not do. What elements, he asked, do they have for building this new apparatus instead of the prebourgeois, bureaucratic serf-culture which they had? "Only two." What were these?

First the workers who are absorbed in the struggle for Socialism. These elements are not sufficiently educated. They would like to build a better apparatus for us, but they do not know how to do it. They cannot do it. They have not yet developed the culture that is required for this; and it is precisely culture that is required for this.

That was for Lenin the end of a road. The workers on whom he depended for everything creative, everything new, were incapable of initiating this mighty reorganisation. He had indicated in what way the energies of peasants could be channelled into the social reconstruction of Russia. But neither peasant nor proletariat could reconstruct, reorganise the prebourgeois, bureaucratic, serf-culture with which Soviet Russia was still saddled.

"Secondly, we have the element of knowledge, education and training, but to a degree that is ridiculously small compared with all other countries." Lenin recognised very clearly what he was saying and what he was leaving unsaid. What he was saying was this:

> For this purpose the very best of what there is in our social system must be utilised with the greatest caution, thoughtfulness and knowledge in building up the new Commissariat.
>
> For this purpose the best elements in our social system, such as firstly the advanced workers, and secondly the real enlightened elements, for whom we can vouch that they will not take the word for the deed, and will not utter a single word that goes against their conscience, must not shrink before any difficulties, must not shrink from any struggle, in order to achieve the object they have seriously set themselves.

This utter dependence on the subjective element, on the personal qualities of individuals, for so gigantic a social task, that was something new and this perhaps explains Lenin's desperation: if you are not going to tackle it with a full consciousness of the magnitude of the efforts required, it would be better not to tackle it at all.

But what you will look for in vain in these three articles is any reference to the Soviet structure of government. This had been Lenin's constant indication of what Russia had brought new into the world, of what was the strength of the Russian revolution. Now that was gone. For the new peasantry, he was looking to the cooperatives, for the new apparatus of government he was looking not even to the party as a whole but to the best elements in both government and party. Perhaps the illusionary character of these ideas, the last explosion so far of what had begun in 1789, is proved by the fact that not only did they make no impact on the Russia of Lenin's time. They have completely disappeared from the estimates and details about what was Lenin's real contribution to modern politics and modern thought. And yet the article, "Better Fewer, but Better", is to this day one of his famous articles. It was in this article that he wrote the famous words: "the outcome of the struggle will be determined by the fact that Russia, India, China etc. constitute the overwhelming majority of the population that, during the past few years, has been drawn into the struggle for its emancipation with extraordinary rapidity, so that in this respect there cannot be the slightest shadow of doubt what the final outcome of the world struggle will be. In this sense the final victory of socialism is fully and absolutely assured."

Russia, he ended, had to build an economic and efficient government and hold on:

> That is how I link up in my mind the general plan of our work, of our policy, of our tactics, of our strategy, with the task of the reorganised Workers' and Peasants' Inspection. This is what, in my opinion, justifies the exceptional attention which we must devote to the Workers' and Peasants' Inspection in order to raise it to an exceptionally high level, to give it a head with the rights of the Central Committee, etc. etc.
>
> And this justification is that, only by purging our apparatus to the utmost, by cutting out everything that is not absolutely necessary, shall we be certain of holding on. If we do that we shall be able to hold on, not on the level of a small-peasant country, not on the

level of this universal narrowness, but on the ever-rising level of large-scale machine industry.

These are the lofty tasks that I dream of for our Workers' and Peasants' Inspection. That is why I am planning for it the amalgamation of the most authoritative party body with an "ordinary People's Commissariat".

Lenin always did his best to guard against being misunderstood. We especially, of the underdeveloped countries, should not misunderstand his views. We may claim that they are utopian, visionary, unrealistic, unworkable, a fantasy. We should bear in mind that these were exactly the charges that the majority of his colleagues made against him in March 1917, when he arrived in Russia, and, almost alone, hurled the masses of Russia at the bourgeois regime and initiated a new epoch in world history, with the slogan, "All power to the Soviets."

1964

23

The People of the Gold Coast

Let us try to form some estimate of the people in 1947. It is a necessary task even if at best it can only be an approximate one. The fundamental difficulty is that only after a revolution or at a certain definite stage in it, as for example in the 1951 elections in the Gold Coast, is one able to estimate what the people were like before the revolution began. The people themselves do not know. The process of the revolution is essentially the process of the people finding themselves. As they scale one height, that girds them to attempt another. It is sufficient to say that this rapid movement is contained in them before they move a step, though it may be only in vague aspirations and thoughts which they do not dare to think to the end. They think by acting.

In 1947 the Gold Coast was a model colony, and despite the upheaval in 1937 and some vigorous journalism by Azikwe and Wallace Johnson, it was accepted that for fifty years the relations between the Colonial Government and the indigenous population had been of the happiest. How to characterise this happy population in December 1947 when Nkrumah landed at Takoradi?

To begin at the most elementary level: It consisted of 327,000 persons directly engaged in labour of various kinds and farming. Of these, by far the largest number were cocoa farmers, for the greater part in Ashanti, 210,000. There were 38,000 workers in the mines, for the most part in the provinces. There were 23,000 workers in various small manufactures; 11,000 in building; 8,000 in transportation; 16,000 in commerce; 8,000 working in hotels and giving personal service. This is a very small number out of a total population of nearly 5 million.

Very small also was the town population in relation to the population in the country. There were about 135,000 in the municipality of Accra, the capital; in the Kumasi municipality, including the suburbs, there were 77,000. In Sekondi-Takoradi there were about 44,000 and in Cape Coast 29,000. For the rest there were a few small towns with about 10,000 people. This, in all, is about 300-400,000. Of the 100,000 wage-earners there were about 30,000 organised in thirteen unions under the general direction of the Trades Union Congress.

The great majority of the people therefore lived in native villages, scattered far and wide, many of them in remote parts not easily accessible.

There were less than 500 miles of railway, and these had been built chiefly in the interests of the European traders, primarily to get raw materials to the Coast, as is usual in colonies, such other benefits as the population got from them being quite incidental.

There were 100,000 children in some 700 primary schools, either Government or assisted by the Government. In the non-assisted schools, chiefly religious, there were the same number of children. In all, there were 28 secondary schools with a total enrollment of 4,000 students. The total enrollment was about 4.5% of the population. Only about 10% of the population could read.

The Central Government was in the hands of the Governor and persons nominated by him to the Legislative and Executive Councils. But local government on a regional, and on a village scale was in the hands of the Chiefs and their supporters who administered under the firm direction of a European representative of the Colonial Government.

By every settled standard of His Majesty's Government's settled policy, these people were totally unfit for self-government and by these standards would continue to be unfit for another generation at least, which was as far as anybody ever cares seriously to think about. They were illiterate, they were tied to the family unit, they were hopelessly divided into tribes. There was a small percentage of educated people but between them and the mass in the village there was a gulf which it would take the Administration decades to bridge. Furthermore the people were quite satisfied. If there was unrest, it was about such simple elementary things as high prices and the shortage of goods.

It was the myth at its most mythical. When you examine this population of the Gold Coast on the eve of the revolution (and not purely in the light of after-events, though this cannot be entirely avoided), the first thing that strikes you is its essential unity.

The basis of this unity is not in its black skin, but the unity of the conditions under which it lives. The population is divided into various tribes, speaking different languages and guarding jealously their own traditions and customs. But these tribal divisions are grossly exaggerated and are not necessarily constituents of a permanent division. In any particular area they are a source of unity; the division which they represent on a national scale can be overcome or adjusted but for the fact that they have been systematically fortified and encouraged by the British Administration. Even when the Administration is not doing this positively for self-interested purposes, it considers tribalism as a permanent feature of the social and political landscape. This is inherent in the situation because the administration has no aim or purpose which can attempt to integrate the divisions of tribalism into a higher unity. Furthermore the divisions of tribalism are an obvious argument for the settled policy of His Majesty's Government which is to introduce self-government only when the people are sufficiently unified to act as a homogenous body.

But transcending these tribal divisions is the essential unity of the Africans in their villages, whether Fanti, Ashanti, Ga or Ewe. There is absolutely nothing here of the caste system that exists in India. The people live in a unified poverty and squalor. Their Chiefs, except for that small number who are big politicians by grace of the Administration, are very close to the people, the majority of them as illiterate as their subjects, and governed by a long tradition of democracy in which the Chief is no more than a representative of his people who could be, and often was, ruthlessly removed if his actions did not accord with their wishes. This was the condition of some 75% of the population.

The workers, particularly in the mining industry and the railways, are united by the very mechanism of the process of production itself. That among the 35,000 miners only 3,000 were actually in the union is of far less significance than the fact that in the United States only fifteen million workers are organised out of a total working population of over sixty million. At any critical moment the large unorganised majority always follows the small organised minority.

The chief towns are Accra, Kumasi, Sekondi-Takoradi, Cape Coast, Koforidua and Tamale, comparatively small but socially effective. Apart from the workers in manufacturing industries, the town population consists mainly of the mass of unskilled and unorganised manual labourers, domestic servants, messengers and casual workers of all kinds. But between 1926 and 1946 the numbers in the schools rose from 60,000 to nearly 200,000. Thus by 1947 there is a substantial body of young people, not only literate but of some educational attainments and occupying thousands of subordinate positions as teachers and clerical assistants of one type or another in government and business. In 1947 a great number of them are in their early twenties and particularly in the Colony are not only educated but Westernised, inheriting the century-old traditions and practices of Western civilisation.

The division between town and country did not, as is usual in more advanced and older civilisations, create a division in the population. On the contrary, these usually divergent elements were knit more closely together. The population in the six large towns had grown from less than 150,000 to over 300,000 since 1931. Thus the inhabitants of the towns were closely connected with the village population, a fact which had had an enormous influence in the Russian revolution. But in the Gold Coast this unity was reinforced by certain special features and here we approach the specifically African.

The fundamental units of African life are the family and the tribe and they persist under all forms of African life. The urban members of the family retain their intimate, social and spiritual connection with the family left behind in the village. The family in the village retains its close sense of relation with the literate urbanised children in the town.

The sense of unity and common social purpose which for centuries has been imbued into the African by the family and the tribe is not lost in the city. In the older European countries the towns centuries ago created new forms and conceptions of social unity in the artisan guilds. Later, large-scale capitalist production recreated another form of unity in the labour process itself, which finally produced the unions and labour organisations of today. Yet in the United States, as late as 1935, one of the most powerful constituents of the meteoric rise of the C.I.O. was the fact that scores upon scores of thousands of Southern workers, on the basis of the discipline imposed upon them by large-scale production, brought a devotion which was rooted in their close sense of bewilderment in the big city, from which the union was a refuge. The urbanised Africans had found neither guild nor large-scale union to organise them. They created their own forms of social unification and they used what came naturally as a basis, the tribe.

On a tribal basis they formed unions and associations of all kinds, mutual benefit associations, religious groupings, literary associations, a vast number of sports clubs, semi-political associations or associations which provide in one way or another for one or some or all of these activities. Sometimes, although some of the members are well educated, they conduct their business in the native language. They maintain close communication with their tribal organisation or village. They raise money and initiate schemes for education and social welfare in the village or tribe. The tribal bond unites both the literate and illiterate members of the town. They often act politically as a unity. Nevertheless these are not tribal organisations in the old sense. They are fundamentally a response to the challenge and the perils of town life in a modern community.

In their variety and multiplicity these organisations are unified by the fact that they serve the same purposes. And thus they make of the city a meeting place and solvent of the ancient tribal differences. It is in this way that , by their own activities, energy and need for organisation, in response to their environment, and making use of their historical past, the basis of national unity between literate and illiterate, between tribe and tribe, between town and country was being laid. The Administration babbled about training the people by stages in order to practise local government in the English manner. When they realised what had been happening, they who had always claimed that tribalism was one of the main obstacles to the implementation of the settled policy of His Majesty's Government, at once began to do their utmost to stimulate and revive the ancient tribalism in its crudest form. But this is to anticipate.

These were the forces making for unity. At the high moment of the revolution, they would require enormous force, and weld the population into national unity, subordinating the very real forces making for disunity. After the revolution, the forces of disunity would recover some of their former strength, but never again as before. The decisive factor in this was to raise the banner high, confident that only the perspective of grand and elevated perspectives would the people be moved out of the age-old divisions and insularity. This was the greatest service Nkrumah rendered to his people.

There was yet another social feature of Gold Coast life, which was specifically African and was to prove of enormous importance in the revolution. For the great mass of the common people the centre of African life has always been the market. The Ewe week consisted of four days, the day before market, market day, the day after market day, and stay at home day. The traders for generations have been the women (Nkrumah's mother was a petty trader), and this function has been maintained and developed until today a large proportion of the retail distribution of goods, and the main channel through which the distribution of commodities flows from the big wholesale importers to the private home is the market in small villages as well as in the big towns such as Accra and Kumasi. Thus in Accra there are thousands of women in action in the market, meeting tens of thousands of their fellow citizens every day. European visitors and officials up to 1947 saw in these markets a primitive and quaint survival in the modern towns. In reality here was, ready formed, a social organisation of immense power, radiating from the centre into every corner and room of the town. Instead of being confined to cooking and washing for their husbands, the market women met every day, dealing with the European and Syrian traders on the one hand and their masses of fellow citizens on the other. The market was a great centre of gossip, of news and of discussion. Where in many underdeveloped communities the women are a drag upon their menfolk, these women of the Gold Coast, although to a large extent illiterate, were a dynamic element in the population, active, well-informed, acute, and always at the very centre of events.

A number of commentators have found the basis of Gold Coast Independence in the founding of Achimota College in 1924 and the resulting formation of a generation of well-educated Africans. Thus *The Manchester Guardian* in its issue of Ghana Independence Day, March 6, 1957, in a special supplement generously spaced and full of good will, writes in its editorial:

> Ghana was born and nurtured on the playing fields of Achimota more surely than Waterloo was won on those of Eton. No men have deserved better the gratitude of today's celebrants than Alexander Fraser and James Aggrey, respectively first principal and vice-principal of this great school, at which Nkrumah himself and many more first drew the breath of finer air. Would that Aggrey could have lived, as Fraser(now 85) has done, to see this crown set upon his work.

Here is the myth in its most liberal and cultivated form. In the struggle for independence one market-woman in Accra, and there were 15,000 of them, was worth any dozen of Achomota graduates. The graduates, the highly educated ones, were either hostile to Nkrumah and his party or stood aside. The social force that made the revolution were the workers, the market-women, and above all, the stratum of youth educated in primary schools who had not been subjected to the influence of British university education. Aggrey understood his people and as far back as 1930 had made his celebrated prediction that a youth movement was coming in Africa which would astonish the world. These were the ones in whom Nkrumah found his ablest and most fearless supporters, and they remain the core of the party of this day.

This was the condition of the people in the Gold Coast in 1947, not in absolute terms, but as a developing process, the process of modernisation. Objectively the most effective single factor in the evolution was in all probability the motor-lorry. Packed to the limit and beyond the limit of safety they sped along such roads as there were, opening up communities at a rate undreamt of in an earlier time. There were 200 licensed in 1923. The number of new ones licensed at the end of the war was 3,467. In the course of the next year it rose to 4,249. By 1955 it was 12,583. These did more to prepare the Gold Coast for independence than all the graduates produced in Achimota during the same period. They reunited the common people.

These strictly objective processes, the movement of a people finding themselves and creating a new social order, were powerfully aided by certain subjective factors whose effect it is impossible to overestimate, once they are seen in relation to the response of the mass to the changing social environment.

The African is a black man, and centuries of Western domination and indoctrination, Western science and Western history, the material privileges and social superiority which those who embody the settled policy of His Majesty's Government have arrogated to themselves; these create in the minds of the great majority of Africans and people of African descent everywhere a resentment which is never entirely absent. It may remain dormant for long periods, but can be depended upon, in a particular population at a particular time, to create and cement a formidable unity and determination, especially when the prospect arises of putting an end to the assumptions of superiority or particularly offensive manifestations of it. Imperialism created this feeling, it has paid and will pay dearly for it. It is a social and political force which seems to grow in power and refinement of expression, as the people of the world, and with them Africans and people of African descent, break down the barriers to racial equality. Thus in Harlem, New York in 1943, the Negroes broke out in long-smouldering resentment against segregation and discrimination in general, and against high prices and the brutal treatment of Negro soldiers in Southern camps in particular. With a systematic and relentless thoroughness they smashed the windows of every shop owned by a white man throughout the area, and it is an established fact that those who did the smashing did not loot—the looting came after and was done by the poor and the hungry and the lumpen-proletarians who could not resist the sight of goods waiting to be taken. But what was most remarkable was that though tens of thousands were in the street participating or sympathising and encouraging, no single Negro attempted any violence to any white person and crowds of white people, many of them from Manhattan, walked, watching and very often talking and exchanging cigarettes and lights with the Negroes in the most amiable manner. The racial consciousness which has been so mercilessly injected into the Negro is today a source of action and at the same time of discipline.

In Montgomery, Alabama, for one year, a Negro population of 50,000 decided not to travel in segregated buses any longer, organised transportation of their own in the form of a car pool, and from the first day of the boycott to the last it was maintained by well over ninety-nine percent of the population, undoubtedly one of the most remarkable manifestations of social consciousness and self-discipline in the long and varied history of revolutionary movements. The actions of the Africans in South Africa are sufficiently similar.

Some such cementing power was most obviously at work during the Gold Coast Revolution. When every objective social factor is analysed and weighed, there remains something over and beyond which alone can fully account for the incredible solidarity, endurance and discipline shown by the Gold Coast population between the years 1947 and 1957, and particularly between 1948 and 1951. Nobody expected it, the Administration was specifically contemptuous of any such possibility, repeatedly the leaders were overcome with wonder and admiration at it, and as we have already seen, it nerved them for a political audacity which time and again seemed to tremble on the edge of a frightful catastrophe, but remained to the end under complete control. They were bound together by the bitter tie of centuries of racial humiliation, and it is to the eternal credit of themselves and their leaders that they were conscious of it, used it with extraordinary confidence, subtlety and finesse and, despite the most extreme provocations, never abused it. The world of today, and still more of tomorrow, owes much to them.

Finally, and perhaps most important, the people of the Gold Coast had lived through the great experience of the second world war. Knit together by the objective environment, conscious in a thousand ways every day that they were in a stage of violent transition from the immemorial past to the modern world, they had heard around them the clash of world conflict, and seen the fall of mighty empires and had heard the slogans and the rhetoric, the promises of an end to age-old injustices, the facile promises of a better world without which it is impossible today to mobilise peoples for war. Particularly they had heard the ringing denunciation of all forms of racial superiority, the simplification of the slogans of democracy, the tears and prayers for national freedom lost, the paeans of triumph for the national freedoms regained, the great liberation. Western politicians promulgated Charters embracing an ocean and enumerated freedoms. Their populations listened with scepticism and fought as a matter of duty or to save themselves from concrete dangers which they saw as imminent and intolerable. Not so the colonial peoples. They took them seriously. For them the postwar world had to be a new world. It would be new only if they were free. The war being ended, there followed in rapid succession the freedom of India, Ceylon, Burma. Thousands of Gold Coast soldiers fought in the Far East and brought home eye-opening information about countries that were on the high road to independence and were not in any way superior to the Gold Coast in literacy and all the other shibboleths of the Colonial Office. What they had done, the Gold Coast could do, had a right to do, owed it not only to themselves but to the world to do.

The Western world as a whole, blinded by the myth, does not yet know what all this means in Africa, and it must. The people of the Gold Coast fought for their own freedom within the context of themselves as a beacon for the rest of tropical Africa, and as part of a world-wide revolutionary movement for a new world. It is in every line of the record. But even if the evidence were not there in such profusion, knowledge of all previous revolutions would show that they always find strength and wisdom and perspective in the most advanced actions and ideas of their time. They always see themselves as leading humanity.

Such in outline were the forces at work, though as late as December 1947 they had not yet overtly manifested themselves in the Gold Coast. The Colonial Office and the Administration knew nothing about all this until it hit them two, three, a dozen times across the face, sent them reeling again and again, never giving them a chance to recover. The idea that they trained the people of the Gold Coast for self-government and independence is the literal reverse of the truth. Here again is the paradox. It is the people of the Gold Coast who trained, bludgeoned, the Colonial Office into the meaning of self-government and independence.

1960

24
The Rise and Fall of Nkrumah

The fall of Dr Kwame Nkrumah is one of the greatest catastrophes that has befallen the minds of Africans in Africa, of people of African descent, and all who are interested in the development and progress of independent Africa.

His dramatic collapse is a thing that many people will find it hard to understand and to place within the context of what is happening in the underdeveloped countries. It will be difficult for people who are genuinely uninstructed about Africa, like the people of the Caribbean (for example, the people of Trinidad and Tobago). But those of us who have been following the developments of Africa and the criticisms of Africans in the European and American press have long been astonished at the confusion and the utter inability to understand of would-be experts on Africa.

Nkrumah's fall is a catastrophe. But it should have been foreseen. In fact it was foreseen, and I shall make that abundantly clear. What must not be lost sight of is that he was one of the greatest leaders of African struggles whom Africa has produced, especially during the last 20 years, the last crucial 20 years.He was not a rogue or a betrayer, or one who lost his head amid the temptations of power.

He was a splendid person, but he was overwhelmed by the economic and political problems which weigh so heavily upon the newly independent countries, particularly the independent countries of Africa. My association with Nkrumah is not only political but it has been personal, although with him, as with me, a personal relation was always governed by political beliefs and perspectives. I met him first in New York about 1941. He saw a great deal of my friends and political associates, and we became very intimately associated. Then in 1943, he said he was going to England to study law, whereupon I wrote a letter that I believe still exists among the archives of George Padmore, and which has become quite famous among us.

Padmore was the leader of an organisation (chiefly of West Indians) devoted to propagating and organising for the emancipation of Africa. Padmore had accumulated an enormous amount of knowledge, a great library of books and papers and a wide international acquaintance of people who were devoted to the emancipation of Africa, and, in fact, of the whole colonial world. I therefore wrote to Padmore telling him about Francis (Nkrumah's English name). This letter said that Nkrumah, a young African, was coming to live in England. I said that he was not very bright but that he was determined to throw the imperialists out of Africa. I asked Padmore to see him and do his best for him, in other words, educate him politically as much as possible.

I am not in the least bothered at having written that Nkrumah was "not very bright." At the time he used to talk a great deal about Imperialism, Leninism and similar data, with which my friends and I were very familiar. Nkrumah used to talk a lot of nonsense about these matters. As a matter of fact, he knew nothing about them.

But as far as I know, Padmore met him at a London railway station. The two of them began to collaborate closely, and about a year later I read an address by Nkrumah on Imperialism which was a masterpiece. In one year he had learnt what had taken us so many years to learn and prepare. But he not only learned. He contributed a great deal of independent knowledge and constructive ideas to Padmore's organisation. And when he left London to go to work in Accra, it would have been difficult to tell of any serious distinction between the two.

How Nkrumah went to the Gold Coast must be remembered for when we come to estimate the cause of his fall this will play a not unimportant role. A body of middle-class Africans of the Gold Coast, lawyers, doctors, retired civil servants, some chiefs, had formed a political organisation called the Convention Party. They aimed at independence, or to be more precise, self-government. They might have been hazy about the name, but they knew what they wanted; to substitute themselves for the British colonial officials wherever possible. This was not an ignoble ambition, but the organisers of this party were too busy with their own affairs to devote themselves to the wearisome task of building the party. So hearing that Nkrumah had taken good degrees in American universities and was actively propagating ideas of freedom and independence for Africa in London, they sent to him and asked him to come and organise their party for them.

Like Caesar, Nkrumah came and saw and conquered, but the first persons he conquered were the people who had employed him. He organised a Youth Party, built a following among the masses, then organised a leadership among the trade unionists and the lower middle class. By the time the educated middle class knew what was happening he had the majority of the country behind him, and organised his own party—The Convention People's Party.

The struggle became extremely bitter between the educated African middle classes whom Nkrumah and his party denounced as stooges of the British Government, and Nkrumah's band of leaders who were derisively labelled "verandah boys". They had no houses of their own and were compelled, so ran the propaganda, to sleep in open verandahs.

Having conquered the middle classes, Nkrumah went on to win independence. It was most brilliantly done and deserves an honoured place in the history of human emancipation.

But you cannot govern a backward country without the co-operation or at least benevolent neutrality of a part of the middle classes. As I heard in London some weeks ago, the middle classes had regained power in the economic and social life of the country. Nkrumah had been balancing now to right and now to left. But as I heard it, he had become more and more dependent upon the leadership of a now huge bureaucracy. In his frantic attempt to modernise Ghana he had been compelled to concentrate more and more power into local hands. I believe that the army has acted on behalf of these.

This, I hasten to say, is *not* similar to what has happened in Nigeria. There the "verandah boys" have never been near to power. The army revolt in Nigeria was aimed at an all-powerful bureaucracy.

But for the time being, and until further evidence comes to hand, we can exercise our minds on the theory that after many years in the darkness and half-light, the middle classes in Ghana are grasping at the power. That is the best we can say now. A journalist so far from the scene cannot *know* anything.

Nkrumah has committed colossal blunders and committed the final blunder of leaving his country in a state where it has to begin all over again to work out an established government. But at a time like this, the one thing observers must never forget is the tremendous political achievements of Nkrumah. If you do not bear those constantly in mind, you will never be able to understand why his government in Ghana lasted so long (fifteen years), created such a great reputation for itself, for Nkrumah, and for Africa; and has now so ignominiously and shockingly collapsed. Nkrumah did three things: He led a great revolution. He raised the status of Africa and Africans to a pitch higher than it had ever reached before. Be prepared for a shock now, Ghana's economic policies were the most dynamic and successful of the new states in Africa.

Let us take them in order. Nkrumah did not win the independence of the Gold Coast by carrying on negotiations with the Colonial Office. He mobilised the population of Ghana and hurled them at the British colonial government. He paralysed the whole working of the state, brought everything to a standstill. This negation of normal life Nkrumah called "positive action" and his main demand was not self-government. Every politician in Ghana was for self-government. What distinguished Nkrumah's politics was the addition of a single word: "now". Thus he agitated for "self-government now" and took drastic steps to force it home. Nobody in Africa has hurled a whole population at an imperialist government.

The Gold Coast government also took a very positive action. They put Nkrumah and his body of leaders in jail. But the government was too late to halt events. Leading his movement secretly from jail, Nkrumah showed his power by an overwhelming victory of his party in elections over one-third of Ghana. He himself from jail ran for Accra and won. By this time his fearlessness, his political courage and political skill, the challenge of this minute David to the huge Goliath, had caught the attention of the world. Journalists from Europe had poured into Ghana. George Padmore, Nkrumah's official agent in London, wrote articles and books, made speeches, ceaselessly informing the world of Nkrumah's policies and events in Ghana. The British pressmen on the spot made it clear that Nkrumah had the mass of the population behind him. And here I write what I have hitherto only said from platforms. The government in Britain was completely baffled by this new apparition of an embattled and revolutionary African population.

It anxiously debated what to do. Some proposed to send force and beat the movement down. Mr Nehru let it be known that if force were used, India would leave the Commonwealth immediately. Whereupon the British government accepted the inevitable and put in power a government headed by Nkrumah. When things began to go wrong in Ghana, some of us stuck by the Ghana government of Nkrumah almost to the very end. It was not friendship nor sentimentality. We knew what had been done and the man who had done it.

This is what Nkrumah now went on to do. It took him six years to win independence by 1957. He could have gone on to independence in 1951. He preferred to wait. But one day he told me that he didn't know whether he was right to wait, or if he should have gone forward in 1951 as George Padmore and Dorothy Padmore were urging him to do. I did not know what to think at the time, but today I am of the opinion that he should have gone straight ahead. That six-year delay was one cause of the deterioration of his party and government. A revolution cannot mark time for six years.

Nkrumah followed Nehru (a great friend of his) and declared Ghana a republic, setting a pattern followed by nearly all the African states. He sent for George Padmore and Padmore organised the first International Conference of African Independent States. He also organised the first Conference of African fighters. Banda, Nyerere, Tom Mboya, Lumumba, all were there. When Sekou Touré of Guinea defied De Gaulle and refused to be part of the new French community, Nkrumah came to his assistance, lent him money and united the state of Ghana to the state of Guinea. He declared that only a United Independent Africa could save Africa from a new colonialism. He wrote in the constitution of Ghana that the Ghana government would subordinate its sovereignty to the government of a United Africa. But more than that, by magnificent speeches and dramatic actions he made the world see Africa and Africans as contenders for liberty, equality and if not fraternity, respect.

Nkrumah is one of the great men of our day. What then went wrong? *He attempted to do too much, particularly in his drive to make Ghana a country of an advanced economy*. That we shall go into most carefully for it brings out two things: the difficulties of all newly independent states; and the vast difference between Africa and the Caribbean.

For many years no political collapse has unloosed among our people—and many others—the dismay that the fall of Nkrumah has caused. A sense of politics being an insoluble mystery has increased and that is bad for democracy; above all, people must understand. We all accept, I hope, that Nkrumah was no commonplace, incompetent person, a grabber at the profits and prerequisites of power, his personal degeneration at last discovered and exposed. No. His fall is deserved. He had become a disease in the blood of Ghana and of Africa. For us in the Caribbean to understand and learn the lesson of his fall we have to appreciate the immense differences between the territory and the population of Ghana and the territory and population of Trinidad and Tobago. Walk about in Accra, the capital of Ghana. A modern city, fine, concrete, American-style structures. The buildings where the trade union is housed; the party headquarters built by Nkrumah are among the finest in formerly colonial Africa. Motorcars of various styles shoot about the streets. Everywhere, activity, modernism. Outside Accra, a university; at Kumasi (inland), a scientific technological institute planned for the highest standards. Much of this was built by Nkrumah or his government.

But drive five miles from the centre of Accra. Get out and walk around. There is a mud-walled village, houses of a type that could have been there 500 years ago, an elementary school in the process of being constructed by the villagers themselves. Go on for 50 miles. You meet small villages of a few score houses. After 150 miles, mainly of thick forest, with small concentrations of people living African lives and for the most part speaking one of a few tribal languages, you come to Kumasi. Kumasi is quite a modern town. But it is the capital of the Ashanti, a people different from the Africans of the coast in language, religion, tribal practices, and outlook, *and very conscious of these differences*. We are not finished yet.

On our journey we have often seen walking on the road a few dozen cattle, with some cattlemen walking behind them. They are on their way to Accra, where the cattle, thin and exhausted, will be fattened up for beef. Men and beasts have come hundreds of miles from the third area of Ghana, the Mohammedan North with its centre, Tamale. When I was in Ghana in 1957 many of them went without clothes. In 1960 I enquired about them. Elementary education was fighting hard against a primitive past, bad roads, remote villages.

And the famous cocoa industry? The cocoa plantations were deep inside the forests, often miles from each other. To sum up: in a Caribbean island, "All o'we is one." In an African state, and Ghana, by and large, is the most advanced of them, "All o'we is many."

That was what Nkrumah faced. In the struggle for "self-government now" the Convention People's Party had knit the population closer together into one people than even before. *Now, however, in Nkrumah's drive to build a modern economy and create a sense of nationhood, he found himself splitting the new nation into far more intractable divisions than the ancient tribalism*. Let us state the problems as they developed and have finally overwhelmed him.

The first problem was a state, a government. To begin with, he had no independent African government. Like all these new African rulers, he had inherited a British colonial government organised for purposes quite different from his own. Further, in a new government, it is people, personnel, who are an urgent priority. Nkrumah had to find people to create a modern economy and run a modern government.

This put a premium on education so that the educated in every area began rapidly to develop into an aristocracy, or to use a contemporary term, a meritocracy. In this drive for modernisation, the only sure source of discipline and loyalty to the regime was the party. The party gradually acquired enormous power and control. But, try as he would, Nkrumah could not prevent the party becoming the party of the new bureaucracy and no longer the party of the masses, as in the days of the struggle for "self-government now". Sharp and persistent conflicts and grave corruption develop in *all* (I repeat, *all*) new and growing bureaucracies. Nkrumah found himself more and more having to decide between honest and dishonest; between groups and individuals fighting often with inter-tribal weapons.

In spite of himself, he had personally to assume dictatorial powers, or to give such powers to individuals whom he could trust or thought he could. In 1960 I warned him of the imminent crisis. By that time he could not understand. He had at the same time, amid these troubles, to battle with the decline in the price of tropical commodities such as cocoa. These prices had dropped fantastically all over the world. But the prices of the manufactured goods these tropical areas had to buy had risen. This was felt acutely by Ghana, dependent on the sale of cocoa, and frantically buying modern goods to modernise itself. It is within these objective practical realities that Nkrumah had to govern, to build a new state. He developed many personal weaknesses (I know quite a few).

But I know that unless you are acutely aware of the economic and social milieu in which a politician is functioning, you get mixed up resignedly in the speculation and analysis of pure personality, and end by shaking your head on the weakness of human, especially political, nature. We can now see Nkrumah the man, fighting with those problems and breaking politically (and personally) under them. As we watch him, we are seeing not merely an individual but a continent, the continent of Africa.

Nkrumah over the years committed what we can now call blunder after blunder. They may not have been seen clearly as blunders at the time, but the way in which his enemies have got rid of him show that there had been accumulating in various sections of the population a great deal of antagonism to him. Unless people are certain that the minds of the population have turned against the political leadership, they do not plot and act in the way they have acted in Nigeria and Ghana. First of all Nkrumah had the greatest contempt for what in democratic countries is known as the parliamentary opposition. A parliamentary opposition, he said, was a luxury which only wealthy and advanced countries could afford. What is needed in Ghana was that everybody should devote himself to developing the country and building the new nation. Nkrumah used to say this openly, and it was a conception of government entirely and utterly false.

Where you have around you only a lot of yes-men, the first victim is yourself. You have no means of judging and testing the information that you get and, most important of all, no means of judging the state of mind of the population. It is perfectly clear that Nkrumah hadn't the faintest idea of what was going on in the minds of the people and in the heads of his chief officials. The first victim of a dictatorship is usually the dictator himself. He cannot govern properly and ensures only the disorder attendant on his removal. Elections were a farce. He ended with a one-party state.

Nkrumah's best known opponents were Danquah, Busia and Appiah. Busia fled. Danquah and Appiah were in and out of jail without trial. The argument that Nkrumah and his supporters used was that Danquah was in reality a city intellectual who, purely for political purposes, had formed an alliance with some of the most reactionary elements in the country, chiefly the rulers of Ashanti. So that when Appiah returned from England he became a leader of the opposition, strongly Ashanti, and was frequently in jail without trial.

Nkrumah's greatest political error was this. He believed that the question of democracy was a matter between him and Danquah and Busia and Appiah and such. He never understood that democracy was a matter in which the official leaders and an opposition were on trial before the mass of the population. It is not a question of conflict between rivals for power, as so many who shout "democracy" believe.

In reality, the concept and practice of democracy is very difficult for people who are just starting it. The new rulers believe that as long as they have a majority in Parliament they can do anything. In Britain and other countries where there is a long tradition of democracy, the politicians know that they cannot overstep certain boundaries without bringing the whole of government into discredit and unloosening dangerous currents among the people. Nkrumah was very energetic. He was not one who could point only to some roads, some schools and some foreign investments. Nkrumah was busy with his truly magnificent Volta scheme for the production of aluminium locally, with building and developing a new town, Tema. But, overwhelmed with work, Nkrumah depended more and more upon the party and less and less upon Parliament. But here his shallow concept of democracy found him out.

When I was in Ghana in 1960 he was engaged in building a special school for the training of party members. The year before he had declared that the party was the real ruler of the country. But having destroyed democracy in Parliament, if even he wanted to, he could not establish democracy in the party. He had made the Parliament into a body of stooges and the party also became the same, a body of stooges. This dual degeneration of the Parliament and of the party had one terrible result. The ablest, the most qualified, and the intellectuals of finest character turned their backs on Nkrumah. Some of them, an astonishing number, went abroad and took jobs elsewhere. Those who stayed at home either devoted themselves to their professions, such as law and medicine, or did their work in the government, drew their pay and let Nkrumah govern or misgovern as he pleased. This abandonment of their own government and their own people by gifted, trained intellectuals of high character is a feature of modern underdeveloped countries. Canadian, British, French, even the United States businesses will take them once their degrees and qualifications are good enough. It is a commonplace that nowhere has a country suffered from the disaffection of its ablest intellectuals as Ghana has suffered.

One strong current of opinion is that they refuse to be governed by "the party". All sorts of ignoramuses, gangster-types, only had to prove their loyalty to the regime, i.e. to Nkrumah, and they could go places in the party and in the country. A notoriously ignorant and even more flagrantly corrupt minister had to be fired. But he had influence among the Ashanti. The Ashanti were restless and he was brought back, to the scandal of the whole country.

A false policy persisted in causing a brilliant politician to deteriorate personally. Nkrumah had himself called "Osagyefo" or Saviour. He bought planes, small warships, wasted public money on prestige building, and on prestige diplomacy. He became the advocate of the policy of a United Africa, a profound and far-seeing policy, but he advocated it crudely and with an intolerance that labelled all who disagreed with him as fools or cranks. Posing as an authority on all sorts of historical and philosophical subjects, he began to publish book after book. Years ago I ceased to read them. The drive towards economic expansion continued but now with a huge and self-seeking bureaucracy and the inevitable heavy taxation of the mass of the population. Ghana began to go bankrupt.

At such times all who are not sharing in the spoils begin to draw near each other and to think in terms of a new regime. Nkrumah was shot at two or three times. I wrote to him hinting that where a head of state is threatened so often with assassination something is vitally wrong with his regime; it is the ruler's business to find out what is wrong and correct it. I told him what to do. Nkrumah replied that he was a revolutionary and had to expect that his life was in constant danger. When I read that, I knew that he was no longer the dynamic, sensitive politician of the old days.

Soon he had publicly to accuse the secretary of his party of plotting to murder him, an accusation which discredited him as much as it discredits the accused. Any politician could now divine that there was surely building up in the country a secret opposition. Then came the dismissal of the Chief Justice, for giving a decision Nkrumah did not approve of. I learnt that he was now compelled to lean heavily on heads of the civil service, police and army. They were not only in charge of governmental departments. They were seeping back into the party. The party, led by the "verandah boys", and then by those whom I call the party gangsters, was coming to an end. With its end has come Nkrumah's end. He says he will return. Maybe. I doubt it. If he does the mess will be bloody.

When he dismissed the Chief Minister, I wrote to him at once and when he did not reply I publicly broke off the relations of twenty-five years. You can poison a Chief Justice, you cannot dismiss him for a decision from the Bench. You destroy the concept of law and order. I knew then that his regime was doomed. I sat down and prepared a book which I called *Nkrumah Then and Now* (published later as *Nkrumah and the Ghana Revolution)*. In it I did at length what I am doing here briefly: I showed the former grandeur and present decadence of Nkrumah. I not only prophesied the end of his regime but showed the necessity for bringing it to an end.

What exactly is happening there today I don't know and can't know. Nkrumah studied, thought and knew a lot. But one thing he never mastered: that democracy is not a matter of the rights of an opposition, but in some way or other must involve the population. Africa will find that road or continue to crash from precipice to precipice.

1966

25
Black Power

Mr Chairman, Ladies and Gentlemen, Black Power. I believe that this slogan is destined to become one of the great political slogans of our time. Of course, only time itself can tell that. Nevertheless, when we see how powerful an impact this slogan has made it is obvious that it touches very sensitive nerves in the political consciousness of the world today. This evening I do not intend to tell you that it is your political duty to fight against racial consciousness in the British people; or that you must seek ways and means to expose and put an end to the racialist policies of the present Labour government. If you are not doing that already I don't see that this meeting will help you to greater political activity. That is not the particular purpose of this meeting though, as you shall hear, there will be specific aims and concrete proposals. What I aim to do this evening is to make clear to all of us what this slogan Black Power means, what it does *not* mean, *cannot* mean; and I say quite plainly, we must get rid, once and for all, of a vast amount of confusion which is arising, copiously, both from the right and also from the left. Now I shall tell you quite precisely what I intend to do this evening. The subject is extremely wide, comprising hundreds of millions of people, and therefore in the course of an address of about an hour or so, we had better begin by being very precise about what is going to be said and what is not going to be said.

But before I outline, so to speak, the premises on which I will build, I want to say a few words about Stokely Carmichael: I think I ought to say Stokely because everybody, everywhere, calls him Stokely which I think is a political fact of some importance. The slogan Black Power, beginning in the United States and spreading from there elsewhere, is undoubtedly closely associated with him and with those who are fighting with him. But for us in Britain his name, whether we like it or not, means more than that. It is undoubtedly his presence here, and the impact that he has made in his speeches and his conversations, that have made the slogan Black Power reverberate in the way that it is doing in political Britain; and even outside of that, in Britain in general. And I want to begin by making a particular reference to Stokely which, fortunately, I am in a position to make. And I do this because on the whole in public speaking, in writing (and also to a large degree in private conversation), I usually avoid, take great care to avoid placing any emphasis on a personality in politics.

I was reading the other day Professor Lévi-Strauss and in a very sharp attack on historical conceptions prevalent today, I saw him say that the description of personality, or of the anecdote (which so many people of my acquaintance historically and politically live by) were the lowest forms of history. With much satisfaction I agreed; I have been saying so for nearly half a century. But then he went on to place the political personality within a context that I thought was misleading, and it seemed to me that in avoiding it as much as I have done, I was making a mistake, if not so much in writing, certainly in public speech. And that is why I begin what I have to say, and will spend a certain amount of time, on one of the most remarkable personalities of contemporary politics. And I am happy to say that I did not have to wait until Stokely came here to understand the force which he symbolizes.

I heard him speak in Canada at Sir George Williams University in March of this year. There were about one thousand people present, chiefly white students, about sixty or seventy Negro people, and I was so struck by what he was saying and the way he was saying it (a thing which does not happen to me politically very often) that I sat down immediately and took the unusual step of writing a letter to him, a political letter. After all, he was a young man of twenty-three or twenty-four and I was old enough to be his grandfather and, as I say, I thought I had a few things to tell him which would be of use to him and, through him, the movement he represented. I will now read to you parts of this letter:

> I was glad to hear you because I wanted to know for myself what had lifted you up to the pinnacle on which you now stand. It is a pinnacle and one that is very rare in my experience or even historically. You are just twenty-four and you are not only one of the people on the American continent who is to be reckoned with, but you are a world-famous figure. At twenty-four. That fact is something very special and seems to offer immense possibilities both for the cause and the advancement, or rather I should say the development, of the personality. I am profoundly aware of the dangers of being in such a position at such an early age. I propose therefore in this letter to deal of course with the movement, because everything depends on that, but also with the specific dangers that beset you as a leader, perhaps the most prominent leader today, of this great movement in the United States.

I then explained why in particular I had been so struck by him. The letter continues:

> One of my most important and pregnant experiences is my experience both personal and otherwise of West Indians and people of West Indian origin who have made their way on the broad stage of Western civilization. Some of them I knew very well personally and others I have studied, am very familiar with their work, and have systematically added to my information and knowledge about them from people who knew them well. They are Marcus Garvey, George Padmore, Aimé Césaire, Frantz Fanon. These are West Indians who have played a role on the world political stage that is not even properly understood by their own people. One of the tasks I have set myself is to make people understand what these men have done and their significance in world politics. In a substantial respect I am

one of them, although I have not played the concrete role that they have played: I say that I am one of them because it means that I understand the type very well. And you are one. I suspected it when I was reading some of your writings and having heard you I am absolutely certain of it. Let me briefly state at once some of the points that brought this home to me with extreme force, particularly at that meeting.

We need not go further into that now. I went on to say (it was a rather lengthy letter) that there were certain doubtful points in his speech which he should bear in mind. I went on further to indicate in the letter that there were grave weaknesses in the whole Negro struggle in the United States; for one, that it lacked a sound historical and theoretical basis. And I suggested to him, that if he did not see his way to initiate this study himself, he should see to it that others take it up and take it up seriously. *So large and far-reaching a struggle needed to know where it was, where it had come from, and where it was going.*

I received a reply in which he took up the points I had made and said he recognized their importance. That was in March and April of this year, 1967. The year has not ended and now he speaks with a scope and a depth and range of political understanding that astonishes me. That the Stokely whom I heard in March and whose conspicuous political ability and character I recognized (that is why I wrote to him) in less than a year should have developed into the political leader we are hearing and seeing, this to me is a testimony not merely to him but to the speed with which the modern world is moving politically. I have to add that much that I shall now say to you I knew before, but I could never have said it in the way that you will hear, unless I had been able to listen and to talk to the new Stokely, the Stokely that we have been hearing.

Now, Black Power. A political slogan and yet not a political slogan: rather a banner. We see that at once the moment we look at previous statements which have captured the political imagination and guided the activity of people all over the world during past centuries and up to today. I shall take some of the best known ones and that will enable us to put Black Power in the proper place to which it belongs.

You remember about the middle of the eighteenth century Rousseau's statement with which he began his famous book *The Social Contract*? "Man was born free and is everywhere in chains." Listen to it again: "Man was born free and is everywhere in chains." It was written two hundred years ago and yet today, in classes in political philosophy, in universities all over the world, in articles and books that are daily published, the debate rages: what did Rousseau mean by saying that man was born free and is everywhere in chains? Some people draw the conclusion about Rousseau that he was the originator of the totalitarian state, others that we have not yet reached the kind of democracy which he had in mind. It is not our business this evening to come to any decision about that (although I know where I stand). The point is that the phrase has been a banner under which men have struggled for liberty and freedom, a phrase under which that struggle goes on today. Without Rousseau's "Man was born free and is everywhere in chains", the world would be a poorer place.

Let us take another statement almost two hundred years old, the statement by Jefferson that "We hold these truths to be self-evident, that all men are created equal . . . that they are endowed by their Creator with certain inalienable rights . . ." the beginning of one of the most famous documents in history, the Declaration of Independence of the United States, declared in Congress on the fourth of July 1776. Self-evident! Jefferson had a nerve. Nothing like that was "self-evident" anywhere. In Britain, all over Europe, all over Asia, all over the known world, people were being governed by kings who were supposed to have been placed on the throne by God; there were nobles, aristocrats; there were the clergy with special rights, in every part of the known globe. In the United States itself there was a solid mass of people who did not believe that even in the United States all men were created equal. Yet Jefferson had the nerve to begin the famous document by saying that this was a truth that he held to be self-evident, i.e. everybody could see it. At the time there were very few people who accepted it. To this day there are vast numbers of people who don't believe it. Nevertheless it is one of the greatest political statements ever made. It is a banner by which and under which tremendous struggles have been waged for liberty, for democracy, for democratic freedom. I hope that you are following me in my view that it is only by placing it historically that we can begin to see what Black Power signifies and avoid gross and dangerous blunders. In fact, it is not a slogan at all. Rather it is a banner for people with certain political aims, needs and attitudes, a banner around which they can rally, a banner which I believe many millions already today see and in the not too distant future will see, as the symbol of a tremendous change in life and society as they have known it.

Let us now leave these slogans (I prefer to think of them as banners) and go directly to the origin and ancestry of this world-shaking movement, Booker T. Washington. For, yes, it is with Booker T. Washington that we have to begin. Today the name of Booker T. is not often mentioned in regard to the development of Negro struggles. Most often people mention with a certain disdain his famous concession, or I can call it his infamous capitulation to race prejudice in the South. It is part of the history of the Negro and of the history of the United States that Booker T., in a famous speech in Atlanta, Georgia, told the South: "In all things purely social we can be as separate as the five fingers, and yet one as the hand in all things essential to mutual progress."

Today we ought to be able to see first that Booker T. Washington faced a situation in which he was seeking desperately for a way out, and he could see no way out except capitulation. But Booker T. did something else. He said that Negroes should prepare themselves for the work of artisans and labourers; everybody could not be a scholar or do a skilled clerical job; the Negro had to prepare himself for manual labor. But, added Booker T., he should also seek to educate himself in the humanities. So it was that Tuskegee, which was the centre of Negro education in the South for many years, became a great pioneer of modern education, i.e. education for the members of a modern community, education of body and mind for manual and intellectual labor. So that today Booker T. Washington's *method* of education, *forced upon him by race prejudice*, has become an educational ideal which is more and more widely accepted as a necessity for the world in which we live.

But Booker T. is also remembered for the fact that he drew upon himself a devastating attack by another great pioneer in Negro struggles, Dr W.E.B. Du

Bois. Du Bois marked a great stage in the history of Negro struggles when he said that Negroes could no longer accept the subordination which Booker T. Washington had preached. On it Booker T. had built a base not only for himself but for a certain type of Negro educator and social functionary. Dr Du Bois declared the absolute right of the Negro for whatever task he was fitted. And we can see how history changes in that, looking at the qualifications and weaknesses of American Negroes in his day, Du Bois championed specifically the Negroes of "the talented tenth", that tenth of the Negro community which he believed was already fitted to exercise fully the qualifications it had already attained. We can see how history moves when we understand that this, which was a legitimate demand by one of the great pioneers of Negro emancipation, would today be repudiated by Stokely and all supporters of Black Power. They do not seek to advance claims, rights for one-tenth of the present Negro population of the United States. They say that it is this tenth of the Negro population which has been and is being given special positions which corrupt it and act as a deadweight on the development of the great mass of the Negro people as a whole. So that "the talented tenth" in the days of Du Bois fifty years ago represented an advance, while today it is the main enemy of all those who fight under the banner of Black Power.

But if we wish properly to understand *the advanced position which Stokely Carmichael and the advocates of Black Power hold today*, we have only to see that Dr Du Bois was not a man whose reputation rested only on the fact that he was one of the great leaders of Negro emancipation. Not only white journalists have thus circumscribed him. I have had to protest to leading people in the coloured community in the United States about what they said when Du Bois died. I am glad to say that I had had the opportunity to point out that in organizing the National Association for the Advancement of Coloured People and founding its periodical *The Crisis*, Dr Du Bois took the lead in making the United States and the world recognize that racial prejudice was not a mere matter of Negroes being persecuted but was a cancer which poisoned the whole civilization of the United States. Secondly, in the Pan-African Conferences that he organized all over the world, he first made people in the United States and elsewhere recognize that Africa could not be left in the state of stagnation and exploitation in which it had entered the twentieth century. Thirdly, in his study of the American slave trade and in his studies of the Civil War he was undoubtedly one of the most penetrating and effective historians of his time: there is no noteworthy American historian writing today and during the last fifty years who does not owe a tremendous debt to Du Bois's work in history. So that in all these respects he was far more than "a leader of our people". In fundamental respects he was a generation in advance of most American thinking of his time and he is one of the great citizens of the United States in the twentieth century. We must bear that mistake in mind and not make it again as we are on the way to doing in regard to the advocates of Black Power. *Think of this seriously, please.*

Now the foundation having been firmly laid, we can move a little faster. Next on the list is Marcus Garvey, of whom we need say only a few sentences. Before Garvey the great millions of Africans and people of African descent simply did not exist in the political consciousness of the world in general, of the general public, and of politicians in particular. After less than a decade this Jamaican had placed them there. He had placed them there in a manner that they could never be removed again. Garvey had placed them not only in the consciousness of the oppressors but as a constituent part of the minds and aims of the great mass of Africans and people of African descent.

We can now go still faster. After Garvey came Padmore, who added a new dimension. Padmore was the originator of the movement to achieve the political independence of the African countries and people of African descent. That is why he is increasingly known as the Father of African Emancipation. So that a certain stage of African emancipation had arrived, very soon after the independence of Ghana, by actually achieving political independence, i.e. rule by local and native politicians over large areas.

There follows automatically the rise and significance of the activities and writings of Frantz Fanon. We must see Fanon as the political activist and writer who is saying that now we have actually achieved independence we have to fight against not only the old imperialism creeping back: we have to carry on a desperate all-out struggle against those native leaders who may have fought for independence. Many do not represent the forward movement of the underdeveloped peoples to some new stage of economic and political progress. Says Fanon: after independence those become the enemy. We do not see Fanon correctly if we do not see him as a natural development after what Padmore represented, and Padmore as the political stage of the wide avenue opened by Du Bois and Marcus Garvey.

It is only now that we are able to see what Stokely and the advocates of Black Power represent. They stand on the shoulder of their ancestors. I have not mentioned all. For example, I have had to leave out Aimé Césaire, the man of Négritude, and I have had to leave out Malcolm X, that great fighter whose potentialities were growing so fast that his opponents had to get rid of him by plain murder. So then, it is now that we can see what Stokely and the concept of Black Power represent.

Stokely and the advocates of Black Power stand on the shoulders of all that has gone before. To too many people here in England, and unfortunately to people in the United States too (you remember I had mentioned this in my letter to Stokely), too many people see Black Power and its advocates as some sort of portent, a sudden apparition, as some racist eruption from the depths of black oppression and black backwardness. It is nothing of the kind. It represents the high peak of thought on the Negro question which has been going on for over half a century. That much we have to know, and that much we have to be certain other people get to know.

Now, as in any political manifestation on a world scale, there is involved not only a general principle. As far as any particular country is concerned, we have to see it not only in its general but in its particular application. Now you notice that Booker T. Washington was from the South of the United States. W.E.B. Du Bois was South and North, everywhere, and in the world outside: his was a universal mind. But the West Indians, Garvey, Césaire, Padmore and Fanon, all worked abroad, away from home, and much of their work, in fact most of it, was concerned with Africa. And taking advantage of this immense political experience which has been accumulated, and the advanced stage of American society, we find that it is in the United States that the Negro struggle has advanced and is now taken to the highest peak it has ever reached. For note that whereas the others on the whole concentrated on Africa and peoples of African descent, in the voice of Stokely we can hear that they are laying the basis of a mortal struggle to the death for what black people believe to be their rights.

They have further extended that struggle to what they call the Third World. By that phrase, the Third World, they embrace what is today the majority of mankind. There are people who say that the Stokely they heard in England here, and the Stokely they have read about, is racist. The falsity of that, or if not falsity, its dishonesty, can be easily exposed. You all have heard him say that as far as he is concerned Tshombe is a white man. Black though his skin may be, he is the servant of what Malcolm X called the white power structure. He tells us specifically that the concept of the Third World includes the population of Latin America. He says specifically that they are not in the majority coloured but he includes them in the Third World. How can one call this racism except through ignorance or malice? And he embraces the concept of the Third World under the slogan Black Power because blacks are the ones who have suffered longest and most from the crimes of imperialism.

Furthermore, there are special conditions in the United States to some of which I shall now draw your attention. First there are districts in the South where Negroes are prevented from exercising the elementary rights of parliamentary democracy by the guns which the white racists keep pointed at their heads. The advocates of Black Power say that they intend (if necessary by using guns) to restore to the blacks in these areas the political power which is theirs by right. Secondly, they say what has long been noted and commented upon in the United States, that as the whites have moved out to the suburbs, the centers of all the big cities of the United States are increasingly populated by Negro majorities. This is a source of power which they propose to organize, and use as key positions in the struggle for Negro rights in the United States as a whole. Note and note well how precise is their concrete use of the term Black Power. And finally, the Negro people in the United States are not a people of a backward colonial area; they are Americans in what is in many ways the most advanced country in the world. The kind of impact the Negroes are making is due to the fact that they constitute a vanguard not only to the Third World, but constitute also that section of the United States which is most politically advanced.

So for the time being, that is what we know. I hope we know it. That is what Black Power means, and when we consider where that banner is being advanced and held aloft, and the kind of people who are carrying it, we can recognize that it is a banner which has come to stay, a banner which the twentieth century will need in the great efforts it will need to overcome the crisis that imperialist domination has imposed upon the whole world. Not only upon the Third.

So far I have been dealing with what we know *or what we ought to know*. That is, I now inform you, the answer to the first of the three famous questions asked by Kant: "What do I know?" The second question is "What must I do?", and here I will take the liberty of reminding you of another profound warning by a famous philosopher: *every determination is negation*. That is to say: every time you do something, every time you *determine* on something, you *do not do* something else. That is very important for us here. The things that I believe we ought to do are very much in opposition to the things we ought not to do. They are, I would suggest, two in number.

Number one, we support the fighters for Negro rights and for Black Power in the United States. That means we *do not* apologize or seek to explain, particularly to British people (and in particular to British Marxists), or give any justification or apologize for whatever forms the struggle in the United States may take.

It is over one hundred years since the abolition of slavery. The Negro people in the United States have taken plenty and they have reached a stage where they have decided that they are not going to take any more. Who are we here to stand, or rather to sit in judgment over what they decide to do or what they decide not to do? I want to take in particular Mr Rap Brown, who makes the most challenging statements. He is prepared to challenge American racial prejudice to the utmost limit of his strength and the strength of the Negroes who will follow him. Who are we to say, "Yes, you are entitled to say this but not to say that; you are entitled to do this but not to do that"? If we know the realities of Negro oppression in the USA (and if we don't we should keep our mouths shut until we do), then we should guide ourselves by a West Indian expression which I recommend to you: *what he do, he well do*. Let me repeat that: what the American Negroes do is, as far as we are concerned, well done. They will take their chances, they will risk their liberty, they risk their lives if need be. *The decisions are theirs*.

A word more about Rap Brown. Whether he is what "they" call a racist, or he is not one, does not interest me at all. I am interested in Rap Brown as a political leader. And I know what Rap Brown is doing. He is not a Garveyite: Garvey's doctrine was suitable for his time. What Brown is doing is this: he is taking care that the total rejection of second-class citizenship, the single-mindedness, the determination to fight to the death if need be, which now permeates the Negro movement, will not be corrupted, modified, or in any way twisted from its all-embracing purpose by white do-gooders and well-wishers of whom the United States is full. Even when whites go down to the South to face blows and bullets from the Southern police and gangsters, the Negro movement finds that they cause difficulties which impede the struggle. If you want to know the facts about this you will have to go and look for it in the August 1967 number of the Negro magazine *Ebony*. There they are stated in full. And there you will see certain sections of the movement declare that they do not want white people in their organizations. It is not racism, it is politics, and the rapidity with which they are learning politics is proved by the masterly solution of this problem that they have arrived at. They say to whites who want to fight, "We welcome the addition of your forces to the struggle. But there up in the North, in your own town, there are areas where a Negro is not allowed to own a house or even to rent. There is an opportunity to fight American race prejudice. You want to fight? Go *there* and fight *there*. We can manage down here without you."

No, that is not racism. Racism is on the decline in the United States. Yes, on the decline. Years ago you used to have white people fighting against black people. Not today. Stokely insists and all the violence points to the fact that what is taking place in American city after American city is black people fighting against the *police*. In other words, they are challenging an ancient enemy which is one wing of the state power. That is not racism. That is revolutionary politics.

They will decide and we support. But if we do that we do not do something else. We do not go around seeking to explain away what they have done, or to prove that they are not good Marxists in that they are not waiting for the American proletariat to move. We know the first thing we must do, and that tells us what we do not do.

The second thing is that we miss no opportunity to make the British public and the public at large know that we consider the life and safety of Stokely Carmichael to be in the greatest danger in the United States. A number of people here, and all over the world, realize that the simple way out for the racists in the United States (or the men of peace, peace at any price) is to murder him out of hand. They did it to Malcolm X, and today the progress of the struggle, building on what Malcolm X began, makes Stokely a person who is a mortal danger to those who wish to preserve the old way of life of the United States. We have not only to let the people in the United States know what we think, but we have to let the people know, and understand, that Stokely is not a person to be shot at by trigger-happy racists, or by deep thinkers who believe that the best black man is a dead black man. Let us, therefore, to personal friends and acquaintances, to unions, to whatever political parties we belong, let us tell them that it is their duty to register, by resolution and motion, the fears that all have for Stokely's safety; and so make those in the United States who want to kill him realize that such an action will make the public opinion of the world question not only the attitude of America to the coloured races, but the American attitude to elementary democracy and respect for the human person. We can do no better than take note of what Fidel Castro said about Stokely's safety at the closing of the OLAS Conference:

> And our people admire Stokely for the courageous statements he has made in the OLAS Conference, because we know that it takes courage to do this, because we know what it means to make such statements when you are going to return to a society that applies the most cruel and brutal procedures of repression, that constantly practices the worst crimes against the Negro sector of the population, and we know the hatred that his statements will arouse among the oppressors.
>
> And for this reason, we believe that the revolutionary movements all over the world must give Stokely their utmost support as protection against the repression of the imperialists, in such a way that everyone will know that any crime committed against this leader will have serious repercussions throughout the world. And our solidarity can help to protect Stokely's life.

Castro is a revolutionary, one of the greatest revolutionaries history has ever known, but the sentiment that he there expresses, you can participate in and take action upon even though you may be a Liberal or, it is not impossible, a Conservative. And we in Britain have a special task to perform in regard to the role that Stokely is playing. I want to read for you a notable piece of historical literature which, though written nearly two hundred years ago, was never so much apropos as it is today. It is a proclamation by the King of England for suppressing rebellion and sedition. It reads as follows:

Whereas many of our subjects in divers parts of our Colonies and Plantations in Northern America, misled by dangerous and ill designing men, and forgetting the allegiance which they owe to the power that has protected and supported them; after various disorderly acts committed in disturbance of the public peace, to the obstruction of lawful commerce, and to the oppression of our loyal subjects carrying on the same; have at length proceeded to open an avowed rebellion, by arraying themselves in a hostile manner, to withstand the execution of the law, and traitorously preparing, ordering and levying war against us: And whereas, there is reason to apprehend that such rebellion hath been much promoted and encouraged by the traitorous correspondence, counsels and comfort of divers wicked and desperate persons within this realm: To the end therefore, that none of our subjects may neglect or violate their duty through ignorance thereof, or through any doubt of the protection which the law will afford to their loyalty and zeal, we have thought fit, by and with the advice of our Privy Council, to issue our Royal Proclamation, hereby declaring, that not only all our Officers, civil and military, are obliged to exert their utmost endeavours to suppress such rebellion, and to bring the traitors to justice, but that all our subjects of this Realm, and the dominions thereunto belonging, are bound by the law to be aiding and assisting in the suppression of such rebellion, and to disclose and make known all traitorous conspiracies and attempts against us, our crown and dignity; and we do accordingly strictly charge and command all our Officers, as well civil as military, and all others our obedient and loyal subjects, to use their utmost endeavors to withstand and suppress such rebellion, and to disclose and make known all treasons and traitorous conspiracies which they shall know to be against us, our crown and dignity; and for that purpose, that they transmit to one of our principal Secretaries of State, or other proper officer, due and full information of all persons who shall be found carrying on correspondence with, or in any manner or degree aiding or abetting the persons now in open arms and rebellion against our Government, within any of our Colonies and Plantations in *North America*, in order to bring to condign punishments the authors, perpetrators, and abettors of such traitorous designs.

Given at our Court at *St. James's* the twenty-third day of *August*, one thousand seven hundred and seventy-five, in the fifteenth year of our reign.

GOD *save the* KING.

Now the curious thing about that piece is that it had in mind George Washington, Jefferson and others, as the men who were being rebellious and seditious. Today, however, the very same proclamation can be signed by Harold Wilson, the Labour Party Prime Minister of Great Britain. In banning Stokely Carmichael from reentry into Great Britain, he is acting in the identical spirit with which George III issued this proclamation, and helped the people of the United States towards independence. And with Harold Wilson we have to link another Prime Minister, Eric Williams of Trinidad and Tobago. Instead of being proud that Trinidad and Tobago was the birthplace of so distinguished a citizen of our age, Williams hastened to follow in the footsteps of George III and Harold Wilson, and has declared Stokely's presence in the country where he was born to be undesirable. To Williams no doubt it is.

We have lived to see a statue of George Washington in the heart of London.

History moves very fast these days, and we may yet live to see Stokely, not only welcomed in Britain, but given the honor of a public statue. That, I am sure, is not as extravagant as some of you might think. Remember: history moves very fast these days and can quickly leave the dull behind. I doubt if we shall hear of Stokely getting married to a daughter or any relation of the Secretary of State (and in any case, that is Stokely's business, not ours). But this much I can say with confidence, that today, over half the world, Stokely, not as anybody's son-in-law but as the Secretary of State for the United States, would be more welcome than the gentleman who today obscurely fills that high position.

Now we come to Kant's last question. The first one, you remember, was: what do I know? Second: what must I do? And now, third: what may I hope? And here I have to deal with a personal experience which I shall share with you. Needless to say, it is completely political. I went to the US from England in 1938 and found them in a rare confusion as to what a Marxist policy should be on the Negro question. What for them, as Marxists, was a difficult social situation was further complicated by the fact that the Stalinists for years had been preaching that Marxism demanded the advocacy of an independent Negro state within the confines of the US. And the Trotskyist movement from top to bottom, at home and abroad, simply did not know where it stood in regard to this fundamental question for a socialist party in the US. I had no difficulty whatever in telling them what I was quite certain was the correct policy. And this I knew not because I was a Negro, not because I have studied closely the situation in the US. No. From the very beginning I put forward what I conceived to be a very simple, straightforward Leninist policy.

I had studied Lenin in order to write *The Black Jacobins*, the analysis of a revolution for self-determination in a colonial territory. I had studied Lenin to be able to write my book on *World Revolution*. I had studied Lenin to be able to take part with George Padmore in his organization that worked for the independence of all colonial territories, but particularly the territories of Africa. I therefore was in a position from the very beginning to state my position and to state it in a discussion that some of us had with Trotsky on the Negro question 1939.

The position was this: the independent struggle of the Negro people for their democratic rights and equality with the rest of the American nation not only had to be defended and advocated by the Marxist movement. The Marxist movement had to understand that *such independent struggles were a contributory factor to the socialist revolution*. Let me restate that as crudely as possible: the American Negroes in fighting for their democratic rights were making and indispensable addition to the struggle for socialism in the US. I have to emphasize this because it was not only a clarification in the darkness of the Trotskyist movement on the Negro struggle in 1938-39. Today, 1967, I find in Britain here a confusion as great as I found in the US in 1938, and nowhere more than among the Marxists.

Now I am going to quote for you one statement by Lenin in which he states the basis of his argument. His actual political programme you will find in the resolutions which he presented to the Second Congress of the Third International on the question of self-determination, and in that resolution specifically you will find that he mentions the Negroes in the US. But the basic argument which was the foundation of Lenin's policy is stated many times in the debates that he carried on before 1917 on the right of nations to self-determination, and I will quote particularly from his sharp observations on the Irish rebellion of 1916:

> To imagine that social revolution is conceivable without revolts by small nations in the colonies and in Europe, without the revolutionary outbursts of a section of the petty bourgeoisie *with all its prejudices*, without the movement of non-class-conscious proletarian and semi-proletarian masses against the oppression of the landlords, the church, the monarchy, the foreign nations, etc. . . . to imagine that in one place an army will line up and say, "we are for socialism", and in another place another army will say, "we are for imperialism", and that this will be the social revolution, only those who hold such a ridiculously pedantic opinion could vilify the Irish rebellion by calling it a "putsch".

Lenin is very angry and though often very sharp he is not often very angry. He explains how the Russian revolution of 1905 came:

> The Russian revolution of 1905 was a bourgeois-democratic revolution. It consisted of a series of battles in which *all* the discontented classes, groups, and elements of the population participated. Among these there were masses imbued with the crudest prejudices, with the vaguest and most fantastic aims of struggle; there were small groups which accepted Japanese money, there were speculators and adventurers, etc. *Objectively*, the mass movement broke the back of tsarism and paved the way for democracy; for that reason the class conscious workers led it.

Now it is necessary to continue straight on with Lenin, because he seems to me to have had some experience, some feeling, that people would not understand what socialist revolution was. And this is one of his sharpest passages. I give it to you in full so that you may see how strongly he feels on what is for him a vital constituent of the phrase, but the way in which he underlined what he considered absolutely necessary to the understanding of what a socialist revolution was:

> The socialist revolution in Europe *cannot be anything else* than an outburst of mass struggle on the part of all oppressed and discontented elements. Sections of the petty bourgeoisie and of the backward workers will inevitably participate in it—without such participation, *mass* struggle is impossible, without it *no* revolution is possible—and just as inevitably will they bring into the movement their prejudices, their reactionary fantasies, their weaknesses and errors. But *objectively* they will attack *capital*, and the class conscious vanguard of the revolution, the advanced proletariat, expressing this objective truth of a heterogeneous and discordant, motley and outwardly incohesive, mass struggle, will be able to unite and direct it, to capture power, to seize the banks, to expropriate the trusts (hated by all, though for different reasons) and introduce other dictatorial measures which in their totality will amount to the overthrow of the bourgeoisie and the victory of socialism, which however, will by no means immediately "purge" itself of petty-bourgeois slag.

Now the moment Trotsky agreed that the independent Negro struggle for its democratic rights was part of the way to the social revolution, the Trotskyist movement accepted it. They accepted it but I don't think they really understood it. At any rate, in 1951 my friends and I broke irrevocably and fundamentally with the premises of Trotskyism, and as independent Marxists, we advocated this policy, this Leninist policy, on the Negro question, and we believed that at any rate we understood this question thoroughly. We did not know what this policy contained in it. I began by telling you that early this year I listened to Stokely Carmichael and was immediately struck by the enormous revolutionary potential which was very clear to me. But I had no idea that before the end of the year I would hear from him the following:

> We speak with you, comrades, because we wish to make clear that we understand that our destinies are intertwined. Our world can only be the third world; our only struggle for the third world; our only vision, of the third world.

Stokely is speaking at the OLAS Conference, and the Negro movement in the US, being what it is, he makes very clear that this movement sees itself as a part of the Third World. But before very long he says what I knew was always inherent in his thoughts, if not always totally plain in his words. I wish you to appreciate the gravity and the weight which a man who speaks as Stokely has been speaking must give to the following words:

> But we do not seek to create communities where, in place of white rules, black rulers control the lives of black masses and where black money goes into a few black pockets: we want to see it go into the communal pocket. The society we seek to build among black people is not an oppressive capitalist society—for capitalism by its very nature cannot create structures free from exploitation. We are fighting for the redistribution of wealth and for the end of private property inside the United States.

In the opinion of myself and many of my friends no clearer or stronger voice for socialism has ever been raised in the US. It is obvious that for him, based as he is and fighting for a future of freedom for the Negro people of the US, the socialist society is not a hope, *not what we may hope*, but a compelling necessity. *What he or any other Negro leader may say tomorrow, I do not know*. But I have followed fairly closely the career of this young man, and I leave you with this very deeply based philosophical conception of political personality. He is far away out, in a very difficult position, and I am sure there are those in his own camp who are doubtful of the positions he is taking, but I believe his future and the future of the policies which he is now advocating does not depend upon him as an individual. It depends upon the actions and reactions of those surrounding him and, to a substantial degree, not only on what you who are listening to me may hope, but also on what you do.

1967

26

Black People in the Urban Areas of the United States

The title may seem a mere geographical or demographic statement. It is not. It is, in reality, a statement of profound importance in America today. All over the country, in key areas of city after city, black people dominate in numbers; and the general opinion is that within a few years they will dominate to a degree that will make them the persons who matter in those areas. This imposes heavy responsibilities and it is a responsibility which strikes at the very heart of black thinking about its particular future within the United States.

The people who dominate the inner cities numerically cannot possibly work out a plan or have any programme by which they can improve their own situation which does not take into consideration the city as a whole. A new situation has arisen for the urban black, for thinking in terms of the whole city means that you are automatically thinking in terms of the state and from the state you find yourself facing the whole nation.

America is a continental area which is very strikingly regional—both geographically and historically. At the present time the different regions can be distinguished by their particular economies and particular political past. There is one unit of people, however, which is only on the surface divided by the regional areas in which it lives. The black people in the United States are the most socially united group in the country; they all have one unifying characteristic—they suffer from that historical development which has placed them in the role of second class citizens. There is no other national group which automatically constitutes one social force with a unified outlook and the capacity to make unified moves in politics and to respond to economic problems.

Here we must go further and place the situation within the context of an international perspective. It is from America's urban blacks that many people all over the world have historically gained a consciousness of the problems that black people suffer and their attempts to overcome them. It was from the urban areas of the United States that Marcus Garvey, one of the greatest propagandists and organisers of the twentieth century, and Dr DuBois, whose historical and sociological work has not only been of original and far-reaching quality, but continues to grow today—it was from here that they and those who followed them had the opportunity to get experience and make contact with the people and things that matter. Today the situation is not too different in that many of the general international ideas come from America, from people who have immense opportunities—financial, social, scholastic—open to them which other territories, particularly black territories, have not got.

The whole situation of blacks has been altered by the achievements in Mozambique and Angola. The Africans are now able to halt the attempt of imperialists to dominate the continent; and not only to halt it, but to actually take charge of their own affairs. But to take charge of the affairs of a continent is not a continental matter—it is a matter which concerns the whole world. The future of Africa is not solely dependent on the African people, just as the emancipation of Africa cannot be understood as purely an African matter. There should be no misunderstanding about that. All problems today, particularly the emancipation of the underdeveloped countries, are matters in which the world in general is involved; and at the centre of African emancipation, particularly in the development of ideas and international strategy, are the urban blacks of America.

If you want to find proof of this fact with respect not only to theoretical ideas, but to what has actually happened, look at the political figures that have dominated political life in the United States during the last two decades. Who have they been? Martin Luther King, Malcolm X (it is to be noted that his reputation and the power of his ideas are much greater today than when he died), Eldridge Cleaver, the movement of the Black Panthers, and that young man, George Jackson, whose achievement is rooted in black urban America. How that young man, going into prison at the age of eighteen and being in solitary confinement for a number of years, how he managed to develop the political and social ideas that he did is due to the surroundings and experiences of urban blacks. Furthermore, there is evidence that in those urban areas there are today being developed political persons, not of the literary type of which DuBois is the most notable example; but rather there are black people who, living in the midst of one of the most developed societies of the world, develop an understanding and penetration into the fundamental realities of their own particular situation and of the world in general.

I want to draw your attention to the fact that in Europe today the young politically minded people and those who feel that the present crisis of modern society cannot continue without resolution, read books written by Fidel Castro, Martin Luther King, Eldridge Cleaver, Stokely Carmichael, Angela Davis, George Jackson. These are the people who are read in the advanced political circles in the universities of western civilization. Whereas formerly the works of Marx and Lenin—and particularly their ideas about the development, freedom and emancipation of nationally oppressed people—were the key works studied by political theorists, there is another movement today. The great upheavals in France in 1968, one of the most tremendous political upheavals that has taken place in Europe, was organised under the slogans of Ho Chi Minh. The students had nobody else that they could think about. In other words, people of the Third World and particularly the writings and speeches of blacks from America's cities, are occupying a key place in the revolutionary thinking of European students. I believe that black people in America must recognise the opportunities which history has placed in their hands, not only in regard to the advancement of their own situation but in regard to the ideas and activities of oppressed people the world over.

I lived in the United States from 1938 to 1953. Never did it once cross my mind or the minds of my highly educated political colleagues that within a few years the mayor of Los Angeles, the second largest city, would be a black man; or that black men would be mayors in St Louis, Newark and Detroit, that great industrial city. These are extraordinary events for a person like myself who has always been keenly aware of the situation of black people in America. What all this means is that these people have been elected, not because black people dominated the areas, but because both black and white people felt that something new was required. I don't think too many people believe that these black men are going to fundamentally alter the situation of the cities; but nevertheless they are going to make changes and the fact that they have become mayors will have a great political effect upon the thinking of white people as well as black. I tell my friends that the thing I look forward to seeing is a black mayor of New York. They tell me that it is impossible. I don't agree with them at all because it is to ignore what has taken place over the last few years. The fact is that the possibility arises from the manoeuvres, combinations and rejections which can create the possibility in the tangled and complicated political developments of United States politics.

It was the black people beginning agitation in Montgomery, Alabama which started what was known as the New Left movement in the United States. Whether this New Left movement has developed or not developed, whether the Black Panther movement has failed or not, does not matter to me. What matters is that these events took place and came to the attention of many people who are not readers of books but who are moved by events. It demonstrated that a great political development was taking place in the sense of what was actually happening and it showed what possibilities were opening up for future developments in the population.

Black people have emerged as a prominent feature in the social and political life of America. Everyone is affected by that. But there is much more involved—the women's movement, the Chicanos and many other groups have followed the dynamism of black people. Only one notable section has not moved, the proletariat—the great body of working people whose movement in politics has such decisive significance today. It is absolutely certain, though, that they will have been affected by what is going on around them in society.

In the recent past it used to be dynamic elements, revolutionary elements in Europe which stimulated the organisation of movements in Africa. I am not saying that there were not Africans fighting for many generations against imperialism in Africa; but it used to be the ideas growing out of the political developments of western civilisation which were taken up by leaders in Africa. Today something new has emerged. Portugal which dominated areas of Africa for 500 years has not only lost control over them; but the revolutionary developments in Africa have affected the future of Portugal itself. In other words the movement is in the opposite direction—instead of movements from Europe stimulating revolutionary developments in Africa, liberation struggles in Africa have unleashed movements of tremendous importance in Europe itself. I wish to draw it to the attention of blacks, students and others who do political work, because this is part of the new world we are living in. Portuguese soldiers have said that in their contact with African fighters in Angola and Mozambique, either the prisoners they captured or when they themselves were taken prisoner, they talked to one another, they exchanged ideas and they found that the average Portuguese peasant was not in a very different situation from the peasants in Africa whom they were fighting. This meant that there existed a close association of ideas among not only thinkers, writers and historians, but among ordinary people.

I believe that if black people in American cities watch what is happening to them, observe also what is taking place among the white people and familiarise themselves with the situation in European countries where great numbers of people from the underdeveloped areas are filling important positions in the workforce, they will find that there is a unified experience and a unified conception of future development which puts them, the urban blacks of the United States, in the very forefront of those who are thinking and working out the kind of life they wish to live in the future.

1970

27

Garfield Sobers

The pundits colossally misunderstand Garfield Sobers—perhaps the word should be misinterpret, not misunderstand. Garfield Sobers, I shall show, is a West Indian cricketer, not merely a cricketer from the West Indies. He is the most typical West Indies cricketer that it is possible to imagine. All geniuses are merely people who carry to an extreme definitive the characteristics of the unit of civilization to which they belong and the special act or function which they express or practise. Therefore to misunderstand Sobers is to misunderstand the West Indies, if not in intention, by inherent predisposition, which is much worse. Having run up the red flag, I should at least state with whom I intend to do battle. I choose the least offensive and in fact he who is obviously the most wellmeaning, Mr Denys Rowbotham of *The Guardian* of Friday, 15 December 1967. Mr Rowbotham says of Sobers: "Nature, indeed, has blessed Sobers liberally, for in addition to the talents and reflexes, conditioned and instinctive, of a great cricketer, he has the eyes of a hawk, the instincts and suppleness of a panther, exceptional stamina, and apparently the constitution of an ox."

I could not possibly write that way about Garfield Sobers. I react strongly against it. I do not see him that way. I do not see Hammond that way. I see Sobers always, except for one single occasion, as exactly the opposite, the fine fruit of a great tradition. That being stated, let us now move on to what must always be the first consideration in writing about a cricketer, what he has done and what he does: that is, a hard look at Sobers on the field of play.

For Sobers the title of all-rounder has always seemed to me a circumspection. The Sobers of 1966 was not something new: that Sobers of 1966 had been there a long time. The truth is that Sobers for years now has had no superior in the world as an opening fast bowler.

Here are some facts to substantiate this apparently extravagant claim which even today many of the scribes (and there are among them undoubted Pharisees) do not yet know.

It is the business of a fast bowler, opening the innings, to dismiss for small scores two or three of the first-line batsmen on the opposing side. If he does this and does it dramatically, then good captaincy will keep him in trim to make short work of the last two or three on the side, so ending with five or six wickets.

In 1964, his last session for South Australia, Sobers, against Western Australia, bowled batsman No. 1 for 12, and had batsman No. 2 caught by wicket-keeper Jarman for 2. Against Queensland Jarman caught No. 2 off Sobers for 5, and Sobers bowled No. 3 for 1. Against the history-making New South Wales side, Sobers had Thomas, No. 1, caught by Lill for 0. He had No. 2, Simpson, caught by Jarman for 0. He then had Booth, No. 4, caught by Jarman for 0. He thus had the first three Australian Test players for 0 each. In the second innings he bowled Thomas for 3.

South Australia's last match was against the strong Victoria side. Sobers had Lawry, No.1, caught by Jarman for 4; Potter, No.3, caught by Lill for 0; Stackpole, No.5, caught by Lill for 5. In the second innings Redpath, No.2, was caught by Jarman for 0; Cowper, No.4, was caught by Hearne for 0; Lawry, No. 1, was caught by Jarman off Sobers for 22. (Let us note in passing that in this match against Victoria, Sobers scored 124 and had also scored 124 in the game against New South Wales, the same in which he dismissed the three Test batsmen each for 0.)

It is impossible to find within recent years another fast bowler who in big cricket so regularly dismissed for little or 0 the opening batsmen on the other side.

His action as a pace bowler is the most orthodox that I know.

It is not the classical perfection, above all the ease, of E.A. McDonald. Sobers gathers himself together and is obviously sparing no effort (a rare thing with his cricket) to put his whole body into the delivery. The result is that the ball leaves the ground at a pace quite inconsistent with what is a fast-medium run-up and delivery. It would be worthwhile to get the pace of his delivery mechanically timed at different stages, as well as the testimony of observant batsmen and observant wicketkeepers.

There is nothing of the panther in the batting of Sobers. He is the most orthodox of great batsmen. The only stroke he makes in a manner peculiar to himself is the hook. Where George Headley used to face the ball square and hit across it, Denis Compton placed himself well outside it on the off-side, and Walcott compromised by stepping backwards but not fully across the hitting, usually well in front of and not behind square leg, Sobers seems to stand where he is and depend upon wrist and eyesight to swish the short fast ball square to the leg boundary. Apart from that, his method, his technique is carried to an extreme where it is indistinguishable from nature.

You see it in both his defensive and offensive strokes. He can, and usually does, play back to anything about which he has the slightest doubt. More rarely he uses a forward defensive stroke. But he never just plays forward to put the bat on the ball and kill it. He watches the ball off the pitch and, even in the most careful forward defensive, plays the ball away; very different from that modern master of the forward defensive, Conrad Hunte. Hunte from the advanced front foot (never advanced too far) plays what Ranjitsinhji used to insist on calling a back stroke. His type of mastery of the forward defensive gives us the secret of the capacity of Sobers to punish good length bowling on anything like a reasonable wicket. He does not need the half-volley of a fast or fast-medium bowler to be able to drive. From a very high backlift he watches the ball that is barely over the good length, takes it on the rise and sends it shooting between mid-on and mid-off. That is a later acquisition to a stroke that he has always had: to move back and time the good length through the covers.

The West Indian crowd has a favourite phrase for that stroke: "Not a man move." That stroke plus the ability to drive what is not a half-volley is the basis of the combination that makes Sobers the orthodox attacking player that he is. His aggressive play is very disciplined, which is shown by his capacity to lift the ball straight for six whenever he feels like it. But as a rule he reserves these paroxysms for occasions when the more urgent necessities of an innings have been safely fulfilled. It is possible that Sobers at times plays forward feeling for a slow ball, more often to a slow off-spin bowler, pitching on or just outside his off-stump, going away. But I have to confess that I saw this and remembered previous examples when I was searching for a way in which as a captain I would plan to get him out.

Yet I have seen the panther in Sobers. Not when he opened in a Test and hit Miller and Lindwall for 43 runs in fifteen minutes. The balls were just not quite there and this neophyte justly put them away. No. The panther one day saw the cage door open. In 1959-60, MCC visited Trinidad in the course of the tour of the West Indies. In between the match against the territory and the Test match the players of the Test side had a practice game, Hall on one side and Sobers on the other. Ramadhin was on the side of Sobers and Hall bowling to him was extremely careful to bowl not too slow but not too fast and always at a good length: he was not going to run the risk of doing damage to one of the main West Indies bowlers. But when he bowled at Sobers, Hall made up for the restraint enforced when bowling to Ramadhin. He ran to the wicket and delivered as fast as he could, obviously determined not to forgo the pleasure of sending Sobers's wicket flying.

Sobers returned in kind. I have never seen a fast bowler hit back so hard. It was not a forward push, it was not a drive. It was a hit. Sobers lifted his bat right back and did not lift the ball. He hit one or two of these balls to the on-boundary, almost straight drives. Hall did not fancy it and bowled faster. Sobers hit him harder.

But in competitive cricket Sobers did not play that way. I saw on the screen shots of the famous century in the first Test against Australia in Brisbane in 1961 and also in the latter part of a day's play at Sydney in the third Test. All have agreed, and I agree with them, that at no time was there anything but orthodoxy carried to the penultimate degree when orthodoxy itself disappears in the absolute. There is no need here to give figures. One episode alone will show what the batting of Sobers can mean not only to spectators but to seasoned Test players. The episode will, I am certain, live in the minds of all who saw it. In a recent series, West Indies were striving to force a win against Australia in Barbados. On the last day with less than an hour to go, West Indies had to make some 50 runs.

Sobers promoted himself in the batting order, and as he made his way to the wicket, as usual like a ship in full sail, the feeling in the crowd grew and expressed itself that if this was to be done, here was the man to do it. But somebody else was thinking the same. Simpson, the.Australian captain, put Hawke on to bowl;

he himself stood at slip and he distributed the other eight men about the boundary. Obviously Simpson felt that if he left one gap in the field unprotected, Sobers would be able to find the boundary through it. I have never seen or heard before of any such arrangement or rather disarrangement of a cricket field.

Sobers had a look at the eight men strewn about the boundary, then had a look at Simpson standing at slip. He accepted Simpson's homage with a great grin which Simpson suitably acknowledged, altogether quite a moment. And an utterly spontaneous obeisance before the fearsome skill of the super batsman.

Two more points remain of Sobers on the field, his close fielding and his captaincy. Sobers has one most unusual close fielder. The batsman is probably aware of him at short leg, most probably very much aware of him. But the spectator is not. Constantine in the slips and at short-leg prowled and pounced like a panther. Sobers did not. Of all the great short-legs, he is the most unobtrusive that I can bring to mind. To Gibbs, in particular, he seems to stand where there is no need for him to move; in making the catch he will at most fall or rather stretch his length to the right, to the left or straight in front of him. But he is so close and so sure of himself that I for one am not aware of him except to know that he will be there when wanted.

His captaincy has the same measured, one might say classical character. Don Bradman has written how embarrassing it is for a junior cricketer, even a Bradman by 1938, to captain a side containing his seniors. Sobers has had to contend with similar pressures native to West Indies society.

I awaited his handling of the captaincy with some trepidation. Not in any doubt about his strategic or tactical ability, not at all. I could not forget a conversation (one of many) with Frank Worrell, immediately after the return from Australia. We had talked about the future captaincy of the West Indies. Worrell was as usual cautious and non-committal: yes, so-and-so was a good man and capable; and so on. Then, when that stage of the conversation was practically at an end, he suddenly threw in: "I know that in Australia whenever I had to leave the field, I was glad when I was able to leave Sobers in charge." The timing, the style of the remark was so pointed that I felt I could push the unlocked door right open.

"He knows *everything*?" I asked.

"Everything," Worrell replied. For me that settled one aspect of the question. The other I would be able to see only on the field. I saw it at Sabina Park at the first Test against Australia in 1965. Sobers was completely master of the situation from the moment he stepped on to the field, most probably before. He was aware of everything and at no time aware of himself. He was more in command of his situation than the far more experienced Simpson, though he did not have to face the onslaught that Simpson had to face, a problem not only collective but personal, Hall at one end and Griffith on the other. To see in the course of one day Sobers despatch the ball to all parts of the field with his bat, then open the bowling, fielding at slip to Hall or Griffith, change to Gibbs and place himself at short-leg, then go on to bowl slows, meanwhile placing his men and changing them with certainty and ease, this is one of the sights of the modern cricket field. I cannot visualize anything in the past that corresponds to it.

It was jealousy, nay, political hatred which prompted Cassius to say to Caesar:

Why, man, he doth bestride the narrow world,
Like a Colossus, and we petty men
Walk under his huge legs and peep about,
To find ourselves dishonourable graves.

Certainly in the press-box watching Sobers a mere scribe is aware of Hazlitt's: "Greatness is great power, producing great effects. It is not enough that a man has great power in himself, he must show it to all the world in a manner that cannot be hid or gainsaid." Of a famous racket-player: "He did not seem to follow the ball. But the ball seemed to follow him." Hazlitt would not have minded the appropriation of this acute simplicity for Sobers at short-leg to Gibbs.

At the end of 1966 Sobers had scored over 5,000 runs in Tests and taken well over 100 wickets. Prodigious! Is Sobers the greatest all-rounder ever? The question is not only unrhetorical. It is unhistorical. Is he? I do not know. And nobody knows. I go further. Alert I always am to the reputation of West Indian cricketers: about this I do not even care. Sobers exceeds all I have seen or read of. That for me is enough, but I keep that well within bounds. There are pedants who will claim that he does not face bowling or batting of the temper and skill of previous generations. The argument errs on the side opposite to that which bravely asserts "the greatest ever". Sobers has so far met and conquered all opposition in sight. How can anyone say that if he had met this bowling quartet or that batting trio he could not have conquered them too? My presumption is that he would have dealt adequately with whatever problems he faced. Sir Donald Bradman is reported to have contested strongly Sir Stanley Jackson's dictum that George Lohmann was the greatest of medium-pace bowlers. Sir Donald gave first place to O'Reilly because O'Reilly bowled the googly and Lohmann did not. Despite the eminence of these two gentlemen I beg to disagree with both. Lohmann had no need to bowl the googly. He had enough in his fingers to dismiss the men whom he bowled at. He needed nothing else. To compare him with other bowlers who had other problems and solved them can lead to missing what really matters and what cries for comparison. And what really matters is this: I believe Garfield Sobers has it in him, has already done enough to become the most famous, the most widely known cricketer of the century and of any century barring of course the Telstar of all cricket, W.G. This is not so much a quality of Sobers himself. It is rather the age we live in, its material characteristics and its social temper.

Let us go back to the weekend, more precisely the Sunday following the first three days of the Oval Test in 1966. West Indies, in their second innings, had lost wickets and still had to make runs to avoid an innings defeat.

On that Sunday over half the world, was that a topic of discussion? Not at all.

The topic was: would Sobers make 200, vitalize his side and so enable West Indies to win? That he could no one doubted, a situation that only one word can express—the word *formidable* as the Frenchman uses it, vocally and manually.

I borrow here a thought from Sir Neville Cardus. Visualize please. Not only in the crowded towns and hamlets of the United Kingdom, not only in the scattered villages of the British Caribbean people were discussing whether Sobers would make 200 or not. In the green hills and on the veldt of Africa, on the remote sheep farms of Australia, on the plains of Southern and the mountains of

Northern India, on. vessels clearing the Indian Ocean, on planes making geometrical figures in the air above the terrestrial globe. In English clubs in Washington and in New York, there that weekend at some time or other they were all discussing whether Sobers would make the 200 required from him for the West Indies to win the match.

Would he? No one knew. But everyone knew that he could. And this was no remote possibility. It was not even 50-50. It was nearer 60-40. I have never known or heard anything like it, though I suspect that in 1895 when W.G. approached the hundredth century the whole cricket world stood on its toes and held its breath. But the means of communication in 1895 were not what they were in 1966. A man must fit into the expanded technicalities of his age. Garfield Sobers does. We are the second half of the twentieth century, heading for the twenty-first, and the word global has shrunk to a modest measure.

In 1967 I saw Garfield Sobers captaining a World XI at Lord's. He not only had been appointed. He fitted the position. No one would challenge either his competence or his moral right to the distinguished position. I confess I was profoundly moved as he led his team on to the ground and fixed his field.

I thought of cricket and the history of the West Indies. I cannot think seriously of Garfield Sobers without thinking of Clifford Goodman, Percy Goodman, H.B.G. Austin (always H.B.G. Austin), Bertie Harragin and others "too numerous to mention" (though not very numerous). They systematically built up the game, played inter-island matches, invited English teams to the West Indies year after year, went to England twice before World War I. I remember too the populace of Trindad & Tobago subscribing a fund on the spot so that "Old Cons" would not miss the trip to England; and that prodigious St Vincent family of the Ollivierres. The mercantile planter class led this unmercantile social activity and very rapidly they themselves produced the originator of West Indian batting, George Challenor. In 1906 he was a boy of eighteen and made the trip to England. He saw and played with the greatest cricketers England has ever known, the men of the Golden Age. Challenor returned to set a standard and pattern for West Indian batting from which at times it may have deviated, but which it has never lost. That history is a history of its own, going deep, too deep for the present area of discourse.

The local masses of the population, Sobers's ancestors and mine, at first looked on; they knew nothing about the game. Then they began to bowl at the nets, producing at that stage fine fast bowlers. Here more than anywhere else all the different classes of the population learnt to have an interest in common.

The result of that consummation is Garfield Sobers. There is embodied in him the whole history of the British West Indies. Barbados has established a tradition that today is the strength, not only of Barbados, but of the West Indian people. But if there is the national strength there is also the national weakness. Sobers, like the other great cricketers of the present-day West Indies, could develop his various gifts and bring them to maturity only because the leagues in England offered them the opportunity to master English conditions, the most varied and exacting in the world. Without that financial backing, and the opportunity systematically to consolidate potential, to iron out creases, and to venture forth on the sea of experiment, there would be another fine West Indian cricketer but not Garfield the ubiquitous. When Sobers was appointed captain of the West Indies he was the first genuine native son to hold that position, born in the West Indies, educated in the West Indies, learning the foundations of his cricket there without benefit of secondary school, or British university. And there he was, just over thirty, with no serious challenge as the greatest cricketer of his generation.

The roots and the ground he now covers (and can still explore further) go far down into our origins, the origins of all who share in the privileges and responsibilities of all who constitute the British version of Western civilization.

For to see Sobers whole one must place him in a wider framework than meets the eye. Research shows that cricket has been a popular game in England for centuries, but the modern game that we know came into its own at the end of the eighteenth century, and the beginning of the nineteenth. It was part of the total change of an agricultural type of society that was developing into what are now known as the advanced countries. Perhaps a most unexpected and therefore arresting exemplification of the change is to be found in a famous piece of writing.

Few books in English literature are more noteworthy than *The Lyrical Ballads*, a joint publication in 1798 of William Wordsworth and Samuel Taylor Coleridge. In addition to the poems, known today to every schoolboy, Wordsworth wrote a preface, now classical, in which he said what he and Coleridge were trying to do and what had impelled them to do it. Civilization had reached a certain stage of decay and they set out to offer an alternative. It reads as if written yesterday:

> For the human mind is capable of being excited without the application of gross and violent stimulants and he must have a very faint perception of its beauty and dignity who does not know this, and who does not further know, that one being is elevated above another in proportion as he possessed this capability.
>
> It has therefore appeared to me, that to endeavour to produce or enlarge this capability is one of the best services in which at any period a writer can be engaged; but this service, excellent at all times, is especially so at the present day.
>
> For a multitude of causes unknown to former times, are now acting with a combined force to blunt the discriminating powers of the mind and unfitting it for all voluntary exertion to reduce it to a stage of almost savage torpor.
>
> The most effective of these causes are the great national events which are daily taking place and the increasing accumulation of men in cities where the uniformity of their occupations produces a craving for extraordinary incident, which the rapid communication of intelligence hourly gratifies.

To meet these new chaotic conditions, Wordsworth and Coleridge wrote about simple things with a simplicity that sought to counteract these new dangers. Wordsworth was certain that there were "inherent and indestructible qualities of the human mind" which would survive "this degrading thirst after outrageous stimulation".

That was the period and those the circumstances in which modern cricket was born. In its own way it did what Wordsworth was trying to do.

And this is the enlargement of our historical past and the savannahs of the future which this young man now impels into our vision of ourselves. For he is one of us. We are some of him. I have met his people, listened to his mother talk about her son; he is a West Indian of the West Indies. But he is also a citizen of the world today. Sobers has played not only in the cricketing countries of the wide, wide world. E.W. Swanton has taken him to Malaya and, the other day, Yorkshire took him to play in Canada and the United States.

More than ever today the English game is a most powerful resistant to the "outrageous stimulation" of our age, stimuli far more powerful and far more outrageous than they were in Wordsworth's time.

And of all those who go forth the world over to maintain and develop the beauty and dignity of the human mind which Wordsworth was so certain would survive all challenges, cricketers are not the least. This is the age of Telstar and whatever the engineers do for cricket, there is one all-rounder whom we may be certain will meet their challenge. Such is the social temper of our age that of all cricketers, the ubiquitous all-rounder Sobers, native West Indian, sprung from the people and now treading the purple with unfaltering steps, is the cricketer with whom people living over thousands and thousands of far-removed square miles, in London, Birmingham, Sydney, Calcutta, Nairobi and Capetown, can most easily identify.

In writing about cricket you have to keep an eye on the game, your own eye on the game that is before you, not on any other. Sometimes it is, it has to be, play and players reconstructed in the imagination. Garfield Sobers as a small boy most certainly played cricket barefooted in the streets with a sour orange for a ball and a piece of box or a coconut branch hacked into an approximation of a bat. All of us in the West Indies did that. I have owned a bat since I was four years of age and I do not remember ever being in a situation where I did not own a pair of shoes. But in the early years of this century there were not many, if any, motor cars about, cork balls were easily lost and could be bought only at the nearest small town; and to this day, far less than thirty years ago when Sobers was a boy, from convenience or necessity, future players at Lord's may be seen playing barefooted with a piece of wood and a sour orange in some village or the back street of a small town in the Caribbean. In the larger islands, once you show unusual capacity, people begin to watch you and talk about you. Sobers stood out easily and people have told me that even as a lad he conferred distinction on his club and people were on the lookout to help in any way he needed. In the West Indies the sea divides us and, in any case, when Sobers at the age of sixteen played for Barbados, I could not possibly see him because I was far away in England. Though as a personality he could mean little to me, I read the accounts, as I always did (and always will if I live in Tierra del Fuego). I couldn't help noting that he was only sixteen years old and that he had taken seven wickets. The scores showed that all were bowled or lbw. Very interesting but no more.

Later, however, I saw what I did not see at the time. In the second innings he bowled 67 overs with 35 maidens for 92 runs and 3 wickets, this when India scored 445 for 9. This was a boy of sixteen, obviously someone that would attract special notice. But in those days Valentine filled the bill for slow left-arm bowling. He took 28 wickets in the series so that one could not take Sobers very seriously as a slow left-arm bowler.

Followed the visit of MCC to the West Indies. Sobers did little for Barbados with the ball, but this youth, it seemed, could bat. His 46 in the first innings was the second highest score and he made 27 in the second. After the third Test, Valentine did not play and Sobers came into the fifth Test, taking four wickets in one innings and scoring 14 and 26 not out. So far, very useful but nothing to strike the eye of anyone far away. He goes into the list of youngest Test players. When he played at Kingston he was only seventeen years and 245 days.

So far there was to the reading eye only promise, but now against the Australians in the West Indies there could be no failure to see that a new man had arrived. Sobers took only six wickets in 93.5 overs. But Valentine in 140 had taken only five. Ramadhin in 139 had taken the same paltry number, Sobers was second in the bowling averages and in batting, in eight innings, had scored 38.50 runs per innings. One began to hear details about his style as a batsman and as a super slip more than as a bowler. In the last Test in Jamaica he made 35 not out and 64. I was informed that from all appearances he would have gone on to the century in a partnership with Walcott which added 79 runs. Sobers was completely master of the bowling but not of himself. Lindwall with a new ball bumped one short at him, Sobers could not resist the hook and found deep square-leg waiting for the catch.

Then came a setback that startled. Sobers went to New Zealand as one of the bright stars of the junior Test players. In four Tests his average was 16 runs and with Valentine doing all that was needed from a left-hander he took only two wickets. In first-class matches his batting average was below 30 and in all first-class matches he took four wickets: far below the boy who had done so well against the full strength of Australia before he was twenty. But for a West Indies team in Port of Spain against E.W. Swanton's team, Sobers had three for 85 and three for 49, and made 71, second only to Weekes with 89. New Zealand was a distant dot on the Sobers landscape.

West Indies came to England in 1957 and obviously Sobers was someone I had to see as soon as possible. I went down to Lord's to see the team at the nets but this was my first glimpse of the three Ws and I don't remember noticing Sobers, except for his fine physique. I missed the Worcester match but found myself at Northampton to see the second game. Curiously enough, as he did often that year, he played second fiddle to Worrell, in a stand of over a century of which his share was only 36. But great batsman was written all over him, and I think it was Ian Peebles who referred to him in terms of Woolley. I remember noting the stroke off the back foot that sent the length ball of the pace bowler past cover's right hand. There was another stroke, behind point off a pitched-up fast ball. The ball was taken on the rise and placed behind point to beat the covers, now packed. Here obviously was that rare phenomenon, in cricket or any other form of artistic endeavour, someone new, who was himself and like no one else. There are vignettes in 1957 that are a permanent part of my cricket library. There was an innings against MCC at Lord's in which Sobers came as near as it was possible for him to look like Constantine in that with monotonous regularity the ball flew from his bat to all parts of the field. In the first Test at Birmingham, he made over 50 in little more than an hour and I remember in particular my being startled at the assured manner in which he glanced—I think it was Bailey—from the middle stump to square-leg and so beat the man at long-leg. The same determination to thumb his fingers at the covers lifted Lock or Laker overhead to drop in front of the pavilion for four; batsmen didn't do these things in 1957.

In the last Test at the Oval West Indies collapsed before Lock and Laker and there came fully to the surface the element of stubbornness which Sobers had shown in the last innings at Kingston in 1953 in his partnership with Walcott, and which I had glimpsed at his batting with Worrell at Northampton. Out of a total of 89 he made 39 and in the second innings out of 86, 42. I believe I saw how famous men of old made runs on impossible wickets. To Laker in particular Sobers played back, always back. When Laker had him playing back often enough, he would drop a ball just outside the off-stump going away from Sobers to cut: there was a long list of West Indian casualties to this particular disease which appeared most often in the records as "Walcott c. Evans b. Laker". Sobers, however, it would appear was waiting for Laker. Time and again he could get across and cut the ball down past third man.

In a review of the season Skelding, former county fast bowler and now umpire, was reported in one of the annuals as saying that the Sobers he saw in 1957 would be one of the greatest batsmen who ever lived. I could not go quite so far but I have it down in writing of 1958 that if Sobers developed as he promised in 1957, he would be the greatest of living batsmen. So that the 365 which exceeded Hutton's 364 and the tremendous scoring which followed filled out a portrait whose outlines had been firmly drawn. No need to go through 1963. I saw and felt what I expected to see and feel. However, there was one piece of play in the field which I have seen mentioned only in *Wisden* and not commented upon elsewhere. That was his bowling in the Oval Test. The famous feat of fast bowling in 1963 was Wesley Hall at Lord's in the second innings when his figures read 40 overs, 9 maidens, 4 wickets for 93 runs. He bowled during the three hours and twenty minutes which play was in progress on the last day. I believe that on that last day he bowled 35 overs.

Now in the Oval Test Sobers bowled in the first innings 21 overs, 4 maidens, for 2 wickets, 44 runs. I remember these two wickets. He had Bolus caught by keeper Murray (33) and Edrich, caught Murray, for 25. Hall and Griffith had tried in vain to break that partnership and Sobers, struggling mightily, dismissed both of them well set. In the second innings he did even better; again he dismissed Bolus at 15, again well set, and Dexter when at 27 he seemed poised for one of his great innings. Sobers bowled 33 overs and took 3 wickets for 77 runs. At the time and to this day I measure that performance and Sobers as a fast bowler by his approximation at the Oval to Hall's far more famous feat in the Test at Lords.

There is one episode on the field which for some reason or other sticks in my mind as representative of Sobers. He came out to bat at the Oval against Surrey early in 1963. He came to the wicket and some Surrey bowler bowled him a short ball. It went to the square-leg boundary. A dead metaphor can sometimes be made to live again: that ball went like a flash. As far as I remember the same over saw another ball, short, but this time outside the off stump and rising higher than usual. That ball streaked to the off boundary. Sobers had not scored any runs in the south and everybody including myself believed that here was the beginning of one of the great innings. It was not to be. Two or three balls later he was out to the almost audible lamentation of the crowd which had been keyed up to a pitch in the belief that we were going to see what we had come forth to see.

Sobers today is a captain and I believe it would be worth-while to give some hint of what I have been able to detect of the personality behind that play. I do not know Sobers as well as I knew Constantine, George John and Headley and the men I have played with. But there are certain things that one can divine. I saw Sobers in 1957 make 27 at Leeds and then get run out not through anybody's fault but by some superb fielding by Tony Lock. Finer batting it is impossible to imagine and that day nothing was more certain than a century before lunch in a Test. But this is not why I remember that day. What remains in my mind is the fury, the rage of Sobers at having been dismissed when he obviously felt that history was in his hands for the making. His walk back to the pavilion made me think of those hurricanes that periodically sweep the Caribbean. I caught a glimpse, by transference so to speak, of the aggressive drive which expresses itself in his batting and fast bowling. I have already referred to the demonic hits with which he greeted Hall's attempt to bowl him out in a practice game. In the Test which followed that practice game Sobers drove too early at a wide half-volley and was caught for 0. Again on his way back to the pavilion I saw the gleam of the damped-down furnace that raced inside of him. Therefore when I read his detailed protests against what he considers the unfairness of British reporters and commentators in their diatribes against his team of 1966 in general and Griffith in particular, I take it much more seriously than most. The protest is not a formality, or something that ought to be put on record, parliamentary fashion. He feels it personally, as a man feels a wound. I suspect that that is the personality which expresses itself as ubiquitously as it does on the field because it needs room. A man of genius is what he is, he cannot be something else and remain a man of genius.

I think of Sobers walking down the pavilion steps at Lord's, captain of an international cricket team. Sixty years ago it would have been Pelham Warner, another West Indian, and thirty years before that it would have been Lord Harris, yet another cricketer of Caribbean connotation. Whoever and whatever we are, we are cricketers. Garfield Sobers I see not as a fortuitous combination of atoms which by chance have coalesced into a superb public performer. He being what he is (and I being what I am), for me his command of the rising ball in the drive, his close fielding and his hurling himself into his fast bowling are a living embodiment of centuries of a tortured history.

1969

28

Black Studies and the Contemporary Student

I have to make certain things clear from the beginning. I do not recognize any distinctive nature of black studies—not today, 1969. However, the history of the United States being what it has been and what it still is, there is a serious struggle going on between the advocates of one lot of black studies and advocates of another lot. And, therefore, I am compelled for the time being to take sides; but for myself, I do not believe that there is any such thing as Black Studies. There are studies in which black people and black history, so long neglected, can now get some of the attention that they deserve. But when you look at what is taking place under the guise of black studies in the United States today, you realize what a fundamental position ought to be. . . .

I have my own views. But I want to take what is going on because we cannot come with views and say, "Oh, look at this," and wave a flag, with other people talking about other things and people talking about them seriously. There is one serious person—they have down here in *The New York Times Magazine* as W. Arthur Lewis. He is a very able man. He used to be Principal of the University of the West Indies and when the West Indian Federation broke up, Lewis left. He is now at Princeton and he has been knighted by the Queen for his services to scholarship. Now he has written that "The Road to the Top is Through Higher Education—Not Black Studies" *(New York Times Magazine*, 11 May 1969, pp. 344 ff.). I want to go into some detail about Arthur Lewis, who is a very distinguished black scholar.

He says that there is no clear line and that a great deal of error is also inevitable; and then he goes on to say:

> America is really not a melting pot but a welding shop. It is country in which many different groups of people live and work together side by side, without coalescing. There are Poles, and Irish, and Chinese, and Jews, and Germans, and many other ethnic groups.

Now Lewis is an extremely able man with a lot of experience and yet he says there are Poles, Irish, Chinese, Jews, Germans, and many other ethnic groups—so he takes black people and he puts them among those. How a man can do that, with all honesty, I can't understand.

> But their way of living together is set by the clock; there is integration between 7 o'clock in the morning and 5 o'clock at night, where all mingle and work together in the center of the city, in the banks and factories, department stores and universities.

Now how long have all been working together and mingling in the banks, department stores and universities?

> But, after 5 o'clock each ethnic group returns to its own neighborhood. There it has its own separate social life. There Poles do not marry Italians, even though they are both white Catholics . . . But in the meantime this voluntary self-segregation shelters those who are not yet ready to lose themselves completely in the American mainstream.

So you see, that's what is happening to the Negro. He lives by himself voluntarily because he is not ready to lose himself completely in the American mainstream.

> An American neighborhood is not a ghetto. A ghetto is an area where members of an ethnic group are forced by law to live, and from which it is a criminal offense to emerge without the license of the oppressing power. That is what apartheid means in the Union of South Africa. An American neighborhood is not a place where members of an ethnic group are required by law to live. . . .

So these people are living in the ghetto because they like it, or they're getting ready to plunge into the diversity of American life. They're sheltering there, but when they get stronger, they will go.

I know this man. He says that you have apartheid in South Africa, but not here. He says that at this minute Negroes have 11 per cent of the population. Our minimum objective must be to capture 11 per cent of the jobs in the middle and 11 per cent of the jobs at the top. That must be the aim and objective of black people in the United States—to get 11 per cent of the jobs in the middle and 11 per cent of jobs at the top, corresponding to the 11 per cent of the population. Rising from the bottom to the middle or the top in the face of stiff white competition, prejudice and so on takes everything that a man can give to it. And those are the people who should be praised. The road to the top in the great American corporations and other institutions is how? Through higher education. That's all we have to do to get to the top. Through higher education: scientists, research workers, engineers, accountants, lawyers, financial administrators, presidential advisors; all these are people recruited from the university. So if we want to be able to get to the top and get our 11 per cent, we have to take advantage of the education that is offered to us. That is all that is wrong up till now. We haven't chosen the type of education which will get us to the top. And there are some people who are bitter enemies of the Negroes. "The trade unions are the black man's greatest enemy in the United States." And our greatest task in terms of numbers is to conquer the middle, through better use of apprenticeships, of the high schools and of technical colleges.

> What can the good white college do for its black students that Howard or Lincoln or Fisk cannot do? It can open the road into the top jobs. It can do this only by giving our people the kinds of skills and the kind of polish which are looked for by people filling top jobs.

They should go to the college where they can scrub a black man to make him white. That would be one skill that would be needed, if he could find a college to do that.

> Any Afro-American who wishes to become a specialist in black studies should be absolutely free to do so. But I hope that the . . . proportion who want to specialize in black studies may . . . turn out to be rather small, in comparison with our scientists, or engineers, accountants, economists or doctors. Another attitude which puzzles me is that which requires black students in the white college to mix only with each other, to have a dormitory to themselves; to eat at separate tables in the refectory, and so on. . . . These colleges are the gateway to leadership positions in the integrated part of the economy, and that what they can best do for young blacks is to prepare them to capture our 11 per cent share of the best jobs at the top—one of every nine ambassadorships, one of every nine vice-presidencies of General Motors, one of every nine senior directors of engineering laboratories, and so on.

So the black people will have to go to schools and learn that and not bother with black studies, and they will get these positions. How does he think somebody is going to get some black man to become one of the nine vice-presidents of General Motors? It was the devil himself to get into the trade unions. And he actually says one out of every nine vice-presidents of General Motors.

An Attorney General once said that in fifty years a black man could become President of the United States. Well, he meant well—that's all that we can say. But, we can say that in twenty-five years, one might become a vice president of General Motors, and he will become a vice president of GM, not because of passing examinations, but by the number of people who attack the offices of GM. They take one in and they say, "You be a vice president. Now the rest of you go home. You see you can get on." I have known Lewis for many, many years, and that he has descended to this is completely beyond me because Lewis knows better than this. He has written this for a purpose.

> How is one to be ambassador to Finland or Luxembourg—jobs which American Negroes have already held with distinction—if one is uncomfortable in white company?

Please, I am not responsible, I am only reading it. I see in your face great distaste for it. Mine is equally great. He is a countryman of mine, so what is to be done? Nevertheless. So that is why we are not trained: that is why we do not have one job out of every nine ambassadorships.

> No doubt a few Negroes, born with the special talents which success in a highly competitive

business world demands, will succeed in establishing sizeable and highly competitive concerns.

But they wouldn't.

President Nixon says he is for black power in the black neighborhoods and he is for black capitalism. Yes, he will have some people who will make cloth—some small manufacturing. But steel, modern industry, engineering, the big ships and the rest—no black people are going to have companies that deal with those. And do you think that Lewis doesn't know that?

> Neither is black America going to be saved by a Marxist revolution. Revolution takes power from one set of persons and gives it to another, but it does not change the hierarchical structure of the economy. Any kind of America that you can visualize, whether capitalist, Communist, Fascist, or any other kind of ist is going to consist of large institutions like GM under one name or another.

He is teaching political economy at Princeton.

> Any kind of America that you can visualize, whether capitalist, Communist, Fascist, or any other kind of ist is going to consist of large institutions like GM under one name or another. It will have people at the top, people in the middle and people at the bottom. Its leading engineers, doctors, scientists and administrators . . .

will be essentially the same. So the problem of the Negro is whether he is going to be mostly in the bottom job or whether he will also get his 11 per cent share at the top and in the middle, in a socialist or communist or fascist United States.

This is very mischievous indeed. I intend before this weekend is over to deal with what I have found out after having lived in the United States in a very crucial area for some weeks—that numbers of Negroes, important people, who are not committed to American bourgeois society, are extremely doubtful in the back of their minds whether a socialist society can fundamentally change the position of black people in American society. And, in my opinion, they have a lot of justification for thinking so. Because the people who say they are socialists, I don't wish to be rude, but SDS (Students for a Democratic Society) and all these people—what they put forward is nothing at all. A black man is entitled to say, "Well, what is that?" They tell me that SDS means, as far they see, to make a better America. Some faults and mistakes—they want to correct those; but to change fundamentally the social structure, they don't see that, and that's why they say what Lewis is saying here. Whatever changes there are, black people are going to be down at the bottom or have to fight to get to the top. And Lewis is encouraging them by saying that whatever kind of society it is, whatever revolution takes place, it will consist of people at the top, in the middle, at the bottom, and the Negro will be at the bottom unless he goes to the schools and gets his best opportunity to go forward. This appears in *The New York Times*. I will inflict you no more with it. That is the kind of black studies that some of the schools are putting forward. They are saying, "Well, you want to study black studies; what you really need to do is to get the kind of education which will fit you for your 11 percent of the top jobs and your 11 per cent of the middle jobs, too."

Now, opposed to that is what is taking place at Federal City College. They have a view of black studies which is not mine. But I would be glad to go back there, and I would join the black studies' faculty and do what they say. It is not for me to live in the Caribbean, to live in London for a number of years and to come here and to tell some black people what they should do for black studies. If in private they ask me, I will give them my opinion. But what they want to do, they will do. I will not interfere with that. Because they have ideas, they have experiences, they have lived from childhood, their parents and their grandparents have told them things, and they have a certain conception of the black man in this society. A man like Rap Brown says things that I can't imagine my saying. But if anybody wants to criticize him, especially people in England, I tell them, "You shut up and leave him alone. What he says and what risks he chooses to run, that is his business, comes from his past and his experience of the people around him."

But these people I am talking about have put forward an idea of black studies, and this is what they say in a document (I have told them, and I don't think they would object to my telling you, I didn't see why they had to say this): "Black education must take these forces into consideration and seek to make these forces a reality." This is what they submit to the authorities that see after Federal City College. And they have to submit this to Congress to get the money. And this is what they say: "These forces are revolution and nation-building." And I say, "Now how do you expect the head of the college to accept a program which says that it aims at revolution and nation-building and then take this document and go to Congress and say, 'Give us the money'?" But, anyway, these forces are revolution and nation-building. "Education which does not seek to achieve these goals is irrelevant to black people. Although these forces fuse, they have separate characteristics. Revolution must give definition to the nation. Revolution is the process of struggle toward the objective—nation. Revolution must give definition to the nation. Revolution must call for an act to end white supremacy, colonialism and oppression embodied in Western ideas and individuals which affects and infects the existence of black people. The process of nationhood must conceptualize and structure the conceptions and possibilities of future black existence. The nation must be defined in terms of human and material and historical cultural resources of the people. The Black Education program has as its purpose the sustenance and revitalization of the black values which include undying love for black people." I said to them, "I meant to say, between us, you can't expect the head of the college to accept this, and then to Congress and say, 'give me the money for black studies'."

I was wrong. They got together at a meeting at which there were the Board of Education and the man in charge, nine or ten of them. Two thousand people came to the meeting to hear. They began to ask the Board questions. And ultimately the two thousand of them got up and walked out. Two thousand of them saying what they're going to have; so that when I told some of them that they were a little bit rash in stating it, they were more right than I was.

What is happening is this. The Board said, "No! We can't have this. We don't like your course. We are not going to allow you to hire any more people and we will go into this thing with you when we are ready." But, after this meeting of 2,000 people, and the determination of most of those who were doing Black Studies not to capitulate, the Board started to give way. It said, "You cannot hire anybody." Now it says, "You can hire whom you like." It said, "We don't like the course. But go ahead for the time being." But the Board is told, "No, we are going to leave." It says, "you were to get one-half million dollars and we promise you $700,000." And it is told, "No. We don't want it." And it says, "Well, what is it you want?" And it is told, "We don't want to be under your authority at all." And the Board says, "Well—where will you go?" And it's told, "We are going to the community." So that is the situation at Federal City College. They are deadly serious about this program. And they are going to refuse to stay in Federal City College unless they fail to get the support of the students. I have told them, "If you go away with a program that a majority of the students do not accept, you will discredit the whole business." But they are prepared to fight Congress with its $700,000, and its right to hire and fire, and they say, "We are not concerned about that. We want to go." And they have told the Board of Education, "We want to go." So, when I told them that I couldn't imagine how they could have written a document like this and given it to the Board, they were quite right and they knew what they were about. So the situation now is quite uncertain. What is to be done?

The Black Studies program as now presented is autonomous to the point of being a separate college. At Federal City College the office of the Provost says, "Yes, that is exactly what we want." The goal of the program is clearly outside the role of a public university: to provide centers of indoctrination for true believers, whether that belief is black nationalism, or Catholicism, or Nazism. That is what the authorities have said and that is exactly what we want to do—to teach people that black studies is something that concerns black people and the future of black people. I couldn't say that. That is to say, I didn't know how to say that. I could say, "overthrow the bourgeois society and so on." But to tell some people, and they offer you the money to run it, and to say, "We don't care, we don't want the money, we'll go to the community," that is really something! So that is the situation. That is what is going on.

Now, as I say, that is not exactly my view of black studies. And I have to go into certain questions; first of all I have to tell you what is still my view, a view that I arrived at with my various socialist friends—Glaberman and others were among them—and I put it forward at a meeting in 1948:

> We need a careful systematic building up of historical, economic, political, literary ideas, knowledge and information, on the Negro question inside the party. Because it is only where you have Bolshevik ideas, Marxist ideas, Marxist knowledge, Marxist history, Marxist perspectives, that you are certain to drive out bourgeois ideas, bourgeois history, bourgeois perspectives which are powerful on the question of the races in the United States.

That is what I said in 1948; I still believe it. I don't say so at all times—I don't go about Federal City College and say this and that Marxism, but sitting on this platform, that is what I have said. . . .

Now I am going to speak on some of the ideas. First of all, I think I may have said this before; it doesn't matter. There are certain things, and I have to repeat them. I follow Mr Lévi-Strauss. I am not a mad follower of human anthropology but I like certain ideas that he has of history. And he says: from the time the Neolithic man began to cultivate the soil, to domesticate animals, to make pottery and to live in a house with his wife and family, or his wives and families, he says civilization of a certain type began and to this day it has not changed. He says the cultivation of the soil, the domestication of animals, the making of pottery and the living in a house with his family, he says they began then, and nothing has changed. Some people challenge him but I know what he means.

However, he says that there is one period in history which offers some serious change from what began ten thousand years ago, the period known as the Industrial Revolution. He says that when man began to use power in industry, it creates a change in the development of human history and society which had not taken place in the previous nine thousand years of human existence.

Now it didn't change only human life, human nature; it changed human society. I have said before, and I want you to understand, that it is no use talking about black studies unless you make it perfectly clear that the wealth which enabled the bourgeoisie to challenge those who were in charge of society and institute the power-building industrial regime came from slavery, the slave trade, and the industries which were based upon that. Now if you agree that the first serious change in the fundamental features of human society came with the Industrial Revolution, if you agree—because at times Lévi-Strauss writes as if to say nothing has changed really, people act to this day no better—if you agree that the wealth which went toward the building up of the bourgeoisie so that they could challenge the ancient regime came from the slave trade and slavery, then I wonder if you realize that to be doing black studies is to be able to get that into your head and then teach that to all the people who listen to you: that the vast change in human society came from the slave trade and slavery. All the historians tell you that. Marx also. His *Poverty of Philosophy* has the section on slavery. It was slavery that built up the bourgeois society and enabled it to make what Lévi-Strauss thinks is the only fundamental change in ten thousand years of human history. The blacks not only provided the wealth in the struggle which began between the old society and the new bourgeois society: the black people were foremost in the struggle itself.

This struggle had two great examples. The first was the French revolution; the second was the American Civil War. And, in both of those, not only did the wealth that enabled them to move to a new type of society come from slavery, but the slaves were in the very forefront of the battle. Now tonight I'm going to use a kind of proof that isn't often done. The French slaves, when they became free, formed an army and they fought and defeated some fifty thousand Spaniards, about sixty thousand Englishmen who tried to take over the colony and another sixty or seventy thousand Frenchmen. They defeated them in battle. Lemmonier-Delafosse wrote some memoirs forty years after, and I quoted in *The Black Jacobins* what he said about these soldiers fighting in the Civil War. I will give you the two passages and you will see how peculiarly alike they are. This is Lemmonier-Delafosse: "But what men these blacks are! How they fight and they die!" I am not boasting about black is beautiful. Please, I don't go in for that. If other people want to, that's their affair, if they say "Black is beautiful", "Black is ugly", black is whatever they like. I am concerned with historical facts.

> . . . but what men these blacks are! How they fight and how they die! One has to make war against them to know their reckless courage in braving danger when they can no longer have recourse to stratagem. I have seen a solid column, torn by grapeshot from four pieces of cannon, advance without making a retrograde step. The more they fell, the greater seemed to be the courage of the rest. . . . Three times these brave men, arms in hand, advanced without firing a shot and each time repulsed, only retired after leaving the ground strewed with three-quarters of their troop. One must have seen this bravery to have any conception of it. French courage alone could resist it: Indeed large ditches, an excellent artillery, perfect soldiers gave us a great advantage—But for many a day that massed square which marched singing to its death lighted by a magnificent sun, remained in my thoughts, and even today after more than forty years, this majestic and glorious spectacle still lives as vividly in my imagination as in the moments when I saw it. *(The Black Jacobins*, pp. 368-9)

Good. Now here is a description of black soldiers—also former slaves—in the Civil War by W.E.B. Dubois:

> The deeds of heroism performed by these colored men were such as the proudest white men might emulate. Their colors are torn to pieces by shot, and literally bespattered by blood and brains. The color sergeant of the 1st Louisiana, on being mortally wounded, hugged the colors to his breast, when a struggle ensued between the two color-corporals on each side of him, as to who should have the honor of bearing the sacred standard, and during this generous contention, one was seriously wounded. One black lieutenant actually mounted the enemy's works three or four times, and in one charge the assaulting party came within 50 paces of them. Indeed, if only ordinarily supported by artillery and reserve, no one can convince us that they would not have opened up a passage through the enemy's works. *(Black Reconstruction*, New York, 1935, pp. 107-8)

It is practically the same thing that Lemmonier-Delafosse is stating about the ex-slaves in the French revolution. This is what happened in the Civil War. And, that is not because their skins are black, or any special bravery of blacks. It is that men who are fighting for freedom and to whom freedom is a reality fight much better.

This is what I want you to bear in mind. Number one: The wealth that enabled society to make the big transition was rooted in the slave trade, slavery, and the industries that came from it. And, secondly, in the struggle by which the bourgeois established the political and social structure of this new form in the very front line, fighting as well as anybody else and better than most, in France in the French revolutionary war, and in the American Civil War, were the ex-slaves.

Now to talk to me about black studies as if it's something that concerned black people is an utter denial. This is the history of Western Civilization. I can't see it otherwise. This is the history that black people and white people and all serious students of modern history and the history of the world have to know. To say it's some kind of ethnic problem is a lot of nonsense.

Now I am going to switch over to some modern problems and some modern individuals. I can't stay to deal with French literature from 1820 to the present day, 1969, nearly 150 years of history. It is impossible to write the history of French literature without stage after stage noting the tremendous roles that West Indians in particular have played during that whole period. You cannot write the history of French literature without having to deal with some ten black men from the Caribbean. I am going to choose one—Victor Hugo—because Hugo was not a man of the Caribbean, he was a white man. But he was the man of whom André Gide said, when they asked him who was the greatest poet of France, "*Malheureusement* (Unfortunately), Victor Hugo." Victor Hugo used to write a lot of liberal, revolutionary stuff and they didn't like it but he was a fine poet. And Victor Hugo was the dominant figure in French literature from 1820 after Napoleon right up to about 1880. When Dumas died, Hugo said that one of the greatest men of the Romantic movement was Alexandre Dumas. This is what he wrote, and I translate:

> No popularity in this century has surpassed that of Alexandre Dumas. His successes were more than successes; they were triumphs. They have the éclat of a fanfare of trumpets. The name of Alexandre Dumas is more than French; it is European; it is universal.

And so forth and so forth. That is one of the greatest figures in French literature.

I am in London and I see some of the students and I ask one of them, "What are you doing?" He says, "I am doing a study of T.S. Eliot." I say, "Fine." I ask another West Indian student, "What are you doing?" He says, "I am working for my Ph.D." I say, "What are you doing?" He says, "I am studying D.H. Lawrence." I say, "Very nice." The most fantastic of them all is another fellow who tells me he is doing Joseph Conrad. Conrad is a Pole who wrote in the English language and wrote very well indeed. But why should these West Indian students be doing D.H. Lawrence, Joseph Conrad, and T.S. Eliot when a man like Alexandre Dumas, the father, is there? One of the most remarkable figures of the nineteenth century. He didn't only write Romantic novels. I suppose you know some of the novels, *The Count of Monte Cristo*, *Louise de la Vallière*, *The Three Musketeers*, *Twenty Years After*, *Chico the Jester*. Now I want to tell you what those novels did. After the French revolution, Europe and the rest of the world broke out into what was known as the Romantic period which meant a tremendous expansion of the individual personality of the ordinary man. Previous to the French revolution, men lived according to a certain discipline, a certain order. The French revolution broke that and people began to live more individual, more experimental, more Romantic lives—Personality. Among the forces which contributed to that were the Romantic poets and novelists of the day. And not one of them stands higher in the popular field, in the expectation and understanding of the people of those days, than Alexandre Dumas. He was translated into every language. *The Count of Monte Cristo* and *The Three Musketeers* and the collected novels are European and universal novels. What I am saying is, not only did the black people contribute, not only did they fight in the ranks, but forging the kind of lives which people lived afterwards, one of the foremost men is a man from the

Caribbean. How do I make that into black studies? I can't. No! I can understand some university saying, "We are going to study the lives and works of black men who have not been done before." That I understand, but to make it black studies! And I have asked, "Allow me to come into your black studies program." I am ready to go, but I can't do it in those terms at all.

Now, I want to take one or two other individuals. I want to take some men whom I knew personally. I'll do that at once before I go back to some other men. I want to take Paul Robeson and Richard Wright. Those are two men whom I knew quite well. I knew Richard Wright very well indeed. I may have mentioned this to some of you. Dick fancied himself as a cook. He would cook rice and chicken or something in some Southern way and say, "Come over, I'm going to cook today." I used to eat it. But he was a remarkable man. One day I went to the country to spend a weekend with him. He had gone to the country to spend the summer. I came into the house and he showed me twenty-five books on a shelf. He said, "Look here, Nello, you see those books there? They are by Kierkegaard." I said, "Yes, he's very popular these days." He says, "I am not concerned about his popularity. I want to tell you something. Everything that he writes in those books, I knew before I had them." I never spoke to him about it after. I knew what he meant to tell me.

Kierkegaard is one of the great writers of today. He is one of the men who, during the last twenty or thirty years, modern civilization has recognized as a man whose writings express the modern temperament and the modern personality. And Dick assured me that he was reading Kierkegaard because everything he read in Kierkegaard he had known before. What he was telling me was that he was a black man in the United States and that gave him an insight into what today is the universal opinion and attitude of the modern personality. I believe that is a matter that is not only black studies, but is white studies too. I believe that that is some form of study which is open to any university: Federal City College, Harvard, etc. It is not an ethnic matter. I knew Wright well enough to know that he meant it. I didn't ask him much because I thought he meant me to understand something. And I understood it. I didn't have to ask him about that. What there was in Dick's life, what there was in the experience of a black man in the United States in the 1930s that made him understand everything that Kierkegaard had written before he had read it and the things that made Kierkegaard the famous writer that he is today? That is something that I believe has to be studied.

There is Paul Robeson. I knew Paul very well. He was a remarkable person. He wasn't only a singer and an actor, that was something else, but a personality. And you get some idea of the personality that he was because he took his profession, his fame, his money and everything and he committed it completely to the Communist Party. That ruined him. But he wasn't alone, there were many who were ruined by it. What I want you to know is the complete commitment to the idea that something that was organized in Moscow and that came from Moscow was the only thing that could change the lives of black people in the United States. That is worth examination, you know. To know his life, what led him to that, what he turned away from—and he didn't sway, go to and come: he joined up and he went all the way. I had a lot of fun with Paul. I always used to laugh at it. He was going to Moscow. I was going away from Moscow. But I like him very much. He acted in my play, *Toussaint L'Ouverture*. And I think he liked me too. We used to meet: "Hello, Paul." "Hello, James." "How are you?" "Are you living in the United States, too, and I haven't seen you?" "Look, I am going over to San Francisco but when I come back I will get in touch with you and I will look forward to it." And he knew I wasn't going to do it, and I knew he wasn't going to do it, but we expressed some good feelings for the time being. There was too much between us politically, but, apart from that, a very fine person. And I believe that an examination should be made of what it was that drew Paul to the Communist Party and made him the man he was, break completely with his past, throw everything into the dustbin with the idea that there was only Communism that could save his black people in the United States from being what they were and where they were.

But you can't sit down and make it up as Harold Cruse has done, you know. Cruse finds that the problem of Negroes in the Communist Party was due to Jews. The man does not understand that the Communists have a line that in Switzerland, in Albania, in India, in China, in Moscow, in London, in Paris, has nothing to do with Jews. That is the Stalinist line. And, therefore, you have to begin to explain what the Stalinists do in regard to the Negroes in the United States by means of the line. But to say it's the Jews, well, I mean! No, there was more to it and I believe we will get a good understanding of what happened to an educated black man in the United States in the '30s, a man of great natural gifts—he didn't inherit money, a man of international fame, a man with worldwide contacts, a man loved and respected all over the world, that he would give it all up and commit himself to Moscow and the policies of Moscow. I believe that is worth examination. That will tell us much about black men in the United States; it will tell us much about the mental attitude of people in the States; it will tell us much about the mental attitude of people in the '30s. It will tell us much about the impact white civilization made upon a very distinguished, splendid man. That I believe is worth examining, more than T.S. Eliot and D.H. Lawrence, much as I like both of them.

And now I have three more to do. I prefer to deal with them at the last because they are historical figures. They are three men of the nineteenth century, Wendell Phillips, Frederick Douglass and Abraham Lincoln. Now Wendell Phillips is one of the most remarkable men of the nineteenth century. He was a man who received a first-class education. He was a lawyer. He inherited a lot of money, but Phillips committed himself to the abolition of Negro slavery in the United States and for thirty or forty years was completely devoted to that. And the personality that he developed cannot be seen except from the connection of the highest classical education that the United States could give. He was a New England Brahmin; he inherited a lot of money; he was trained as a lawyer; he had a fine education at Harvard—and he committed himself completely to the abolition of Negro slavery. That I believe is something that has to be studied. I read some biographies of Phillips—they are not aware of the kind of change that must have made in this man, this educated man, this man with all the wealth and all the prestige and power, intellectual power, of a New England Brahmin who gave it up and turned away and went and fought in the struggle for the abolition of slavery. By the way, he was a great revolutionary. I don't want to go into that but he's a man who has to be studied. I believe—I may be wrong, Professor Rawick here will tell me if I'm wrong—I believe that it is in a black university or a university by black people who are committed to the black struggle that Phillips helped start and which they have continued that they can really read his life and work out what really was decisive. I believe that. I don't think that the Harvard professor, or the Columbia professor or Lewis at Princeton would be able to do that. No, I think at Federal City College they would be able to do that in time. (They can't do that now; they don't do enough—and not at Howard either. I hear that Howard is a very peculiar kind of an institution.) But an institution that is concerned with the development of black studies can handle a man like Wendell Phillips. I think so. That is what I intend to say at any rate. That is what I intend to say at the Socialist Scholars Conference and that, for me, is black studies. And Phillips was no black.

Another man who I believe is an important man of black studies is Frederick Douglass. I believe that there was a greater orator in the English language in the United States at the same time. That was Abraham Lincoln, because during Lincoln's greatest speeches, especially during the Presidency, he outlined and explored areas not then reached by philosophers, politicians and other persons of the kind. Frederick Douglass didn't do that. There is nothing in Douglass like the Second Inaugural or the Gettysburg Speech by Lincoln. But, beyond that, within the limits of a man agitating and making propaganda, I do not know a finer handler of the English language than Frederick Douglass. He was a man of exceptional qualities of mind, and he learned to read by begging little white boys in the street to teach him. Some of those speeches, to this day, I read them and I know nothing superior to them in the nineteenth century. Nothing. There is Abraham Lincoln, there is Demosthenes, there is Edmund Burke—they are in a category above. Edmund Burke on the American Independence. But just below, among the men who agitated and propagandized for a particular cause and did all that could be done within that cause, nobody stands higher than Frederick Douglass, nobody. And that is a matter for black studies and white studies too.

He was foremost among the propagandists for the abolition of slavery. And he was recognized as such, not only in America but in England. I remember, in particular, a statement by Mr Higginson, an army commander and New England Brahmin. Douglass, it seems, was a man over six feet, an extremely handsome man, a man who carried himself with great dignity and ease. Higginson, a New England Brahmin who had fought in the Civil War, said that he had walked down the road with a man whom one did not often meet, and have the opportunity to meet in public, that he had enjoyed it because it was an opportunity that he hadn't had before and didn't know when he would have again. This opportunity consisted in walking down the road with Frederick Douglass. I have repeatedly met that sort of thing in people who heard of Douglass and saw him. I think it is worth examining him properly. Foner has written four volumes of his speeches and so on, but Frederick Douglass, the particular man, who wrote in the middle of the nineteenth century—I haven't seen him stated anywhere. I believe a great deal can be got from a serious study of Frederick Douglass.

Before I touch Abraham Lincoln, President of the United States and a very interesting character, I want to say something else. Jaspers, the German philosopher, and Heidegger both agree: they say that there are many philosophers who go and write and get their doctorate on Plato, Aristotle, Kant, Leibniz and such like, but they say that these fellows are merely writing books out of books, that unless a man is taking part in the philosophical struggles of the times in which he lives it is impossible for him to understand what Kant and Aristotle and Plato and these were doing, because when they were busy doing philosophy it was a part of them. And I know that unless you are busy actively taking part in politics, you read the history of these revolutions but you don't understand. So the people who are today taking part in the struggle, in the kind of struggle that Frederick Douglass and Wendell Phillips took part in, they will be able to write about them and they can understand. But the professor sitting down in his office and giving out his lectures two or three times a week and not involved in this kind of struggle, he cannot understand them. I know that from personal experience and I am sure that when Jaspers and Heidegger say that, they know what they're talking about. They say that all these people writing about philosophy—they don't know what they're saying. Because for them philosophy is something that they write from books; they read Kant and they read Plato and Aristotle and they write about it. They say that is nothing. And I know that can be applied to politics. And it is people in the midst of a struggle today who can write about Frederick Douglass and Wendell Phillips and really illuminate them. And that is not black studies. That is study of society.

Now, the last man I want to speak about is Abraham Lincoln. I'm getting into a lot of trouble at Federal City College over what I am saying about Lincoln. But they don't bother me. They like to say that Lincoln fought the Civil War to keep the country united, and he said that if he could keep the country united and keep the blacks as slaves, he would do that too. Yes, he said so, undoubtedly. But I want to end this talk about black studies by telling you something that I have discovered about Abraham Lincoln.

Now Abraham Lincoln some time when he was a young man, some thirty-odd years old, wrote a letter to a friend of his saying that he was on board a boat going down South and he saw on board some ten or twelve black slaves who were being sold to the South. One of them had been sold because he was too much concerned about his wife and he was not doing his work properly so they separated him from her and were sending him down South. In those days it meant that you were being sent to murder, prison, sickness, death of all kinds. What Lincoln noted was that these fellows were singing and dancing and behaving in a way that he could not understand—how people in that situation could behave in the way that they were behaving. He wrote this letter to his friend telling him exactly what he thought.

Now some time afterwards Lincoln was speaking to some young men somewhere in Michigan or Missouri and he told them what it meant in his mind to be an American citizen. Lincoln said that he and his generation knew the men and the children of the men who had fought in the American War of Independence. He said they were magnificent men. He said they had made a great historical experience and that had transformed their quality so that they were exceptional people. Lincoln implied that there were no such people in other parts of the world because none of them had that great experience. Then he went on to say, what about those people who have come from foreign countries and come to the United

States, the Germans in particular? He said the Declaration of Independence and what it states and the experience of living alongside those people who were descendants of those who had fought in the War of Independence—that was making the Germans into citizens worthy of being members of the great American Republic. You see, what he's saying is that to be an American citizen and part of the American democracy demands an exceptional type of person. He wasn't speaking about color. And when Lincoln was arguing with Stephen Douglas and he said he didn't think that blacks were the equal of white people, that is what he had in mind. He was saying the American citizen was a special kind of person who had a special kind of experience and the blacks—he didn't think they were up to it. It's difficult for me to get angry about that today. I understand his position because I understand his conception of what it was to be a citizen of the great American Republic. He had made that perfectly clear. To be that, you had to be descendants of those who had fought in the War of Independence and you had to be a part of that, and the Germans who came had to live with them and study the Declaration of Independence. They could become incorporated. But he said he didn't think the slaves could be.

Then the situation developed where Lincoln had to give black people a part in the war. Lincoln wrote another letter in which he said that the time will come when we shall see, we shall be celebrating, the preservation of the Republic and there will be black men who, with rifle in hand and clenched teeth, helped to save it while there will be white men who had fought against the democratic Republic. He changed his mind when he saw the black people fighting in the war; he felt that they, just as the people who had fought in the War of Independence, were now proving that they were perfectly able to be citizens of the Republic in the tradition which had been established by the men who had fought in the War of Independence. And that is the reason for that famous sentence in Lincoln's Second Inaugural Address:

> Fondly do we hope—fervently do we pray—that this mighty scourge of war may speedily pass away. Yet, if God wills that it continue, until all the wealth piled by the bondman's two hundred and fifty years of unrequited toil shall be sunk, and until every drop of blood drawn with the lash shall be paid by another drawn with the sword, as was said three thousand years ago, so still it must be said "the judgments of the Lord are true and righteous altogether".

Lincoln was not making a speech, he wasn't writing an article, he wasn't seeking votes. He was the President of the United States elected for a new term and he was making it clear that he was going to settle his business; and if I understand politics all right, he wasn't talking so to the South—he was telling people around him: Now I am going to settle it. And government of the people, by the people, for the people means, if it means anything, government of the people, including the black people; by the people, including black people; for the people, including the people, including the black people; because four score and seven years ago without the black people it was OK. He understood that something important had been established. So the Gettysburg Address and the Second Inaugural contain his new conception of what black people were and their fitness to become citizens of the famous Republic and his readiness to do all that he could to see that that was done. That's why, in my opinion, they shot him. There were some who knew that he meant what he said, that he had enormous power and prestige, and he was making a declaration. He wrote a letter to somebody who wrote him and said, "I congratulate you on your Second Inaugural," and Lincoln said, "Yes, I think it's one of the best things that I've ever done, but a lot of people are not too sympathetic to it. But time will tell."

Frederick Douglass says that he was in Washington when Lincoln said that he trembled at what he saw around him. I believe that is an important part of black studies. I cannot think of black studies in any other way. I will end by telling you two things. Before the election in 1864 (I haven't told them this at Federal City College. I have a certain amount discretion, you know. Not too much, but a certain amount), before Lincoln took part in the election of '64, Lincoln suspected that he was going to lose. Lincoln called Douglass and told him, "I want you to go down to the South; I want you to get twenty-five men who can go into the South among the blacks. I will give you the money and we will raise the black slaves in revolt." The main idea of that is very unpleasant to certain people. He was prepared to send people down to raise the slaves in revolt because he says, "I'm going to lose the election and if I lose it, nobody is going to carry it through." But as he won the election, he made clear what his policy was going to be. And I believe that he would have managed it. He would have managed something. I will go so far as to say if anything could have been done, Lincoln could have done it. Nobody else could. That's why he was shot.

So, my friends, that's where I stand in regard to black studies. I do not know, as a Marxist, black studies as such. I only know the struggle of people against tyranny and oppression in a certain social and political setting, and, particularly, during the last two hundred years, it's impossible to me to separate black studies from white studies in any theoretical point of view. Nevertheless, there are certain things about black studies that need to be studied today. They have been ignored; we are beginning to see a certain concern about them. I believe also that certain of these studies are best done by black people, not by professors as such, but by the same people who are engaged in the struggle in which those people were engaged then. That will make them better understand them and illustrate them. And that is how I see black studies at the Socialist Scholars Conference, although I am ready to submit myself to the black studies department at Federal City College and do what they have to do. Life presents you with some strange difficulties and, at times, you have to run with the hare and hunt with the hounds.

1969

29

Picasso and Jackson Pollock

When I was in Washington some months ago, a friend of mine took me to see some pictures by Jackson Pollock. They interested me. I bought some books and spent a long time over them. I have now come to the conclusion that the paintings of Picasso dominated the first half of the twentieth century and that the painter of the second half is Mr Jackson Pollock.

Now this must sound very strange because I am an amateur when it comes to painting, but I have spent some hours on this business and I believe that I have discovered the connection between Picasso and Pollock. Pollock, as you know, worshipped Picasso; and there was a relationship between Picasso's painting and himself that lasted fifteen years.

It is necessary to bear in mind the kind of mentality which we bring to a work of art. There are two fundamental elements that meet. First there is the work of art itself. Secondly there is the mind that you bring to it. I am going to spend some time on the mind that one brings to the work of art, in this case Picasso's *Guernica* and secondly, the work of Jackson Pollock. The range I bring to these works is not comprehensive, but rather wide.

I begin with the great artist in literature. I begin with the European writers, yes, writers—starting with Dante, who avoids living in the Inferno by going up to heaven and meeting Beatrice there, sitting next to God, Jesus, the Virgin Mary, etc.; then on to Shakespeare. A few years ago a critic from the totalitarian states reinforced the general view that in *King Lear*, Shakespeare expressed his total disillusionment with society. *That is not true*. In *Lear*, Shakespeare introduces the character Edgar who before the play is ended has appeared in six different roles; that is to say he has represented all the different stages in society. That is not accidental.

In one of his disguises, his blinded father asks Edgar:

> Now, good sir, what are you?

And Edgar replies:

A most poor man, made tame by fortune's blows;
Who, by the art of known and feeling sorrows,
Am pregnant to good pity. Give me your hand
I'll lead you to some biding.[1]

Shakespeare, at any rate, has reached the very depth of disillusionment with society and only a man who has been tempered with hard experiences in every sphere of society is fit to rule. Edgar will rule.

The next great writer I move to is Pushkin, who as a creative artist and man of letters has no superior in European literature. Pushkin's last and greatest poem is *The Bronze Horseman.* Here Pushkin places in conflict, certainly in direct opposition, the founder of the city of St. Petersburg, Peter the Great and all the appurtenances of a great capital on the one hand; and on the other, an ordinary member of the city, a man without any status whatsoever, who in the course of the poem has to fly from Peter. But, before he flies, he shakes his fist at the statue and utters words of defiance.

I shall not go any further, but I merely mention Tolstoy and Dostoyevsky at the head of the greatest national literature of the twentieth century. I think that it is sufficient to show what has been the tendency of the great writers in literature.

Now to go to the artists themselves. I begin, of course, with the Renaissance, Leonardo Da Vinci and Michelangelo. The lady with the smile has distorted the public appreciation of Leonardo. The ordinary public is not aware that in the last years of his life, Leonardo painted a world being overcome by storms, floods and hurricanes. My regret is that the equestrian statue that he had prepared was destroyed. I think that we would have seen something there of Leonardo, similar to, or rather going further than, the sketches that he made for the Town Hall in Florence.

It is easier with Michelangelo. It might seem that his last word as a painter was stated in *The Last Judgement*, the death of a civilisation. But that is not so. Michelangelo in the two frescoes that he did in the Capella Poalina took great pains to show that *The Last Judgement* was not his last word. In *The Conversion of St. Paul*, in the top right hand corner, there is a man and a woman and a boy absolutely cut away from the rest of the painting. One wonders what they are doing there. But they appear again in *The Crucifixion of St. Peter*. The end of that painting from the viewer's point of view is what appears to be a line of ordinary people on the right led by what is quite rightly believed to be a portrait of Michelangelo himself. These people have nothing at all to do with the rest of the painting. There something is taking place of great importance.

This line of citizens is passing along and they do not know what is happening—so it would appear at first glance. But when you look again, you see the pair at the top right of *The Conversion*, at the top right of *The Crucifixion*. Of all those in that line, the man knows what is happening and he is explaining it to the woman. To his left is a youth full of fire and rebellion; and behind them is an old man who has obviously seen the battle for many years and is quite undisturbed. He is absolutely different from the man who is leading this procession.

I think it is fairly obvious that, like Shakespeare in *King Lear*, Michelangelo was saying that in young people with some experience there was the possibility of re-building a world in which truth and justice would emerge over the destruction or punishment of the evil and of the innocents.

Now to the painters of our time. The Impressionists rejected all that the Renaissance had discovered and which had been developed. *They went back to nature*. Nature, they thought, would give them all that was required, but nature didn't. In the end came Cézanne, who wanted to combine the Impressionist return to nature with the artistic discoveries of the great painters. From Cézanne came Cubism. Picasso and Braque come from Cézanne and African art.

I don't intend to spend any time here on African art and its influence on French painting because, waiting for us there, is a morass of debate and confusion. Picasso's high peak is *Guernica*. In preparation for *Guernica* and for many years before, Picasso had been unable to make up his mind.

The decisive question for our investigation is that Picasso could not make up his mind about the human personality. When I say could not make up his mind, I mean as a painter. Like all the great artists (and that is why I have dealt with them), Picasso was aware of the antagonistic forces in human nature. For the time being, he obviously came to the conclusion that a man as such could not express, in paint or sculpture, the true nature of a human being. He therefore began to paint the Minotaur; and up to the time that he prepared to paint *Guernica* he could not come to any decision as to whether the Minotaur was an evil character or a good one.

Picasso's difficulty can best be understood by a celebrated passage in Karl Marx's *Capital*, where Marx tackled the same problem with great confidence:

> Along with the constantly diminishing number of magnates of capital, who usurp and monopolise all advantages of this process of transformation, grows the mass of misery, oppression, slavery, degradation, exploitation; but with this too grows the revolt of the working class, a class always increasing in numbers and disciplined, united, organised by the very mechanism of the process of capitalist production itself.[2]

Marx could be as confident and untroubled as he was by those violent antagonisms in the same unit because he had been tracing each of them separately and in unity for many hundreds of pages. But to put them both into one character on the canvas, that was a problem that troubled Picasso for years.

His Minotaur was at one time the personification of evil; at another time, the embodiment of kindness and even tenderness. That was the situation when the destruction of the town of Guernica faced Picasso with the necessity of painting a picture of historical symbolism—as he himself has stated for the first and only time in his painting career. He began his sketches for *Guernica* on May 1st. But on April 19th it seemed that he had come to some sort of conclusion about his general problem. In Barr's *Picasso: Fifty Years of His Art*, Barr reproduces on page 198 a reproduction of a painting entitled *Negro Sculpture Before A Window*. There Picasso seems to have come to a conclusion about the Minotaur. The face, and it is only a face, is that of a human being of strongly marked features, but with the horns presumably of a bull. In the face there are hints of enormous power, but if there is evil, it is firmly controlled by the strongly disciplined features.[3]

On May 1st, Picasso began his preliminary sketches for *Guernica*. In the very first one, from the right, he has the extended arm with the lamp in his hand. Small and faint at first he does another one on the same day where that extended arm with the lamp in his hand is most clearly and powerfully drawn. There on May 1st, at the very beginning of his preparations for *Guernica*, Picasso has placed himself in what will turn out out be an insoluble difficulty. He has isolated wisdom, nobility, elevated character in the Greek face and extended arm. This means that the unified antagonism which has troubled him for many years is now definitively split. He has isolated one aspect of it and he has to get the other in somehow.

Here I have to give some analysis of *Guernica*. I have never had any difficulty whatever with this picture. I have to say this because in his book on Picasso (1975), Mr Hilton, in a work obviously aimed at putting Picasso in his place (not the place which the world had given him), says of *Guernica* (page 246)"Nobody knows what is going on in it . . ." He soon adds, "there is no possible reading for the bull, the dominant figure, because it is always possible that the bull might stand for something else." To the statement that nobody knows what is going on in it, I have not to make any answer here. Hundreds of thousands, if not millions, of people know. But when he says there is no possible reading for the bull etc., that is a double blunder—of common sense and of criticism.

Guernica is to be looked at from the right and the whole picture moves visually from right to left. You did not have to be a great painter to realise as Picasso realised that the bull could no longer be moved from the right to the left as it had done in all the preliminary sketches. To make a picture at all, some figure had to be placed in opposition to this movement from right to left. So Picasso turned the bull around and made the picture into an acceptable structure.

So far, so good. But what could he do with the bull? In the preliminary drawings he had, as usual, wavered between the evil of Minotaur and the Greek aspect of high civilisation. The uncertainty which had characterised his work on the Minotaur for the last five years tormented him in his preparation for *Guernica*. What he finally did was this: he made the bull into a fighter against the decay that the picture represented. That is expressed in the aggression, in fact, the battle signal, of the tail. He went still further and emphasised that procreation could not be defeated. That is in the testicles of the bull. But what to do with the head and the face of the bull? The antagonism to a society in irreversibly decay is in the very place of the bull in the structure of the painting. The woman with the child makes it clear that the only hope of a continuing humanity is in the bull. But what to do with the face of the bull? Picasso chooses the easiest and the obvious way out. He does nothing in particular with it. He ignores all the preliminary drawing and basically he goes back to the structure that he had worked out in the drawing of April 19th. He increases the militancy of April 19th. He introduces uncertainty in the nostrils and in the thumb. He makes the bull a part of the total uncertainty that is in all the heads in the painting. But more than that he does not do. In opposition to the decay of society, he places sexuality (pro-creation), militancy and high civilisation; but he cannot join them. They remain separate in the bull, on the one hand; and the extended arm holding the lamp on the other.

It is this with which Pollock lived, as his wife tells us, for fifteen years. By this time he had absorbed all that Picasso had to tell him.

We come to the great paintings of the period 1947. In *The Enchanted Wood* we see what Pollock is going to do. *The Enchanted Wood* is a combination of the immense diversity of the world and scattered all over it are the beginnings and development of human personality in the human face. That is what is going to be for some years Pollock's central activity. The world is not a chaos. He goes on, the diversity becomes more and more structured and organised, not according to previous organisations, but independently according to the designs which have emerged or are implied in the drippings. But Pollock does not remain with originality of design and types of the human face which seem to emerge without system from his intricate linear structures.

In paintings, *One* (1950) and *Autumn Rhythm*, there is clearly discernible walking fee from the knee down including the foot. What this means, I am not prepared to speculate upon. But in these two paintings in particular there is the intricacy of design, the emergence of human faces and there is unmistakably the sense of feet walking along. I must say that I am astonished that in the critiques that I have read, there is insistence on the absence of representation and no statement whatever on these walking feet that are so fundamental a part of the structure of these paintings. In painting *Seven* of 1950, there is not only the foot from the knee, but from the top right hand of the painting there is an indication of a back continued to the waist right down to the toes. In the painting *Lucifer*, there is a human being standing, legs, chest, arms and face.

In all great artists, as Max Raphael has said, there is an excess. I indicate the following. There is a *Self-Portrait* in 1933, then there is a *Head* in 1938. I personally cannot think of these separately, but the *Head* of 1938 cannot be eliminated from *Ocean Greyness* in 1953.

But the final debt to Picasso is to be found in two paintings of 1951 and 1952. In *Number 10* of 1951, Pollock has returned to linear representation. I find it impossible to separate *Number 10* of 1951 from the head of the bull in Guernica. It is equally impossible to separate the famous drawings of a woman's face which followed Guernica from *Number 10* of 1951. Having exhausted, or at least completed what he was doing from 1947 to 1950, Pollock then went back. To me it is, to say the least, instructive not only about Pollock, but about art on the whole that he went back to tackle in his own way the problems that Picasso was tackling in 1937 and 1938.

What conclusion can one draw from all this? Dangerous as such conclusions really are I shall not run away from mine. In the bull of *Guernica*, Picasso, having already established the civilisation represented by Greece, could find only procreation and struggle as the future of human society. A great painter starting from there found his way to the infinite diversity and basic, though hitherto unrepresented order in the world. But he insisted that from this structural diversity there emerged the human face (not high civilisation as in *Guernica*); and more than mere sexuality and struggle. He found the beginnings of humanity in that men, or rather human beings, walked.

There I have to stop. I have to because I can go no further. I have seen the Pollock's at the Museum of Modern Art and I must say that when I left the room where they are and passed *Guernica*, a painting which I have admired and seen any number of times, *Guernica* looked dull to me in comparison with the blazing impact that the Pollock paintings had just made.

1980

30

Three Black Women Writers: Toni Morrison, Alice Walker, Ntozake Shange

I have chosen three books to discuss: *Sula* by Toni Morrison; *Meridian* by Alice Walker; and *Nappy Edges* by Ntozake Shange. These books are by three Black women, though I haven't chosen them because they are Black women, but because they are very fine Black writers. They are first-class writers. *Meridian* and *Nappy Edges* I would place in the very front rank of books being published in the United States today. There is another reason, also, that I was particularly interested in these: they represent a social movement in the United States.

Women all over the world seem to have realised that they have been exploited by men. Marx pointed out many years ago that women were more exploited than the proletariat. (This is a remarkable thing for him to have said.) Now women are beginning to say: "Who and what are we? We don't know. Hitherto we have always tried to fit ourselves into what men and what masculine society required. Now we are going to break through that." These three women have begun to write about Black women's daily lives. Black women in America for hundreds of years have been scrubbing, sweeping, cleaning, picking up behind people; they have been held in the background; kept for sex. And now Toni Morrison, Alice Walker and Ntozake Shange have taken these Black women and put them right in the front of American literature. They can't be ignored any more. So it seems that in the women's movement, as usual in the United States, Black people took part; and they have taken a part in it which, as I hope to show you, is important not only to Blacks, but to society as a whole.

I'm going to talk about these books one by one. I'm not going to read from them too much; except for the poetry, because poetry must be read. Then I will talk about writing, because that is what you are concerned with; and because it is an important part of the Black struggle today.

I will begin with *Sula* by Toni Morrison. *Sula* is the story of Black women; this in itself is an unusual topic for an American writer, so far as I know. The story begins with a description of the Bottom, a black slum of the southern town Medallion; and with the story of a World War I soldier who is released from an army hospital while still having problems with hallucinations, is arrested for his peculiar behaviour, and is finally sent home to the Bottom, which he had not seen since going into the army. He seems to be crazy, and doesn't know what has happened to him. He establishes an annual holiday in the Bottom called National Suicide Day: on this day every year people can let out their anger and their violence acceptably. He lives alone, and generally celebrates the holiday alone. He supports himself by catching fish twice a week and selling them. This is how the book begins. It begins this way to register that the people in it, and the work they do, and the life they lead, are not normal. But this is the life of the vast majority in the South; from 1971, when the book was published, until this very day.

We are introduced to two girls; Sula and Nell. They are very good friends. The level of their lives is very low, and they go through much together. There is something harmonious between them. They are not separated even by the accidental death of a small boy who drowns while playing with them; even by the bizarre incinerations of two of the people Sula lives with. They grow up around and in spite of the daily poverty and tragedy. Nell gets married to a man named Jude. Sula sees that he is a handsome, hard-working, well-meaning young man. She helps with the wedding and reception, and then leaves town.

Ten years pass between the wedding and the beginning of the next chapter; 1927-37. Nell is still with Jude; they are living well, and have two or three children. Sula returns well-dressed, sophisticated, and college-educated. She and Nell seek to rediscover that friendship which they had before, but Sula is unable to accommodate herself to the old society. One day Nell comes home to find Sula and Jude together in the bedroom, and Jude leaves her that day. Sula does not particularly want Jude; she begins sleeping with men in the town and is further distanced from the other townspeople. She becomes, at one point, really attached to a man; but it is, of course, at that point that he leaves her.

Sula and Nell see each other only once more in their lives. In 1940 Sula becomes seriously ill and Nell visits to offer help. She finally asks, "Why did you do it? . . . We were friends. . . . And you didn't love me enough to leave him alone. To let him love me. You had to take him away."

To which Sula replies, "What do you mean take him away? I didn't kill him, I just fucked him. If we were such good friends, how come you couldn't get over it?" As Nell is leaving, she asks her, "How do you know . . . who was good? . . . I mean maybe it wasn't you. Maybe it was me."

After Nell leaves, Sula dies. At the end of the book, at Sula's grave, Nell comes to a significant and painful realisation: that it is not Jude but Sula that she has missed so much in the years since they all parted.

This is a fantastic book. Now, I want to quote a particularly significant passage, from the chapter just following Sula's return:

> It had surprised her a little and saddened her a good deal when Nell behaved the way the others would have. Nell was one of the reasons she had drifted back to Medallion, that and the boredom she found in Nashville, Detroit, New Orleans, New York, Philadelphia, Macon and San Diego. All those cities held the same people, working the same mouths, sweating the same sweat. The men who took her to one or another of those places had merged into one large personality: the same language of love, the same entertainments of

love, the same cooling of love. Whenever she introduced her private thoughts into their rubbings or goings, they hooded their eyes. They taught her nothing but love tricks, shared nothing but worry, gave nothing but money. She had been looking all along for a friend, and it took her a while to discover that a lover was not a comrade and could never be—for a woman. And that no one would ever be that version of herself which she sought to reach out and touch with an ungloved hand. There was only her own mood and whim, and if that was all there was, she decided to turn the naked hand toward it, discover it and let others become as intimate with their own selves as she was. (pp. 104–5)

Now, this Black woman has gone to all of these most important towns and places of social life in the United States, found them no good, and has gone back to Medallion. That is a very bold thing to write about. She tells us why Sula returns—because everywhere she goes the men and the problems and emptiness with them are always the same. The important thing about that is that it could, and would, be said by women on every level of society in the world today, from the highest to the lowest. This woman could not find a man who would treat her as another human being, and she got tired of it and went back to her home town. So on the one hand, the friendship between women, that is so often ignored, is really of great importance; and on the other hand, no matter how hard she tries, she just learns that friendship with a man is impossible.

Toni Morrison is saying that in this society, with the lives they lead, this is what happens to men and women; this becomes characteristic of the love relationship. I find it astonishing and revealing that Toni Morrison should insist that this tremendous insight come from a poor Black woman, on the lowest level of American society. She is also saying that the real fundamental human difference is not between white and Black, it is between man and woman.

Now we come to *Meridian* by Alice Walker, whom I have found to be one of the finest writers in the United States. Near the beginning of the book, Meridian is told by a group of her friends that she can only join the movement if she makes up her mind that she can kill for the Revolution. Meridian is not so sure about this; she is willing to die, but not to kill. It goes against her upbringing and her heart. She goes off on her own to work and live with the people in the South. The story goes on and Meridian becomes very involved with a Black man named Truman, who eventually becomes involved with a white woman named Lynne. The personal, sexual and racial interrelations of these three people, and the context of the civil rights movement, are treated very well indeed. They have a lot of difficulties. Again we have a picture of the significance of friendship between women:

As they sat they watched a television program. One of those Southern epics about the relationship of the Southern white man to madness, and the closeness of the Southern black man to the land. It did not delve into the women's problems, black or white. They sat, companionable and still in their bathrobes, watching the green fields of the South and the indestructible (their word) faces of black people much more than they watched the madness. For them, the madness was like a puzzle they had temporarily solved (Meridian would sometimes, in the afternoon, read poems to Lynne by Margaret Walker, and Lynne, in return, would attempt to cornrow Meridian's patchy short hair), they hungered after more intricate and enduring patterns. Sometimes they talked intimately, like sisters, and when they did not they allowed the television to fill the silences. (p. 173)

This is tremendous. These two women have quarrelled over a Black man; he has gone with both of them, and generally made a mess of things; but they have become friends. This is beautifully expressed. This is a serious and difficult topic; not many books deal with the relationship of a Black man and a white woman, or even with two women getting together and understanding one another. This is an astonishing thing, but it is not the most astonishing thing in the book by far.

I'm going to deal now with another part of the book which makes it one of the most extraordinary books I have ever read. A young man has been killed; a Black church is having a service for him, to help the father and so on. Meridian is there, and as she follows the service, and hears the people singing, suddenly, after all her troubles, Meridian comes to this conclusion:

There was a reason for the ceremony she had witnessed in the church. And, as she pursued this reason in her thoughts, it came to her. The people in the church were saying to the red-eyed man that his son had not died for nothing, and that if his son should come again they would protect his life with their own. "Look," they were saying, "we are slow to awaken to the notion that we are only as other women and men, and even slower to move in anger, but we are gathering ourselves to fight for and protect what your son fought for on behalf of us. If you will let us weave your story and your son's life and death into what we already know—into the songs, the sermons, the 'brother and sister'—we will soon be so angry we cannot help but move. Understand this," they were saying, "the church" (and Meridian knew they did not mean simply "church" as in Baptist, Methodist or whatnot, but rather communal spirit, togetherness, righteous convergence), "the music, the form of worship that has always sustained us, the kind of ritual you share with us, these are the ways to transformation that we know. We want to take this with us as far as we can."

In comprehending this, there was in Meridian's chest a breaking as if a tight string binding her lungs had given way, allowing her to breathe freely. For she understood, finally, that the respect she owed her life was to continue against whatever obstacles, to live it, and not to give up any particle of it without a fight to the death, preferably not her own. And that this existence extended beyond herself to those around her because, in fact, the years in America had created them One Life. She had stopped, considering this, in the middle of the road. Under a large tree beside the road, crowded now with the cars returning from church, she made a promise to the red-eyed man herself: that yes, indeed she *would* kill, before she allowed anyone to murder his son again.

. . . Meridian's dedication to her promise did not remain constant. Sometimes she lost it altogether. Then she thought: I have been allowed to see how the new capacity to do anything, including kill, for our freedom—beyond sporadic acts of violence—is to emerge, and flower, but I am not yet at the point of being able to kill anyone myself, nor—except for the false urgings that come to me in periods of grief and rage—will I ever be. . . .

. . . But at other times her dedication to her promise came back strongly. . . . On those occasions such was her rage that she actually felt as if the rich and racist of the world should stand in fear of her, because she—though apparently weak and penniless, a little crazy and without power—was yet of resolute and relatively fearless character, which, sufficient in its calm acceptance of its own purpose, could bring the mightiest country to its knees. (pp. 199-201)

In other words, these people hadn't to be trained or taught Marxism; these Black people in this Southern church had built up a sense of community, and of right and wrong, so strong that if the need came, they would join any revolutionary movement that meant to kill those who were oppressing them. This is a major problem, this feeling that there are certain people who are revolutionaries but the great mass of the population is not, is filled with God and Christ. Alice Walker shows instead that they, in their church, with what they have learned there, with the togetherness they have, with the songs they have sung, and the beliefs they have, would be ready to join anything to overthrow the mightiest nation on earth; to overthrow the United States. Whether you agree or not, it is a tremendous notion and a successful book.

I lived in the United States for twenty-five years, and I had no idea that this kind of community could be built in the Southern Black churches; but, of course, this was the source of Dr King's power. It would not be the same in the West Indies. The Black church does not have the same role to play, because the Bishop of Trinidad is a Black man, his son is a member of the revolutionary trade-union movement; the result is that Blacks do not feel that terrific separation and persecution that has driven those Blacks to form those churches in the South. The Black church also could not have the same revolutionary significance in Britain.

The friendship between women; the impossibility of women getting on with men, as long as men see them chiefly as sexual instruments; the church; the lowest levels of Black life in America: these Black women are arriving at conclusions that are filling the minds of the most advanced and hard thinking people today.

There is a poem called "Advice" by Ntozake Shange, and it's from her book, *Nappy Edges*. It begins:

people keep tellin me to put my feet on the ground
i get mad & scream/there is no ground
only shit pieces from dog horse & men who dont live
anywhere/they tell me think straight & make myself
somethin/i shout & sigh/i am a poet/i write poems/
i make words/cartwheel & somersault down pages
outta my mouth come visions distilled like bootleg
whiskey/i am like a radio but i am a channel of my own
i keep sayin i do this/& people keep askin what am i gonna do/
what in the hell is going on?
. . .

people keep tellin me these are hard times/what are you gonna be
doin ten years from now/what in the hell do you think/i
am gonna be writin poems/i will have poems/inchin up the
walls of the Lincoln tunnel/i am gonna feed my children poems on
rye bread with horseradish/i am gonna send my mailman off

with a poem for his wagon/give my doctor a poem for his heart/
i am a poet/i am not a part-time poet/i am not an amateur
poet/. . .

She says, "I am a poet, and I'm going to be a poet." It can't be better stated, and she says it for you and me and other people; a person who is not educated can well understand what she writes. She is a very serious and a very funny woman. She can also be very mad. "With No Immediate Cause", I think, is her finest poem:

every 3 minutes a woman is beaten
every five minutes a woman is raped/
every ten minutes
a lil girl is molested
yet i rode the subway today
i sat next to an old man who
may have beaten his old wife
3 minutes ago or 3 days/30 years ago . . .

She is telling me things that I had no idea of. I read these things in the paper and I pass on, but she says: "It happened to me. That man over there who served me coffee, he might have done it."

. . . i took the coffee
& spit it up/i found an
announcement/not the woman's
bloated body in the river/floating
not the child bleeding in the
59th street corridor/not the baby
broken on the floor/
"there is some concern
that alleged battered women
might start to murder their
husbands & lovers with no
immediate cause"
i spit up i vomit i am screaming
we all have immediate cause
every 3 minutes
every 5 minutes
every 10 minutes
every day
women's bodies are found
in alleys & bedrooms/at the top of the stairs
before i ride the subway/buy a paper/drink
coffee/i must know/
have you hurt a woman today
thrown a child across a room

are the lil girl's panties
in yer pocket
did you hurt a woman today
i have to ask these obscene questions
the authorities require me to
establish
immediate cause
every three minutes
every five minutes
every ten minutes
every day

She makes it personal. She doesn't speak about "it" in general, like a politician; she says, "It happened not to the public in general, but to me, and that's what I think about it." Only first-class poets write this way.

Now I want to say a few words to the writers. You must be able to write what you think—and maybe what you write about your day-to-day, everyday, commonplace, ordinary life will be some of the same problems that the people of the world are fighting out. You must be able to write what you have to say, and know that that is what matters; and I hope you can see that you can begin anywhere and end up as far as anybody else has reached. I hope you are not scared to write about what concerns you, what you know—these things matter.

Write what you have to say, and think about it. Read as much as you can, don't limit yourself. Gather knowledge. Copy down a phrase that strikes you or a passage that matters. But when you get down to write something, concentrate on it. That is my advice. Concentrate on it and read it over. And if it takes you two weeks, you have to settle down and get it right. That is the way to write poetry. But the point is, to express your knowledge, concentrate on special writing.

1981

Notes

Introduction C.L.R. James: A Revolutionary Vision for the Twentieth Century

1 Reviewers at the time, while noting Robeson's contribution to the play, found *Toussaint L'Ouverture* rather stilted. Some thirty years later, the playwright Arnold Wesker wrote to James about the revised version of his play, now called *The Black Jacobins*: "Your canvas is enormous and I was fascinated to read the way you handled it. . . . But there is a spark which is missing from the whole work. Forgive me, but there does seem to be something wooden about the play. The construction is dramatic; the dialogue carries the story and the dialectic of what you want to say, but when all the component parts are put together, it doesn't work." (Wesker to James, 16 May 1968).

2 Letter to Constance Webb, 4 February 1944.

3 See *Discussions with Trotsky* (1939), reprinted in *At the Rendezvous of Victory* (Allison and Busby, 1984).

4 Notes for an autobiography, see under section VII. in *The C.L.R. James Archive: A Reader's Guide* by Anna Grimshaw (C.L.R. James Institute, New York 1991).

5 Ibid.

6 Johnson was James's pseudonym; Forest, the pseudonym of Dunayevskaya.

7 Letter to Constance Webb, 1945.

8 For a detailed analysis of this work and the circumstances of its writing, see *C.L.R. James and The Struggle for Happiness* by Anna Grimshaw and Keith Hart (C.L.R. James Institute, New York 1991).

9 *Mariners, Renegades and Castaways*, p.76, Allison and Busby, London 1985.

10 The intensity of this personal struggle was revealed in James's letters to Constance Webb in the late 1940s.

11 The fusion of the particular and the universal, the real and the symbolic, the actual and the potential. See my *Popular Democracy and the Creative Imagination: The Writings of C.L.R. James 1950-1963* (C.L.R. James

Institute, New York 1991)

12 James explored the connections between great works of art through an analysis of character. He was particularly interested in those characters which were continuations of a certain general type, e.g. the rebel or the intellectual, and yet revealed the specificities of a particular historical moment. Thus he understood Prometheus, Lear and Ahab, in situating their rebellion against the prevailing order *outside* society, to be part of a single tradition. But each of these original characters also revealed something new and specific about the age from which they emerged.

13 *Mariners, Renegades and Castaways*, p.77, Allison and Busby, London 1985. This was a theory which James borrowed from Melville's *The Confidence Man*.

14 Letter from James to Frank Kermode, September 1982 (my emphases), see under section III. in *The C.L.R. James Archive: A Reader's Guide*.

15 To Whom It May Concern, 20 September 1955. See under section II. in *The C.L.R. James Archive: A Reader's Guide*.

Chapter 4 The Case for West Indian Self-Government

1 Lord Olivier: Secretary of the Royal W.I. Commission of 1899, Governor of Jamaica (1907-13); Chief Commissioner W.I. Sugar Commission, 1930.

2 Italics my own.

3 Served in many colonies, including the Windward Islands; at one time Governor of British Guiana.

4 Many of the West Indian islands are cosmopolitan, and East Indians form about twelve per cent of the total population, though concentrated in Trinidad. But there is no need to give them special treatment, for economically and educationally they are superior to the corresponding class in India, and get on admirably with the Negroes.

5 Alas! It did not save him. He has been omitted from the new nominations.

Chapter 7 Stalin and Socialism

1 No finer volume on the realities of English politics and history exists than his occasional articles collected in the volume *Lenin on Britain*.

2 See the early chapters of *Stalin* by Souvarine.

3 Zinoviev and Kamenev have exposed it all. What was not so clear in 1927, when Trotsky was expelled from the Soviet Union, is clear today when one by one Stalin has destroyed every member of the old Central Committee.

4 As far back as December 1923, Trotsky had pointed out the immense political dangers lurking behind party bureaucracy. See *The New International*, January, 1935.

5 This and other relevant documents are given in full in appendices to Eastman's *Since Lenin Died*. See also *Le Cours Nouveau*, by L. Trotsky, Paris, 1925.

6 *Since Lenin Died*. Fully documented with the important references easily verifiable in a file of *Pravda*.

7 Seven Years in Soviet Russia, p. 143.
8 *Since Lenin Died.*
9 *The American Nation*, May 2, 1934.
10 *I Write As I Please*, 1935, p. 218.
11 I Write As I Please, by Walter Duranty.
12 *Leninism* by Joseph Stalin, vol 1.
13 Ibid.
14 Ibid.
15 *Leninism* by Stalin.
16 *Stalin.*
17 Marxism badly needs a careful study of this period. Trotsky's account of it in his autobiography suffers from an over-emphasis on the economic and social forces at work. Lenin's Testament, one of the key documents to the understanding of historical materialism holds a perfect balance. He states early in it that there are two classes in Russia between whom harmony must be maintained or the Soviet regime would collapse. It is against this solid background that he then considers the personal characteristics of the Central Committee. Selecting Trotsky and Stalin as the dominating personalities, he asks for the removal of Stalin. It seems that he thought, with Stalin out of the way, the Central Committee would regroup itself around Trotsky and, with a larger membership, be linked closer to party and masses. What he seemed most afraid of was an even split, behind the two halves of which a conflict might develop which would imperil the whole State. It is doubtful if he ever dreamt of the possibility that within six months Trotsky would be practically isolated in the Central Committee. On p. 414 of his autobiography Trotsky tells us what he said to Kamenev about this time. "I am against removing Stalin, and expelling Ordzhonikidze, and displacing Dzerzhinsky from the commissariat of transport. But," he goes on to say, "I do agree with Lenin in substance." The contradiction between word and deed was fatal. Still more revealing are his words on Stalin to Kamenev, "Let him not overreach himself." That is Trotsky's own confession, and if that is the way he approached this initial struggle he had lost before he had begun. We today can see that clearly. But it is of profound importance to understand that whereas Lenin, sensitive to the role of strong personalities in the flux and reflux of social forces, realised the danger of Stalin and the necessity of his removal, Trotsky, with all his gifts, did not, even after Lenin had urgently pointed it out to him.

Chapter 8 Letters to Constance Webb

1 James often spent time in Northport, Long Island, at the summer home of Freddie and Lyman Paine. The Paines were members of the Johnson Forest Tendency and close friends of James.
2 James was referring to his lengthy review of Harold Laski's *Faith, Reason and Civilization.* It was published in the June 1944 issue of *The New International.*

Chapter 9 Dialectical Materialism and the Fate of Humanity

1 Dialectic as a mode of thought had its origin among the Greek philosophers. In fact, the more one penetrates into dialectics, the more one is astonished at the colossal impudence and ignorance which passes for exposure of it. Lenin was very conscious of its historic significance. As he wrote in 1915: "The division of the one and the cognition of its contradictory parts (see the quotation from Philo on Heraclitus at the beginning of Part III, 'Knowledge', in Lassalle's book on Heraclitus) is the *essence* (one of the 'essentials', one of the principal, if not the principal, characteristics or features) of dialectics. This is precisely how Hegel also puts the matter (Aristotle in his *Metaphysics* continually grapples with it and combats Heraclitus and Heraclitan ideas)." But although Hegel learnt more about dialectic from Aristotle than from any other single philosopher, he himself accepts Christianity as the starting-point of our civilisation.

Chapter 11 The Class Struggle

1 A similar process in Germany led straight to Hitler.
2 This was the order issued in the attempt to get the completely disorganized railroad system to function. The railroads were placed under almost military rule, subordinating the ordinary trade union democracy to "Chief Political Departments" which were established in the railway and water transport workers' unions. As soon as the critical situation had been solved, the transport workers demanded the abolition of the "Chief Political Departments" and the immediate restoration of full trade union democracy.
3 *Subbotniks* were the workers who on their own initiative volunteered to work five hours' overtime on Saturdays without pay in order to help the economy of the workers' state. From the word Subbota, meaning Saturday.

Chapter 14 Notes on *Hamlet*

1 Referring to the players who had been performing before the court.

Chapter 15 Popular Art and the Cultural Tradition

1 T.S.Eliot, "Burnt Norton" from *The Four Quartets.*
2 This is not true of his other better known works.
3 What would happen to them there is another matter.

Chapter 19 From Toussaint L'Ouverture to Fidel Castro

1 Baudelaire and Rimbaud, Rilke and D.H.Lawrence. JeanPaul Sartre has done the finest of critical appreciations of *Cahier* as poetry, but his explanation of what he conceives Négritude to mean is a disaster.
2 None will dare to say so publicly. He or she would be driven out of the territory.

3 Study Conference of Economic Development in Underdeveloped Countries, August 5-15, 1957. University of the West Indies, Jamaica.
4 *Season of Adventure*, by George Lamming.
5 *Palace of the Peacock*, *The Far Journey of Oudin*, *The Whole Armour*, *The Secret Ladder*. London: Faber & Faber.

Chapter 20 'What is Art?'

1 If I do Mr Berenson any injustice it can be corrected in the reprint of his story, third edition, 1954, and his *Des Arts Visuels* (Esthetique et Histoire), Paris, 1953, where the original thesis is restated. (I am not being pedantic. In these metaphysical matters you can misplace a comma and be thereby liable to ten thousand words of aesthetic damnation.)
2 Mr Berenson's aesthetics do not by any means exhaust the subject. Mr Adrian Stokes, for example, on Michelangelo, is suggestive of much that is stimulating to any enquiry into the less obvious origins of a game like cricket. Further I find it strange that (as far as I know) so ardent an apostle of mass culture and non-representational art as Sir Herbert Read has never probed into the question of whether the physical modes so beloved by Michelangelo and the physical movements of popular sports and games so beloved by the millions do not appeal to the "collective unconscious" more powerfully than the esoteric forms of, for example, Mr Henry Moore. The difficulty here, it seems to me, is not merely the habit of categorizing into higher and lower. The aesthetics of cricket demand first that you master the game, and, preferably, have played it, if not well, at least in good company. And that is not the easy acquisition outsiders think it to be.

Chapter 22 Lenin and the Problem

1 *World Revolution: the Rise and Fall of the Communist International, 1917-1936*, London 1937.
2 *Selected Works*, Vol. VII, pp. 351-78.
3 *Selected Works*, Vol. VIII, pp. 165-76.
4 *Selected Works*, Vol. IX, p. 406.
5 "Under the conditions prevailing in Russia at present, freedom and rights for the cooperative societies mean freedom and rights for capitalism. It would be stupid and criminal to close our eyes to this obvious truth."

Chapter 29 Picasso and Jackson Pollock

1 *King Lear*, Act IV, Scene VI.
2 *Capital*, volume 1, chapter 32.
3 I shall say no more of this drawing of April 19th because of the fact that I never see any reference to it.

Notes on the Chapters

PART I TRINIDAD 1901-1932

1. *La Divina Pastora* (1927). This was one of the first pieces of fiction which James had published before he left the Caribbean in 1932. It originally appeared in the *Saturday Review*; and was later included in E.J. O'Brien's collection, *Best Short Stories* (London 1928).

2. *Triumph* (1929). During the 1920s James was part of a circle of Caribbean writers (including Mendes, Gomes and de Boissiere) responsible for the foundation of two literary journals, *Trinidad* and *The Beacon*. *Triumph* appeared in the first issue of *Trinidad*. The story is suggestive of the full-length novel, *Minty Alley*, which James later published in England.

PART II BRITAIN 1932-1938

3. *Bloomsbury: An Encounter with Edith Sitwell* (1932). Shortly after James's arrival in England in the spring of 1932 he wrote a six-part series of articles, *London: First Impressions*, for the *Port of Spain Gazette* in Trinidad. For others in the series, see the Bibliography.

4. *The Case for West Indian Self-Government* (1933). This essay appeared as number 16 in the Hogarth Press series, *Day to Day Pamphlets*. It was a shortened version of James's biography, *The Life of Captain Cipriani*, which had been privately published, with Constantine's help, a year earlier in Nelson, Lancashire.

5. *Abyssinia and The Imperialists* (1936). During the early part of the 1930s James was a contributor to *The Keys*, the journal of Harold Moody's League of Coloured Peoples. His essay on the Ethiopian crisis appeared in volume 3, number 5.

6. *The Black Jacobins*: the play (1936). James originally wrote his play about the 1791 slave revolution under the title *Toussaint L'Ouverture*. It was produced by Peter Godfrey of the Stage Society at the Westminster Theatre, London in

March 1936. Later, the drama was revised and re-titled, *The Black Jacobins*. This is the version published here. It was produced by Dexter Lyndersay at the University of Ibadan, Nigeria in 1967; by the BBC, in the radio series *Monday Play*, 1971; and, in 1986, by Yvonne Brewster of the Talawa Theatre Company at the Riverside Studios, London.

7. *Stalin and Socialism* (1937). This essay is taken from James's book, *World Revolution 1917-1936: The Rise and Fall of the Communist International*, originally published in England by Secker and Warburg. At the time of his death, James was working with the London-based group Socialist Platform to produce a new edition of the book.

PART III AMERICA AND AFTER 1938–1956

8. *Letters to Constance Webb* (1943-1946). James's correspondence with the woman he eventually married began in 1939 and continued until his death in 1989. The early letters, particularly up to his marriage in 1948, are extraordinarily revealing; they cast an entirely new light on James's life and work in the United States. The correspondence may be read at the Schomburg Center for Research Into Black Culture, New York.

9. *Dialectical Materialism and the Fate of Humanity* (1947). It was written by James under the pseudonym, J.R. Johnson and was originally published in pamphlet form. The following year, while seeking a divorce in Reno, Nevada which would enable him to marry Constance Webb, James developed and expanded the themes of this essay. A full-length study of the dialectic, based on the Nevada documents, was later published as *Notes on Dialectics*.

10. *The Revolutionary Answer to the Negro Problem in the USA* (1948). James first presented this document the Socialist Workers Conference in 1948. It was the culmination of many years of work on the race question, much of it stimulated by the 1939 discussions with Trotsky in Mexico.

11. *The Class Struggle* (1950). This essay is taken from *State Capitalism and World Revolution*, a collaborative work of the Johnson Forest Tendency. It was one of several critical political documents to appear at the end of the 1940s. Others included *The Invading Socialist Society* and *The Balance Sheet*. They marked James's break with the Trotskyist movement.

12. *Whitman and Melville* (1950). In late 1949 James began to draft his manuscript on American civilization. His chapter on the nineteenth century writers, although carefully woven into an intricate argument, also stands as an essay by itself. Many of the ideas were later used by James for his critical study of Melville *(Mariners, Renegades and Castaways)*. At the end of his life, James was preparing his work on America for publication.

13. *Letters to Literary Critics* (1952/53). James put aside his work on American civilization to focus upon his struggle with the US immigration authorities. He used his critical study of Melville in his battle to avoid deportation; but his exchanges with critics were part of a bigger project, largely unfinished, which the

James archive now reveals. In this selection, the full name and identity of Bell is unknown, Jay Leyda was a Melville scholar, Meyer Schapiro is a poet, editor, and critic, and Frank Kermode is a prominent British literary critic.

14. *Notes on* Hamlet (1953). As part of his case to be allowed to remain in America, James gave many public lectures on American and European literature. The best known series were held at the Institute of Arts and Sciences, Columbia University, New York. This essay on *Hamlet,* a fragment found in the archive, probably comes from the Columbia series *Human Personality in Great Tragedy*.

15. *Popular Art and the Cultural Tradition* (1954). This was a lecture James gave in Paris at a conference on Mass Culture. It was organised under the auspices of the Congress for Cultural Freedom and was held at the offices of Preuves. It was reprinted in the London journal, *Third Text* spring 1990.

16. *Preface to Criticism* (1955?). This is an extract from one of the major unpublished documents in the James archive. It is undated, but was probably drafted in the early to mid 1950s. It has four parts: 1. The principles of literary criticism; 2.The dramatic performance, *The Oresteia*; 3. Shakespeare: *Julius Caesar* and *King Lear*; 4. Beyond Aristotle. The essay included here is taken from parts 1 and 3.

PART IV THE AFRICAN DIASPORA 1957-1989

17. *Letters on Politics* (1956/60). James retained close ties with a number of his former associates in the Johnson Forest Tendency. Members of the group, re-named Correspondence, and, later, Facing Reality, exchanged many documents on contemporary political movements, questions of organisation, recruitment and so on. The letters included here are taken from the James archive. Maxwell Geismar, an American literary critic, was a major correspondent with James after his return to the Caribbean in 1958.

18. *Writings from* The Nation (1958/60). In 1958 James accepted an invitation from Eric Williams, leader of the Peoples' National Movement in Trinidad, to return as editor of the *PNM Weekly*. James reorganised the newspaper, publishing it as *The Nation.* He served as its editor until the autumn of 1960 when political differences with Williams forced him to resign from the post.

19. *From Toussaint L'Ouverture to Fidel Castro* (1962). James prepared this long essay as an appendix to the new Random House edition of *The Black Jacobins* (published in 1963). It reflected his experiences of the independence politics of the Caribbean. Two companion pieces, reflecting in different ways the general themes of James's appendix, are *Modern Politics* (1960) and *Party Politics in the West Indies* (1962).

20. *'What is Art?'* (1963). This essay is taken from James's classic book, *Beyond A Boundary*. James had drafted his manuscript (originally entitled, *What do they know of cricket who only cricket know?*) before he returned to the Caribbean in 1958. Nevertheless the final form of the book was influenced by James's participation in the historic moment of decolonisation. At first its very originality

made it hard for James to find a publisher. *Beyond A Boundary* was published in 1963, the year after Trinidad gained independence.

21. *Lenin and the Vanguard Party* (1963) was published in *Controversy*, a left wing journal in Britain.

22. *Lenin and the Problem* (1964) originally appeared in a Ghanaian publication; later James included it in his collection of writings, *Nkrumah and the Ghana Revolution.*

23. *The People of the Gold Coast* (1960). James visited Ghana several times in the late 1950s. He planned to write a political study of the Ghana revolution; but in the course of the next decade his book was shaped by Nkrumah's fall and the growing problem of government in the new nations. This piece was published in *The Nation*. James wrote it for a Caribbean audience, mindful of the approach of Trinidadian independence.

24. *The Rise and Fall of Nkrumah* (1966) was originally published as a four part series in the *Daily Mirror*, Trinidad.

25. *Black Power* (1967). This is a transcript of a talk James gave in London.

26. *Black People in the Urban Areas of the United States* (1970) is taken from the documents in the James archive. It was originally a speech, probably given in 1970, location unknown.

27. *Garfield Sobers* (1969). Towards the end of the decade in which James's output as a cricket writer was impressive (both in substance and volume) he wrote this essay on Sobers for the collection, *The Great All-Rounders*, edited by John Arlott.

28. *Black Studies and the Contemporary Student* (1969). James was eagerly sought out by younger generations of political activists, particularly black activists in America during the 1960s. He responded to their immediate concerns; and *Black Studies* was an important, if controversial, intervention into that debate. It was originally delivered as a talk while James was teaching in Washington.

29. *Picasso and Jackson Pollock* (1980). This essay was found among papers in the James archive. It was written in a letter to Sura Devine in Chicago while James was living at the headquarters of the Oilfield Workers Trade Union in Trinidad.

30. *Three Black Women Writers* (1981). In the early 1980s James began to speak and write on the new literary movement in America—the emergence of Black women writers. He was influential in their work becoming known to audiences outside the United States; and this essay is a transcript of a talk he gave at the Black Ink writers' collective in London. It was originally published in *Cultural Correspondence* magazine.

C.L.R. James: Bibliography

The material listed below is a revised and updated version of the James bibliography published in volume three of his selected writing, *At the Rendezvous of Victory* (Allison and Busby, 1984). I wish to acknowledge my great debt to Margaret Busby whose dedicated work made available for the first time valuable information concerning James's writing career and upon whose careful original compilation I have drawn for this book. The *Reader* bibliography is confined, however, to James's published writings: that is, his books, pamphlets, reviews, texts of public lectures and talks. It does not encompass the corpus of unpublished papers and manuscipts which comprise the James archive. For the interested reader, these materials are listed and annotated in: *The C.L.R. James Archive: A Reader's Guide* by Anna Grimshaw, the C.L.R. James Institute, New York, 1991.

Information concerning James's published work is arranged chronologically and the entries are divided into four sections which correspond to the divisions within the *Reader* itself. Books are highlighted in capitals. Items which have appeared in the Allison and Busby series are indicated as follows: *Future* (Future in the Present, 1977), *Spheres* (Spheres of Existence, 1980), *Rendezvous* (At the Rendezvous of Victory, 1984), *Nkrumah* (Nkrumah and the Ghana Revolution 1977), and *Cricket* (1986). Those readers requiring more details of James's cricket articles should consult the bibliography at the end of his collected volume, *Cricket*. The cities where journals were published are listed at the end of this bibliography.

The secondary literature on James is steadily growing. Of particular significance are the following volumes: *C.L.R. James: His Life and Work*, ed. Paul Buhle, Allison and Busby, London 1986; *C.L.R. James: The Artist as Revolutionary* by Paul Buhle, Verso, London 1988; *C.L.R. James: A Political Biography* by Kent Worcester, forthcoming; and the pamphlet series of the James Institute, New York, which includes *C.L.R. James and The Struggle For Happiness* by Anna Grimshaw and Keith Hart; *Popular Democracy and the Creative Imagination: The Writings of C.L.R. James 1950–1963* and *The C.L.R. James Archive: A Reader's Guide* by Anna Grimshaw.

PART I TRINIDAD 1901-1932

"The Meaning of Philosophy", in *The Royalian*, magazine of Queen's Royal College, Port of Spain, 1920s.

"La Divina Pastora", in *Saturday Review*, 15 October 1927; reprinted in *Best Short Stories*, ed. E.J. O'Brien, London, 1928, in *Stories from the Caribbean*, ed. Andrew Salkey, London, 1965, in *West Indian Narrative*, ed. Kenneth Ramchand, Nelson, London, 1966, in *Caribbean Prose*, and in *Spheres*.

"Triumph", in *Trinidad*, vol. 1, no. 1, Christmas 1929; reprinted in *Island Voices*, Liveright, New York, 1930, in Salkey, *Stories from the Caribbean*, op. cit. 1965, in R.W. Sander (ed) *From Trinidad: an Anthology of Early West Indian Writing*, London, 1978, and in *Future*.

"Turner's Prosperity", in *Trinidad*, vol. 1, no. 1, Christmas 1929; reprinted in *Spheres*.

"The Problem of Knowledge", in *The Beacon*, vol. I, no. 1, Port of Spain, March 1931. (*The Beacon* reprinted by Kraus, New York and Lichtenstein, 1977, with introduction and index by Reinhard Sander.)

"Revolution", in *The Beacon*, vol. I, no. 2, May 1931; reprinted in *Rendezvous*.

"The Star that Would Not Shine", in *The Beacon*, vol. I, no. 3, June 1931; reprinted in *Rendezvous*.

"Books and Writers" column (on Arnold Bennett), in *The Beacon*, vol. I, no. 4, July 1931.

"The Intelligence of the Negro: A few words with Dr Harland", in *The Beacon*, vol. I no. 5, August 1931; reprinted in R.W. Sander (ed.), *From Trinidad*, op.cit., London, 1978.

"Books and Writers" column (including review of Mahatma Gandhi—His Own Story), in *The Beacon*, vol. I, no. 5, August 1931.

"Michael Maxwell Philip: 1829-1888", in *The Beacon*, vol. I, no. 6, September 1931. Reprinted in Sander, *From Trinidad*, op.cit.

PART II BRITAIN 1932-1938

"Tribute to Lord Harris", *The Times*, 29 March 1932.

"The greatest of all bowlers: an impressionist sketch of S.F. Barnes", *Manchester Guardian*, 1 September 1932, reprinted in *Cricket*.

"Barbados and the Barbadians", 2 parts, *Port of Spain Gazette*, 20 and 22 March 1932.

"A visit to the Science and Art Museums", *Port of Spain Gazette*, 22 May 1932.

"London: First Impressions", 6 parts, *Port of Spain Gazette*, 21 and 22 June, 27 July, 4, 11, 28 August 1932.

"Proconsuls, Beware: a cautionary tale", *Port of Spain Gazette*, 11 September 1932.

THE LIFE OF CAPTAIN CIPRIANI: an account of British Government in the West Indies, Cartmel & Co., Nelson, Lancs, 1932; three chapters published as pamphlet "The Case for West-Indian Self-Government", London, no. 16 in the *Day to Day* series, Hogarth Press, London 1933; reprinted University Place Bookshop, New York, 1967; and Facing Reality Publishing Co., Detroit, 1967, 32pp; extract in *Future*.

Cricket reports in the *Manchester Guardian*, 1933: April 17, 18, 19; May 8, 9, 10, 22, 24; June 24.

"West Indies cricket", *The Cricketer*, Volume 14, 6/13/20/27 May, 3/10/17/24 June 1933, reprinted in *Cricket*.

"Chances of West Indians in First Test", *Port of Spain Gazette*, 15 June 1933, reprinted

in *Cricket*.
"A Century of Freedom", *Port of Spain Gazette*, 17 June 1933.
"The West Indies Cricket Team, 1933" in *The Keys* (organ of Dr Harold Moody's League of Coloured Peoples), vol. 1, no. 1, July 1933.
"Slavery Today : A Shocking Exposure"; *Tit-Bits*, 5 August 1933.
"West Indies Self-Government", in *The Keys*, vol. 1, no. 4, April-June 1934.
Cricket reports in the *Manchester Guardian*, 1934: May 7, 8, 14, 15, 16; June 7, 8, 9, 11, 12, 14, 15, 16, 22, 23, 25, 26, 28, 29; July 5, 6, 9, 10, 11, 12, 13, 14, 16, 17, 18, 19, 23, 24, 25, 26, 27, 28, 30, 31; August 1, 17, 18, 20*, 21*, 22*, 23, 24, 25; September 10*, 11*, 12*. (* indicates that the piece was reprinted in *Cricket*.)
Cricket reports in the *Manchester Guardian*, 1935: May 21, 27, 28, 29; June 4, 6, 7, 15, 17, 18, 20*, 22, 24, 25; July 1, 2, 3, 9, 10, 11, 12, 15, 16, 17, 18, 19, 20, 20, 26, 27, 29, 30, 31; August 8, 9, 10, 19, 20, 21, 22, 23, 26, 27, 28; September 3, 4, 5, 6, 7, 9, 10, 11. (* reprinted in *Cricket*.)
"Is This Worth a War? The League's Scheme to Rob Abyssinia of its Independence", in *New Leader* (weekly paper of Independent Labour Party, edited by Fenner Brockway), 4 October 1935; reprinted in *Rendezvous*.
"The Game at Geneva: Behind the scenes in the 'Thieves Kitchen'", in *New Leader*, 18 October 1935.
"The Workers and Sanctions: Why the ILP and the Communists take an opposite view", in *New Leader*, 25 October 1935.
"National Stay-in Strike? How the miners could win an increase—What I learned in Wales", in *New Leader*, 1 November 1935.
"Truth about 'Peace Plan': Britain's Imperialist Game", in *New Leader*, 20 December 1935.
"'Honest' Stanley in a Fix—What next in the Abyssinian Dispute?", in *New Leader*, 27 December, 1935.
"Baldwin's Next Move: Parliament has become a nuisance to the ruling class—look out for Fascist Developments!", in *New Leader*, 3 January 1936.
"Abyssinia and the imperialists", in *The Keys*, vol. 3, no. 5, January/March 1936.
"Toussaint L'Ouverture", letter in *New Statesman*, 28 March 1936.
"Economic Organisation in the Tropics", lecture delivered to Third Annual Weekend Conference of the League of Coloured Peoples, Hoddesdon, 4 April 1936.
"The Abyssinian Debate: Conference supports independent working-class action", in *New Leader*, 17 April 1936.
"'Civilising' the 'Blacks': Why Britain Needs to Maintain her African Possessions" (review of George Padmore, *How Britain Rules Africa*, and Prince Nyabongo, *Africa Answers Back*) in *New Leader*, 29 May 1936.
"Italy and Abyssinia. Should British workers take sides?", originally advertisement in *New Leader*, 8 May 1936, reprinted in *Controversy* (journal of Independent Labour Party), special supplement, no. 1, 1936 (with Fenner Brockway, Bob Edwards, James Maxton, John McGovern and Joseph Southall).
"Towards the New Workers' Party" (with Arthur Ballard), *Fight*, December 1936, Volume 1 no. 2.
Toussaint L'Ouverture, the play, produced by Peter Godfrey at the Westminster Theatre (Stage Society), London, in March 1936, with Paul Robeson in the title role. Revised under the title, *The Black Jacobins* and first performed by the Arts Theatre Group, lbadan, Nigeria, 1967. Play text published in *A Time . . . and a Season*, 8 Caribbean

Plays, ed. Errol Hill, University of the West Indies, Extra-Mural Studies, Trinidad, 1976.

MINTY ALLEY, Secker & Warburg, London, 1936, 320pp; new edition with 1969 introduction by Kenneth Ramchand, New Beacon Books, London and Port of Spain, 1971, reprinted in 1975, 1981 and 1989, 244pp.

Preface to Juan Brea and Mary Low, *Red Spanish Notebook* (first-hand account of the Spanish revolution), 1937.

"Letters to us", letter from James to the Editor, *New Leader*, 23 April 1937.

"The Second Moscow Trial", 2 parts, *Fight*, April and May 1937, Volume 1 nos. 5 & 6.

Cricket articles in the *Glasgow Herald*, 1937: April 28*; May 5, 12*, 19, 26; June 2, 9, 16, 24; July 7, 14, 21, 28*; August 4, 11, 18, 25. (* reprinted in *Cricket*.)

"Trotskyism", in *Controversy* vol. 2, no. 1, October 1937.

WORLD REVOLUTION 1917-1936: The Rise and Fall of the Communist International, Secker & Warburg, London, 1937, 429pp., Pioneer Publications, New York, 1937; reprinted Kraus, Nendeln, 1970, Hyperion Press, Westport, Conn., 1973; to be reprinted by Humanities Press/Socialist Platform in 1992; extracts "Stalin Ruins the Chinese Revolution" in *Future*; "After Hitler, Our Turn" in *Spheres*; "The Revolution Abandoned" in *Rendezvous*.

"Six Questions to Trotskyists—and their answers", in *Controversy*, vol. 2, no. 17, February 1938.

"Revolutionary Socialist League", in *Fight*, (organ of the Revolutionary Socialist League, edited by C.L.R. James), vol. 1, no. 1, London, April 1938.

"British Barbarism in Jamaica! Support the Negro Workers' Struggle", in *Fight*, vol. 1, no. 3, June 1938; reprinted in *Future*.

"The Voice of Africa" (review of *Facing Mount Kenya* by Jomo Kenyatta), *International African Opinion*, August 1938, Volume 1, no. 2.

"Whither the ILP: Centrist Circle about to be completed—The only road to revolutionaries", in *Workers Fight*, October 1938.

"French 40 Hour Week Attacked", in *Workers Fight*, October 1938.

Cricket articles in the *Glasgow Herald*, 1938: April 27; May 11*; June 16, 27, 30; July 6, 14, 20, 25, 28; August 10, 17*, 23, 26. (* reprinted in *Cricket*.)

THE BLACK JACOBINS: Toussaint L'Ouverture and the San Domingo revolution, Secker & Warburg, London, 1938, 328pp., Dial Press, New York, 1938; revised edition with 1962 preface and appendix "From Toussaint L'Ouverture to Fidel Castro", Vintage Books/Random House, New York, 1963; new British edition with foreword, Allison & Busby, London, 1980, reprinted 1989, 440pp. French edition *Les Jacobins Noirs*, translation and preface by Pierre Naville, Gallimard, Paris, 1949; new edition, Editions Caribéennes, Paris, 1983. Italian edition, *I Jacobini Neri: La Prima Rivolta contro L'Uomo Bianco*, Feltrinelli, Milan, 1968. German edition, Pahl, Rugenstein, Cologne, 1984. (The libretto of David Blake's opera *Toussaint*, produced by the English National Opera in 1979 and 1983, used *The Black Jacobins* as its basis.)

A HISTORY OF NEGRO REVOLT, Fact monograph no. 18, London, September 1938, 97pp. New York, 1967, 1969; revised and reissued as A History of Pan-African Revolt, with introduction by Marvin Holloway and Epilogue "The History of Pan-African Revolt: A Summary of 1939-1969", Drum and Spear Press, Washington, 1969, 160pp.; reprinted by Race Today Publications, London 1985; extracts "Revolts in Africa" in *Future*; and "Always out of Africa" in *Nkrumah*, 1982 edition.

PART III AMERICA AND AFTER 1938-1956

James wrote under a variety of pseudonyms while living and working in the United States. The name he used most frequently was J.R. Johnson; but others included A.A.B., G.F. Eckstein, Evans, J. Meyer and Brother Williams.

"The Negro Question", a column by J.R. Johnson in *Socialist Appeal*, 26 November 1938.

"Self-Determination for the American Negroes", "A Negro Organization" and "Plans for the Negro Organization" (discussions with Trotsky, Coyoacan, Mexico, 4/5/11 April 1939), in *Internal Bulletin*, Socialist Workers Party, no. 9. June 1939. Reprinted in *Documents on the Negro Struggle*, Pioneer Publishers, New York, 1962, in *Leon Trotsky on Black Nationalism and Self-Determination*, 2nd edition, Pathfinder Press, New York, 1978 (1st edition Merit Publishers, 1967), and in *Rendezvous.*

"Fighting Against the Stream" (discussion with Trotsky, April 1939), published in uncorrected typescript in SWP's *Internal Bulletin*, vol. II, no. 4, 20 December 1939, under title "The Fourth International in Europe", with Trotsky identified as "Crux", James as "Johnson"; reprinted in *Fourth International*, May 1941, minus final three paragraphs and James's introductory statement, in *Writings of Leon Trotsky, 1938-39*, Pathfinder Press, New York, 1974 (Merit Publishers, 1969), and in *Rendezvous.*

"On the History of the Left Opposition" (discussion with Trotsky, early April 1939), uncorrected transcript by James in SWP's *Internal Bulletin*, vol. II, no. 7, January 1940; reprinted in *Writings of Trotsky, 1938-39*, op. cit., and in *Rendezvous.*

"The SWP and Negro Work" (resolution presented to and adopted by SWP national conference, New York, 1-4 July 1939), reprinted in *Documents on the Negro Struggle*, 1962, and in *Leon Trotsky on Black Nationalism and Self-Determination*, op.cit..

Translation of Boris Souvarine's *Stalin* (from French), Secker and Warburg, London, 1939; Longman, Green, New York, 1939; Alliance Book Corps; 690pp.

"The Negro Question", a column in *Socialist Appeal* (J.R. Johnson: 1939—August 15, 22, 25, 29; September 1, 5, 6*, 9*, 11*, 13*, 15*, 18*, 20*, 26*, 29*; October 3*, 6, 10, 13, 17, 20**, 24**, 27, 31; November 3, 7, 10, 14, 17, 21, 24; December 1, 9, 16, 23**, 30**. (* indicates pieces reprinted as pamphlet "Why Negroes Should Oppose the War", issued by Pioneer Publishers, New York, October 1939, 32pp.; reprinted in *Fighting Racism in World War II*, Monad Press, New York, 1980. ** indicates piece was reprinted in *Fighting Racism in World War II*, op.cit.)

"Labor and the Second World War", series of articles by J.R Johnson in *Socialist Appeal*: 1939—October 27, 31; November 3, 7, 10, 14, 17, 21.

"Revolution and the Negro" (J.R. Johnson), *The New International*, December 1939.

"The Negro Question", a column in *Socialist Appeal* (J.R. Johnson): 1940—January 6, 13, 20, 27; February 3*, 10, 17, 24; March 9. (* reprinted in *Fighting Racism in World War II*, op.cit..)

"Capitalism and the War", *The New International*, July 1940.

"Trotsky's Place in History", *The New International*, September, 1940.

Column in *Labor Action* (J.R. Johnson): 1940—May 27; June 10, 19, 24; July 28; August 5, 12; September 16, 23.

"Russia—a Fascist state", *The New International*, April 1941.

Column in *Labor Action* (J.R. Johnson): 1941—March 10, 14, 27, 31; April 7, 28; May 5, 12, 19, 26; June 2, 9, 16, 23; July 7, 14, 21; September 22, 29; October 6, 13.

Column in *Labor Action* (J.R. Johnson): 1942—November 16; December 7, 14, 28.

Labor Action, unsigned columns probably by James on Missouri sharecroppers fight: 1942—April 12; May 11, 18, 25; June 1, 8, 15, 22, 29; July 6, 13; September 28.

"Down with Starvation Wages in South-East Missouri" (Local 313, UCAPAWA-CIO), St Louis, 1942, 12pp.; reprinted in *Future*.

"Education, Propaganda and Agitation", 1943, mimeographed; reissued, Facing Reality, 1968.

"The Way Out for Europe", *The New International*, April 1943 and May 1943.

"Production for the Sake of Production—A reply to Carter" (J.R. Johnson), in *Internal Bulletin*, SWP, No.2, April 1943 (in Raya Dunayevskaya Papers).

"The Philosophy of History and Necessity: A few words with Professor Hook" (as A.A.B.), *The New International*, July 1943; reprinted in *Spheres*.

"Socialism and the National Question", *The New International*, October, 1943.

Column in *Labor Action* (J.R. Johnson): 1943—January 4, 11; May 3, 24.

"In the International Tradition: Tasks Ahead for American Labour", *The New International*, January 1944.

"The American People in 'One' World", *The New International*, January 1944.

"Laski, St Paul and Stalin: A prophet in search of new values", *The New International*, June 1944; reprinted in *Future*.

"The French Rats and the Sinking Ships: A grave-digger indicts his fellows", *The New International*, September 1944.

"German and European Civilisation", *The New International*, November 1944.

Column in *Labor Action* (J.R. Johnson): 1944—June 19, 26; July 3, 17, 24; August 21, 28; September 4, 20, 25; October 2, 4, 23; November 27; December 4, 11*, 18*, 25. (* One Tenth of the Nation, column on Black politics and history.)

"The Americanization of Bolshevism", *The New International*, 1944.

"Negroes and the Revolution", *The New International*, January 1945.

"The Resolution of the Minority", *The New International*, January 1945.

"The British Vote for Socialism: The rise of British Labour", *The New International*, September 1945; reprinted in *Future*.

Column in *Labor Action* (J.R. Johnson): 1945—January 8*, 22*, 29*; February 12*, 19*; March 5*, 12; April 2*, 9*, 23*; May 7*; June 4*, 11*, 18*, 25*; July 2*; August 13*, 27*; September 3*, 24*. (* One Tenth of the Nation.)

"Historical Retrogression or Socialist Revolution", *The New International*, January and February 1946.

"After Ten Years: On Trotsky's The Revolution Betrayed", *The New International*, October 1946; reprinted in *International Socialism*, 16, Spring 1964, and in *Spheres*.

Column in *Labor Action* (J.R. Johnson): 1946—January 6; February 4*, 18*, 25*; March 11, 18, 18*, 25; April 1, 1*, 8, 8*, 15*, 22, 22*; May 20*, 27*; July 1, 1*, 8*, 22*; August 5, 5*, 19, 19*, 26*; September 2, 2*, 9, 16*, 23, 23*, 30; October 7*, 21, 21*, 28*; November 4, 4*, 18, 18*; December 23*, 30. (* One Tenth of the Nation.)

Introduction to first English translation of *Essays by Karl Marx Selected from the Economic-Philosophic MSS* (J.R. Johnson, Freddie Forest, Ria Stone), Johnson Forest Tendency, New York, 7 August 1947; reprinted in *Rendezvous*.

The Balance Sheet: Trotskyism in the United States 1940–47 (J.R. Johnson, F.Forest and Martin Glaberman), Johnson Forest Tendency, New York, August 1947, 32pp.

Dialectical Materialism and the Fate of Humanity, New York, September 1947; edited and reprinted as *Dialectic and History: An Introduction*, with introduction by P. Buhle and D. Wagner, Cambridge, Mass., 1972; reprinted in *Spheres.*

"We join the SWP", *Bulletin of the Johnson Forest Tendency* number 12, September 1947.

THE INVADING SOCIALIST SOCIETY (with F. Forest and Ria Stone), Johnson Forest Tendency, New York, 1947; reprinted with new preface by James, Bewick Editions, Detroit, 1972, 72pp.

Column in *Labor Action* (J.R. Johnson): 1947—January 6*, 13*, 20*; February 24*; March 3, 24; April 7*, 14, 21; June 2. (* One Tenth of the Nation.)

Column in *The Militant* (J.R. Johnson): 1947—July 1, 28; August 4, 11, 18, 25; September 1, 8, 15, 22, 29; October 6, 13, 20; November 3.

"The Revolutionary Answer to the Negro Problem in U.S."(J. Meyer), report delivered in presenting draft resolution on the Negro Question to 13th Convention of SWP, 1-5 July 1948; reprinted in *Documents on the Negro Struggle*, Pioneer Publishers, New York, 1962, in *Radical America James Anthology*, May 1970, in *Marxism and Black Liberation*, Hera Press, Cleveland, 1980, and in *Future.*

NOTES ON DIALECTICS: Hegel, Marx, Lenin. Written in 1948 and circulated within Johnson Forest Tendency, photo-offset by Facing Reality 1965; mimeographed as *Notes on Dialectics*, published by Friends of Facing Reality, Detroit, 1970; new edition with introduction, Allison & Busby, London 1980, Lawrence Hill, Westport, Conn., 1980, 232pp.

Column in *The Militant* (J.R. Johnson): 1948—February 2, 9, 16; March 1*, 29*; April 12*, 17*, 26*; May 3*, 17*. (* G.F. Eckstein.)

Column in *The Militant* (J. Meyer): 1949—January 3, 17; February 7, 14*; April 25; May 2, 23; October 3, 10; November 7. (* G.F. Eckstein.)

Reply to Louis Menard's review of *Les Jacobins Noirs*, in *Les Temps Modernes*, March 1950.

"Two Young American Writers", in *Fourth International*, March/April 1950; reprinted in *Spheres.*

"Negro Liberation through Revolutionary Socialism: The Socialist Workers Party Position on the Negro Struggle" (SWP 1948 convention resolution, as amended and adopted in February 1950), in *Fourth International*, May/June 1950; reprinted in *Documents on the Negro Struggle*, op. cit..

Column in *The Militant*: 1950—January 23*; February 13.** (* G.F. Eckstein; ** J. Meyer.)

STATE CAPITALISM AND WORLD REVOLUTION, originally published anonymously, as collective statement of Johnson Forest Tendency, 1950; 2nd edition, with preface signed by Johnson, Christianson, Chaulieu, Brendel, Maassen and Hughes, Welwyn Garden City 1956; 3rd edition with preface by Martin Glaberman, Facing Reality, Detroit, 1969, 108pp; extracts in *Radical America James Anthology*, May 1970, and in *Future*. New edition with foreword by James and introduction by Paul Buhle, Charles H. Kerr, Chicago 1986.

NOTES ON AMERICAN CIVILIZATION, unpublished typescript, 330pp, 1950. To be published by James, edited and introduced by Anna Grimshaw and Keith Hart as *The Struggle For Happiness*, extract in *The Times Higher Education Supplement*, March 1989; now to be issued as *American Civilization*, Blackwell 1992.

Column in *The Militant* (J. Blake): 1951—(as J. Blake) March 12; April 30; May 7, 14, 21; June 11, 25.

"The Balance Sheet Completed: Ten Years of American Trotskyism" (with F.Forest), Johnson Forest Tendency, New York, August 1951.

"On Organization", "On Proletarianization" and "Summary on Proletarianization" (Evans), in *Towards a Workers Organization*, March 1952.

MARINERS, RENEGADES AND CASTAWAYS: The story of Herman Melville and the world we live in (written in 1952), privately published, New York, 1953, 215pp.; new edition with introduction by George P. Rawick and Afterword, but omitting last chapter which dealt with James's deportation, Bewick, Detroit, 1978, 168pp.; extracts in *Radical America James Anthology*, May 1970, and in *Future*; reprinted by Allison & Busby, London, 1984.

"Return of a wanderer: comparisons between 1938 and 1953", *Manchester Guardian*, 7 October 1953, reprinted in *Cricket*.

"Popular Art and the Cultural Tradition", translation of talk sponsored by Congress of Cultural Freedom, *Preuves*, March 1954; reprinted *Third Text*, spring 1989.

"Britain's New Monthlies", *Saturday Review*, Feb/March 1954.

Cricket reports in the *Manchester Guardian*, 1954:

May 3, 7, 8, 10*, 11*, 12*, 13, 14, 15, 17, 18, 19, 20, 21, 22, 24, 25, 26, 27, 28; June 7, 14, 15, 21, 22, 23, 24, 25; July 5, 6, 12, 13, 14, 15, 16, 17, 19, 20, 21, 22, 23, 24. (* reprinted in *Cricket*.)

PART IV THE AFRICAN DIASPORA 1957-1989

"Every Cook Can Govern: A Study of Democracy in Ancient Greece, and Negro Americans and American Politics"(reprinted from *Correspondence*, vol. 2, no. 12), Correspondence Publishing Co., Detroit, June 1956, 24pp.; reprinted in *Future*.

Debate with John Arlott, "In the opinion of this house, neither toss, weather nor wicket were decisive elements in the defeat of Australia last season", 12 March, 1957, reprinted in *Newsletter of the Cricket Society*, no. 48 (3) and in *Cricket*.

"Cricket and Contemporary life", *The Cricketer*, vol. 28, no. 5, June 1957 (appears in *Beyond A Boundary*).

FACING REALITY (authorship originally given as J.R. Johnson with Grace C. Lee and Pierre Chaulieu), Correspondence, Detroit, 1958; republished by Facing Reality, later by Bewick Editions, Detroit 1974, 174 pp.; extracts in *Radical America James Anthology*, May 1970, "The Workers' Councils in Hungary" in *Future*, and "New Society: New People" in *Rendezvous*.

"Nationalist Strain", *New Statesman*, 18 January 1958.

"Without Malice", a column in *The Nation*, Trinidad: 1958—December 20, 27.

"Discovering Venezuela", 3 parts, *The Nation*, December 1958.

"Federation"(West Indies and British Guiana) (lecture delivered at Queen's College, Demerara, June 1958), with preface by L.F.S. Burnham, British Guiana Argosy Co., 1959, 25pp.; reprinted in *Rendezvous*.

"The Artist in the Caribbean" (text of lecture at University of the West Indies, Mona, Jamaica), 1959, 8pp.; reprinted in *Radical America James Anthology*, May 1970, and in *Future*.

"Without Malice", a column in *The Nation*, Trinidad: 1959—January 10, 17, 24, 31; February 7, 14, 21, 28; March 13, 20; April 10, 17; May 15*, 22, 29; June 5; July 3, 17; August 7; September 25; October 2, 23, 30; November 13, 20, 27; December 4, 18, 24, 31. (* reprinted in *Cricket*.)

Other articles by James in *The Nation*, 1959:
"Tobacco and Tobago", 31 January 1959.
"Abraham Lincoln", 7th February 1959.
"Preliminary report on the Carnival", 14 February 1959.
"Independence, Energy and Creative Talent of Carnival Can Do Wonders", 21 February 1959.
"Frank Worrell must be captain", 28th February 1959.
"This lynching-rape business", 15 May 1959.
"Looking back at the crisis", 5 parts, 17, 24, 31 July and 7, 14 August 1959.
"Federal Matters: the politics and personality of Dr Eric Williams", 25 September 1959.
"Notes on the life of George Padmore", 11 parts, September/October/November 1959, January 1960.
"Nehru", 20 November 1959.
"Gilchrist before and Gilchrist after", 20 November 1959, reprinted in *Cricket*.
"Some of the MCC players as I knew them, 2 parts, 24 and 31 December, 1959.
"Without Malice", a column in *The Nation*, Trinidad: 1960—January 3, 15, 22, 29; February 5, 12, 26; March 4, 11, 18; April 1, 8; May 27; June 3, 17, 24; July 1, 8.
Other articles by James in *The Nation*, 1960:
"Homage to English Cricket", 3 parts, 15/22 January/5 February 1960.
"Notes on the Evans Report", 22 January 1960.
"Make Worrell Captain", 2 parts, 5 and 12 February, 1960.
"Divertimento or How the Masters Teach the Pupils to Ensure a Complete Mess", 5 February 1960.
Open letter to Queen's Park Cricket Club, 12 February 1960 (in *Beyond A Boundary*).
"The Jamaica Test", 19 February 1960.
"The West Indies—Trinidad, Jamaica", 19 February 1960.
"The Same Wretched Story" (West Indian captaincy), 26 February 1960.
"That Open Letter to Queen's Park—was it too sharp?", 26 February 1960.
"Why is Amery Coming Here?", 3 parts, 26 February, 4, 11 March 1960.
"The People of the Gold Coast—they created Ghana", 4 March 1960.
"West Indian Board of Control: the captain for Australia", 4 March 1960; reprinted in *Cricket*.
"West Indies to Ghana", 4 March 1960.
"The Press, the Party and the People", 3 parts, 11, 18 March, 8 April 1960.
"Dr Eric Williams—PNM Political Leader: A Convention Appraisal", 18 March 1960.
"West Indies v. Australia", 8 April 1960.
"England v. The West Indies", 8 April 1960.
"Without any Malice Whatsoever" (Chaguaramas—some facts), 29 April 1960.
"Trinidad Families—the James family", 4 parts, 17, 24 June, 1, 15 July 1960.
"As Long as Possible" (the oilfield workers' strike), 1 July 1960.
"Ghana Celebrations", 5 parts, 15, 22, 29, July, 5, 12 August 1960.
"Dr Eric Williams, First Premier of Trinidad and Tobago—A Biographical Sketch", PNM Publishing Co., Port of Spain, 1960, 16pp.
"Federation: We Failed Miserably—How and Why" (text of lecture to Caribbean Society, Kingston, Jamaica, November 1959 with Message to the People of Jamaica, Foreword and letter to Norman Manley dated 1960), Vedic Enterprises, San Juan, Trinidad, 1961, 32pp.; extracts reprinted in *Rendezvous*.

"Resemblance to Scott and Shaw", *Trinidad Guardian*, 1962.

Marxism and the Intellectuals (J.R. Johnson; includes a two-part essay, "The creative power of the working class" and "The American working class", written in 1961 for Correspondence but then unpublished), Facing Reality, Detroit, May 1962, 32pp.; reprinted in *Spheres.*

"Arthur Andrew Cipriani", Independence Supplement, *Sunday Guardian*, Trinidad, 26 August 1962.

Documents on the Negro Struggle (*Bulletin of Marxist Studies*, no. 4; includes text of discussions with Trotsky, 1933 and 1939, and Socialist Workers Party convention resolutions, 1939 and 1948), 1962; condensed in *Leon Trotsky on Black Nationalism*, Merit Publishers, New York, 1967; extracts in *Rendezvous.*

MODERN POLITICS (subtitled "A series of lectures on the subject given at the Trinidad Public Library, in its Adult Education Programme"), PNM Publishing Co., Port of Spain, 1960; new edition, with introduction by Martin Glaberman, Bewick Editions, Detroit, 1973, 176pp.; extracts in *Radical America James Anthology*, May 1970, "The Battle for Survival" in *Rendezvous.*

PARTY POLITICS IN THE WEST INDIES, Port of Spain, 1962, 176pp.; extracts in *Radical America James Anthology*, May 1970, "The Mighty Sparrow" in *Future*, and "The West Indian Middle Classes" in *Spheres.*

Letters on Organization (J.R. Johnson; written 3 December 1962—20/26 January 1963), mimeographed, Facing Reality, Detroit, 1963.

Lenin, Trotsky and the Vanguard Party: A Contemporary View (originally published in *Controversy*, London 1963), Facing Reality, Detroit, 1964, 8pp.

Foreword to *Cricket Quarterly*, vol. 1, 1963.

"Lenin and the Vanguard Party", in *Controversy*, Spring 1963.

"Cricket in West Indian culture", *New Society*, 6 June, 1963, reprinted in *Cricket.*

"West Indies v. Australia", in *Cricket Quarterly*, London, vol. III, no. 3, Summer 1963.

"The West Indies and the Vote", in *New Society*, 5 September 1963.

"The 1963 West Indians" (address given to the Cricket Society in the Tavern at Lord's on 5 September 1963), in *Journal of the Cricket Society*, vol. II, no. 2, 1963, reprinted in *Cricket.*

"The departure of the West Indians", 1963, first published in *Cricket.*

"Dexter and Sobers", 1963, first published in *Cricket.*

"Indomitable Rebel", review of Isaac Deutscher's, *The Prophet Outcast: Trotsky 1929-1940*, in *New Society*, 28 November 1963.

Talks on Shakespeare: Hamlet, Macbeth, Othello (reprinted in *Spheres*), The Merchant of Venice (in *Spheres*), King Lear, "The Man Shakespeare", written in 1963, broadcast on BBC Caribbean Service, London, 1963-4.

BEYOND A BOUNDARY, Stanley Paul/Hutchinson, London, 1963, reprinted 1966, 1969, 1976, 1980, 1986 with new foreword by Mike Brearley, 256pp.; extracts "What is Art?" in *Radical America James Anthology*, May 1970; and "Against the Current" in *Caribbean Essays*, ed. Andrew Salkey, Evans, London, 1973; new edition Pantheon, New York, 1984.

Towards a Caribbean Nation (first published as "Parties, Politics and Economics in the Caribbean" in *Freedomways*, Summer 1964), Caribbean Conference Publication, 1967; reprinted in *Spheres.*

Series of columns in *Evening Bulletin*, San Fernando, Trinidad, January-April 1964. "But where are the snows of yesteryear?", 22 January; "The letter I felt compelled to write (to Nkrumah)", 29 January; "We Anglo-Saxons", 19 February; "Why I complain about my people", 4 March; "Emperor Haile Selassie", 24 April; undated—"A Universal Declaration of Human Rights", "The West Indian Vote"; "Miss Jamaica"; "De Gaulle and the West Indies"; "Politics as I see it"; "Man I met on Harley Street".

Review of *Frank Worrell: The Career of a Great Cricketer* by Ernest Eytle, *Cricket Quarterly*, vol. 2, no. 1, January 1964.

"Sir J.B. Hobbs", *The Cricketer*, vol. 45 February 1964, reprinted in *Cricket.*

"Lenin and the Problem", article in Ghanaian political journal, 1964, reprinted in *Nkrumah*, 1982 edition.

"Slippery Descent" and "They never should have let this young man die" (on Nkrumah), in *Trinidad Evening News*, February 1964, reprinted in *Nkrumah*, 1982 edition.

"A National Purpose for Caribbean Peoples", talk given to the West Indies Students' Association in Edinburgh, Scotland, 26 February 1964; reprinted in *Rendezvous.*

"Race Relations in the Caribbean", in *Newsletter*, Institute of Race Relations, London, April/May 1964.

"Rastafari At Home—and Abroad", in *New Left Review*, no. 25, May/June 1964; reprinted in *Caribbean Conference Bulletin*, vol. 1, no. 2, September 1967; and in *Rendezvous.*

"Sobers' greatest days are ahead of him", *The Cricketer*, vol. 45, no. 11, July 1964, reprinted in *Cricket.*

"Parties, Politics and Economics in the Caribbean", in *Freedomways*, IV:3, Summer 1964; reprinted as pamphlet "Towards a Caribbean Nation", 1967, in *C.L.R. James Symposium Document* no. 4, and in *Spheres.*

"Nationalisation talk hints of immaturity", in *Trinidad Guardian*, 30 August 1964.

"Race: the unmentionable issue", contribution by James, *Peace News*, London, 25 September 1964.

"The inheritors", in souvenir programme commemorating Sir Frank Worrell's West Indies XI Tour, 1964.

'Negro Americans take the lead: A statement on the crisis in American civilization", Facing Reality Publishing Committee (chairman Martin Glaberman), Detroit, September 1964, 44pp.

"Reflections on the late series", in *Cricket Quarterly*, vol. II, no. 4, October 1964, reprinted in *Cricket.*

"Black Sansculottes", in *Newsletter*, Institute of Race Relations, October 1964; reprinted in *Rendezvous.*

"Heart of the Matter" (review of Wilson Harris's *Heartland*), in *New Society*, 22 October 1964.

"Colour: another view", in *New Society*, 10 December 1964.

'Marxism for the Sixties" (delivered to Solidarity Group in London, 1963), mimeographed, Facing Reality, Detroit May 1965.

"West Indians of East Indian Descent", IBIS Pamphlet No.1, Trinidad, 1965, 10pp.

"Wilson Harris: A Philosophical Approach" (text of speech delivered in April 1960), General public lecture series: West Indian literature, no. 1, University of the West Indies Extra-Mural Department,Port of Spain, 1965, 15pp.

"Home is where they want to be", in *Sunday Guardian* Magazine, 14 February 1965.

"Wilson Harris and the Existentialist Doctrine", lecture at University of the West Indies, Trinidad, 1965; in *Spheres.*

"Marxism for the Sixties" (based on address "Marxism 1963" delivered to Solidarity Group in London, November 1963), in *Speak Out*, no. 2, May 1965.

"Mackenzie and Hawke rout West Indies", *The Times*, 18 May 1965.

"Open letter on Butler", *Vanguard*, organ of the Oilfield Workers' Trade Union, Trinidad, 19 June 1965.

Introduction to reprint of W.E.B. Du Bois's *The Souls of Black Folk*, Longmans, London, 1965; reprinted in *Future*.

Perspectives and Proposals (based on three talks delivered to a small audience in London, August 1963), mimeographed, Facing Reality, Detroit, 1966.

"Dr Williams's Trinidad: An attack", in *Venture* (monthly magazine of Fabian Society), January 1966.

"The Rise and Fall of Nkrumah", in *Daily Mirror*, Port of Spain, 28 February and 2/3/4 March 1966; reprinted in *Speak Out*, no. 4, Detroit, March 1966, and in *Rendezvous*.

"First Test at Old Trafford", *The Vanguard*, 10 June, 1966.

Cricket Articles in *Sunday Guardian*, Trinidad, 1966: "Long may Windies flourish",* 26 June; "After that Nottingham defeat, England must find 12 new players to battle WI",* 10 July; "A question of cricket approach . . .",* 14 August; "Why Windies fade in the end",* 28 August; "Two cricketing societies",* 4 September; "Sobers—a man who fits into the expanded technicalities of his age", 11 September; "From the spectators came Sobers", 18 September. (* reprinted in *Cricket*.)

Articles from *The World of Cricket*, edited by E.W. Swanton (Michael Joseph, London): "Australia v. West Indies"; "West Indies";* biographies of Challenor, Goddard, Gomez, Hall, Headley, Kanhai, Ramadhin, Smith, Sobers, Stollmeyer, Valentine, Walcott, Weekes, Worrell. (* reprinted in *Cricket*.)

"Kanhai: a study in confidence", *New World*, Georgetown, Guyana Independence issue, 1966, reprinted in *C.L.R. James Symposium Document* no. 4, in *Rendezvous*, and *Cricket*.

"Tomorrow and Today: A Vision", in *New World*, Guyana Independence Issue, Georgetown, 1966.

"James Baldwin's attack on *Native Son*", in *Trinidad Guardian*, 23 and 30 October 1966.

"Why Nkrumah Failed", in *Encounter*, 1966.

"The argument about Nkrumah—a reply", *Encounter*, November 1966.

"Monarchy or Republic?", Independence Anniversary Magazine, *Sunday Guardian*, 1966.

Introduction to Wilson Harris's *Tradition and the West Indian Novel*, pamphlet based on lecture by Harris at West Indian Students' Union, London, 15 May 1965; reprinted as an appendix in Wilson Harris's *Tradition, The Writer and Society*, New Beacon Books, London, 1967, and in *Spheres*.

"World Politics Today", speech at Windsor, Ontario, 14 January 1967; reprinted in *Speak Out*, no. 10, March 1967.

"Document: C.L.R. James on the Origins" (portion of speech delivered in Detroit, January 1967), in *Radical America*, vol. II, no. 4, July/August 1968.

Review of *King Cricket* by Gary Sobers, *Cricket Quarterly*, 1967, vol. 5, no. 3.

Obituary: Sir Frank Worrell, "The man whose leadership made history", *The Cricketer*, vol. 48, 5 May, 1967, reprinted in *Cricket*.

"George Headley", in J.Arlott (ed.), *Cricket: The Great Ones* (Pelham Books, London), 1967, reprinted in *Cricket*.

Review of James R. Hooker's *Black Revolutionary: George Padmore's path from Communism to Pan-Africanism*, for "Caribbean Magazine" of BBC Caribbean Service, London, 16

August 1967.

"How West Indies cricket was built", *The Cricketer*, Winter Annual, vol. 48, no. 12, 1967/68.

"The Gathering Forces", mimeographed, Facing Reality, Detroit, November 1967.

"The Caribbean Rejection", address to conference on "Politics, Philosophy and Creative Literature" at Makerere University College, Uganda, 23-25 August 1968.

"Ancient and Modern" (review of *The Growth of the Modern West Indies*, by G.K. Lewis), *New Society*, London, 26 September 1968.

"Not Cricket" (on d'Oliveira affair), in *Transition*, 37, 1968, reprinted in *Cricket*.

"The Making of the Caribbean Peoples" (lecture to Second Conference on West Indian Affairs in Montreal, Canada, Summer 1966), mimeographed, London, October 1968, 18pp.; reprinted in *Radical America James Anthology*, May 1970, and in *Spheres*.

"Black Power: Its Past, Today and the Way Ahead" (text of speech delivered in London, August 1967), mimeographed, Marcus Garvey Institute, 1969; reprinted in *Spheres*.

"African Development", in *Speak Out*, vol. II, no. 4, April 1969.

"The West Indian Intellectual", introductory essay to new edition of J.J.Thomas's *Froudacity*, New Beacon, London, 1969.

"Black Studies and the Contemporary Student" (text of a talk), mimeographed, Facing Reality, Detroit, June 1969, 36pp.; edited version in *Rendezvous*.

"Discovering Literature in Trinidad: The Nineteen Thirties", in *Journal of Commonwealth Literature*, no. 7, July 1969, reprinted in *Savacou*, no. 2, September 1970, and in *Spheres*.

"The State of the Movement: Caribbean, Africa and America", speech to Africa and American Teachers Association, New York, 7 September 1969.

"Driving the ball is a tradition in the West Indies", *The Cricketer*, vol. 49, no. 12, reprinted in *Cricket*.

"Sir Learie Constantine", in *Cricket: The Great All-Rounders*, ed. John Arlott, Pelham Books, London, 1969; reprinted in *Spheres* and *Cricket*.

"Garfield Sobers", in Arlott, *Cricket* . . ., op. cit., 1969; reprinted in *Future* and *Cricket*.

"West Indian Cricketers in County Cricket", 1960's, first published in *Cricket*.

"Sobers and the future", *The Cricketer*, Winter, 1969/70 vol. 50, no. 12.

"Walter Hammond: an anniversary tribute", *The Cricketer*, 1970, vol. 51, no. 8, reprinted in *Cricket*.

Introduction to Rowland Bowen's, *Cricket: A History of its Growth and Development throughout the World* (Eyre and Spottiswoode, London), 1970, reprinted in *Cricket*.

"Sir Frank Worrell", in J.Arlott (ed.), *Cricket: The Great Captains* (Pelham Books, London), 1970, reprinted in *Cricket*.

"The Atlantic Slave Trade and Slavery: Some Interpretations of their Significance in the Development of the United States and the Western World", in *Amistad* I, ed. John A. Williams and Charles F. Harris, Vintage Books, New York, 1970; reprinted in *Future*.

"From Du Bois to Fanon", (text of a talk), Michigan, 1970, 4pp.

"The Olympia Statues, Picasso's Guernica and the Frescos of Michelangelo in the Capella Paolina", lecture prepared for television, 1970; first published in *Future*.

Review of H. Rap Brown's *Die, Nigger, Die* and Julius Lester's *Look out, Whitey! Black Power's Gon' Get Your Mama*, in *New Society*, 6 August 1970.

"On Black Power in Trinidad", *Race Today* 1970.

"Paul Robeson: Black Star", *Black World* no. 1, November, 1970, reprinted in *Spheres*.

"The Old World and the New", 70th birthday speech on 4 January 1971 in Ladbroke

Grove, London; reprinted in *Rendezvous.*

"On Paul Robeson", in *Freedomways*, 1971.

Letter about George Athan Billias and Gerald N. Grob's *American History, Retrospect and Prospect*, to *Free Press*, New York, 12 March 1971.

"La société contemporaine et les Noirs", in *Partisans*, no. 59/60, mai/aout 1971.

"The Way Out: World Revolution", in *Radical America*, vol. 5, no. 6, November/December 1971.

"George Jackson", in *Radical America*, vol. 5, no. 6, November/December 1971, reprinted in *Future.*

"Peasants and Workers" (excerpts from unpublished *The Gathering Forces*, written in 1967 as a draft for document to appear on 50th anniversary of the Russian revolution, sections written in collaboration with Martin Glaberman, William Gorman and George Rawick), in *Radical America*, vol. 5, no. 6, November/December 1971, reprinted in *Spheres.*

"Colonialism and National Liberation in Africa: The Gold Coast Revolution", in Norman Miller and Roderick Aya (eds), *National Liberation in the Third World*, Free Press, New York, 1971.

Text of lecture at University of Texas, in *Kas-Kas: Interviews with Three Caribbean Writers in Texas*, ed. Ian Munro and Reinhard Sander, occasional publication of the African and Afro-American Research Institute, University of Texas, Austin, 1972.

"Kwame Nkrumah: Founder of African Emancipation", in *Black World*, July 1972, reprinted in *Rendezvous.*

"George Padmore: The Man and His Work", and "Sir Frank Worrell, 1924–67", in publication of Caribbean Conference Committee for symposium "West Indian Nation in Exile", 6–8 October 1967, Montreal.

"The Man whose Leadership Made History", obituary of Sir Frank Worrell, in *The Vanguard*, 24 June 1967.

"The West Indian" (address at Graduation Ceremony at University of the West Indies, Cave Hill, Barbados, 1 February 1972), in *Bim*, vol. 14, No.55, July/December 1972.

"The Middle Classes", in David Lowenthal and Lambros Comitas, *Consequences of Class and Color: West Indian Perspectives*, Doubleday, New York, 1973.

"The Commune in 1971", in *Revolution and Reaction: The Paris Commune 1871*, ed. J. Hicks and R. Tucker, 1973.

"African Independence and the myth of African inferiority", in *Education and Black Struggle: Notes from the colonized world*, ed. Institute of the Black World, Harvard Education Review Monograph No.2, 1974.

"Black Intellectuals in Britain", in Bhikhu Parekh, *Colour, Class and Consciousness*, Allen and Unwin, London, 1974.

"The Role of the 6th Pan-African Congress", interview, with Julius Nyerere, in *Race Today*, vol. 6, no. 4, April 1974.

Review of TANU, The Arusha Declaration and TANU, Tanzania: Party Guidelines, in *Falling Wall Book Review*, No.2, June/July/August 1974.

"TANU, The Arusha Declaration and Party Guidelines", in *Race Today*, vol. 6, November 1974.

"Beyond the Boundary", in *Race Today*, vol. 7, no. 7, July 1975.

"Not just cricket", review of *Learie Constantine*, by Gerald Howat, *New Society*, vol. 34, no. 689, 18 December 1975, reprinted in *Cricket.*

"Cricket and Race", 1975, first published in *Cricket.*

"The Presence of Blacks in the Caribbean and its impact on our culture", in *Amsterdam News*, June/July 1975; reprinted in *Rendezvous.*

Review of Jean Fouchard's *The Haitian Maroons* (included as introduction and critique in Blyden Press edition, 1976), in *Black World*, November 1975.

"Blacks in the police force?", letter in *Race Today*, vol. 8, no. 1, January 1976.

"Towards the Seventh: The Pan-African Congress—Past, Present and Future", address delivered at First Congress of All African Writers, Dakar, Senegal, 8 January 1976, and at Homecoming, Federal City College, Washington, DC, 19 October 1976; repeated in *Ch'indaba* (formerly *Transition*; ed. Wole Soyinka), 2, July/December 1976, and in pamphlet *Not For Sale*, Editorial Consultants, San Francisco, 1976; reprinted in *Rendezvous.*

"George Padmore: Black Marxist Revolutionary", talk given in North London, 1976; in *Rendezvous.*

Review of Alex Haley's *Roots* (reprinted from *Caribbean Contact*), in *Race Today*, vol. 9, no. 2, London, March/April 1977.

"A view of Africa", in *Race Today*, vol. 9, no. 5, London, July/August 1977.

NKRUMAH AND THE GHANA REVOLUTION (referred to before publication as *Nkrumah Then and Now*; Part I written in 1958, Part II includes "Government and Party", speech delivered in Accra in July 1960, "1962: Twenty Years After", letter to Nkrumah dated 21 July 1962, "Slippery Descent", two articles first published in Trinidad Evening News, February 1964, "Lenin and the Problem" written for Ghanaian political journal in 1964, and ". . . Always out of Africa", extract from *A History of Pan-African Revolt*), with introduction, Allison & Busby, London, 1977; revised paperback edition with new preface, 1982, 224 pp.; Lawrence Hill & Co., Westport, Conn., 1977; extracts "Lenin and the Problem" in *Radical America James Anthology*, May 1970, and "Colonialism and National Liberation in Africa: the Gold Coast Revolution", in *National Liberation*, ed. Norman Miller and Roderick Aya, New York, 1971.

THE FUTURE IN THE PRESENT, Selected Writings vol. 1, with biographical introduction, Allison &. Busby, London, 1977, Lawrence Hill, Westport, Conn., 1977, 272pp.; reprinted in new paperback format, 1980.

Review of *Paul Robeson Speaks: Writings, Speeches, Interviews 1918-74*, in *New Society*, 8 February 1979.

Review of Wenda Parkinson's *This Gilded African: Toussaint L'Ouverture*, in *New Society*, 15 February 1979.

"Whither Trinidad and Tobago?" (based on an interview), in *Race Today*, vol. 11, no. 4, November/December 1979.

"Australia v. West Indies", with Tony Crozier, in E.W. Swanton (ed.), *Barclays' World of Cricket* (Collins, London), 1980.

"West Indies", with P.D.B. Short, in E.W. Swanton (ed.) *Barclays' World of Cricket* (Collins, London), 1980.

Review of Maurice Nyagumbo's *With the People: An autobiography from the Zimbabwe struggle*, in *New Society*, 9 October 1980.

Text of speech at memorial rally for Walter Rodney in Conway Hall, London, 20 October 1980, in *Race Today*, vol. 12, no. 2, November 1980.

Review of Michael Thelwell's *The Harder They Come*, in *New Society*, 27 November 1980.

Review of *Norman Manley: A biography*, in *New Society*, 11 December, 1980.

SPHERES OF EXISTENCE, Selected Writings vol. 2, with biographical introduction, Allison & Busby, London, 1980, Lawrence Hill, Westport, Conn., 1980, 272pp.

Review of Earl Lovelace's *The Dragon Can't Dance*, in *Race Today*, vol. 13, December 1980/January 1981.

"How free was free?" (review of *Been in the Storm So Long* by L.F.Litwack), *New Society*, 19 February 1981.

"Feet First" (on Mugabe and the 1980 Zimbabwe vote), in *Cultural Correspondence*, 12-14, Summer 1981.

Review of Ralph de Boissière's *Crown Jewel*, in *New Society*, 11 June 1981.

"Birth of a Nation", abridged version in Susan Craig, *Contemporary Caribbean* (2 vols.), College Press, Maracas, Trinidad and Tobago, 1981, vol. 1.

"Black Women in America: In Fact and in Fiction", two lectures on the work of Ntozake Shange, Alice Walker and Toni Morrison, at Riverside Studios, London, 29 and 30, August 1981; extract "I'm a Poet"(on Ntozake Shange's collection *Nappy Edges*) from first lecture, in *Race Today Review*, vol. 14, no. 1, December 1981/January 1982.

Review of V.S. Naipaul's *Among the believers: An Islamic journey*, in *New Society*, 22 October 1981.

"After Scarman: An accumulation of blunders", in *New Society*, 3 December 1981.

Preface to reprint of George Lamming's *Season of Adventure*, Allison & Busby, London, 1982.

"Ignoring History" (on V.S. Naipaul), in *Vanguard*, 5 March 1982.

Review of Alice Walker's *You Can't Keep a Good Woman Down*, in *Race Today*, vol. 14, no. 3, May/June 1982.

"The nine-year-old leader", in *Race Today*, vol. 14, no. 3, May/June 1982; reprinted as "Free for All" (on the British riots), in *Cultural Correspondence*, Winter 1983.

"Missouri Sharecroppers: The workers who opened the door", reprinted in *Socialist Worker*, June 1982.

"Zenith" (review of Alice Walker's *Meridian*), in *Race Today*, vol. 14, no. 4, August/September 1982.

"A majestic innings with few peers: Sandip Patel", *South*, September 1982, reprinted in *Cricket*.

Introduction to Ron Ramdin's *From Chattel Slave to Wage Earner: A History of Trade Unionism in Trinidad and Tobago*, Martin Brian & O'Keefe, London, 1982.

"Cricket Notes" column, in *Race Today Review*, vol. 14, no. 5, January 1983.

"Cricket Notes", in *Race Today*, vol. 14, no. 6, March/April 1983.

"Mama Was There", review of Ntozake Shange's *Sassafrass, Cypress & Indigo*, in *Race Today*, vol. 14, no. 6, March/April 1983.

"Cricket Notes: Gower to lead England", in *Race Today*, vol. 15, no. 1, May/June 1983, reprinted in *Cricket*.

"Cricket Notes: Gower & Richards", in *Race Today*, vol. 15, no. 2, August/September 1983.

"Cricket Notes: The Captain and his Team—An injustice to Gower", in *Race Today*, vol. 15, no. 3, October/November 1983, reprinted in *Cricket*.

"Address on Poland: Speech at Solidarity Support Rally, November 1981", in *Cultural Correspondence*, new series 2 (ed. Jim Murray and Susan McCarn), Winter 1983, reprinted in *Rendezvous*.

"C.L.R. James at Black Ink: A talk on Toni Morrison, Alice Walker and Ntozake Shange", in *Cultural Correspondence*, Winter 1983, reprinted in *Rendezvous.*

Review of Adolfo Gilly's *The Mexican Revolution*, in *Third World Book Review*, pilot issue, November 1983.

"Walter Rodney and the Question of Power" (delivered at memorial symposium "Walter Rodney, Revolutionary & Scholar: A Tribute", University of California, Los Angeles, 30 January 1981), Race Today Publications, London, 1983, 16pp.

80th BIRTHDAY LECTURES (text of three public lectures, on "Socialism or Barbarism", "Britain and America: Two English-Speaking Democracies" and "Immigrants to Britain: Formerly Colonial Peoples", delivered at Princeton College, London, 6/9/12 January 1981), Race Today Publications, London, 1983.

"Some observations on George Lamming", in *South*, January 1984.

"Reminiscences" (review of *Everything Under the Sun*, by Jeffrey Stollmeyer), *Race Today Review*, January 1984.

"Carribean Views from the Top" (review of *Everything Under the Sun*, by Jeffrey Stollmeyer), *The Guardian*, 6 January 1984.

"A princely gift to England's game", *South*, July 1984.

Foreword to *Apartheid: The story of a dispossessed people*, by Motsoko Pheto, Moram Books, London 1984.

Preface and introduction to new edition of *Mariners, Renegades and Castaways*, Allison and Busby, London 1984.

Review of *Ranji, Prince of Cricketers*, by Alan Ross, *South*, London, July 1984.

"The Grenadian Revolution: from self-defence to self-destruction", *Communist Affairs*, July 1984.

Review of *As I Said At the Time*, by E.W. Swanton, *Race Today*, July/August 1984.

"West Indies cricket team in England 1984", *Sunday Tribune*, August 1984.

"It's still cricket, lovely cricket", *The Times*, 26 September 1984.

"MacGregor", *Journal of the Cricket Society*, vol. 12, no. 1, September 1984, reprinted in *Cricket.*

"West Indies v. England", *Race Today*, vol. 16, no. 2, October/November 1984, reprinted in *Cricket.*

"A United Carribean", (review of *Grenada: Revolution, Invasion and Aftermath* by Hugh O'Shaughnessy and *Grenada: Revolution and Invasion* by Anthony Payne, Paul Sutton and Tony Thorndike), *London Review of Books*, September 1984, vol. 6 no. 16.

"Personal reflections on centenary of publication of *Huckleberry Finn*", *New York Times*, September 1984.

"Africans and Afro-Caribbeans: a personal view", *Ten:8*, November 1984, issue 16.

"Pot a Greens" (review of *A Daughter's Geography*, by Ntozake Shange), *Race Today*, December 1984.

AT THE RENDEZVOUS OF VICTORY, Selected Writings vol. 3, with biographical introduction and bibliography, Allison & Busby, London, 1984, 320pp.

"The decline of English cricket", *Race Today Review*, January 1985, reprinted in *Cricket.*

"Paul Robeson" (review of London exhibition), *Race Today*, May/June 1985.

"Caution in Comparisons", *Race Today*, May/June 1985.

"Botham still hitting sixes", *Race Today*, vol. 16, no. 5, August/September 1985, reprinted in *Cricket.*

"Botham and Gower", *Race Today*, July 1986.

"Fully and absolutely assured", new introduction for reissue of *State Capitalism and World*

Revolution, Charles H. Kerr, Illinois, 1986.

"My First Cricketing XI", *New Community*, autumn 1986, Vol XIII, no. 2.

CRICKET, edited by Anna Grimshaw, Allison and Busby, London 1986, 319pp.

"Anyone for Cricket", *Southside*, January 1987.

"The Politics of Emancipation", *Capital Issues*, August 1987.

"Garvey in Retrospect", *Capital Issues*, August 1987.

Foreword to *An Introduction to the Philosophy of Marxism* by R.S. Baghavan, Socialist Platform, London, 1987.

"C.L.R. James and British Trotskyism: an interview", Socialist Platform, pamphlet, London 1987.

Foreword to *Carribbean Reflections: The Life and Times of a Trinidadian Scholar* (1901-1986), an oral history narrated by William Besson, edited and introduced by Jean Besson, Karia Press, London 1989.

PERIODICALS' PLACE OF PUBLICATION

Accra: *Ch'indaba*, *Transition*; **Barbados:** *Bim*; **Bristol:** *Falling Wall Book Review*; **Cleveland:** *Socialist Worker*; **Detroit:** *Bulletin of the Johnson Forest Tendency, Correspondence, Speak Out*; **Dublin**: *Sunday Tribune*; **Georgetown:** *New World*; **Glasgow:** *Glasgow Herald*; **Jamaica:** *Savacou*; **London:** *Black World, Bulletin of Marxist Studies, Capital Issues, Communist Affairs, Controversy, Cricket Quarterly, The Cricketer, Encounter, Fight, The Guardian, International Africa Opinion, Journal of Commonwealth Literature, Journal of the Cricket Society, The Keys, London Review of Books, New Community, New Leader, New Left Review, New Society, New Statesman, Newsletter of the Cricket Society, Newsletter, Institute of Race Relations, Peace News, Race Today, Race Today Review, Saturday Review, South, Southside, Ten:8, Third Text, Third World Book Review, The Times, Times Higher Education Supplement, Tit-bits, Venture*; **Madison:** *Radical America* (Somerville after 1971); **Manchester**: *Manchester Guardian*; **Montreal:** *Caribbean Conference Bulletin*; **New York:** *Amsterdam News, Cultural Correspondence* (Providence before 1982), *Fourth International, Free Press, Freedomways, Internal Bulletin of the SWP, Labor Action, The Militant, The New International, New York Times, Socialist Appeal*; **Paris:** *Partisans, Preuves, Les Temps Modernes*; **Trinidad:** *The Beacon, Daily Mirror, Evening Bulletin*; **San Fernando**: *The Nation, Port of Spain Gazette, The Royalian, Saturday Review, Sunday Guardian, Trinidad, Trinidad Guardian, The Vanguard*

Index of Names

Anna Grimshaw is a writer who teaches Anthropology and Film at Manchester University. Her other publications include:

Cricket by C.L.R. James (editor)
C.L.R. James: Man of the People, exhibition catalogue
The C.L.R. James Archive: A Reader's Guide
The Fontana Dictionary of Modern Thought (editor)
Servants of the Buddha